PIERRE LAVAL
and the eclipse of France

Pierre Laval in 1934

PIERRE LAVAL

and the eclipse of France

GEOFFREY WARNER

The Macmillan Company · New York

IN MEMORY
OF GRAHAM

Contents

Illustrations

Pierre Laval in 1934   *Frontispiece*

Following page 238

Maps

drawn by W. H. Bromage

Acknowledgments for the Illustrations

Acknowledgements and thanks for permission to reproduce photographs are due to Roger Viollet for plates 1(a), 1(b), 10(b), 12, 14(a), 14(d), and 15; Ullstein Bilderdienst for 2(b), 3, 4(a), 5(a), 9(a), 13 and 14(b); Keystone Press for 6, 11(b), 14(c), and 16(a); Associated Press for 9(b), 11(a), and 16(b); Central Press for the *Frontispiece*, and 10(a); United Press International for 5(b); *History Today* for 4(b); Paul Popper Limited for 2(a). Plate 7 (cartoon 30 October 1940) is reproduced by permission of *Punch*; Plate 8(a) (cartoon 30 October 1940) is reproduced by permission of the *Daily Mirror* and Syndication International; Plate 8(b) (cartoon by David Low, 15 April 1942) is reproduced by arrangement with the *Evening Standard*.

Preface

In 1931, France was at the peak of her power. As the historian Arnold Toynbee put it, '. . . France was the dominant military power in Europe in the air as well as on land; she was executing a naval programme . . . which was causing uneasiness to the Admiralty in Whitehall. Above all, she had extended her potency into the field of international finance. In 1931, the Bank of England was shocked to find itself dependent on the Bank of France, and the Federal Reserve Bank [of the United States] to find itself not altogether independent of French good will . . .'[1] In 1944, at the time of the Liberation, the position was very different. A French journalist and historian has described the situation as follows: 'Anarchy reigned. The liberation committees sought to supplant the town councils and the prefects. . . . The patriotic guards took over from the police. Summary executions multiplied. Neither law nor justice was universally respected. Finally, misery threatened the ruined towns, where transport chaos hampered food supply at the start of a bitter winter.'[2]

This book attempts to tell the story of the thirteen years in between through the career of one man: Pierre Laval. I do not mean to suggest by this that Laval was solely, or even mainly, 'to blame' for the decline in France's fortunes. The basic reasons for what happened lie in a whole series of complex economic, social, cultural and political circumstances which are largely beyond the scope of this study. Nevertheless, individuals are important, both as actors in the historical process and as reflections of the broader environment in which they live, and Laval played a crucial part at several important points during this period. While a book which focuses mainly upon him will inevitably offer only a partial view of what happened, it may still clear some of the ground for a more definitive history of these years.

[1] Arnold J. Toynbee, *Survey of International Affairs 1931*, London, Oxford University Press for the Royal Institute of International Affairs, 1932, p. 22.
[2] Jacques Fauvet, *La Quatrième République*, Paris, Fayard, 1959, p. 30.

Even though this book is essentially a 'life and times', there is perhaps rather more 'times' than 'life'. The trouble is that Laval, although a fascinating personality, provides very little help to the biographer. Apart from his death-cell defence, he wrote very little and, as a result, his personality has to be reconstructed from the accounts of third parties, most of whom have axes to grind. His formative years are an almost complete blank and one can really only guess at the decisive influences which shaped his early life. It says something for him that, in spite of these limitations, he does emerge from the sources as a character of some force, and I can only hope that I have managed to convey something of this to the reader.

Domestic affairs were of course important during this period, but the availability of the sources and the fact that, for good or ill, Laval's major impact was in the field of foreign affairs inevitably made foreign policy the centre of attention. Within this framework, the main focus is upon Franco-German relations, and here no explanation is necessary beyond the fact that this was how Laval saw things too.

Anyone working on the period covered by this book soon realizes how much he owes to the pioneers who have gone before him. The names of Robert Aron, Edward Bennett, Günter Geschke, Adrienne Hytier, and General Georges Schmitt immediately spring to mind. Full reference to the work of these and other scholars will be found in the bibliography, although this is an inadequate recompense for the labours they have spared me and the errors from which they have saved me. I hope that they, together with the other readers of this book, will not take my occasional disagreements with their conclusions as any reflection upon the quality of their work.

No student of contemporary history can fail to understand how little he would be able to accomplish without the facilities provided by the specialist libraries and their staffs. I would like to record my immense debt to the following individuals and institutions: the staffs of the Archives Nationales, the archives of the Prefecture of Police, the Bibliothèque Nationale, the Centre de Documentation Juive Contemporaine and the Bibliothèque de Documentation Internationale Contemporaine in Paris; Miss Judith Schiff and Miss Bess Henkin of the historical manuscripts division of the Yale University library; Miss Anne Abley and her colleagues at the library of St Antony's College,

Oxford; Miss Elisabeth Campbell and her staff at the press library of
the Royal Institute of International Affairs (Chatham House), London;
Miss Dorothy Hammerton and her staff at the Institute's printed
library; and last, but by no means least, Mr Kenneth Hiscock, the
ever-cheerful custodian of the German records at the Foreign Office
Library, London.

I am indebted to the Warden of St Antony's College, Oxford, for
permission to consult and quote from the Italian documents deposited
in his college's library, which proved so valuable a source for Chapter
4, and to the Stimson Literary Trust for permission to consult and
quote from the Stimson diary at Yale University library, without
which Chapter 1 could not have been written. I would also like to
thank all those who have kindly permitted the reproduction of copy-
right material. Full details of books and articles from which excerpts
have been taken will be found both in the body of the book, on the
occasion of the first reference, and in the bibliography. I should add at
this point that all translations, except those from the published collection of *Documents on German Foreign Policy*, are my own.

I owe a very special debt of gratitude to M. René de Chambrun,
who is the son-in-law of the subject of this book. From the moment I
first wrote to him, M. de Chambrun has been unfailingly helpful in
providing me with information and rare source material. I know that
he will not agree with all that is written in this book, a fact which
saddens me in view of all the help I have received from him.

The Rockefeller Foundation provided me with a generous grant
for the academic year 1963-4, which enabled me to accomplish much
of the preliminary research for the book. I am grateful to the Foundation, and particularly to Mr Gerald Freund, the head of the Social
Science division, for their help. During that same year, my wife and I
were privileged to enjoy the hospitality of the Yale Law School while
I was working on the Stimson material, and I would like to thank the
Dean, together with Mr Robert Stephens and Mrs Rosalyn Higgins,
for making our stay possible.

Although the captured German documents were a mine of information for this book, they would have been less so for one so unskilled in
calligraphy and the nuances of diplomatic and National Socialist
German as myself without the assistance of several individuals, notably
Professor Pickering and Mrs Black of the Department of German at

Reading University, and Herr Hans Abendroth of the University of Leicester.

Many others have helped me by providing references and/or discussing parts of the book with me. In particular, I should like to thank the following: Mr Tony Adamthwaite, Mr John Chapman, Mr Ian Colvin, Mr David Dilks, Mr Martin Gilbert, M. André Guénier, Mr Paul Ricard, Mr Douglas Todd, Mr Neville Waites, Mr Donald Watt, Mr Ronald Wheatley and M. Georges Wormser.

I must also express my thanks to my publishers who displayed an almost Job-like patience in waiting for the manuscript from an author who is determined to revolutionize his working methods on future occasions. The fact that it arrived in a fit state at all is largely due to the professional skill and industry of my typist, Mrs Rita Smith.

Finally, like most married authors, I suspect, I would have been completely lost without my wife. Not only did she make life bearable during the five-and-a-half years in which this book was written, she actually helped to bring the long travail to an end by assisting me at several stages during my research. It may be a cliché to say that this book could not have been written without her, but it happens to be true.

In conclusion, I must add that while the individuals and institutions mentioned in these paragraphs must claim a considerable share of the credit for any merits this book may possess, they are in no way to blame for its faults, which are mine alone.

GEOFFREY WARNER

Reading, January 1968

Postscript

It is one of the hazards of writing contemporary history that one's work runs the risk of being overtaken by new material becoming available. Thus, no sooner was this book completed than the Public Records Act (1967) came into force, releasing all British official records up to the end of 1937. There is no doubt that the use of this material would have improved the documentation of Chapters 1, 2, and 3, but I decided that, rather than delay the appearance of the book, it would be better to publish it as it was and leave any revisions occasioned by the new material for a subsequent edition.

May 1968

Abbreviations

C.E. *Les Evénements survenus en France de 1933 à 1945. Rapport de M. Charles Serre, Député, au nom de la Commission d'Enquête Parlementaire*, 2 volumes, and *Témoignages et Documents Receuillis par la Commission d'Enquête Parlementaire*, 9 volumes, Paris, Presses Universitaires de France, n.d. The two series are cited C.E. *Rapport* and C.E. *Témoignages*.

D.B.F.P. *Documents on British Foreign Policy, 1919–39*, London, H.M.S.O., 1947 *et seq.* They are cited by series, volume and document numbers.

D.D.I. *I Documenti Diplomatici Italiani*, Rome, La Libreria dello Stato, 1952, *et seq.* They are cited by series, volume and document numbers.

D.G.F.P. *Documents on German Foreign Policy, 1918–45*, London, H.M.S.O. 1949 *et seq.* They are cited by series letter, volume and document numbers.

F.R.U.S. *Foreign Relations of the United States, Diplomatic Papers*, Washington, U.S. Government Printing Office, 1870 *et seq.* They are cited by year and volume and page numbers.

GFM Documents of the German foreign ministry and chancellery, available in the form of photostats at the Public Record Office or Foreign Office Library, London. They are cited by serial and frame number(s). A complete list of serials cited will be found in the bibliography.

GMR   German military records available on microfilm from the National Archives in Washington. They are cited by microcopy, roll and frame number(s). A complete list of files cited will be found in the bibliography.

H.C. Deb.   U.K. House of Commons Debates (Hansard). They are cited by series, volume and column number(s).

H.L. Deb.   U.K. House of Lords Debates (Hansard). They are cited by series, volumes and column number(s).

Italian Documents   Miscellaneous Italian records available in the form of photostats at St Antony's College, Oxford. They are cited by Job and frame number(s).

J.O.   *Journal Officiel de la République Française*. This official gazette of the French government and parliament is published in various series. The two used in this book are the *Débats Parlementaires* (a stenographic record of parliamentary debates) and the *Lois et Décrets* (containing the texts of laws, decrees, etc.). The parliamentary series is further divided according to whether it deals with the Chamber of Deputies or the Senate. In this book, the two series are cited as J.O. Chambre (or Sénat), *Débats*, followed by the date of the debate and the page number(s); or J.O., *Lois et Décrets*, followed by the date of issue and the page number(s). The J.O. is invariably printed three columns to a page and, in order to facilitate reference, column numbers (reading from left to right) are sometimes added.

Laval Parle   *Laval Parle. Notes et mémoires rédigés par Pierre Laval dans sa cellule, avec une préface de sa fille et de nombreux documents inédits*, Geneva, Editions du Chevail Ailé, 1947.

ND   Documents presented at the Nuremberg war crimes trials. They are cited by document number.

Procès Laval   *Le Procès Laval. Compte Rendu Sténographique*, Paris, Albin Michel, 1946.

Procès Pétain   République Française, Haute Court de Justice, *Procès du Maréchal Pétain. Compte Rendu in extenso des Audiences*, Paris, Imprimerie des Journaux Officiels, 1945. This is in effect a special edition of the J.O. and is cited by page and, where necessary, column number(s).

R.I.I.A.   *Documents on International Affairs*, London, Oxford
Documents   University Press for the Royal Institute of International Affairs, 1929 *et seq*. They are cited by year and, where necessary, by volume number.

*La Vie de la   Institut Hoover, *La Vie de la France sous l'Occupation
France   (1940–44)*, 3 volumes, Paris, Plon, 1957.

The Apprentice

June 1883 – January 1931

Pierre Laval was a man whose deepest roots lay in his native village. 'Don't you know Châteldon?' he asked one of his lawyers while he was awaiting trial for treason in 1945. 'There's no other place like it in the world. . . . It's a village in a valley, with hills all around and vineyards on the hills. They make a fine wine there. It's no Burgundy certainly, but it's good and I like it. It's an old village is Châteldon, with medieval houses. In the valley there's a knoll with an old castle on it. That's where I live.'[1]

Laval had not always lived in the castle. He bought it in February 1932 at the end of his first term as prime minister of France. Although it was very dilapidated and cost him relatively little, the purchase was convincing proof that the local boy had made good and that he was deeply attached to the surroundings in which he had grown up.[2]

Châteldon is situated in the northern part of the Auvergne deep in the heart of France. Laval was born on 28 June 1883, the youngest of four children. The two eldest were boys. One died before the outbreak of the First World War and the other was killed in the bloody fighting of 1914. The third child, the only girl, married an ex-army officer and settled in the town of Bayonne. His brothers and sister do not seem to have exercised any great influence upon Laval.

His father, the village innkeeper, café proprietor, and butcher, was an important member of the local community. He was also the local postmaster and arranged for the mail to be brought by cart from the

[1] Yves-Frédéric Jaffré, *Les Derniers Propos de Pierre Laval*, Paris, Editions André Bonne, (hereafter cited as Jaffré), p. 57.

[2] Ibid., pp. 57–8; *Procès de M. Pierre Laval. Enquête sur la Fortune, 1945. Rapport Caujolle* (hereafter cited as *Rapport Caujolle*), p. 75. This unpublished report gives the results of a detailed inquiry, ordered by the examining magistrates in 1945, into the sources and development of Laval's wealth over the years. A copy was kindly communicated to me by M. René de Chambrun.

I

nearby railway station at Puy-Guillaume. 'Laval *père*,' wrote one of Laval's biographers, 'was something more than a peasant. Socially he was situated between the rural artisans and the petty bourgeoisie. . . . He was moderately well-to-do; he owned a few acres of vineyard and six horses.'[1]

Young Pierre was educated at the village school, but his father took him away at the age of twelve after he had passed his elementary school certificate and put him in charge of the mail-cart which ran between Châteldon and Puy-Guillaume. He was an intelligent youngster and his father intended him to take over the family business. But even at that age, Laval had more ambition. He had set his heart upon obtaining the *baccalauréat*, or secondary school certificate, and used to work on his own as he drove the mail-cart backwards and forwards. He was encouraged in his studies by several local dignitaries, including the village magistrate, the parish priest, and his former schoolmistress. Most important, however, was the encouragement given by the mayor of Châteldon, Dr Claussat, and his son Joseph, who was some nine years older than Laval. The Claussats were the key political figures in the area and it was undoubtedly Joseph's influence which helped to propel Laval into the Socialist party. But this was still some years in the future.

By the time he was fifteen, Laval had to enter a *lycée* if he was to take his *baccalauréat*. At first, his father was reluctant, but after some pressure from his mother he finally agreed and Laval went to Paris to stay with a friend of the family and commence his studies at the Lycée Saint-Louis.[2]

His childhood in Châteldon had implanted in Laval a sense of deep attachment to the countryside. 'I love the soil,' he was to say later, 'for it is the source of everything.'[3] He was to go in for farming on quite a large scale in later life and was proud of his agricultural expertise. This attachment to the very soil of France undoubtedly provides a clue to his

[1] Maurice Privat, *Pierre Laval*, Paris-Neuilly, Les Documents Secrets, 1931 (hereafter cited as Privat), p. 21; Henry Torrès, *Pierre Laval*, London, Gollancz, 1941 (hereafter cited as Torrès), p. 11. Written in war-time, Torrès' book is a vicious attack upon Laval. Most of it is completely untrustworthy, but as the author was an acquaintance of Laval's for some years, it occasionally contains useful information lacking in other sources.

[2] Privat, pp. 32–6; Torrès, p. 12; Alfred Mallet, *Pierre Laval*, 2 volumes, Paris, Amiot Dumont, 1954 (hereafter cited as Mallet), Vol. I, pp. 13–14. For Joseph Claussat and his influence on Laval, see Jaffré, p. 141, and the article on Claussat in Jean Jolly (ed.), *Dictionnaire des Parlementaires Français*, Vol. III, Paris, Presses Universitaires de France, 1963, pp. 1060–61.

[3] Jaffré, p. 97.

subsequent career and, in particular, to his decision to remain in France in 1940 in order to try and preserve some of the fabric of the country he loved so much.

Another legacy of his rural upbringing was his legendary tight-fistedness. 'To Laval a *sou* remains a *sou*, and that whether it belongs to him or to the state,' wrote someone who was to work with him closely when he became a minister. This careful attitude towards money was linked to his mistrustfulness,[1] which was in turn related to his undoubtedly superstitious nature. He occasionally consulted an astrologer and, in the words of M. Jaffré, while 'he clearly only believed half of it, he did believe half of it'.[2]

For reasons which are obscure, Laval did not remain in Paris to complete his *baccalauréat*. Instead, he returned south and spent a year in Bayonne, followed by a year in Moulins. He then decided to read for a degree in zoology and, in order to spare his parents any further expense, he took up a series of posts as a *pion*, or supervisor, in a number of *lycées*. This took him in turn to Lyon, Autun, Saint Etienne, Dijon and, finally, back to Paris again in 1907.[3]

During this period, he was called up for military service, and after serving a spell in the ranks he was discharged on account of varicose veins. To judge by his remarks in a speech in April 1913, the experience was not a particularly happy one. Barrack-based armies, he declared, were 'incapable of the slightest effort, because they are badly-trained and, above all, badly commanded'. He favoured the outright abolition of the army and its replacement by a citizens' militia.[4]

This, of course, was socialist doctrine. Laval had joined the socialists at Saint Etienne in 1903. 'I was never a very orthodox socialist,' he explained in 1945. '. . . By which I mean that I was never much of a Marxist. My socialism was much more a socialism of the heart than a doctrinal socialism. . . . I was much more interested in men, their

---

[1] A probably apocryphal, but none the less indicative, story of Laval's mistrustfulness was told me by a member of the French diplomatic service. It was to the effect that Laval used to sign official documents as close as possible to the last line of text so that no additional material could be inserted afterwards.

[2] Pierre Tissier, *I Worked with Laval*, London, Harrap, 1942 (hereafter cited as Tissier), p. 36; Jaffré, p. 59. The astrologer was his biographer, Maurice Privat. See the latter's account in *La Vie de la France*, Vol. III, pp. 1300–11.

[3] Unpublished note, dictated in December 1945, by Madame Pierre Laval on her husband's career; Privat, p. 55; Mallet, Vol. I, p. 14; Torrès, pp. 12–14.

[4] Privat, pp. 67–8; Prefecture of Police report, 20 April 1913, Archives Nationales, F7/13337.

jobs, their misfortunes and their conflicts than in the digressions of the great German pontiff.'[1] This was undoubtedly so, and Laval's 'unorthodoxy' was the long-term reason behind his eventual estrangement from the party.

But it was for political reasons that, after having obtained his zoological qualifications, Laval turned to the law. He became a member of the Paris bar in 1909 and, according to a contemporary, was already thinking along classical French lines of using the legal profession as a stepping-stone to parliament.[2] Later that same year, he married one of Joseph Claussat's sisters and they set up a small home in Paris. Their only child, a daughter, was born in 1911. Madame Laval, although coming from a very active political family, never meddled in politics herself. She belonged to a generation, she said, which believed that a woman's place was in the home. It was a happy home too, for Laval was devoted to his family, a fact which even his enemies have never denied.[3]

The years immediately before the First World War in France were characterized by widespread labour unrest, and Laval made his mark by defending strikers, trade-unionists, and left-wing agitators against attempts by the authorities to prosecute them. 'I am proud to be what I am,' he declared. 'A lawyer in the service of manual labourers who are my comrades, a worker like them. I am their brother. Comrades, I am a manual lawyer.'[4]

His first great success came in September 1911, when he defended a man called Manhès, who was accused of being a member of an anarchist gang which had been cutting telegraph wires. According to the prosecution, Manhès had been found on a patch of waste ground near where the saboteurs had been operating. Manhès claimed that he had gone there to meet an ex-army friend and had fallen asleep, but the police said that they had chased one of the gang on to the waste ground, from which there was only one way out, and left him there to pursue the others. Manhès had not been asleep, they maintained, but unconscious. A revolver and two cartridges were conveniently 'found' on the site

---

[1] Jaffré, p. 141; Privat, p. 55.
[2] Lucien Lamoureux in *La Vie de la France*, Vol. III, p. 1288; Privat, p. 67.
[3] Mallet, Vol. I, pp. 14–15; Privat, p. 77; Madame Laval's testimony to the examining magistrates in 1945, cited in Jacques Baraduc, *Dans la Cellule de Pierre Laval*, Paris, Editions Self, 1948 (hereafter cited as Baraduc), pp. 104–5; Tissier, pp. 37–8.
[4] Torrès, pp. 17–20.

the next day and, to cap it all, the police said that they had discovered a portrait of Bakunin in Manhès' flat. Laval made short work of the prosecution's case. He proved conclusively that there was more than one way out of the piece of waste ground, so that no saboteur would have been forced to remain there. The prosecution had attempted to discredit Manhès' story by suggesting that, as his friend's name did not figure in army records, he did not exist. In that case, Laval pointed out, neither did Manhès, for his name did not figure in the records either. As for the incriminating portrait, Laval was able to show that it was not of Bakunin, but of Manhès' father. The defendant was acquitted.[1]

Perhaps because of his success in the Manhès case, Laval was invited to stand as the socialist candidate in a by-election in the Neuilly-Boulogne constituency of the Paris region, which took place in November. On the first ballot, he came just over a hundred votes behind the radical candidate, who was in turn well behind the right-wing candidate, the mayor of Neuilly. According to the normal rules of the French political game, Laval should have stood down for the second ballot in order to give the radical, who counted as a left-winger, a straight fight against his right-wing opponent. But the radical was an unashamed supporter of the prime minister, M. Joseph Caillaux, whom the socialists strongly opposed, and Laval therefore maintained his candidature. The result was a foregone conclusion. The mayor of Neuilly won handsomely and Laval came last.[2]

As a result of his activities during the next few years, a profile in the socialist newspaper *L'Humanité* subsequently stated, Laval's name would 'remain associated with all the great labour trials'. His devotion to the cause brought its reward, and in the general election of April–May 1914 he was chosen to contest the working-class constituency of Aubervilliers, to the north of Paris. On the first ballot, he led the right-wing candidate by just over 2,000 votes and, in contrast to his own action two and a half years earlier, the radical candidate stood down for the second ballot and urged his supporters to vote for Laval. To judge by the result, most of them appear to have done so and he won comfortably. He entered the Chamber of Deputies shortly before his 31st birthday, the 'Benjamin' of the socialist parliamentary group.[3]

[1] *La Bataille Syndicaliste*, 19, 20, 21 September 1911.
[2] *Le Temps*, 7, 21 November 1911.
[3] *L'Humanité*, 29 April, 7, 11, 26 May 1914.

Together with the rest of his colleagues, Laval was soon to face the traumatic experience of the outbreak of the First World War. In accordance with Marxist theory, the French socialists had always condemned wars between nations as a consequence of capitalism and a diversion from the only legitimate conflict, the class struggle. As late as the middle of July 1914, when the international crisis was building up to flashpoint, the Socialist party congress passed a resolution which declared that 'the French party considers the spontaneous general strike of the workers of all countries, combined with anti-war propaganda among the masses, as the most workable means in the hands of the workers to prevent war and to force international arbitration of the dispute'. A number of anti-war demonstrations were held during the last week in July and, on the 31st, a right-wing fanatic, incensed by these manifestations of a lack of patriotism, shot and killed the socialist leader, Jean Jaurès.[1]

But when war was declared on 3 August 1914, the Socialist party, and its trade union allies, placed no obstacle in the way of mobilization. In face of the German danger, it adhered to the *union sacrée* of all Frenchmen, voted war credits, and even delegated two of its members to participate for the first time in a 'bourgeois' government.[2] There were four main reasons for this almost incredible *volte-face*. In the first place, it seemed even to many socialists that France had genuinely been the object of German aggression. Secondly, there was none of the international socialist action against the war which had been expected: the German socialists, in particular, had remained completely passive. Thirdly, events had moved so rapidly in the final few days that the socialists were taken almost by surprise. Finally, in the face of the wave of patriotic fervour which swept the nation, they realized that their theoretical attitude towards the problems of peace and war was not even shared by a majority of their own supporters, let alone French public opinion as a whole.[3]

One factor which undoubtedly helped to disarm socialist opposition to the war was the decision of the minister of the interior, Louis-Jean

[1] R. A. Markoff, *Opposition to the War in France, 1914–18*, unpublished Ph.D. thesis, University of Pennsylvania, 1962 (hereafter cited as Markoff), pp. 10–19, 22–5. Dr Markoff's thesis, which is the best analysis of the French Socialist party's changing attitude to the First World War known to the author, can be obtained from the Ann Arbor University Microfilms service (Ref. no. 63–4164).
[2] Ibid., pp. 45–8.
[3] Ibid., pp. 37–41.

Malvy, not to arrest the people whose names figured on the notorious *Carnet B*, which was a list of persons, mostly left-wing extremists, who were thought likely to try and interfere with the process of mobilization. Malvy was under strong pressure from the minister of war to arrest those on *Carnet B* but he felt that, after the assassination of Jaurès, such a step would be an intolerable provocation to the socialists. In any case, his own conversations with left-wing leaders had convinced him that no real trouble was to be expected.[1]

Only two members of parliament were on *Carnet B* and one of them was Laval. In view of his subsequent attitude, it is hard to see why he was singled out as a dangerous pacifist. Others were to display much more extremism than he ever did. His own explanation, which he gave in an interview in 1933, seems the most likely. He was the lawyer of the *Confédération Générale du Travail* (C.G.T.), the national trade union federation, and all the C.G.T. leaders were on *Carnet B*. 'As their lawyer,' Laval supposed, 'I would have been included in the round-up.'[2]

In a speech to an audience of mayors nearly thirty years later, Laval claimed, 'I have always been against war. By my political origins, I come from the parties of the left. I was a socialist in my youth . . . and, from my progress through this environment, I retained the hatred of war. It never pays.'[3] But such statements are liable to convey a false impression of his action during the First World War. For example, he was not one of the hard-core pacifists who supported the international socialist meeting at Zimmerwald in Switzerland in September 1915 and which called for immediate negotiations to end the war. Indeed, at a socialist meeting on 20 November 1915, Laval implicitly condemned the 'Zimmerwaldians' when he declared that, while 'there is not a single socialist who could not put his name to the Zimmerwald resolution, the meeting was held at neither the right time nor in the right place'.[4]

In fact, Laval seemed to steer deliberately clear of such controversial issues as socialist support of the war effort. To judge by the surviving

[1] Louis-Jean Malvy, *Mon Crime*, Paris, Flammarion, 1921, pp. 35–42.

[2] Paul Allard, *Les Enigmes de la Guerre*, Paris, Editions des Portiques, 1933 (hereafter cited as Allard), p. 44.

[3] Speech at a reception for the mayors of the Marseilles region, 6 November 1943. The unpublished text was kindly supplied to me by M. René de Chambrun.

[4] 'Chamoix' report, 21 November 1915, Prefecture of Police Archives, Ba/1535 (79). For the Zimmerwald meeting, see Markoff, pp. 118–23.

evidence he was a 'bread-and-butter' deputy, a constituency member, confining himself to such issues as rents, food and fuel supplies, and the cost of living.[1] It is perhaps significant that his comment upon Zimmerwald was more or less forced out of him. He had been invited to speak on 'socialism before, during and after the war', but he had spoken instead on the rents question, to the obvious irritation of some members of the meeting.[2]

It is interesting to speculate how far this concentration upon basic issues was influenced by the vicious press campaign which was being waged against him by the local newspaper in his constituency, the *Journal de Saint-Denis*. In April 1915, the paper published a letter from a serviceman asking why Laval had not volunteered to join the army.[3] The editor offered to print any reply, but none was forthcoming. This was too good an opportunity to miss for so violently anti-socialist a paper and, during the following months, its pages were full of references to Laval's failure to enlist. Finally, in February 1916, the paper coined the nickname '*Pierre loin-du-front*', with which it continued to belabour him for the rest of the war.[4] Laval's preoccupation with the kind of practical issue which was closest to the experience of his constituents may have helped to offset this constant stream of hostile propaganda.

As the war dragged on, however, the Socialist party's traditional pacifism began to reassert itself. Zimmerwald had been a symptom of this, and so was a resolution passed by the federation of the Haute-Vienne *département* in May 1915, which opposed the party's full support of the war effort and called upon it to make greater efforts to obtain peace through the medium of the Socialist International. Although, on 14 July 1915, the party's national council voted unanimously in favour of continuing to support the *union sacrée*, it was to be the last unanimous vote on an issue of peace and war.[5]

---

[1] In 1915, Laval's major interventions in the Chamber of Deputies concerned the supply of gas in the suburbs (J.O. Chambre, *Débats*, 20 July 1915, pp. 1139–40) and the rising costs of foodstuffs and fuel (ibid., 23 November 1915, pp. 1850–52). See also 'Chamoix' reports, 1 February and 19 July 1915, Prefecture of Police Archives, Ba/1535(7) and Ba/1535(75); Sûreté Nationale report, 4 February 1915, Archives Nationales, F7/13574.

[2] 'Chamoix' report, 21 November 1915, Prefecture of Police Archives, Ba/1535(79).

[3] Members of parliament had the choice of whether to enlist or not.

[4] *Journal de Saint-Denis*, 18–24 April, 25 April–1 May, 23–9 May, 25–31 July, 8–14 August, 12–18 September and 25 September–2 October 1915; 5 February 1916.

[5] Markoff, pp. 102, 110–12.

The split emerged into the open at the congress of the Seine federation of the party in December. In Dr Markoff's words, 'A "majority" resolution supporting the war of national defence was presented by Renaudel. Longuet introduced a resolution which differed from Renaudel's in that it declared that *all* capitalistic governments were responsible for the war and that the socialists should negotiate with their German opposite numbers for an eventual international conference, provided the German Social Democrats would agree to certain conditions, e.g. Alsace and Lorraine must be returned to France. A pure Zimmerwaldian motion was offered by Bourderon which also blamed the capitalists, but which demanded an immediate international conference *without conditions*. The Renaudel resolution received 6,121 votes; Longuet's got 3,826 votes; and 545 ballots were cast for Bourderon's motion.'[1]

A hard fight in the resolutions committee, in which Laval had played a considerable part, had preceded the tabling of these motions. After three meetings of the committee, the members had divided practically 50–50, with Laval supporting Longuet. Then Laval called a special meeting of the committee to try and get a compromise, but neither side would budge. His tactics laid himself open to the charge of having deserted Longuet, but he strenuously denied this at the congress itself. 'If both sides support the resumption of relations [between the socialist parties],' he said, 'it will be easy to reach agreement.' He wanted the party to extend 'a fraternal hand' to the German and Austrian socialists.[2]

The Seine federation congress was a preliminary to the national congress of the Socialist party, which was held over Christmas. There, the Longuet group did rally to a compromise motion put forward by Renaudel, 'doubtless through fear of incurring responsibilities' as a police report unkindly put it. It was left to Bourderon and the Zimmerwaldians to divide the congress, and their resolution obtained a mere 76 votes compared with Renaudel's 2,736. At a meeting of his constituents on 26 December, Laval explained his own position. 'The present war was forced upon us by Germany when we had no notion of conquest or annexation,' he declared. 'There can be no question of peace until the evacuation of northern France, Belgium, and Serbia. Moreover,

---

[1] Ibid., p. 133.
[2] 'Chamoix' reports, 7, 9, 10, 11 and 19 December 1915, Prefecture of Police Archives, Ba/1535(7), Ba/1536(89).

according to the German chancellor's last speech, our enemies do not want a peace which will deprive them of the advantage they have acquired. It is for this reason that we must persevere in order to secure victory and destroy Prussian militarism.'[1]

It was during 1916 that one can detect the first stirrings of the ambition which eventually led to Laval's break with the Socialist party. He was seen in the company of Malvy, the minister of the interior who had saved him from arrest in 1914, and there were rumours that he was about to be offered a post in the government. He was also in close touch with Joseph Caillaux, the man whom his party had opposed so strongly on the occasion of his first venture into national politics in 1911, and it subsequently transpired that Caillaux had earmarked him as a promising candidate for office should he return to power.[2]

Both Malvy's and Caillaux's attitude towards the war was, to say the least, ambiguous. Both men were later to be arrested by the Clemenceau government on charges of defeatism and treasonable activities and, while most of these charges were without foundation, there can be little doubt that Caillaux, if not Malvy, would have welcomed some form of compromise peace.[3] It was perhaps not surprising, therefore, that Laval, as a member of the Longuet faction of the Socialist party, should have been associated with them.

But he also seems to have had a foot in the opposition camp, that of Georges Clemenceau, the proponent of war to the bitter end. Thus, when Renaudel warned a meeting of the socialist parliamentary group on 25 May 1916 that the supporters of Clemenceau might use a forthcoming secret session of the Chamber of Deputies to overthrow the government, Laval replied that he 'did not see the trap . . . [and] declared in a loud voice that one should not be preoccupied with personalities and that, as far as he was concerned, he much preferred Clemenceau to Barthou'.[4] These were outspoken words to use at a

[1] Ibid., 25–6, 28–30 December 1915 and 26 December 1915, Ba/1535(7), Ba/1535(3).
[2] Mallet, Vol. I, p. 18; Hubert Bourgin, *Le Parti Contre la Patrie*, Paris, Plon, 1924, p. 122; Georges and Edouard Bonnefous, *Histoire Politique de la Troisième République*, 5 volumes to date, Paris, Presses Universitaires de France, 1956–62 (hereafter cited as Bonnefous), Vol. II, p. 371.
[3] There is no good modern study of Malvy. His own defence, *Mon Crime*, Paris, Plon, 1921, is the fullest account, but is naturally somewhat biased. For Caillaux, see Rudolph Binion, *Defeated Leaders*, New York, Columbia University Press, 1960, Part I.
[4] Hubert Bourgin, op. cit., pp. 95–6. While not a deputy himself, Bourgin attended socialist group meetings.

meeting of socialists, for whom Clemenceau was still the chief public enemy as a result of his strike-breaking activities as prime minister before the war.

'I was pro-Clemenceau and I did not disguise the fact,' Laval subsequently told Paul Allard.[1] He could claim that this was not inconsistent with his desire for a compromise peace in so far as he believed France must negotiate from a position of strength,[2] but one cannot help thinking that there was a common element in Laval's support of Caillaux and Clemenceau: namely, a desire for office.[3] As the prolonged, bloody, and static trench warfare failed to resolve the stalemate into which the war had drifted, it became increasingly evident that France faced the choice between a negotiated peace and an even more ruthless prosecution of the war. Rightly or wrongly, these alternatives were associated with the names of Caillaux and Clemenceau, and Laval was merely keeping a foot in both camps. It may seem strange, and even outrageous, that the same man could apparently support two such contradictory policies, but Laval was merely displaying his early mastery of the French parliamentary system. As one of its most perceptive critics had written on the eve of the First World War, 'there is less difference between two deputies, one of whom is a revolutionary while the other is not, than between two revolutionaries, one of whom is a deputy while the other is not.'[4]

The crisis which compelled France to choose between Caillaux and Clemenceau was prompted by two events: the first Russian revolution of March 1917 and the French army mutinies which followed the disastrous Nivelle offensive in April.[5] The Russian revolution gave rise to new demands for a negotiated peace, and a proposal, originally put forward by the neutral Dutch Social Democrats, calling for a full meeting of the Second International in Stockholm, won considerable support. The French socialists agreed to send delegates, but the Ribot government, terrified in case rumours of peace should further demoralize the French army, refused to grant the necessary passports.[6]

[1] Allard, p. 40.
[2] Privat, p. 115.
[3] Bourgin described Laval's statement of support for Clemenceau as 'a declaration of candidature' (Bourgin, op. cit., p. 96).
[4] Robert de Jouvenel, *La République des Camarades*, 2nd edition, Paris, Bernard Grasset, 1934, p. 17. The first edition appeared in 1914.
[5] For the best analysis of the army mutinies, see Markoff, Chapter IX.
[6] Ibid., pp. 253–5.

On 1, 2, and 4 June, the Chamber of Deputies debated the government's refusal to grant passports in secret session. It was on the last day of the debate that Laval, reading from a letter he had received from the front, gave the Chamber its first news of the army mutinies. Linking these events with a recent ugly incident in Paris, in which Indo-Chinese soldiers had fired upon a crowd of French women, he made a passionate plea for the right of the socialists to send delegates to Stockholm to discuss the possibility of peace. '. . . After three years of war, after so many thousands of deaths and after so much sacrifice endured with the prospect of peace still distant and uncertain,' he declared, 'one can understand that the country is weary and an effort will be made to find the best way of restoring the morale of this great country.' Speaking not as a party man but as a Frenchman, he concluded, 'I ask you whether the means of restoring hope to the troops and confidence to the working population would not be found in the political context and in the political conduct of the war. Whether you like it or not, Stockholm is the pole star!' Despite his eloquence, however, the government obtained a vote of confidence.[1]

Ribot's respite was, however, only a temporary one. He resigned in September after Clemenceau's violent attack in the Senate upon M. Malvy's 'defeatism' had led to the resignation of the minister of the interior. Caillaux was tarred with the same brush as Malvy and it became increasingly clear that things were moving very much Clemenceau's way. In its determination to exclude him from power, the socialist parliamentary group took the unprecedented step of calling a special meeting on 10 November which passed a resolution 'debarring M. Clemenceau' and pledging support to the existing government led by M. Painlevé. 'Many believe,' it was stated in a police report, 'that [this resolution] was only passed to compel certain socialists "who believe in a Clemenceau government and would be fairly well-disposed towards joining one" to refuse their support to M. Clemenceau.' Laval's absence from the meeting was specifically noted by the author of the report.[2]

Clemenceau did indeed want a socialist in his government. It was not Laval, however, but Albert Thomas, who had earlier been a minister of

[1] J. O. Chambre, *Comité Secret du 1er juin 1917*, pp. 541–2. The quotation comes from p. 542, col. 3. The debates in this secret session were printed as a special supplement to the J.O. of 16 May 1925.

[2] Sûreté Nationale Report, 10 November 1917, Archives Nationales, F7/13575.

munitions. He had already approached Thomas directly, telling him that 'only two men could save the country – himself and M. Thomas', and had invited him to join the government which he would soon be forming. Thomas had replied that he could take no action without consulting his party.[1]

In spite of the socialists' pledge of support, the Painlevé government fell on 13 November and President Poincaré sent for Clemenceau. The latter still wanted Thomas in his government, and the socialists met again on 14 November to examine the situation. The meeting was indecisive and it was afterwards that Laval, who once again had not been present, entered upon the scene. Georges Mandel, Clemenceau's right-hand man, approached Laval, whom he knew quite well, and asked him to urge his fellow-socialists to agree to Thomas's participation in the government. According to Georges Wormser, who was Clemenceau's secretary at the time, 'Laval let it be understood that he would gladly do this if he could hope for an under-secretaryship of state; that in any case Clemenceau's offer ought to be more substantial than one portfolio, as the socialists would rightly require more in view of the importance of their group. Yielding to this consideration, Clemenceau had a substantial offer transmitted unofficially to the socialists: namely one minister (Thomas) and two (at the most three), under-secretaries of state. The latter could be nominated, not by himself for whom [the socialists] were practically all unknowns, but by their colleagues in the parliamentary group.'[2]

At the next meeting of the parliamentary group on 15 November, Laval argued strongly in favour of the acceptance of Clemenceau's offer. It seems he had almost succeeded in convincing his colleagues when Léon Jouhaux, leader of the C.G.T., intervened in the name of the trade unions to say that 'the latter still considered Clemenceau as "the enemy of the working class".' His intervention carried the day and the group reaffirmed its unqualified opposition to a Clemenceau government. 'Due to this tactical error,' Laval told them, '. . . you are going to alter the axis of political control in this country for at least twenty

---

[1] Ibid.; Wickham Steed in *The Observer*, 28 June 1938. Wickham Steed knew Clemenceau well in 1917.

[2] Georges Wormser, '*Note sur le rôle de Pierre Laval lors de la formation du 2ème cabinet Clemenceau* (November 1917),' which M. Wormser was kind enough to send me on 19 February 1963. The dates of the socialist group meetings, which are not in M. Wormser's note, come from *Le Temps*.

2

years. Clemenceau will survive to finish the war and he will win it!' But his real grievance was personal. 'The comrades have stymied me,' he indignantly exclaimed to a fellow-deputy after the meeting. 'The next time I won't be in the party. That way I can accept a post.'[1]

An element of mystery surrounds this event, for Georges Wormser is quite categorical in denying that Clemenceau offered Laval a post, or even proposed any names apart from that of Albert Thomas.[2] Laval, on the other hand, was always equally categorical that he had been offered a post – under-secretary of state at the ministry of the interior – and that Compère-Morel, Groussier, and Bouisson were also offered posts in addition to Thomas.[3] One explanation is that Mandel and Laval came to some private arrangement beforehand in order to give the impression that certain deputies had been designated by name. Otherwise, what was Laval to get out of it, for it was by no means certain that he would have been chosen in a free vote? Whatever the truth of the matter, however, it is quite clear that Laval took the parliamentary group's decision as a blow to his personal ambition and, while he was prepared to abide by party loyalty for the moment, his remark to Jobert shows the direction in which his mind was moving.

Following his rebuff, Laval seems to have been relatively inactive while Clemenceau fulfilled his prophecy of surviving to finish the war and winning it. There is, however, an interesting report in the police files of a speech which he made at Drancy in March 1918, in which one can perhaps detect the first hint of that policy of Franco-German *rapprochement* for which he was to become notorious. '. . . We would like the war to be waged with rapid decisions and realistic ideas,' he said. 'We demand that our war aims should be proclaimed every day, but without condemning a people with whom we do not want to be forever at war.'[4]

After the armistice of November 1918, Laval's parliamentary activity centred upon two issues. One was electoral reform, and, in September 1919, he was put up by Georges Mandel to try and draw the government out of its non-committal attitude towards the bastardized system

---

[1] Wormser note, loc. cit.; Allard, p. 41; Aristide Jobert, *Souvenirs d'un Ex-Parlementaire*, Paris, Editions Eugène Fignière, 1933, pp. 154–5.

[2] Wormser note, loc. cit.

[3] Allard, p. 41.

[4] Sûreté Nationale report, 10 March 1918, Archives Nationales, F7/13372.

of proportional representation which had been passed by both houses of parliament earlier in the year by tabling an amendment calling for the postponement of the implementation of the new law for the period of one legislature. But Clemenceau refused to be drawn, taking the view that electoral law was a matter for parliament rather than the government.[1]

The other issue was that of an amnesty for political and military offences committed during the war. As many of their supporters were involved, the socialists were among the most enthusiastic advocates of an amnesty and Laval was one of their chief spokesmen. The first bid to enact legislation failed in May 1919. The second succeeded in the following October, although the Chamber's text was drastically altered by the Senate. 'We thought,' Laval complained bitterly in the Chamber on 19 October, 'that in the aftermath of victory and in conformity with public opinion, the government would consider it a duty – and parliament would follow – to grant as large an amnesty as possible. My socialist friends and I can only regret that, instead of this amnesty which was desired by the country, we see a restricted and incomplete amnesty which is incompatible with the victory of this country and the state of mind to which it should have given rise.' They would have to wait until after the elections, he concluded, to tackle the problem anew.[2]

Unfortunately, Laval was not to be in the Chamber to continue his campaign after the elections. The Bolshevik revolution was well under way in Russia and had led, in France as in many other countries, to a struggle for power within the Socialist party between its supporters and opponents. The fear of revolution – epitomized in the famous election poster depicting 'the man with the knife between his teeth' – led to the virtual isolation of the Socialist party during the election campaign. Under the new electoral law, this spelt doom for the party's chances. Laval knew which way the wind was blowing, but for the moment had no alternative but to enter the lists under the socialist banner. His campaign, which concentrated upon the amnesty issue,

[1] For this incident, see Georges Wormser, *La République de Clemenceau*, Paris, Presses Universitaires de France, 1961, pp. 363–7. For Laval's intervention, see J. O. Chambre, *Débats*, 19 September 1919, pp. 4454–6. For the electoral law of 1919 see P. W. Campbell, *French Electoral Systems and Elections since 1789*, 2nd edition, London, Faber and Faber, 1965, pp. 90–5.

[2] For Laval's speeches on the amnesty issue, see J. O. Chambre, *Débats*, 22 May 1919, pp. 2379–80; 18 October 1919, pp. 5184–6, 5190–91; 19 October 1919, p. 5273.

was very effective if we are to believe one witness. 'The brute!' complained Paul Faure, one of his colleagues, after an election speech. 'That's the seventh time I've heard it and that's the seventh time he's made me cry.' But Paul Faure's tears were to no avail. Although Laval obtained slightly more votes than the rest of his colleagues on the socialist list, the list as a whole was beaten by the right-wing *Bloc National* by 2,102,411 votes to 1,576,602.[1]

Following his defeat, Laval reverted to his pre-war profession of lawyer. At the end of 1920, he helped secure a notable triumph when the C.G.T. was prosecuted by the government for exceeding its powers in connection with the May-day strikes of that year. The court dissolved the C.G.T. and punished its leaders, but the union's chief counsel, Joseph Paul-Boncour, ably assisted by Laval, 'dragged out the appeal until a change of policy extinguished a matter which was purely political'.[2]

But Laval still had his eye on a political career. His opportunity came at the end of 1922, in his old constituency of Aubervilliers. In the same month that he and Paul-Boncour had defended the C.G.T., the Socialist party had finally split into communist and socialist wings at the congress of Tours. In January 1921, most of the socialist-controlled municipalities in the Paris suburbs went over to the communists. As the former deputy for Aubervilliers, Laval was under pressure from both socialists and communists, but he preferred to retain his independence. He explained one day to a group of friends that 'he had desired this independence for some time when, during the course of his term as a socialist deputy, he had to vote . . . according to the party's dictates in a way which did not coincide with his own opinions'. By October 1922, communist intransigence had produced fresh divisions in the *banlieue* and Laval emerged from a long period of silence to call for the formation of an autonomous group of socialist municipalities in the Seine *département*. The suggestion was adopted, but at Aubervilliers, where they remained in the majority, the communists staged a counter-attack on 9 November by refusing to vote the municipal

---

[1] For the 1919 election in general, see Bonnefous, Vol. III, pp. 63–72. For the campaign in Laval's constituency, see Ludovic-Oscar Frossard, *De Jaurès à Léon Blum: Souvenirs d'un Militant*, Paris, Flammarion, 1943, pp. 77–81. For the results, see *Presse de Paris*, 21 November 1919.

[2] Joseph Paul-Boncour, *Entre Deux Guerres*, Volume II, *Les Lendemains de la Victoire 1919–34*, Paris, Plon, 1945, pp. 74–8. See also *Le Temps*, 19 December 1920.

budget presented by the 'dissident' mayor, Georgen. The prefect of the Seine was forced to dissolve the council and hold fresh elections to break the deadlock. Laval, who had taken the precaution of buying a small plot of land in the *commune* so that he could become eligible for election, emerged as the leader of the 'independent socialist' list, which was affiliated to neither the Communist nor the Socialist party. It was this list which triumphed in the elections which took place on 25 February and 4 March 1923. A few days later, Laval was elected mayor.[1]

The reasons which prompted Laval's brilliant re-entry into Aubervilliers politics have been analysed by M. André Guénier, who was the *commune's* municipal treasurer at the time and who subsequently became Laval's private secretary. 'He foresaw,' Guénier writes, 'that in 1924 there would be a swing of the pendulum away from the "horizon blue"[2] Chamber elections of 1919 and that a left-wing coalition would be formed. Given the large number of ambitious men, places would be hard to find on this coalition's list. This is what Laval was thinking of when he decided to stand in the Aubervilliers elections of 1923. The office of mayor held no attraction for him at this date. The interest he saw in it was that the office of mayor in a large working-class *commune* was a "platform" (his own expression) from which he could impose himself on the *Cartel des Gauches* list which would be drawn up for the whole of the Paris suburbs.'[3] It was sound strategy.

Nevertheless, Laval did not neglect his mayoral duties. Indeed, his punctilious fulfilment of them served to strengthen his position. Every evening in those early days, writes M. Guénier, Laval would leave the Palais de Justice for the *mairie* at Aubervilliers. There, he would see, on average, about fifty people who had come to seek information or present a grievance. Two typists were employed to type the letters which had to be sent to a higher authority and, in order to avoid the impression that complaints were being shelved, the interested parties posted the letters themselves. There was no need for an appointment to see the mayor on these occasions. As in a doctor's surgery, one simply awaited

---

[1] *Journal de Saint-Denis*, 14, 21, 28 October 1922; 11, 18, 25 November 1922; 6 January 1923; 3 March 1923; '*Réponses de M. André Guénier au questionnaire de Mr Geoffrey Warner*,' kindly sent me on 13 September 1965.

[2] 'Horizon blue' was the colour of the French army uniform. Compare the phrase 'khaki election' in British politics.

[3] '*Réponses de M. André Guénier . . .*', loc. cit.

one's turn.[1] Although Laval was able to devote less and less time to the *mairie* as his political star rose nationally, he retained the post of mayor until 1944, when he was deprived of it by General de Gaulle's provisional government.

Laval's 'takeover' of Aubervilliers was a bitter blow to the communists, who controlled it before he re-entered the scene and who have controlled it ever since the end of the Second World War. While it is impossible to prove, it is quite likely that the mutual antagonism which existed between Laval and the communists and which eventually came to distort completely the former's political outlook during the late 1930s and the Vichy period had its origins in this struggle for power in a Paris suburb in the early 1920s.

Laval duly won a place on the *Cartel des Gauches* list for the general election of 11 May 1924 and was re-elected to the Chamber of Deputies. He carefully refrained, however, from joining any of the party groups and sat as an independent.[2] His ministerial experience began about a year later, when he was appointed minister of public works in the second Painlevé government, which lasted from April to October 1925. Thereafter, he was under-secretary of state to the prime minister in the eighth Briand government from November 1925 to March 1926 and minister of justice in the ninth and tenth Briand governments, which lasted from March to July of the same year.[3] He does not seem to have made much of an impression in any of these posts. They were merely rungs on the ladder of political advancement.

In July 1926, however, the *Cartel des Gauches* majority was smashed as a result of a financial crisis and the former president, Raymond Poincaré, returned to power as the leader of a predominantly right-wing government. This shift of power from left to right in the middle of a legislature was to become characteristic of French politics in the inter-war years. It occurred again in 1934 and 1938.

The shift in the Chamber's centre of gravity towards the right was followed by a corresponding change in Laval's own position when, in January 1927, he stood for election to the Senate. Although a skilful politician, he does not seem to have enjoyed the cut-and-thrust of the hustings and preferred the quieter atmosphere of the indirect senatorial

---

[1] Ibid.
[2] *Le Temps*, 13 May 1924; J. O. Chambre, *Débats*, 26 June 1924, p. 2378.
[3] Bonnefous, Vol. IV, pp. 387, 389–90.

elections.[1] Yet this does not explain his desertion of the *Cartel des Gauches* for the right-wing National Republican Union list. There is no obvious reason for this. It probably reflected his age (43), his increased wealth, and his personal position in Aubervilliers as the communists' number one enemy. But if we must agree with David Thomson that 'it is 1927, rather than 1920, which marks his real desertion from the left',[2] the results of the election indicate that he enjoyed considerable personal support, some of it coming from left-wing electors.[3] Indeed, this ability to retain old ties, even when they cut across present political allegiances, was one of Laval's greatest assets.

It was not until March 1930 that Laval re-entered the government, as minister of labour and social security in the second Tardieu cabinet. His trade union background and his skill at handling people came in very useful when dealing with labour disputes. Pierre Tissier, who was a member of his secretariat, subsequently recalled the reception of a deputation of dockers on strike. 'The deputation . . . [was] determined to make a first-class row and to tell the "turncoat" Laval just what it thought of him,' Tissier wrote. 'Before five minutes had passed, Laval, who began to *tutoyer* each of the delegates, and called them by their first names, had the whole delegation in his pocket. With the help of his smile and his easy good nature, within half an hour he had obtained the ending of the strike, and yet had only given way to the dockers' demands on a few minor points.'[4] Similar techniques enabled him to settle the great textile strike in the Nord in August and September 1930.[5]

But Laval's greatest achievement in this period was in supervising the passage of the social insurance bill through parliament. Originally passed by the Chamber of Deputies in 1928, it needed extensive amendment if it was to be successfully implemented and the prime minister, André Tardieu, had promised that it would be on the statute book by 1 July 1930. The bill was one of immense complexity and Laval had to reconcile the frequently divergent views of Chamber and Senate. 'Had

[1] '*Réponses de M. André Guénier* . . . ,' loc. cit.; Odette Pannetier, *Pierre Laval*, Paris, Denoël et Steele, 1936, p. 37.
[2] David Thomson, *Two Frenchmen: Pierre Laval and Charles de Gaulle*, London, The Cresset Press, 1951, p. 30.
[3] *Le Temps*, 10 January 1927.
[4] Tissier, pp. 53–4.
[5] Ibid., p. 54; Jean-Stéphane Guille in *La Vie de la France*, Vol. III, p. 1329.

it not been for Laval's unwearying patience,' Tissier wrote, 'an agreement would never have been achieved,' and when the bill had passed its final stages, Tardieu paid a glowing tribute to his minister of labour, whom he described as 'displaying at every moment of the discussion as much tenacity as restraint and ingenuity'.[1]

During the years 1927–30 Laval began to accumulate the sizable personal fortune which later gave rise to the unjustified charge that he had used his political position to line his own pockets.[2] There was, it is true, a link between wealth and political power in Laval's mind, but it was not the one his enemies alleged. 'I have always thought,' he wrote to the examining magistrate on 11 September 1945, 'that a soundly-based material independence, if not indispensable, gives those statesmen who possess it a much greater political independence.'[3] Until 1927 his principal source of income had been his fees as a lawyer and in that year they totalled 113,350 francs, according to his income tax returns. Between August 1927 and June 1930, however, he undertook large-scale investments in various enterprises, totalling $5\frac{1}{2}$ million francs. Not all this money was his own by any means. It came from a group of financiers who enjoyed the backing of an investment trust, the *Union Syndicale et Financière* and two banks, the *Comptoir Lyon Allemand* and the *Banque Nationale de Crédit*.[4]

Two of the investments which Laval and his backers acquired were provincial newspapers, *Le Moniteur de Puy-de-Dôme* and its associated printing works at Clermont-Ferrand in his native Auvergne, and the *Lyon Républicain*. The circulation of the *Moniteur* stood at 27,000 in 1926 before Laval took it over. By 1933, it had more than doubled to 58,250. Thereafter it fell away again and never surpassed its earlier peak. Profits varied, but over the seventeen years of his control, Laval obtained some $3\frac{1}{2}$ million francs in income from the paper and the printing works combined, and the renewed plant was valued at 50 million francs, which led the high court expert to say with some justification that it had been 'an excellent affair for him'. Laval did not retain control over the *Lyon Républicain* for any length of time, selling

---

[1] Tissier, p. 48; Bonnefous, Vol. V, pp. 28–9. (Bonnefous is in error, however, in stating that the minister involved was Loucheur, who was Laval's predecessor.) J. O. Chambre, *Débats*, 23 April 1930, p. 2165, col. 2.

[2] See the *réquisitoire définitif* at his trial in 1945, *Procès Laval*, p. 27.

[3] *Laval Parle*, p. 21.

[4] *Rapport Caujolle*, pp. 259, 288–91.

his controlling interest in 1931 and 1932 to M. Raymond Patenôtre. The newspaper itself was not very profitable, but its sale brought him a capital gain of about 3 million francs.[1]

Another lucrative investment was Radio-Lyon, which Laval acquired in December 1928 for just under 400,000 francs. It was some years, however, before it began to make money and the turning-point in the station's fortunes seems to have occurred in 1936 when it began broadcasting advertisements in English.[2]

Although Laval made no attempt to use his radio station for political propaganda, leaving its director in full control,[3] he did use *Le Moniteur* as a vehicle for his political opinions on the principle that 'local newspapers make domestic politics'.[4] The editor of the paper, René Bonnefoy, has recalled how, in his daily editorials, he did no more than 'translate President Laval's thoughts and expand upon his own public statements'.[5] At the same time, politics were not allowed to stand in the way of circulation. Laval helped to choose the serials and increased the sports coverage. 'If I did put the *Moniteur* on its feet again,' he claimed, 'it was not by making it a political paper, but above all by making it a well set-out *news*paper.'[6]

The secret of his business successes, Laval later maintained, was in taking over run-down concerns like the *Moniteur* and Radio-Lyon and making them pay. But one had to be careful. 'A business which is in a bad way is only a good business if you know how to set it up. That doesn't happen by itself. You need work, discipline, will, and perseverance. I think I possess those qualities.'[7] When added to his Auvergnat tight-fistedness, the combination proved irresistible and Laval was undoubtedly one of the wealthiest men in French politics between the wars.

When the right-wing majority returned in the Chamber elections of 1928 showed signs of breaking up at the end of 1930, Laval, fresh from his triumphs as minister of labour and with his contacts ranging practically all the way across the political spectrum, was a natural choice as

[1] *Rapport Caujolle*, pp. 122–3, 133–4, 137–8, 144–6, 153–3 *bis*, 156–7.
[2] Ibid., pp. 174–8.
[3] Adolphe Anglade (Radio-Lyon's director) in *La Vie de la France*, Vol. III, pp. 1187–8.
[4] Laval made this remark to two Nazi party press officials in 1937. See unsigned memorandum, 14 May 1937, GFM/7657/E547235.
[5] René Bonnefoy in *La Vie de la France*, Vol. II, p. 928.
[6] Jaffré, pp. 47–8, 51.
[7] Ibid., p. 47.
2*

one of the potential prime ministers who might be able to form a government. But the radicals would not agree to serve in the same cabinet as members of the right-wing *Union Républicaine Démocratique* – mainly on account of the age-old clerical issue – and his first attempt to enter the Hôtel Matignon therefore failed.[1] At the end of January 1931, however, the interim government led by senator Théodore Steeg fell and President Doumergue invited him to try again. Once more, his efforts to secure radical participation proved fruitless, although he offered the party no less than five portfolios. One of his radical friends, Lucien Lamoureux, told him that there was no choice other than to base his government on the right, but that 'he would have a chance to appease feelings on the left and provoke a relaxation of tension which was desirable in every respect' if he did not appoint any extremists and tried to obtain the support of a few centre-left moderates. He suggested the names of a couple of the latter and Laval followed his advice and took them into his government. The formation of the cabinet was completed on 27 January and it received the approbation of the Chamber of Deputies on the 31st.[2] At the age of 47 and after nearly twenty years in politics, Pierre Laval had reached the summit.

[1] Bonnefous, Vol. V, p. 49; Michel Soulié, *La Vie Politique d'Edouard Herriot*, Paris, Armand Colin, 1962, p. 331.
[2] Bonnefous, Vol. V, pp. 60–62; Michel Soulié, op. cit., p. 332; Lucien Lamoureux in *La Bourbonnais Républicaine*, 26 June 1955. Lamoureux serialized his memoirs in this newspaper, which he owned.

I

Prime Minister

January 1931 – February 1932

Laval's reputation, prior to 1931, lay almost exclusively in the field of domestic politics, but the main interest of his first government lies in the light it throws upon what was to become the central preoccupation of the rest of his life: the problem of Franco-German relations. He always liked to believe that his approach to this question was pragmatic. 'We will always be neighbours of Germany,' he told his private secretary in 1931. 'We face the alternative of reaching an agreement with her or of clashing every twenty years on the battlefield.'[1] He had not changed his mind fourteen years later, after the Second World War. 'It has been said that I lacked idealism,' he wrote in his prison cell in 1945, 'doubtless because I believed and still do believe that, while politics must not neglect the imponderables, it must be based upon realities, especially in the foreign field. Régimes follow one another and revolutions take place, but geography remains unchanged. We will be neighbours of Germany for ever.'[2]

But there was rather more to it than this. 'M. Laval believed that world-wide peace hinged on keeping peace in Europe,' the American ambassador to France in 1931 wrote in his memoirs; 'that European peace hinged on cordial relations between France and Germany; and that France and Germany could work out their differences only if the British would refrain from interfering in European affairs in execution of their traditional balance-of-power policy. . . . He envisioned a future where Europe would be more or less united, Russia would be thrust back into Asia, and the Anglo-Saxon world would lead an

---

[1] André Guénier in *La Vie de la France*, Vol. III, p. 1346.
[2] *Laval Parle*, p. 89.

autonomous existence with the United States and France serving as the point of contact between the European and Anglo-Saxon world.'[1] Justifying the French refusal to disarm on the grounds of the danger of bolshevism, Laval told the German foreign minister in September 1931 that 'just as war was originally waged between towns, then between countries and recently between empires, so, in future, it would be waged between continents. He did not believe in a Franco-German conflict . . . but sooner or later the Russians and the Chinese would launch an attack upon Europe. We had to make ourselves safe against this.'[2] All the elements of Laval's future policies are to be found here: the anti-communism, the suspicion of Britain, and the desire for European unity based upon a Franco-German *entente*. It was the tragedy of his career that this vision was to find its apotheosis in Adolf Hitler's phoney European 'new order'.

Was this tragedy inevitable? The fascination of 1931 lies not so much in the course of events as in the tantalizing possibility that they contained the seeds of a Franco-German understanding which might have been reached before Hitler came to power and which might even have prevented him from doing so. Certainly, at first sight, Laval seemed ideally suited to break through the tangled web of mutual suspicion which enveloped Franco-German relations. He did not fight in the First World War, and he had no commitment to the treaty of Versailles which was the source of so much antagonism between the two countries. He had, in fact, voted against the treaty in the Chamber of Deputies and, to judge by his description in October 1931 of one of its major creations – the Polish corridor – as 'a monstrosity', his views on this subject had not changed as much as they had on some others.[3] He was, moreover, blessed with a frank and charming manner which impressed all those who came into contact with him. This may seem at odds with the reputation he now enjoys as a devious intriguer, but it is well attested in contemporary sources. 'Laval stands in a class by himself for frankness and directness and simplicity,' the American secre-

---

[1] Walter E. Edge, *A Jerseyman's Journal*, Princeton, N.J., Princeton University Press, 1948 (hereafter cited as Edge) p. 207.

[2] Curtius memorandum, 28 September 1931, GFM/2406/D51041–45.

[3] W. E. Scott, *Alliance Against Hitler*, Durham, N. C., Duke University Press, 1962, p. 23; Henry L. Stimson, *Diary* (typescript deposited in Yale University library), entry for 25 October 1931. This source is cited hereafter as Stimson, *Diary*, followed by the date of the entry.

tary of state, Henry L. Stimson, noted in his diary, 'and he is different from all other Frenchmen with whom I have negotiated in those respects.'[1] 'He impressed me strongly as a man of directness and solidity of mind,' wrote the British foreign secretary, Sir John Simon, 'with whom it was possible to pursue a subject consecutively in a way which Englishmen understand.'[2]

However, his direct approach could sometimes be a liability. 'In his opinion,' wrote a colleague who knew him well during this period, 'a frank exchange of views on a personal level, unencumbered by the formal language, the absurd discretion, and the childish precautions of diplomacy – about which he entertained the usual prejudices – must surely produce results. It was true that he was hampered neither by a knowledge of these problems nor by a desire to study them more closely. He freely admitted . . . that he possessed a rare talent for persuasion, which those with whom he spoke were unable to resist.'[3] However successful this technique may have been in dealing with the voters of Aubervilliers, his business acquaintances, and even deputies and senators of the French parliament, something more was needed for negotiations with the world's statesmen.

Even more important, Laval was working in an atmosphere of considerable constraint. Outwardly, France was all-powerful in Europe, with the largest army and air force and tremendous financial resources. But, in reality, her position was much less secure. Time and time again, she found herself isolated from Britain and the United States and left to face Germany alone in the company of her motley collection of east European client states, and while there was no doubt that she could easily overpower Germany in the immediate future, time was not on her side. Thus, her population was only 40 million compared with Germany's 60 million, and Germany's was increasing at a faster rate. In the five years 1926–30, France's coal and lignite production had averaged 52.8 million metric tons a year compared with Germany's 185.7 million, and, over the same period, her output of steel had averaged 9.1 million metric tons annually compared with Germany's

[1] Stimson, *Diary*, 23 October 1931.
[2] Enclosure in Simon to Vansittart, 17 November 1931, D.B.F.P., 2nd Series, Vol. II, No. 293.
[3] André François-Poncet, *Souvenirs d'une Ambassade à Berlin*, Paris, Flammarion, 1946, p. 21.

14.0 million.[1] In ten or twenty years time, it could be argued, the relative strengths of the two countries could, and probably would, be very different.

This contrast between France's apparent and real strength goes some way towards explaining the intransigence of the French right-wing parties towards Germany. They would have agreed with Henry Stimson's diagnosis that 'the Versailles treaty froze an extreme oscillation which was unfavourable to Germany at the point of furthest unfavourability', but they would not have accepted his conclusion that 'any attempt to perpetuate such an oscillation would meet with failure'.[2] Indeed, they would have taken the view that the Versailles settlement needed to be preserved intact precisely because it placed Germany in a position of perpetual inferiority. Any relaxation of its terms would send the pendulum, which was already weighted against France demographically and economically, swinging too far in the opposite direction.

In these circumstances it was unfortunate that the Laval government depended upon the right-wing parties for its parliamentary majority. Indeed, it included some of their most notable spokesmen among its members: men like André Maginot, the minister of war, Pierre-Etienne Flandin, the minister of finance, and André Tardieu, whose influence was far greater than his post as minister of agriculture would suggest. Laval lacked the strength, and possibly even the desire, to break away from the tutelage of his political supporters, and, as the elections which were scheduled to be held in the spring of 1932 grew nearer, their baneful influence upon his conduct became more and more evident. Reflecting upon the situation in December 1931, both the permanent head of the French foreign ministry, Philippe Berthelot, and the German ambassador in Paris, Leopold von Hoesch, were agreed that Laval seemed 'orientated in a purely negative direction'. Government statements, Hoesch commented, were replete with such phrases as 'France will never allow . . .' and 'France could not forgo . . .', and contained no constructive ideas whatever. 'The development of the domestic political situation here,' he explained, '. . . has

---

[1] The figures are from the *League of Nations Statistical Yearbook, 1932–33*, Geneva, 1933, pp. 22, 107, 118.

[2] Hoover/Stimson memorandum, 24 October 1931, attached to Stimson, *Diary*, 23 October 1931.

made [Laval] more and more a straightforward exponent of his majority, while the left – and even the radical left up to the left flank of his majority – has finally abandoned him.'[1]

There were similar obstacles to a *rapprochement* on the other side of the Rhine. For all his admiration of Laval – he subsequently described him as 'an humanitarian . . . and a great French patriot'[2] – the German chancellor, Heinrich Brüning, knew that unless he pursued a policy of narrow German self-interest, regardless of the effect this would have upon France, others would be only too glad to pursue that policy in his place. Like so many of the shaky governments of the Weimar period, Brüning's was largely dependent upon the support of the army and the latter's representative in the cabinet, the war minister General Gröner, was a nationalist and Francophobe. Outside the government were even more virulent extremists. In the elections of September 1930, Hitler's Nazi party had obtained nearly 6½ million votes (18 per cent of the total) and 107 out of 577 seats in the *Reichstag*, and they were by no means the only powerful right-wing extremist group in German politics. If anything, Brüning had even less room for manœuvre than Laval.

The three questions which dominated Franco-German relations during 1931 were Austria, reparations, and disarmament, with the ever-present problem of Germany's frontier with Poland never far below the surface. The fact that Austria came to loom so large was due to a misguided attempt by the German government to present France and her allies with a *fait accompli* in the shape of an Austro-German customs union. Various international agreements, notably the Versailles and Saint-Germain treaties and the Geneva protocol of 1922, forbade Austria and Germany from taking any steps which might compromise the former's independence or, in other words, lead to union or *Anschluss* between the two countries. But plans for a customs union, which the Germans certainly saw as the prelude to an *Anschluss*, had been in the air for some time and, when the German foreign minister visited Vienna at the beginning of March 1931, the two governments decided to go ahead with the scheme. Unfortunately, news

---

[1] Letter, Hoesch to Bülow, 17 December 1931, GFM/4620/E199842-8.
[2] In a letter, dated 3 January 1950, to M. René de Chambrun, a copy of which the latter kindly communicated to me.

of their agreement leaked out and precipitated an international crisis.[1] Its effects were not limited to Franco-German relations. On 1 March 1931, after months of patient negotiation, 'bases of agreement' had been reached between France and Italy on the question of naval construction, on which they had been unable to agree at the London naval conference of January–April 1930. When British, French, and Italian experts met in London on 19 March to work out the details, however, they were unable to do so. It was the French who were creating difficulties and it was widely believed that the reason for their intransigence was to put pressure on Italy to come out unequivocally against the Austro-German customs union. If this was so, the gambit failed and naval rivalry was still an issue between France and Italy when Laval made his better-known attempt to cement an understanding between the two countries four years later.[2]

There were also domestic repercussions inside France. Aristide Briand, the French foreign minister and veteran proponent of Franco-German reconciliation, had made the mistake of telling the Chamber of Deputies on the very day that the German foreign minister arrived in Vienna that 'although it had not entirely disappeared, this danger [of an *Anschluss*] at any rate no longer presents the urgency which was pointed out to me two years ago. If it had been as imminent as people tried to make out, it would already have taken place.'[3] For years, right-wingers had been arguing that Briand was blind to the threat of German revisionism; now they had their proof. In an embarrassed attempt to get rid of his foreign minister, Laval zealously promoted his candidature for the forthcoming election to the presidency of the republic, but other influential figures – including Tardieu – thought that Briand's election to the highest office in the land, even though its duties were largely symbolic, would only encourage the Germans still further, and they backed a rival candidate, the president of the Senate, Paul Doumer. When the election took place on 13 May, Doumer beat

---

[1] For the background of the Austro-German customs union plan, see Jürgen Gehl, *Austria, Germany and the Anschluss 1931–38*, London, Oxford University Press, 1963, pp. 1–10; F. G. Stambrook, 'The German-Austrian Customs Union Project of 1931: A Study of German Methods and Motives', *Journal of Central European Affairs*, April 1961, pp. 15–44.

[2] Gehl, op. cit., pp. 14–15; Arnold J. Toynbee, *et al.*, *Survey of International Affairs 1931*, London, Oxford University Press for the Royal Institute of International Affairs, 1932 (hereafter cited as Survey for 1931), pp. 259–78.

[3] J. O. Chambre, *Débats*, 3 March 1931, p. 1525, col. 3.

Briand into second place on the first ballot and the latter withdrew from the contest. He stayed on as foreign minister until January 1932, but his authority was shattered and, in the field of Franco-German relations in particular, the lead was henceforth taken by Laval and other ministers.[1]

France did not find an effective means of blocking the Austro-German customs union until May 1931, when the collapse of Austria's largest bank, the *Credit-Anstalt*, created a desperate need for liquidity which she was one of the few countries in a position to fulfil. It was probably this factor more than any other which induced the Austrian foreign minister, Dr Schober, to promise the League of Nations council on 18 May that 'no further progress would be made towards the establishment of the proposed [customs union] régime' before the international court had pronounced upon its legality. This promise was made without consultation with the Germans.[2] A month later, when the financial situation had deteriorated still further, the Austrian ambassador was summoned to the Quai d'Orsay and presented with an ultimatum. The French government agreed to put up the money to cover the Austrian government's advance to the *Credit-Anstalt* on the following conditions: the Austrian government had to issue a declaration, the text of which was provided, stating that it had decided to ask the League of Nations council to proceed to an immediate examination of Austria's economic and financial situation and that it was ready to accept, in advance, whatever the council recommended. Secondly, the Austrian government was to send a note to the French government, the text of which was also provided and which the French intended to publish, declaring that its decision to appeal to the League council 'implies the formal renunciation on its part of any combination, either economic or political, which is capable of modifying the international status of Austria', or, in other words, the customs union with Germany. Dr Schober indignantly told the French ambassador in Vienna that 'neither he nor any other Austrian minister would ever accept such a

---

[1] For the French presidential election, see Bonnefous, Vol V, pp. 84–8; Edge, pp. 189–90; Henry Lémery, *D'une République à l'Autre*, Paris, La Table Ronde, 1964, pp. 135–7; Jacques Debû-Bridel, *L'Agonie de la Troisième République*, Paris, Editions du Bâteau Ivre, 1948, pp. 138–50; Lucien Lamoureux in *La Bourbonnais Républicaine*, 10 July 1955; *Le Temps*, 10, 11, 12, 13, 14 and 15 May 1931. The accusation, made by Bonnefous and Edge amongst others, that Laval deliberately sabotaged Briand's chances while at the same time encouraging him to stand for election, is not substantiated by the bulk of the evidence.

[2] Survey for 1931, pp. 316–17; Curtius to Bülow, 19 May 1931, GFM/3086/D615760–62.

capitulation',[1] but he might have had to swallow his pride had not the Bank of England agreed to advance the necessary sum instead.[2] But it was only a short-term loan and, as the French ambassador in London cynically remarked to Sir Robert Vansittart of the Foreign Office, 'Austria would in any case have to address herself to the League; . . . the question of a new loan would arise and that would be the occasion for his government to renew the condition they had laid down as to renunciation of the customs union; but that the condition might be put in a milder and more tactful form.'[3] This was exactly what happened.[4]

In the meantime, however, the financial crisis had spread to Germany and set in train a process which threatened to engulf the entire capitalist world. H. V. Hodson has described it in the following words: 'An individual bank, or the banking system of a country or of the world as a whole, has to remain liquid or perish. If one item among its assets, which had been regarded as liquid, becomes unrealizable for the time being, it must improve its proportion of liquidity by realizing other assets. What happened in this case was that the failure of the *Credit-Anstalt* involved a complete loss of confidence in Austrian finance and therefore a "standstill" upon all banking assets held in Austria. In order to cover their position, banks were forced to encash other foreign balances. . . . It was natural that the attempt to liquidate foreign assets should have seized upon Germany as its next victim. Her financial houses were closely associated with those of Austria. . . . Unprecedented sums had been invested in Germany by foreigners within the space of a few years, both at short term and at long term. Her obligation to pay reparations, at a time when commodity prices were low and were still falling, and when the inflow of capital had been completely stopped, caused the creditors grave uneasiness.'[5]

Reparations were the crucial link between the financial crisis and Franco-German relations. They had been repeatedly scaled down during the 1920s, but still stood at 110,735.7 million gold marks payable in 59 annual instalments according to the Young plan[6] of 1930,

---

[1] Clodius to Foreign Ministry, 17 June 1931, ibid., D615862–4.
[2] Atherton to Stimson, 17 June 1931, F.R.U.S., 1931, Vol. I, pp. 23–4.
[3] Enclosure in Henderson to Tyrrell, 23 June 1931, D.B.F.P., 2nd Series, Vol. II, No. 76.
[4] See below, p. 40.
[5] Survey for 1931, p. 211.
[6] So named after the American banker, Owen D. Young, who chaired the committee responsible for devising it.

which was the latest revision. 59,845.5 million marks of this total sum was payable to France.[1] It was one of the major aims of German foreign policy to get rid of reparations altogether, while France was equally determined that her 'sacred right' to these payments should be upheld. After the failure of the *Credit-Anstalt*, the German government began to contemplate a temporary suspension of payments within the framework of the Young plan, but as the run on the mark increased during June, it began to wonder whether this was enough. At crisis talks on 19 June, Hoesch, the German ambassador in Paris, told Brüning and his advisers that, while there was 'considerable sympathy' for Germany's difficulties in France, 'he could not conceive that the idea of a revision of the Young plan could have a real chance of success. None of the European creditors would be prepared to renounce any of their claims if their obligations to America remained the same. In practice, none of the creditor nations wanted to abandon the connection between reparations payments and the debt agreements with America. In the final analysis, it was once again a question of what effect the declaration of a moratorium would have upon America, and he was compelled to recommend in this connection that top priority be given to making special contact with America.'[2]

Hoesch had put his finger on the major difficulty facing a further revision of the reparations settlement. The only condition upon which France would conceivably accept a permanent reduction in the amount of reparations due to her was if there was a corresponding reduction in the amount of war debt, totalling nearly $7,000 million,[3] which she owed the United States. The American government, however, had consistently refused to recognize any connection between reparations, to which it had never laid claim, and what it regarded as perfectly legitimate inter-governmental obligations.

But unknown to Hoesch, and indeed to everyone else outside a small circle of his closest advisers, President Hoover of the United States had already decided upon a dramatic initiative which seemed to offer a way out of the dilemma. No less than 41 per cent of Germany's foreign debt was owed to American creditors and it was thus evident

---

[1] See the schedule of repayments set out on p. 15 of *Economist*, Supplement on 'Reparations and War Debts', 23 January 1932.

[2] Curtius to Hoesch, 13 June 1931, GFM/3243/D729102–10; Vogels memorandum, 19 June 1931, ibid., L170/L045623–36.

[3] *Economist*, Supplement on 'Reparations and War Debts', 23 January 1932, p. 6.

that any collapse of the German financial system would have the gravest repercussions upon the United States, which was already in the depths of economic depression. After much soul-searching, Hoover decided that the best contribution he could make to the situation was to propose a year-long moratorium on all inter-governmental obligations, reparations and war debts alike. In order to avoid the risk of subsequent congressional repudiation, he canvassed the idea with a number of influential senators and representatives. The inevitable press leak followed and, in order to avoid further speculation, Hoover released the full text of his plan on 20 June.[1]

It might be thought that the French government would have welcomed the proposed Hoover moratorium, with its implicit recognition of the link between reparations and war debts, but not a bit of it. In the first place, France stood to lose financially under the proposal because the sum due to her in reparations exceeded by far the amount of war debt she had to repay.[2] Secondly, the proposal had been sprung on the French without prior consultation. 'It is not so much the content of President Hoover's proposal that has aroused our people,' Laval told the American ambassador, but 'the shock tactics which have been employed in presenting [it] to us'.[3] Thirdly, unlike the moratorium which could be claimed under the Young plan and which, as we have seen, the German government was thinking of claiming, the Hoover proposal made no distinction between the so-called 'conditional annuities', which could be suspended in time of economic difficulty, and the 'unconditional annuities', which had to be paid at all times. 'Essentially,' Hoesch cabled from Paris on 24 June, 'France sees what she has interpreted as her completely hallowed right to her conditional claims for reparations called into question.' She was 'enraged' that this claim should be placed on a par with American war debt claims and 'staggered' that it was being modified so soon after the entry into force

[1] Richard Ferrell, *American Diplomacy in the Great Depression*, New Haven, Yale University Press, 1957, p. 117, fn. 17; Louis P. Lochner, *Herbert Hoover and Germany*, New York, The Macmillan Company, 1960, pp. 83–95; Charles G. Dawes, *Journal as Ambassador*, New York, The Macmillan Company, 1939, pp. 350–51; Stimson, *Diary*, 5, 8, 13, 15 and 19 June 1931; *The Times*, 21 June 1931.
[2] The figures were: receipts from reparations – £39·7 million; war debt repayments – £23·6 million; i.e. a net loss of £16·1 million. It should be added, however, that the United States was proposing to forgo £53·6 million (*Economist*, Supplement on 'Reparations and War Debts', 23 January 1932, p. 7).
[3] Edge, p. 195.

of the Young plan. The president's proposal was seen as 'a scandalous presumption and an unparalleled interference with French rights', motivated solely by America's self-interest in wishing to protect her investments in Germany. The whole thing, in fact, was looked upon as a 'German–Anglo-Saxon plot'.[1] Finally, the French saw the proposal as the thin end of the wedge. 'If we do renounce our right to reparation payments,' Laval asked the American ambassador, '. . . what guarantee will be given to us by the United States and Great Britain that these payments will be resumed at the end of one year?'[2] Events were to prove that this was an entirely justified concern.

It took nearly three weeks of feverish negotiation in Paris before a settlement was reached on 7 July, whereby the German government was to continue to pay the unconditional annuities, but only in the form of guaranteed bonds of the German railways, and not to France, but to the Bank of International Settlements in Basle.[3] What may have compelled the French to come to terms was the repeated threat from the American side that, if they did not agree, the president would simply repeat his proposal to each country individually.[4] As the major countries involved, including Germany, Britain, and Italy, had already accepted it, this would have left France in a position of more or less complete isolation. In the meantime, Laval's government only managed to survive a vote of confidence in the Chamber of Deputies due to the unaccustomed support of the socialists.[5]

The French government desperately sought to use the breathing-space provided by the Franco-American negotiations to try and reach a direct understanding with Germany. On 22 June, for example, the Berlin representative of the Lee Higginson banking firm, a Mr Courtney, approached Brüning with a number of suggestions which he claimed emanated from the French government and which were designed to facilitate French acceptance of the Hoover moratorium. The core of these suggestions was that Brüning should make a public speech before the French parliament rose for the summer recess in which he

---

[1] Hoesch to Foreign Ministry, 24 June 1931, GFM/3243/D29233–6. The reference to an 'Anglo-Saxon' plot was doubtless due to the fact that the British government had never made any secret of its belief that reparations should be abolished.
[2] Edge, p. 192.
[3] The negotiations can be followed in F.R.U.S., 1931, Vol. I, pp. 42–164.
[4] Castle to Edge, 29, 30 June, 4 July 1931, ibid., pp. 88–91, 117–18 and 133.
[5] Le Temps, 28 June 1931.

would state, among other things, 'that it was his intention to leave the study of problems arising out of the war to the appropriate machinery, sheltered from the passion of public opinion and political parties . . . that time will bring easier solution to these problems, made all the more easier of solution if in the meanwhile there have been established between nations a real basis of co-operation in the work of European reconstruction . . . that Germany should now devote herself to the study of co-operation and to that end recognizing the important role France could play . . . is ready to examine various financial and economic problems which are disturbing Europe in collaboration with French leaders.'[1] To have accepted a dialogue on this basis would have been tantamount to abandoning all Germany's claims for the revision of the Versailles treaty, at any rate for the moment. Brüning was simply not interested and told Courtney outright that 'a continuation of the discussion on the basis of [these] points did not seem practicable in any direction, especially since, from the German point of view, an objective discussion of individual points along these lines was quite impossible'.[2] Another approach, made by Laval's undersecretary of state, André François-Poncet, at Geneva on 25 June was similarly ignored.[3] There were two reasons for German intransigence. In the first place, as Brüning told his closest advisers on 30 June, 'political concessions of any kind with respect to France were quite out of the question. . . . In the existing situation, no German government which yielded on these points would be able to survive.'[4] Secondly, the Germans were fully apprised of the American threats to France and they must have felt that they could afford to hold out.[5]

But the delay in French acceptance of the Hoover proposal aggravated the German financial crisis. A temporary credit of $100 million had been granted the *Reichsbank* by the B.I.S., the Bank of England, the Bank of France, and the Federal Reserve Bank of New York, but this proved insufficient, especially after the failure on 3 July of one of Germany's largest corporations. Foreign speculation against the mark

[1] Curtius to Hoesch, 23 June 1931, GFM/3243/D729164-9. The quotation is from Courtney's own handwritten notes in English, ibid., D729170-74.
[2] Pünder memorandum, 24 June 1931, ibid., L170/L045658-9.
[3] Lammers to Brüning, 25 June 1931, ibid., 3243/D729294-6.
[4] Berger memorandum, 30 June 1931, ibid., L170/L045691-2.
[5] Leitner to Foreign Ministry, 1 July 1931, ibid., 3243/D729377; Curtius memorandum, 1 July 1931, ibid., D729398-400.

was now reinforced by domestic withdrawals, and, on 9 and 10 July alone, the *Reichsbank* had to provide 100 million *Reichsmarks* of foreign exchange.[1] The efforts of the bank's president, Dr Hans Luther, to raise an additional loan met with no success. The British and Americans were unable to help and the French continued to attach political strings to any offer they made. They were now talking about a generalized 'moratorium' on all Germany's political demands.[2]

Suddenly, however, there took place what appeared to be a complete change in the French position. In one more desperate appeal for help, Hoesch saw Laval on 12 July. He was surprised when the French prime minister, while expressing his scepticism about the possibility of financial assistance, made no mention of political conditions. Indeed, he said that 'the question of political conditions, which had never in fact been formally demanded by France, had been overtaken by events. . . . He realized full well that there was only one thing that mattered now: whether Germany could be saved and how.'[3] This may have been nothing more than a subtle ploy to entice Brüning to Paris, which was something the French had been trying to do for some time. If so, it worked, although the Germans went into it with their eyes wide open.[4] The situation was complicated by the British government's almost simultaneous proposal for a conference of heads of government in London to examine the financial crisis. British zeal in taking up what had originally been an American suggestion is partly explained by the fact that the pound was now beginning to show unmistakable signs of weakness. This was of little concern to the French, however, who refused to come to London until they had seen the Germans in Paris. In addition, they wanted a preliminary meeting of all the interested powers in Paris to lay the foundations for the London conference. It took three days of complicated negotiations just to settle the sequence of events, and it was finally agreed that Brüning and Curtius, his foreign minister, would come to Paris on 18 and 19 July and that the London conference would open on the 20th.[5]

---

[1] Survey for 1931, pp. 212–13.

[2] Planck memorandum, 11 July 1931, GFM/L170/L045829–46; Hoesch to Foreign Ministry, 11 July 1931, ibid., 3375/D731769–73.

[3] Hoesch to Foreign Ministry, 13 July 1931, ibid., D731789–92.

[4] See, for example, Bülow to Hoesch, 14 July 1931, ibid., D731821–3.

[5] Survey for 1931, pp. 215–17; Henderson memorandum, 20 July 1931, D.B.F.P., 2nd Series, Vol. II, No. 193; Bülow memoranda, 16 July 1931, GFM/3375/D731857–63, D731864, D731865, D731868, D731869, D731870.

But this still did not settle the scope of the preliminary discussions in Paris. Laval took advantage of the presence in the French capital of both the British foreign secretary, who had been *en route* for Berlin, and the American secretary of state, who had arrived on the second leg of a long-planned European tour, to unveil a new French proposal for a ten-year loan of $500 million to Germany. In spite of Stimson's initial impression that the French proposal, which contained no hint of political conditions at this stage, was 'not as bad as [he] had feared', it was rejected outright by both the United States and British governments on the grounds that neither was in a position to back it. Hoover's view was that existing lines of credit were sufficient, provided they could be maintained. As the American under-secretary of state put it in a message for Stimson, 'if present lines of credit are maintained, the proposed $500 million is not needed. If these lines are not maintained, $500 is merely a drop in the bucket.' As for the British, prime minister Ramsay Macdonald warned his foreign secretary, Henderson, that 'it seems to us essential that conversations in Paris should not . . . assume appearance of replacing or even prejudging London conference.'[1]

Thus, when Laval announced plans for a conference with the Germans in Paris at an Anglo-French-American meeting on 17 July, Henderson made what Stimson called a rather stiff speech warning the French that he would refuse to participate in any meeting which might prejudge the London conference. Laval replied that the purpose of these conferences was to help him float his loan in Paris. He said that if he tried to present to the French a loan which had been made in London it would be represented by the press as having been imposed upon the French by the London conference. This would not succeed and therefore he wanted to have these preliminary conferences first. Stimson interposed to say that while he sympathized with anything that would help raise money for the Germans, these preliminary discussions must not result in decisions and he warned Laval that if the press was informed that decisions had been reached, he would be compelled to issue a denial. Laval agreed to make no statement to the press.[2]

[1] Unsigned memorandum, 16 July 1931, F.R.U.S., 1931, Vol. I, pp. 265–8; Castle to Edge, 16, 17 July 1931, ibid., pp. 268–9, 275–8; Tyrrell to Vansittart, 16 July 1931 (twice), D.B.F.P., 2nd Series, Vol. II, Nos. 199, 205; Vansittart to Tyrrell, 16 July 1931, ibid., No. 208; Stimson, *Diary*, 16 July 1931.
[2] Stimson, *Diary*, 17 July 1931.

But no one present apparently saw fit to tell Laval that his loan plan was unacceptable in any case. There was no such reticence, however, in informing the Germans, before they set out for Paris.[1]

At 2 p.m. on 18 July, Brüning and Curtius arrived in Paris. The German chancellor had an hour-long tête-à-tête with Laval, of which no record is available, before the main Franco-German talks got under way at 4.30. At these, Brüning began as requested by outlining his country's financial plight. The French finance minister, Flandin, then described the broad outlines of the French loan proposal and set out the purely financial conditions which Germany would have to accept to obtain the loan. Laval then proceeded to enlarge the basis of the discussion. '. . . Any financial help by France did not depend solely upon financial guarantees,' he said, 'but must be based upon an overall improvement of the atmosphere in relations between the two countries.' He then listed some of the things which had been disturbing this atmosphere of late, such as the Austro-German customs union, Germany's proposal to build a second 'pocket battleship',[2] recent speeches by right-wing extremists and the attitude of the Nazis. Laval said that 'he readily appreciated the difficulties which could arise for the chancellor out of these questions as far as the German people were concerned, but stressed at the same time the difficulties which would accrue to the French government without a thorough improvement in the atmosphere in respect of all these contentious matters. He therefore put forward the idea of a political moratorium and declared repeatedly that it was a question of finding a formula which was still tolerable for Germany and yet would offer France the possibility of negotiating the loan which . . . Flandin had proposed. In this connection he mentioned the suggestion, put forward in his personal conversation with the chancellor by the latter, to implement such a moratorium for one year.' While stressing the difficulties in reaching an agreed formula, especially if it contained references to specific questions, Brüning made no attempt to deny that he had in fact suggested a period of one year for Laval's proposed political moratorium. It

[1] Louis P. Lochner, *Herbert Hoover and Germany*, New York, The Macmillan Company, 1960, pp. 114–15.

[2] 'Pocket battleships' were relatively lightly-armoured vessels with heavy calibre guns which the Germans were building to get around the restrictions imposed by the Versailles treaty.

was agreed that an attempt should be made to draft a joint statement and that another meeting would take place the following afternoon to examine the results.[1]

From what took place at this second meeting, however, it seems that both Laval and Brüning had made more concessions than their colleagues were prepared to accept. Flandin took the lead in insisting that the political moratorium must last for as long as the proposed loan – i.e. ten years – while the Germans replied that 'even a temporary sacrifice of their legal rights was out of the question'. Realizing that the gulf between the two sides was unbridgable, Laval brought the meeting to a close with a realistic and sympathetic statement of the position which greatly impressed his German listeners. 'If he committed himself to the negotiation of a loan to Germany without clear guarantees,' he said, 'it would mean the end of the French government. Similarly, Chancellor Brüning would be brought down if he complied with the French demands. He therefore wanted to exact nothing at all from the German minister, although he must preserve complete freedom of negotiation in the matter of financial assistance.' He proposed to shelve the question of a loan and a political moratorium and to refer only to the friendly nature of the German visit in the communiqué. 'At the very least, this would not prejudice the atmosphere of the London negotiations,' he concluded. 'Besides, he had no right to persist in negotiating the French conditions for a loan when it was by no means certain that a loan would materialize in London at all.'[2]

Laval, of course, was right. What the London conference did was to accept President Hoover's proposal for the stabilization of existing credits and set up a committee of experts 'to enquire into the immediate further credit needs of Germany and to study the possibilities of converting a portion of the short-term credits into long-term credits'.[3] When this committee reported on 18 August, however, all it could do, apart from announcing the imminent conclusion of an agreement to prolong Germany's short-term credits for a period of six months, was to reaffirm the well-known fact that the real obstacles to the granting of long-term credits were political rather than financial and urge

[1] Unsigned memorandum, 18 July 1931, GFM/3375/D731920–26.
[2] Undated von Häften memorandum, GFM/5724/H025928–30; Curtius to Foreign Ministry, 20 July 1931, ibid., 3375/D731954–5.
[3] The full records of the London conference are printed in D.B.F.P., 2nd Series, Vol. II, pp. 435–84.

the governments concerned to get together and do something about it.[1]

On the face of it, therefore, the Paris and London conferences did not achieve very much. In concrete terms this was undoubtedly so, but at the psychological level they did produce an improvement in Franco-American and, above all, in Franco-German relations which seemed to augur well for the future. Stimson, for example, was tremendously impressed by Laval. 'My impression of Laval has steadily risen during this series of conferences from the first time I met him in Paris,' he noted in his diary. 'He has shown himself to be an able, forceful man and I think also a sincere man. . . . His speeches in the conference were always to the point, clear and forceful. In his talks with me he was extremely frank and towards the end of our acquaintance mani-fested the utmost friendliness.'[2] In a letter to President Hoover he wrote, 'My present impression is that in Laval we have a hopeful figure for the future in respect to French foreign policy. Briand is failing, but unless I am greatly mistaken we can hope for Laval to give to moderate French policy a new leadership. His attitude . . . was in refreshing contrast to the viewpoint of Tardieu with whom I also talked.'[3] In view of the strain to which Franco-American relations had been subjected as a result of the wrangling over the Hoover moratorium, the fact that Stimson and Laval had got on so well with one another was of con-siderable importance.

As far as Germany was concerned, Hoesch noted in a lengthy report which he sent to Berlin on 21 August that 'the improvement in the atmosphere of Franco-German relations . . . and the personal rela-tions of trust which have so happily been established between the leading statesmen of both countries constitute a valuable new factor in so far as the mutual understanding of the possibilities and the limita-tions of both governments has been noticeably enhanced and the danger of fundamental discord over differences of opinion has been significantly reduced.'[4] The most obvious consequence of this change of mood was the visit which Laval and Briand paid to Berlin at the end

[1] The report of the experts' committee is printed in ibid., pp. 485–94.
[2] Stimson, *Diary*, 24 July 1931.
[3] Letter, Stimson to Hoover, 11 August 1931, F.R.U.S., 1931, Vol. I, pp. 315–23. The quotation is from p. 321.
[4] Hoesch report, 21 August 1931, GFM/K936/K240776–89. The quotation is from frame K240779.

of September.[1] It was the first official visit of leading French statesmen to the German capital since the congress of Berlin in 1878.

Unfortunately, by the time the visit took place, a number of events had occurred which either threatened to jeopardize its success or else seemed to reduce its significance.

The first concerned the Austro-German customs union. Just a month after its ultimatum to the Austrian government in June had been rejected, the French government returned to the charge, but in a much more subtle way. It was freely admitted that the earlier approach had been 'too direct and brutal' and it was now suggested that the whole question of an enquiry into Austria's financial and economic position and Austria's acceptance of its findings should be left to the League of Nations and that, as far as the customs union itself was concerned, it was up to the Austrian government to make whatever statements it saw fit. Freed of the ultimatum, the Austrians clearly felt more able to oblige the French, especially as they knew that the bulk of any financial assistance they received would have to come from France in any case. On 3 September, therefore, the Austrian foreign minister announced at Geneva that his government no longer intended to go ahead with the customs union. Two days later, the International Court, to which the matter had been referred, ruled that the proposed union was in any case incompatible with the Geneva protocol. The Germans sat through all this with a stiff upper lip, but it was clearly a great blow to their prestige. Indeed, it forced the resignation of foreign minister Curtius, who had been the driving force behind the scheme. He had already made up his mind to resign before Laval and Briand arrived in Berlin, but agreed to stay on for their visit. He was then replaced by Brüning himself.[2]

The second event was the British financial crisis, which led to the replacement of the second Labour government by the 'national' government, and the decision, announced on 20 September, that Britain was leaving the gold standard. 'After first shock,' the British ambassador reported from Berlin on the 22nd, 'it is thought that latest development may hasten measures necessary to restore the world to health and in

[1] The visit was originally planned for August but had to be postponed because of Briand's ill health.
[2] Curtius memoranda, 31 August, 4 September 1931, GFM/3086/ D616009–14; D616041–57; Curtius to Rieth, 1 August 1931, ibid., 5002/E285292–301; Survey for 1931, pp. 319–22; Rumbold to Reading, 6 October 1931, D.B.F.P., 2nd Series, Vol. II, No. 262.

particular help Germany by compelling revision of reparations and war debts.'[1]

Thirdly, only a few days before the visit, the French war minister, André Maginot, had written to Briand claiming that the Germans had infringed the disarmament clauses of the Versailles treaty by setting up a number of new motorized detachments in the German army.[2] German

[1] Rumbold to Reading, 22 September 1931, D.B.F.P., 2nd Series, Vol. II, No. 252. For the background to the British government's decision, see Survey for 1931, pp. 223–30.

In parenthesis, it is interesting to note that when, in later years, he was accused of Anglophobia, Laval always liked to recall how he came to Britain's rescue during the financial crisis of September 1931. '. . . Called upon in the middle of the night to receive Mr Campbell, the *chargé d'affaires*, immediately,' he subsequently wrote, '. . . I agreed, without consulting the cabinet so as not to damage Great Britain's credit through indiscretions, to grant her that very morning a credit of 3,000 million francs from the French treasury. The coffers of the Bank of England were empty and payments would have had to have been suspended without the spontaneous assistance of France. Mr Campbell thanked me with emotion and, shaking me by the hand, said, *"Monsieur le Président*, my country will never forget".' (*Laval Parle*, p. 26.) In a preface to the English edition of Laval's prison notes, his daughter adds the important detail that he advised the British to approach the United States to put up half the required credit, but that if – as he suspected – it would not do so, then France would provide the lot (*The Unpublished Diary of Pierre Laval*, London, Falcon Press, 1948, p. 11.)

All his biographers have accepted his version of what happened, apparently not stopping to wonder why, if it is true, Britain still had to go off gold. In fact, the documents which are carefully reproduced in Laval's post-war apologia do not quite support his own assertions. One, a memorandum from the Chancellor of the Exchequer, refers to the tremendous drain on Britain's gold reserves and warns that 'in the absence of further credits the government reluctantly will have no alternative but to suspend gold payments'. British bankers did not believe it would be possible to obtain sufficiently large banking credits to prevent this. 'In these circumstances,' the memorandum concludes, 'I think that it is only right to inform you in confidence of the position in case your government can help.' (English text in The *Unpublished Diary of Pierre Laval*, pp. 192–5.) This document, together with a French translation, was handed over to Laval on the night of 18–19 September (see Campbell's letter, dated the 18th, printed in the *Unpublished Diary*, p. 187 and *Laval Parle*, p. 233). The other document reproduced is a letter from Campbell to Laval dated the 19th. This states that the United States government had been approached for credits, but had been unable to help. 'In these circumstances,' the letter continued, 'the British government is compelled to put into force the measures foreseen in the Chancellor of the Exchequer's message.' Parliament would take the necessary action on Monday, 21 September. 'At the same time,' the letter concluded, 'I am requested to express to you . . . the very sincere thanks of the British government for the very friendly way in which you received its appeal, which is greatly appreciated. The doubt which you expressed as to the effectiveness of any expedient at the present time has been entirely confirmed by the fact that the total of withdrawals in the last four days has reached £40 million or 5,000 million francs' (*Unpublished Diary*, pp. 196–8; *Laval Parle*, pp. 238–40).

This would surely suggest that Laval did not offer to put up the whole sum regardless of the attitude of the United States, and that, on the contrary, he did not think any measures could prevent Britain from going off gold. He may have offered some money, and plenty of sympathy, but he did not save the pound. An interesting final point is that there is no record whatever of any of these transactions in the published documents on British foreign policy.

[2] Forster to Bülow, 24 September 1931, GFM/2406/D510092–3.

rearmament was an extremely sensitive issue for both politicians and public opinion in France and the incident can only have strengthened the hand of those in the government who felt that Germany was not to be trusted and that not much was to be expected from the visit.

Finally, the visit was to a large extent overshadowed by the news that Laval had accepted an invitation to go to Washington in the near future for talks with the United States government.[1] Britain's decision to leave the gold standard had underlined the pre-eminent position of France and the United States in world affairs and it was clear that new initiatives, particularly in the field of reparations and war debts, were more likely to come from the talks in Washington than from those in Berlin.[2]

The effect of all these factors was apparent in Laval's first tête-à-tête with Brüning in Berlin on the morning of 27 September. Although the chancellor felt that the conversation was 'very harmonious' and 'obviously completely frank' on Laval's part, he did not feel that it was 'as fruitful as his corresponding discussion two months previously in Paris'. Laval seemed to Brüning 'to have become much more solemn' and freely admitted at the outset of the conversation that 'he had no authority from his cabinet to discuss any of the important unsolved questions between France and Germany'. Thus he would not allow himself to be drawn into any discussion of reparations or war debts and, when it came to the question of disarmament, he took the line that 'rearmed France constituted precisely the only *bloc* inside Europe against what was perhaps imminent bolshevist chaos. If France, too, had disarmed, there would be no other country at all in Europe which could offer resistance.'[3] This well-worn argument cut very little ice with the Germans who knew full well that it was their country, and not Russia, which was the object of French precautions.

This conversation, therefore, together with the subsequent plenary sessions dealt mainly with the one subject which Laval was empowered to discuss: the establishment of a Franco-German economic committee. The origin of this proposal was a scheme put forward by the French government as a reply to the Austro-German customs union. Devised

[1] Edge to Stimson, 19 September 1931, F.R.U.S., 1931, Vol. II, p. 237; Stimson to Edge, 19 September 1931, ibid., p. 238; Edge to Stimson, 21 September 1931, ibid., pp. 239–40; Edge, p. 205.
[2] Luther note, 26 September 1931, GFM/2406/D510116–17.
[3] Pünder memorandum, 27 September 1931, GFM/K2083/K553539–46.

essentially by François-Poncet, then under-secretary of state to the prime minister and now the new French ambassador to Berlin and owing much to his connections with the world of big business, the French scheme called among other things for increased cartellization of European industry to combat the depression.[1] It had temporarily dropped out of sight during the financial crisis, but in the euphoria which followed the Paris and London conferences, it was revived in a purely Franco-German context both by the French government and private industry. On 13 August Laval told Hoesch that one of the things he hoped to see come out of the French visit to Berlin was the 'setting up of a Franco-German study group, composed of high officials and economic leaders, working under the aegis of ministers, and having as its task the formulation of a programme for the organization and sharing of production'.[2] A decision to set up such a joint committee was in fact announced in the communiqué issued at the close of the Franco-German talks. The committee met for the first time in Paris on 13 November, with Laval himself in the chair. Four sub-committees – dealing with trade and cartels, transport, general economic policy, and external co-operation – had already been set up and it was agreed that these should meet, either in Paris or Berlin, later the same month or in December.[3] The Franco-German economic committee produced some modest achievements, but never became the foundation-stone of Franco-German co-operation which some of its most fervent advocates hoped. Its history clearly shows that economic co-operation does not of itself lead to political co-operation. There has to be a basic community of political interests.

Just how wide the gap still was between France and Germany on political questions can be seen from what happened on the one occasion when Laval tried to go beyond the narrow brief he had been given by his cabinet colleagues and discuss some of the real issues which divided the two countries. During a car journey with Brüning, 'he casually alluded to the fact that there were many different plans in

---

[1] For the text of the French plan, see Enclosure in Henderson to Tyrrell, 4 May 1931, D.B.F.P., 2nd Series, Vol. II, No. 31. For François-Poncet's business connections and political views, see the memorandum of the German foreign ministry protocol department, 22 September 1931, GFM/K2083/K553521–5.

[2] Hoesch to Foreign Ministry, 13 August 1931, ibid., 2406/D509925–31.

[3] *The Times*, 29 September 1931; *Le Temps*, 9, 16, 31 October, 5, 14 and 15 November 1931. Much information on the genesis of the Franco-German economic committee and its subsequent development is contained in files GFM/5762 and ibid.,/K2086.

existence to settle the sharply opposed standpoints of Germany and Poland [over the Polish corridor] in the direction of a benevolent compromise,' whereupon the chancellor brusquely cut him short with the observation that 'in this national question, in which the whole of Germany – regardless of party – was happily of one mind, a compromise was completely out of the question. Every German government must and would continue to insist that the wrong done to the German people by the delineation of the frontier in the east be put right without compromise.'[1] So much for conciliation!

If the visit to Berlin failed to produce any significant step forward in the political field, could that to Washington provide anything more substantial? Although he was worried by President Hoover's lack of interest – 'the Laval meeting was evidently just a nuisance to him' – Stimson, for one, certainly hoped that it might. He told Hoover that 'in my opinion, on the whole it was a great opportunity. I wanted him to get acquainted with Laval. I wanted to get Laval talking with him in the way he talked to me about European problems, and I thought it was a great opportunity for the president to put in a good stroke on what are really the underlying and fundamental problems in the European question.'[2]

But even Stimson's enthusiasm must have been dampened by what Paul Claudel, the French ambassador in Washington, told him on his return from France on 9 October. 'He told me,' Stimson noted in his diary, 'that Briand is very much peeved because Laval is coming without him, also Flandin. Laval is tickled to death but the other two don't like it. Consequently Maginot is not allowed to come by Briand, and Laval will not have anybody from the foreign office with him. . . . He said everybody in France was afraid of Laval's going wrong here, so far from home on new untried land; that they don't want to have anything determined; that they are willing to have matters opened not finished.' Stimson agreed that nothing could be settled by the president and the prime minister on their own, but added that he wanted 'to have as much opened, as frankly opened, and as widely opened as possible'. Claudel retorted that 'we shouldn't expect to get very far

[1] Pünder memorandum, 10 October 1931, GFM/K2083/K553564. The 'plans' which Laval had in mind were apparently those of the pan-European enthusiast, Count Richard Coudenhove-Kalergi. See the latter's memoirs, *An Idea Conquers the World*, London, Hutchinson, 1953, pp. 145–6.

[2] Stimson, *Diary*, 30 September 1931.

with disarmament. He said frankly that the munition manufacturers in France were very powerful and controlled the press; and while the depression had hit them, they retained sufficient power to make it very difficult to disarm against their wishes. Also, Laval regarded the French army as a great safeguard against Communism. So [he] thought we had better talk first about economic questions, at any rate leave disarmament to the end.'[1] It was the same old story over again.

To make matters worse, the weeks preceding Laval's arrival in the United States witnessed a round of speculation against the dollar, triggered off by French press reports that the United States was about to follow Britain off the gold standard. Between 19 September and 31 October, the gold holdings of United States reserve banks fell by $748 million, or just over 20 per cent.[2] Stimson noted that he was beginning to see the truth of Claudel's remarks about the arms manufacturers and the press. 'Apparently,' he added, 'Laval's rivals are trying to make the visit not a success and the press are helping them.' Hoover was furious at the speculation and the secretary of state was hard put to it to convince him that Laval was not personally responsible.[3]

Laval arrived in New York on 22 October. After the traditional procession down Broadway to the City Hall – he was 'tremendously impressed by the high buildings' Stimson recalled – the party left for Washington. That evening President Hoover gave a dinner at the White House for Laval and another distinguished Frenchman who happened to be in the United States at the same time. The paths of the president's two French guests were to cross again in later years in very different circumstances. The other visitor was Marshal Philippe Pétain.[4]

Serious political discussions began the following afternoon in a conversation which began at 3.30 p.m. and lasted until midnight with only a short break to enable the participants to get ready for dinner. Hoover began with a classic synthesis of the American isolationist viewpoint. 'He said that the [ordinary] American would sum up the situation in this wise. We had started with a hundred and fifty years of isolation from Europe. Fifteen years ago we were dragged by Europe

[1] Ibid., 9 October 1931.
[2] *Economist*, Banking Supplement, 14 May 1932, p. 7.
[3] Stimson, *Diary*, 13, 20 October 1931.
[4] Ibid., 22 October 1931.

into the war for the first time. And he would sum up the results of the following fifteen years as follows: that we had lost the lives of some 75,000 men and disabled over 200,000 more. We had spent in loans, or war payments, something like $40,000 million; and that as a result Europe was now more unstable than it was in 1914. It would, therefore, be very difficult to do more unless it was connected with some improvement in the stability of Europe.'

In his reply, Laval pinned the blame for this lack of stability fairly and squarely upon Germany. 'So long as Germany continued to excite people with a view to revising the treaties,' he said, 'the unrest would continue. France stood for the morality, or preservation of treaties. And that was all there was to it.' What he suggested was 'a political moratorium, perhaps for ten years, and that possibly in that time French minds would cool down and possibly some solution could be made then'. Stimson interposed to remind the French prime minister of his own statement the previous July that, if only the question of the Polish corridor could be solved, there would be no more trouble between Germany and France. Laval did not deny this, but pointed out that 'he had subsequent talks both with the Germans and with the Poles. As a result he thought any question of the eastern boundary was a political impossibility.' When Hoover commented that 'a political moratorium wouldn't be any good unless there was some hope given of a solution afterwards,' Laval calmly replied that 'the giving of such a hope would merely perpetuate the agitation during the meanwhile and make it impossible.'

No more progress was made in the discussions on disarmament and security. Laval 'dilated on the real pacific feeling of France, of horror at any war at all, and the fact that the French army under the present situation in Europe, the unsettlement in middle Europe and Sovietism in Russia, was after all the defence against bolshevism'. France, he said, would have to have security before disarmament, 'but . . . a promise of consultation with us [the United States] such as we had already given as to the Pacific, would be taken in France as a great gesture which would help very much the possibility of any disarmament'. What did the president think of this? Hoover 'replied at once that he thought it was a political impossibility'. He then brought forward his own suggestion 'for a basic size for an army, based upon a size large enough merely for an internal police force and then giving other nations additions to the basic need based upon their respective different needs'. This time it was Laval's turn to shoot down a proposal. He 'at once brought up the question of the impracticability of carrying out such a plan, what measure would they have to determine the different needs of the different countries, or what guarantees that they were not larger than they needed. It would be impossible for instance to appraise the danger from the political unrest in Germany; how could we measure that?'

It was only on the question of reparations that any progress could be made. Hoover put to Laval the suggestion that 'a commission determine the immediate capacity of Germany to pay during this time of depression'. Laval replied that 'it depended on whether the new arrangement would be made under the Young plan or outside of it'. He also asked whether, if the commission reported in favour of a reduction in reparations, the United States would 'co-operate', that is, in the matter of war debts. Hoover 'replied that we would co-operate, of course, *but in the sense of the depression only and subject of course to Congress*'. Laval raised no objections, but emphasized that 'he would never be in favour of an entire abolition of reparations'. His reason was a far cry from the usual French tale of woe about what had happened to the devastated regions of France during the war. Abolition 'would put German industry in such a favourable position compared with France, England, or America that we would all regret it'.[1]

Laval's overall intransigence brought out all the latent Francophobia in Hoover. He told Stimson the following day over lunch that 'France always goes through this cycle. After she is done and begins to recuperate . . . she gets rich, militaristic, and cocky; and nobody can get on with her until she has to be thrashed again.' Although Stimson, too, was 'very much discouraged with the tightness with which Laval is tied to his people's military ideas', he tried to stress the brighter points of the conversation. '. . . In the reparations point,' he noted, 'we had made great progress. The French agreed that Germany must be helped by reparations during the period of depression. Laval admitted this very frankly. He was only anxious that it be so stated in the communiqué so as not to make it unnecessarily difficult for him at home.' On the American side, Hoover had 'admitted that if Germany

[1] Stimson/Hoover memorandum, 24 October 1931, attached to Stimson, *Diary*, 23 October 1931. The words in italics were added by Hoover.

was helped in their reparations, we have to help our debtors on debts during the depression, and, in view of the past, that was quite important'.[1]

The point about the communiqué was an important one. In the event, it took the two sides a day and a half to agree on its terms. When it was issued on 25 October, the crucial passage read, 'In so far as intergovernmental obligations are concerned, we recognize that prior to the expiration of the Hoover year of postponement, some agreement regarding them may be necessary covering the period of business depression, as to the terms of which the two governments make all reservations. The initiative in this matter should be taken at an early date by the European powers principally concerned within the framework of the agreements existing prior to 1 July 1931.'[2] This last reference, of course, was to the Young plan.

In the meantime, another incident had occurred which did not augur well for the success of the visit. Senator Borah, the influential chairman of the Senate foreign relations committee, had issued a statement on European affairs to the press which Stimson described as 'coming out vigorously and in an embarrassing way on pretty nearly all the embarrassing points there were'. Laval had promptly issued a tart counterstatement in which he declared that he had come to talk with Hoover and not Borah. Both men were due to attend a dinner at Stimson's Washington home, where Laval was staying, on the evening of 24 October, but as a result of this incident there was considerable speculation as to whether either would attend. In the end, Stimson was able to record the following outcome: 'Borah . . . had not taken offence. Laval had a great sense of humour, and on his part had enjoyed it. So they both agreed to debate in my study and fight it out. . . . They sat on the sofa and continued it so long that it pretty nearly busted up the rest of the conversation. I couldn't get them away, and I couldn't bring all the rest in to hear him, because the . . . room was not large enough.'[3]

To judge by his own account, however, Borah remained unconvinced by Laval's arguments. 'Do you see any chance anywhere in the future of a revision in respect to the treaty of Versailles?' he asked Laval. The

[1] Stimson, *Diary,* 24 October 1931.
[2] Ibid., 24 October 1931; Survey for 1931, p. 125.
[3] Stimson, *Diary,* 24 October 1931.

latter replied that while 'he could not speak for all time', he 'could see no chance for revision'. Did he then see any chance for disarmament before the treaty was revised, Borah enquired. Laval replied that this was possible, provided there was a security pact which, as Borah understood it, 'would make inviolate and eternal the Versailles treaty'. It was during the course of this conversation that Laval told the assembled company, 'If you Americans will quit lending money to Germany and quit encouraging Germany, we can take care of Germany and we can bring about an adjustment, or settlement, which ought to obtain.' Borah and another senatorial colleague left the dinner, 'agreeing that the outlook was discouraging'.[1]

Stimson had his opportunity for a quiet talk with Laval on the following morning before breakfast. The secretary of state was delighted to find him 'much more amenable' than he had been during the full-dress conversations with Hoover. The two men 'talked over [Laval's] real attitude towards the German eastern boundary' and Stimson found him 'asking questions as to what we could possibly do to soothe down the friction which had arisen'. Stimson repeated his objections to the 'political moratorium' which Laval had proposed in his conversation with the president and said that 'the whole point was to try to get some concessions, some smoothing out of the irritation which would be an earnest to the Germans that we really meant to treat them fairly'. He alluded to 'the irritations and frictions of the customs of the various transports across the corridor' and Laval showed himself 'very much interested and took it down evidently in his memory'. He told Stimson that he agreed with him 'that the corridor was a monstrosity'.[2]

Personally, the Washington visit was another success for Laval. The French ambassador reported that he had 'conquered everyone with his occasionally pretty blunt frankness and good grace'. As for the press, with which Hoover himself had never managed to get on good terms, 'it is no exaggeration to say that it was literally "carried away".' On one occasion when the newsmen applauded him, Laval turned to the ambassador and remarked with evident satisfaction, 'I could be in Aubervilliers!' The general opinion was that 'no man could have done more to make himself understood by America'.[3] Politically, however,

[1] C. O. Johnson, *Borah of Idaho*, New York, Longmans, 1936, pp. 448–9.
[2] Stimson, *Diary*, 25 October 1931.
[3] Claudel to Briand, 26 (?) October 1931, cited in Baraduc, pp. 68–9.

the visit was much less productive. Except in his final conversation with Stimson, Laval had taken a line which was virtually indistinguishable from that of Tardieu and other hard-liners in the French cabinet and this had produced a predictable lack of comprehension on the part of men like Hoover and Borah. Even the limited agreement on reparations, it was soon to become clear, was no real agreement at all.

Thus, when as a result of lengthy negotiations,[1] Germany was persuaded against her will to appeal to the B.I.S. under article 119 of the Young plan for the establishment of a special advisory committee to examine her capacity to pay reparations, the French government refused to associate itself in public with the appeal, although it had participated in its drafting practically word by word, and Laval made so many reservations concerning the French attitude in a speech to the Chamber of Deputies on 26 November that his remarks, in Stimson's words, 'tended to put handcuffs on the [special advisory] committee'. He insisted that France would only accept a reduction in reparations for the strictly limited period of the depression, that she would only accept it then to the extent that '*at least* equivalent reductions' were made in war debts, that unconditional reparations continued to be paid, and that private debts must not be accorded priority over reparations.[2]

Fearful lest Laval's speech be interpreted as reflecting a policy agreed in Washington, Stimson summoned the French ambassador on 3 December 'to make it clear to Mr Laval and the French government that some of the things which he asserted as France's policy were not made under any agreement with us but that as to some of them we held an entirely different view'. The secretary of state was particularly critical of Laval's caveat in respect of war debts which, he said, 'meant that America was to pay the whole bill and that France even reserved the right to make a profit out of the transaction.' This, he emphasized,

---

[1] They are summarized in an undated, unsigned memorandum, GFM/3243/D730021–36.

[2] The key passage of Laval's speech to the Chamber is to be found in J. O. Chambre, *Débats*, 26 November 1931, p. 4063, col. 3 (emphasis added). The quotation from Stimson comes from the memorandum cited in the next paragraph. German objections to the use of the Young plan machinery were precisely that it seemed to commit them to continued payment of unconditional reparations and did nothing to solve the problem of short-term debts which was more pressing from their point of view, although not from that of the French who held relatively little of this kind of obligation (see the figures in *The Economist*, Supplement on 'Reparations and War Debts', 23 January 1932, p. 11). The Germans sought to raise both these issues in their appeal to the B.I.S. (see the text in Neurath to Simon, 20 November 1931, D.B.F.P. 2nd Series, Vol. II, No. 299).

was simply not on as far as the United States was concerned. He also told Claudel that there had been no agreement between the two governments as to the continued payment of unconditional reparations and that he believed the French attitude towards private short-term debts 'would mean the entire destruction of German credit'.[1] Later in the month, what was left of the Franco-American accord seemed irreparably shattered by a rider which Congress attached to its ratification of the Hoover moratorium to the effect that it was 'against the policy of Congress that any of the indebtedness of foreign countries to the United States should be in any manner cancelled or reduced'.[2]

The special advisory committee of the B.I.S. reported on 23 December. It concluded that 'the adjustment of all inter-governmental debts (reparations and other war debts) to the existing troubled situation of the world – and this adjustment should take place without delay if new disasters are to be avoided – is the only lasting step capable of re-establishing confidence which is the very condition of economic stability and real peace'. It called upon 'the governments on whom the responsibility for action rests to permit of no delay in coming to decisions which will bring an amelioration of this grave crisis which weighs so heavily on all alike'.[3]

Diplomacy's task during the next few weeks was to arrange an international conference which would deal with these matters. Preliminary exchanges produced agreement on Lausanne as the site and the latter part of January 1932 as the date when, on the 9th of that month, the Germans suddenly dropped a bombshell into the arena. A Reuter despatch from Berlin reported that Brüning had told the British ambassador that Germany could not pay reparations now and would not be able to do so in the future.[4] Later the same day, the chancellor confirmed this in an interview with a German news agency when he said that 'it was perfectly obvious that Germany's position made the continuation of political payments [i.e. reparations] impossible for her'.[5]

---

[1] Stimson memorandum, 3 December 1931, F.R.U.S., 1931, Vol. I, pp. 352–3. To make his government's position crystal clear, Stimson gave Claudel an *aide-mémoire* summarizing it (ibid., pp. 353–4).
[2] The text of the congressional resolution is printed in ibid., pp. 248–9.
[3] The text of the report is printed in D.B.F.P., 2nd Series, Vol. II, pp. 495–514.
[4] *Le Temps*, 10 January 1932.
[5] Rumbold to Simon, 11 January 1932, D.B.F.P., 2nd Series, Vol. III, No. 16.

This was nothing less than a calculated attempt to forestall the conference.[1]

Brüning's statement coincided with a political crisis in Paris. André Maginot, the minister of war, had died as a result of food poisoning on 7 January and Laval was engaged in a ministerial reshuffle in which he sought to get rid of the now very ill Briand. But the old man did not want to go and Laval was compelled to stage a collective resignation of the entire government to force his hand. He seized the opportunity to try and broaden his majority by offering a number of posts to the radicals, including that of foreign minister to their leader Edouard Herriot, but at a party meeting on 12 January the radicals refused to be drawn and Laval was forced to reconstruct his government on the same basis as before. He took the portfolio of foreign affairs himself.[2]

It is impossible to say with certainty how this crisis affected Laval's reaction to the German move, but it can hardly have inclined him towards moderation. In a somewhat heated interview with Hoesch on 11 January, he repeatedly accused the Germans of 'having prejudged the Lausanne conference by a categorical statement and thereby rendering it as it were superfluous'. His government 'could not accept the German statement under any circumstances'. Indeed, 'no conceivable French government would be prepared to do so'.[3]

He did more than protest. On the day Brüning's interview was published, he had a long meeting with General Weygand, the army chief of staff. This was followed by the calling up of key reservists and the transport of troops and ammunition towards the German frontier. The distinguished British military commentator, Captain Basil Liddell Hart, who passed through Paris at this time on his way to Geneva for the opening of the disarmament conference, subsequently recalled how he 'heard from friends . . . that government circles had been considering a mobilization of the army to enforce Germany's continuance of reparations payments and had even discussed the idea of bombing the Rhineland as an enforcement insurance. I was given details of how the French government had gone so far as to assemble

---

[1] In conversations with the French and British, the Germans tried to make out that Brüning's interview had been prompted by the Reuter 'leak' of his remarks to Rumbold. The German documents show quite clearly, however, that the interview had been planned before the 'leak' occurred.

[2] Hoesch to Foreign Ministry, 9, 12 January 1932, GFM/2406/D510336–7, D510383–9; Edge, p. 210; *Le Temps*, 8, 14, 15 January 1932.

[3] Hoesch to Foreign Ministry, 11 January 1932, GFM/3243/D730203–8.

troops on the frontier in readiness for a move into the Rhineland.'[1] In the absence of any French documentation, it is hard to say how seriously these military counter-measures were intended. They may only have been an exercise in bluff, but the fact that they could be taken at all shows the extent to which the undoubted mutual trust and confidence which once existed between Laval and Brüning had been dissipated.

The German initiative effectively torpedoed the early convening of the Lausanne conference. As Laval told Hoesch on 30 January, '. . . there was no hope that [Brüning] would tell him anything other than he had said in his . . . interview or than I [Hoesch] had told him. The conference would, therefore, inevitably turn out to be fruitless at this stage and, in contrast to the German view, he not only did not expect any relaxation of tension to follow such an outcome, but rather a deterioration in the situation.'[2] It was eventually decided to hold the conference in June, after the French elections.[3]

The quarrel over reparations and the French military precautions outlined above were not a good omen for the success of the long-awaited League of Nations disarmament conference, which opened at Geneva on 2 February 1932. But was there any chance of success in any case? On 5 February, André Tardieu, who had succeeded Maginot as war minister and who was the leader of the French delegation, tabled a plan before the conference which, as he freely admitted, was in the tradition of all French plans over the previous decade. In calling for the handing over of bombing aircraft to the League of Nations and the setting up of an international police force within the framework of the existing treaty system, it was nothing less than an attempt to perpetuate the *status quo* by main force.[4] As Colonel Jacques Minart, one of the officers who was well acquainted with the drafting of the plan, subsequently observed, 'The position adopted had the advantage of subordinating French disarmament to conditions which were such that our strength would not be compromised. It maintained, as between Germany and France, the *de jure* and *de facto* military inequality which the

[1] Hoesch reports, 22, 29 January 1932, ibid., K936/K241027–31, K241033–6; Sir B. H. Liddell Hart, *Memoirs*, Vol. I, London, Cassell, 1965, pp. 190–91. There is a great deal of material on the French military preparations in the file GFM/K936 for late January and early February 1932.
[2] Hoesch to Foreign Ministry, 31 January 1932, GFM/3243/D730358–63.
[3] *The Times*, 15 February 1932.
[4] The full text of the French plan is printed in *Le Temps*, 7 February 1932, and Tardieu's speech to the conference commenting on it in ibid., 9 February 1932.

signatories of the Versailles treaty had deemed a necessary precaution. It did not jeopardize the general principles of our military organization in any way and did not involve any proposal for treaty revision on France's part.'[1]

Not surprisingly, this was not a position which appealed to the Germans. Their aim at Geneva was also what it had always been – equality of rights – although they intended to approach it in a way calculated to gain the support of world opinion, by stressing the obligation upon other countries to disarm rather than the right of Germany to rearm. What was more, as General Gröner emphasized to his cabinet colleagues, 'any failure [of the conference] must be attributable to France in the eyes of the world'.[2] From the very beginning, therefore, the disarmament conference seemed set on a course headed for disaster.

This problem was not, however, to exercise Laval for much longer. The French elections were due in the spring of 1932 and a new electoral law needed to be enacted, if only to modify constituency boundaries which had been fixed for a four-year period at the time of the previous elections in 1928. But for some time, the Chamber of Deputies had been discussing a much more far-reaching electoral reform which was the brainchild of Georges Mandel, Laval's old acquaintance of First World War days and now chairman of the Chamber's universal suffrage committee. Mandel's proposal called for a partial return to the one ballot electoral system prevailing in 1919 and abolished in 1927 by declaring any candidate who obtained 40 per cent or more of the votes at the first ballot elected. This was transparently designed to favour the right, who normally put only one candidate into the field, as opposed to the left, who put several and who tended to coalesce behind the most favourably placed one at the second ballot. At first, Laval showed little interest in Mandel's proposal, but when the latter threatened to overthrow the government with its own majority unless it was passed, he quickly changed his tune and forced the new law through the Chamber. *En route* it attracted an amendment which gave the vote to women.[3]

---

[1] Jacques Minart, *Le Drame du Désarmement Français 1918–1939*, Paris, La Nef de Paris Editions, 1959, p. 25.

[2] Planck memorandum, 15 January 1932, GFM/3242/D811404–8. See also the instructions for the German delegation, ibid., D811413–16.

[3] *Le Temps*, 9 January 1932; Bonnefous, Vol. V, pp. 110–11; Lucien Lamoureux in *La Bourbonnais Républicaine*, 2 October 1955.

Both electoral reform and votes for women were anathema to the upper house, however, and on the very day that the law was passed by the Chamber of Deputies, Senator Albert Peyronnet gave notice that he intended to interpellate, or initiate a general debate, on the government's policy. On 16 February, the date of Peyronnet's interpellation came up for discussion in the Senate. Because of the disarmament conference, Laval wanted it postponed until the 26th, but his proposal was defeated. He then suggested the 19th and rashly made the issue one of confidence. 'I appeal to the conscience of M. Albert Peyronnet,' he declared, 'and I turn towards the representatives of the nation, the elected members who must have a sense of proportion. Today, you have a choice between your domestic political passions and the country's higher interest.' The senators chose the former and Laval lost his vote of confidence by 157 votes to 134, thus entailing his government's resignation.[1] 'I was overthrown . . . by a kind of masonic conspiracy,' he was to say in 1945, '. . . because they didn't want me to control the 1932 elections.'[2]

Brüning subsequently claimed that he was sure that a disarmament agreement would have been reached if only Laval had remained prime minister.[3] But this was wishful thinking. Looking back on it, there seems something almost inevitable about the way in which France and Germany failed to resolve any of their basic differences during the thirteen months of Laval's first premiership. After the French collapse of 1940 had underlined this failure, and those of successive governments, Laval recalled how in July 1932 Brüning had sat opposite him bemoaning the fact that 'our peoples are condemned to perpetual disagreement'.[4] It is to Laval's credit that he never accepted this diagnosis, not even in the darkest days of the war. But it does not say much for his political acumen that, having failed to reach an agreement with Brüning, he thought he could achieve one with Hitler.

---

[1] *Le Temps*, 14 February 1932; J. O. Sénat, *Débats*, 16 February 1932. Laval's appeal is on p. 159, col. 2.
[2] *Procès Pétain*, p. 191, col. 2.
[3] In a letter to M. René de Chambrun, dated 3 January 1950, and kindly communicated by the latter to me.
[4] Unsigned, undated memorandum of a conversation between Laval and Dr Grimm of the German embassy on 28 August 1940, GFM/2624/D525934–47.

2

Foreign Minister

May 1932 – June 1935

Although the left-wing parties triumphed in the elections of May 1932, they were unable to agree upon a common policy, particularly in the financial field. As a succession of governments fell in an attempt to balance the budget, the public became increasingly exasperated at the ineptitude of its rulers. This exasperation exploded into violence at the beginning of 1934 when the Stavisky scandal, a large-scale financial swindle in which a number of politicians were involved, came to light. Camille Chautemps, the Radical prime minister who was in office at the time, resigned as a result of hostile demonstrations. After failing to enlist the support of the centre and right-wing parties, his successor, Edouard Daladier, sought to consolidate his position on the left by dismissing the unpopular Paris police chief, Jean Chiappe. This precipitated a large-scale demonstration by fascist and other right-wing groups on the night of 6 February 1934 as Daladier was presenting his government to the Chamber of Deputies. The demonstration degenerated into the bloodiest riots the French capital had seen for many years. Fifteen people were killed and nearly 1,500 injured, more than 300 of them seriously. The consequences of 6 February were far-reaching. Thenceforth, the dichotomy between right and left, between opponents and supporters of the régime, became more marked. The full fruits of this tragic division in the French body politic were not to be reaped until the collapse of 1940, of which it was the underlying cause.[1]

But there was a more immediate problem: the choice of a successor to Daladier who, fearing further bloodshed, had resigned at 1 o'clock

[1] For the Stavisky scandal and the riots of 6 February 1934, see the present author's article in *History Today*, June 1958, pp. 377–85. See also Max Beloff, 'The Sixth of February', in *The Decline of the Third Republic* (St Antony's Papers, No. 5), London, Chatto and Windus, 1959, pp. 9–35.

56

in the afternoon on 7 February. Leading a delegation of members of parliament and municipal councillors from the Paris area, Laval burst into President Lebrun's office and 'called upon [him] to take a decision and to do his duty as president of the Republic'.[1] The delegation demanded that he send for the former president, Gaston Doumergue, and Laval went so far as to telephone the latter at his country retreat in an effort to force Lebrun's hand.[2]

Doumergue, whose fatherly image would provide the necessary reassurance in this time of crisis, was indeed the name on many people's lips and, after some hesitation, he agreed to come to Paris and try to form a government. By the evening of 9 February, he had succeeded. It was a government of 'national union', with its centre of gravity well to the right, and was a complete repudiation of the left-wing majority which had won the 1932 elections and failed so conspicuously to govern the country thereafter. Of course, it could not have survived without the support of the Radicals, but the party as a whole, shattered by the traumatic experience of the Stavisky scandal and the riots, was only too pleased to give it when asked. Herriot neatly balanced Tardieu as the two ministers of state in what Doumergue himself called 'a government of truce, appeasement, and justice'. Laval did not go unrewarded for his part in the affair, becoming minister of colonies. Marshal Pétain was minister of war.[3]

The continued reverberations of the Stavisky affair were a serious threat to the unity of the Doumergue government. Tardieu, who was accused of being implicated in the scandal, took the opportunity of his appearance before a parliamentary committee of enquiry on 18 July 1934 to make a long and bitter attack upon M. Chautemps and other Radicals. This threw a considerable strain upon the loyalty of a party which had no less than six ministers in the government. Herriot, the most senior, wanted Tardieu to resign, but Doumergue would not hear of it. Probably through fear of incurring the responsibility for further disorders, the Radicals decided not to force the issue. Yielding to the

---

[1] This was how Laval put it at his trial in 1945. *Procès Laval*, p. 77.

[2] Jean Fabry, *J'ai Connu, 1934–45*, Paris, Editions Descamps, S.E.P.H.L., 1960 (hereafter cited as Fabry), p. 35.

[3] Accounts of the formation of the Doumergue government may be found in Bonnefous, Vol. V, pp. 215–18; Lebrun in C.E., *Témoignages*, Vol. IV, pp. 983–4; Edouard Herriot, *Jadis*, Vol. II, *D'une Guerre à l'Autre, 1914–36*, Paris, Flammarion, 1952 (hereafter cited as Herriot, *Jadis*), pp. 378–82.

promptings of Laval among others, they agreed to postpone further consideration of the matter until their congress in October.[1]

By then, Herriot, who seems to have harboured a burning resentment against Doumergue as a result of his exercise in political blackmail, had found the perfect weapon with which to exact his revenge: the prime minister's proposals for constitutional reform. First announced in a broadcast address to the nation, thus seeming to devalue parliament, the reforms centred upon a proposal to enable the prime minister to dissolve the Chamber of Deputies. It was easy to represent this as a bid for personal power on the part of Doumergue, and Herriot lost no opportunity of doing so. He was helped considerably by the prime minister's own pig-headedness. When the final draft proposals came before the cabinet on 2 November, Laval, who could see which way the wind was blowing, declared, 'The greatest man will be he who makes the most concessions tonight.' 'I am quite happy to be the least great,' Doumergue replied tartly. Somewhat surprisingly, he agreed to the Radicals reserving their right to oppose the reforms, but promptly precipitated another crisis by demanding three months of provisional financing in case he decided to dissolve the Chamber. Herriot practically forced the other Radical ministers into submitting their resignations on 8 November. Doumergue tried to call his bluff by submitting the resignation of the rest of his cabinet and blaming it upon the Radicals. This might have worked in February, or even in June, when he was still the indispensable figure. But this time there was an alternative prime minister to hand in the person of Pierre-Etienne Flandin, who had indicated his readiness to collaborate with the Radicals only a few days before. Flandin formed a new goverment in record time.[2]

During the Doumergue government an important change took place in Laval's political fortunes. On 9 October 1934, Doumergue's foreign minister, Louis Barthou, was assassinated in Marseilles as he was accompanying King Alexander of Yugoslavia on the start of the latter's

[1] Bonnefous, Vol. V, pp. 271–7; Herriot, *Jadis*, pp. 445–9. Laval, too, was accused of complicity in the Stavisky affair, but he managed to clear himself. Cf. *Le Temps*, 3 May 1934.

[2] For the fall of the Doumergue government, see Bonnefous, Vol. V, pp. 279–83, 2‿3–301; Herriot, *Jadis*, pp. 455–80; Peter Larmour, *The French Radical Party in the 1930's*, Stanford, Stanford University Press, 1964 (hereafter cited as Larmour), pp. 156–60.

first state visit to France. The assassin was a Croat terrorist and the king, who was also killed, had been his intended victim. Doumergue hesitated between Flandin, François Piétri, and Laval as Barthou's successor, finally choosing Laval on the somewhat curious grounds that he had been prime minister.[1] The decision was to lead to one of the most crowded and controversial periods in Laval's career.

The international scene in October 1934 was, of course, very different from what it had been in February 1932, when Laval had last been responsible for French foreign policy. The great issue with which his government had wrestled throughout 1931 – reparations and war debts – had been settled. The long-awaited conference on reparations at Lausanne in the summer of 1932 had resulted in a decision to absolve Germany from further payments. True to form, the United States government refused to renounce its war debt claims as a corollary to the Lausanne agreement, despite the promptings of Stimson. But having forgone reparations, France was in no mood to continue paying war debts, and the Chamber brought down the Herriot government in December 1932 when the latter had the temerity to suggest that the next debt instalment should be paid. No further payments were ever made.[2]

In January 1933, Franco-German relations were completely transformed by Hitler's accession to power in Germany. While recent scholarship has rightly emphasized the basic continuity of Germany's foreign policy under Weimar and the Nazis,[3] there can be little doubt that Hitler was much more virulently anti-French than his predecessors. He had described France in *Mein Kampf* as 'the mortal enemy of our nation' and had advocated her 'destruction' as 'a means of subsequently and finally giving our nation a chance to expand elsewhere'.[4] He took advantage of France's growing domestic difficulties to achieve some striking diplomatic successes. In October 1933, after failing to secure acceptance of his conception of 'equal rights', he ostentatiously

---

[1] Herriot, *Jadis*, p. 459.

[2] The best accounts, from the French side, of the settlement of the reparations and war debts issue may be found in ibid., pp. 307–49; Michel Soulié, *La Vie Politique d'Edouard Herriot*, Paris, Armand Colin, 1962, pp. 361–71, 407–17. See also Henry L. Stimson and McGeorge Bundy, *On Active Service in Peace and War*, London, Hutchinson, 1949, pp. 62–8.

[3] e.g. A. J. P. Taylor, *The Origin of the Second World War*, London, Hamish Hamilton, 1961.

[4] Adolf Hitler, *Mein Kampf*, New York, Reynal and Hitchcock, 1940, pp. 966, 978–9.

withdrew Germany from both the disarmament conference and the League of Nations. Three months later, in January 1934, he opened a breach in France's security system by concluding a non-aggression pact with Poland.[1]

At the same time, Hitler was a genius at offsetting hostile actions with honeyed words. He told the *Reichstag* on 30 January 1934 that 'the struggle for German equality of rights . . . could in my opinion find no better end than by a reconciliation of the two great nations which have in the last few centuries so often shed the blood of their best sons on the field of battle without bringing about any essential change in the ultimate state of affairs'. In the same speech, he repeated what amounted to a renunciation of Germany's claim to Alsace-Lorraine. The Saar, he said, 'is the only territorial question which is still open between the two countries. After it has been settled, the German government is prepared not only to accept the letter but also the spirit of the Locarno pact, since there are no other territorial questions outstanding between France and Germany.'[2]

Laval hoped that the *Reichstag* orator of January 1934, and not the author of *Mein Kampf*, was the 'real' Hitler. On practical grounds, he could accept many of the Führer's criticisms of the Versailles treaty, including the restrictions placed upon Germany's right to rearm. Basically, however, his attitude was an emotional one and was rooted in his horror of another war. In the circumstances, he had no alternative but to accept Hitler's protestations of peace and declarations of readiness to come to terms with France at their face value. 'War means the end of us all,' he told a German visitor shortly before he became foreign minister. 'Mankind is morally incapable of enduring another war, the horrors of which will surpass everything that has occurred hitherto. War would mean the end of Christian civilization.'[3] Many politicians said similar things; Laval, more than most, believed them.

This meant, among other things, a reversal of his predecessor's policy, for Louis Barthou had made little attempt to disguise his

---

[1] For Hitler's early foreign policy, see Alan Bullock, *Hitler: A Study in Tyranny*, Harmondsworth, Penguin Books, 1962, pp. 312–29; Esmonde Robertson, *Hitler's Pre-War Policy and Military Plans*, London, Longmans, 1963, Chapters 1–5.

[2] For Hitler's speech, see R.I.I.A. Documents, 1934, pp. 328–9.

[3] Undated von der Ropp memorandum, GFM/5708/H021980–96. The conversation, which took place on 25 September 1934, is a valuable source for Laval's opinions.

fundamental hostility towards Germany. However, Laval could not have carried out such a reversal single-handed. Cabinet responsibility in France, where several ministers might be waiting to head the next government, may have been weaker than in Britain, but it was not so weak as to enable Laval to pursue a policy of his own making in defiance of his colleagues. Flandin's post-war claim that he had opposed Laval's policy and had only retained him as foreign minister for domestic reasons[1] may therefore be discounted. Those responsible for French policy in the 1930s have always been assiduous in their search for scapegoats, and there are few more eligible candidates than a man who was shot for treason.[2]

An early indication of Laval's determination to seek a 'direct, honourable and effective *rapprochement* with Germany'[3] was his policy over the Saar question. Under the terms of the Versailles treaty, the Saar territory had been detached from Germany and placed under the control of the League of Nations. The control of the territory's rich coal mines was vested in France. At the end of 15 years – that is, in 1935 – a plebiscite was due to be held offering the Saarlanders the choice of union with France, reunion with Germany, or the preservation of the *status quo*. The accession to power of Hitler, who regarded the position in the Saar as a classic example of the Versailles *diktat*, was bound to aggravate tension, especially as the date for the plebiscite grew near. The League council began to discuss arrangements for the plebiscite in January 1934 and, as the discussions proceeded, so Nazi intrigue and intimidation increased.

Whether Barthou seriously believed that the Saarlanders would vote against reunification with Germany is not certain, but Laval subsequently claimed that a great deal of money was spent on propaganda to persuade them to do so, and the Germans certainly regarded the memorandum which Barthou presented to the League council on 31 August 1934 as a bribe for the retention of the *status quo*. Similarly, his public threat to send French troops to help maintain order during the campaign, which was made in a speech to the council on 27

[1] C. E. *Témoignages*, Vol. IX, p. 2559.
[2] This is not to say that Laval did not sometimes run ahead of his colleagues, or that he had no opponents within the cabinet. As we shall see, Herriot was particularly critical of Laval's policies, but he was in a minority.
[3] The phrase was used by Laval in his conversation with von der Ropp.

September, was seen by the German government as an attempt to exert influence upon the result.[1]

Laval was much more reassuring. He stopped the flow of money for anti-German propaganda and told the German ambassador in Paris on 7 November that 'in his opinion, the Saar was one hundred per cent German and . . . he personally desired nothing more sincerely than that [it] should return to Germany. Once this had been effected, it would be possible to strike a useful balance in mutual relations and thus create the basis for a programme for the future.' Although he realized that France was under an obligation to send troops into the Saar if the need should arise, he assured the German government that 'she was not in the least interested in doing so'. In fact, he hoped that other members of the League, particularly Britain and Italy, would send police forces. He 'did not expect any advantage from the use of French troops but only confusion and discord'.[2]

A few days later at Geneva, Laval told Anthony Eden, then a junior minister at the Foreign Office, that 'he would take no step in the Saar that was not internationally sanctioned, and if France were asked to send police in an emergency, then he would invite the League council to ask other countries, notably Britain and Italy, to do the same'. Under pressure from Laval and Eden, the British government, which had hitherto been reluctant to play any part in policing the Saar, agreed to contribute to an international force. The Italian government did likewise. Both Laval and the Germans gladly agreed to the British government's condition that French troops should not form part of the force. Sweden and the Netherlands also agreed to send troops, and the international force, under a British commander, was operational by Christmas.[3]

Simultaneously, French negotiators in Rome were concluding an

---

[1] Laval's speech to a meeting of youth leaders, 4 August 1943 (unpublished text kindly communicated to me by M. René de Chambrun); Neurath to Köster, 5 November 1934, D.G.F.P., Series C, Vol. III, No. 297. The text of the French memorandum of 31 August is in R.I.I.A. Documents, 1934, pp. 30–36; that of Barthou's speech of 27 September in ibid., pp. 55–7.

[2] Laval speech, 4 August 1943, loc. cit.; Köster to Foreign Ministry, 7 November 1934, D.G.F.P., Series C, Vol. III, No. 307.

[3] Lord Avon (Sir Anthony Eden), *Facing the Dictators*, London, Cassell, 1962 (hereafter cited as Eden), pp. 102–6; Baron Pompeo Aloisi, *Journal, 25 juillet 1932–14 juin 1936*, Paris, Plon, 1957 (hereafter cited as Aloisi), pp. 232–3; Krauel to Foreign Ministry, 6 December, 1934, D.G.F.P., Series C, Vol. III, No. 375; Neurath to Krauel, 6 December 1934, ibid., No. 378.

agreement with Germany which covered, among other things, the tricky problem of compensation for France for relinquishing control of the Saar coal mines in the event of the plebiscite favouring reunification with Germany. 'On the whole,' a senior German foreign ministry official commented, 'it emerges from the Rome negotiations that the present French government do not intend to take a settlement of the Saar affair as a pretext for quarrelling with Germany but that, on the contrary, they are prepared, while safeguarding their financial interests, to withdraw from the Saar venture.' Hitler's comment was more cynical. The agreement was 'a clear success, for which credit must go to Germany's resurgence as a great power', he told a cabinet meeting on 4 December. 'The French had definitely missed the opportunity for a preventive war.'[1]

The Saar plebiscite took place on 13 January 1935. It resulted in an overwhelming victory for Hitler, with more than 90 per cent of the electorate voting for reunification with Germany.[2] Unfortunately, however, it was not followed by that improvement in Franco-German relations which Hitler had predicted in his *Reichstag* speech of the year before and upon which Laval had set his heart.

While the Saar plebiscite campaign was in its final stages, Laval was cementing an agreement with France's other totalitarian neighbour, Italy. Barthou had taken advantage of a growing coolness between Mussolini and Hitler – a coolness intensified by the attempted Nazi *putsch* in Austria in July 1934 – to try and draw Italy into an anti-German coalition. Laval continued the negotiations, but with a different end in view. 'I tried to organize peace in Europe,' he told an audience of teachers in September 1942, 'and I thought that the first thing to do was to bring France and Italy closer together. I thought that this was the first link in a chain which would one day lead us to an agreement with Germany.'[3]

The issues which required settlement before France and Italy could come to an agreement were many and complex. Some, which were of long standing, were essentially colonial in character and stemmed from

[1] Köpke circular telegram, 4 December 1934, D.G.F.P., Series C, Vol. III, No. 372; Cabinet Protocol, 4 December 1934, ibid., No. 373. The text of the Franco-German agreement is in R.I.I.A. Documents, 1934, pp. 51–5.
[2] *The Times*, 15 January 1935.
[3] Laval's speech to teachers, 3 September 1942 (unpublished text kindly communicated to me by M. René de Chambrun).

the fact that Italy had not done so well out of the 'scramble for Africa' as the other powers. The French protectorate in Tunisia, which dated from 1881, was a particularly bitter blow to Italy in view of the large numbers of Italians who had settled in the country. Continued disputes concerning the legal status of these settlers served to keep this old antagonism alive. Italy's ruffled feelings might have been soothed by the concessions promised in the London treaty of April 1915 as a bribe to persuade her to enter the First World War on the side of the Entente, but successive Italian governments never considered the territory actually handed over by France in 1919 – a few hundred square miles on the borders of Libya – as an adequate recompense. Finally, France seemed determined to play the role of protector of one of the few remaining independent African states, Abyssinia, upon whose territory Italy had gazed with eyes that were both greedy and revengeful after her first attempt to take over the country had ended in the humiliating defeat at Adowa in 1896.

Equally difficult problems were raised by France's alliances in eastern Europe which, despite their primarily anti-German intention, had taken on something of an anti-Italian aspect. The countries of the so-called Little Entente (Czechoslovakia, Roumania, and Yugoslavia) were all to a greater or lesser extent succession states of the defunct Austro-Hungarian empire and, as such, they took strong exception to Italy's support of Hungarian revisionist claims. Even more important was the direct antagonism between Italy and Yugoslavia, based ultimately upon rival claims to the territory at the head of the Adriatic. Politically, Laval could not afford to reach an agreement with Italy at the expense of the Little Entente, so he was compelled to try and include the latter in it. This was to prove a difficult task.[1]

Negotiations began in earnest in November 1934, but the most urgent task was to avoid a clash at the League of Nations, where Yugoslavia was expected to charge Hungary, and possibly Italy as well, of complicity in the assassination of King Alexander. Laval told Eden that he had come to Geneva deliberately 'to try and calm Jevtić [the Yugoslav foreign minister] and the Yugoslav delegation'. In the event,

[1] This account of Franco-Italian problems is based upon the following sources: A. J. Toynbee (ed.), *Survey of International Affairs, 1935*, Vol. I, London, Oxford University Press for the Royal Institute of International Affairs, 1936, pp. 94–103; Hubert Lagardelle, *Mission à Rome: Mussolini*, Paris, Plon, 1957 (hereafter cited as Lagardelle), pp. 93–104; C. A. Macartney and A. W. Palmer, *Independent Eastern Europe*, London, Macmillan, 1962.

the Yugoslavs were persuaded not to accuse Italy directly, but there was still the possibility that she might become involved in attempting to protect her Hungarian *protégé*. While Laval worked upon Jevtić and the other Little Entente delegates, Baron Aloisi, the Italian representative and a keen supporter of Franco-Italian *rapprochement*, did his best to influence the Hungarians. They both received invaluable assistance from Eden, who drafted the resolution which was finally voted by the League council on 10 December. This did not accuse the Hungarian government directly, but merely suggested that 'certain Hungarian authorities may have assumed, at any rate through negligence, certain responsibilities relative to acts having a connection with the preparation of the crime of Marseilles'. By means of this involved formula, *amour-propre* was spared and a crisis averted.[1]

France and Italy could now concentrate upon settling their own differences. From the instructions which Laval gave Count Charles de Chambrun, the French ambassador in Rome, on 14 November 1934, it is clear that he was trying to obtain a promise of Italian support in the event of a German breach of the disarmament clauses of the Versailles treaty in return for territorial concessions in Africa. The Little Entente were to be brought into the agreement by making them a party to a collective guarantee of Austrian independence, and Laval further insisted that there must be a positive improvement in Italo-Yugoslav relations before any agreement could be reached.[2]

De Chambrun's discussion of the French proposals with Mussolini on 20 November produced a considerable measure of agreement. Thus, it was decided that, if Germany publicly denounced the disarmament clauses of the Versailles treaty, France and Italy 'would agree on joint action'. If she merely requested the legalization of her rearmament, Italy would support France's claim for a margin of superiority. Italy was also ready to take part in the collective guarantee of Austrian independence and to accept full Little Entente participation. In Tunisia, Italy proposed and France accepted a ten-year prolongation of the *status quo*, but the former also indicated a readiness to enter into immediate negotiations concerning the situation thereafter. Issues which remained to be settled included Italian territorial claims in Africa – and

[1] Eden, pp. 111–19; Aloisi, pp. 232–7. The text of the resolution is in R.I.I.A. Documents, 1934, pp. 112–14.
[2] Herriot, *Jadis*, pp. 483–4.

the precise definition of France's economic interests in Abyssinia. According to Robert de Dampierre, a member of the French embassy in Rome, it soon became clear that this last issue was 'the key to the agreement'.[1]

Mussolini had long realized that any venture in Abyssinia, for which military preparations were already in hand, would require what his advisers termed 'adequate international preparation'. In his view, a Franco-Italian *rapprochement* was an essential part of this 'preparation', in so far as it would obtain French support for, or at any rate benevolent neutrality towards, Italian aims in Abyssinia. Aloisi's diary makes it quite clear that, in order to secure this end, Mussolini was prepared to make substantial sacrifices. Little Entente participation in the Austrian guarantee was a case in point. After having accepted the idea in his conversation with de Chambrun on 20 November, the Duce evidently had second thoughts, for we find him telling Aloisi on 14 December that he could not possibly inflict such a humiliation upon Austria. By Christmas Day, however, he was saying that 'this Abyssinian business will come to fruition after we have reached agreement with France and . . . we must now speed things up'. Four days later, he instructed his negotiators to rally to the original French proposals and include the Little Entente in the Austrian guarantee.[2]

Laval wanted to come to Rome to sign the agreement as early as possible in the new year. This led to a frantic last-minute round of talks between 27 December and 1 January aimed at persuading the Austrians to accept a guarantee from the Little Entente and the Italians to accept the proposed French concessions in Africa, which were only communicated to them on 28 December, as a basis for discussion. Enough agreement was reached to enable Laval to announce, after a cabinet meeting on 2 January, that he would leave for Italy on the following day. But some of the key issues remained to be settled.[3]

---

[1] Robert de Dampierre, *'Dix Années de Politique Française à Rome'*, Part II, *La Revue des Deux Mondes*, 15 November 1953, p. 279.

[2] Aloisi, pp. 200–201; 224, 238–40.

[3] Ibid., pp. 240–41; Robert de Dampierre, op. cit., pp. 280–81; Jean-Paul Garnier, *'Autour d'un Accord'*, *Revue de Paris*, September 1961, pp. 105–6; Herriot, *Jadis*, p. 493. Flandin subsequently claimed that he compelled Laval to go to Rome 'to put an end to the sabotage, in which the officials of both foreign ministries were indulging'. See Pierre-Etienne Flandin, *Politique Française*, 1919–40, Paris, Les Editions Nouvelles, 1947 (hereafter cited as Flandin), p. 104, fn. 2. If this is true, it is further proof of Flandin's support for Laval's policies.

In retrospect, it can be seen that it was a mistake for Laval to have gone to Rome before a detailed agreement was ready for his signature. While M. de Dampierre was probably correct in writing that, once he was on his way, 'the agreement could not fail to be effected',[1] this does not mean that it was bound to be a satisfactory one. In fact, it was to prove something of a deception for both sides.

After lunching with King Victor Emmanuel, Laval began his talks with Mussolini at the Palazzo Venezia in the afternoon of 5 January. The Duce was somewhat scathing about the proposed French concessions in Africa. 'I'm not a collector of deserts,' he said. '. . . I sent Marshal Balbo to take photographs of the areas you are prepared to cede us. I have them here for you. They are lunar landscapes.' 'All the same,' replied Laval, alluding to a couple of oases, 'there are two towns.' 'Two towns!' exclaimed Mussolini. 'Of course,' Laval added, 'I'm not saying they are on a par with Rome or Aubervilliers.' Mussolini laughed and the ice was broken.[2]

Nevertheless, there was much hard bargaining to come and as late as the evening of the 6th, de Chambrun thought the talks might fail. Mussolini attended a dinner at the French embassy that night and negotiations continued after the meal. Laval and the Duce were closeted alone together in one room with their advisers in another. M. Garnier, who acted as liaison, has written that the officials, who were discussing Abyssinia, were completely bogged down. 'On the Italian side, they stuck to their guns: the French formula of economic disinterestedness in Abyssinia must be made explicit on the political level, so that complete freedom of action for the Italian government with regard to the Negus's empire would indisputably result from it. The French delegation did not want to agree to this. The negotiations marked time. Suddenly, between midnight and 1 a.m., the Duce ordered his representatives, who felt as though they had been betrayed, to rally to the French formula.'[3]

Mussolini had clearly been given a verbal assurance by Laval which he considered an effective substitute for the written assurance his advisers had been trying to obtain. But what kind of assurance? Mussolini subsequently claimed that it was nothing less than the promise of a

[1] Robert de Dampierre, op. cit., p. 281.
[2] Jean-Paul Barnier, op. cit., p. 109.
[3] ibid., pp. 110–11.

completely free hand to Italy to satisfy her ambitions in Abyssinia.[1] While not denying that he might have used the expression 'a free hand', Laval always insisted that he had meant it to apply only to the economic sphere and that, above all, he had never condoned the use of force.[2] A partial explanation of this divergence of opinion may be found in one sentence of a letter which Mussolini wrote to Laval on 25 December 1935. After a lengthy justification of his interpretation of the agreement that had been reached the previous January, the Duce added, 'Of course, I do not mean by this that you gave your consent to this war, which subsequent circumstances have made inevitable.'[3]

'This war', it should be recalled, was not a straightforward Italo-Abyssinian conflict, but a full-scale international confrontation in which the League of Nations was involved and in which Britain was on the brink of hostilities with Italy. Mussolini had certainly not envisaged this kind of situation in January 1935. Indeed, there is evidence to suggest that he thought he might be able to get what he wanted in Abyssinia as the result of some kind of joint agreement between Italy, France, and Britain. Thus, having as he thought 'squared' the French, he invited the British government on 29 January 1935 'to proceed to an exchange of views in order to ensure the mutual and harmonious development of Italian and British interests in Abyssinia', and a month later, the Italian ambassador in London suggested to Sir Robert Vansittart, the permanent head of the Foreign Office, that 'Abyssinia should be considered as an object of the colonial policy of the three powers and not as an object of international policy'.[4] It was not until

---

[1] For Mussolini's claim, see his letters to Laval dated 25 December 1935 and 19 February 1936, in Lagardelle, pp. 278–84, 286–7; and his statement to Eden on 24 June 1935 in Eden, p. 224. See also Rafaele Guariglia, *Ricordi, 1922–46*. Naples, Edizioni Scientifiche Italiane, 1949 (hereafter cited as Guariglia), pp. 220–21 (Guariglia was head of the Abyssinian section of the Italian foreign office from April 1935); Italian foreign office report, '*Francia: Situazione politica nel 1935*', Italian Documents, 321 (3) (hereafter cited as Francia), p. 16. Some extracts from this report have been translated and published by William C. Askew in the *Journal of Modern History*, March 1953, pp. 47–8.

[2] For Laval's assertion, see his letters to Mussolini, dated 22 December 1935 and 23 January 1936, in Lagardelle, pp. 275–8, 284–6; his statement to Eden on 21 May 1935 in Eden, p. 209; his declaration to the Chamber of Deputies, J.O. Chambre *Débats*, 28 December 1935, p. 2865; his declaration to the Senate, J. O. Sénat, *Comité Secret du 14 mars 1940*, published as a special supplement to the *Journal Officiel* on 2 August 1948 (hereafter cited as J. O. Sénat, *Comité Secret*), p. 7, col. 2; and his testimony at the Pétain trial on 3 August 1945, *Procès Pétain*, p. 184, col. 1.

[3] Lagardelle, p. 279.

[4] Guariglia, pp. 214–15, 218.

the summer of 1935 that Mussolini finally realized that the British government was not going to acquiesce in his schemes.

If he could labour for so long under the misapprehension that the Abyssinian question could be settled on a three-power basis, why not Laval also? Such self-deception was all the more easy in that the precise extent of Italian ambitions was by no means clear in January 1935, not even to the Duce himself. Nevertheless, the real misunderstanding between Laval and Mussolini was not over the latter's aims, but over the support which Italy could expect from France in the event of those aims proving incapable of fulfilment by relatively peaceful means. Mussolini blandly assumed that he could count upon French support whatever happened. Laval, mesmerized by the prospect of using the Franco-Italian agreement as 'a link in the chain' to a *rapprochement* with Germany, hardly seems to have considered the problem at all.

This emerges very clearly from his reaction to the agreement. He triumphantly telegraphed to Paris at the conclusion of the negotiations that he had conceded less than he had been authorized to do by the cabinet.[1] Upon his return to France he told an American journalist that, although 'on paper he felt that he had lost his shirt to Italy for he had given Mussolini land in the Sahara and near Djibouti and had received nothing much in exchange . . . Mussolini could not raise a dozen bananas on that 117,000 square kilometres of African soil and from now on Italy will have to pay for its policing instead of France. [He] felt . . . that in getting Mussolini to drop Germany's arms demands and Hungary's revisionist claims he really came away with Mussolini's shirt and studs.'[2] These are hardly the comments of a man who had bothered to work out the possible implications of the agreement on Abyssinia. As the Italian foreign office subsequently put it, 'In the beginning, the French government did not fully realize what the "free hand" it had given could and must mean in the near future.'[3]

On 8 January 1935, an official summary of the agreements which had been reached was published by the two governments. It showed that rectifications in Italy's favour had been agreed in the frontiers

---

[1] Guariglia, p. 221. Laval's telegram was intercepted by the Italians.
[2] Straus to Hull, 16 January 1935, F.R.U.S., 1935, Vol. I, pp. 173–5.
[3] Francia, p. 16.

between French West Africa and Libya and between French Somaliland and Eritrea. In Tunisia, children of Italian parents born after
1945 would be able to opt for French nationality and those born after
1965 would automatically become French. Italian schools in the country
would become subject to French law after 1955. On the question of
Austria, the two governments agreed 'to recommend to the states
principally concerned the conclusion of an agreement of non-inter-
ference in their respective internal affairs, and a reciprocal pledge not
to foment or support any action aimed at forcibly attacking the territorial integrity and the political or social régime of any of the contract-
ing parties'. This agreement was to be concluded, in the first instance,
by Austria and her immediate neighbours (Italy, Germany, Hungary,
and Czechoslovakia), but was later to be open to France, Poland, and
Roumania as well. Pending its conclusion, France and Italy would
consult with one another and with Austria if and when the latter's
independence seemed threatened. On armaments, the official summary
stated that the two governments were in agreement that 'no country
can modify its obligations in the sphere of armaments by unilateral
action and that, in the event of such action, they would consult one
another'. Finally, the summary spoke of proposals to improve economic
relations between French and Italian colonies, mentioning in this connection Italian participation in the French-owned Djibouti–Addis
Ababa railway.[1]

A secret protocol on disarmament and a confidential exchange of
letters on Abyssinia went further than the published summary. The
protocol on disarmament referred specifically to Germany as the potential transgressor and stated that 'in the event of circumstances per-
mitting a resumption of international negotiations with a view to the
conclusion of a general disarmament agreement, the two governments
will concert their efforts so that the figures of limitation inscribed in
the agreement will ensure the two countries, in relation to Germany,
the advantages which will be justified for each of them'. The exchange
of letters on Abyssinia recorded the French government's declaration
that it did not 'look in Abyssinia for the satisfaction of any interests
other than those economic interests relating to the traffic of the

---

[1] The official summary and the full texts of the treaties relating to the territorial changes
in Africa and the Tunisian question are printed in R.I.I.A. Documents, 1935, Vol. I,
pp. 19–24.

Djibouti–Addis Ababa railway' and the rights it enjoyed under the Franco-Abyssinian treaty of 1908. The amount of Italian participation in the Djibouti–Addis Ababa railway was specified as 2,500 shares.[1]

Laval subsequently made much of the fact that the Rome agreements were the prelude to Franco-Italian staff talks, culminating in June in what he called 'a veritable military alliance'.[2] But the initiative for the talks seems to have come from the Italians and the French government displayed no sense of urgency until after the German denunciation of the armaments clauses of the Versailles treaty in March.[3] Laval was anyway more interested in using the Rome agreements as a means of coming to terms with Germany than as the first step in a military alliance against her. The Germans themselves were informed of this as early as 6 January, when Laval told their ambassador in Rome in Mussolini's presence that 'to join the Italo-French agreement would provide the best opportunity of proceeding from the stage of proclaiming a desire for peace and understanding, to deeds'. Turning to the Duce, Laval added that 'Franco-German understanding was the corner-stone of any policy of peace. After the settlement of the Saar question and the conclusion of the Rome agreements, the disarmament question could be tackled. In this question, Germany could no longer play hide-and-seek; on the other hand equality of rights could not be denied her in principle: this opportunity should not be allowed simply to slip by, and a settlement must be found.'[4]

Before leaving Rome, Laval had an audience with Pope Pius XI. This was the first time that a French foreign minister had paid an official visit to the Vatican. Laval had to be coached in the elaborate ritual required for the audience and this gave rise to some amusing stories concerning his rustic ignorance. 'With your usual bad faith,' he is said to have complained to a group of journalists, 'you reported me as having addressed the Pope as "Mr Pope", as if I did not know that

[1] The secret agreements have been published with a commentary by D. C. Watt in *The Middle East Journal*, Winter 1961, pp. 69–78.

[2] J. O. Sénat, *Comité Secret*, pp. 6–7. See also *Procès Pétain*, p. 184, col. 1.

[3] General Georges Gamelin, *Servir*, Vol II, *Le Prologue du Drame, 1930–août 1939*, Paris, Plon, 1946 (hereafter cited as Gamelin), pp. 163–7. Flandin's denial (C.E. *Témoignages*, Vol. IX, pp. 2571–3) that military co-operation was envisaged during the Rome conversations is unconvincing.

[4] Von Hassell to Foreign Ministry, 6 January 1935, D.G.F.P., Series C, Vol. III, No. 413.

one had to call him "Holy See".' In fact, the meeting seems to have passed off very well, even if there is no need to believe the holy father's reputed remark to Cardinal Verdier that, after God, he relied upon M. Laval to save the world from war.[1]

The alacrity with which Laval and the French government pursued the goal of an agreement with Italy contrasted sharply with their attitude towards the Franco-Soviet negotiations. Russo-German relations, which had been very cordial during the Weimar period, cooled off considerably after Hitler's accession to power. Soviet negotiations with the French had begun in the summer of 1933 and had gathered momentum after Germany's withdrawal from the League of Nations and the disarmament conference in October of that year. At first the Russians had proposed a straightforward bilateral alliance, but this was unacceptable to the then French foreign minister, M. Paul-Boncour, and M. Barthou, who both wanted to include France's eastern allies in any agreement. The French also insisted that they should not be compelled to go to Russia's aid in the Far East and that the Soviet government must become a member of the League of Nations.

By June 1934 an elaborate compromise had been worked out which consisted of two interrelated parts. The first was a proposed mutual assistance pact between the U.S.S.R., Germany, Czechoslovakia, Poland, Lithuania, Latvia, Estonia and Finland, which, because of its similarity to the agreement signed in 1925 between Germany and her western neighbours, became known as the 'eastern Locarno'. The second part was a separate treaty between France, who was not of course one of Germany's eastern neighbours, and the U.S.S.R. Under the terms of this treaty, France would assume the same obligations towards the Soviet Union as any other member of the 'eastern Locarno' while the Soviet Union would accept the same obligations towards France as if she had signed the original Locarno agreement. Neither agreement would come into force until the U.S.S.R. had joined the League of Nations.

The major drawback to this scheme was the likelihood that the 'eastern Locarno', at least in its original form, would fail to materialize.

[1] François Charles-Roux, *Huit Ans au Vatican, 1932–40*, Paris, Flammarion, 1948, pp. 188–97 (M. Charles-Roux was French ambassador to the Vatican); Alexander Werth, *The Destiny of France*, London, Hamish Hamilton, 1937 (hereafter cited as Werth), p. 100 (Werth was *Manchester Guardian* correspondent in Paris); Maurice Vallet in *La Vie de la France*, Vol. III, p. 1530.

This was for two main reasons. The first was that, while it was quite clear to everybody that the agreement was primarily directed against Germany, she was being invited to join it. The British government proposed a partial solution to this difficulty by suggesting that Germany should also become a party to the separate Franco-Soviet treaty, thus giving the latter 'the necessary element of reciprocity', but the German government turned down this idea on the grounds that it 'cannot consider it a practical reality that Germany, one day, should be defended in her own territory by Soviet Russian troops against an attack from the west or by French troops against an attack from the east'. The second reason was the attitude of Poland. Under the aegis of her foreign minister, Colonel Josef Beck, Poland had to some extent abandoned her close ties with France and was attempting a precarious balancing-act between Germany and Russia. From the Polish viewpoint too, therefore, the 'eastern Locarno' was unacceptable because it was too anti-German.[1]

In the event of the breakdown of the 'eastern Locarno', the Russians hoped that the French would go ahead and conclude a separate treaty with them. Moreover, Barthou appears to have told them on 4 June 1934 that, if Germany and Poland refused to take part, it was his 'personal opinion' that 'some sort of agreement between the U.S.S.R. and France' would be concluded.[2] But in October Barthou was replaced by Laval and, in November, the Flandin government was formed. The attitude of the new team was to be somewhat different.

Laval had been an opponent of an agreement with the Russians from the very beginning. When the 'eastern Locarno' came up for discussion at a cabinet meeting on 5 June 1934, Herriot, who was the most notorious Russophile in the government, noted that Laval declared himself 'categorically in favour of an agreement with Germany and hostile to a *rapprochement* with Russia, which would bring us the Internationale and the red flag'. In the fervour with which Laval argued, Herriot recognized a man who, only a few days before, had been

[1] The preceding three paragraphs are based upon W. E. Scott, *Alliance against Hitler*, Durham, N. C., Duke University Press, 1962, chapters 6-9. The quotations are from pages 179 and 186.

[2] 'The Struggle of the U.S.S.R. for Collective Security in Europe during 1933-35', Part I, *International Affairs* (Moscow), June 1963, p. 113. This article is the first of four based upon and frequently citing the Soviet foreign ministry archives. The articles will be hereafter cited as 'The Struggle . . . for Collective Security', followed by the month and page number(s). See also W. E. Scott, op. cit., p. 209.

roughly handled by the communists at Aubervilliers. 'Small causes, large results,' the Radical leader commented.[1]

When he took over the foreign ministry, Laval certainly left the Russians in no doubt about his real aim. At his first meeting with the Soviet ambassador on 19 October 1934, he said that his appointment had aroused hope in Germany because he was known to be striving for an agreement with that country, without which peace in Europe was impossible. Still, he realized that there were difficulties and if agreement with Germany were possible only in a roundabout way, as the result of prior agreement with Russia, then he was willing to try that method as well! Four days later, he told a Soviet embassy official that 'peace is the main thing and that without the enlistment of Germany the cause of peace will be unstable.' 'Of all the French political leaders,' he added, 'he . . . had done most for a *rapprochement* with Germany.'[2]

In the circumstances, it was not surprising that the Soviet government took fright and put forward a proposal that, pending the conclusion of the 'eastern Locarno', the two countries should pledge not to enter into any other agreement which might jeopardize it and to keep each other informed of any proposals for such an agreement. Laval was reluctant to enter into any such commitment, especially if it was to be made public, but he finally gave in to Russian pressure. A Franco-Soviet protocol, incorporating the Russian proposal, was signed at Geneva on 5 December by Laval and Litvinov, the Soviet commissar for foreign affairs.[3]

The Russians were also highly suspicious of the Rome agreements, especially in view of Laval's admission to the Soviet ambassador in Paris on 9 January that 'he had agreed "in principle" with Mussolini . . . on certain conditions to recognize the completion of German remarmament'. The ambassador indignantly retorted that 'before making any concessions to Germany on the question of armaments, it is a matter of priority to conclude an eastern pact'.[4]

Russian concern was shared by the Little Entente governments. Meeting at Ljubljana on 11 January, their representatives publicly

[1] Herriot, *Jadis*, pp. 437–8.
[2] 'The Struggle . . . for Collective Security', July 1963, pp. 119–20.
[3] Ibid., pp. 120–21. The text of the protocol is printed in R.I.I.A. Documents, 1934, pp. 184–5.
[4] 'The Struggle . . . for Collective Security', July 1963, pp. 122–3.

promised 'to collaborate with all the interested powers to put the principles of the Rome agreements into practice in the most sincere spirit', but privately warned France that they would do so only 'in the event of a close entente with the U.S.S.R. and the conclusion of an eastern pact'. A week later, M. Titulescu, the Roumanian foreign minister, told Laval point-blank in the presence of representatives of the Balkan Entente (Turkey, Yugoslavia, and Greece) and of the Soviet Union that 'Roumania will side with France only if a Franco-Soviet agreement is concluded and that, if in the absence of such agreement the U.S.S.R. again joins up with Germany, the Roumanians will follow suit. Yugoslavia will act similarly. Neither the Little Entente nor the [Balkan] Entente can exist without a Franco-Soviet agreement. That is why they insist that an eastern pact should be concluded as a priority.' The American adviser to the disarmament conference was right when he cabled to the State Department that 'the Soviets, the Little Entente, and the Balkan Entente have put a pistol at Laval's head'.[1]

One thing which Laval was constantly being urged to do was to exert pressure upon France's recalcitrant ally Poland to make her more favourably disposed towards the eastern pact. He promised to do so and informed the French ambassador in Warsaw on 23 January 1935 that he had taken advantage of Colonel Beck's presence at Geneva to warn him that, whatever Poland's attitude, he would continue to negotiate the pact. But Polish sources are much less emphatic than this. Beck told Count Szembek, the permanent head of the Polish foreign office, that Laval 'confined himself to remarking, in a very mild fashion, that he hoped our attitude would not force France to sign the eastern pact without us'. Beck's own record of his conversations with Laval is even less categorical. When the Polish foreign minister described the proposed pact as anti-German, Laval is said to have replied that 'he is in no way conducting an anti-German policy and that he only considers the pact as a general problem. . . . As far as he is concerned, the agreement is, at rock bottom, designed to ensure collective security at a time when the question of German armaments is coming up for discussion once again.' During the course of the discussions, Beck noted, that 'matters relating to western Europe and Germany interest Laval to a much greater extent than Russian policy, in which

[1] Ibid., p. 123; Mayer to Hull, 22 January 1935, F.R.U.S., 1935, Vol. I, p. 6

connection he repeated on two occasions that, in the final analysis, it was not he who was the author of the proposed eastern pact'.[1]

This 'western orientation' of French foreign policy was illustrated in the communiqué which was issued at the conclusion of Flandin's and Laval's visit to London on 3 February. With its talk of the Rome agreements, the possibility of new armaments negotiations with Germany, and a west European air pact, the communiqué led the Soviet commissariat for foreign affairs to suspect 'a desire to drown the proposed eastern pact in some general European arrangement which should cover a wide range of problems, including disarmament'. It was true that the communiqué did speak of the eastern pact as one element in 'a general settlement' which would be negotiated simultaneously with all the others, and the French made much of this in their subsequent dealings with the Russians. But there was room for doubt as to whether the French really attached as much importance to the principle of 'simultaneity' as they professed and, in any case, 'simultaneity' was not enough for the Russians. They wanted the eastern pact accorded priority.[2]

After a series of conversations with Laval, however, the Soviet ambassador in Paris was compelled to report to Moscow that there was little hope of this. 'Laval is not disposed to really single out an eastern pact as an independent and priority action,' he wrote. 'He is not thinking at the moment of activating the negotiations. . . . [He] has not yet made up his mind whether it is worth while concluding such a pact, in the event of Germany's refusal, without her and Poland. [He] has by no means given up the thought of replacing the mutual assistance obligations in an eastern pact with non-aggression and consultations [and he] has not yet made up his mind whether, after releasing Germany and Poland of mutual assistance, France should give undertakings concerning mutual assistance in regard to us and Czechoslovakia.'[3]

---

[1] Jules Laroche, *La Pologne de Pilsudski, Souvenirs d'une Ambassade, 1926–35*, Paris, Flammarion, 1953, p. 191; Comte Jean Szembek, *Journal, 1933–39*, Paris, Plon, 1952 (hereafter cited as Szembek), p. 23; Joseph Beck, *Dernier Rapport, Politique Polonaise, 1926–39*, Neuchatel, Editions de la Baconnière, 1951 (hereafter cited as Beck), pp. 284–5.

[2] For the text of the Anglo-French communiqué, see R.I.I.A. Documents, 1935, Vol. I, pp. 25–7. For French views on 'simultaneity', see Enclosure in Hoesch to Foreign Ministry, 6 February 1935, D.G.F.P., Series C, Vol. III, No. 483. For the Soviet attitude and Franco-Soviet exchanges, see 'The Struggle . . . for Collective Security', August 1963, pp. 132–3.

[3] Ibid., p. 133.

If the German government had played its cards right, it might have succeeded in keeping the Franco-Soviet negotiations in the doldrums indefinitely, but, thanks to two singularly inept actions, it actually hastened the conclusion of an agreement. The first was the invitation to the British government on 14 February to negotiate the question of a west European air pact with Germany direct. As Laval complained to the German ambassador on 22 February, this tactic 'had created the impression amongst the French public and also in certain British circles that [the Germans] wished to separate France from Britain'.[1] The second, and more important, action was the German government's decision, which was made public on 16 March, to renounce the disarmament provisions of the Versailles treaty and reintroduce conscription. The justification given for these measures was the strength of the Soviet armed forces and the French government's recent decision to increase the period of compulsory military service from one to two years.[2]

On the face of it the reaction to the German decision was an impressive one. On 9 April Laval completely reversed his earlier delaying tactics and agreed, albeit reluctantly, upon the need to conclude a bilateral pact with the U.S.S.R. by 1 May at the latest.[3] An Anglo-Franco-Italian 'summit' conference was held at Stresa from 11 to 14 April and its final declaration stated that 'the three powers . . . find themselves in complete agreement in opposing, by all practical means, any unilateral repudiation of treaties which may endanger the peace of Europe, and will act in close and cordial collaboration for this purpose.'[4] Three days after the end of the conference, the League of Nations council, meeting in extraordinary session, passed a resolution sponsored by the same three powers roundly condemning the German government's unilateral action and calling for a strengthening of the Covenant.[5] 'Stresa and Geneva,' wrote André François-Poncet, the

[1] For the German invitation, which was contained in the reply to the Anglo-French communiqué of 3 February, see R.I.I.A. Documents, 1935, Vol. I, pp. 35–6. For Laval's complaint, see Köster to Foreign Ministry, 22 February 1935, D.G.F.P., Series C, Vol. III, No. 502.

[2] The texts of the conscription law and Hitler's accompanying proclamation are printed in R.I.I.A. Documents, 1935, Vol. I, pp. 58–64. The French decision to double the period of military service was taken in order to offset the decline in the number of recruits caused by the falling birth-rate. See Herriot, Jadis, pp. 502–20; Gamelin, pp. 152–9.

[3] 'The Struggle . . . for Collective Security', October 1963, pp. 112–13; Herriot, Jadis, pp. 523, 525.

[4] For the text of the Stresa declaration, see R.I.I.A. Documents, 1935, Vol. I, p. 82

[5] For the text of the three-power resolution, see ibid, pp. 98–9.

French ambassador in Berlin, 'were the high-water mark of European solidarity against the ambitions of the *Reich*. . . . Never did her leaders, her diplomats, and her official journalists seem to me to be more confused and discouraged.'[1]

But this solidarity was more apparent than real. The British government had nearly ruined it at the start by refusing to cancel or postpone the proposed visit of the foreign secretary, Sir John Simon, and Mr Eden to Berlin. During that visit, which took place on 25 and 26 March, Simon invited the German government to take part in 'informal conversations . . . about naval armaments' with the British government. These 'informal conversations' led to the notorious Anglo-German naval agreement of 18 June, by which Britain agreed, without effective consultation with her allies, to Germany's constructing a navy 35 per cent the size of her own.[2]

Mussolini's aim at Stresa seems to have been less the formation of an anti-German front in Europe than the obtaining of a blank cheque for his proposed venture in Abyssinia. The statement in the conference's final declaration that the three powers opposed 'any unilateral repudiation of treaties which may endanger the peace of Europe' acquires a sinister ring when it is recalled that Mussolini deliberately suggested the addition of the words 'of Europe'. For some inexplicable reason, the British did not appear to catch on, although Flandin subsequently wrote that 'M. Laval and I, and doubtless Mussolini also, gained the impression of a tacit acquiescence on the part of the British government in Italian ambitions, in Abyssinia, if not in the means of realizing those ambitions, which only became apparent . . . after Stresa.'[3] When the British government finally did adopt a positive

[1] André François-Poncet, *Souvenirs d'une Ambassade à Berlin*, Paris, Flammarion, 1946, p. 235.

[2] For Simon's invitation, see the unsigned, undated memorandum of Hitler's conversations with Simon and Eden, D.G.F.P., Series C, Vol. III, No. 555, p. 1064. For the best account of the Anglo-German naval agreement and its repercussions, see D. C. Watt, 'The Anglo-German Naval Agreement of 1935: an Interim Judgement', *Journal of Modern History*, June 1956, pp. 155–75.

[3] On this incident at Stresa, see Flandin, p. 178; Undated letter from Pirelli to Lord Salter in Guariglia, p. 782; Mussolini's interview with Ward Price, 16 September 1935, in E. and D. Susmel (eds), *Opera Omnia di Benito Mussolini*, Vol. XXVII, Florence, La Fenice, 1959 (hereafter cited as Mussolini), pp. 139–40. In spite of the promptings of Eden and the British ambassador in Rome, the Abyssinian question was not placed upon the Stresa agenda by the British government for fear that it would rupture the inter-allied front. In Vansittart's words, it was considered better 'to land Mussolini first and lecture him later'. Discussions did take place, however, at official level between British and Italian

attitude towards Mussolini's Abyssinian policy, it was a hostile one, and the resultant conflict blew the so-called 'Stresa front' wide open.

On the French side, Laval made it clear as early as 22 March that his reaction to Germany's renunciation of the armaments clauses of the Versailles treaty was one of sorrow rather than anger. 'A generous effort has been made to organize peace in Europe,' he told the Chamber of Deputies, alluding to the Rome and London meetings. 'By her gesture, Germany will, I hope, merely have slowed down the task to which we remain passionately devoted.' France had no intention of excluding anybody from 'the solid and lasting peace which all people demand,' he went on. '. . . The policy which France is pursuing in conjunction with her allies and friends is not a policy of aggression. It is not directed against any country.'[1]

He still hoped to persuade Germany to enter into some kind of agreement to guarantee the peace and was therefore greatly encouraged by a remark which Hitler had made to Simon and Eden during their visit to Berlin to the effect that, while he would continue to oppose the mutual assistance provisions of the 'eastern Locarno' – it being out of the question for national socialists to call upon bolsheviks for support – 'he was prepared to join a system of non-aggression pacts and to include the bilateral treaties concluded or to be concluded by Germany in a multilateral treaty'.[2] Mindful of his newly-acquired obligation to sign a bilateral pact with the Soviet Union by 1 May, Laval asked the British during the Stresa conference to find out whether Germany would still take part in a multilateral pact if some of its members had signed separate bilateral pacts which included mutual assistance provisions. When the German foreign minister replied, on 12 April, that his government would have no objection provided there was no reference to such bilateral pacts in any pact which Germany signed, Laval

---

experts. See Lord Vansittart, *The Mist Procession*, London, Hutchinson, 1958 (hereafter cited as Vansittart), pp. 520–21; Eden, p. 179; Viscount Templewood (Sir Samuel Hoare), *Nine Troubled Years*, London, Collins, 1954 (hereafter cited as Templewood), p. 156; Guariglia, pp. 226–7; Sir Geoffrey Thompson, *Frontline Diplomat*, London, Hutchinson, 1959, pp. 96–8.

[1] J. O. Chambre, *Débats*, 22 March 1935, p. 1209, cols. 2–3.

[2] Unsigned, undated memorandum of Hitler's conversations with Simon and Eden, D.G.F.P., Series C, Vol. III, No. 555, p. 1051. The Germans later handed the British ministers some draft suggestions for the conclusion of a ten-year non-aggression and consultative pact. See Enclosure to von Neurath's circular telegram, 29 March 1935, ibid., No. 564.

must have been overjoyed. He was free to resume his quest for peace and, as we shall see, the multilateral non-aggression pact became something of an obsession with him during the next few weeks.[1]

During the final negotiations for the Franco-Soviet pact, which began at Geneva on 15 April, the French insisted upon two important restrictions to the mutual assistance provisions. The first specified, in effect, that France could not go to the assistance of the Soviet Union without the approval of Britain and Italy. This was because, under the Locarno treaty of 1925, Britain, France, and Italy had all guaranteed Germany's western frontier against attack. The second restriction delayed the implementation of the mutual assistance provisions until the League council had given its verdict on the dispute which had arisen. Thus, although articles 2 and 3 of the pact were clear enough about the obligation of both countries to go to one another's assistance in the event of 'unprovoked aggression on the part of a European state', the protocol to the pact, which contained the restrictions mentioned above, placed a strict limitation upon this obligation.[2]

Laval's motives in emasculating the Franco-Soviet pact were mixed. To some extent undoubtedly, he shared the suspicion of other western statesmen[3] that the Soviet Union wanted to embroil other countries in war for her own selfish purposes. But he also had a somewhat peculiar conception of the role of pacts in general. For him, they were not alliances designed to preserve the balance of power, but rather public pledges of international good behaviour. Finally, of course, he wanted to reassure Germany that France harboured no hostile intentions towards her. All these reasons were reflected in a remark to his private secretary at the conclusion of the laborious negotiations for the pact. 'You want to know why it's so difficult?' he asked. 'It's because *they* want a treaty to make war, and *I* want one to avoid it.'[4] The old dictum that, if you want peace you must prepare for war, was a contradiction in terms for Laval.

[1] Von Neurath memorandum, 12 April 1935, ibid., Vol. IV, No. 24; *Correspondence showing the course of certain diplomatic discussions directed towards securing an European settlement, June 1934–March 1936* (Cmd. 5143), London, H.M.S.O., 1936, pp. 23–5.

[2] For the final negotiations concerning the pact, see 'The Struggle . . . for Collective Security', October 1963, pp. 115–19; Herriot, *Jadis*, pp. 529–34. The text of the pact and the accompanying protocol is printed in Herriot's memoirs and R.I.I.A. Documents, 1935, Vol. I, pp. 116–19.

[3] e.g. Neville Chamberlain.

[4] André Guénier in *La Vie de la France*, Vol. III, p. 1347.

Nevertheless, the final text of the pact was not solely the work of Laval. It was adopted without objection, as far as is known, by the entire cabinet, and Flandin told an American scholar in 1950 that he saw it primarily as 'a guarantee of Russian non-intervention against the neighbours of Germany', adding that, 'we never wanted to give Russia a guiding hand in our destinies [or] . . . bring the Russian army into the centre of Europe'.[1] There was nothing in this statement with which Laval would have disagreed and it is therefore somewhat surprising to find Flandin in his memoirs claiming that he 'succeeded in imposing' the signature of the pact upon a reluctant Laval.[2] By his own admission, there was nothing to impose.

Litvinov came to Paris on 2 May to sign the pact, and Laval paid a return visit to Moscow on the 13th. He stopped off in Warsaw *en route* for two days of talks with the Polish government, during which he did his best to explain away the document he had just signed. It was, he claimed, the best method of preventing a return to the Rapallo policy of Russo-German co-operation, and he emphasized that paragraph four of the protocol to the pact, for which he claimed the credit, meant that France would not come to Russia's aid in the event of a Russo-Polish conflict. In any case, Laval made it clear that he was more interested in the multilateral non-aggression pact which Hitler had suggested to Simon and Eden than in the Franco-Soviet pact. Indeed, he told the Poles that 'if the multilateral pact was actually constituted, the Franco-Soviet agreement . . . would become quite useless'.[3]

Needless to say, he did not employ this language in Moscow. Instead, he concentrated upon extracting a public acknowledgement from Stalin of the need for France to strengthen her armed forces, thus spiking the guns of the communist opposition at home. Laval told William Bullitt, the American ambassador in Moscow, how he had obtained Stalin's agreement. He said that 'he had begun his conversation . . . in the usual vague diplomatic manner and that Stalin had interrupted him saying "I cannot talk in diplomatic language, I am not a diplomat", whereupon he had replied "all right, you will get it straight", and had at once told Stalin the French could not understand the camouflage of the actual dictator of Russia and world communism pretending

---

[1] W. E. Scott, *Alliance against Hitler*, Durham, N.C., Duke University Press, 1962, p. 245 and fn. 86.
[2] Flandin, p. 170.
[3] For Laval's conversations in Poland, see Szembek, pp. 70–78; Beck, p. 288.

that he had nothing to do with the Comintern and foreign communists and that French public opinion certainly would not understand if Stalin did not now give orders to the communists in France to cease opposition to the army budget and to the two-year service law. He said that Stalin had replied "I agree" . . .' As a result of this agreement, the communiqué which was issued at the conclusion of the visit contained a sentence which read, 'M. Stalin understands and fully approves of the policy of national defence carried out by France in order to maintain her armed strength at the level required for her security.'[1] 'The communist campaign against the "two years" ceased immediately,' a British observer noted.[2]

Laval was greatly impressed by Stalin, especially by his self-control. Contrasting him later with Hitler, whom he had not met in 1935, he said, 'If Stalin is a fanatic, and I'm not altogether sure of it, he is at any rate a lucid fanatic.'[3] But if anything his visit to Moscow deepened his hatred of communism. Eight years later, in a private speech, he recalled that, when he had recrossed the frontier into Poland, the journalists accompanying him had asked him what he thought of the bolshevik régime. 'I hope with all my heart that my country never experiences this system,' he replied. It struck him that he had never seen a smile on the faces of the people in the streets.[4]

In view of Laval's attitude to the Franco-Soviet pact, it is not surprising that he tried to side-step Stalin's proposal to give it teeth by initiating immediate staff talks between the two countries. At first he argued that it would be better to wait until after the conclusion of the complementary Russo-Czech pact, but when Litvinov pointed out that this agreement had already been concluded, he promised to propose to the French government 'the opening of these staff conversations in the usual conditions of discretion'.[5] They never took place.

While Laval was in Moscow, Marshal Pilsudski, the head of the Polish state, suddenly died. On his way home, Laval attended the state funeral at Cracow on 18 May and had a long conversation with

[1] Bullitt to Hull, 15 May 1935, F.R.U.S., 1935, Vol. I, pp. 278–9. The text of the communiqué is printed in R.I.I.A. Documents, 1935, Vol. I, pp. 137–8.
[2] Werth, p. 140.
[3] Jaffré, p. 136.
[4] Speech at the Hôtel de Ville in Paris, 29 September 1943 (unpublished text kindly communicated to me by M. René de Chambrun).
[5] Laval to Flandin, 16 May 1935, cited by Flandin in C.E. *Témoignages*, Vol. I, pp. 142–3. For the Russo-Czech agreement, see R.I.I.A. Documents, 1935, Vol. I, pp. 138–9.

the German representative at the ceremony, Hermann Goering. According to the French record of the meeting, which is the only one that has survived, the conversation was not very productive. Goering mainly confined himself to attacking the Franco-Soviet pact and suggested more than once that peace in Europe would be better served by a direct Franco-German understanding. Laval told Goering point-blank that 'peace can only exist if it exists in all parts of Europe'. If Germany was as peaceful as Goering maintained, he concluded, she must be prepared to rest content with her present frontiers and give guarantees against aggression in eastern Europe as well as in the west.[1]

None the less, both participants seemed favourably impressed by the meeting. Goering shared his interpreter's view that, together with the British ministers' visit to Berlin, it reflected a desire 'not to let things come to a final break with Germany, but to try and draw the *Reich* out of her isolation and back into the community of nations'.[2] As for Laval, he told Count Szembek that Goering had made 'an incontestably favourable impression upon him' and he was more than ever determined to press ahead with the multilateral non-aggression pact, which he described as 'the only means of guaranteeing peace'. 'You mustn't think I'm a thoughtless chaser after pacts,' he said. 'I'm a realistic politician. But there's such an atmosphere of excitement in the world that, in all seriousness, I can see no other way of reducing this scheme to order. Otherwise, we shall be invaded by bolshevism.'[3]

Laval promised Goering he would take up the question of the multilateral pact with his government as soon as he returned to Paris, and on 3 June he gave the German ambassador a personal memorandum in which he suggested the opening of preliminary discussions between the two countries. The occasion was somewhat marred by a recent German statement, putting forward the view that the Franco-Soviet pact was incompatible with Locarno,[4] and Laval sought first of all to set the ambassador's mind at rest. He told him that 'he . . . regarded

---

[1] Undated Rochat memorandum, printed in Jacques Baraduc (ed.), *Tout ce qu'on vous a caché*, Paris, Editions de l'Elan, 1949, pp. 299–311. Rochat's authorship emerges from his testimony in *La Vie de la France*, Vol. II, p. 1107.

[2] Paul Schmidt, *Statist auf Diplomatischer Bühne, 1923–45*, Bonn, Athenäum-Verlag, 1949, p. 310. Schmidt had been the interpreter at Laval's meetings with Brüning in 1931 and Laval saw this as a good omen.

[3] Szembek, pp. 82–4, 85–6.

[4] Enclosure to von Neurath circular telegram, 25 May 1935, D.G.F.P., Series C, Vol. IV, No. 107.

the Franco-Russian treaty as primarily a factor in assuaging the Russian fear of a German attack and thus inducing Russia to co-operate effectively in restoring conditions to normal in Europe'. The Russians had, it was true, tried to persuade France 'to take up a position which would not have accorded with her peace policy, but . . . in the end [they] had had to be satisfied with the present treaty'. But in any case, Laval went on, this was not the purpose of his visit. Germany had stated her readiness to sign a multilateral non-aggression pact and, as the ambassador could see from his memorandum, 'France was making Germany's proposed course of action her own.' He had been greatly encouraged by his conversation with Goering, although he had been compelled to point out that a Franco-German understanding 'could not be realized by means of bipartite negotiations, but only on an international basis which would guarantee Germany's intention of remaining at peace with all the countries of Europe'. All his hopes, he concluded, 'rested on Germany's accepting these proposals.'[1]

A cabinet crisis had prevented Laval from handing over his memorandum sooner. A disastrous run on the franc had been precipitated, and the Flandin government was overthrown by the Chamber of Deputies on 30 May when attempting to obtain emergency powers to deal with the situation. Only the day after Laval saw the German ambassador, the Bouisson government, which had succeeded that of Flandin and in which Laval remained foreign minister, was overthrown on the same issue. It was Laval himself who succeeded in forming a government to succeed Bouisson's. Thenceforth he was called upon to deal with a grave internal situation in addition to the far from promising outlook abroad.

[1] Köster to Foreign Ministry, 3, 4 June, 1935, ibid., Nos. 127, 129.

3

The Second Government

June 1935 – January 1936

'It is in order to combat speculation and save the franc that our government has been formed,' Laval told the Chamber of Deputies on 7 June 1935.[1] The most obvious symptom of the financial crisis with which he had to deal was the outflow of gold from the Bank of France. Between 10 and 31 May the bank lost 8,500 million francs' worth of gold, or a little over 10 per cent of its holdings.[2] The underlying cause of this outward movement of gold was that for over three and a half years the French government had been fighting to preserve the parity between gold and the franc established by the Poincaré government in 1928. Until Britain left the gold standard in September 1931 there had been little difficulty in doing so. In fact, the franc was actually under-valued compared with other major international currencies, which more than any other factor, explains why the world economic depression affected France so late. After September 1931, however, the position began to deteriorate and the process was accentuated by the continued depreciation of sterling, especially during 1934, and even more by the devaluation of the dollar in 1933. Now, instead of being undervalued in relation to other currencies, the franc was overvalued. One estimate put the disparity between the franc and the pound as high as 12 to 15 per cent in October 1934.[3]

When a currency is overvalued, bankers and other dealers in foreign exchange fear devaluation and this is liable to lead to a run on the currency, which is what happened in the case of France in the spring of 1935. The run on the franc was preceded by runs on the currencies

---

[1] J. O. Chambre, *Débats*, 7 June 1935, p. 1807, col. 1.
[2] 'Letter from Paris', *Economist*, 13 June 1935, p. 1361.
[3] This diagnosis follows that in 'France's Economic Problem', ibid., 27 April 1935, pp. 943–5.

of other countries which, in 1933, had joined with France in forming the so-called 'gold bloc'. Triggered off by the planned devaluation in Belgium (hitherto a member of the 'gold bloc') at the beginning of April, speculation attacked, with gathering momentum, the Swiss franc in April and the Dutch guilder in April and May before turning to France.

Closely connected with the weakness of the franc was the onset of the world depression in France. As French prices rose relative to those of other countries, so French exports fell: from a monthly average of 2,536 million francs in 1931 to 1,487 million in 1934. This helped to produce an all-round decline in economic activity, and the index of industrial production, which stood at 100 in April 1931, fell to 76 by April 1935.[1] An important consequence of the depression as far as the central government was concerned was the decline in tax receipts. Revenue from all taxes had been 3,570 million francs in 1931; by 1934 it had fallen to 2,896 million. Expenditure had not been reduced correspondingly and this gave rise to the problem of budgetary deficits with which successive governments had grappled in vain since 1932.[2]

Most present-day economists would probably agree that the best solution for France's ills would have been a large programme of public spending designed to stimulate home demand, coupled with a devaluation of the franc sufficient to improve the country's competitive position in world markets. But this would have been a very unorthodox approach in the pre-Keynesian days of 1935. Then, the best remedy was held to be deflation. Government expenditure and wages and salaries were held down, or even cut back, in an attempt to wipe out budgetary deficits and lower costs. It was thereby hoped to reduce or even eliminate the gap between French and world prices while at the same time preserving the parity of the franc. This policy had not worked before, but such was the fear of deficit financing and devaluation that, on 7 and 8 June, parliament voted Laval's government full powers to make one more attempt to implement it by decree-law.

The political context in which the government was called upon to tackle these difficult economic problems was an unstable one. The riots of 6 February 1934 produced a polarization of French political life to

---

[1] Etat Français, Statistique Générale et Institut de Conjoncture, *Mouvement Economique en France de 1929 à 1939*, Paris, Imprimerie Nationale, 1941, pp. 146–7, 165.

[2] Ibid., p. 205.

a degree unknown since the Dreyfus affair. The process was not quite complete when Laval became prime minister; it was one of his achievements to make it so. On the left, 6 February led to a *rapprochement* of those arch-enemies, the Socialist and Communist parties. Pressure from below and from the Soviet Union, which was interested in building up strong left-wing coalitions in the democracies as a barrier against German expansionism, compelled the communist leadership to abandon its prejudices and campaign with the socialists against the fascist threat at home and abroad. On 27 July 1934, the two parties signed a 'unity of action' pact for this purpose.

With that almost unbelievable access of enthusiasm which always seems to characterize communist parties when they change their line, the French party took the lead in calling for an extension of the unity pact to other anti-fascist forces. In October 1934 the party secretary, Maurice Thorez, invited the socialists to explore the possibility of re-unifying the French labour movement, which had also split in 1920 into communist and socialist factions. By the beginning of 1935, he was even calling for approaches to 'local organizations of the radical party or the League of the Rights of Man which are opposed to the policy of national union and the misdeeds of fascist bands'. He even coined a name for this vast regrouping of the forces of the left: 'the Popular Front of labour, freedom, and peace'.[1]

Thorez's appeal to the radical party was a shrewd one. Although the party had rallied to the national union formula of the Doumergue and Flandin governments, there was always a strong current of feeling against such a combination, and it was strengthened by such factors as Tardieu's attack upon the radicals at the Stavisky enquiry, Doumergue's proposals for constitutional reform, and his alleged tenderness towards the right-wing bands which had taken part in the riots of 6 February 1934. A coalition with Flandin's *Alliance Démocratique*, which seemed to offer a centrist alternative to reliance upon right or left, was tried in the municipal elections of May 1935, but it was not a great success. At the same time, a hitherto insuperable obstacle to co-operation with the communists was removed by Stalin's declaration at the conclusion of Laval's visit to Moscow that he approved of the French defence

---

[1] The previous two paragraphs closely follow Georges Dupeux, *Le Front Populaire et les Elections de 1936*, Paris, Armand Colin, 1959, Chapter IV. The two quotations from Maurice Thorez may be found on pp. 82–3.

effort.[1] Previously the most bitter opponents of French defence policy, the communists now joined its most vociferous supporters. Indeed, the transformation had gone so far that, on the day the Flandin government was overthrown, Thorez openly appealed to the radicals to form a left-wing government with his party's support. This was a real option open to the radicals during the week of crisis that followed, but it was ruled out, not only by the attitude of their leadership, but also by the deliberately obstructionist tactics of the socialists, who posed impossible conditions for their support. As a result, the radicals had virtually no alternative but to support Laval. Herriot again figured in the new cabinet as a minister of state and radicals were given the key ministries of finance and the interior as well as three other portfolios. Nevertheless, the lukewarm nature of radical support for Laval is clearly indicated by the abstention of half the party's members in the Chamber of Deputies in the vote granting his government full powers. Less than a fortnight later, the party accepted the invitation to take part, along with the socialists and communists, in the *Front Populaire* demonstration planned for 14 July.[2]

The chief factor which propelled the radicals towards the *Front Populaire* was undoubtedly the activity of the leagues, those right-wing paramilitary organizations which had been the spearhead of the riots of 6 February 1934. By mid-1935, the most dangerous looked to be the *Croix de Feu*. Originally founded as an association for decorated ex-servicemen in 1927, it was gradually taken over by Lieutenant-Colonel de la Rocque, a retired army officer who at one time had been on Marshal Foch's staff. De la Rocque widened the membership of the organization, admitting men who had not even fought in the war, and also transformed it into an overtly political movement. Although vague, the *Croix de Feu*'s programme, with its call for some form of corporatism and the reinforcement of the executive at the expense of the legislature, had suspiciously fascist overtones.[3]

Even more alarming than its programme was the style of its meetings and the tone of its leader's pronouncements. Alexander Werth, the Paris correspondent of the *Manchester Guardian*, subsequently gave a

---

[1] See above, p. 82.
[2] This paragraph is based upon Larmour, Chapter 6. For the list of members of Laval's government, see Bonnefous, Vol. V, pp. 444-5. For the party breakdown of the vote on full powers, see *Le Temps*, 9 June 1935.
[3] For the *Croix de Feu* and the other leagues, see my essay on France in S. J. Woolf (ed.), *European Fascism*, Weidenfeld and Nicolson, 1968.

THE SECOND GOVERNMENT · 89

vivid picture of this side of the movement's activities just at the time of
the formation of the Laval government. '. . . Once Laval was safely
in the saddle,' he wrote, 'the fun started. "Giant" rallies and mobilisa-
tion exercises began to be held in various parts of France. . . . [De
la Rocque] swore that the *Croix de Feu* had been "on their guard"
during the cabinet crisis, and that there would have been some
fun – *il y aurait eu du sport* – if *le fusilleur* Daladier[1] had been included
in the new government . . . and, becoming bolder and bolder, the
Colonel proclaimed that "he did not care a hang for legality", and that
the *Croix de Feu* would "take command" at the appropriate moment.
The most impressive rally – in the course of which many ominous
speeches were made – took place at Algiers [on 10 June], complete with
thirty aeroplanes belonging to the *Croix de Feu* organisation; and
there were also many other rallies mostly held on the estate of some
wealthy patron. . . . On several occasions the roads leading to these
"secret rallies" were policed by *Croix de Feu* men.'[2]

It is doubtful whether the conditions for a right-wing *coup* did exist
in France in mid-1935, but many radicals saw the danger as a very real
one. Moreover, they contrasted the violence of the leagues with the
relatively peaceful demeanour of the communists. 'Does the communist peril even exist in Eure-et-Loir?' one deputy asked rhetorically
in his local newspaper. 'Even if it did, it would not [like the *Croix de
Feu*] mass thousands of individuals at the very gates of Chartres.'[3]

Laval got off to a bad start as far as the leagues were concerned. On
20 June he adopted a very high-handed tone with a radical deputy,
Marc Rucart, who was seeking to get a debate on proposals to curb the
leagues, threatening to cut short the parliamentary session unless the
government's agenda was immediately voted.[4] Five days later, he told
a deputation from the *délégation des gauches*, the informal liaison group
of all left-wing parties, that he 'would use every means at his disposal
in order to ensure respect for the republican institutions which were
in his charge'. But he also made it quite clear that he blamed the communists as much as the leagues for any disorders which had occurred.[5]

[1] This was an allusion to his responsibility for the police opening fire on the rioters on
6 February 1934.
[2] Werth, pp. 158–9.
[3] Larmour, pp. 173–5.
[4] J. O. Chambre, *Débats*, 20 June 1935, p. 1871, col. 3.
[5] *Le Temps*, 27 June 1935.

By his attitude, he was to lay himself open to the charge that he secretly sympathized with leagues and their aims.

A more charitable explanation is that he was obsessed by the need to take action to deal with the financial crisis. Already, on 15 June, he had obtained the services of Raoul Dautry, the director of the state railways, Claude-Jean Gignoux, editor of the business newspaper *La Journée Industrielle* and a minister in Laval's 1931–32 government, and Jacques Rueff, then a finance ministry official, as 'a brains trust' to advise him and his finance minister Marcel Régnier. 'All three,' commented the *Economist*, 'hold "orthodox" economic views and are staunch supporters of budgetary deflation.'[1] The first fruits of their advice were seen in the decree-laws published on 16 July. The details are extremely complicated, but broadly speaking the decrees provided for a ten per cent reduction in all central and local government expenditure and cuts of up to ten per cent in the wages and salaries of all public employees. In order to make this seem more equitable, income tax on the highest incomes was increased by half and reductions were made in rents, mortgages, bread, coal, gas and electricity prices over which the government exercised control.[2]

In a broadcast to the French people on 17 July, Laval explained the measures in simple, homespun language. In the past five years, he explained, the national debt had increased from 260,000 to 340,000 million francs. 'You don't have to be an expert or a financier to realize that if you want to spend more than you have, you soon end up bankrupt. What is true for individuals is also true for the national community.' Both devaluation and inflation were ruled out. Advocates of the former, he said, 'forget, or pretend to forget, that our currency has already lost four-fifths of its value'. Advocates of inflation 'are suggesting that we should coin false money'. The government had chosen other methods. 'The decrees we have signed demand heavy sacrifices from you,' Laval declared. '. . . None [of the measures] is beyond criticism . . . but they achieve that equality of sacrifice which corresponds to the deepest aspirations of our country.'[3]

There was no parliamentary reaction to the decree-laws, for both

---

[1] Ibid., 17 June 1935; 'Letter from Paris', *Economist*, 22 June 1935, p. 1422.
[2] The full texts of the decree-laws are in J.O., *Lois et Décrets*, 17 July 1935, pp. 7658–80. For a convenient summary, see 'France and Stabilisation', *Economist*, 20 July 1935, pp. 112–13.
[3] *Le Temps*, 19 July 1935.

the Chamber and the Senate had gone into recess at the end of June, but there was an immediate explosion of indignation from the left, which was not convinced of the 'equality of sacrifice' allegedly imposed by the measures, and indeed complained that they favoured the rich at the expense of the poor. 'Down with the decree-laws of misery!' proclaimed a joint socialist-communist manifesto on 18 July, and the next few weeks were punctuated by a series of demonstrations against the government's policy. These culminated in two very ugly incidents at Brest and Toulon on 6 and 8 August, when workers from the naval arsenals who had gone on strike against the decree-laws were involved in violent clashes with the police. Many people were injured and three killed.[1]

As if to illustrate its determination, however, the government issued a second series of eighty-three decree-laws on the very day of the Toulon disturbances. They were designed mainly to stimulate economic activity, and included an increase in the public works programme, the stabilization of some wholesale prices, and the establishment of a committee to examine ways and means of expanding trade.[2] The amount of work which went into the preparation of the decrees was impressive, but as the *Economist* remarked, there seemed too many contradictions in a policy which combined budget reductions with loans for public works, cuts in the cost of living with increased farm support, and expansion of trade with the protection of an overvalued franc. 'M. Laval,' it commented, 'might have set himself the task of defending the franc *à tout prix*, or of increasing foreign trade, or of stimulating internal trade by public works, or of reducing the cost of living, or of balancing the budget. But to attempt all five at once is not a policy at all – it is a desperate muddle.'[3]

Whatever the faults of the policy, agitation against it died down as France went on her summer holidays. With parliament in recess and the most urgent economic decisions behind him, Laval was now free to concentrate once more upon foreign policy, where the situation was, if anything, even more complicated than before he formed his government.[4]

---

[1] *Le Populaire*, 19 July 1935; Bonnefous, Vol. V, pp. 346–7.
[2] The texts of the decree-laws may be found in J.O., *Lois et Décrets*, 9 August 1935, pp. 8674–717.
[3] 'A Desperate Defence', *Economist*, 17 August 1935, pp. 313–14.
[4] It should be noted that Laval retained the post of foreign minister in his own government.

In his negotiations with the Germans, Laval continued to press for the signature of a multilateral non-aggression pact, multiplying his assurances that this would replace the Franco-Soviet pact to which they took such exception. Thus, François-Poncet told state secretary Bülow on 25 June that the Franco-Soviet pact would become 'invalid' just as soon as the multilateral pact was concluded,[1] and on 27 July Laval told the German ambassador in Paris that 'if the view obtained in Germany that, through her treaty, France wanted to lend herself to playing the Russian hand, it was an entirely mistaken view. France's object in signing the Franco-Russian treaty had been quite the reverse. She had wanted to induce Russia to abandon the idea of bolshevizing Europe and to adopt the active European policy which was essential for general peace and, above all, for economic reconstruction. This had, however, been made possible only by France's giving Russia security against unprovoked attacks by third parties, particularly by Germany in her new incarnation.' The fact that the Franco-Soviet pact had only been concluded for a period of five years, Laval added, 'showed that in the long run France did not want to engage in a Franco-Russian policy of the old style.' If only Germany would guarantee not to attack Russia, he concluded, 'France would "hand her paper back to Russia".'[2]

Words were supported by deeds, for Laval continued to resist Russian attempts to put teeth into the Franco-Soviet pact. On three separate occasions during the first month of Laval's premiership, his war minister, Colonel Fabry, was approached by the Soviet ambassador to initiate military conversations. Fabry, who, as a rabid anti-communist, needed little incentive to go slow, was instructed by Laval to keep the talks 'unofficial' and the ambassador soon gave up trying.[3] Laval also deliberately delayed the ratification of the Franco-Soviet pact by laying it before parliament instead of having it ratified by the President of the Republic. Having done this, he refused to allocate time for a debate and the pact was not in fact ratified until after he had left office.[4]

But if Laval believed that his attitude to the pact would make the

---

[1] Bülow memorandum, 25 June 1935, D.G.F.P., Series C, Vol. IV, No. 172.
[2] Köster to Foreign Ministry, 27 July 1935, ibid., No. 231.
[3] Fabry, pp. 76–81.
[4] 'The Struggle . . . for Collective Security', October 1963, pp. 119–20.

Germans more willing to sign a multilateral agreement, he was doomed to disappointment. The German view, as expressed in a Bülow memorandum of 25 July, was that the Stresa declaration in favour of a multilateral pact was 'no longer of any significance',[1] and a few days later, Bülow was writing to Neurath, the foreign minister, suggesting various procedures whereby the negotiations could be delayed.[2] Neurath accepted his main proposal – that, because of the holiday season, Germany would not be ready for serious negotiations until October – and the embassies concerned were instructed on 9 August to pass this information on to the governments to which they were accredited. Laval saw through this transparent excuse.[3]

As well as official channels, Laval used an unofficial envoy to sound out German intentions. He was the pro-German journalist, Fernand de Brinon, who much later was to become the Vichy ambassador to the German occupation authorities in Paris. De Brinon visited Germany in July 1935 to find out whether it would be possible for Hitler to meet Laval to discuss, and possibly settle, the outstanding issues between the two countries. But Hitler and Ribbentrop, whom he saw personally, both insisted that any negotiations must be 'seriously prepared', and that no meeting could be held before the end of September or the beginning of October at the earliest. The serious preparation which Hitler and Ribbentrop had in mind was more of a psychological than a diplomatic matter. Laval had to get it into his head that, while Germany 'had no intention of infringing' the territorial clauses of the Versailles treaty, the possibility of peaceful revision must remain open and all other forms of discrimination against Germany contained in the treaty must be considered null and void. In particular, the Germans gave notice of their intention to raise the colonial issue. But the great obstacle to Franco-German agreement was, of course, the pact with Russia. Communism, the Nazi leaders maintained, was such a pernicious doctrine that it should render the traditional Franco-German rivalry obsolete. 'All countries of European culture' should unite against the red peril, but as long as France continued 'to hinge its

---

[1] Bülow memorandum, 25 July 1935, D.G.F.P., Series C, Vol. IV, No. 223. See also Neurath to Bülow, 26 July 1935, ibid., No. 225; Bülow to Köster, 23 July 1935, ibid., No. 218.

[2] Bülow to Neurath, 30 July 1935, ibid., No. 234.

[3] Neurath to Bülow, 7 August 1935, Köster to Foreign Ministry, 9 September 1935, ibid., Nos. 252, 289.

policy upon what the Russians and their Slav allies do', there was no possibility of agreement.[1]

The results of Laval's soundings, both official and unofficial, must have been a considerable disappointment to him. In the circumstances, France's new-found friendship with Italy took on added importance, both as a means of bringing Germany back into the fold and as a re-insurance in case the attempt failed. This was all the more so as two of France's traditional allies, Britain and Poland, were showing, by such actions as the conclusion of the Anglo-German naval agreement and Colonel Beck's visit to Berlin at the beginning of July, a disturbing tendency to pursue their own interests regardless of those of their partner.[2] It is therefore important at this stage to examine how far the Franco-Italian co-operation envisaged in the Rome agreements had gone in order to be able to assess its influence upon Laval's subsequent policy.

At the secret session of the Senate in March 1940, Laval disclosed that his visit to Rome in January 1935 had been followed in May and June of that year by military agreements between France and Italy which, in his words, constituted 'a veritable military alliance'. The texts of these agreements have never been published, but it is possible to reconstruct their general outline from a number of sources. They were based on the desire expressed at both the Rome and Stresa meetings to protect Austria's independence. As far as ground forces were concerned, the French agreed to send an army corps to north-east Italy to act as a link between the Italian and Yugoslav armies in the event of a joint drive upon Vienna. In return, the Italians agreed to send an army corps to take part in operations against Germany on France's north-eastern front. An added bonus was that, because of the *rapprochement* between the two countries, this latter front could also be reinforced by the transfer of ten French divisions from the Alps and seven from north Africa, where they had hitherto been stationed to deter possible Italian aggression. Finally, the intelligence services of both armies agreed to a large-scale programme of co-operation directed against Germany. The army agreements were supplemented by agreements between the two countries' air and naval staffs. Little is known

[1] Long extracts from de Brinon's report, from which the quotations are taken, are printed in his *Mémoires*, Paris, L.L.C., 1949, pp. 29–33.

[2] The Italian foreign office noted the influence of British and Polish policy upon Laval. See Francia, pp. 17–18.

about the naval agreement, but, in the air, operational zones in the event of war with Germany were delineated, intelligence was to be exchanged, and there was agreement on technical co-operation.[1]

These were staff agreements, however, subject to confirmation by the respective governments, and Laval made it clear that, as far as he was concerned, confirmation was dependent upon a *rapprochement* between Italy and Yugoslavia.[2] Mussolini did make a serious attempt to improve relations with his neighbour,[3] but it was bound to take time, especially after Yugoslavia joined the sanctionist powers during the Abyssinian crisis. Laval subsequently claimed that an agreement could have been reached before then but for the replacement, in June 1935, of the Yugoslav prime minister, Jevtić, by Stoyadinović. Moreover, he also made the somewhat surprising accusation that Britain, who for some unspecified reasons was alleged to be opposed to the Italo-Yugoslav *rapprochement*, had deliberately engineered Jevtić's dismissal with this end in view.[4] While it is true that Nevile Henderson, the British minister in Belgrade, did recommend Stoyadinović to the Regent as Jevtić's successor, there is no evidence that he was behind the latter's overthrow. Indeed, this was a purely internal affair.[5] Laval's charge, therefore, is an indication of his feelings towards England after the failure of the Hoare–Laval plan and his subsequent fall from power. Ironically enough, Stoyadinović did conclude an agreement with the Italians in March 1937, but it was one which marked Yugoslavia's break with the French camp. The upshot of all this was that, throughout the period of Laval's premiership, the

[1] This paragraph is based upon the following sources: Laval's speech to the secret session of the French Senate in March 1940, J. O. Sénat, *Comité Secret*, pp. 6, col. 3, 7, col. 1; Gamelin, pp. 168–9; Fabry note, 18 January 1936, in Fabry, pp. 233–8; evidence of Roatta (head of Italian army intelligence), Baistrocchi (Italian under-secretary for war) and Valfré di Bonzo (of Italian army intelligence) in *Il Processo Roatta*, Rome, Donatello de Luigi, 1945, pp. 30–31, 81, 93, 200–201.

[2] Gamelin, p. 169; J. O. Sénat, *Comité Secret*, p. 6, col. 3.

[3] He began, for example, by sending a new diplomatic representative to Belgrade with special instructions to reach an agreement. See Von Heeren to Foreign Ministry, 16 March 1935, GFM/6038/E445356–60. France also sent a new representative to Belgrade and his recollections (Robert de Dampierre, '*Une Entente Italo-Yugoslave, Mars 1937*', in the *Revue des Deux Mondes*, 1 September 1953, pp. 126–36), are an extremely valuable source for the whole complex of Italo-French-Yugoslav relations.

[4] J. O. Sénat, *Comité Secret*, p. 6, col. 3; speech to National Assembly, 10 July 1940, C. E. Rapport, Vol. II, pp. 488–9.

[5] C. A. Macartney and A. W. Palmer, *Independent Eastern Europe*, London, Macmillan, 1962, p. 338. I am indebted to Mr Palmer who, in a letter dated 21 October 1963, provided me with further details about Stoyadinović's appointment.

French condition for the confirmation of the military agreements remained unfulfilled, let alone the unspoken Italian one of unconditional support for her Abyssinian adventure.[1]

Nevertheless, even if the co-operation envisaged in the Rome agreements had not progressed as Laval sometimes liked to believe, it undoubtedly constituted a factor of the highest importance in French foreign policy. It should be remembered, for example, that there had not even been staff conversations between France and Britain at this date. Although partly of his own making, therefore, the dilemma in which Laval was placed by the Abyssinian crisis was a very real one. It was heightened by the fact that it was not simply a case of choosing between Britain and Italy. The League of Nations was also involved and, as Laval put it in a telegram to the French ambassador in Rome on 19 July 1935, 'France's entire European policy is based upon the League of Nations. The League of Nations is the basis of the Locarno treaty, which is an essential element of French security, and it is within a League framework that the agreements which bind us to our friends in central Europe are inserted.'[2] Support of Italy over Abyssinia meant rejection of the League; support of Britain meant support of the League. This then was the real choice: the whole system of French security as it had evolved since 1919; or a new, perhaps more effective but as yet untried, system. Laval sought to avoid the choice and ended up with nothing.

The first stirrings of the Abyssinian crisis had taken place in December 1934, when Italian and Abyssinian forces had clashed at the oasis of Wal-Wal, which was situated in disputed territory along the border with Italian Somaliland. The Abyssinian government appealed to the League, but, at a meeting of the Council in January 1935, it was decided to postpone discussion of the question when both sides agreed to bilateral negotiations on the basis of the Italo-Abyssinian treaty of 1928. By March, however, the negotiations had got nowhere and, in the light of a rapid Italian military build-up in Eritrea and Italian Somaliland, the Abyssinian government again referred the matter to the League. Following further discussions at Geneva in April and

---

[1] An additional problem was that Austria, the object of all the concern, did not want a guarantee in which Germany did not participate, especially one which involved the succession states. See Macartney and Palmer, op. cit., pp. 329-30.

[2] Laval to de Chambrun, 19 July 1935, quoted in J. O. Sénat, *Comité Secret*, p. 8, col. 1.

May, it was finally agreed to set up a four-man arbitration committee under the auspices of the League to examine the Wal-Wal and succeeding incidents.[1]

Mussolini, of course, was not really interested in arbitration. He was resolved upon revenging Adowa and grabbing as much of Abyssinia as he could in the process. As early as 8 March 1935, he wrote to his representative in East Africa, Emilio de Bono, of his 'profound conviction' that the initiative must be taken 'at the end of October or the end of September', and he kept to his timetable.[2] The British government were well aware of Mussolini's intentions. 'You realize, don't you, that the Italians intend to take Abyssinia?' the foreign secretary, Sir John Simon, told one of his advisers in January 1935.[3] Two months later, the Foreign Office stated in an official internal communication that what the Italian government was aiming at in Abyssinia was probably not 'pure and simple economic predominance, but the virtual absorption of as much Abyssinian territory as can be achieved without prejudice to Italian interests and influence in other parts of the world'.[4]

Laval must have been equally aware of Italian aims, but he allowed his eagerness to secure a Franco-Italian agreement to blind his judgment of the consequences, apparently sharing the Duce's belief that the whole thing could be 'arranged' between Britain, France, and Italy.[5] In spite of subsequent attempts to whitewash himself, Flandin seems to have been a more cynical member of the French government. According to one source, he went so far as to advise the Italians to provoke an armed rebellion by the *Rases*, Abyssinia's tribal chiefs, in order to justify their intervention.[6]

British government pussyfooting lent support to Mussolini's and Laval's illusions about its reaction to an Italian move into Abyssinia. The Italians were warned several times during the spring and summer of 1935 of the dangers inherent in a policy of aggression, but as Eden

[1] This account is based upon the report of the League Council (Committee of Thirteen) to the League of Nations, dated 7 October 1935. Large extracts from this report are printed in R.I.I.A. Documents, 1935, Vol. II, pp. 120–50.

[2] Mussolini to de Bono, 8 March 1935, in Mussolini, p. 275.

[3] Sir Geoffrey Thompson, *Front Line Diplomat*, London, Hutchinson, 1959, p. 95.

[4] Foreign Office letter, dated 6 March 1935, to the inter-departmental committee headed by Sir John Maffey to examine the Italian request for an elucidation of Anglo-Italian interests in Abyssinia. A copy of the committee's report, which was completed in June, fell into Italian hands and was published in the *Giornale d'Italia*, 20 February 1936.

[5] See above, pp. 67–9.

[6] Galeazzo Ciano, *1937–38 Diario*, Bologna, Cappelli, 1948, entry for 24 December 1938.

commented, '. . . we were resting our case on the effect of Italian action on British opinion. No firm indication was given of how His Majesty's government would have to react against an Italian aggression in Abyssinia, not from choice but because we were pledged under the Covenant, upon which our alignment with France and Italy and peace in Europe were based.'[1] The inexplicable silence at the Stresa conference, which has already been mentioned,[2] only made matters worse.

It was not until June 1935, when Sir John Simon was replaced by Sir Samuel Hoare at the foreign office and Anthony Eden entered the cabinet as minister for League of Nations affairs, that the British government gave serious consideration to the possible consequences of the Abyssinian question. The result was a plan to buy off the Italians, by persuading Abyssinia to cede some territory in the southern Ogaden province in exchange for a small area of British Somaliland which included the port of Zeila. Eden was deputed to take this proposal to Rome, where it was rejected out of hand by Mussolini during talks on 24 and 25 June.[3] A particularly tactless aspect of the British proposal was that it was communicated to the Italians without prior consultation with the French, obviously with the intention of presenting them with a *fait accompli*. The Italians lost no time in informing Paris that the proposal to give Abyssinia the port of Zeila would damage French interests in Djibouti, which, thanks to the railway to Addis Ababa, had hitherto been the country's chief port.[4] When Eden returned to Paris on 27 June, Laval justifiably complained that 'Britain had very nearly played' a trick on France by offering to cede Zeila to Abyssinia'.[5] Coming on top of the Anglo-German naval agreement, the British plan was bound to make co-operation between Britain and France even more difficult.

'It is clear after Eden's visit to Rome,' the chancellor of the exchequer, Neville Chamberlain, wrote in his diary on 5 July, 'that Mussolini has made up his mind to eat up Abyssinia, regardless of

[1] Eden, p. 204. See also Guariglia, pp. 215–19, 230–38.
[2] See above, p. 78.
[3] For the Eden mission to Rome and its antecedents, see Eden, pp. 220–28; Templewood, pp. 149–55; and the Italian records printed in Mario Toscano, '*Eden a Roma alla vigilia del conflitto italo-etiopico*', in his *Pagine di Storia Diplomatica*, Vol. II, Milan, A. Giuffrè, 1963, pp. 142–4, 147–8, 150–51.
[4] Suvich to Pignatti, 26 June 1935, cited in Toscano op. cit., p. 152.
[5] Eden, p. 232.

treaties, covenants, and pacts.'[1] The British government had two alternatives. The first was to make it plain to Italy that Britain would not tolerate aggression, from wherever it came, and that she was prepared to go to the limit of her own resources and those of the League of Nations to stop it. This was the course advocated by Eden and, to a lesser extent, by Chamberlain. It was also a popular policy if one is to judge by the results of the so-called 'peace ballot', which were announced on 27 June. The 'peace ballot' was the largest public opinion poll ever conducted in Britain and the final question which was put to respondents asked them whether, 'if a nation insists on attacking another, the other nations should combine to compel it to stop by (a) economic and non-military measures? (b) if necessary, military measures?' Ten million people answered part (a) in the affirmative, with only 635,000 against. The majority in favour of military sanctions – 6,784,000 for 2,351,000 against – was less overwhelming but still decisive.[2] It was the kind of expression of public opinion which democratic governments, especially those about to face a general election, ignore at their peril.

The second choice open to Britain was to admit the sorry state of her armaments, the ill-will of the French, and the need to keep Mussolini in the 'Stresa front' against Germany and let Italy have her way in Abyssinia. This was the view of Sir Robert Vansittart, the permanent under-secretary of state at the foreign office. It received support from the Dominion governments, who made it clear that they were not prepared to go to war over Abyssinia, from the chiefs-of-staff, and from the dying King George V, who repeatedly told Hoare, 'I am an old man. I have been through one world war. How can I go through another? If I am to go on, you must keep us out of one.'[3]

Unfortunately, the British government chose neither course. Instead, it relied upon what Hoare called 'the double line', a policy of 'negotiation with Italy and respect for our collective obligations under the League Covenant, based on Anglo-French co-operation'.[4] Not surprisingly, it reaped the worst of both worlds.

[1] Keith Feiling, *Neville Chamberlain*, London, Macmillan, 1946 (hereafter cited as Feiling), p. 265.
[2] Eden, p. 237; Templewood, p. 128; C. L. Mowat, *Britain Between the Wars, 1918–40*, London, Methuen, 1955, pp. 541–42.
[3] Templewood, pp. 159–60.
[4] Ibid., p. 161.

If the British government had followed Vansittart's policy, there would have been no difficulty with Laval. Even if it had followed Eden's, Laval would probably have been forced to toe the line in the end. As it was, he did not know where he stood and hedged accordingly. Eden's memoirs are replete with expressions of exasperation at Laval's conduct, but the fault was as much the British government's lack of resolution as the French prime minister's deviousness.

The most immediate problem facing the British and French governments after the failure of the Eden mission was the breakdown of the arbitration procedure agreed upon at the League council meeting in May.[1] On the eve of the meeting which was to examine the next step, Eden suggested to the British cabinet that he be empowered to give a private warning to the Italians that Britain would live up to her obligations under the Covenant if Italy attacked Abyssinia. 'Unhappily,' he wrote later, 'my colleagues did not accept my recommendation.'[2] Instead, the Foreign Office sent a memorandum to Laval which pointed out, in general terms, the consequences of allowing Italian aggression to go unchecked. When Eden, *en route* for Geneva, saw Laval in Paris on 30 July, the Frenchman 'immediately fastened upon [the memorandum's] weakness, remarking that he agreed with its principles, but had sought in vain for any practical suggestion for solving the difficulty'.[3] Unknown to Eden, he also communicated the document to the Italians, which, in view of its harsh comments upon Italian policy, did little to improve a steadily worsening atmosphere.[4]

There is no need to go into the details of the negotiations which took place in Geneva between 31 July and 3 August.[5] It suffices to say that the Italians, whose military preparations were not yet complete, agreed to the appointment of a fifth arbitrator to add to the panel of four who had so far been unable to agree on the responsibility for the Wal-Wal and succeeding incidents. The council also decided to meet on 4 September to discuss the whole question, whatever the results of the arbitration. Parallel to the arbitration procedure, it was further decided that the three powers which had signed the 1906 treaty

---

[1] For the arbitrators' declarations, dated 9 July 1935, see R.I.I.A. Documents, 1935, Vol. II, pp. 39–41.
[2] Eden, pp. 242–4.
[3] Ibid., pp. 245–6.
[4] Guariglia, pp. 249–50; Aloisi, p. 290.
[5] Full accounts may be found in Eden, pp. 247–8; and Aloisi, pp. 290–92.

guaranteeing Abyssinia's political and territorial integrity – Britain, France, and Italy – should meet 'at the earliest possible date' to examine the wider issues between Italy and Abyssinia which were not being dealt with by the arbitrators.[1]

But of course, Mussolini was not interested in compromise. 'I want no agreements unless I am conceded everything,' he told one of his senior advisers on 9 August, less than a week before the tripartite conversations were due to open in Paris.[2] Four days later, he launched into a bitter attack upon the British in a conversation with Comte de Chambrun, the French ambassador in Rome. 'They want to drive me to a Fashoda at any price,' he declared, 'but they won't succeed. . . . My victory in Abyssinia is certain. . . . Whatever the cost, I will revenge Adowa.' If Britain, in defiance of international agreements, sought to cut his supply lines by closing the Suez canal, he would reopen it. 'In the last resort, I shall not hesitate, if need be, to make war upon her. She is more vulnerable than she thinks.'[3]

Laval's reaction to this outburst shows both the dilemma in which he was placed and his failure to recognise the fundamental incompatibility of his policies. In a conversation with the new Italian ambassador, Cerruti, on 15 August, he said, 'Tell Mussolini that I am determined to do everything for Italy, who must be able to extend her own control over the territories she needs. But there must be no talk of war and the existence of the League of Nations must not be jeopardized.' As the Italian foreign ministry commented, Laval was advocating 'squaring the circle'.[4]

The tripartite conversations began on 16 August. Laval suggested that an acceptable solution might be for the League to entrust France, Britain, and Italy with the task of introducing reforms in Abyssinia and that the first two countries could then delegate their responsibilities to Italy. Aloisi did not rule out this suggestion, but according to his diary account, 'Eden showed himself unyielding and only wanted to make concessions on the economic plan, confining himself on the political plane to accepting what the Negus would concede.' The British counter-proposal was in part a reversal to the plan Eden had

---

[1] For the texts of the various resolutions, see R.I.I.A. Documents, 1935, Vol. II, pp. 43-4, 47.
[2] Aloisi, p. 293.
[3] De Chambrun, pp. 217-19.
[4] Francia, p. 19.

taken to Rome, in that it included a suggestion that Abyssinia should cede territory to Italy in exchange for an outlet to the sea. But it added a proposed zone of Italian economic influence and a League of Nations framework within which the entire plan would operate. The plan was sent to Rome, but it was not nearly far-reaching enough to satisfy Mussolini. Adding insult to injury, the Duce studiously waited twenty-four hours before rejecting it. The talks were over.[1]

Laval's dilemma must have been sharpened by the news his war minister brought him on 19 August, immediately after the breakdown of the talks. According to information received, the Germans might seek to profit from the growing disagreement between the other major signatories of the Locarno treaty – Britain, France, and Italy – by re-militarizing the left bank of the Rhine. Fabry subsequently wrote that Laval did not share these fears and 'persisted in his belief that the Franco-Italian *entente* was paving the way for a *rapprochement* with Germany'.[2] But even Laval must have wondered how long the Franco-Italian *entente* would survive an invasion of Abyssinia.

Such considerations were clearly uppermost in his mind when he told the cabinet on 28 August that he intended to continue trying to persuade Britain to 'restrict' her demands upon Italy. Both he and the service ministers stressed the importance of the Italian alliance and cast doubt upon the ability of Britain to back up her strong language with force. Herriot, however, indignantly refused to accept the trend of Laval's argument. He was in favour of negotiation too, he said, 'but if, when the time comes, we must choose between Great Britain and Mussolini, I shan't hesitate for ten seconds: I'm with Great Britain. I don't want to abandon the League of Nations, the keystone of our security.' But for Laval, it was the alliance with Italy which was the more important. 'I shall never vote for sanctions,' he declared. 'I shall never part company with Britain or the League of Nations,' Herriot retorted. It was not only the British cabinet which was divided, but the French as well.[3]

The League council was due to meet on 4 September to discuss the Italo-Abyssinian dispute. Just a few days before, on 30 August, Laval

---

[1] Aloisi, pp. 295–8; Eden, pp. 250–51; Templewood, pp. 161–2; Vansittart, p. 531. There are some divergences between these various accounts of the tripartite meeting and I have tried to give what seems to me the most plausible reconstruction.

[2] Fabry, p. 64.

[3] Ibid., pp. 64–5; Herriot, *Jadis*, pp. 574–5.

sent a long telegram to the French ambassador in Rome instructing him to urge restraint upon Mussolini while the French government pursued its policy of conciliation. He would do his utmost, he said, 'to ensure that the legitimate pride of the Italian government is safeguarded in the most complete way and that Italian aspirations receive every possible satisfaction.' He therefore hoped that the Duce would instruct his representatives not to reject out of hand proposals which might be made for a settlement and that 'outside Geneva, no Italian initiative will interrupt the supreme effort of conciliation which has just been attempted'.[1]

At the same time, Laval sought to reassure himself that his policy was correct. When Eden stopped off in Paris on his way to Geneva, Laval asked him point-blank whether 'Britain would be as firm in upholding the Covenant, to the extent of sanctions in Europe in the future, as she appeared to be today in Abyssinia.' Eden hedged. 'If the Covenant were upheld over Abyssinia,' he said, 'the authority of the League would be immediately strengthened and our own moral obligation to assist in supporting and enforcing the Covenant correspondingly increased. If, however, the Covenant were now violated with impunity, the authority of the League would be so impaired that its future influence must be negligible in Europe or anywhere else.' It was the kind of evasive answer Laval had expected.[2]

Although Eden admitted that his cautious attitude had been dictated by 'the British government's wariness and the state of our defences', he was furious at what he considered to be Laval's effrontery. The United States minister in Switzerland reported on 4 September that 'Eden felt strongly that it would be incredible to pay a price to France to induce France to carry out its obligations under the Covenant. What Great Britain was working for was even more for the benefit of France than Great Britain and he spoke in a tone of rather humorous exasperation of the possibility of entering into a bargain to build up a system of collective action for which France had pushed for the past fifteen years.'[3] He omitted to add that, for the same period, successive British governments had consistently resisted the French pressure. This gives

---

[1] Laval to de Chambrun, 30 August 1935, cited in J. O. Sénat, *Comité Secret*, p. 8, cols. 1–2.
[2] Eden, pp. 257–8.
[3] Ibid., p. 258; Wilson to Hull, 4 September 1935, F.R.U.S., 1935, Vol. I, pp. 640–41.

Laval some justification for his enquiry, even if one strongly suspects that its real purpose was less to extract a genuine commitment than to convince his cabinet colleagues that it was pointless to rely upon British support.

A few days later, on 8 September, he returned to the charge in writing. In a *note verbale* to the British government, which referred specifically to the possibility of German aggression against Austria, the French government asked whether, if sanctions were applied against Italy, Britain would give the guarantee of Austrian independence which she had hitherto refused.[1] In his reply, dated 26 September, Sir Samuel Hoare referred to his speech to the League assembly on the 11th – of which more will be said below – and reaffirmed that Britain stood 'for the collective maintenance of the Covenant in its entirety, *and particularly for steady and collective resistance to all acts of unprovoked aggression*'.

Hoare immediately proceeded, however, to add a whole host of qualifications to this seemingly categorical statement which took on a particular importance in the context of the Austrian situation, to which the original French note had referred. 'Your Excellency will observe,' he told the French ambassador, 'that I spoke, as I am now writing, of all acts of unprovoked aggression. Each word in that sentence must have its full value. It is at once evident that procedure under article 16 of the Covenant, appropriate as regards a positive act of unprovoked aggression, is not made applicable as regards the negative act of the failure to fulfil the terms of a treaty.' It was the treaties of Versailles and Saint-Germain, of course, which guaranteed Austrian independence. 'Further, in the case of a resort to force', the Foreign Secretary went on, 'it is clear that there may be degrees of culpability and degrees of aggression, and that consequently, in cases where article 16 applies, the nature of the action appropriate to be taken under it may vary according to the circumstances of each particular case.' This must have caused the French to wonder what the British response would be to, say, a Nazi *putsch* inside Austria. Finally, Hoare restated the need for collective action in the very words he had used at Geneva. 'If risks for peace are to be run they must be run by all.'[2] In the circumstances, it is hard to see why Herriot derived as much satis-

---

[1] Laval to Corbin, 8 September 1935, cited in Herriot, *Jadis*, pp. 576–8.
[2] Hoare to Corbin, 26 September 1935, R.I.I.A. Documents, 1935, Vol. II, pp. 300–302.

faction from Hoare's note as he evidently did.[1] The public could perhaps be excused for thinking the British commitment was more far-reaching than was in fact the case, for the original French note was not published at the time. But Herriot knew about it; indeed, he published it in his memoirs.

Nor was Hoare's speech to the League of Nations assembly on 11 September, and to which continual reference was made in the British note, quite the clarion call to collective security which Herriot and some others assumed, for it was made under special circumstances. On 3 September, the five-man arbitration committee reported that neither side was responsible for the Wal-Wal and succeeding incidents.[2] In so far as their report was not a clear-cut condemnation of the Abyssinians, it was unacceptable to Italy and, on 4 September, when the council meeting began, the Italian government presented a long memorandum which was designed to show, in the words of its conclusion, both 'Abyssinia's failure to fulfil the obligations undertaken in her special agreements with Italy . . . [and her failure] to live up to the undertakings assumed on becoming a member of the League of Nations.' The chaotic conditions in Abyssinia, where slavery and barbarism were undoubtedly rife, placed the country – or so the Italians argued – beyond the protection of the Covenant. 'Italy can no longer tolerate a similar state of affairs,' the memorandum concluded, 'and must defend her own security, rights and dignity. In so doing she is also defending the prestige and name of the League of Nations.'[3] Naturally enough, the Abyssinian delegate denied these charges. As soon as he rose to speak, Aloisi walked out of the chamber, followed by the rest of the Italian delegation. On 6 September, the council referred the dispute to yet another committee, with Salvador de Madariaga of Spain as its chairman and Laval, Eden, and representatives of Poland and Turkey as its members. The Italians refused to have anything to do with it.[4]

It was against this background that Hoare arrived in Geneva on 10 September for the sixteenth meeting of the League's assembly. He had brought with him a speech drafted in close collaboration with

[1] Herriot, *Jadis*, pp. 590–91.
[2] Extracts from their report are printed in R.I.I.A. Documents, 1935, Vol. II, pp. 55–60.
[3] Extracts from the Italian government's memorandum are printed in ibid., pp. 60–84.
[4] Eden, pp. 258–9; Aloisi, pp. 300–301.

Neville Chamberlain, which surprised both Eden and his under-secretary, Lord Cranborne. 'Its strength,' Eden subsequently re-called, '. . . surpassed anything that the tone of the discussions with our colleagues had revealed up to the time when I left London a fort-night before.'[1] Hoare's own explanation was that he hoped to put 'new life into [the League's] crippled body [and] accordingly determined to make a revivalist appeal to the assembly. At best, it might start a new chapter of League recovery, at worst, it might deter Mussolini by a display of League fervour. If there was any element of bluff in it, it was a moment when bluff was not only legitimate but inescapable.'[2] This was a disastrous miscalculation. The worst that could happen was not the possible deterrence of Mussolini, but the effective collapse of the League when the Duce's actions exposed the soft centre behind the hard words. As Eden remarked, 'Mussolini was a man to practise bluff, not to be its victim at faltering hands.'[3] Bluff it was, however, as is clear from Hoare's own account of his conversations with Laval imme-diately before the speech was delivered. 'We both . . . excluded the idea of war with Italy as too dangerous and double-edged for the future of Europe,' Hoare wrote. 'We also agreed that as we must, if possible, avoid provoking Mussolini into open hostility, any economic pressure upon which the League collectively decided should be applied cautiously and in stages, and with full account of the unescapable fact that the United States, Japan, and Germany were not member states of the League.'[4]

After these private agreements, Hoare mounted the tribune of the assembly to declare in public that 'in conformity with its precise and explicit obligations, the League stands, and my country stands with it, for the collective maintenance of the Covenant in its entirety, and par-ticularly for steady and collective resistance to all acts of unprovoked aggression'.[5] The speech created a sensation. The Belgian foreign minister, M. Hymans, was heard to comment, 'The British have decided to stop Mussolini, even if it means using force.' 'To this day,' Eden wrote later, 'I consider that this was the only possible interpre-

[1] Eden, p. 260.
[2] Templewood, pp. 165–6.
[3] Eden, p. 261.
[4] Templewood, pp. 168–9.
[5] Extracts from Hoare's speech are printed in R.I.I.A. Documents, 1935, Vol. II, pp. 100–102.

tation of the speech, if the words meant what they said.'[1] But as we have seen, the words did not mean what they said; and Laval knew it.

The committee of five reported on 18 September. It recommended that the League, in agreement with the Emperor Haile Selassie, should appoint a team of experts to carry out reforms in Abyssinia. The British and French governments also made known their willingness 'to facilitate territorial adjustments between Italy and [Abyssinia] by offering [Abyssinia], if necessary, certain sacrifices in the region of the Somaliland coast and to recognize a special Italian interest in the economic development of [Abyssinia].'[2] Both Aloisi and Riccardo Astuto of the Italian colonial ministry, who were very impressed by Hoare's speech and the equally dramatic despatch of units of the British home fleet to the Mediterranean which followed it, urged their government to accept the committee's proposals as a basis for discussion. As Astuto pointed out, 'the sphere of competence of the experts would cover at least 90 per cent of any conceivable governmental activity.' Although Italians would not, of course, make up the whole of the League mission, it would suffice for them to be in a majority to exercise a very real control over the country.[3] Although he had tried to obtain even more favourable terms for Italy,[4] Laval, too, urged Mussolini to accept the committee's proposals as a basis for discussion. 'By outright rejection of the five's proposal or by his refusal to negotiate,' he cabled the French ambassador on 19 September, 'M. Mussolini would justify the already too widespread suspicion of systematic opposition to any peaceful solution of the conflict.' If on the other hand, he agreed to negotiate, he could count upon Laval's wholehearted support. 'I will leave no stone unturned to support Italian claims in so far as they are compatible with respect for the Covenant.'[5]

But Mussolini was no more ready to compromise now than he had been before. 'I am certain,' he told de Chambrun on 20 September, 'that England wants war. . . . In reality, it's a question of compelling me to surrender. Nothing has been neglected in order to humiliate me.' The proposals of the committee of five did not go far enough, he went on, and, in any case, they had appeared in the press before they

[1] Eden, pp. 261–2.
[2] The committee's proposals are printed in R.I.I.A. Documents, 1935, Vol. II, pp. 106–10.
[3] Guariglia, pp. 265–9.
[4] Aloisi, p. 304; Eden, pp. 263–4.
[5] Laval to de Chambrun, 19 September 1935, cited in Herriot, *Jadis*, pp. 586–7.

had been submitted to him. 'I might not have rejected them, and asked for clarification at the Geneva committee. But it would mean losing face to reply in this way, when the offers which have been made to us have already been made public and the British press itself has made up its mind to say that they are unacceptable to me.' It was all Britain's fault, he repeated, and the consequences would be to see 'Germany march upon Vienna and the Little and Balkan Ententes under her thumb, which will extend as far as the Bosphorus'.[1] The following day, the Italian council of ministers formally rejected the proposals.[2] On 29 September, Mussolini ordered de Bono to invade Abyssinia in the early hours of 3 October. There was to be no preliminary declaration of war.[3]

A measure of the sense of desperation which Laval felt in the face of the threatened collapse of the entire foreign policy which he had been pursuing since October 1934 is provided by the unusual step which he took after the Italian rejection of the committee of five's proposals. He appealed directly to King George V over the head of the British government. According to his subsequent accounts, he had two lengthy conversations about Abyssinia with the Prince of Wales, who was on a brief visit to France. He stressed the need for a peaceful settlement and asked the prince to try and persuade his father to use his influence upon the British government in that direction. 'My father does not involve himself in politics,' the prince is said to have replied, '. . . but I will speak to [him] about it.' There was no immediate response to this strange *démarche*, but Laval always believed that the Hoare–Laval proposals of the following December owed something to royal intervention.[4]

[1] De Chambrun to Laval, 20 September 1935, cited in J. O. Sénat, *Comité Secret*, p. 9, cols. 1–2. In his speech to the Senate, Laval misdated this telegram, saying that it was sent on the 21st.
[2] The text of the communiqué is printed in R.I.I.A. Documents, 1935, Vol. II, pp. 119–20. The Abyssinian government had agreed to negotiate on the basis of the committee's proposals. See ibid., pp. 114–17.
[3] Mussolini to de Bono, 29 September 1935, Mussolini, pp. 297–8.
[4] *Procès Pétain*, p. 184, cols. 2–3; Laval's speech to youth leaders, 4 August 1943 (unpublished text kindly communicated to me by M. René de Chambrun). Laval met the Prince of Wales on 1 and 2 October (see *The Times*, 2, 3 October 1935). When Laval first alluded to this contact in public, at the Pétain trial, the Duke of Windsor as he had then become immediately issued a denial through the British embassy in Washington, saying that no discussions of a political nature had taken place on the occasion of his visit to France (*The Times*, 6 August 1945). It is hard to see why Laval should have made up the story.

Once the Italians had invaded Abyssinia, the question of sanctions came to the forefront. On 7 October, the League of Nations council voted that Italy had committed an act of aggression. On the 10th, the assembly passed a resolution which set up a co-ordinating committee to discuss sanctions under article 16 of the Covenant. Between the 11th and the 19th, this committee drew up proposals for embargoes on the export of arms, ammunition, and certain strategic raw materials to Italy, the suspension of credit facilities, and a ban on all imports from Italy. These proposals were then communicated to both member and non-member governments.[1]

There was no serious attempt by the French government to block any of these moves. Laval told the Italian ambassador on 15 October that 'he had been forced to accept the economic sanctions, but had obtained in return, despite enormous difficulties, Britain's abandonment of recourse to the second part of article 16: namely, military sanctions, the closing of the Suez canal and blockade and the boarding of ships. A French veto of any sanctions whatever would have induced the British government to withdraw from the League, putting Britain in a position of isolation vis-à-vis Italy and making war inevitable.' As we know, Laval was claiming too much credit, for Hoare was no keener on military sanctions than he was. The Italians may have guessed as much, and they attributed the French attitude to a need for solidarity with Britain in the event of a German attack, and to internal pressure.[2]

There was another reason. As Laval explained to Cerruti, he hoped that the sanctions would never have to be implemented, for a new attempt at conciliation was under way. This seems to have been based upon proposals drawn up by Mussolini on 13 October, which called for an Italian mandate over the non-Amharic regions of Abyssinia plus those parts of the Tigré province which had been overrun by Italian forces since the fighting started, a joint mandate – in which Italy would play an important, if not predominant, rôle – over the Amharic core of the country, the settlement of the disputed frontiers with Eritrea and Italian Somaliland in Italy's favour, and the disarmament of Abyssinia.[3] It was in order to discuss these proposals that the British

[1] The relevant documentation may be found in R.I.I.A. Documents, 1935, Vol. II, pp. 168–9, 201–11.
[2] Francia, p. 25.
[3] Ibid., pp. 25–7.

government sent Maurice Peterson, head of the Abyssinian department of the Foreign Office, to Paris at the end of October. In co-operation with M. Saint-Quentin of the Quai d'Orsay, Mr Peterson worked
out a scheme which, while it did not give Mussolini everything he
wanted, went a long way to meet him. The Peterson–Saint-Quentin
proposals were, however, rejected by the British government on 30
October and were thus never formally presented to Mussolini.[1]
Three days later, on 2 November, the co-ordinating committee resolved that sanctions would come into force on the 18th.[2] But still
Laval did not give up. On the 12th, he made a last-minute suggestion
by telephone to the French ambassador in Rome. It called for a suspension of hostilities in exchange for the non-implementation of sanctions. But the Italian advance was going too well and the proposal
came to nothing.[3]

On 15 November, Laval saw the German ambassador. The timing
of this meeting strongly suggests that it was not unconnected with
developments in the Abyssinian crisis. The alliance with Italy had
become, as we have seen, a cornerstone of Laval's foreign policy. Now
that sanctions threatened to subject it to considerable strain, the
French prime minister desperately sought to take out a reinsurance
policy with the Germans. He suggested that the time had come 'to
publish a "diplomatic document" which should once again stress the
desire of both the German and the French governments to remain on a
good neighbourly footing and to cultivate relations of mutual trust.
. . . It would be of particular value to him if the Führer and Chancellor could repeat, in the document addressed to France, that it was not
Germany's intention to attack Russia.' He felt that such a document
'would constitute a "preamble" to the negotiations on concrete questions, such as, for instance, the limitation of armaments and the air
pact. Public opinion in France, and indeed all over the world, would
undoubtedly be favourably affected and, above all, the present extremely tense atmosphere would give way to a calmer assessment of
the overall situation.' In an audience with Hitler on 21 November, the
French ambassador, André François-Poncet, put forward a similar
proposal. But the Germans were not very sympathetic. Hitler told

[1] Ibid., pp. 27–8; Eden, p. 285; Köster to Foreign Ministry, 16 November 1935, D.G.F.P.,
Series C, Vol. IV, No. 412.
[2] R.I.I.A. Documents, 1935, Vol. II, pp. 211–12.
[3] Aloisi, p. 321; Francia, p. 28.

François-Poncet that 'a *rapprochement* between Germany and France on the basis of the Russo-French assistance pact was out of the question', while the German foreign minister cabled the ambassador in Paris that 'a worthwhile *rapprochement* cannot be introduced by the mere abstract expression of the desire for an understanding, but only by negotiating on concrete problems'.[1] Laval was back at square one.

Meanwhile, on 14 November, there had been a general election in Britain. The government, campaigning on a pro-League and pro-sanctions platform, was returned with a reduced but still sizeable majority. Almost immediately it was called upon to decide whether the sanctions against Italy should be extended to cover oil. The League's co-ordinating committee had adopted a resolution in favour of oil sanctions on 6 November,[2] but so far no firm decision had been taken. Eden and Neville Chamberlain were in favour of oil sanctions; Hoare, and other members of the government, were less certain.[3] On the other side of the Channel, there was no doubt where Laval stood. He was informed by the Italian ambassador towards the end of November that Italy would regard an oil embargo as a military sanction which would provoke a very strong reaction and endanger the peace of the world.[4] Thoroughly alarmed by this Italian warning, Laval told his cabinet on 26 November that he intended to oppose oil sanctions, and he urged caution upon the British.[5] Eden was not impressed by Mussolini's veiled threats, but, at a meeting of senior British ministers on 29 November, Hoare 'was inclined to hold up the embargo long enough to allow further conversations in Paris to test out the possibility of a general settlement', and his view was evidently accepted.[6] Independently, Laval supplied a few days' grace by arguing that a parliamentary crisis made it impossible for him to attend a League meeting to discuss oil sanctions until 12 December, six days after the date suggested by Eden.[7] The latter evidently believed that Laval was

---

[1] Köster to Foreign Ministry, 18 November 1935, D.G.F.P., Series C, Vol. IV, No. 415; Neurath memorandum, 22 November 1935, ibid., No. 425; Neurath to Köster, 3 December 1935, ibid., No. 440.

[2] For the text, see R.I.I.A. Documents, 1935, Vol. II, p. 214.

[3] See the extract from Chamberlain's diary in Iain Macleod, *Neville Chamberlain*, London, Frederick Muller, 1961 (hereafter cited as Macleod), pp. 188–9.

[4] Francia, p. 28.

[5] Herriot, *Jadis*, pp. 613–14; Eden, p. 293.

[6] Eden, pp. 293–4; Macleod, p. 188.

[7] Eden, pp. 293–4.

inventing these domestic political difficulties in order to gain time, but this was not in fact the case. His government had been coming under increasingly heavy pressure and it was only by the most astute management of parliamentary time that it managed to survive at all.

To understand the position it is necessary to go back to the end of September. It was then that the *Croix de Feu* made a tremendous come-back after the summer holidays with a series of ever more spectacular rallies and demonstrations. The left-wing press was full of the organization's activities and even published what were said to be plans for a *coup d'état*.[1] It is clear that all this publicity was aimed at influencing the crucial Radical party congress, which took place in Paris from 24 to 27 October. In an effort to appease the delegates, the government issued three decrees on the eve of the congress, increasing the strength of the *garde mobile*, making it compulsory to notify the authorities of meetings in public places, and regulating the ownership of firearms.[2] But this was not enough for the party's left-wing militants and the final declaration of the congress asked the government 'not to forget that the most rigorous texts are seen to be ineffectual without the spirit to interpret them and the will to apply them'.[3]

This was the nub of the left-wing radicals' grievance against Laval: he was thought to be too 'soft' towards the leagues because, at heart, he sympathized with them. Alexander Werth quotes some remarks he is said to have made to a friend about this time. 'Yes, I am on good terms with the *Croix de Feu*. They are real Frenchmen. They include some of the finest elements of the youth of France. They will become some day the backbone of a real big anti-capitalist, though non-Marxist, party. I like them. What would you have me do? . . . My old socialist and communist comrades will not have anything more to do with me. Who can I fall back on in the circumstances?'[4] If there is not much evidence that he really did hold such views, there is no doubt that he was beginning to find parliament something of an encumbrance in the pursuit of his policies. In the first place, he failed to recall it until the very end of November, thus setting a record for the length of the summer recess. Secondly, in a broadcast speech summarizing the

---

[1] Werth, pp. 183–7.
[2] J.O., *Lois et Décrets*, 25 October 1935, pp. 11202–4, 11214.
[3] For a full account of the Radical congress, see *Le Temps*, 26, 27, 28 and 29 October 1935.
[4] Werth, p. 160.

government's achievements during the recess, he declared that 'five hundred decree-laws[1] bear witness to the enormity of the task, the accomplishment of which would have required several years of parliamentary deliberations'.[2] Finally, on the first day of the new session, the socialist leader, Léon Blum, extracted from him the admission that he would have promulgated the budget by decree if he had been able to do so.[3] These were not the sentiments of a man who was enamoured of France's institutions; they were more like those of one who envied Germany's and Italy's.

Meanwhile, the *Front Populaire* was steadily growing in strength. Laval was so worried by it that, when his Senate term expired in October 1935, he decided to stand for re-election in his home constituency of Puy-de-Dôme as well as in Paris, because of the threat from a *Front Populaire* coalition in the capital. As it happened, he was elected in both constituencies, but he was the only non-*Front Populaire* candidate to be elected in Paris and he came well down the list in terms of the number of votes received.[4]

It looked, too, as though the government's financial policy was running into trouble. When its budget proposals were presented to the finance committee of the Chamber of Deputies at the end of October, they were, in Herriot's words, 'cut to pieces' by the opposition. There is little doubt that the government would have been overthrown on this issue when the Chamber reconvened had not the radical leadership, and Herriot in particular, made it clear that they were not yet ready for a *Front Populaire* government which might lead to devaluation. A compromise was, therefore, finally worked out.[5]

But there was still the question of the leagues, upon which all the left-wing parties could agree. When the Chamber reconvened, therefore, Laval sought to postpone discussion of this issue until after it had pronounced upon the government's financial policy. Léon Blum bitterly attacked these Machiavellian tactics. 'There is a republican

[1] A further colossal total of 317 decree-laws were promulgated on 30 October, the day before the government's emergency powers expired (see J.O., *Lois et Décrets*, 31 October 1935, pp. 11407–720). Many, if not most, of these had little to do with the economic and financial crisis which had prompted the granting of the powers.

[2] *Le Temps*, 28 November 1935.

[3] J. O. Chambre, *Débats*, 28 November 1935, p. 2143, col. 1.

[4] *Le Temps*, 22 October 1935. Laval opted to sit for Puy-de-Dôme (ibid., 31 October 1935).

[5] Herriot, *Jadis*, pp. 607, 611; Larmour, pp. 186–7; *Le Temps*, 22, 23, 24 November 1935.

majority in this Chamber,' he declared, '. . . It can come into existence against you, but only on one issue: that of the defence of the republic . . . You accept M. Rucart's interpellation [on the leagues], but you accept it by choosing a time for its discussion when you hope to have been fortified by two successive majorities and to have weakened [the republican majority] on two occasions by discussions on procedure and by a split in the financial debate.'[1] As if to prove Blum's point, Laval began the debate on the leagues on 3 December with two substantial victories behind him: the first (345 votes to 225) on the procedural issue of fixing the date of the various debates, and the second (324 votes to 247) on the government's financial policy.[2] But the prime minister was not out of the wood yet. Speaking on behalf of the *délégation des gauches*, Marc Rucart launched a powerful attack on his alleged tenderness towards the leagues. He referred, as did other speakers, to the authoritarian sentiments expressed in Laval's recent broadcast, but what really annoyed him was the latter's admission that he would have liked to have passed the budget by decree. 'No real republican will be able to stomach that affront to the sovereign people,' he declared, and he warned Laval that 'republicans can no longer have any faith in you.'[3]

The outcome of the debate was still in doubt on the morning of 6 December, when a right-wing deputy, M. Jean Ybarnégaray, rose to speak on behalf of the *Croix de Feu*. In the middle of his speech, an astonishing event took place. When Ybarnégaray suggested that there should be all-round disarmament, Blum interrupted to say that this was not the real issue. 'What is vital,' he said, '. . . is the existence of formations which, by their recruitment, their method of command and obedience, and the training exercises to which they are subjected, possess a military character.' Although there was nothing in common between the 'self-defence' groups of the socialists and the leagues, he was ready to dissolve the former if the leagues would do the same with their paramilitary units. Maurice Thorez, on behalf of the communists, immediately associated himself with Blum's offer. Choosing his words very carefully, Ybarnégaray accepted on behalf of the *Croix de Feu*. Laval, whom some suspected of having stage-managed Ybarnégaray's

---

[1] J. O. Chambre, *Débats*, 28 November 1935, p. 2143.
[2] *Le Temps*, 30 November, 1 December 1935.
[3] J. O. Chambre, *Débats*, 3 December 1935, p. 2325.

speech, intervened at once to 'note with satisfaction this triple declaration, which does honour to the Chamber and from which the government will draw the necessary conclusions'. At the beginning of the afternoon session, he tabled three bills: one dissolving all paramilitary formations, another prohibiting the carrying of arms in public, and the third amending the press laws so that incitement to murder would be accorded the same harsh treatment as anarchist propaganda. He won his vote of confidence by 351 votes to 219, an even larger majority than his earlier triumphs.[1] It was the support of 76 radicals which carried the day for him, as the socialists and communists had voted *en bloc* against the government. To the charge that the whole incident was like the 'kiss of Lamourette'[2] and that the goodwill would not last, he is said to have replied, 'What will they think of next? We shall see. Let's go and eat a dozen oysters. Tomorrow I have to work for peace; I am meeting Sir Samuel Hoare.'[3]

Laval had been trying to arrange a meeting with Hoare during the previous few days in order to discuss the implementation of oil sanctions, which, as we know, he wanted to avoid. At first, he proposed that he should go to London, but, in the event, it was Hoare who came to Paris. The Foreign Secretary's health was, in his own words, 'alarmingly precarious' at this time and his doctors had ordered him to take a rest. He had arranged to take a few weeks' holiday in Switzerland after speaking in the House of Commons on 5 December and agreed to stop over in Paris on the way.[4] The result of the stop-over was the Hoare–Laval plan.

So much myth encrusts the Hoare–Laval proposals that it is important to examine in some detail how they were reached. In the first place, what were the precise circumstances of Hoare's visit to Paris? Lord Halifax's explanation, given on behalf of the British government in the House of Lords on 19 December 1935, was as comforting as it was inaccurate. 'Sir Samuel Hoare was ordered – imperatively ordered –

---

[1] J. O. Chambre, *Débats*, 6 December 1935, *passim* (Ybarnégaray's speech and the interventions of Blum, Thorez and Laval can be found on pp. 2389–92); Herriot, *Jadis*, pp. 617–18; Bonnefous, Vol. V, pp. 358–9; Werth, pp. 195–200; Larmour, pp. 187–8.

[2] This was a famous incident during the French Revolution when a speech in the legislative assembly by the *Abbé* Lamourette in favour of reconciliation led to political enemies kissing and embracing one another. The reconciliation did not last and Lamourette himself was eventually guillotined.

[3] Bonnefous, Vol. V, pp. 359–60.

[4] Eden, pp. 294–5; Templewood, pp. 177–8.

by his doctors to seek rest and health abroad,' Halifax stated. '. . . On his way abroad he went to Paris. There was very little pre-designed about it. He was passing through Paris, and it natural was that he should meet the French prime minister. He did not go there to discuss terms of conciliation; he went to discuss matters, quite other, though still connected with the Italo-Abyssinian dispute. . . . But when he reached Paris he found the French government urgently anxious to make progress as rapid as might be with the proposals for conciliation and, at great personal sacrifice of convenience and health, he agreed to take personal part with M. Laval in their examination.'[1] From here it is but a short step to the pathetic vision of a sick Englishman being bamboozled by a wicked and unscrupulous foreigner.

Unfortunately, Lord Halifax's attempt to impart an almost fortuitous character to the Paris meeting does not stand up to examination. Indeed, it was destroyed by the disclosures of other government spokesmen during the very debates in which he spoke. The opposition in both houses of parliament had made much of the conversations which had been taking place at official level between the British and French governments and which we will examine in detail in due course. Lord Halifax did not deny the existence of these conversations, but Earl Stanhope, the under-secretary of state for foreign affairs, went further. Hoare, he admitted, 'went out [to Paris] knowing that these points' – i.e. the terms being discussed at official level – 'might be raised', but, as it was not expected that agreement would be reached, he carried no specific instructions apart from 'a general instruction that conversations should go on'.[2] Neville Chamberlain, winding up for the government in the House of Commons, went further still. The cabinet had hoped, he said, that 'through the conversations between my right hon. friend [Hoare] and M. Laval, the discussions [at official level] might be conducted further towards a favourable conclusion'.[3] In a private letter to his sisters on 15 December, Chamberlain was even more candid. 'I believed, and so far as I know, my colleagues believed also,' he wrote, 'that [Hoare] was going to stop off at Paris . . . to get the discussions with the French into such a condition that we could say to the League, "don't prejudice the chances of a favourable issue by

---

[1] H.L. Deb., 5th series, Vol. 99, col. 278.
[2] H.L. Deb., 5th series, Vol. 99, col. 346.
[3] H.C. Deb., 5th series, Vol. 307, col. 2114.

thrusting in a particularly provocative extra sanction [i.e. oil] at this moment".[1]

The Anglo-French conversations at official level to which reference has been made were a continuation of the Peterson–Saint-Quentin talks of October.[2] 'The election over,' as Eden cynically put it, 'His Majesty's government were free to continue the discussions with the Quai d'Orsay and it was decided that Mr Maurice Peterson should go to Paris again.'[3] To judge by Eden's and Hoare's subsequent accounts, as well as the statements of Earl Stanhope and Neville Chamberlain in parliament at the time, one would gather that the British and French were still poles apart in these conversations at the time Hoare arrived in Paris.[4] A completely different impression is gained from Peterson's own account. 'We were agreed as to the main lines of demarcation [between Italy and Abyssinia]', he wrote, 'the nature of the assistance to be given to the emperor in ruling the truncated, but ethnically consolidated, territory which was to remain to him, the compensation Abyssinia was to receive by the cession of a port in either British or Italian Somaliland.' The two points upon which there was still disagreement were the precise extent of that portion of the Amharic Tigré province which was to be ceded to Italy and the restrictions which might need to be placed upon Abyssinia's use of another port in order to avoid conflict with French interests in Djibouti and the Addis Ababa railway.[5] Peterson sent off a telegram to London asking for further instructions on these disputed points. He received no reply, but was informed instead that Hoare and Vansittart were coming to Paris.[6] What other impression could he – and, even more important, Laval – have received than that the British foreign secretary and his senior official adviser were coming to settle the remaining points at issue? This was certainly the impression of Vansittart himself, who arrived in Paris a day or so before Hoare. Sir Samuel, he subsequently wrote, 'was apparently authorized by his colleagues to evolve a provisional scheme *ad referendum* both to cabinet and League.'[7]

---

[1] Feiling, p. 274.
[2] See above, p. 110.
[3] Eden, p. 291.
[4] Ibid., pp. 291–2; Templewood, pp. 174–5; H.L. Deb., 5th Series, Vol. 99, col. 346; H.C. Deb., 5th series, Vol. 307, cols. 2113–14.
[5] Sir Maurice Peterson, *Both Sides of the Curtain*, London, Constable, 1950, pp. 118–19.
[6] Ibid., p. 119.
[7] Vansittart, p. 538. Vansittart generally confirms Peterson's account.

Even more interesting than the Peterson–Saint-Quentin conversations, perhaps, were those which had taken place at the end of November and beginning of December between Vansittart and the Italian ambassador in London, Count Dino Grandi. According to a subsequent report of Grandi's, 'the bases of the Paris agreements were halfway between the proposals which Vansittart made him on 3 December and the concessions which Vansittart had been induced to accept on 5 December.' Sir Robert explicitly told Grandi that he had kept both Baldwin and Hoare informed daily of these conversations and that they had encouraged him to continue.[1] 'These conversations,' Aloisi noted in his diary, 'made a good impression on Mussolini.'[2] It is therefore somewhat strange to find Eden writing in his memoirs that '. . . three visits to the foreign office by Grandi at the beginning of December gave no indication that the Duce's appetite was moderating *or that we could satisfy it*.'[3] If one accepts the Italian evidence – and there is no obvious reason why one should reject it – the second part of Eden's statement is revealed as untrue. There are three possible explanations for this: either Eden is being less than frank; or Vansittart, who was deeply attached to the idea of the 'Stresa front' against Germany, was playing some kind of subtle personal game and offering Grandi concessions which he was not reporting to his superiors; or Eden was not being told the full facts about the conversations. In the present state of the evidence, it is impossible to say which, if any, of these explanations is the more likely.[4]

---

[1] Guariglia, pp. 289–90.

[2] Aloisi, p. 327.

[3] Eden, p. 298 (emphasis added).

[4] There are a few scraps of evidence which, perhaps, ought to be considered in connection with this problem. As far as Vansittart is concerned, we have Eden's testimony that he was 'much more a secretary of state in mentality than a permanent official' (Eden, p. 242) and that, before Hoare's departure for Paris, Eden warned the foreign secretary, 'Don't forget that in Paris Van can be more French than the French' (ibid., p. 298). Vansittart's biographer also discloses that, on the eve of the Paris meeting, he asked the head of the press department of the Foreign Office how long it would take to change public opinion on the Abyssinian issue. The reply was three weeks. 'We have only three days', Vansittart replied (Ian Colvin, *Vansittart in Office*, London, Gollancz, 1965, pp. 74–5). As far as the question of Eden's knowledge of what was going on is concerned, there are two somewhat cryptic passages in his memoirs which could suggest that he felt something was going on behind his back. The first concerns discussions which took place before Hoare left for Paris. 'We all agreed,' he writes, 'that Hoare should try to clear this matter [of French military support in the event of war with Italy] up with Laval when they met on 7 December . . . We did not, however, discuss any possible terms of peace, either at cabinet or, *so far as I know*, between ministers, because the meeting with Laval was not expected to reach conclusions about

There can be little doubt, however, that Hoare went to Paris to discuss peace terms, albeit among other things, and that those terms were
much nearer fruition than the British government subsequently led its
public opinion to believe. As Hoare wrote later, 'Laval and I plunged
into the details of the joint plan that we were preparing for the League'
shortly after conversations began at the Quai d'Orsay on the evening
of Saturday 7 December. By the time the discussions ended, very late
at night, the two statesmen had agreed upon one of the points which
Peterson and Saint-Quentin had been unable to settle: the amount of
the Tigré province to be ceded to Italy. The question of the port to be
ceded to Abyssinia remained and 'very reluctantly' Hoare agreed to
remain in Paris on the following day in order to continue the discussions and reach agreement. 'By the evening of 8 December,' Hoare
wrote, 'agreement had been reached between us on a threefold basis.
First, an effective outlet to the sea with full sovereign rights for
Abyssinia. Secondly, in exchange for this outlet, the cession of some,
but not all, of the territory in Tigré occupied by Italy, and a frontier
rectification in the east and south-east. Thirdly, a large zone in the
south and south-west in which Italy, acting under the League, would
have the monopoly of economic development.' Abyssinia would retain
her sovereignty over the areas not actually ceded to Italy and the plan
would be referred to the League for approval or rejection.'[1]

It is true that the British negotiators were subjected to considerable
pressure from the French. Although Laval agreed to the opening of
Franco-British staff talks to discuss ways of dealing with possible
Italian aggression – a step he had so far refused – Hoare noted that he
'avoided any undertaking to make military preparations, and obviously
assumed that French co-operation would depend upon Anglo-French
agreement as to our immediate policy'. According to Vansittart, Laval
went even further. After pointing out that France could not support an
oil embargo, he added that 'if the imposition of oil sanctions led to a
state of war France might be unable to support Great Britain even with
naval strength in the Mediterranean. A mobilization of the French

---

them' (Eden, p. 297). The second concerns his first reaction to the Hoare–Laval proposals
themselves. 'It did not seem to me to be possible,' he writes, 'to reconcile these proposals
with those of the committee of five, nor with the instructions given to Peterson. *I knew of no
other basis agreed upon in London*' (ibid., p. 300). I have italicized the passages in question.
[1] Templewood, pp. 179–81.

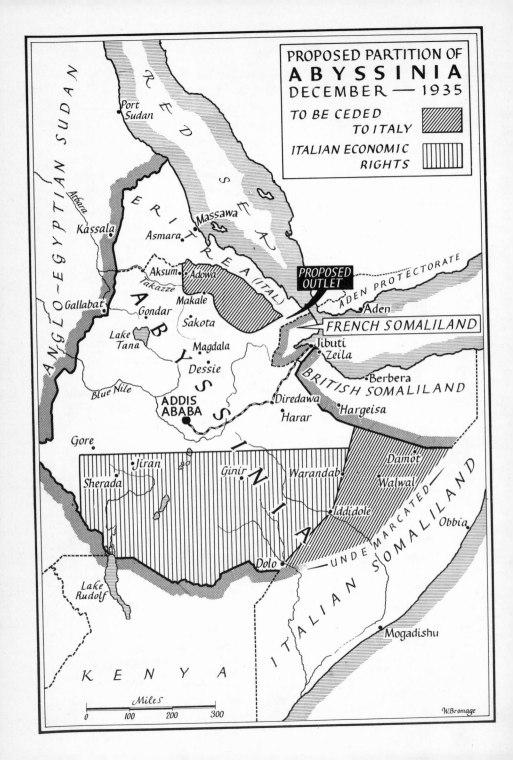

PROPOSED PARTITION OF
ABYSSINIA
DECEMBER — 1935

TO BE CEDED
TO ITALY

ITALIAN ECONOMIC
RIGHTS

fleet would require a mobilization order which [he] believed might result in disorders in Toulon and Marseilles, and this the French government could not afford to contemplate at this time.'[1]

This does not mean, however, that sudden and unexpected revelations of French unwillingness to fight compelled Hoare's acquiescence in the Paris peace proposals, as both he and Vansittart would have us believe. Laval's reluctance was well known before Hoare went to Paris, and the French admiralty had already refused to discuss co-operation between the British and French fleets in the Mediterranean.[2] Most important of all, of course, Vansittart had already been discussing peace terms with Count Grandi which were every bit as favourable to Italy as those contained in the Hoare–Laval plan.

Two events, it is generally agreed, helped to kill the Hoare–Laval plan. The first was the publication, on the evening of Sunday 8 December, of a joint communiqué in which Hoare and Laval stated that agreement had been reached.[3] 'Looking back,' Lord Halifax wrote to Neville Chamberlain on 26 December, 'it seems to me that the initial mistake was [Hoare's], in publishing his (and therefore, except at great price, *our*) assent in the Paris communiqué.'[4] The communiqué, wrote Halifax to Eden, 'was the *fons et origo* of all our troubles. And I think it's an amazing mistake for [Hoare] to have made.'[5] The burden of Halifax's complaint, it should be noted, was not the nature of the proposals, but the fact that Hoare had prematurely disclosed their existence. The foreign secretary's conduct is, indeed, very hard to explain – except on grounds of ill-health – if one accepts the claim which was subsequently made by British government spokesmen that he did not keep them informed of the progress of his talks. '. . . There was an absence of liaison . . . during that Sunday,' prime minister Baldwin told the House of Commons on 19 December, 'We were not aware until it had been accomplished that an agreement had been come to. It was not until breakfast time on Monday morning that I received a letter from my right hon. friend [Hoare] urging that the cabinet

---

[1] Bingham to Hull, 16 December 1935, F.R.U.S., 1935, Vol. I, p. 713.
[2] Eden, p. 282; Vansittart, p. 533; Viscount Simon, *Retrospect*, London, Hutchinson, 1952, p. 212.
[3] For the text, see R.I.I.A. Documents, 1935, Vol. II, p. 350. The editors have, however, misdated it 9 December.
[4] Feiling, p. 275.
[5] Eden, p. 303.

might endorse what he had done. . . .'[1] Earl Stanhope, in the House of Lords, maintained that there had been no telegraphic or telephonic communications from Paris about the peace proposals on either the Saturday or the Sunday.[2]

Eden belies Earl Stanhope's statement. It is clear from his memoirs that there were enough communications from Paris on both Saturday and Sunday to make him feel distinctly uneasy about what was going on.[3] Other sources go even further. On 11 December, the United States ambassador in London, Mr Bingham, reported that Hoare had 'on Sunday, *with the prime minister's specific consent*, accepted the general content of the French-Italian proposals'. Five days later, Vansittart told Bingham of the reasons which had led him and Hoare to agree to the Paris proposals, adding that 'these arguments were the basis used in obtaining *Baldwin's acquiesence on Sunday* and cabinet agreement on Monday for the proposed terms to be sent off to Rome and Addis Ababa'.[4] At the Pétain trial in 1945, Laval also maintained that the British negotiators had been in touch with London. 'Every hour or half-hour,' he said, Sir Robert Vansittart 'telephoned London to inform Mr Baldwin of the progress of our negotiations.'[5] An enterprising British newspaper confronted both Hoare and Vansittart with this statement of Laval's. Hoare refused to comment while Vansittart issued a long statement, the main burden of which was that he was merely an official and knew nothing about Hoare's dealings with the cabinet prior to or during the Paris visit.[6] One is left to draw one's own conclusions.

The second event which helped to kill the Hoare–Laval plan was its premature leakage to the press. Geneviève Tabouis, one of the journalists concerned, has given a vivid account of how she obtained the gist of the plan and deliberately published it in the hope that she 'might be able to ruin its chances' by inflaming opinion in France, Britain, Italy, and the League against it.[7] Laval himself was convinced that it

[1] H.C. Deb., 5th series, Vol. 307, cols. 2031–2.
[2] H.L. Deb., 5th series, Vol. 99, cols. 346–7.
[3] Eden, pp. 299–300.
[4] Bingham to Hull, 11, 16 December 1935, F.R.U.S., 1935, Vol. I, pp. 700, 713 (emphasis added).
[5] *Procès Pétain*, p. 184, col. 2.
[6] *News Chronicle*, 4 August 1945.
[7] Geneviève Tabouis, *They Called Me Cassandra*, New York, Charles Scribner's Sons, 1942, pp. 266–70.

was Sir Charles Mendl, the press attaché at the British embassy in Paris, whom he firmly believed to be in the pay of the secret service, who leaked the details, also with the intention of wrecking the plan.[1]

As the story broke, Hoare arrived in Switzerland for his holiday. His movements are, of course, quite understandable if one accepts the view that he went to Paris with a fairly clear idea of what he was going to do there and had obtained Baldwin's support, not only beforehand, but throughout the negotiations themselves. It is only if one accepts the British government's subsequent explanation that Laval 'sprang' the plan upon him and that no one in London knew anything about it until after it was initialled that his journey to Switzerland seems so incomprehensible.

The British cabinet met at 6 p.m. on Monday 9 December to discuss the peace proposals. Eden was totally opposed to them. 'My wish,' he subsequently wrote, 'was to have nothing to do with these proposals and resign.'[2] But his colleagues evidently did not agree and, while they may not all have liked the plan, they decided to press both Mussolini and the Emperor of Abyssinia to accept it. Eden was able, however, to win two minor victories. Laval's suggestion that the League meeting to discuss oil sanctions should be postponed still further, pending examination of the peace proposals, was rejected. So was his other suggestion that Mussolini should be informed of the plan before Haile Selassie. Eden correctly divined Laval's intention of using the Duce's acceptance and the emperor's probable subsequent refusal as an excuse for not imposing sanctions, at least in respect of oil.[3]

On 10 December, in the light of fairly full press reports on the Hoare–Laval plan, the British government was placed in an awkward position in the debate on the address in reply to the king's speech. Baldwin made a characteristic contribution to the discussion. 'I have seldom spoken with greater regret,' he said, 'for my lips are not yet unsealed. Were these troubles over I would make a case, and I guarantee that not a man would go into the lobby against us.'[4] Early in January 1936, he told his friend Thomas Jones that he had had the poor

[1] Unpublished notes by Madame de Chambrun (Laval's daughter) on Lord Templewood's memoirs, kindly communicated to me by M. René de Chambrun. A few years later, Laval told the Italian press attaché in Paris that Sir Charles Mendl had been heard to boast that his government had spent more money to bring the Laval government down than on a colonial war (Landini to Luciano, 18 March 1938, Italian Documents, 148/043539–41).

[2] Eden, p. 302.

[3] Eden, pp. 304–5; Templewood, p. 181; Herriot, *Jadis*, p. 621.

[4] H.C. Deb., 5th series, Vol. 307, col. 856.

state of British armaments in mind. 'Our fleet would be in real danger from the small craft of the Italians operating in a small sea,' he said. 'Italian bombers could get to London. I had also Germany in mind. Had we gone to war our anti-aircraft munitions would have been exhausted in a week.'[1] In 1940 – after the French collapse no doubt – he felt it safe to offer an alternative explanation for his words. '. . . What of course I meant,' he told a friend, 'was that I was morally sure that Laval had been bought by Mussolini, and I could not very well say that to the house. After all, we had to remain on good terms with the French.'[2] Poor Laval had yet another explanation for the 'sealed lips' phrase. Bearing in mind his meetings with the Prince of Wales, he thought it referred to royal intervention. 'I wondered, "What is it that he cannot say?" ' he told the court at the Pétain trial. ' "Perhaps he cannot say that he has received advice from the king".'[3]

When the French cabinet met on 10 December, it was decided to accept the Hoare–Laval plan as a basis for negotiation, provided that both the emperor and the League agreed to it. That night, the British and French representatives in Rome and Addis Ababa were instructed to inform the governments to which they were accredited of the peace proposals. The British ambassador in Addis Ababa was further asked to 'use [his] utmost influence to induce the emperor to give careful and favourable consideration to these proposals and on no account lightly to reject them'. Laval sent a personal appeal to Mussolini urging him to 'moderate his demands and not to assume, by his refusal, the responsibility for prolonging and exacerbating a crisis during the course of which French friendship could henceforth hardly make its influence felt'.[4]

In spite of this appeal, Mussolini's initial reaction to the Hoare–Laval plan was negative. In his opinion it did not go far enough. But he did not reject it outright. Instead, he decided to call a meeting of the Fascist Grand Council on 18 December, after which he promised to make known his reply.[5] The reasons for the Duce's attitude are not

---

[1] Thomas Jones, *A Diary with Letters, 1931–50*, London, Oxford University Press, 1954 pp. 158–60.

[2] A. W. Baldwin, *My Father: The True Story*, London, Allen & Unwin, 1955, p. 291.

[3] *Procès Pétain*, p. 184, col. 2.

[4] Herriot, *Jadis*, pp. 620–21; Hoare to Barton, 10 December 1935, printed in R.I.I.A. Documents, 1935, Vol. II, pp. 358–60.

[5] Aloisi, pp. 328–9; Herriot, *Jadis*, p. 622.

clear. Perhaps he wanted to try and extract more concessions;[1] perhaps he wanted to see whether the British and French governments would stand by the plan in the face of growing hostility on the part of public opinion; perhaps he was quite simply unable to make up his mind. Whatever his motives, the delay almost certainly knocked the final nail into the coffin of the plan. In the first place, it gave public opinion, especially in Britain, time to make its influence felt. Secondly, and even more important, it enabled those who opposed the proposals to set about sabotaging them. On the British side, Eden was the most dedicated of these opponents. He now saw his chance and seized it with both hands. Arriving in Geneva on 11 December, after the press leakages had taken place, he found that 'the impression which the Paris proposals have made upon opinion here is even worse than I anticipated'. This gave him the opportunity to state, in public, that 'the proposals now put forward are neither definitive nor sacrosanct. They are suggestions which it is hoped may make possible the beginning of negotiations. If the League does not agree with these suggestions, we shall make no complaint. Indeed, we should cordially welcome any suggestions for their improvement.'[2] Herriot, who was present when Eden made his speech, noted that the British minister seemed 'to be asking for a disavowal'. Acting on the principle of 'anything you can do I can do better', this French opponent of the plan delivered a speech at Montbéliard on 15 December which was so effective in its condemnation that it was subsequently quoted by the Abyssinian government to justify its own refusal to accept the plan.[3]

There is some evidence that, by 18 December, Mussolini was prepared to accept the Hoare–Laval plan as, at any rate, a basis for negotiation.[4] But it was already too late. The British government had decided to abandon it the previous day. If Hoare, who was by his own account still convinced that he had done the right thing, had been able to put up more of a fight, the outcome might have been different. But he had broken his nose while skating in Switzerland and, although he

---

[1] On 15 December he telegraphed Grandi and Cerruti, asking them to sound out Vansittart and Laval on a number of suggested amendments (Guariglia, pp. 292–4).

[2] Eden, pp. 307–8.

[3] Herriot, *Jadis*, pp. 623–5; declaration of the Abyssinian government, 18 December 1935, in R.I.I.A. Documents, 1935, Vol. II, pp. 371–81.

[4] Guariglia, pp. 296–7. Aloisi, however, says that Mussolini was still undecided (Aloisi, p. 331).

returned to London on 16 December, he was still confined to bed. On the evening of the 18th, while the Fascist Grand Council was in session, he resigned.[1]

Laval, of course, was bitterly disappointed. He complained to Eden that 'he never seemed to have much luck in his negotiations with the English',[2] and, in a letter to Mussolini, he 'deeply regretted that the Italian government did not reply with an immediate and spontaneous acceptance of our proposals which, as events have shown, were as far as we could go.' In October, he said, Mussolini had told him that the European, and perhaps even the world, political situation depended upon France. 'Do I not have the right today, after all I have done,' he asked, 'to tell you that the outcome of European peace henceforth rests, above all, in the hands of Italy ?'[3]

The Chamber of Deputies debated Abyssinia on 27 and 28 December. The *Front Populaire* coalition was in full cry against Laval, having found a foreign policy issue to add to their many grievances against his domestic policy. Léon Blum for the socialists told Laval, 'You have tried to give and to keep. You wanted to have your cake and eat it. You cancelled your words by your deeds and your deeds by your words. You have debased everything by fixing, intrigue and slickness. . . . Not sensitive enough to the importance of great moral issues, you have reduced everything to the level of your petty methods.' For the *Front Populaire* radicals, Yvon Delbos was no less scathing. 'Your plan is dead and buried,' he declared. 'From its failure, which is as total as possible, you could have – but you have not – drawn a personal conclusion. Two lessons emerge. The first is that you were in a dead end because you upset everyone without satisfying Italy. The second is that we must return to the spirit of the Covenant by preserving agreement with the nations gathered at Geneva.' Nor was criticism confined to the left. From the centre benches, Paul Reynaud attacked the government for playing Hitler's game by wrecking the Anglo-French alliance.

In his long speech at the end of the debate, Laval sought to justify his actions by disclosing some of the details of the diplomatic negotiations of the previous months. For those who criticized his attitude to-

[1] Eden, p. 309; Templewood, pp. 184–5; Macleod, pp. 188–9.
[2] Eden, p. 309.
[3] Laval to Mussolini, 22 December 1935, in Lagardelle, pp. 275–8.

wards Britain, he revealed the agreement with Hoare at Geneva in September that the two countries would not apply military sanctions. To those who accused him of encouraging Italy, he replied that he had never given Mussolini a 'free hand' in Abyssinia and had continually warned him that, if he attacked that country, France would live up to her obligations under the Covenant. He then outlined the various attempts at compromise which had been made and concluded that the path of conciliation was still open. 'France will continue to apply the sanctions in force,' he said, 'but she will also continue . . . to seek conciliation.'[1]

In the division on Delbos' motion of censure, the government scraped home by a majority of 296 votes to 276. In the light of the debate it was a surprising – and some thought a fraudulent – result. One radical deputy claimed that 'legions of honour, palms of agricultural merit and public instruction were handed out by the ministers in the lobbies; the deputies in difficult electoral situation were promised that they would not be opposed by right-wing candidates; subsidies were granted for bringing water to rural communities, and agricultural credits were widely distributed; and during the vote in the Chamber, the ballot boxes were stuffed.'[2] On this last point Alexander Werth has commented, 'There was . . . some talk of the *armoire à confiture* – the "jam cupboard" at the Chamber – where the ballot papers of half a dozen chronic absentees are kept – and which may, in a great emergency, be discreetly raided by government supporters.'[3] But however the votes were obtained, the key factor was that a third of the radicals voted for the government. If they had followed the majority of their colleagues, Laval would have been out.[4]

Having survived this crisis, it looked as though the government could survive anything. Such, indeed, was the opinion of the political correspondent of *Le Temps*, who wrote on 10 January 1936 that 'the government's position . . . now seems more solid than in the days which preceded . . . 28 December. Victorious on all issues in succession – financial policy, the maintenance of public order, foreign policy – M. Pierre Laval's government could only find itself in difficulties in the

[1] J. O. Chambre, *Débats*, 27 and 28 December 1935, *passim*.
[2] Octave Crutel in *L'Eveil*, 5 January 1936, cited in Larmour, p. 191.
[3] Werth, p. 207.
[4] 37 radicals voted for the government and 93 against. 14 abstained and 8 were absent (*Le Temps*, 30 December 1935).

near future as the result of an internal crisis, which no longer appears very likely. . . .'[1] But the task of a political tipster in pre-war France was a difficult one. Less than a fortnight after that comment appeared, the Laval government had fallen as the result of just such an internal crisis as the *Temps* correspondent had discounted.

Not surprisingly, the radicals were at the bottom of it. Herriot had resigned from the chairmanship of the party on 18 December in a fit of pique and had been succeeded by Edouard Daladier, the most enthusiastic supporter of the *Front Populaire*.[2] On 10 January 1936 the programme of the *Front Populaire*, in the drafting of which radicals had taken part, was published. With its attack upon the decree-laws, its call for 'effective' measures against the leagues, its hostility towards 'secret diplomacy', and its emphasis upon collective security and the League of Nations, it was an unremitting condemnation of the government's policies.[3] The pressure upon the radical ministers to resign and for the party to associate itself wholeheartedly with the *Front Populaire* was growing all the time.

Herriot, it seems, had more or less made up his mind to go. His motives are not clear. No great admirer of the *Front Populaire*, he may simply have been tired of the continual abuse to which he was subjected – for different reasons – from both right and left. At any rate, he told Laval on 16 January that he intended to resign. Laval 'understands my position and accepts it,' he noted. 'He simply asks me to delay my departure.' The following day, he saw two other radical ministers, Georges Bonnet and William Bertrand, who, he claims, approved his intention. 'Either I resign and the executive committee of our party authorizes them to remain in the cabinet,' Herriot commented, 'or, wanting more, the committee compels us all to resign.' This in fact was what happened. At the meeting of the executive committee on 19 January, a motion was passed condemning the government's policies and calling upon all members of the parliamentary group to accept a common discipline. On the 22nd, Herriot, Bonnet, Paganon, and Bertrand handed in their resignations to the prime minister. Two radicals, Marcel Régnier and Henri Maupoil, stayed on.

---

[1] *Le Temps*, 11 January 1936.
[2] Larmour, p. 194; Herriot, *Jadis*, p. 626.
[3] The full text of the *Front Populaire* programme is printed in Georges Dupeux, *Le Front Populaire et les Elections de 1936*, Paris, Armand Colin, 1959, pp. 179–83.

But Laval decided that he had had enough. He resigned without even going before parliament.[1]

Upon leaving office, Laval took the somewhat unusual step of issuing a personal statement to the press. 'I did not seek power,' it said. 'I accepted the burden last June as a duty towards the country. I am conscious of having carried out my task. The franc . . . is intact. The budget, reduced by a fifth, has been voted. The measures taken in all fields are beginning to bear fruit and the preliminary signs of an upturn in economic and agricultural activity are visible. During parliamentary debates themselves, the divisions among Frenchmen have been softened. We have seen the onset of the dawn of national reconciliation.' In spite of the many difficulties he had had to face, he listed the government's achievements in the realm of foreign policy as follows: 'Peace has been maintained. Our obligations towards the League of Nations have been kept. Our friendships and our alliances are intact. The independence of our foreign policy is assured and strengthened . . . France remains mistress of her destiny.'[2]

The success of Laval's domestic policy is debatable. The franc, it is true, had not been devalued, although many present-day economists would undoubtedly argue that it should have been. As for the overall state of the economy, it has been shown that the upturn in economic activity, which did indeed take place during the second half of 1935, antedated the Laval government's measures. It is also quite clear that some of the decree-laws – those designed to hold down prices, for example – did not have the desired effect.[3] On the other hand, supporters of Laval's policies can always claim that they helped in the process of recovery and that they provided that elusive, but apparently so necessary, ingredient of 'confidence'. As in so many analyses of economic problems, one pays one's money and one takes one's choice.

[1] This account of the fall of the Laval government is based upon Herriot, *Jadis*, pp. 635–7; and Larmour, pp. 191–6. Lucien Lamoureux (cited in Bonnefous, Vol V, p. 371) claims that the issue which prompted Herriot to leave the government was Laval's sympathy with a proposal to postpone the 1936 elections for two years. He also claims that Herriot exercised considerable pressure upon his radical colleagues to leave the government with him. The latter may be true, but the former is not. Herriot mentions Laval's interest in prolonging the life of the legislature in October 1935 (Herriot, *Jadis*, p. 606), but by January 1936 the issue was quite a different one. At that stage, the government was considering *advancing* the date of the elections. See ibid., p. 635; *Le Temps*, 15 January 1936.

[2] *Le Temps*, 24 January 1936.

[3] Etat Français, Statistique Générale et Institut de Conjoncture, *Mouvement Economique en France de 1929 à 1939*, Paris, Imprimerie Nationale, 1941, pp. 126–9.

There can be no such doubts about Laval's foreign policy. It was a failure and his resignation statement was, to put it bluntly, a verbal camouflage in that respect. The alliance with Italy, which had been its centre piece, was no more. Mussolini told the German ambassador in Rome on 7 January 1936 that 'basically . . . [the Franco-Italian military agreements] were, in view of the present situation, pretty well liquidated. . . . Stresa he regarded as dead and buried once for all.'[1] The French government had already been forced to draw its own conclusions. In a note for the chiefs of staff, M. Fabry the minister of war pointed out that, since the outbreak of the Abyssinian conflict, it had been necessary to retain where they were 14 out of the 17 divisions on the Alpine frontier and in North Africa, which it had been intended to transfer to the north-eastern frontier with Germany.[2]

No progress whatever had been made in seeking an alternative counterweight to Germany. Laval's policy in the Abyssinian crisis had thrown the League of Nations into disarray and brought Anglo-French relations to a new low point of mutual suspicion and recrimination. Admittedly, it was not all his fault, but he must bear a considerable share of the blame. The Franco-Soviet pact remained unratified and Russian proposals for staff talks had been cold-shouldered. The pact would be ratified, Laval told the German ambassador on 18 December 1935, but 'he . . . would not . . . allow himself to be dragged into the adventurous policy which Russia desired, and he knew that the French people, too, rejected any such idea.' The ambassador must have seen, he continued, 'that French public opinion was increasingly coming to realize that the French army should only be used in defence of French soil, and in no circumstances beyond France's own frontiers.'[3] This was a terrible admission to make, especially in view of the mounting evidence that Hitler was thinking of taking advantage of the international situation to jettison the Locarno agreement and remilitarize the Rhineland.[4] It was also virtually a declaration of abandonment of France's eastern European allies, most

[1] Hassell to Foreign Ministry, 7 January 1936, D.G.F.P., Series C, Vol. IV, No. 485.
[2] Fabry note, 18 January 1936, in Fabry, pp. 233-8.
[3] Köster to Foreign Ministry, 18 December 1935, D.G.F.P. Series C, Vol IV, No. 467.
[4] For evidence on Hitler's designs on the Rhineland, see the testimony of Jean Dobler, the French consul in Cologne, in C.E. *Témoignages*, Vol. II, especially pp. 470-80, 502-3; and the documents printed in Ministère des Affaires Etrangères, *Documents Diplomatiques Français 1932-39*, 2nd Series, Vol. I, Paris, Imprimerie Nationale, 1963, especially Nos. 37, 77 and 91.

of whom had already been subjected to great difficulties as a result of his policies towards Russia, Germany, and Italy, and whom he still had the nerve to ask to get together with Austria in order to preserve the latter's independence.[1]

The real tragedy was, however, that Laval seemingly believed a great deal of what he said in his resignation statement. He remained convinced that he had been on the right lines and that if it had not been for the British, the Germans, the Italians, the *Front Populaire*, the radicals, or some other convenient scapegoat, he could have preserved European peace and set his country on the road to prosperity. During 1935, in fact, something had happened to Laval to convince him of his own infallibility. It cannot be dated nor analysed with precision, but its symptoms were to become increasingly evident in the years that followed, with disastrous consequences.

---

[1] Laval to Puaux, Naggiar, d'Ormesson and Dampierre, 11 January 1936, ibid., No. 34.

4

In the Wilderness

January 1936 – September 1939

A casual observer might be forgiven for thinking that Laval virtually disappeared from the French political scene between 1936 and 1939. After the fall of his government in January 1936, he did not speak in the Senate again until 2 September 1939 and he made very few public statements outside it. This seems to suggest a voluntary and almost total withdrawal from public life rather than the normal transition from government to opposition. Yet, in fact, he was by no means inactive. His attendance and voting records in the Senate were good. His interventions in the proceedings of its foreign affairs committee were frequent and often controversial. In addition, he continued to be very active in the lobbies.

Laval's choice of privacy was really dictated by the victory of the *Front Populaire* at the general elections of 26 April and 3 May 1936. This coalition of left-wing parties, ranging from the Radicals to the Communists, had been finally cemented during the period of his premiership, and its programme had been inspired by opposition to his policies, both at home and abroad. For Laval, then, the 1936 elections were much more than the customary swing of the political pendulum; they were a personal defeat. He himself admitted as much in June 1940 when, referring to the Chamber of Deputies elected four years earlier, he exclaimed, '*Cette Chambre m'a vomi.*'[1]

It is difficult for the outsider to appreciate the bitterness engendered in the French body politic by the triumph of the *Front Populaire*. It would hardly be too much of an exaggeration to say that, for many of its opponents, it represented a Moscow-led conspiracy bent upon wholesale revolution and war, while its supporters in their turn tended to regard its opponents as fascist or Nazi sympathizers, determined to

---

[1] Paul Baudouin, *Neuf Mois au Gouvernement*, Paris, La Table Ronde, 1948, p. 219.

132

destroy France's traditional Republican liberties. The fact that the accession to power of France's first socialist prime minister, Léon Blum, coincided with a wave of sit-down strikes, in which nearly two million workers were involved at one stage, did nothing to appease spirits on either side. Rather it seemed to herald the outbreak of revolution. The atmosphere is vividly described by an opposition deputy, who was by no means an extremist, in his diary entry for 11 June. 'Many foreigners have left Paris in a hurry,' he wrote. 'They believe in an imminent revolution. In spite of the enforced prudence of the press and radio, the news which reaches us from abroad is heartbreaking, for many consider that France is lost and are making their arrangements accordingly. . . There is talk of the collapse of the franc and even the taking over and looting of private dwellings, of the hoarding of money and flight to the provinces or abroad. [A friend], who is very worried, asks me if I think he ought to allow his family to remain in Paris.'[1]

But there was no bloody revolution. Instead the *Front Populaire* government passed a series of social and economic reforms, including the introduction of paid holidays and a forty-hour week, the nationalization of the Bank of France, and the establishment of a National Wheat Office, which was designed to manage the market of this key agricultural commodity in a way more favourable to the farmers. Due to the lack of confidence in business and banking circles, however, it was not long before the Blum government was in financial difficulties, and on 26 September 1936 it was compelled to devalue the franc, thereby breaking the prime minister's personal pledge on this issue which he had made in his ministerial declaration less than four months previously. But devaluation proved to be only a temporary palliative and speculation against the franc continued. On 13 February 1937, Blum announced the need for a 'pause' in the *Front Populaire*'s programme of social reform, and when, in June, he failed to obtain emergency powers from the Senate to deal with the ever-worsening financial situation, his government resigned. Almost inevitably, it seemed, the pattern of the 1924 and 1932 legislatures was to be repeated, with a left-wing majority transforming itself into a right-wing one. But the transformation was not a sudden one, as it had been in 1926 and 1934,

---

[1] Abbé Desgranges, *Journal d'un Prêtre-Député*, Paris-Geneva, La Palatine, 1960 (hereafter cited as Desgranges), p. 34.

and it was not until the accession to power of Daladier in April 1938 that it was really completed. Even then it was preceded by a tragicomic three-week interlude, during which Blum, after having failed to form a genuinely 'national' government, presided over what was almost an exact replica of his 1936 ministry.[1]

In common with many other right-wing senators, Laval either voted for or prudently abstained in the early divisions on the *Front Populaire*'s social and economic reforms. But everyone knew that the Senate, which was indirectly elected and which did not therefore reflect the *Front Populaire* majority in the country, was voting under the threat of militant action by the government's working-class supporters. After the devaluation of the franc, however, Laval was already calling in the lobbies for the immediate overthrow of the government, although he had at least taken the precaution of safeguarding his own financial interests by transferring some of his assets from francs into gold dollars when the *Front Populaire* came to power.[2]

If Laval's experience as prime minister in 1935–36 had given rise to a certain scepticism about the virtues of French parliamentary democracy, the triumph of the *Front Populaire* only reinforced it. In an interview with two American journalists, he told one of them that 'he was convinced that the era of popular government by parliaments was doomed on account of the inherent weakness of assemblies composed of political parties'. When *he* returned to power, he told Signor Landini, the Italian press attaché in Paris, on 4 April 1938, he intended to use 'every means' to keep himself there. Furthermore, 'he wanted to deprive parliament of the capacity to do harm.'[3]

These were fascist sentiments, but it is only fair to add that Laval had no desire to work through France's home-grown fascist parties. In an earlier conversation with Landini on 8 March 1938, he conceded that de la Rocque's and Doriot's groups were 'useful because they prevented many people . . . from sliding or straying into other

---

[1] For the achievements of the Blum government and the subsequent decline of the *Front Populaire*, see Werth, pp. 315–51; Alexander Werth, *France and Munich*, London, Hamish Hamilton, 1939, pp. 98–143; Louis Bodin and Jean Touchard, *Front Populaire 1936*, Paris, Armand Colin, 1961, pp. 137–227.

[2] Desgranges, pp. 35, 60; Baraduc, p. 27.

[3] Ralph Heinzen in *La Vie de la France*, Vol. III, p. 1736. Heinzen does not give a precise date for this interview, merely stating that it took place 'between 1936 and the outbreak of the war'. Landini to Luciano, 6 April 1938, Italian Documents 148/043545–54. Luciano was *capo di gabinetto* to the Italian minister of popular culture.

dubious and dangerous formations.' However, he emphasized that 'they will not be the ones to save France'. The reference to 'dubious and dangerous formations' is an interesting one, for it almost certainly meant the *Cagoule*, an extremist right-wing organization which had been plotting an armed *coup d'état* before its discovery by the government in 1937. It was suggested at the time in some quarters that Laval was involved with the *Cagoule* in some way, and he had the occasion to protest indignantly to the minister of the interior when one of the organization's leaders was questioned by the police about his relations with Laval. Similar allegations were made after the war, notably at Marshal Pétain's trial in 1945, but no reliable evidence was ever produced and the matter was not even raised at Laval's own trial two months later. Whatever his political views, Laval's antipathy towards violence would almost certainly have made it impossible for him to belong to an organization like the *Cagoule*.[1]

As early as April 1937, Laval's alternative to the *Front Populaire* was a national government headed by Marshal Pétain. This emerges quite clearly from a report of a conversation between Laval and one of General Franco's agents. After voicing his fears about Communism in France, Laval told the Spaniard that he was 'in touch' with Doriot, de la Rocque and Pétain, that he believed 'the salvation of France lay in a Pétain government and that the Marshal was determined to assume this responsibility'. His subsequent assertion that he was 'secretly working' with Blum towards the same end but that the prime minister was reluctant might seem to cast doubt on the accuracy of the entire report, but Laval was prone to exaggeration, especially when he wanted to impress. He may not even have secured Pétain's support, let alone Blum's. In any case, talk of a Pétain government in April 1937, when the *Front Populaire* majority was still fairly solid, was clearly premature.[2]

A year later, however, the position was very different and we again find Laval discussing the possibility of a Pétain government in two

[1] Landini to Luciano, 9 March 1938, ibid., 148/043531–8; *Procès Pétain*, p. 7, col. 3; Laval's evidence, ibid., p. 197, cols. 1–2. For details on the *Cagoule*, see my essay on France in S. J. Woolf (ed.), *European Fascism*, London, Weidenfeld and Nicolson, 1968.
[2] Enclosure in Faupel to Foreign Ministry, 14 April 1937, D.G.F.P., Series D, Vol. III, No. 244.

conversations with Landini during Blum's precarious three-week administration. After stressing the need for the utmost secrecy, he confided to the Italian press attaché on 17 March 1938 that 'he was in the process of forming a national government, of which he would be the driving force and which would be headed by Marshal Pétain, who had decided to accept from patriotic motives'. One obstacle to the success of this plan, said Laval, was President Lebrun, whom he described as 'trembling with fear'. Laval and his supporters were accordingly sending politicians of various persuasions to discuss the plan with the president of the Republic and 'to give him the impression that [it] enjoyed widespread support in the country.'[1]

Landini was sceptical about the prospects of success for Laval's plan, and rightly so in view of what the latter told him during their next recorded conversation on 4 April. Laval told the Italian that 'his Pétain formula was continuing to develop, but I was not to believe that the affair was going so smoothly. The Marshal had a will and prejudices of his own and it required considerable tact to make him see reason.'[2] Whether Laval succeeded in getting Pétain to 'see reason' is not known. In any event, the Daladier government was formed six days after this conversation took place and Laval voted for it when it came before the Senate on 13 April.

The available evidence makes it extremely difficult to discover the exact nature of the relationship between Laval and Pétain during these years, but it is necessary to explore the question in some detail, if only to assess the validity of the countless accusations bandied about during and after the Second World War to the effect that the actual Pétain–Laval government of 1940 was the result of a deeply-laid conspiracy.

The two men were colleagues for the first time in the Doumergue government of 1934. At first sight, there might seem little in common between the 78-year-old war hero making his political début and the experienced 50-year-old career politician who had flirted with pacifism at the very time when Pétain was acquiring his military reputation. Yet the Marshal seems to have been favourably impressed by Laval. Commandant Loustaunau Lacau, who served on the Marshal's staff

---

[1] Landini to Luciano, 18 March 1938, Italian Documents, 148/043539–44.
[2] Landini to Luciano, 6 April 1938, ibid., 148/043545–54. Pétain apparently expressed the fear that the proposed government, even if it were formed, would end up like Doumergue's in 1934.

from October 1934 until March 1938 and who kept in close touch with him afterwards, testified in 1945 how Pétain, 'in that obstinate way old men have of repeating things', frequently used to recall how one day Doumergue had told him, 'The Republic is rotten; they don't have anyone left.' Then, pointing to Laval, he had added, 'But there is still that one.' Whatever the truth of this anecdote, it is worth emphasizing that Pétain did not see fit to become a member of Laval's own government in 1935, although he was apparently asked to do so.[1]

A common opposition to the *Front Populaire* probably created a much stronger bond of sympathy between the two men. Pétain kept his views more to himself than did Laval, but it is clear from his right-wing contacts and, of course, from his attitude in 1940 what those views were.[2]

There was a more personal link between Pétain and Laval in the person of the latter's son-in-law, Count René de Chambrun. He knew Pétain quite well through his father, General de Chambrun, and when the Marshal visited the United States in 1931 he had prepared his speeches and acted as his interpreter. In 1935, René de Chambrun founded the French Information Centre in the United States and managed to persuade Pétain to become the organization's president. From then until the outbreak of the war, he has written, he saw Pétain 'regularly, at least once a week' on business connected with the Centre. But he has emphatically denied acting as an intermediary between his father-in-law and the Marshal. 'I have always practised my profession of independent international lawyer,' he writes, 'and never worked in any way during those pre-war years as either assistant to my father-in-law or intermediary between him and Marshal Pétain.' Indeed, he cannot even remember a meeting of the two men at which he was present.[3]

But meetings between Laval and Pétain did take place and politics were discussed. Laval freely admitted this at the Marshal's trial in 1945. He had taken the view, he said, that 'governments which want to bother about the internal régimes of other countries' — a reference to the *Front Populaire* was no doubt intended — 'are a threat to peace,

[1] *Procès Pétain*, p. 121, col. 1; Mallet, Vol I, p. 135.

[2] For Pétain's right-wing connections, see Robert Aron, *Histoire de Vichy*, Paris, Fayard, 1954, pp. 31–2.

[3] Unpublished memorandum by M. René de Chambrun for the French Public Prosecutor on his relations with Marshal Pétain, dated 22 January 1946; letter from M. de Chambrun to the author, dated 23 February 1963.

and I thought that the Marshal, who enjoyed considerable authority and prestige, could perhaps rectify our position abroad. . . . This was the key idea which guided me. I had a right to it. I was a member of parliament, I had frequently been a minister and head of government, and . . . I was concerned to do and try everything to prevent the worst. . . . That is how I arrived at the idea of having Marshal Pétain in power. I made no secret of it at the time. I said it in the Senate and discussed it with my colleagues. There was nothing sinister. There was no plot. What's more, my conversations with the Marshal were very infrequent, but what interested me was that, for the same reasons as I have just outlined . . . he seemed disposed to accept the responsibility of power if the opportunity were presented to him.'[1]

In the light of the evidence, therefore, the most that one can safely say about the Laval–Pétain relationship is as follows: Laval hoped to return to power as 'the driving force' of a government headed by Pétain, who would provide the necessary prestige. He discussed this possibility with the Marshal, who 'seemed disposed to accept the responsibility of power'. But the project never got off the ground. Not only was the political climate unfavourable, but Pétain 'had a will and prejudices of his own' and, although Laval did not mention it, these included a stubborn determination not to be used by politicians for their own purposes. 'Politicians try to make use of me,' the Marshal subsequently told a colleague. 'They are making a mistake.'[2]

Perhaps it was Pétain's refusal to play Laval's game that led the latter to oppose his candidature for the presidency of the Republic in April 1939. At the end of February, the Marshal had accepted Daladier's offer of the post of ambassador to the newly-recognized Franco government in Spain, but, as France's most distinguished old soldier, it was not surprising that his name began to be mentioned as a possible presidential candidate. One of his supporters, Senator Henry Haye, has related how, 'together with a number of other senators and deputies belonging to the most diverse political parties and including several Socialists,' he was convinced that 'a grave warning would be given to Hitler' – whose troops had just marched into Prague – 'if the representatives of the French people were to affirm their unity by elevating

---

[1] *Procès Pétain*, p. 185, col. 3.
[2] Armand Gazel in ibid., p. 73, col. 3. M. Gazel was on the staff of the French embassy in Spain when Pétain was ambassador.

the man of Verdun . . . to the highest office of the Republic.' However, recalls Henry Haye, he had 'the most lively arguments' with Laval, whom he described as 'the most inveterate opponent of the Marshal's supporters'. In the event, Pétain refused to be considered as a candidate, explaining to some that his task in Spain was more important and to others that he was too old for the job, and M. Lebrun was re-elected for a further term.[1]

Laval's attitude was not purely negative, for he had a candidate of his own in the person of Fernand Bouisson, the former president of the Chamber of Deputies. By supporting Bouisson, he explained to Landini on 6 March 1939, he hoped 'to obtain the post of prime minister on a suitable occasion'. Another source makes his support of Bouisson part of a larger and much more sinister design. Testifying at the Pétain trial, a Mlle Petit, a former secretary of an Italian journalist, Mirko Giobbe, who worked in Paris, told the court that on 26 January 1939 Laval asked to see her employer, whom she described as 'an unofficial agent of the Palazzo Chigi', so that the two men could 'work together at a policy which was the one the Axis wanted France to follow'. Inside France, this policy involved the setting-up of a dictatorship, while in the field of foreign affairs, Laval was said to favour a reversal of alliances which 'could go as far as joint military action by France, Spain, Italy, and Germany against the British empire'. Laval claimed that this policy had the support of 'a high-ranking military personage, nine-tenths of the general staff, and an important minority in the Chamber and Senate'. He preferred that his return to power should be effected constitutionally and hoped to use the forthcoming presidential election for that purpose. If he were elected, Bouisson, whom Mlle Petit described as being 'completely won over' to Laval's plan, would cover up by confirming Daladier in office, but he, Laval, 'undertook to slip an orange peel under the prime minister's feet and bring down his government in a way which would appear normal to public opinion'.[2]

[1] Henry Haye in *La Vie de la France*, Vol. III, pp. 1428–9; evidence of M. de Chayla in *Procès Pétain*, p. 153, cols. 1–2 (M. de Chayla was counsellor of the French embassy in Spain when Pétain was ambassador); Louis Noguères, *Le Véritable Procès du Maréchal Pétain*, Paris, Fayard, 1955 (hereafter cited as Noguères), pp. 14–16. M. Noguères, a former president of the high court, based this book almost exclusively upon hitherto unpublished documentation in the Pétain trial dossiers, much of which he reproduces in full.

[2] Landini to Luciano, 8 March 1939, Italian Documents 148/043630–34; *Procès Pétain*, p. 107, col. 2.

Fantastic as this story may sound, enough documented statements by Laval compel us to take it seriously. He wanted to maintain himself in power by 'every means'. This certainly suggests that he favoured some form of dictatorship. At the same time, he opposed violent methods of seizing power. In foreign affairs, we shall see his Anglophobia and his desire for a 'Latin bloc' consisting of France, Italy, and Nationalist Spain, together with a Franco-German *rapprochement*. On the other hand, his claims of support, if indeed he ever made them, were pure hyperbole, and it is unlikely that he ever suggested joint military action against Britain. Nor is there any confirmation of the attitude of Bouisson, who withdrew his candidature at the last moment. As for Giobbe, while his paper was subsidized by the Italian government and while he occasionally passed on information to the Italian embassy, it seems a little melodramatic to describe him as 'an unofficial agent'. In short, therefore, Mlle Petit's story boils down to an embroidered version of what was probably little more than an elaborate pipe-dream of Laval's. In so far as it reflects his thoughts, however, it is an indication of how early he supported the policies which were to gain him notoriety in 1940.[1]

An essential ingredient of these policies was Laval's conception of a 'continental' foreign policy for France. There was nothing new about this: he was already talking in these terms during his premiership in 1931.[2] But the British attitude over the Abyssinian crisis had given a new urgency to the need for a continental orientation of French policy, based upon a *rapprochement* with both Germany and Italy. Unfortunately, there were two major obstacles to Laval's ideal. One was the persistently unreasonable attitude of Hitler's Germany and the other was the ideological prejudice of the *Front Populaire*.

The reoccupation of the Rhineland in March 1936 was a bitter blow to the policy of an understanding with Germany which Laval had pursued throughout his tenure of the Quai d'Orsay. This comes through very clearly in a statement which he made to his own newspaper, *Le Moniteur de Puy-de-Dôme*, and which was reproduced in many other papers. In it, he described the German action as 'an

---

[1] For Giobbe's own account of his relations with Laval, see *La Vie de la France*, Vol. III, pp. 1364–9. Laval's account, which attempts to belittle the relationship in general and Mlle Petit's evidence in particular, is in *Laval Parle*, pp. 32–3.

[2] See above, pp. 23–4.

initiative and a gesture which bring out everything that divides us from Germany'. Nevertheless, provided France took the precaution of remaining strong, he felt that she should continue to seek agreement with Germany. This might invite further disappointments, but, he argued, 'we must demonstrate and prove our enduring desire for the construction of peace.' Naturally, France could not act without her allies. 'The peace we desire is not a selfish peace for ourselves alone,' he maintained. 'We desire it for everyone, both in the east and the west.' Laval urged that the diplomats should not be rigidly bound by formulae. 'If proposals were made in the past and failed,' he said, 'we must seek and find others. . . . In the state of anxiety and disorder in which Europe finds itself, we must act and act quickly. In particular, we must try and settle all the problems which exist between France and Germany. . . . Stable frontiers and respect for the internal régimes of the two countries is the condition, the real condition, of a lasting peace.' Bemoaning the failure of the Hoare–Laval plan, he said that there was no peace in Abyssinia and that it remained to be constructed in Europe. He thought it paradoxical that while France invoked the Locarno Treaty at the time of the Rhineland reoccupation, thus calling upon Italy for help, she was still applying sanctions against her. He had done all he could to keep the flame of Stresa from going out. 'The time has come to rekindle it,' he declared. 'Once sanctions are lifted and a just and honourable peace concluded in Ethiopia, we shall then be able to envisage the future of Europe and organize peace with more confidence.'

The absence from this statement of any call for a new initiative to improve Franco-British relations is significant. Laval's references to Britain, apart from a tribute to Sir Samuel Hoare, who was described as having fallen 'in the cause of peace', were essentially expressions of regret that the British government had failed to understand what he was trying to do. Equally important was the absence of any positive reference to the Soviet Union. Indeed, that country was only mentioned when Laval attempted to refute Hitler's assertion that the re-occupation of the Rhineland was justified by the ratification of the Franco-Soviet pact. 'The precautions I took,' he said in a revealing sentence, '. . . were such that it is impossible for Germany to maintain that the pact which I negotiated and signed can be considered as aggressive.' While Laval wanted peace for 'everyone, both in the east and the west', his statement made it quite clear with which countries he preferred to work to secure it. They were Germany and Italy, and not Britain and Russia.[1]

But Hitler continued to refuse to abide by the rules of Laval's game. The latter displayed his exasperation at a meeting with two Nazi party press officers in May 1937. 'Germany has obtained everything she wanted,' he declared. 'She has ceased to pay reparations, she has rearmed and she has "torn up Locarno".' Waving aside the two Germans' protests, he went on, 'Germany must now say what she wants and that she does not want a war with anyone. . . . It is not enough to say, "We want to be good friends with you" simply in order to be all the more able to proceed in another direction.' He was no longer interested in a declaration promising to keep the peace for ten years, he said. 'It must be for twenty-five years at least.'[2]

This exasperation was also reflected in his attitude at the time of Munich. He was well aware that France was not in a position to fight, but he realized that the agreement was, as he put it, 'the greatest diplomatic humiliation to which France has ever had to submit'. Unable to bring himself to vote for the government and, at the same time, unable to join with the Communists in voting against it, he was one of the odd assortment of 21 senators who abstained in the division of 4 October 1938 which gave full powers to Daladier and which was essentially a vote of confidence in the government's handling of the Czech crisis. Similarly, the day after Hitler's troops marched into Prague on 15 March 1939, he told the Senate foreign affairs committee, 'What is going on is abominable. A cry of indignation goes up at such a situation. Today, Germany, who lost the war, has more territory than she had before 1914. . . . I demand that the government should find the solution. But there's one which is impossible and that is to let Germany go on with what she's doing.'[3]

In these circumstances, Laval pinned his hopes upon Italy, not only as an ally in her own right, but also as a means of restraining and, at

[1] *Le Temps*, 15 April 1936.
[2] Memorandum of a conversation between Laval, Freiherr du Prel and Dr Gruber in the presence of Fernand de Brinon, 14 May 1937, GFM/7657/E547235–44.
[3] Paul Luquet in *La Vie de la France*, Vol. III, p. 1197 (Luquet was lobby correspondent for Laval's newspapers between 1929 and 1932 and kept in touch with him afterwards); J.O., Sénat, *Débats*, 4 October 1938, p. 736; ibid., *Comité Secret*, pp. 10, col. 3, 11, col. 1. For Laval's intervention in the Senate foreign affairs committee on 16 March 1939, see *Laval Parle*, pp. 255–8.

the same time, getting through to Germany. Unfortunately, in Laval's view, the *Front Populaire*, with its anti-fascist ideological prejudice, deliberately prevented a French *rapprochement* with Italy, which Mussolini would otherwise have been only too eager to accept.

Nowhere was this more evident than in the case of the Spanish Civil War. In common with most French right-wingers, Laval favoured a Nationalist victory in Spain and, in addition, he was prepared to do something about it. He told one of Franco's representatives in April 1937 that he was going 'to carry out an intense propaganda in the Nationalists' favour', and he went so far as to offer 'an extremely high-powered radio station which, if set up in San Sebastian, could conduct great propaganda in France in favour of the Spanish Nationalist cause.' He even had no objection to Italian intervention on Franco's behalf, provided Mussolini's sole aim was 'to prevent Spain from becoming Communist' and not to obtain 'concessions on the other side of the Pyrenees'. But the *Front Populaire*, on the other hand, was pro-Republican and continued to provide the Spanish government with arms in spite of the Non-Intervention Agreement. At one meeting of the Senate foreign affairs committee in the summer of 1937, Laval upbraided Yvon Delbos, the French foreign minister, for France's continual breaches of the Non-Intervention Agreement. When the chairman of the committee rebuked him for making accusations without proof, Laval promptly produced a letter from Franco himself in which the Nationalist leader gave full details of the *matériel* supplied to the Republicans by the French government.[1]

Laval described, in his speech in the secret session of the Senate on 14 March 1940, how the *Front Populaire*'s policy towards Spain damaged France's relations with Italy. At the end of January 1937, he said, the Italian ambassador in Paris had approached Blum to inform him that Italian support for Franco was not motivated by any feeling of hostility towards France, but simply by a refusal to tolerate the existence in the Mediterranean of 'a republic which was either Communist or tending towards Communism and which would be, moreover, as dangerous for France as for Italy'. If Blum gave the word, the Italian ambassador was alleged to have said, the Italian government was

---

[1] Enclosure in Faupel to Foreign Ministry, 14 April 1937, D.G.F.P., Series D, Vol. III, No. 244; Mirko Giobbe in *La Vie de la France*, Vol. III, p. 1366; Landini to Luciano 17 July 1937, Italian Documents, 148/043489–90; Baraduc, pp. 83–4.

prepared to use its good relations with Franco to obtain an assurance that he would not pursue an anti-French policy. According to Laval, however, Blum replied that 'a *Front Populaire* government could not make such a request to Italy'. In 1947, Blum himself gave more details about the Italian *démarche*. The Italian ambassador, he said, had declared that 'Mussolini detests Hitler' and that, if France and Italy were closely united, 'nothing in the world could resist this bloc of 80 million Latins'. The only question which separated the two countries was Spain, but the Italian government was prepared to ensure Franco's goodwill in exchange for the *quid pro quo*, which Laval did not mention in his account of the incident, that France should stop supporting the Republicans and thereby allow the Nationalists to win the war. Blum explained that he had rejected the Italian proposal because he no longer believed in the possibility of a Franco-Italian *rapprochement* in 1937 and because he saw the Italian *démarche* as 'a pretty childish dodge aimed at pushing us into complete neutrality in the Spanish question and making the support which Mussolini for his part was determined to continue to provide for Franco more easy and more effective'.[1]

A year later, on 16 March 1938, less than a week after the *Anschluss*, there is a record of Laval calling again in the Senate foreign affairs committee for the re-establishment of good relations with Italy, non-intervention in Spain, and the recognition of the Nationalist government. Informing Landini of his intervention, he said, 'I consider agreement between Italy and France, that is to say between the Latin countries, including Nationalist Spain as well, as my life's mission.' This was also the time of Eden's resignation over Chamberlain's policy of a *rapprochement* with Italy and of the second Blum government's decision to reopen the French land frontier with Spain for the traffic of arms to the Republican government, and, in an interview which he gave to the London *Evening Standard* on 21 March, Laval praised the British prime minister and implicitly condemned his French opposite number. 'Mr Chamberlain is right to refuse to intervene in Spain,' he said, 'just as he is right to re-establish good relations

---

[1] J.O., Sénat, *Comité Secret*, pp. 8, col. 3, 9, col. 1; Blum in C.E., *Témoignages*, Vol. I, p. 220. See also Laval's speech in the secret session of the National Assembly at Vichy on 10 July 1940, in C.E., *Rapport*, Vol. II, p. 489, from which it emerges that Laval obtained the details from the Italian ambassador himself.

with Italy. I hope that my country will not delay too long in following England's example.'[1]

Both the interview and the intervention in the foreign affairs committee must be seen as attempts on Laval's part to define the foreign policy of the Pétain government which we know he was trying to form at the time. The formation of the Daladier government temporarily scotched his domestic plans, but Daladier's foreign minister, Georges Bonnet, paid him the compliment of more or less taking over his foreign policy. Although he did not succeed in getting the Franco-Spanish frontier closed again until June, he wasted no time in seeking an understanding with Italy. Chamberlain's Anglo-Italian agreement was signed on 16 April and Bonnet did not want France to be left out of any Mediterranean settlement. He began negotiations, but they were broken off after Mussolini's violently anti-French speech at Genoa on 15 May 1938 in which the Duce declared that France and Italy were 'on opposite sides of the barricade' in Spain and that 'everything of a diplomatic and political nature which went under the name of Stresa was dead and buried and, as far as we are concerned, will never be revived.'[2]

Laval might have drawn the same conclusion from this renunciation of the Stresa policy, with which he had identified himself, as Blum had done more than a year before: namely, that a Franco-Italian *rapprochement* was simply not on the cards. But he did not. Even when Mussolini launched his campaign for the cession of Tunis, Corsica, Nice, and Savoy to Italy in November 1938, when the Italian government specifically denounced the Laval–Mussolini agreements in December, and when it concluded the 'Pact of Steel' with Germany in May 1939, Laval continued to flog the dead horse of a Franco-Italian understanding. In a conversation with Landini on 30 December 1938, he said that his political outlook had not changed. He wanted 'a close agreement with Italy and to repair, if possible, the enormous harm done by the *Front Populaire*'. He could not agree to territorial concessions, but 'he thought

[1] Landini to Luciano, 18 March 1938, Italian Documents, 148/043539–44; *Le Temps*, 23 March 1938. It is perhaps worth noting that, in private, Laval was not so enthusiastic about Chamberlain's approaches to Italy. 'From London's point of view,' he told Landini, 'it's only a matter of gaining time' (Landini to Luciano, 9 March 1938, Italian documents, 148/043531–8).

[2] Mussolini, *Opera Omnia*, Vol. XXIX, pp. 100–101; Georges Bonnet, *La Défense de la Paix*, Vol I, *De Washington au Quai d'Orsay*, Geneva, Les Editions du Cheval Ailé, 1946, pp. 142–8.

that Italy could easily be satisfied in some other way' and he promised
to work for concessions which were 'compatible with French honour
and interests'.[1]

Even more mistaken than the policy itself was the belief that he was
the man to implement it. As early as April 1938, he had hinted to
Landini that he might make a private visit to Italy to see Mussolini, but
the Italian had dissuaded him. Certainly the Duce wanted nothing more
to do with him. When the French government was considering the
appointment of an ambassador to Italy in October 1938, Bonnet told
the Italian *chargé d'affaires* that it had not made up its mind between a
politician and a career diplomat. Laval's name was not mentioned, but
the French authorities tapped a telephone conversation between Ciano
and the Italian *chargé*, in which the former stated that the Italian
government did not want a politician, 'particularly M. Laval'. No one
could have informed Laval of this incident, for in March 1939 he made
a direct approach to Daladier and asked to be sent on a secret mission
to Rome in order to try and negotiate an agreement with Mussolini.
Once again, as soon as the Italians got wind of the scheme, they torpedoed it. On 20 March, Mussolini instructed Ciano to reject the
proposed mission on the grounds that it 'would be of no value except
as a great publicity device for Laval'. Once again, too, Laval was kept
in ignorance of the Italian reaction and it was only when he raised the
matter in the secret session of the Senate a year later that Daladier
informed him, and the rest of the Senate, that Ciano had expressly
warned the French ambassador in Rome against the despatch of 'brash
political personalities noisily simulating the intention of negotiating'.[2]

In the summer of 1939, Laval made a Franco-Italian understanding
the theme of one of his rare public speeches. Addressing a gathering of
provincial newspaper representatives in Paris on 24 June, he maintained that, 'if Germany is in Vienna and Prague and if peace is at
present in jeopardy, this is because co-operation between France and
Italy has been destroyed.' He recognized that the Rome–Berlin Axis

[1] Landini to Luciano, 31 December 1938, Italian Documents, 148/043619–26.
[2] Landini to Luciano, 6 April 1938, ibid., 148/043545–54; Georges Bonnet in C.E.,
Témoignages, Vol. IX, p. 2732; Galeazzo Ciano, *Diario 1939–43*, 2 vols., Milan, Rizzoli,
1946 (hereafter cited as Ciano, *Diario*), 20 March 1939 (to facilitate reference to the many
different editions of Ciano's diaries, entries will always be cited by date rather than page
number); Mario Toscano, *Le Origini Diplomatiche del Patto d'Acciaio*, 2nd edn., Florence,
Sansoni, 1956, p. 172, fn. 23; J.O., Sénat, *Comité Secret*, pp. 10, cols. 1–2, 25, col. 1.

was strong and that relations between France and Italy were bad, but he refused to accept as final 'a situation which is so obviously contrary to the vital interests of the two countries'. The applause which he received from his predominantly right-wing audience shows that his views were by no means unique.[1]

Although he called in his speech for action by the French and Italian governments, he held out little hope that the former would do anything. He admitted as much as the Italian consul at Clermont-Ferrand in July, attributing French intransigence to 'British and Soviet influence, to which some members of the government are particularly susceptible, as well as to the intrigues of freemasonry and international Jewry'.[2] Fascist diplomats often wrote what they thought would please their superiors and it is unlikely that Laval, who was never an anti-Semite, referred to 'the intrigues of . . . international Jewry'. But the mistrust of 'British and Soviet influence' rings true. After all, this conversation did take place at a time when the British, French, and Soviet governments were trying to reach an agreement which would effectively guarantee Poland against the threat of German aggression. Laval doubtless felt that his mistrust was justified when, in August, the Soviet Union concluded an agreement with Germany instead, thus ensuring the rapid success of that aggression.

As war approached, Laval's fundamental pacifism reasserted itself. Already, in his intervention in the Senate foreign affairs committee in March, he had raised the spectre of war and the dreadful image of 'hundreds of thousands of wooden crosses . . . scattered throughout our cemeteries', and, on the day that German troops invaded Poland, he told a friend with a look of horror and revulsion on his face, 'It has begun. There will be millions of corpses.'[3] That same day, 1 September 1939, France mobilized and, on the 2nd, both houses of parliament reassembled in special session.

It was the deputy premier, Camille Chautemps, who laid the critical situation before the Senate. After he had finished his explanation and after the president of the Senate, Jules Jeanneney, had obtained the house's consent to a temporary adjournment in order to give the

[1] *Le Temps*, 26 June 1939.
[2] Enclosure in Guariglia to Ciano, 17 August 1939, D.D.I., 8th Series, Vol. XIII, No. 78. The fact that this conversation, which took place on 14 July, was not reported on until 17 August is, perhaps, a fair measure of Italian interest.
[3] *Laval Parle*, p. 256; Jean-Stéphane Guille in *La Vie de la France*, Vol. III, p. 1334.

Chamber of Deputies time to vote the necessary military credits, Laval rose to speak in public session for the first time in over three years. Jeanneney tried to rule him out of order on the grounds that a government statement could not be the subject of a debate, but Laval ignored him. 'In common with all my colleagues,' he began, 'I have listened to the government's statement with considerable emotion . . .' At this point he was interrupted by several senators who urged him to speak in the debate on the credits themselves. 'In 1935 . . .' he began again, amid mounting noise. Once more Jeanneney tried to stop him, but Laval refused to be deterred. 'In January 1935,' he said, 'I signed the Rome agreements with M. Mussolini in order to safeguard European peace. These agreements have been destroyed. Today I call upon the government to remember that the reason which brought them into existence is more obvious than ever and to bear this in mind as a basis for action.'[1]

'I did not want to refuse military credits,' Laval explained in a speech in November 1943. 'Throughout my public life I have never refused military credits, because they were useful and indispensable for France.' What he had intended to ask the Senate, he said, was 'to meet in secret session and not to vote for war'.[2] Wisdom after the event? Perhaps, for he made no attempt to develop his case in the debate on the credits. Indeed, there was no debate, and they were voted unanimously. It is more likely, however, that in that momentary surge of national unity, he knew he would be wasting his breath. Thus, still pursuing the mirage of an alliance with Italy, Laval reluctantly entered upon a war which was to bring him power, and finally death.

[1] J.O., Sénat, *Débats*, 2 September 1939, p. 640.
[2] *La Vie de la France*, Vol. III, p. 1592.

5

The Fall of France

September 1939 – June 1940

During the so-called 'phoney war', Laval's attitude towards the conflict reflected a cautious ambivalence. While his name was reported to
the commander-in-chief of the armed forces as that of a participant in
a 'peace offensive', he is also on record more than once as saying that,
although the war could have been avoided by diplomatic means, it was
now up to the government to prosecute it with the utmost vigour.[1] His
opposition to the war, in fact, did not come completely into the open
until after the French collapse in 1940.

One view of which he never made a secret, however, was that the key
to the situation lay in Rome. While some of his remarks to the Italian
journalist Giobbe on 11 November 1939 were probably exaggerated to
impress Giobbe's superiors, there is no reason to doubt the genuineness
of Laval's hope that Mussolini would make a peace move 'at the appropriate moment' or of his belief that, as the conflict could not be resolved
without Italy, 'it is France's interest to have [Italy] with her, either
militarily or diplomatically. Otherwise, there is no knowing where she
will go: probably towards Bolshevism.' Equally plausible is Giobbe's
account of how Laval claimed to have English support. 'The English
would not oppose a Franco-Italian *rapprochement*,' he is reported to
have said. 'They have finally realized the precise British function. They
want to prevent German hegemony, but are resigned to leaving Europe
to the Europeans and the Mediterranean to the Mediterranean peoples.
Recent contacts with English personalities enable him to say this with
assurance.'[2] The wish was no doubt father to the thought.

---

[1] Jacques Bardoux, *Journal d'un Témoin de la Troisième*, Paris, Fayard, 1957 (hereafter
cited as Bardoux), pp. 85, 117; Gamelin, Vol. III, p. 107; Elie J. Bois, *Le Malheur de la
France*, London, The Continental Publishers and Distributors Ltd. (*Hachette*), 1941 (hereafter cited as Bois), pp. 111–12.

[2] Guariglia to Ciano, 14 November 1939, D.D.I., 9th Series, Vol. II, No. 217.

Laval's faith in Italy was by no means unusual at this date. Mussolini's last-minute efforts to avert the outbreak of war, and his failure, despite the Pact of Steel, to enter the conflict on Germany's side led many to adopt exaggerated ideas of Italy's importance and goodwill. After all, it was not Laval but two members of the Daladier government who described Mussolini as 'the master of the hour' and said that it was 'Italy's mission to lay the foundations of European reconstruction', while the prime minister himself more or less invited Italy to assume the hegemony of the Balkans in a conversation with the Italian ambassador on 29 September 1939 in an attempt to gain Italian support.[1] Where Laval differed from others was in his persistent refusal to believe that any government, apart from one which he either belonged to or led, could reach agreement with Italy. 'If there's much more delay, it will be too late to negotiate with Rome,' he complained to his fellow-senator from the Puy-de-Dôme, Jacques Bardoux, on 20 December. 'How can you hesitate to vote against Daladier? Nothing is possible as long as he's there. Obviously, he will be replaced by the distinguished conjurer Paul Reynaud, which would be worse, or by Jeanneney, which would be worse still.'[2]

As the patron for the diplomacy which he felt he alone was capable of conducting Laval was once more turning towards Pétain. But the Marshal was beginning to entertain political ambitions of his own and it is important to examine his plans as well as Laval's if we are to reach a proper understanding of the rôles of the two men in the gradually unfolding crisis which eventually brought them both to power.

Pétain had refused to stand for the presidency in April 1939 on the grounds that his task as ambassador in Spain was more important. On the outbreak of war, however, he remarked to his friends, 'I don't intend to vegetate here.'[3] And when he refused to join the national government which Daladier tried to form in September 1939, it was not because he did not want a governmental post, but because he objected to the composition of this particular government. 'After considerable reflection,' he wrote to the prime minister on 11 September, 'I have come to the conclusion that the government which you are proposing to form does not meet the requirements of the present situation. It is

[1] Guariglia to Ciano, 24 September 1939, 30 September 1939 and François-Poncet to Ciano, 4 October 1939, ibid., Vol. I, Nos. 414, 521, and 608.
[2] Bardoux, p. 155.
[3] Noguères, p. 47.

based upon almost exclusively political foundations and therefore seems hardly qualified to assure overall direction of the war.' In particular, Pétain objected to certain politicians, whose presence 'will be an obstacle to proper relations with Spain and Italy and will therefore produce a deplorable effect upon the morale of the country and of the army'. In a conversation with General Gamelin on the day this letter was written, he made it clear that he had Edouard Herriot, whom Daladier intended to make foreign minister, chiefly in mind.[1]

Only the day before, Laval had been criticizing Herriot's attitude towards Italy in the Senate corridors and, if any further proof of the similarity between his ideas and Pétain's is needed, it can be found in Daladier's assertion that the Marshal tried to convince him of the need to bring Laval into his government, as the latter 'possessed the stature to bring Italy into a position more favourable to France'. In the circumstances, it is not too hard to credit the story of one well-informed journalist that it was Laval who persuaded Pétain not to enter the Daladier government.[2]

Be that as it may, just before Pétain's return to Paris after a brief stay at the French embassy in Spain at the end of August 1939, Major Loustaunau Lacau was asked by the Marshal to 'see what Laval thinks about the situation'.[3] He did so and reported back in a letter dated 22 September. According to Loustaunau Lacau, Laval maintained that only he and Pétain, who 'alone enjoyed a greater influence in Italy than his own', could bring about an agreement with Mussolini. A Pétain government was therefore 'indispensable'. Alluding to Pétain's First World War reputation as a field commander, Laval added that such a government would also be extremely popular 'because, above all else, the Marshal's presence would guarantee that French blood would be spared to the greatest possible extent'.

Laval went on to say that the government should include a small war cabinet consisting of 'technicians and important parliamentary figures', which would be presided over by the Marshal and which would relieve him of as many 'short-term anxieties' as possible. Because of his great success in Spain, it would be natural for Pétain to take over the foreign ministry with the help of a career diplomat to relieve him of all the

---

[1] *Procès Pétain*, p. 322, col. 1; Gamelin, Vol. III, p. 106.
[2] Desgranges, p. 319; Daladier in *Procès Pétain*, p. 35, col. 1; Bois, pp. 64–5.
[3] Loustaunau Lacau in *Procès Pétain*, p. 121, col. 1.

routine work. This would automatically spike the guns of those potential critics who were afraid to see him (Laval) as foreign minister and would, at the same time, leave him free to take over the ministry of the interior, 'where his duties as mayor of Aubervilliers would allow him to win over the working class which was in a very hesitant mood after Stalin's treachery.'[1]

M. Noguères, who published this letter, did not think that it was an accurate representation of Laval's views. 'One has only to think of what happened when the Pétain government was formed on 16 June 1940,' he wrote, 'to realize that Pierre Laval would not have accepted any ministry but that of foreign affairs.'[2] The obvious answer to this, of course, is that, although Laval refused to join the Pétain government on 16 June 1940 except as foreign minister, he joined it on 23 June as a minister of state. But more important is the difference between the two situations. In June 1940, Laval knew that the alternative foreign minister, Paul Baudouin, was an active young man whom he might not be able to control.[3] He did not have the same qualms about Pétain. When Elie Bois of the *Petit Parisien* said, on 27 October 1939, that he thought Pétain was too old and mentally enfeebled, Laval interjected, 'That doesn't matter. What will be asked of him? To be a mantelpiece, a statue on a pedestal. His name! His prestige! Nothing more.'[4] Besides, it is clear from the Loustaunau Lacau letter itself that Laval did not intend to neglect foreign affairs. The fact that Pétain was foreign minister and he minister of the interior, he said, 'would not prevent him from helping the Marshal in the field of foreign affairs and possibly accompanying him on a visit to Mussolini.' One of Laval's most serious miscalculations was to under-estimate Pétain's stubborn independence.

As well as reporting Laval's views, Major Loustaunau Lacau's letter contained a general appreciation of the political situation. Pétain's

[1] The full text of the letter is printed in Noguères, pp. 631–4. At Pétain's trial, Laval freely admitted having seen Loustaunau Lacau, but maintained that he could not remember what was said at their meeting. 'If I told [him] that I wanted to see the Marshal as head of the government,' he added. 'I told him what was for me a self-evident truth.' See *Procès Pétain*, p. 186, col. 1.

[2] Noguères, p. 58.

[3] It may also be noted that, when Laval discovered that he could by-pass Baudouin, he made no attempt to manœuvre him out of his post. Indeed, he tried to persuade him to stay on after Montoire. See below, p.246.

[4] Bois, p. 112.

refusal to enter the cabinet, he wrote, had put paid to Daladier's plan for a national government and he had been forced to content himself with a minor reshuffle. This had not been well received by parliamentary opinion, which was unimpressed by Daladier's attempts to put the blame on the Marshal. On the contrary, maintained Loustaunau Lacau, members attributed the Marshal's refusal to his desire 'not to lend his authority to a combination which he considered second-rate and ill-adapted to the circumstances'. As a result, he concluded, 'there is no longer a question of anything but a Pétain government, the effect of which would be enormous at home and even more so abroad.'

This highly exaggerated assessment of parliamentary opinion seems to have strengthened Pétain's desire to assume a more active rôle politically. In October, he tried to get himself recalled from Spain on the grounds that his mission was completed and that he would be of more use in a post where his military experience would be called upon. This request was turned down, as was another that he should be allowed to come to Paris twice a month to attend meetings of the Army Council.[1] Both were clearly prompted by a desire to be at the centre of the political stage in readiness for the inevitable collapse of the Daladier government. In the meantime, he busied himself by drawing up lists of his future ministers. He showed two of these to M. Gazel, a member of his embassy staff, who later recalled that they both contained the names of Henry Lémery, a senator and long-standing friend of Pétain's, and of Laval.[2] Lémery himself paid a secret visit to the embassy in October in the company of Raphaël Alibert, a royalist and former *Cagoulard*. The two men discussed various possible ministerial combinations with the Marshal in which Laval was invariably included as minister of the interior.[3]

Unfortunately for Pétain, and Laval, the Daladier government did not fall, and, by the turn of the year, the Marshal seems temporarily to have shelved his political ambitions. Writing on 15 January 1940 to General Vauthier, a former colleague at the French embassy in Spain, he said that 'the more I think about politico-military questions, the greater becomes my inclination to steer clear of them. I have been

---

[1] Noguères, pp. 18–19, 47.
[2] Gazel in *Procès Pétain*, p. 73, col. 3.
[3] Emmanuel Beau de Loménie, *La Mort de la Troisième République*, Paris, Editions du Conquistador, 1951 (hereafter cited as Beau de Loménie), pp. 170–72.

asking myself for a long time how I could best serve my country and I have come to the following conclusion: my physical strength would no longer permit me to bear the burden of office and I am abandoning the idea.' He thus admitted that he had entertained it. 'There remains the army. Perhaps I could still render some service, at least in the sphere of morale.' Visiting Paris incognito a few days later, he told Lémery to stop his campaign in favour of a Pétain government. 'I want to return to France where I can be of some service to the high command.' he explained. 'But Daladier is opposed to the idea because he sees me as a rival.' Pétain does not seem to have seen Laval during his visit.[1]

Pétain's vacillation had no effect upon Laval. Patiently, he awaited an opportunity to launch a devastating attack upon the Daladier government. It came in March 1940, when Finland was forced to seek peace after her brief but bitter 'winter war' with the Soviet Union. This was widely held to be a moral if not an actual defeat for the allies, who had publicly stated their support for Finland, sent quantities of war *matériel*, and even contemplated the despatch of troops. The sense of defeat was particularly acute in France, where political factors produced a much more intense anti-Soviet feeling than in Britain. Resentment against Daladier for failing to save the Finns threatened and finally succeeded in toppling his government.

The anti-Daladier offensive was launched in earnest in a secret session of the Senate on 14 and 15 March. Laval chose the occasion to attempt a political come-back by putting down an interpellation on 'the government's conception of the conduct of the war' and the long speech which he made in developing it was one of the most powerful of his career.

France, he began, had declared war to save Poland; but Poland was destroyed. She had declared war to protect small nations against aggression; but Finland had just been forced to surrender after a long struggle without adequate assistance. 'What people, what country,' he demanded, 'will in future dare to link its fate with the destiny of our arms? I look around, but I do not see any.'

A compromise peace, he went on, was out of the question. But if the war must be won, it must be won quickly because – and this was the thrifty countryman speaking – it was devouring France's wealth at

---

[1] *Procès Pétain*, p. 342, col. 3; Noguères, pp. 25–7; Beau de Loménie, pp. 192–3. See also the evidence of General Serigny in *Procès Pétain*, p. 173, col. 3.

the rate of a thousand million francs a day. He doubted whether a rapid victory could be gained by the methods which were being employed at present. A frontal assault on the Siegfried Line was out of the question and the Allied blockade was ineffective because supplies continued to reach Germany through Russia and the Balkans. In the meantime, Germany was building up her strength. In July she would have 200 divisions to the Allies' 130 and, if Italy and the Balkans joined her, she would have up to 140 more.

But must Italy and the Balkans join Germany? Laval went on to describe at great length the steps he had taken in 1935 to win Italy to the side of France. The facts are familiar to us now, but many of them, particularly those dealing with the secret military agreements, were a revelation to his audience. At the end of his *exposé*, he pointed out how Italian support would enable France to by-pass the Siegfried Line and exploit the potentialities of the Balkans. He accused Daladier of drawing up 'paper strategies' and advised him to 'take a good look at the map of Europe'. 'You will understand the policy of 1935,' he said, 'the policy which was mistakenly not followed and which must be followed.' He criticized the prime minister for not doing enough to win Italy's support. He had, Laval claimed, missed chance after chance, including his (Laval's) own offer to go to Rome in March 1939. 'The Italian question is delicate and difficult,' Laval agreed, 'but the least I can say is that, in my opinion, its solution by men who once had the chance to solve it and let that chance pass is bound to be difficult.'

Turning to Finland, Laval attacked Daladier for refusing to send troops without a formal appeal from the Finnish government. This was too legalistic an approach. 'I am a lawyer,' he said, 'and I have been to Geneva. But I no longer recognize procedure. When procedure's place is taken by artillery and machine-guns, there is no more procedure!' As for Russia, he wanted to know whether France was at war – *de facto* not *de jure* – with the country which was supplying Germany and which was her ally. He did not say the government should declare war, for he was not in possession of all the facts, but he expected some indication of its policy.

'If my presence at this tribune,' he concluded, 'had no other purpose and no other result than to draw my colleagues' and the government's attention to failings and to what must be done, albeit in a way which could seem irritating, I would be glad to have come here.' One senator was evidently not satisfied. As Laval stepped down, he called out, 'What must be done then?' 'What must be done?' echoed Laval. 'If you were M. Lebrun and you put me in charge of France's affairs, I would have a talk with you about that.' Amid laughter and prolonged applause, he resumed his seat.[1]

When Daladier replied to his critics the following day, he vigorously defended his record and, as far as Laval was concerned, returned the ball into his opponent's court. He disclosed that it was none other than Ciano who had vetoed Laval's proposed visit to Rome the previous year. He sarcastically referred to Laval's diplomatic journeys in 1935 as 'sleeping-car diplomacy' and accused him of doing nothing when, on 16 March 1935, Hitler first denounced a clause of the Versailles Treaty unilaterally. 'There was a protest,' interjected Lémery from the floor. 'Congratulations!' replied the prime minister with obvious irony. Then up jumped Laval himself to remind Daladier that there had also been a resolution at Geneva. The prime minister agreed, but commented, 'When I don't cross Norway and Sweden' – i.e. to help Finland – 'in the difficult conditions which I have just described to the Senate, I lack energy, initiative, and daring. But those who allow the [Versailles] Treaty to be torn up and Germany to rearm, they are men of imagination!'[2]

Daladier may have had the better of the argument on paper, but the Senate was not in a reasonable, let alone a charitable mood, and Jacques Bardoux noted that his speech was less well received than Laval's.[3] The latter returned to the charge in a brief intervention at the end of the debate, answering, among other things, the 'sleeping-car diplomacy' jibe. 'I went to see the Holy Father,' he said. 'I went to see M. Mussolini; I went to see Stalin: I would have gone to see the devil to ensure peace in Europe and the security of my country.'[4] Daladier obtained his vote of confidence, but there were about sixty abstentions. Four days later, he fared even worse in the Chamber, when no less than three hundred deputies abstained in a confidence vote. Judging it impossible to carry on in such circumstances, he resigned and was replaced, as Laval had predicted, by his finance minister, Paul Reynaud.

[1] Laval's speech may be found in J.O., Sénat, *Comité Secret*, pp. 5–12.
[2] Daladier's speech may be found in ibid., pp. 20–27.
[3] Bardoux, p. 246.
[4] Laval's final intervention may be found in J.O., Sénat, *Comité Secret*, pp. 30–31.

An indication of Laval's real motives in wanting to get rid of Daladier can be found in the account of a conversation with the British Conservative M.P., Sir Robert Boothby, at about the same time as the secret session debates. In his speech, Laval had declared that a compromise peace was out of the question and had criticized the prime minister for failing to prosecute the war with sufficient energy. In private with Boothby, however, he took a different line. He described the war as 'a great mistake' and said that, if only Britain and France had been able to come to terms with Mussolini as he had wanted to, 'there might have been a different story to tell'. But this was no longer possible. 'I am a peasant from the Auvergne,' he concluded in terms which expressed, at one and the same time, his fundamental materialism, his profound pacifism, and his basic insularity. 'I love the soil, I want to keep my farm. I want to keep France. Nothing else matters now. . . . We should make peace.'[1] These words make it overwhelmingly clear that Laval's main criticism of Daladier was not that he was waging war with insufficient vigour, but that he was waging it at all.

Whatever he may have said to Sir Robert Boothby, however, Laval had by no means given up the hope of coming to terms with Mussolini. His speech, although made in secret session, gave rise to new and possibly inspired rumours in the press that he would be sent on some kind of mission to Rome. But once again the Italian government acted swiftly to kill them. Ciano instructed the Italian ambassador in Paris to make it known 'in responsible circles' that the despatch of a French plenipotentiary to Rome would not be welcomed by the Italian government, 'even less so if the plenipotentiary concerned were Laval, who would not even be received by the Duce.'[2] In fact, the Italians were not interested in allied approaches of any kind. 'A change of attitude on Italy's part towards England and France was inconceivable,' Mussolini told Hitler at their meeting on the Brenner Pass on 18 March, just four days after Laval's speech. 'Co-operation with these countries was out of the question. "We hate them." Therefore, Italy's entry into the war was inevitable.'[3] The only problem was one of timing: the Duce wanted to be sure that the Germans had already won the war for him.

[1] Sir Robert Boothby, *I Fight to Live*, London, Victor Gollancz, p. 205.
[2] Ciano to Guariglia, 28 March 1940, D.D.I., 9th Series, Vol. III, No. 636. See also Guariglia to Ciano, 1 April 1940, ibid., No, 678.
[3] Schmidt Memorandum, D.G.F.P., Series D, Vol. IX, No. 1.

Unaware of Mussolini's real feelings, Laval also chose to ignore the direct rebuff to himself. Indeed, he managed to explain it away in a speech to the councillors of his home *département* of Puy-de-Dôme on 6 May. He had, he maintained, received a visit from 'a personal representative of Mussolini' and had asked him why the Italian government had declared its unwillingness to receive a special envoy from France, no matter who he was. 'Because he would be representing the present government,' this unidentified Italian was alleged to have replied, 'and we haven't forgotten Paul Reynaud's speech on sanctions in December 1935.' To which story, Laval added, 'In any case I am an optimist. I don't believe that Mussolini will make war on us. Why? Because I can read a map and it would mean that the Duce was off his head.'[1]

No account of Laval's political activities during the 'phoney war' would be complete without an examination of a story which he himself told Admiral Darlan after the French collapse. This was that, in May 1940, he reached agreement with Daladier on the need for a Pétain government, in which both he and the recently resigned prime minister would have important posts. The main task of this government was said to have been to negotiate peace. A similar story also appears in two post-war sources. One is the statement in 1947 of Marcel Guillaume, a member of Laval's private secretariat during the war, and the other is the book by Albert Naud, one of Laval's lawyers at his trial. There are minor discrepancies between these two versions, but both refer to a discussion at the home of Guy la Chambre, Daladier's friend and former air minister, and both state that it was Daladier who took the initiative in suggesting the overthrow of the Reynaud government. Neither of the post-war accounts mentions Pétain and both seem to refer only to a hypothetical Daladier–Laval government.[2]

As all three versions emanated from Laval in the first place, there is no means of checking them. Naud writes that, if Laval's trial had been conducted properly, the defence would have called Guy la Chambre and an unnamed young woman to corroborate the story. By implicating one of the major prosecution witnesses at the Pétain trial in a pacifist plot, such corroboration would certainly have caused a sensation. But,

[1] Bardoux, p. 294.
[2] Alain Darlan, *L'Amiral Darlan Parle*, Paris, Amiot-Dumont, 1952 (hereafter cited as Darlan), pp. 102, 135; Marcel Guillaume in *La Vie de la France*, Vol. II, p. 1145; Albert Naud, *Pourquoi je n'ai pas défendu Pierre Laval*, Paris, Fayard, 1948, p. 242.

on the face of it, the story is very unlikely to be true. The most that can be said in favour of it is that Daladier, who agreed to remain in office as minister of defence in Reynaud's cabinet, disliked his chief and may have expressed a desire to get rid of him to Laval.

If a more definite plan existed, it was rapidly overtaken by events. At dawn on 10 May, the Germans launched their long-awaited offensive in the west by simultaneously invading Holland, Belgium, and Luxemburg. The Belgian and Dutch governments appealed to the Allies for help and British and French troops moved into Belgium. But the main German thrust did not come through the Low Countries as the Allies anticipated; it came through the Ardennes, by-passing the famous Maginot Line. On 15 May, General von Rundstedt's *panzer* divisions broke through the French positions near Sedan and, from then on, disaster followed disaster. The Dutch had already capitulated on 14 May. On 20 May, von Rundstedt's columns, which had made for the Channel instead of Paris in order to cut off the Allied armies in Flanders, reached the sea near Abbéville and then turned northwards along the coast to roll up the Allied rear. Fortunately, however, the German commander temporarily halted his advance, and this made possible the evacuation from Dunkirk which began on 28 May, the day after King Leopold of the Belgians announced the surrender of his forces.[1]

Reynaud's first reaction to the German breakthrough was to re-shape his government. The changes were announced on 18 May. He exchanged portfolios with Daladier, becoming minister of defence while the latter took over the foreign ministry. He transferred Clemenceau's right-hand man, Georges Mandel, from the ministry of colonies to that of the interior. Most important of all, he invited Marshal Pétain to join the government as a second deputy premier, and appointed General Maxime Weygand, then commanding French forces in the Middle East, as commander-in-chief in succession to Daladier's protégé, General Gamelin, with whose conduct of operations he had long been dissatisfied.[2]

[1] This account of the fighting in France is based upon J. R. M. Butler, *Grand Strategy* Vol. II, London, H.M.S.O., 1957, pp. 175–96 and chapters II, III and IV of Winston S. Churchill, *The Second World War*, Vol. II, *Their Finest Hour*, London, Cassell 1949 (hereafter cited as Churchill).

[2] Paul Reynaud, *La France a sauvé l'Europe*, Vol. II, Paris, Flammarion, 1947 (hereafter cited as Reynaud), p. 120. Reynaud has published three separate versions of his memoirs, but I have preferred to use the earliest and will only refer to subsequent versions when they contain important new material.

The prestige of Pétain and Weygand was such that their appointment, as Reynaud had intended, gave an immediate boost to French morale. Subsequently, however, he was to regret his choice and describe it as 'the basic mistake' which he made.[1] The mistake lay in the failure to realize that both men were essentially defeatists and, if Reynaud can be forgiven for not knowing Weygand's views, which did not become apparent until after his appointment, he cannot plead the same excuse with Pétain. The latter's attitude to the war was well known. Even the Italians and Germans were aware of it. As early as 3 November 1939, the Italian ambassador in Paris had informed Ciano that 'Marshal Pétain rightly believes that the continuation of the present conflict is not good for France, even if she succeeds in winning a conclusive victory' and that 'there is no risk in saying that the day when France, either through desire or necessity, feels the need to end the war, she will have to resort to Marshal Pétain if she wishes to avoid the upsurge of violent political and military feelings which may reveal themselves in connection with the *idea* or the *fact* of peace.'[2] And, on 19 March 1940, an official of the German embassy in Spain informed his superiors that Pétain was said to have told his close associates that 'France's greatest mistake . . . had been to enter the war'.[3] Moreover, when the Marshal received Reynaud's request to come to Paris on 16 May, his adjutant, Major Bonhomme, noted in his diary that 'the war may be considered as lost', 'an opinion which,' M. Noguères comments, 'was no doubt not strictly his own.'[4] Reynaud even admitted that 'parliamentary gossip had represented the defeatist faction, headed by Laval, as planning to make use of Pétain,' but added that he felt that, in entering his government, the Marshal 'had made his choice and come down against them.'[5] This was, to say the least, an unwarranted assumption.

It is not possible, in the light of the available evidence, to say why Pétain agreed to serve under Reynaud when he had refused to do so under Daladier. His decision appears to have been taken on 1 May

[1] Ibid., p. 128.
[2] Guariglia to Ciano, 3 November 1939, D.D.I. 9th Series, Vol. II, No. 99. The contents of this telegram were communicated to the Germans. See Weizsäcker Memorandum, 16 November 1939, D.G.F.P., Series D, Vol. VIII, No. 363.
[3] Gardemann to Foreign Ministry, 19 March 1940, ibid., Vol. IX, No. 5.
[4] Noguères, p. 33.
[5] Reynaud, p. 123.

during a visit to Paris[1] – that is to say before the German attack – so it was not simply a matter of coming to the rescue of his country in its hour of distress. Perhaps he anticipated the *débâcle*; perhaps he merely allowed his political ambitions to get the better of any reservations he may have had.

Reynaud was soon to be enlightened as to the views of his new appointees. As early as 24 May, he told the parliamentary committee of enquiry in December 1950, Pétain and Weygand told him that 'if the battle of France is lost, we must seek an armistice'.[2] Weygand said much the same thing at a meeting of the cabinet's war committee, which was held on the following day. His plan, he explained, was to stand and fight on the line of the rivers Somme and Aisne, but he believed that this front might well be broken. If so, each separate unit would 'fight to the end to save the country's honour'. He was bitterly critical of France's entry into the war 'with neither the necessary *matériel* nor military doctrine' and observed that she would in all probability have to pay dearly for this 'culpable rashness'. Both the prime minister and the president realized that the general was hinting at the possibility of an armistice if things got any worse, and drew attention to the agreement which Reynaud had concluded with Britain on 28 March and which forbade a separate peace without prior consultation. Weygand recognized that any cessation of hostilities must be discussed with the British government. He also agreed with the prime minister that the British should be invited to consider what concessions they felt they could make to keep Italy out of the war and what additional help, in the way of troops and aircraft, they could send to France.[3]

The prime minister agreed to go to London the next day to discuss these issues and it is clear from British accounts of his visit that he realized which way the wind was blowing. 'M. Reynaud dwelt not

[1] Noguères, p. 32.
[2] C.E., *Témoignages*, Vol. VIII, p. 2389.
[3] There has been a great deal of controversy about this important meeting, of which three different versions of the minutes have survived. For an excellent analysis of the problems involved, see Paul Dhers, '*Le Comité de Guerre du 25 mai 1940*', *Revue d'Histoire de la Deuxième Guerre Mondiale*, June 1953, pp. 165–83. I have based my account upon what M. Dhers considers to be the most reliable set of minutes, viz. those reproduced photographically as Appendix IX of Weygand's memoirs. It is worth noting, however, that one of the other versions of the minutes makes Weygand much more explicit. He is twice quoted as saying, 'The war must be stopped at once'.

obscurely upon the possible French withdrawal from the war,' Winston Churchill wrote subsequently. 'He himself would fight on, but there was always the possibility that he might soon be replaced by others of a different temper.' Sir Llewellyn Woodward, the official historian of British foreign policy during the Second World War, is even more explicit. Basing his account upon the official records, he writes that 'M. Reynaud . . . told the prime minister and other members of the war cabinet that, if France were "entirely invaded", they must reckon on a move by Marshal Pétain in favour of an armistice.'[1]

Certainly, Weygand and Pétain were acting in concert. While Reynaud was in London, they met to discuss the question of an armistice, and the Marshal approved of the contents of a note which Weygand gave to the prime minister on 29 May and which stated that 'it seems . . . necessary for the British government to realize that a point may come after which France, in spite of her will, would find it impossible to continue a militarily effective struggle for the protection of her territory'. Even the possibility of Pétain's assuming control of the government was under discussion. The Marshal himself told the Spanish ambassador in Paris at about this time that 'a *coup d'état* would be necessary if he wanted to seize power in France'. This, however, was 'a serious matter' and, as the president of the republic – whom Pétain described as 'a servant of the political parties' – would do nothing to help, 'they must therefore wait'.[2]

To what extent was Laval, the man Reynaud described as the leader of 'the defeatist faction', involved in these machinations? In the light of the available evidence, it is impossible to say with certainty. He told Jacques Bardoux as early as 17 May, that is to say before their appointments were made public, that there was 'no other solution apart from a Pétain–Weygand government', and subsequent events did nothing to shake this conviction. Of course, he felt that he ought to be in this government, primarily in order to negotiate with Italy, whose entry into the war was now widely felt to be imminent. He told the merchant navy minister, Alphonse Rio, on 18 May that he thought he could still 'act on the Duce' and that he would 'gladly return to office as a member

---

[1] Churchill, pp. 108–9; Sir L. Woodward, *British Foreign Policy in the Second World War*, London, H.M.S.O., 1962 (hereafter cited as Woodward), p. 48.

[2] Noguères, p. 72; General Maxime Weygand, *Mémoirs*, Vol. III, *Rappelé au Service*, Paris, Flammarion, 1950 (hereafter cited as Weygand), pp. 149–52; Stohrer to Foreign Ministry, 3 June 1940, D.G.F.P., Series D, Vol. IX, No. 376.

of a new team and would accept the foreign ministry in a Pétain government'. Twelve days later, he met Pétain himself, but unfortunately we do not know what the two men discussed.[1]

It is probably safe to assume, however, that the two major topics of conversation were the need for changes in the government and plans for negotiations with Italy. Indeed, as Laval had already explained to Giobbe on 24 May, the success of the latter depended upon acceptance of the former, together with the recognition that Italy's 'main objectives' were 'the expulsion of the English from the Mediterranean and then from Africa'. He repeated this theme to a few senatorial colleagues on the following day, saying that, if Italy entered the war, it would be less on account of her territorial demands upon France than of her desire 'to burst open the three English locks on the Mediterranean: Gibraltar, Suez, and Cyprus–Malta.' He did not think that Reynaud and Daladier were capable of negotiating on this basis and therefore proposed an exchange of portfolios between Reynaud and Pétain, accompanied of course by his own entry into the Quai d'Orsay.[2]

A large-scale reorganization of the government did in fact take place on 5 June. Daladier was finally dropped altogether and Reynaud added the foreign ministry to his other offices. In order to assist him, he appointed Paul Baudouin, whom he had made under-secretary of state to the prime minister in March, as under-secretary of state for foreign affairs as well, and General de Gaulle, whose military theories he had long admired, as under-secretary of state for war. Among the other changes were the replacement of Lucien Lamoureux as minister of finance by the civil servant, Yves Bouthillier; of Albert Sarraut as

[1] Bardoux, p. 310; Noguères, pp. 26, 76–7.
[2] Enclosure in Guariglia to Ciano, 24 May 1940, D.D.I., 9th Series, Vol. IV, No. 565; Bardoux, p. 342. As it happened, Laval was wrong in his assumption that the existing government was incapable of negotiating with Italy on the basis of a sacrifice of British interests. See Zoppi to Ciano, 20 May 1940, D.D.I., 9th Series, Vol. IV, No. 500; Ciano to Zoppi, 20 May 1940, ibid., No. 504; Stohrer to Foreign Ministry, 22 May 1940, D.G.F.P., Series D, Vol. IX, No. 298. These documents refer to a suggested visit by the French minister Ybarnégaray to Spain to discuss 'the freedom of the Latin sea'. Ybarnégaray's proposals, which were put forward without prior consultation with the British, were rejected by Franco and also by Mussolini, at whom of course they were really aimed. See also Churchill, p. 109.
   In the face of British opposition to any concessions to Italy, the French government put forward fresh proposals which would have involved a considerable sacrifice of its own interests in the Mediterranean and Africa. See Guariglia to Ciano, 30 May 1940, No. 665; and also Reynaud, pp. 210, 215–20. These proposals were simply ignored by the Italians. They go to show that, if Laval was prepared to give away a lot in a vain attempt to appease Italy, the French government was prepared to give away as much, if not more.

minister of education by Yvon Delbos; of Anatole de Monzie as minister of public works by Ludovic-Oscar Frossard; and of Frossard as minister of information by Jean Prouvost. Reynaud subsequently sought to justify these changes by claiming that they were designed to isolate Pétain and Weygand, whose prestige ruled out their dismissal, by expelling all other defeatists from the government. But this explanation does not hold water for three reasons. In the first place, by no means all the ministers who were forced to resign can be classified as defeatists. Indeed, only Lamoureux and de Monzie really fall into this category, as Reynaud himself admitted. Secondly, not all the newcomers were free from defeatism themselves. If de Gaulle and Delbos were to be among the bitterest opponents of the armistice, Bouthillier and Prouvost were to be among its keenest advocates. Finally, the changes left several defeatists apart from Weygand and Pétain still entrenched in the government, as the events of the days that followed were to make clear.

The real reasons behind some of the changes are likely to remain a mystery, but there is evidence that Reynaud was under strong pressure from Pétain to get rid of Daladier and Sarraut. The Marshal was particularly hostile towards Daladier, whom he accused of having 'created the *Front Populaire*' and of thus sowing the seeds of France's present misfortunes. The foreign minister was also under fire from the Senate foreign affairs committee, which had instructed its chairman to protest against his continuance in office. Reynaud, who had never got on well with Daladier, was probably glad of the opportunity to drop him. The overall impression created by the ministerial changes does not, in fact, inspire much confidence in the prime minister's judgement.[1]

On the same day that the Government changes were announced, the Germans began their attack upon Weygand's Somme–Aisne line. The French positions held for a while, but on 7 June the enemy's armoured forces punched a hole in the left flank near Hornoy and captured Rouen on the following day. The French were now forced to withdraw to the line formed by the rivers Seine and Marne for a last-ditch stand before Paris. On 9 June, the Germans followed up their attacks in the west and the centre by an assault on the extreme east of

[1] For the government changes of 5 June, see Reynaud, pp. 177–8 and 260–64, as well as his evidence in C.E., *Témoignages*, Vol. VIII, pp. 2407–8; Paul Baudouin, *Neuf Mois au Gouvernement*, Paris, La Table Ronde, 1948 (hereafter cited as Baudouin), pp. 90, 92–3, 115, 119 and 124–6; Bardoux, p. 326; Noguères, pp. 77–9.

the French position in the Argonne region. They were then advancing on a front of more than 200 miles in length across the entire width of France.[1]

As far as Weygand was concerned, if the Germans crossed the Seine and the Marne, it was 'the end'. When General de Gaulle, to whom he said this, reminded him that the French empire and the rest of the world remained to be defended, Weygand laughed despairingly and replied, 'The Empire? That's childish nonsense! As for the rest of the world, if I'm beaten here, England won't wait a week before treating with the *Reich*.' Then he added ruefully, 'If I could only be sure that the Germans would leave me with enough forces to keep order.' Weygand has denied ever making such remarks. Nevertheless, the sentiments expressed are similar to those voiced by him on other occasions.[2]

Simultaneously, Pétain was increasing the pressure upon Reynaud. On the morning of 9 June, he read the prime minister a note in which he called for an armistice, provided that the conditions, which were bound to be hard, were also honourable. Reynaud dismissed the suggestion on the grounds that honourable terms could not be expected from Hitler. Besides, he added, it would be extremely rash of France to break with her ally. 'England got us into this position,' Pétain retorted. 'Don't let us confine ourselves to putting up with it. Let us try and get out of it.'[3]

9 June also witnessed a desperate last-minute effort by Laval to avert Italy's entry into the war. That morning, Count Arduini-Ferretti, an Italian resident in Paris, presented himself at Laval's office in the Champs-Elysées. He said that he had just returned from a visit to Italy and he told Laval that his country was about to declare war on France. Nevertheless, he thought that this 'could perhaps be prevented' and gave Laval some suggestions to pass on to the French government. When Laval asked if these suggestions were official, Arduini-Ferretti replied that they came from Baron Aloisi, with whom Laval had many dealings during the Abyssinian crisis. 'These were doubtless the procedures of Italian diplomacy,' Laval commented subsequently, 'but I realized that the message could also be interpreted as

---

[1] This account of the fighting is based upon Weygand, pp. 168–88.

[2] Charles de Gaulle, *Mémoires de Guerre*, 3 vols., Paris, Plon, 1954, 1956 and 1959 (hereafter cited as de Gaulle), Vol. I, pp. 44–5; Maxime Weygand, *En Lisant les Mémoires de Guerre du Général de Gaulle*, Paris, Flammarion, 1955, pp. 35–6.

[3] Baudouin, pp. 135–6.

coming from Mussolini.' He therefore asked General Denain, who had signed the air agreements with Italy in 1935, to pass it on to President Lebrun. The latter, in turn, referred him to Reynaud, who asked him whether he knew that Ciano had told the French ambassador in Rome that Italy had already fixed the date for declaring war upon France. When Denain replied that he did, Reynaud said that he was sorry to see him lending his support to a manœuvre in which it was obvious that Laval wanted him for a witness. When Laval himself telephoned Reynaud in the afternoon to ask him what had happened, the prime minister told him that 'it was clear that the chips were down and that . . . any new *démarche* would be pointless'. Laval did not insist and merely told Reynaud that he was leaving Paris for his home at Châteldon immediately.[1] The following day, Italy declared war on France.

There is no knowing how seriously Laval took Arduini-Ferretti's message. On the face of it, Reynaud's cynicism seems justified: Laval merely wanted to show that he, unlike the government, had never resigned himself to a war with Italy. After all, Aloisi, who had left office four years before, had no obvious standing and all the facts pointed towards an imminent declaration of war by Mussolini. It would have been naïve to suppose that it could be averted at such a late stage. But Laval *was* naïve where Italy was concerned, and he possessed an uncanny knack of ignoring facts that were unpalatable to him. If he believed Arduini-Ferretti, it was probably because he wanted to.[2]

Laval did not reappear upon the scene until 14 June and what he did, said, and thought during those five days at Châteldon remains a mystery. But while he was there, events of considerable importance were taking place elsewhere. In view of the German advance, the government left Paris for Tours on 10 June. The same day, General Weygand gave Reynaud a second note in which he declared that 'the events of the last two days' fighting compel me to warn the prime minister that the final rupture of our lines of defence may take place at any moment'. If this happened, 'our forces would continue to fight until their strength and resources were exhausted. But their disintegra-

---

[1] *Laval Parle*, pp. 34–5; Reynaud, pp. 224–5.

[2] There is no reference to Arduini-Ferretti in the D.D.I. The Italian ambassador in Paris writes in his memoirs that his approach to Laval 'was clearly a personal idea of Aloisi's and alien to any thought of Mussolini or Ciano' (Guariglia, p. 459, fn. 1). An ardent francophile, Aloisi was probably as keen as Laval to avert a conflict between Italy and France, and equally out of touch with reality.

tion would be no more than a matter of time.' Weygand had avoided mentioning the fatal word in his note, but he told Baudouin later the same day that he agreed with him on the need for an armistice.[1]

The following day, Churchill came to France at Reynaud's request for a meeting of the allied supreme war council. It began at 7 o'clock in the evening at the château of Briare near Orléans. Weygand painted a gloomy picture of the situation, saying that he could not guarantee that the lines would still hold the following day and that he had no more reserves to throw into the fight. At one point in the discussion, although this is not recorded in the French minutes, he declared that France might have to ask for an armistice. 'That is a political affair,' Reynaud snapped back at him. The meeting was adjourned for dinner and, after the meal, Reynaud told Churchill that Pétain had said to him that France would have to seek an armistice and that he had written a note to that effect. 'He has not handed it to me yet,' Reynaud added. 'He is still ashamed to do it.' After further discussions the following morning, the British party returned to London. Churchill was evidently worried by the defeatism of Weygand and Pétain, for he formally requested the French to let their ally know at once if there was any change in the situation so that he could come to France again and discuss the matter before any final decisions were taken.[2]

It was at the cabinet meeting at the château of Cangé on the evening of 12 June that Weygand first told the full government of his opinion that France should seek an armistice. 'If the fighting continues,' he said, 'it means the cutting to pieces of our forces, confusion and disorder: not merely military disorder, but general disorder.' Weygand did not receive much support. Only Pétain and Prouvost spoke in favour of an armistice. Reynaud opposed them. Not only would an attempt to conclude an armistice be contrary to France's honour and to her pledge to Britain, it would also be unbelievably naïve. 'You take Hitler for Wilhelm I,' he told Pétain and Weygand – 'an old gentleman who took Alsace-Lorraine from you and left it at that. But Hitler is Genghiz Khan!' Even if France were occupied, he maintained, the government should go to North Africa and continue the fight from

[1] Weygand, pp. 189–90; Baudouin, p. 143. It may be noted that Baudouin, who was in effect Reynaud's right-hand man, admitted to the parliamentary committee of enquiry in 1949 that he considered the war as lost as early as 16 May. See C.E., *Témoignages*, Vol. VII, p. 2052.

[2] Weygand, pp. 584–96 (French minutes); Churchill, pp. 138–40.

there. These points were taken up by several other ministers and it seemed that the issue was settled. Nevertheless, the government was forced to recognize that, with Weygand's formal request to seek an armistice, there was once again a need for consultation with the British. Camille Chautemps, the deputy premier, proposed that Churchill be invited to attend a meeting of the French cabinet to discuss the situation and Reynaud was instructed to arrange it.[1]

Churchill arrived at Tours at about lunchtime on 13 June. At their subsequent meeting, Reynaud asked him point-blank what Britain's attitude would' be if France had to seek an armistice. The British prime minister was evasive. 'Whatever happens,' he said, 'we will not waste our energy in reproaches and recriminations. But that is a different thing from agreeing to a separate peace, concluded in violation of the agreements that have been reached.' He advised an appeal for help to President Roosevelt. Still persisting, Reynaud asked him what would happen if such an appeal failed. 'If the reply is unfavourable,' Churchill replied, 'and if you then announce your determination to negotiate separately, we will have a whole set of problems to examine.' The matter was so serious that Churchill retired to consider it in private with his colleagues who had accompanied him. When he returned, however, he could only add that they agreed with him and that he thought the British cabinet would do so as well. The first thing to do was to appeal to Roosevelt without delay. The British government would do the same on his return to London.[2]

Contrary to what had been agreed the previous evening, Reynaud did not invite the British prime minister and his party to attend a meeting of the French cabinet. 'We should have been very willing to do so,' Churchill wrote subsequently. '. . . But we were not invited; nor did we know there was to be a French cabinet meeting.' Reynaud's explanation of his failure to make the invitation is confused and con-

[1] For accounts of the first cabinet meeting at Cangé, see the evidence of Weygand, Pernot, and Louis Marin in the Pétain trial dossiers (Noguères, pp. 83–8); Reynaud, pp. 313–16; Albert Lebrun, *Témoignages*, Paris, Plon, 1945 (hereafter cited as Lebrun), pp. 75–6; Yves Bouthillier, *Le Drame de Vichy*, Vol. I, *Face à Ennemi, Face à Allié*, Paris, Plon, 1950 (hereafter cited as Bouthillier, Vol. I), pp. 54–9; Baudouin, pp. 147–51; Camille Chautemps, *Cahiers Secrets de l'Armistice*, Paris, Plon, 1963 (hereafter cited as Chautemps), pp. 125–9.

[2] The French minutes of the Churchill–Reynaud meeting are printed in Paul Reynaud, *Au Cœur de la Mêlée*, Paris, Flammarion, 1951, pp. 770–74; and an extract from the British minutes in Churchill, pp. 160–61. The quotations are from the French minutes.

tradictory. 'Churchill did not ask me if he could come before the cabinet,' he said. This is not surprising as Churchill did not know there was to be a cabinet meeting and as, in any case, it was Reynaud who was supposed to do the asking. What was more, the French prime minister added, 'I saw no reason for obtaining his presence at a cabinet, some of whose members were already beginning to crack up. It was not a very edifying spectacle to offer the leader of an allied country.'[1] But what would have shocked a man like Churchill more: the defeatism of Pétain and Weygand, or the obvious failure of Reynaud to control his own government? One may perhaps be forgiven for thinking that Reynaud felt it might be the latter.

Reynaud's failure to carry out his mandate gave rise to some acrimonious exchanges at the beginning of the cabinet meeting at Cangé that evening, and after the prime minister had reported on his discussion with Churchill, the split in the French government became wider. Two more ministers, Bouthillier and Ybarnégaray, joined those who supported an immediate armistice. Weygand, who described the military situation as 'the same only worse' than the previous day's, hotly opposed any suggestion that the government should leave France. 'As far as I'm concerned,' he declared, 'I am staying whatever happens – with my legs in chains if necessary.' Pétain made the same point in another of his notes which he read to his colleagues. To abandon the country to the enemy, he said, would 'kill the soul of France'. If necessary, he would resign from the government altogether rather than leave. 'I will remain among the French people,' he said, 'to share their sorrows and their miseries.' The government was now hopelessly divided, but it managed to take two decisions. The first was to authorize Reynaud to send an appeal to Roosevelt. The second was to move to Bordeaux the following day to escape the German advance. Weygand, however, left the meeting furious that his advice to seek an armistice had still not been adopted.[2]

Friday 14 June was a crucial day. Before leaving for Bordeaux, Baudouin went to see Pétain. He found the Marshal determined to 'have done with it' and indignant at the 'ignoble and cowardly' attitude

[1] Churchill, p. 162; Reynaud's evidence in C.E., *Témoignages*, Vol. VIII, p. 2411.
[2] For accounts of the second cabinet meeting at Cangé, see Noguères, pp. 91–8 (evidence of Reynaud, Rio, Lebrun, Marin, Rollin, and Weygand); Lebrun, pp. 77–9; Baudouin, pp. 160–64; Bouthillier, Vol. I, pp. 66–71; Reynaud, pp. 322–7; Chautemps, pp. 131–6.

of the cabinet. Things must be settled by the following midday, he said, and he was sending General Weygand a message informing him that his presence in Bordeaux was imperative. The message, which Weygand received at his H.Q. at 5 p.m., read: 'Yesterday evening, the cabinet decided not to take a decision with regard to the request to Germany for an armistice until after a telegram had been sent to President Roosevelt . . . asking him to declare war on Germany. The Marshal believes that the latest moment to take a decision is mid-day on Saturday. To do this, a cabinet meeting must be convened at Bordeaux late tomorrow morning. General Weygand's presence at Bordeaux is necessary. The commander-in-chief must be at M. Bau-douin's address . . . before 10.30 a.m.' In other words, the armistice party were concerting their strategy – behind the prime minister's back it should be noted – for the next and decisive phase of the struggle.[1] As they did so, the Germans entered Paris.

14 June was also the day on which Laval left Châteldon for Bordeaux. Two witnesses who saw him – his daughter's father-in-law, General de Chambrun, and his fellow-senator, Jacques Bardoux – confirm that he was still convinced that Pétain, who he felt would impress the Germans, should lead the country. Bardoux adds that he intended to suggest to the Marshal that he (Laval) be permitted to negotiate the armistice terms with Germany. Reynaud should be left the opprobrium of requesting the armistice, but he could not be allowed to negotiate it. 'Don't you realize,' he said, 'that . . . this man, who talks more often of democracy than of France, and who has insulted Hitler and Musso-lini, can only obtain the worst terms? Franco [sic] and Mussolini have no interest in allowing France to be crushed. They've no grudge against us, only against England, from whom Hitler wants to grab control of the world.'[2]

It is interesting to reflect that Laval might never have had the opportunity to advance these and other ideas during the vital days and weeks that followed. His son-in-law has written that, when the Lavals arrived in Bordeaux, his wife nearly convinced her father of the neces-sity of going to the United States, where he was. 'She felt strongly that he should do this,' M. de Chambrun continues, 'but her mother

---

[1] Baudouin, p. 166; Weygand, p. 224; Reynaud's evidence in C.E., *Témoignages*, Vol. VIII, pp. 2413-14.
[2] General de Chambrun in *La Vie de la France*, Vol. III, p. 1689; Bardoux, p. 363.

dreaded the idea of leaving her native soil. After wavering for a very short time, my father-in-law decided to remain.'[1] Laval's devotion to his wife is unquestioned, but, in view of his political ambitions, it is doubtful whether this was the only reason why he decided to remain in France.

While in Bordeaux, Laval stayed at the home of his friend, Adrien Marquet, a deputy and mayor of the city. Another of Laval's friends, Jean Montigny, has provided a vivid description of his activities during those first few days in Bordeaux. As members of parliament, 'in complete confusion, partly ignorant of what was going on, and exhausted by the terrible exodus' arrived in the city, they sought in vain for news of what was happening. Herriot and Jeanneney, the presidents of the Chamber and Senate respectively, were in favour of leaving France, and refused to summon a meeting of parliament. 'Bewildered' and 'extremely worried by a situation which was deteriorating hourly,' the members of parliament went to the town hall, where Laval had installed himself in a tiny office. There, he and Marquet, together with a few other deputies and senators who 'had remained calm and who were putting their undissipated energy at the service of their threatened country', held briefing sessions. As more and more members of parliament arrived, these sessions had to be held elsewhere and, 'gradually, on account of the abdication of the presidents of the Senate and the Chamber, a sort of Bordeaux "Commune" came to be formed, which was to have a decisive influence upon events.'[2]

Whether 'decisive' or not, there is no doubt that the influence of the 'Bordeaux Commune' was being used, at a lower level, to further the same ends as that of Marshal Pétain and his supporters inside the government itself. This is quite clear from Montigny's account of how Laval told members of parliament that it was 'their duty . . . to remain in France and share the ordeals of the population'. But although we know from Baudouin's diary that Laval was sending 'messenger after messenger' to Pétain on 15 June, there is no evidence that the Marshal paid any attention to them, let alone co-ordinated his

[1] Letter from M. de Chambrun to the author, dated 3 November 1963.
[2] Jean Montigny, *Toute la Vérité sur un Mois Dramatique de Notre Histoire*, Clermont-Ferrand, Editions Mont-Louis, 1940 (hereafter cited as Montigny), pp. 19–20. This little book, which was printed on Laval's printing presses, seems to have been written in the autumn of 1940 to bring home to Pétain how much he owed to Laval. See Montigny's own account of how it came to be written in *La Vie de la France*, Vol. I, p. 378.

campaign with Laval's. He was, in fact, far too preoccupied with his own plans to bother with anyone else's.[1]

His proposed timetable for a decision about the armistice had already been thrown out of joint, as he was unable to arrange for a cabinet meeting to be held before midday. Moreover, General Weygand did not manage to arrive in Bordeaux until after lunch. At the secret meeting which had been arranged the previous day, and which was attended by Admiral Darlan and Bouthillier as well as Pétain, Weygand, and Baudouin, the commander-in-chief apparently did little more than reaffirm that the army was exhausted and that a decision was imperative. In the circumstances, he said, an armistice was the lesser evil. Baudouin backed him up with a completely erroneous version of the conversation between Churchill and Reynaud two days previously, at which he had been present. The British prime minister, Baudouin maintained, had pledged his solidarity in the event of France's seeking an armistice.[2]

When the cabinet eventually met at four o'clock in the afternoon, Reynaud began the proceedings with another proposal which he felt might salvage something of the situation and which he had already discussed with General Weygand earlier in the afternoon. This was that, instead of seeking an armistice, the government should follow the Dutch example, viz. order its armed forces to lay down their arms and then leave the country, thus keeping the flag of resistance flying abroad. Weygand had indignantly repudiated this proposal, interpreting it as a shady political manœuvre to shift the responsibility for an end to hostilities from the government to the high command. On the other hand, the cabinet seemed prepared to accept the proposal. Theoretically, Reynaud could have overruled his commander-in-chief or appointed a more pliant successor, but he lacked the strength of character to do either. Instead, the fatal mistake was made of delegating Pétain, who seemed to have been temporarily won over to the proposal, to try and convert Weygand. Needless to say, he failed.

In an attempt to break the deadlock, Chautemps, whose gift for compromise was unrivalled even among politicians of the Third Republic, put forward a new and ingenious proposal. 'Get an important neutral international authority, either the Pope or the president of the

---

[1] Montigny, p. 21; Baudouin, p. 170.
[2] Ibid., pp. 167–8.

United States, to make a rapid unofficial enquiry about the possible peace terms,' he urged Reynaud. 'If, contrary to our expectations, these terms appear moderate, our English friends will no doubt agree with us to study them. If on the other hand they are, as you and I think they will be, disastrous or dishonourable, then I hope that the Marshal, his illusions clarified, will agree with us that the struggle should be continued. Thus, the division and disintegration of our government will be avoided.' Chautemps added that, in the unprecedented event of the government leaving France, it had a duty to give the country a full account of the circumstances. 'When the country realizes that any honourable peace is out of the question,' he said, 'it will be ready to bear the highest sacrifices which we shall have to demand of it.'

Pétain immediately accepted the Chautemps proposal, emphasizing that he had always thought only in terms of an honourable armistice. He was joined, not only by the rest of the armistice party, but also by the waverers, whose numbers were increasing daily. When Reynaud came to count the voices, he found that no less than 13 ministers were in favour of the proposal and a mere 6 against. The prime minister was fully aware of the major snag in the Chautemps proposal. What is dishonourable to one man may be honourable to another, particularly if he is keen enough to have it. He therefore immediately offered his resignation, but the president of the republic refused to accept it and urged him to fall in with the cabinet's wishes. After some hesitation, he gave in. He took the view, he subsequently wrote in justification, that if the British refused to countenance the proposal, he would at least live to fight another day. If on the other hand he resigned, he was convinced that he would be succeeded either by Chautemps or by Pétain and that an armistice would follow soon afterwards. He therefore agreed to put the proposal to the British, but only on behalf of 'the majority of the cabinet' and not of himself and those who shared his views.[1]

It was after the cabinet meeting had broken up that Darlan told Baudouin that Laval had been sending 'messenger after messenger' to Pétain. The Admiral's own attitude was, of course, a key factor in the

---

[1] For accounts of the cabinet meeting, see Reynaud, pp. 338–42; Chautemps, pp. 143–57; Baudouin, pp. 168–70; Bouthillier, Vol. I, pp. 75–8; Lebrun, pp. 80–81; Noguères, pp. 100–105 (evidence of Lebrun, Julien, Rio, Laurent-Eynac, and Marin). Facing page 367 of his *Mémoires*, Vol. II, *Envers et Contre Tous*, Paris, Flammarion, 1963, Paul Reynaud reproduces a photograph of the piece of paper on which he noted the names of those in favour and those against the Chautemps proposal.

Marshal's plans. There is plenty of evidence to show that, right up until 15 June, Darlan was prepared to sail away with the fleet if any attempt was made to seek an armistice. Had he done so, he would in Churchill's own words have become 'the master of all French interests beyond German control . . . [and] the chief of the French Resistance with a mighty weapon in his hand. . . . The whole French empire would have rallied to him. Nothing could have prevented him from being the Liberator of France.' But, for political motives of his own, Darlan chose instead to throw in his lot with Pétain. In so doing, he not only ensured that an armistice would be sought, but also that it would be effective. Darlan remained suspicious, however, of Laval and his ambitions. 'I have asked the Marshal,' he told Baudouin, 'that if he is called upon to form a government, as appears possible, he will promote you from under-secretary of state for foreign affairs to minister.'[1] Pétain was therefore already discussing the composition of his future government and, from what happened on the following day, it was clear that he had been making very thorough preparations indeed.

These included the drafting of a letter of resignation from the Reynaud government, which he read to the cabinet on the morning of 16 June. An immediate end to hostilities, the letter said, was the only way to save the country and the government's daily discussions were nothing more than 'purely dilatory manœuvres, leading up to the final abdication of French sovereignty'. He could not accept them and was therefore resigning.[2] There is some suggestion that this letter was not written by Pétain himself. One of the members of the Reynaud government, Henri Queuille, testified at the Marshal's pre-trial hearings in 1945 that he had been told that it had been drafted the previous evening at the town hall, in the presence of Laval and Marquet. But this is evidence at third-hand and Pétain's own testimony was singularly unhelpful. When shown the document, he said, 'I think that someone interpreted my thoughts and drafted this letter in my absence. They asked me afterwards to read it to the cabinet. Who was it? I cannot tell you. I cannot tell you if it was Laval who drafted the letter. I know nothing about it.'[3]

[1] Albert Kammerer, *La Passion de la Flotte Française*, Paris, Fayard, 1951 (hereafter cited as Kammerer, *Flotte Française*), pp. 66–71; Churchill, pp. 202–3; Baudouin, pp. 170–71.
[2] Pétain's letter is printed in Noguères, p. 107.
[3] Ibid., pp. 107–8.

Even if the letter was drafted by someone else, there are more likely candidates for the job than Laval. Baudouin and Bouthillier, for example, were fully acquainted with and sympathetic towards Pétain's determination to 'have done with it' and were both present at his meeting with General Weygand the previous day. Then there was Dr Ménétrel, the Marshal's personal physician, who exercised considerable influence over him and who had certainly been consulted in connection with the statement which he read at the second Cangé cabinet meeting.[1] Finally, there was Raphaël Alibert, now director of Pétain's *cabinet civil*, who later boasted of having drafted at least one document on the Marshal's behalf.

Whoever was responsible, Pétain's resignation did not materialize. He was persuaded by Lebrun to wait until the British reply to the Chautemps proposal had been received, although he made it clear that he was not going to wait any longer. The only other major incident at the cabinet meeting was Reynaud's communication of President Roosevelt's reply to his appeal of 14 June. After reaffirming his country's willingness to go on sending war *matériel* as long as France remained in the fight, the president concluded, 'I know that you will understand that these statements carry with them no implication of military commitments. Only the Congress can make such commitments.' The appeal had failed. All that could be done now was to wait for the British government's reply to the Chautemps proposal. The cabinet adjourned until 5 p.m.[2]

The British reply arrived just before lunch. Briefly, it stated that the British government would agree to a French enquiry about armistice terms 'provided, but only provided, that the French fleet is sailed forthwith for British harbours pending negotiations'. A second telegram, giving the British government's conditions in more detail, arrived later in the afternoon. Reynaud did not disguise his disappointment. He had been hoping for a blank refusal which he could use in the cabinet as an argument for continuing the struggle. Moreover, as he pointed out to the British ambassador and to Major-General Spears, Churchill's personal representative, the despatch of the French fleet to British ports would leave North Africa at the mercy of the Italians. While he

[1] Bouthillier, Vol. I, pp. 22–3.
[2] For accounts of the cabinet meeting, see Baudouin, pp. 171–2; Bouthillier, Vol. I, pp. 81–3; Lebrun, p. 82; Reynaud, p. 343; Chautemps, pp. 157–9. Roosevelt's message is printed in Hull to Waterman, 15 June 1940, F.R.U.S., 1940, Vol. I, pp. 255–6.

was discussing the matter with them, the telephone rang. At the other end of the line was Reynaud's under-secretary of state for war, General de Gaulle, speaking from London and dictating the proposed declaration of Franco-British union which had been drafted in the British capital earlier that day. On hearing the declaration, Spears wrote later, Reynaud was 'transfigured with joy. . . . He was happy with a great happiness that France would now remain in the war.' Turning to Spears and the ambassador, he said that he supposed that the proposed declaration of union superseded the British government's earlier telegrams. The two Englishmen correctly surmised that it did. Whereupon, Reynaud went off to his cabinet meeting, determined as he put it to 'die defending these proposals'.[1]

Unfortunately, the cabinet did not share his enthusiasm. Either Chautemps or Ybarnégaray, and perhaps both, said that the proposed Franco-British union would make France a British dominion, while Pétain dismissed it as yet another device to delay the armistice. The majority of the cabinet seemed to feel that, while the proposal was important, it did not meet the needs of the hour. Chautemps repeated his earlier proposal and, to his horror, Reynaud realized that he was back where he had started. What happened then is not clear. Reynaud later claimed that he resigned. Some of his colleagues, including Lebrun, have agreed with him. Others, however, have maintained that he merely adjourned the cabinet so that he could discuss the future with the President of the Republic. What is certain is that in subsequent discussions with Lebrun and the presidents of the Chamber and the Senate, Reynaud refused to implement the Chautemps proposal. Herriot and Jeanneney both felt that Reynaud should be invited to form a new government, but the prime minister advised Lebrun to send for Pétain.[2]

It was shortly before 10 p.m. when the President of the Republic

[1] Churchill, pp. 181–4; Reynaud, pp. 347, 349; De Gaulle, Vol. I, pp. 61–5; Sir Edward Spears, *Assignment to Catastrophe*, Vol. II, *The Fall of France*, London, Heinemann, 1954, pp. 284, 290.

[2] For accounts of the cabinet meeting, see Baudouin, pp. 174–5; Bouthillier, Vol. I, pp. 86–9; Lebrun, pp. 83–4; Reynaud, pp. 352–4; Chautemps, pp. 159–64; evidence of Rio, C.E., *Témoignages*, Vol. VI, pp. 1320–21; Rollin, ibid., pp. 1403–4; Monnet, ibid, pp. 1427–8; Louis Marin, 'Contributions à l'histoire des prodromes de l'Armistice', *Revue d'Histoire de la Deuxième Guerre Mondiale*, June 1951, pp. 17–18. For the subsequent discussions, see Lebrun, p. 85; the evidence of Reynaud in *Procès Pétain*, p. 19, col. 1; Jeanneney, ibid., p. 58, col. 1; Herriot, ibid., p. 111, col. 2.

summoned Marshal Pétain and asked him to form a government. To his surprise, the Marshal produced a ready-made list of his ministers, convincing proof that he had been expecting the president's summons and had prepared for it.[1] One of the names on the list was Laval's, as minister of justice. We do not know who suggested him for the post and, at Pétain's trial, he himself maintained that the invitation came out of the blue. What gives his account a ring of authenticity is what happened afterwards, and here his story is, to some extent at any rate, confirmed by other sources. When informed of his proposed appointment, he said that he told Pétain he would rather be minister of foreign affairs. 'I have already given that post to M. Baudouin,' replied the Marshal, indicating that he had accepted Admiral Darlan's advice. 'I'm sorry,' said Laval. Then, all of a sudden, Pétain added, 'I can let you have it,' and promptly appointed Laval foreign minister in Baudouin's place. Laval probably had to apply a great deal more pressure than he suggested, but there is no doubt that Pétain did change his mind. Baudouin seemed prepared to accept the *fait accompli*, but not so M. Charles-Roux, the permanent head of the French foreign office. He told Weygand, who had been appointed minister of defence in the new government, to tell Pétain that Laval's appointment as foreign minister would place an added strain upon Anglo-French relations. Weygand, who had no liking for Laval, passed on Charles-Roux's message, but was unable to persuade Pétain to reinstate Baudouin. Whereupon, Charles-Roux threatened to resign himself unless Laval was excluded from the foreign ministry. This threat eventually had the desired effect and Laval, after again refusing the ministry of justice as a consolation, stormed out in a temper. Marquet, who was to have been minister of the interior, went with him.[2]

One result of these events was that Laval was later able to claim, quite legitimately, that he had had no part in the government which requested the armistice, although he never attempted to deny that he was in favour of the request. Curiously enough, he did claim that he was responsible for the government's making its approach to Germany through Spain. Pétain, he said, had originally intended to use Switzerland, but during his extremely brief tenure of the foreign ministry, he

[1] Lebrun, p. 85.
[2] Laval's evidence in *Procès Pétain*, p. 186, col. 3; Weygand, p. 237; Baudouin, p. 176; F. Charles-Roux, *Cinq Mois Tragiques aux Affaires Etrangères*, Paris, Plon, 1949 (hereafter cited as Charles-Roux), pp. 49–50.

had managed to persuade the Marshal that Spain would be a better choice. There is no supporting evidence for this somewhat odd contention, but it was indeed the Spanish ambassador whom Baudouin received at midnight on 16–17 June in order to ask the Spanish government 'to transmit to Germany with all speed the request to cease hostilities at once and at the same time to make known the peace terms proposed by Germany'.[1]

In spite of the French government's request, there was still considerable support for a move to North Africa, whence, it was felt, it would be able to negotiate in greater freedom. But the government did not go to North Africa and, at Laval's trial in 1945, it was alleged that he was the man responsible.[2] The sequence of events is complicated, but it is necessary to examine it in some detail to see how justified this accusation was.

On the afternoon of 18 June, Herriot and Jeanneney, who both supported the idea of a move to North Africa, went to see President Lebrun in an effort to win him over to their point of view. They found him far from unsympathetic, but there was still Pétain to convince. The latter was invited to join them, but he reiterated his determination to remain in France whatever happened. Then someone – it is not clear who – suggested that Pétain should delegate his powers to one of his ministers, and that this minister, together with the President of the Republic, other members of the government, and members of parliament, should go to North Africa. Pétain seemed agreeable and it was decided that Chautemps should be the minister concerned. He thought it an excellent idea and the matter seemed to be settled. In fact, Herriot was to declare in 1945 that the decision taken was 'complete, absolute, and without reservation'.[3]

At 6.30 on the morning of 19 June, however, an event took place which put a different complexion on the situation. The Spanish ambassador informed Baudouin that the German government was prepared to receive French plenipotentiaries to discuss armistice terms and invited the French government to designate them. The Germans had not replied before because, on 18 June, Hitler had been discussing

[1] *Laval Parle*, p. 37; *Procès Laval*, pp. 67–8; Laval's evidence in *Procès Pétain*, p. 186, col. 3; Stohrer to Foreign Ministry, 17 June 1940, D.G.F.P., Series D, Vol. IX, No. 459.
[2] *Procès Laval*, p. 27.
[3] Lebrun's evidence in *Procès Pétain*, p. 47, col. 3; Jeanneney, ibid., p. 58, col. 2; Herriot, ibid., p. 111, col. 3; Chautemps, pp. 192–3.

THE FALL OF FRANCE · 179

the French situation with Mussolini at Munich. The French cabinet meeting which began at 9 a.m. on 19 June spent most of its time, therefore, in drawing up a list of French plenipotentiaries, and, according to Baudouin, it was only agreed to *study* the proposed departure to North Africa. This was a very different thing from the complete, absolute, and unreserved decision which, according to Herriot, had been taken the evening before.[1]

Indeed, both Pétain's and Baudouin's attitude to the departure of the government was deliberately ambivalent. While the latter told the British ambassador that the government was preparing to leave France, both he and Pétain conveyed a very different impression to the Spaniards and, through them of course, to the Germans. 'If Germany and Italy are interested in concluding a treaty with the French government *on French soil*,' the Spanish ambassador reported to his government late on 19 June, 'I must again point out . . . that a zone must be established in which the French government can function freely and with security. The Marshal shares this view. The foreign minister, however, would like a stop to be put to hostilities everywhere tonight. If it is considered important to negotiate with France, action must be taken quickly. The foreign minister told me that he was finding only very little support.' What emerges from this telegram is that both the Marshal and his foreign minister were in effect asking the Germans to make it easier for them not to transfer the government abroad.[2]

Meanwhile, Herriot and Jeanneney were pressing on with their plans. These included the evacuation of members of parliament, which was negotiated by Admiral Darlan. At 7.20 in the evening, the Admiral sent Herriot a note in which he informed him that a 600-place passenger vessel, the *Massilia*, would moor in Bordeaux harbour at about midday on 20 June for the subsequent embarkation of members of parliament.[3]

When the French cabinet met again at 9 a.m. on the 20th, there was as yet no news from the Germans as to whether they were prepared to receive the French plenipotentiaries who had been designated the day before. This was because the French government's message had taken

---

[1] Weiszäcker to Embassy in Spain, 18 June 1940, D.G.F.P., Series D, Vol. IX, No. 481; Stohrer to Foreign Ministry, 19 June 1940, ibid., No. 485; Baudouin, pp. 187–8.

[2] Woodward, p. 71; Stohrer, to Foreign Ministry, 20 June 1940, D.G.F.P., Series D, Vol. IX, No. 496 (emphasis added).

[3] Herriot's evidence in *Procès Pétain*, p. 112, col. 1; E. Herriot, *Episodes 1940–44*, Paris, Flammarion, 1950 (hereafter cited as Herriot), pp. 90–91.

the whole of the 19th to reach Berlin, but the cabinet was of course unaware of this, and the lack of news, coupled with the psychological effects of an aerial bombardment of Bordeaux during the night, strengthened the hand of those who wanted to leave for North Africa. There was a fierce argument between supporters and opponents of departure, but it was eventually decided that the government should move to Perpignan, prior to embarkation. Pétain, of course, did not intend to leave France, and he was joined by Baudouin, Bouthillier, and Weygand.[1]

The government's decision was communicated to Herriot and Jeanneney soon after the cabinet meeting, and the latter actually set off for Perpignan. But members of parliament, who were meeting in a school building in the rue Anatole-France, were not told until two o'clock in the afternoon. Moreover, they were also informed, by means of a notice from Darlan posted in the building, that the *Massilia* had not been able to moor in Bordeaux harbour after all, because the river was mined. She was therefore waiting several miles downstream at Verdon. According to Darlan, the government would provide transport to take members to Verdon, but in the event it was the officials of the two chambers who scraped together what transport they could. Such members of parliament as could be collected left the city at about 5 p.m.[2]

Unbeknown to them, however, the government had already reversed its decision to go to Perpignan. At 11.15 a.m., Baudouin heard that the Germans had agreed to receive the French plenipotentiaries at Tours later that day. On hearing the news, General Weygand called a cabinet meeting for 2 p.m. but, apart from Weygand, only two ministers turned up. Learning that President Lebrun was on the point of leaving for Perpignan, Weygand telephoned him and asked him to contact Pétain. He did so and agreed to postpone his departure until six o'clock that evening.[3]

The man who may have been responsible for delaying Lebrun's departure still further was Raphaël Alibert, who was Pétain's undersecretary of state in the new government. In February 1942, he told how he was present at a meeting later that afternoon at which Pétain

[1] Stohrer to Foreign Ministry, 19 June 1940, D.G.F.P., Series D, Vol. IX, Nos. 489, 490. For accounts of the cabinet meeting, see Baudouin, p. 191; Bouthillier, Vol. I, p. 103; Lebrun, p. 90; Weygand, pp. 247–8; Chautemps, pp. 193–5.

[2] Jeanneney's evidence in *Procès Pétain*, p. 58, cols. 2–3; Herriot, pp. 94, 96–7; Edouard Barthe, *La Ténébreuse Affaire du 'Massilia'*, Paris, Imprimerie Dupont, 1945 (hereafter cited as Barthe), pp. 10–13; Gabriel Delattre in *L'Aurore*, 3 October 1944.

[3] Baudouin, p. 192; Weygand, p. 248.

was discussing the arrangements for the transfer of the government with Lebrun and Chautemps. The Marshal nodded his agreement as Chautemps summarized them once more. Realizing that, if Chautemps and Lebrun ever arrived in Algiers, Pétain's authority would be nil, Alibert intervened to say that he had just learned that the news that German troops had crossed the Loire, to which Lebrun attached great importance, was untrue. This, Alibert admitted in 1942, was a lie. 'As the situation is less urgent,' he said to the president, '. . . don't you think we could postpone any final decision until tomorrow morning?' Lebrun reluctantly agreed. What happened when Alibert returned to his office is best told in his own words. 'I took the Marshal's personal notepaper,' he said, 'I dictated to my secretary the order to each member of the government to remain at his home until 8 a.m. the following morning to await instructions and on no account to leave the city before receiving them. I took the Marshal's stamp, stamped the documents and signed. . . . Without that forgery, Pétain would never have been head of state.'[1] By the following morning, in fact, the French plenipotentiaries had crossed the German lines and the armistice negotiations were about to begin.

Laval's name has not so far appeared in this chronicle of events between 18 and 20 June. He and his colleagues of the 'Bordeaux Commune' were certainly active in trying to persuade other members of parliament not to leave France and there is evidence that Alibert intended to try and make use of his known opposition to the government's departure to North Africa.[2] But that is a very different thing from saying that it was Laval who prevented the departure. There were far more influential people working towards that end.

Neverthless, on the evening of 20 June, Laval began to assume a more active rôle. After Edouard Barthe, the *questeur* of the Chamber of Deputies, had supervised the departure of those members of parliament embarking on the *Massilia*, he went to the town hall, where a meeting of the 'Bordeaux Commune' was in full swing. Marquet was in the chair and both he and Laval were bitterly criticizing the government's decision to leave France. After some discussion, it was decided

---

[1] Alibert told this story to the deputy, Fernand-Laurent, who recounted it in his book, *Un Peuple Ressuscite*, New York, Brentano's, 1943, pp. 87–90.

[2] M-M. Tony-Révillon, *Mes Carnets, Juin-Octobre 1940*. Paris, Odette Lieutier, 1945, pp. 49–50; Gabriel Delattre in *l'Aurore*, 3 October 1944; Montigny, p. 21; Noguères, pp. 125–6.

to send a delegation to Pétain to ask him to prevent Lebrun's departure. The delegation was received at ten o'clock that evening. When Laval stated the purpose of the visit, Pétain replied that he had already prevented the president from leaving that afternoon and that he hoped to be able to provide 'useful information' at the following morning's cabinet meeting which would prevent the government's departure altogether. Barthe, who was present, noted that 'he winked mischievously' as he said this. In the light of Pétain's subsequent remarks, it seems likely that the 'useful information' he hoped to impart to his colleagues was German consent to the establishment of a neutralized zone inside France from which the French government could negotiate the armistice more freely. After Laval had digressed on his favourite theme of Franco–Italian relations, the delegation withdrew.[1]

Barthe's account of this meeting seems to cast doubt on Alibert's story of his forged message to members of the government, for it shows that Pétain was fully aware of the decision to postpone the government's departure until the following morning. Of course, Alibert may have been acting on the Marshal's instructions and have tried subsequently to inflate his own role, or he may have let Pétain into the secret later on. But this is immaterial from the point of view of Laval's part in events. Barthe's account shows clearly that Pétain had no need of Laval's prompting to do his utmost to prevent the government from going to North Africa.

But Laval and the 'Bordeaux Commune' were taking no chances. At another meeting at the town hall on 21 June, it was decided to send a delegation to Lebrun himself. Accounts of the delegation's reception vary. Lebrun describes his visitors as 'panic-stricken men, having lost control of themselves, gesticulating and all talking at once', while Montigny conveys the impression that they were business-like and ruthless. All agree, however, that Laval did most of the talking. He began by stating that more than a hundred deputies and senators had charged him with presenting the delegation, which had come to protest against the government's departure. This was quite inaccurate, according to Barthe, who says that there were no more than fifty people present at the town hall meeting. 'You cannot and must not leave,'

[1] Barthe, pp. 15–21. Two messages asking for the creation of a neutralized zone had already been handed to the Spanish ambassador on 20 June for transmission to the Germans. See Stohrer to Foreign Ministry, 20 June 1940, D.G.F.P., Series D, Vol. IX, Nos. 499, 500.

Laval told Lebrun. 'We will not allow the government, by this most fraudulent manœuvre, to go to Africa and continue a struggle which is obviously impossible.' If the President of the Republic and the presidents of the two chambers left France, he went on, the ministers who remained would no longer possess any authority. The Reynaud–Churchill policy stood condemned by the government and he refused to recognize Lebrun's right to resume it by going to North Africa. 'Only two men,' he said, 'are qualified to say whether the war can be continued: General Weygand and Marshal Pétain. If they believe we must stop fighting, then we must all accept their judgement.' All the same, he could not refrain from adding his own justification for an armistice. 'I came from Clermont by road,' he said. 'I saw the spectacle of our defeat. We are beaten!' In the circumstances, all they could do was to salvage what they could. 'It is not by leaving France that you can serve her,' he concluded.

Lebrun tried to point out that he only wished to respect the agreement that had been reached with Pétain on 18 June and asked how the government could possibly remain free and sovereign in a country that was occupied by the enemy. Another member of the delegation promptly chipped in to say that it was Lebrun's government which would no longer be free and sovereign if it left forty million Frenchmen to their fate. The latter would constitute the real government of France, he maintained, and 'we will form it because we will never leave France. What will you be able to do about it where you are going?' He seemed quite oblivious of the fact that he had contradicted Laval's earlier assertion that Lebrun's departure would deprive a metropolitan government of all authority. At that point, however, Laval took over the discussion again. 'If you leave France,' he told the president, 'you will never set foot here again.' Leaving France at the moment of her greatest distress, he claimed, would invite a charge of desertion or even of treason. He advised the president to follow Pétain's example and not to listen to 'those who have led the country to the abyss'. Jeanneney was obviously included in this category, for when Lebrun tried to explain that his constitutional position obliged him to consult certain people, Laval launched into such a bitter attack upon the President of the Senate that the president had to ask him to keep his voice down. He would probably have attacked Herriot with equal vehemence had not Barthe threatened to create an incident if he did so.

Upon this note, and with the somewhat incongruous spectacle of Lebrun and Laval shaking hands, the audience came to an end.[1]

Robert Aron has written that it was Laval's intervention which finally persuaded Lebrun to drop his insistence that the government should leave Bordeaux. But this was not in fact the case. It is clear from Baudouin's diary that the president was still arguing in favour of the government's departure after his meeting with Laval, and he even criticized Pétain for his indecision. Baudouin tried to frighten Lebrun by suggesting that, if the Pétain government left Bordeaux, it would be immediately replaced by a *de facto* administration under Laval. But the president refused to believe that Laval harboured any such sinister design. Exactly when and why Lebrun changed his mind about going to North Africa is uncertain, but it is in any case an academic point. When Baudouin told Pétain later the same evening that Lebrun still seemed determined to leave Bordeaux and asked him what he proposed to do about it, the Marshal replied, 'It's quite simple. I shall have him arrested.'[2] By the evening of 21 June, in fact, only a full-scale revolt inside the cabinet could have forced Pétain to change his mind and carry out the promise he had made on 18 June. Such a revolt might have taken place if the German armistice terms, which were received at Bordeaux between 8.30 and 10 in the evening, had been impossible to accept. But while General Huntziger, the head of the French armistice delegation, described them as 'harsh', he said that they 'contained nothing which directly offended against honour'.[3]

The terms certainly were harsh. They provided for the occupation by Germany of two thirds of metropolitan France, including Paris and the whole of the Channel and Atlantic coasts (article 2). The French government was to pay the maintenance costs of the German troops (article 18). All French forces, with the exception of some units necessary for the maintenance of order – the figure of 100,000 men was mentioned in the discussions – were to be disarmed and demobilized and the Germans were empowered to request the surrender intact of all their weapons and equipment (articles 4 and 5). The French battle-

---

[1] For accounts of the meeting, see Lebrun's evidence in *Procès Pétain*, p. 48, cols. 1–2; Lebrun, pp. 91–3; Montigny, pp. 25–30; Barthe, pp. 22–3, 25–6.

[2] Robert Aron, *Histoire de Vichy*, Paris, Fayard, 1954, p. 73; Baudouin, pp. 194–5.

[3] Weygand, pp. 249–57; Memorandum on the telephone conversation between General Huntziger and General Weygand, 21 June 1940, D.G.F.P., Series D, Vol. IX, No. 513. This telephone conversation was monitored by the Germans.

fleet, the third largest in the world, was to be assembled in its peace-time ports and disarmed under German and Italian supervision, except for those vessels allowed the French government to protect its colonial interests (article 8). The French government was also obliged to hand over to Germany any Germans living in France whom the German government requested (article 19). This provision was aimed at anti-Nazi refugees who had fled to France before the outbreak of the war. Finally, the armistice with Germany was not to take effect until a parallel agreement had been reached with Italy (article 23).

On the credit side, the French empire was left untouched and the French government was to be allowed to administer the occupied, as well as the unoccupied, zone. Even an eventual return to Paris by the French government was envisaged (article 3). And, as far as the fleet was concerned, the German government solemnly pledged that 'it does not intend to use for its own purposes in the war the French fleet which is in ports under German supervision, with the exception of those units needed for coastal patrol or minesweeping. Furthermore . . . it has no intention of raising any claim to the French war fleet at the time of the conclusion of peace' (article 8).

The German terms were thoroughly debated by the French government at Bordeaux during the night of 21–22 June and again the following morning. In addition to a preliminary request that the German advance be halted during the negotiations, it was decided to ask for seven modifications to the terms themselves. The first was that Paris should not be occupied and that it should be attached to the unoccupied zone by a corridor. The second was that military aircraft should be exempted from the equipment which could be demanded by the Germans under article 5. As General Huntziger explained, 'for the Air Force an obligation to hand over aircraft was just as hard as for an officer to have to surrender his sword.' The third request was that the French fleet be allowed to sail to French African ports with half its peace-time complement after demobilization and landing of ammunition under German and Italian supervision. The French government had been under continuous pressure from the British and American governments not to allow its fleet to fall into Axis hands at any price, and it is clear that it realized that full possession of the fleet would be one of its most important assets in future negotiations. The fourth request concerned the position of foreign nationals, chiefly

Poles, who had fought in the French armed forces. The fifth proposed that the German government should make a specific undertaking to facilitate the transfer of all products and foodstuffs essential to the population from the occupied to the unoccupied zone. The sixth request was that the section of article 19 referring to the extradition of German nationals should be completely deleted on the grounds that it was dishonourable. Finally, the French government requested a change of words in article 23 in order to make clear its opposition to linking the armistice with Germany to one with Italy. 'Although Italy had declared war on France,' General Huntziger indignantly exclaimed, 'she had not waged war on France. . . . As regards Germany France accepted the consequence of the fact that the fortunes of war had decided in Germany's favour, but as regards Italy she refuses to do so. . . .'

When the French requests were discussed on 22 June, the head of the German delegation, General Keitel, accepted the amendment to article 5 and agreed to some expression of German responsibility for the essential needs of the population in the unoccupied zone, but he flatly refused to consider any of the other proposed French amendments. On hearing the news, the government instructed General Huntziger to ask that the French requests and the German replies be appended to the text of the armistice in the form of a protocol. Huntziger and the rest of the French delegation opposed this suggestion on the grounds that it might lead to a break in the negotiations. Finally, at about 6.30 in the evening, Keitel presented the French delegation with an ultimatum: either they sign in an hour's time or the negotiations would be broken off. In these circumstances, Huntziger requested the French government to order him to sign and the signature took place at ten to seven.[1]

[1] The above account of the armistice negotiations is based on the following sources. German memoranda on the armistice negotiations, 21, 22 June 1940, D.G.F.P., Series D, Vol. IX, Nos. 512, 522, 524; German memoranda on the telephone conversations between Huntziger and Weygand, 21 June 1940, and Huntziger and Colonel Bourget (Weygand's adjutant), 22 June 1940, ibid., Nos. 513, 521; abbreviated French records of the negotiations published in Appendix XXXI of Albert Kammerer, *La Vérité sur l'Armistice*, 2nd edn., Paris, Editions Médicis, 1945, pp. 422–42; Baudouin, pp. 196–202; Bouthillier, Vol. I, pp. 104–7; 109–11; Charles-Roux, pp. 83–8, 90; Chautemps, pp. 207–11; Lebrun, p. 94; Weygand, pp. 249–64.

The quotations from General Huntziger are taken from the German memorandum on negotiations of 22 June. An English text of the armistice, from which the quotation is taken, is printed in D.G.F.P., Series D, Vol. IX, No. 523.

It was still possible, however, that the Italian terms would be so unreasonable as to compel the French government to go to North Africa and continue fighting, in spite of the opposition of Marshal Pétain and his closest colleagues. 'It was clear,' wrote Baudouin of the cabinet meeting which took place on the morning of 22 June, 'that a section of the government has transferred its hopes of a breakdown to the armistice with Italy. The President of the Republic stated that the Italian conditions would break off everything.' The attitude of Admiral Darlan was particularly crucial. When the German terms were first received, he had indignantly repudiated them and demanded a continuation of the struggle and, while he failed to press home this initial opposition, he issued orders that the Italian coast was to be shelled if the Italian terms proved 'unacceptable'.[1]

A measure of the government's indecision was its continued exploration of the possibilities of further resistance in North Africa, even while negotiations with the Germans were still in progress. On 21 June, General Weygand telegraphed General Noguès, the French commander-in-chief in North Africa, asking him to come to Bordeaux. In reply Noguès begged to be excused on the grounds that his departure might seem to the inhabitants like desertion. In a second telegram, sent at 12.50 p.m. on 22 June, Weygand accepted Noguès' arguments and asked him his opinion of the possibility of resistance in Algeria, Tunisia, and Morocco, and of an offensive against the Italians in Tunisia, 'given the almost complete impossibility of the home country's reinforcing you and supplying you with munitions.'

Weygand's own pessimism is clearly shown in the passage quoted and he must have been all the more surprised, therefore, when Noguès replied the same day that 'with the help of its existing resources, the aerial reinforcements which are taking place and which are of prime importance, and the support of the fleet, North Africa is capable of resisting enemy operations for a long time'. As well as requesting Noguès' opinion, Weygand had also informed him that he was sending a staff officer, General Koeltz, to North Africa to obtain 'all additional information' from him. Koeltz subsequently explained that, when he arrived in Algiers, he received the impression that further resistance had already been decided between Noguès and Weygand and that his

---

[1] Baudouin, pp. 197, 199; C.E., *Rapport*, Vol. II, p. 461 (Darlan's orders).

188 · PIERRE LAVAL

task was merely to transmit the former's requests for *matériel* to the defence ministry.

Looking at the accounts of these transactions as recorded by Baudouin and Bouthillier, however, one can see how Noguès' telegram and Koeltz's mission were distorted in the perspective of those who wanted an armistice at almost any price. As far as Noguès' reply to Weygand's query was concerned, attention was focused upon his statements that he could not take the offensive in Tunisia until the autumn and that an Axis attack through Spanish Morocco was a real danger which could only be met by a counter-attack, whose chances of success would be greatly enhanced by the immediate despatch of armoured, anti-tank and anti-aircraft reinforcements. These statements, together with the more precise requests for reinforcements which General Koeltz conveyed to the government on his return to Bordeaux on 23 June, were taken as proof of the essential weakness of Noguès' position, and his overall optimism was completely ignored.[1]

By the time that General Koeltz had returned to Bordeaux, the armistice with Germany had already been signed and the initial contacts with the Italians had taken place. The Italian armistice terms reached Bordeaux during the evening of 23 June and they were surprisingly moderate. Baudouin was particularly glad to see that the Italians had made no excessive territorial demands upon France, a step which might well have ruined all hopes of a settlement. He attributed Italy's moderation to the firm stand which Huntziger had taken with the Germans, but in fact it was due to Mussolini himself. At the Munich meeting between Hitler and Mussolini on 18 June, it had been agreed that Italy could occupy metropolitan France as far as the Rhône, as well as Corsica, Tunis, and Djibouti. When he was informed of the German armistice terms, however, the Duce decided that it would be wiser not to press these claims for the moment. 'This might provoke a rupture in the negotiations and lead to a real rift in our relations with Berlin,' Ciano noted in his diary. Instead, Mussolini contented himself with a demilitarized zone, 50 kilometres in width, along the Franco-Italian frontier, and shelved his territorial demands until

---

[1] The telegrams exchanged between Weygand and Noguès are printed in C.E., *Rapport*, Vol. II, pp. 418–20. General Koeltz's evidence is in ibi d., *Témoignages*, Vol. IX, pp. 2810–16. See also Baudouin, pp. 200, 207–8; Bouthillier, Vol. I, pp. 107–8.

the peace. Like Hitler, he did not think he would have to wait very long.[1]

In addition to General Koeltz's return from Algiers and the receipt of the Italian armistice terms, 23 June witnessed another important event: the entry of Laval into the French government. The previous day, records Lebrun, 'a person from the prime minister's office' had asked him to sign a decree nominating Laval and Marquet as members of the government. The president indignantly refused to do so, pointing out that the proper procedure was for the prime minister himself to present the decree for his signature. Accordingly, the following morning, Marshal Pétain appeared and the decree appointing Laval and Marquet as ministers of state was duly signed. Four days later, they were given enhanced status, Laval becoming deputy-premier and Marquet minister of the interior.[2]

The arrival of Laval and Marquet at their first cabinet meeting on the morning of 23 June was a complete surprise to many members of the government, who knew nothing of what was going on. Even Baudouin had only been informed a matter of minutes beforehand. Justifying Laval's appointment, Pétain told his foreign minister that Laval had recognized his mistake in not accepting the ministry of justice. Besides, he added, 'I must bring him into the government, where his intrigues will be less dangerous than if he were fomenting opposition outside.' In fact, the truth was a little more complicated. Laval had indeed 'recognized his mistake' in not entering the government when he had had the chance and he asked Lémery to help him 'pick up the pieces', as he put it. At first Pétain turned a deaf ear to Laval's pleas, but on 22 June he finally gave in, apparently with the help of some pressure from Alibert, who at that time agreed with Laval's authoritarian conception.[3]

In spite of Laval's previous interest in Franco-Italian relations, no intervention of his is recorded in the accounts of the government's discussion of the Italian armistice terms on 23 and 24 June. The principal disagreement between the two sides lay in the Italian demand that the French forces in North Africa, French Somaliland, and Syria

---

[1] Baudouin, p. 208; Letter from Mussolini to Hitler in Memorandum by Weiszäcker, 22 June 1940, D.G.F.P., Series D, Vol. IX, No. 525; Ciano, *Diario*, 21 June 1940.

[2] Lebrun, p. 95; Beau de Loménie, p. 355.

[3] Weygand, p. 298; L.-O. Frossard in *L'Aurore*, 14 February 1949; Baudouin, p. 204; Beau de Loménie, p. 340; Mallet, Vol. I, p. 162.

should be disarmed and demobilized. The French refused to accept this, but a satisfactory compromise was eventually reached. The Franco-Italian armistice was signed at 7.15 p.m. on 24 June and both it and the Franco-German armistice were scheduled to come into effect at 12.35 a.m. on the night of 24–25 June.[1] With the entry into force of these two documents, the first stage of the transformation of France's role in the second world war was complete. Laval was determined that the second stage should be no less revolutionary.

For Laval, the fall of France provided both proof and an opportunity: proof that his diagnosis of France's problems had been right all along, and an opportunity to apply his remedies. On the domestic front, it confirmed his belief, which had been growing ever stronger since 1935, that parliamentary democracy was incapable of responding to the country's needs. 'Since parliamentary democracy wished to enter into a struggle with Nazism and fascism,' he told an audience of members of parliament on 8 July 1940, 'and since it lost that struggle, it must disappear. A new régime – one that is bold, authoritarian, social and national – must take its place.'[2] The disappearance of the 'old order' aroused no regrets in him, he told an American diplomat the following November. 'The word "democracy", which is so often repeated, as far as France is concerned leaves him completely cold. . . . He had seen enough of so-called democracy in France in the past few years and the state to which it had brought his country, the vile and criminal demagogy into which it had degenerated under the *Front Populaire* ever to wish to see it again.'[3] The shift to the right, which had begun with his departure from the Socialist party in 1920, was now complete.

An authoritarian régime was necessary to enable Laval to implement his foreign policy without the constraint of domestic criticism. This policy was to be based upon his old idea of a Franco-German *entente*, the necessity for which had merely been underlined by the French collapse. 'Whether, in the last resort, Germany wins the war or not,' he told a friend in June 1940, 'we now have less choice than ever. We

[1] For the armistice negotiations with Italy, see the abbreviated French records printed in Appendix XXXV of Albert Kammerer, op. cit., pp. 448–54; Baudouin, pp. 208–10; Charles-Roux, pp. 100–101; Weygand, pp. 268–9. The text of the Franco-Italian armistice is printed in Kammerer, op. cit., pp. 454–8.
[2] Montigny, p. 62. See below, p. 204.
[3] Matthews to Hull, 14 November 1940, F.R.U.S., 1940, Vol. II, p. 404.

must reach an agreement with her.' If Germany won, he went on, such an agreement would be France's only hope of survival. It was important to seize the opportunity, not only for her sake, but also for that of the rest of Europe. '. . . I don't believe in the permanence or even the long life of Nazism,' he explained. 'In fifteen or twenty years' time – and that's nothing in history – Europe will have a new thirst for freedom. If the French flame has been kept alight, albeit dimly, it is to her that they will come to rekindle the extinguished torches . . . for there will be no one else.'

But even if Germany lost the war, a Franco-German *entente* was essential, not only to prevent a revival of militant German nationalism, but also to exorcize Laval's permanent bogey: Bolshevism. For Germany to lose the war, he maintained, both the United States and Russia would have to enter it and, if this happened, 'the latter would be so monstrously strong and aggressive that we would be on the threshold of a new war after having barely emerged from the previous one. The only possible basis for world equilibrium would still be the Franco-German *entente*, for a Germany which remained smashed after her defeat would put the Russians on the Rhine and therefore in Paris.'[1]

In the meantime, Laval did not intend that France should play a self-effacing role in the German-dominated Europe which Adolf Hitler was creating. On the contrary, he told the American *chargé d'affaires* that he was convinced that the Germans had no intention of crushing France, 'but that their plan contemplates a European federation of states in which France will play an important role compatible with its dignity and traditions.'[2] When talking to Hitler and Ribbentrop, he said on another occasion, he spoke 'as a proud Frenchman', who believed that 'considerations of the future impose a collaboration that may lead to France regaining her rightful place in Europe as the first Latin power'. Like many others before him, he felt that Hitler was 'a man he could deal with'.[3]

There was, of course, no place for Britain in this scheme of things. Laval was not alone in thinking, in the summer of 1940, that Britain's defeat at the hands of Germany was only a matter of time. Where he

[1] Claude Lewy in *La Vie de la France*, Vol. III, p. 1580.
[2] Murphy to Hull, 29 July 1940, F.R.U.S., 1940, Vol. II, p. 378.
[3] Matthews to Hull, 15 November 1940, ibid., p. 410; Matthews to Hull, 14 November 1940, ibid., p. 404.

differed from most was in actually rejoicing at the prospect. Thus, he told the American *chargé d'affaires* on 29 July 1940 that 'he had announced it before and did not hesitate again to say that "he hoped ardently that the British would be defeated".' France, he said, 'had suffered too often as a result of British dishonesty and hypocrisy.'[1] The seeds sown during the Abyssinian crisis had indeed brought forth bitter fruit.

Following his appointment to the Pétain government, therefore, Laval set out to do two things. The first was to create the domestic base for his foreign policy by depriving parliament, as he had put it to Landini in April 1938, 'of the capacity to do harm'.[2] The second was to implement that foreign policy, which was predicated on both the likelihood and the desirability of a German victory. It is the task of the following two chapters to explore, successively, his progress in each of these two fields.

[1] Murphy to Hull, 29 July 1940, F.R.U.S., 1940, Vol. II, p. 379.
[2] See above, p. 134.

6

The End of the Third Republic

June – July 1940

It was generally recognized that the Pétain government, formed as it was in exceptional circumstances, could not be expected to function subject to the normal controls of parliament and public opinion. But while men like Baudouin and Bouthillier were content to make use of the amazing flexibility of the 1875 constitution to prorogue parliament indefinitely and govern by means of decree-laws, this was not enough for Laval. Nothing less than a completely new constitution would satisfy him.

Although Laval frequently justified this view by pleading the necessity of adapting French institutions to the German and Italian pattern, one cannot help feeling that the real basis of his attitude was personal animosity. It was impossible to govern with parliament, he told Baudouin and Bouthillier on 26 June 1940, especially with the *Front Populaire* Chamber of 1936. 'That Chamber spewed me up,' he added with characteristic coarseness, 'now I'm going to spew it up.' A couple of months later, he boasted to a member of the German embassy of how he had got rid of parliament 'without revolution and without bloodshed.' 'I'm very pleased about it,' he said, 'because . . . that was the self-same parliament which came into being as a result of the *Front Populaire* elections of 1936, under the leadership of Léon Blum and with the slogan, "Hang Laval!" These same members of parliament have now freely shaken hands with me and returned home contented.' It was indeed an achievement.[1]

But Laval's triumph was by no means a foregone conclusion. When discussed at a meeting of himself, Baudouin, Bouthillier, Alibert, and Pétain on the afternoon of 30 June, his proposed constitutional reform

[1] Baudouin, p. 219; Unsigned Memorandum of conversation between Laval and Dr Grimm, 28 August 1940, GFM/2624/D525934–47.

193

met with considerable opposition. He wanted to convene a meeting of the National Assembly as soon as possible and undertook to persuade the assembled deputies and senators to vote Marshal Pétain the power to promulgate a new constitution. Baudouin disagreed. It could only happen, he maintained, 'if 480 senators or deputies agreed to commit suicide.' Besides, he added, 'you do not change the constitution of a country whose capital is in enemy hands.' Pétain tended to agree and, in the face of Laval's insistence, raised the problem of President Lebrun. 'I undertake to obtain Albert Lebrun's full agreement to his disappearance,' replied Laval and immediately left the meeting to seek out the president. He returned an hour later, claiming to have secured Lebrun's agreement to a change in the constitution. Full of admiration at his minister's self-confidence and at his powers of persuasion, Pétain gave way. 'Very well then,' he said, 'try.'[1]

The following day the government moved to the spa town of Vichy, having already moved from Bordeaux to Clermont-Ferrand on 29 June. Laval had hoped that the government would remain in Clermont, where his newspaper and printing press were located, but perhaps for this very reason it was decided otherwise. Pétain refused to go to Lyons, where Herriot – as mayor – exercised considerable political influence, so Baudouin suggested Vichy, where the large number of hotels could be used to provide accommodation for the various government departments. It was thus that 'the Vichy régime' entered the history books.[2]

When the constitutional reform came before the 'inner cabinet' of Pétain and his closest advisers on 2 July, the Marshal reaffirmed his support of Laval's views. But General Weygand, to whom everything which emanated from Laval was suspect, was opposed, while Baudouin reiterated his fear that the manœuvre would fail. 'You've no experience,' retorted Laval scornfully. 'Through fear you get everything from men, because they are cowards.' The 'inner cabinet' endorsed the Marshal's earlier decision to allow the deputy premier to proceed with his plans, and two days later the full cabinet took note

[1] Baudouin, pp. 227–8. Lebrun (Lebrun, p. 102) states that Pétain was present when Laval first informed him of the proposal to change the constitution. However, he adds that he said nothing 'as if he was not there. He seemed to be uninterested in this serious matter.' Lebrun claims that he merely took note of what Laval said and awaited a definite text.

[2] Baudouin, p. 226; Paul Luquet in *La Vie de la France*, Vol. III, p. 1199.

of the text which he proposed to put before the National Assembly. This simply gave Pétain the power to promulgate 'the new constitution of the French state' subject only to the two provisos that it must 'guarantee the rights of labour, the family and the fatherland' and that it must be 'ratified by the assemblies which it creates'.[1]

It is important to emphasize at this point that few of the members of Marshal Pétain's government had any objections to the demise of the Third Republic as such. Baudouin and Bouthillier were both in favour of governing without parliament. General Weygand had written a memorandum in which he maintained that 'the old order of things, that is to say a political régime of masonic, capitalist, and international compromise, has brought us to our present state. France wants no more of it.' Pétain himself had told Admiral Darlan before the armistice 'how sickened he was by the . . . government's incapacity to take any decision whatsoever' and how what was needed was 'a sort of Consulate'. Such objections as there were were to the fact that it was Laval, a product of 'the old order of things' if ever there was one, who was mounting the operation and that he had chosen a particularly inopportune moment to do so. Baudouin was the strongest exponent of this view. He was worried in case the project was defeated and the discredit rebounded on to the Marshal and the other members of his government. He told both Pétain and President Lebrun that, if the National Assembly did reject the proposed reform, the blame must be laid fairly and squarely on Laval's shoulders. Indeed, it would provide a good excuse for excluding him from the government. On the other hand, if the reform were adopted, then Pétain must ensure that he was 'the sole beneficiary'.[2]

External events were, however, already adding grist to Laval's mill. On 3 July a British naval task force shelled that part of the French fleet which was anchored off Mers-el-Kébir near Oran in Algeria, sinking one battleship, disabling two more, and killing 1,300 French sailors. This action, which was accompanied by less extreme measures against French naval units at Alexandria and in British ports, was prompted by the British government's fear that, notwithstanding Article 8 of the

---

[1] Baudouin, pp. 228–9; Weygand, p. 303, fn. 1; Lebrun, p. 103; Montigny, pp. 56, 61.
[2] Baudouin, pp. 224–5, 229–30; Weygand, pp. 298–9; Bouthillier in C.E., *Témoignages*, Vol. VIII, pp. 2537–8; Robert Aron, *Histoire de Vichy*, Paris, Fayard, 1954 (hereafter cited as Aron), p. 89.

Franco-German armistice convention, the French fleet would be taken over and used by the Axis powers.

The detailed story of this episode has been told many times.[1] What is important here is the repercussions of Mers-el-Kébir at Vichy. Admiral Darlan, it seems, virtually lost control of himself. He had repeatedly informed the British that he would sink the fleet rather than allow it to fall into Axis hands and had even issued an order to that effect. But the British had not trusted his word, and he clamoured for reprisals. Baudouin, supported by Bouthillier, claims that he did his utmost to dissuade Pétain from following Darlan's advice and, indeed, the breaking-off of diplomatic relations with Britain, a bitter broadcast speech by Baudouin, and a welcome German decision to suspend temporarily that part of Article 8 which called for the disarmament of the French fleet, in order to enable it to face up to further British attacks, were the only immediate results of the British action. Laval is generally held to have supported Darlan's demand for reprisals, but the evidence is in fact contradictory. Both his daughter and Jacques Guérard, who was a member of Baudouin's *cabinet* at the time, emphatically deny that he favoured reprisals. 'Isn't one defeat enough for you then?' he is alleged to have asked the more belligerent members of the government. Whatever the truth, however, there is no doubt that Mers-el-Kébir was a useful weapon in Laval's armoury when it came to persuading members of parliament to support his policy of collaboration with Germany, and to support the reform of the constitution, which was the first step in that policy.[2]

'Through fear,' Laval had boasted, 'you get everything from men,' and, in accordance with this precept, he began his campaign with a brutal attempt to cow his opponents into submission. Observers noted that he was a changed man. No longer was he concerned to persuade,

---

[1] See, for example, Aron, pp. 102–12; Churchill, pp. 203–11; Kammerer, *Flotte Française*, pp. 145–77. See also P. M. H. Bell, 'Prologue de Mers-el-Kébir' in *Revue d'Histoire de la Deuxième Guerre Mondiale*, January 1959, pp. 15–36.

[2] Baudouin, pp. 231–5; Bouthillier, Vol. I, pp. 149–52; Lebrun, pp. 102–3 (Lebrun misdates the discussions as taking place on 3 July); Hencke to Foreign Ministry, 3 July 1940, D.G.F.P., Series D, Vol. X, No. 93; Kramarz Memorandum, 4 July 1940, ibid., No. 111; Note from Huntziger to von Stülpnagel, 3 July 1940, *La Délégation Française auprès de la Commission Allemande d'Armistice*, 5 vols., Paris, Alfred Costes-Imprimerie Nationale, 1947–59 (hereafter cited as La Délégation Française), Vol. I, pp. 38–9; Huntziger Memorandum, 3 July 1940, ibid., pp. 39–40; Note from von Stülpnagel to Huntziger, ibid., pp. 40–41; Josée de Chambrun in *La Vie de la France*, Vol. III, p. 1637; Jacques Guérard, *Criminel de Paix*, Paris, Nouvelles Editions Latines, 1953 (hereafter cited as Guérard), p. 27.

but merely to dictate, as Léon Blum found out when he discussed the suppression of the Socialist party's newspaper with him on 4 July. '*Le Populaire* will not appear,' stated Laval. 'Until when?' asked Blum. 'Until I've decided otherwise,' replied Laval. 'Tell me frankly,' said Blum, 'is it on my account? If my name were to disappear from the top of the paper and if I were to abandon the editorship, would it appear?' 'Don't bother yourself,' Laval retorted, 'you won't alter the position in any way.' He explained that no newspaper would be allowed to appear as long as it showed 'the slightest hesitation' towards his policy. 'I must be followed totally and without reservation,' he concluded, 'and I will not let the wool be pulled over my eyes.'[1]

Similar tactics were employed at the 'briefing sessions' for members of parliament. Parliament, he told a meeting of senators on the afternoon of 4 July, must be dissolved and the constitution 'modelled upon the totalitarian states'. Concentration camps might even have to be introduced! If they did not agree to these changes, he warned, 'Germany will impose them upon us, with the occupation of the whole of France as an immediate consequence.' The next day, it was the turn of the deputies. When the right-wing deputy, Marcel Héraud, asked him to prevent General Weygand from making statements to his troops which could be construed as attacks upon the régime, Laval retorted. 'You've made a fine speech. But do you imagine that we still have time to listen to speeches? You're wrong! We're through with speeches! We're not here for you to make them or for us to listen. Our task is to rebuild France.'[2]

This injunction did not, however, prevent Laval from making a speech of his own, which lasted for about one-and-a-half hours. 'It is not a matter of the government applying any old remedy or carrying out any old reform within the existing framework,' he declared. 'No. We want to destroy the whole set-up.' He repeated the warning he had given the senators the previous day. 'There are two alternatives,' he said: 'either you agree to what we ask and model yourselves on the German and Italian constitutions, or Hitler will force you to do so.' Referring to Mers-el-Kébir, Laval launched into a bitter attack upon

[1] Léon Blum, *L'Œuvre de Léon Blum*, 1940–45, Paris, Albin Michel, 1955, pp. 68–9.
[2] Jean Taurines in C.E., *Témoignages*, Vol. VIII, p. 2330; Joseph Paul-Boncour, *Entre Deux Guerres*, Vol. III, *Sur les Chemins de la Défaite 1935–40*, Paris, Plon, 1946 (hereafter cited as Paul-Boncour), p. 254; Louis Noguères in C.E., *Témoignages*, Vol. VII, pp. 2230–31.

Britain. 'France has never had and never will have a more inveterate enemy than Great Britain,' he maintained. 'Our whole history bears witness to that. We have been nothing but toys in the hands of England, who has exploited us to ensure her own safety. Today we are at the bottom of the abyss where she led us. . . . I see only one way to restore France . . . to the position to which she is entitled: namely, to ally ourselves resolutely with Germany and to confront England together.'

Only on one point did Laval appear to pay any heed to the views expressed by other speakers. A socialist, Georges Monnet, had said that while the deputies would gladly support Marshal Pétain, they wanted to know what would happen if he had 'an accident' after being granted full powers. Other considerations apart, this was a very pertinent question in view of the Marshal's advanced age. Laval explained that after the National Assembly had voted Pétain full powers to promulgate a new constitution, he would publish various constitutional 'acts'. The first of these would give him all the powers at present exercised by the president of the republic, the prime minister, and the cabinet, while a second would designate a successor who would exercise these powers if he were prevented from doing so. Laval was very careful, however, not to reveal to his audience what he confided to Baudouin the following day: that he hoped to be that successor himself.[1]

In addition to the deputies, Laval sought to browbeat Jeanneney. 'I received a sudden visit from Pierre Laval,' the president of the Senate told the High Court in 1945. 'He came . . . to ask me – although, in view of the tone he employed, it is more true to say that he told me – to convene the Senate on the following Tuesday [9 July] in preparation for a meeting of the National Assembly the following day and for a purpose about which, moreover, he was none too clear.' Jeanneney took the view that more time was needed to enable senators to reach Vichy and find out what was going on, and he therefore refused Laval's request. But the deputy premier simply carried on as if he had granted it and, during the next few days, decrees appeared in the *Journal Officiel* closing the ordinary sessions of both Chamber and Senate and reconvening them in extraordinary session on the desired dates. 'From then on,' Jeanneney concluded lamely, 'my only concern

---

[1] Louis Noguères in C.E., *Témoignages*, Vol. VII, pp. 2231–2; Baudouin, p. 238.

was to guide the debates of the two assemblies with impartiality . . . and the greatest possible clarity.'[1]

But Laval was not having everything his own way. A group of ex-service senators, who had been deeply disturbed by his remarks on 4 July, held a meeting of their own on the afternoon of the 5th to examine the situation. They agreed unanimously that, while they were prepared to support Marshal Pétain, they wanted further clarification of Laval's plans. They decided to send a delegation to Pétain in order to obtain this clarification, and one of the senators, Jean Taurines, telephoned the prime minister's office to arrange an appointment. Unfortunately, he was put through to Alibert, who appears to have been working hand in glove with Laval. By first pigeon-holing the request and then becoming 'unavailable', Alibert succeeded in stalling the senators until midday on 6 July, when, in exasperation, they tried another channel.

The meeting finally took place at 6.15 p.m. that evening and Pétain was most reassuring. According to their report of the meeting, he told the senators that, until peace was signed, he merely wanted to avoid the 'snags and difficulties' which beset President Lebrun and 'not to have to pay any more attention to outmoded groups and parties'. He had no intention of assuming an attitude of secrecy and, when full powers were given to him, 'he did not intend to use them to transform the nation without consulting [members of parliament] in the process.' Paul-Boncour expressed the general relief of the delegation upon hearing these words and said that, in these circumstances, the senators would not hesitate to suspend the constitution and 'confer upon him, and him alone, a dictatorship in the way that Roman law had done on several occasions'. Pétain replied with a smile that 'he was not a Caesar and had no desire to be one'. All the same, Paul-Boncour insisted that he and his colleagues would be delighted to vote a bill suspending the constitution until the peace and empowering the Marshal to govern by decree and to work out the bases of a new constitution in collaboration with parliament. 'But that's a proposal,' said Pétain. 'Let me have a text.' Overjoyed at the apparent identity of views between themselves and the Marshal, the delegation withdrew to prepare one.[2]

In the meantime, Laval himself seems to have realized that his

[1] Jeanneney in *Procès Pétain*, pp. 58, col. 3, 59, col. 1.
[2] Jean Taurines in C.E., *Témoignages*, Vol. VIII, pp. 2331–3; Paul-Boncour, pp. 261–3.

hectoring attitude was gaining him more enemies than friends and he began to revert to his more usual, and more effective, tactics of persuasion and guile. Marcel Héraud, for example, whom he had taken to task so severely when he had addressed the deputies on 5 July, was invited to meet him privately after the meeting. Héraud found the deputy premier much more accommodating than he had been a few hours earlier. 'You understand,' Laval told him, 'there's Hitler and Mussolini. We must take up a position between them. As you know, I'm well in with Mussolini and, by playing one off against the other, I might manage to do something. But, in order to do it, there must be a strong government and I must be in it. Your criticisms are unjustified. Let me get on with it. I'm working in the interests of France.' He denied that he had any dictatorial ambitions. He only wanted 'the trappings' so that he could 'speak in France's name and on an equal footing with these people'. Héraud replied that Hitler and Mussolini were two conquerors with powerful parties. Laval did not have a party, but, if he wanted to be strong, he needed supporters. 'There is only one way to get them immediately,' Héraud argued, 'and that is to collaborate with parliament and to base yourself upon it in order to give yourself the strength which you lack.' 'Of course,' Laval assured him, 'that's how I should act and that's how I'm going to act.' His subsequent actions showed how much he meant it.[1]

Sunday 7 July saw the height of the counter-offensive against Laval's plans to reform the constitution. It was aided by the arrival in Vichy of one of his former ministerial colleagues, Pierre-Etienne Flandin. Addressing the deputies in their meeting-place at the Petit Casino, Flandin argued that it was a waste of time discussing constitutional reform when there were so many other important things to be done. Everybody, he maintained, wanted Marshal Pétain at the head of the country in order to negotiate with the Germans and to guarantee, with his name and prestige, the reorganization of France. But, he asked, 'why do we need to alter the constitution for that? . . . In the circumstances, there could be no simpler solution than to ask the president of the Republic to resign and elect Marshal Pétain in his place. In that way, we will obtain the desired result and respect the constitution at the same time.' Flandin's proposal met with universal

[1] Marcel Héraud in C.E., *Témoignages*, Vol. VI, pp. 1511-12.

approval and he himself was appointed head of a delegation whose task was to see Lebrun and persuade him to resign.[1]

Flandin, however, decided to see Laval first. The latter trotted out his usual arguments in favour of constitutional reform and was 'extremely annoyed' when Flandin put forward the objections he had expressed to the deputies. 'That's not the Marshal's view,' snapped Laval. Calling the deputy premier's bluff, Flandin promptly called on Pétain to find out for himself and was gratified to discover that the Marshal apparently had no objection whatever to his proposal. In terms reminiscent of those he had used when speaking to the senators on the previous day, he said that 'all he wanted was to be granted full powers until the conclusion of peace, without being accountable to parliament in the meantime'. Flandin replied that this would not be very different from the position during the 'phoney war', when parliament had scarcely met. The powers granted to Daladier and Reynaud should suffice. Pétain agreed.[2]

Armed with the Marshal's blessing, Flandin and his delegation hurried off to see President Lebrun. But if they expected their mission to be a success, they were doomed to disappointment. The president of the Republic, punctilious observer of constitutional practice that he was, would do nothing until he had consulted the presidents of the Chamber and Senate. He admitted that he personally saw no need to resign and, apparently, Herriot and Jeanneney agreed with him. Moreover, he was told by a deputy that Flandin's delegation did not enjoy the support of all those at the Petit Casino meeting and that it had been formed privately. This piece of news made up Lebrun's mind and, when he saw Flandin again 24 hours later, he rejected his proposal. The Flandin plan was dead.[3]

The ex-service senators also met on 7 July to draft the text they had discussed with Marshal Pétain the previous evening. As finally worded, it consisted of three short articles. The first suspended the 1875 constitution until the conclusion of a peace settlement. The second gave Pétain full powers to promulgate by decree 'measures necessary for the maintenance of order, the existence and recovery of the country, and

[1] Noguères in ibid., Vol. VII, p. 2237.
[2] *Le Procès Flandin devant la Haute Cour de Justice, 23–26 juillet 1946*, Paris, Librairie de Médicis, 1947 (hereafter cited as *Procès Flandin*), p. 122.
[3] *Procès Flandin*, pp. 123–34; Lebrun, pp. 105–6.

the liberation of its territory'. The final article entrusted him with 'the task of preparing, in collaboration with the competent committees, the new constitutional laws which will be submitted to ratification by the nation as soon as circumstances permit a free consultation'.[1]

When the senators brought their text to Pétain the same evening, he accepted it after a brief discussion. 'But,' he added, dropping an unexpected bombshell, 'you must now convince M. Laval who, as you know, is representing the government in these discussions.' In the twenty-four hours which had elapsed since the senators first saw Pétain, Laval had clearly been to work upon the latter. 'Here come the conspirators!' he exclaimed when the senatorial delegation, in accordance with the Marshal's wishes, submitted their text for his approval – a remark which showed that he was well aware of their activity. Not surprisingly, he refused to accept the text, saying that he would make a statement to the National Assembly in Pétain's name which would give the senators satisfaction. 'The National Assembly has not been convened to listen to statements,' retorted Taurines. 'The government has convened us to vote a bill. We are tabling the amendment.' 'Very well,' replied Laval, growing progressively more irritated, 'if your amendment is voted, I shall resign, and then you'll have a Weygand dictatorship.' '*Monsieur le Président,*' said Taurines wearily, 'during your so-called unofficial meetings of the Senate, you brandished the spectre of the Germans in order to obtain the revision of the 1875 constitution. This evening, you are brandishing the spectre of General Weygand. Whom will you find tomorrow?' The senators, he concluded, had every right both to table and to discuss their amendment and they intended to do so. Upon this note of defiance, the delegation withdrew.[2]

His experiences with Flandin and the senators convinced Laval that he needed something more than the Marshal's verbal pledge of support if he was to succeed in his self-appointed task. Pétain, of course, knew that he would get what he wanted whether Laval was successful or not. When he told Baudouin of Flandin's opinion that the deputy premier's scheme would fail, he commented that he was 'indifferent' and that 'the main thing [was] to govern and to govern quickly by getting down to work without delay'. Laval may or may not have been aware of

---

[1] Taurines in C.E., *Témoignages*, Vol. VIII, p. 2339.
[2] Ibid., pp. 2333–4; Paul-Boncour, pp. 267–8.

these views, but he was determined to have his own position reaffirmed once and for all. Immediately after the senators' departure, he went to see Pétain. Referring to the latter's conversations with Flandin and the senators, he said, 'I will not go before the National Assembly unless you let me have a letter in which you write that I am speaking in your name and that you agree with my text.' Presented with this ultimatum, the Marshal gave in and penned the following letter:

'*Monsieur le Président*,
    The constitutional measure tabled by the government which I head will come up for discussion before parliament on Tuesday 9 and Wednesday 10 July.
    As it is difficult for me to take part in the debates, I ask you to represent me.
    The passing of the measure which the government is putting before the National Assembly appears to me to be essential to ensure the salvation of our country.
    Please accept, etc.,

Philippe Pétain'

Laval now had the weapon he needed.[1]

On 8 July, Laval made another appearance at the Petit Casino, this time to acquaint the deputies with the text of the proposed constitutional reform bill and the *exposé des motifs*, or explanatory memorandum, which went with it. The latter, which called for a 'national revolution' to reinvigorate the defeated France, seems to have been the work of Alibert. After reading it, Laval went on to add a commentary of his own. He was, an observer noted, much less arrogant than he had been three days previously. 'We are beaten,' he began, '. . . [and] we are meeting today in a casino a few miles away from the occupation forces. This is very sad. But we can recover. We must face the future bravely, draw lessons from our misfortunes and create the conditions most favourable to our recovery.' He had reason to believe, he went on, that Hitler would accord France an honourable peace, but to secure it, 'we must collaborate loyally with Germany and Italy and become integrated, sincerely and in good faith, in a reorganized continental

---

[1] Baudouin, p. 239; Laval in *Procès Pétain*, p. 189, col. 1, and *Procès Laval*, pp. 134–6. A photographic reproduction of the letter from Pétain to Laval may be found at the end of Noguères' book.

Europe.' This, he reminded his audience, was a policy he had always advocated. France's institutions would, of course, have to be modified in the process. Parliamentary democracy had lost the war, and so it must go. 'A new régime – one that is bold, authoritarian, social and national, – must take its place.'

This time, however, Laval was careful to sweeten the pill. Did the deputies fear a military dictatorship? He would be there to guarantee the supremacy of civilian authority and to see that the traditional freedoms were safeguarded. Were they concerned about their own futures? Some of them would be called upon 'to undertake tasks of all kinds'. The Senate and Chamber would not disappear until the new constitution came into force, a process which would take 'some time'. In the meantime, they would continue to benefit from all their existing privileges and even to draw their salaries. Not everyone, of course, was satisfied with these soothing reassurances. A number of socialists, in particular, tried to put some questions, but they were shouted down by Laval's supporters. He took the opportunity to excuse himself on the grounds that he had to address a meeting of the Senate.[1]

The Socialist party was the largest in the Chamber and its united opposition might have gravely embarrassed Laval. But some of its pacifist wing had already gone over to his camp and the rest were placed in the awkward position of having to defend a constitution they had always opposed in order to spike his guns. At a party meeting which was held later on the 8th, they compromised by agreeing not to oppose the principle of constitutional reform, which was to be debated by the Chamber and Senate separately, but only Laval's text, which was to be debated by the National Assembly. In addition, Marcel Rivière, who was one of the party's two representatives in the government, was instructed to support the ex-service senators' amendment at the next cabinet meeting. Rivière duly carried out his mandate at the cabinet meeting which was held at half-past nine that evening, only to be told by Laval that during the course of 'several conversations' with the senators, he had managed to give them 'every satisfaction'. This was completely untrue, as the unfortunate Rivière was to find out the following day, but for the moment he failed to press his

[1] For the text of the *exposé des motifs*, see Montigny, pp. 129–32. For Alibert's role, see Beau de Loménie, pp. 384–5. For the Petit Casino meeting, see Montigny, pp. 61–3; Noguères in C.E., *Témoignages*, Vol. VII, pp. 2239–40; Vincent Auriol, *Hier . . . Demain*, Paris, Charlot, 1945, Vol. I, pp. 104–9.

point. Thus, the last chance of opposition at government level was lost.[1]

There was still the Chamber and Senate where, in addition to the ex-service senators, a new current of opposition was forming. It crystallized around the 'Badie motion', which was named after Vincent Badie, the right-wing radical who drafted it. The motion recognized the urgent need 'to bring about . . . the moral and economic recovery of our unfortunate country . . . to conduct negotiations with a view to a lasting and honourable peace' and to grant Marshal Pétain, 'the perfect embodiment of traditional French virtues in these difficult times', all necessary powers to accomplish these tasks. But it firmly rejected the imputation, contained in the *exposé des motifs* of the government's bill, that the present system was in any way to blame for the catastrophe and opposed the bill itself on the grounds that it 'would inevitably lead to the disappearance of the republican régime'. Drafted soon after the Petit Casino meeting on the 8th, the Badie motion soon attracted the signatures of some twenty-eight senators and deputies from various parties.[2]

At 9.30 a.m. on Tuesday 9 July, Edouard Herriot took the chair for the first formal meeting of the Chamber of Deputies since 16 May. The Chamber's task, like that of the Senate, which met for the first time formally since 21 May the same afternoon, was to debate a simple resolution expressing the need for constitutional reform. This was a necessary preliminary to the meeting of the National Assembly, which was due to take place on the following day, and which would debate the government's bill. Laval did not intend that there should be any discussion of the government's plans at these preliminary meetings. Instead, he suggested that there should be a secret and informal joint meeting of the Chamber and Senate the following morning, when 'the matter will be thrashed out thoroughly'. Anyone who wished to speak, Laval said, could do so then, and he promised to reply to 'all questions and all objections'. The Chamber adopted his proposal by 395 votes to 3 and the Senate by 229 votes to 1, the only dissentient in the upper house being his son-in-law's uncle, the Marquis de Chambrun.[3]

---

[1] Ibid., pp. 116–19 (Auriol misdates the Socialist meeting), 125–6; Léon Blum, *L'Œuvre de Léon Blum, 1940–45*, Paris, Albin Michel, 1955, pp. 75–81; Noguères in C.E., *Témoignages*, Vol. VII, p. 2243; Lebrun, pp. 106–7; Montigny, p. 56.

[2] Vincent Badie in C.E., *Témoignages*, Vol. VIII, pp. 2269–72; Noguères in ibid., Vol. VII, pp. 2240–41; Gaston Manent in ibid., *Rapport*, Vol. II, p. 509.

[3] J.O., Chambre, *Débats*, 9 July 1940; ibid., Sénat, *Débats*, 9 July 1940.

The secret and informal joint session of the Chamber and Senate began at 9.15 a.m. on Wednesday 10 July. It was preceded by one significant change in the situation. As the result of a long discussion with Herriot the night before, Laval had agreed to amend the text of the government's bill to allow for the ratification of the new constitution by the nation instead of by the assemblies which were to be set up under its terms. It is hard to see why Laval agreed to this change unless he hoped to appease the ex-service senators, who had included the same provision in their amendment. Even before the session began, however, Taurines made it clear to Laval that he and his colleagues intended to press for the acceptance of their full text.[1]

Indeed, it was Taurines and one of his colleagues, the war-maimed Maurice Dormann, who opened the debate, the former explaining the background to the senators' amendment and the latter its purpose. While agreeing with the broad outlines of the government's text, Dormann said that the senators' amendment differed from it in that they wanted to preserve the 'republican image' of France which made her beloved throughout the world. To loud applause he went on, 'We wish to preserve that freedom which has been conquered at the price of so much blood and we wish to continue the traditions of our country. We want all our fellow-citizens to understand, to be conscious of, and to see what can be done.' He could not understand why Laval had refused to accept their amendment which, after all, gave him all he wanted, and paraphrasing Kipling, he warned the deputy premier, 'Riding a tiger is not difficult, it's getting off. You are riding the tiger, *M. le vice-président du conseil*, be careful when you dismount.'

Remaining seated in order – so he said – to give the debate 'a more informal character', Laval began his reply by reading out the letter he had extracted from Pétain three days before. Having thus established his credentials, he went on to describe at great length the sad plight of France and the follies that had brought her to it. He described the declaration of war as 'the greatest crime which has been perpetrated in our country for a long time' and he deplored the ideological basis of the conflict. 'I was hurt in my little village in the Auvergne,' he said, 'when, tuning in [my radio] in the evenings, I heard talk of democracy,

---

[1] Herriot in *Procès Pétain*, p. 112, cols. 2–3; Taurines in C.E., *Témoignages*, Vol. VIII, p. 2334; Laval in *Procès Pétain*, p. 189, cols. 1–2. Laval claimed that the change in the text was resented by Weygand.

but little of France.' He launched into yet another attack upon England, giving highly-coloured and inaccurate accounts of the various British naval actions against the French fleet. But France would not declare war on England, he promised. Indeed, she would not declare war on anyone. 'But we shall respond to blows with blows, to the extent of our resources.' He repeated his account of how he had negotiated the Rome agreements in 1935 and how his policy had been sabotaged by the ideological prejudice of the *Front Populaire*. He spoke of the need to revive the old-fashioned virtues of discipline and patriotism – 'it is the excesses of liberty which have led us where we are' – but insisted that this did not mean that the new constitution would be reactionary. He ended where he had begun, by calling the absent figure of Pétain to his support. Alluding to the great impression the Marshal had made upon Goering at Cracow in 1935, he concluded, 'If today we are beaten, the whole world – friend and foe alike – respects this man who embodies the finest hours of our history. We are fortunate to have him, to shelter and to walk behind him in order to try and make the soil of our country safe. This is what I am asking you to do and I am certain that there will not be a single vote lacking for the adoption of the [government's] bill this evening, for you will be voting for France.'

After this rhetorical *tour de force*, the debate degenerated into an argument about the nature of the ratification of the new constitution by the nation. Laval said that the nation would be consulted on the broadest possible basis. Someone asked whether this meant a plebiscite. He replied that it did not, for he had always held that a plebiscite was a Bonapartist device. He refused, however, to amplify what (if anything) he had in mind until Gaston Bergery, who was one of his supporters, pointed out that 'the nation' could be taken to mean the existing Chamber and Senate. Laval at once hastened to make it clear that this was not the government's view. 'Obviously we don't mean the existing assemblies,' he said, 'but a vote by the entire nation.' Quite how 'a vote by the entire nation' differed from a plebiscite, he would not elaborate.

The debate was wound up by Flandin. His was a curious speech which hovered between approbation and condemnation of what the government was trying to do. He refused to accept the belief that parliament alone was to blame for the present catastrophe and, while he agreed that reforms were necessary, he maintained that nothing would be worse than 'a slavish imitation' of Nazi or fascist institutions. At the same time, he reminded his audience that France was still technically at war and that they had 'no right to weaken in any way whatever the position of the government, which, tomorrow, will have to represent France in the peace treaty negotiations'. This entailed complete confidence in the men who were ruling France, a confidence that was justified because of the presence of Marshal Pétain at their head.[1]

When the National Assembly finally met at 2 o'clock that afternoon, it was immediately presented with two important procedural proposals. The first, put forward by Fernand Bouisson, was that the Assembly's standing orders should be modified to enable the government's bill to be voted on before any of the amendments. This would mean that neither the ex-service senators' amendment nor the Badie motion would be debated unless the government's own proposal was defeated first. The second proposal, which was put forward by Emile Mireaux, was that, in view of the special circumstances in which the Assembly was meeting a simple majority of those present should suffice to pass the government's bill instead of the constitutionally required majority of all members entitled to attend. Laval welcomed both these proposals. Indeed, as they would make his own position virtually impregnable, he may well have inspired them himself.

But this does not explain the docility of the Assembly in accepting them. Badie, as we shall see, tried to register his protest, but Taurines and the ex-service senators seem to have capitulated completely. It is true that the former asked to appear before the joint committee to which the government's bill was referred, but, according to the minutes of the meeting, he confined himself to asking the members to 'take note of' his amendment, whereupon it would be withdrawn. He later denied having said anything of the sort, claiming that Laval had tampered with the record, but he gave no indication of what he was really supposed to have said. The one certain fact is that, when it came to the point, only a quarter of the senators who signed the original amendment voted against the government. Perhaps the others, who included both Taurines and Dormann, simply felt that further resistance was futile.

After the joint committee's discussions, the Assembly reconvened

[1] The full stenographic record of the secret joint session of the Chamber and Senate is printed in C.E., *Rapport*, Vol. II, pp. 479–97.

at ten to six. M. Boivin-Champeaux, the *rapporteur* of the committee, recommended adoption of the government's bill, and it was agreed to proceed to a vote immediately. It was at this point that Vincent Badie jumped up, determined to state his case. He pushed his way through a noisy crowd of government supporters and clambered upon the dais to speak. Just as he was about to begin, however, he was grabbed by two or three men – led by Bouisson – who tried to force him off the platform. He managed to fight them off, but it was too late. During the scuffle, Jeanneney had put the government's bill to the vote. It was carried by 569 votes to 80. 'Gentlemen,' said Laval, after the result had been declared, 'in the name of Marshal Pétain, I thank you on behalf of France.' The Third Republic, the longest-lasting régime in France since the Revolution, was dead.[1]

What was the secret of Laval's triumph? In a famous description of the scene, Léon Blum put it down to fear. 'During those two days,' he said, 'I saw men change and become corrupt as if before my eyes, as though they had been plunged into a poisonous bath. The agent was fear: fear of Doriot's gangs in the streets, fear of Weygand's troops at Clermont-Ferrand, and fear of the Germans who were at Moulins.' The revolutionary assemblies must have been like that at times, he went on. He could certainly understand why the frightened majority of the Convention had been nicknamed 'the Marsh'. 'It was indeed a human swamp in which you could see, before your eyes as I've said, all the courage and loyalty which you knew to exist in some men melt away, crumble, and disappear.'[2]

There was undoubtedly an element of truth in Blum's account – we have seen how Laval played upon fears of the Germans and Weygand – but it does not tell the whole story. Similarly, while there is evidence that Laval and his supporters hinted at the possibility of government jobs for the more amenable members of parliament and sanctions for the more recalcitrant,[3] it would be a gross over-simplification to attribute

---

[1] J.O., Assemblée Nationale, *Débats*, 10 July 1940. The minutes of the joint committee's meeting are printed in C.E., *Rapport*, Vol. II, pp. 498–502. The comments of seven members on the minutes' authenticity are in ibid., pp. 502–7. Taurines' explanation is in ibid., *Témoignages*, Vol. VIII, pp. 2357–9. There is no trace of the Badie incident in the *Journal Officiel*, but there is no doubt it took place. Badie's own account is in C.E., *Témoignages*, Vol. VIII, p. 2274. It is supported by Paul Boulet, ibid., Vol. VII, pp. 2218–21; Noguères, ibid., p. 2254; and Manent, ibid., *Rapport*, Vol. II, p. 510.

[2] *Procès Pétain*, pp. 77, col. 3, 78, col. 1.

[3] See Badie's evidence in C.E., *Témoignages*, Vol. VIII, pp. 2272–3.

his success to a mixture of bribery and threats. Laval's greatest ally was, in fact, neither fear nor patronage, but Marshal Pétain. In moments of supreme crisis, the French people, whose customary individualism is legendary, have a capacity for abdicating all responsibility in favour of one man. The parallel in this respect between Marshal Pétain in 1940 and General de Gaulle in 1958 may be unpopular, but it is none the less striking. However critical men like Taurines, Herriot, Flandin, Jeanneney, and the signatories of the Badie motion were of Laval, they had nothing but praise for Pétain. Indeed, like Baudouin and his friends inside the government, they realized that the only way to defeat the deputy premier was to isolate him from the Marshal. Unfortunately, Pétain's letter to Laval of 7 July, which left no doubts as to the identity of views between the two men, rendered this task virtually impossible. In the light of its contents, to vote against Laval was to vote against Pétain, and this was a step which only the most determined were prepared to take.

The remainder of Laval's constitutional revolution was accomplished quickly enough. On 11 July, the cabinet were invited to approve three constitutional acts, which had been drafted by Alibert in close collaboration with Laval. The first appointed Marshal Pétain head of state in place of President Lebrun. The second gave him full executive and legislative powers until the promulgation of the new constitution. Even then, he would be entitled to assume full powers if he judged that the external or internal situation warranted it. The only restriction upon his power, and it was an important one, was that he could not declare war without 'the prior assent of the legislative assemblies'. Laval had promised this concession to the joint committee of the National Assembly, and he kept his word. This provision was to come in useful during subsequent negotiations with the Germans. The third constitutional act declared that the Senate and Chamber would remain in being until the assemblies envisaged in the new constitution were set up, but at the same time it adjourned them both until further notice. Although all three texts were quite new to most members of the cabinet, no objections were raised and they duly appeared in the *Journal Officiel* the following day.[1]

Laval had rather more difficulty with the fourth constitutional act,

[1] Beau de Loménie, p. 410; Baudouin, pp. 242–43; Bouthillier in C.E., *Témoignages*, Vol. VIII, pp. 2539–40; Weygand, p. 303, fn. 1; J.O., *Lois et Décrets*, 12 July 1940.

which concerned the Marshal's successor. As we have seen, he told Baudouin as early as 6 July that he wanted this position for himself. But when Baudouin passed on this information, he noted that the Marshal was 'not very enthusiastic' and, on 12 July, the latter told his foreign minister that he had devised a formula whereby his successor would be chosen by a vote of the cabinet. Baudouin was extremely surprised, therefore, when, later the same evening, Pétain announced that he had changed his mind and that he was appointing Laval his successor after all. When Baudouin asked the deputy premier how he had managed it, Laval would only say that 'he had made his request firmly and that had been enough'. The argument he used seems to have been that a civilian was needed to 'balance the ticket' and, in particular, to allay fears that General Weygand might be the successor, but his case was no doubt strengthened by the genuine sense of gratitude Pétain felt towards him. 'I could have done nothing without Laval,' the Marshal was to tell the head of his civilian secretariat when discussing the constitutional changes some time later. '[He] was extraordinary.'[1]

Constitutional Act No. 4, appointing Laval the Marshal's successor, appeared in the *Journal Officiel* on Saturday 13 July. 'I never expected,' commented the disgruntled Weygand somewhat bitterly, 'that the marriage of a Marshal of France with the Republic would produce Pierre Laval as its offspring.'[2] There were, indeed, some curious features to the new régime. Pétain prefaced his decrees with the royal plural, he enjoyed the powers of an absolute monarch, and now he had appointed a Dauphin. But for the humiliation of their defeat, Frenchmen could have been forgiven for thinking that they had returned to the *Grande Époque*.

---

[1] Baudouin, pp. 238, 244–5; *Procès Laval*, pp. 157–8; Admiral Jean Fernet, *Aux Côtés du Maréchal Pétain*, Paris, Plon, 1953 (hereafter cited as Fernet), pp. 6–7; Henri du Moulin de Labarthète, *Le Temps des Illusions, Souvenirs (Juillet 1940–Avril 1942)*, Geneva, Les Editions du Cheval Ailé, 1946 (hereafter cited as Du Moulin), p. 106.

[2] J.O., *Lois et Décrets*, 13 July 1940; Charles-Roux, p. 164.

7

The Dauphin

July – December 1940

Following the liquidation of the past in the shape of the Third Republic, Laval was free to look forward towards the future in the shape of a European 'new order' based upon Franco-German co-operation. In order to implement his plans, Laval sought first to corner the field of Franco-German relations for himself, even though this meant usurping the powers of the titular foreign minister, Paul Baudouin. As early as 5 July he suggested that Fernand de Brinon, who had performed similar services for him in 1935,[1] should be employed to make contact with the Germans. Although the cabinet rejected the suggestion, this did not prevent Laval from summoning de Brinon to Vichy, where he arrived shortly after the meeting of the National Assembly. Laval told him that 'he would like to enter into contact with the German authorities in order to lay the foundations of a policy which was useful to France', and took him to see Pétain, who also declared his willingness to co-operate with the Germans. At about the same time, Laval asked another journalist, Jean Luchaire, to get in touch with the Germans on his behalf. The man whom both de Brinon and Luchaire were to contact and whom they both knew before the war was Otto Abetz, the newly-appointed representative of the German foreign ministry with the military command in France.[2]

Abetz had had an interesting past. Born in 1903 near Mannheim, he began his career as a secondary school art teacher. Before Hitler came to power he was actively engaged in youth work and, firmly convinced

---

[1] See above pp. 93–4.

[2] Baudouin, p. 236; Fernand de Brinon, *Mémoires*, Paris, L.L.C., 1949 (hereafter cited as de Brinon), p. 20; Jean Luchaire in *Les Procès de Collaboration: Fernand de Brinon, Joseph Darnand, Jean Luchaire*, Paris, Albin Michel, 1948 (hereafter cited as *Procès de Collaboration*), pp. 354–5, 370. In addition to de Brinon and Luchaire, there seems to have been a third intermediary between Laval and Abetz: Jean Fontenoy, another journalist. However, Laval subsequently claimed that it was Abetz who sent Fontenoy to him. See *Laval Parle*, p. 64; de Brinon, p. 20; Luchaire in *Procès de Collaboration*, p. 370.

of the need for Franco-German friendship, worked towards this end by helping to arrange meetings between French and German youth organizations in his native Baden. At one of these meetings he met and fell in love with a French girl, and they were married in 1932. After a brief spell in the Hitler youth Abetz became head of the French section of the *Dienststelle Ribbentrop*, the future German foreign minister's personal research and information bureau. This was in the autumn of 1934, but he did not actually join the Nazi party until 1937. In this capacity he was closely associated with the activities of the *Comité France-Allemagne* and other organizations which sought to improve Franco-German relations. In the summer of 1939, however, he was expelled from France for alleged fifth-column activities. In June 1940 he was asked by Ribbentrop, who was determined that the foreign ministry should play a part in the formulation of occupation policy, to return to France as his personal representative.[1]

Although Laval had not known Abetz before the war, it was typical that he should try and contact him rather than the military authorities. Apart from the personal link through de Brinon and Luchaire, Abetz was a civilian and Laval was never at his ease with soldiers, possibly as a result of his socialist past. In any event, the two men got on well together. Laval described Abetz after the war as being 'more human and also more intelligent than most of the other German leaders who operated in France'. Abetz's tribute to Laval was even more generous. In his memoirs he described him as 'one of the greatest statesmen of our time and certainly its last truly great liberal statesman'. In fact, as Luchaire was to state in 1945, Abetz was 'completely won over by Laval . . . because Laval had given him the impression of being essentially a patriot, and Abetz liked that.'[2]

Nevertheless, the first Laval–Abetz meeting, which took place in Paris on 19 July, was not very fruitful from the French point of view. Laval, according to Abetz, wanted 'to attempt, in his country's interest, to collaborate with the *Reich* government on French soil'. He said that 'Germany could inflict considerable harm upon France and the French people, but she could not possibly destroy them. Every abuse of German power would one day rebound against the Germans themselves,

---

[1] The information on Abetz's early career comes from the first eight chapters of his memoirs: Otto Abetz, *Das Öffene Problem: ein Rückblick auf zwei Jahrzehnte deutscher Frankreichpolitik*, Cologne, Greven Verlag, 1951 (hereafter cited as Abetz).

[2] Jaffré, p. 133; Abetz, p. 146; Luchaire in *Procès de Collaboration*, p. 373.

8*

for the works of mankind were only transitory.' He did not believe that the importance of 'this historical moment' was fully appreciated in France any more than it was in Germany; but, he asked, 'was an intransigent attitude in Germany's interest now that he had offered the *Reich* government unreserved collaboration for the benefit of Europe?' Abetz was sympathetic, but not very forthcoming. He stressed the weakness of his own position and even asked Laval to treat his visit as unofficial and to refrain from issuing any communiqué to the press. While he assured the Frenchman that he could count upon his support, he warned him that 'it seemed virtually impossible to make up the ground that had been lost in the sphere of Franco-German understanding since the war'.[1]

Indeed, about the only positive result of the Laval–Abetz meeting was the latter's promotion to the rank of ambassador, 'solely responsible for dealing with all political questions in occupied and unoccupied France'. Laval's opponents in the French government indignantly reflected that it was probably due to his choice of Abetz as interlocutor that the promotion was made.[2]

Abetz's pessimism about the future of Franco-German relations was as justified as Laval's optimism was not. If the terms of both the German and Italian armistice agreements had been relatively moderate, this was due partly to the Axis powers' desire to prevent the French government from leaving France, and, even more, to prevent the French fleet from going over to the British. 'The fact that even though there was a French sham government in London [i.e. de Gaulle's], there was on French territory a government under Pétain, to which the French colonies had also adhered, was doubtless a great advantage for Italy and Germany,' Hitler told Ciano in Berlin on 7 July. But there was no mistaking his real feelings. 'Basically,' he continued, 'Italy and Germany should realize . . . that France was now playing the part of an unfortunate and innocent victim of British wiles. Actually, however, that was not the truth of the matter. If France were now in a position to do so, she would immediately attack Germany and Italy and destroy these countries. . . . Just as there was an eternal England with a definite political orientation, there was also an eternal

---

[1] Abetz, pp. 149–50; *Laval Parle*, p. 64.

[2] Ribbentrop to Keitel, 3 August 1940, D.G.F.P., Series D, Vol. X, No. 282; Baudouin, p. 279; Bouthillier, Vol. I, pp. 171, 174.

France with an equally definite anti-Axis attitude.' He was determined, adds Ciano's record of the conversation, that 'France must pay, and pay dearly, for her responsibilities'.[1]

There was no need, however, to be an eavesdropper at top-level conferences to discover the real German attitude towards France. The French were remarkably well-informed of Hitler's intentions and what they did not know they could deduce from German actions. As far as France's territorial integrity was concerned, Alsace and Lorraine were treated as part of Germany from the very beginning of the occupation, the two *départements* of the Nord and Pas-de-Calais were attached to the German military administration in Belgium instead of to that in France, and a large area in the north and east of the country was declared a 'prohibited zone' to which French refugees were forbidden to return and in which German farmers were settled. This formed part of a Wagnerian concept of Hitler's to extend Germany's frontier westwards in order to take in much of what had been the kingdom of Lothair after the partition of Charlemagne's empire in the year 1843! As for the French empire, Ribbentrop told Ciano in June that Germany intended to claim 'all her [former] colonies', such as Togo and the Cameroons, together with certain other undefined areas in French West Africa. In addition, he declared, 'it is Hitler's plan to create a free Jewish state in Madagascar, to which the several million Jews who inhabited the territory of the old Reich as well as the recently conquered areas could be compulsorily sent.' On top of this, of course, were Italy's own claims, which had been temporarily shelved at the time of the armistice. These included Nice, Corsica, Tunisia, Algeria, and French Somaliland.[2]

In the economic sphere, one of the most pressing problems was that

[1] Schmidt memorandum, 8 July 1940, D.G.F.P., Series D, Vol. X, No. 129; Ciano memorandum, 7 July 1940, in Galeazzo Ciano, *L'Europa verso la Catastrofe*, Milan, Mondadori, 1948 (hereafter cited as Ciano, *L'Europa*), pp. 566–72.

[2] On the situation in Alsace-Lorraine, see the memorandum prepared for the French delegation to the armistice commission, dated 25 November 1940, in *La Délégation Française*, Vol. III, pp. 90–103. For the Nord and Pas-de-Calais, see Huntziger's instructions for the French delegation, dated 16 October 1940, ibid., Vol. II, pp. 167, 169. For the 'prohibited zone' and Hitler's plans, see the following: Globke affidavit, 14 January 1947, ND NG–3540; Klas affidavit, 18 November 1947, ibid., NG–3572; Himmler to Lammers, 17 July 1940, ibid., NG–3455. For German colonial ambitions and Italian territorial claims, see Ciano memorandum, 19 June 1940, in Ciano, *L'Europa*, pp. 562–5; Roatta memorandum, 19 June 1940, in Francesco Rossi, *Mussolini e lo Stato Maggiore: Avvenimenti del 1940*, Rome, Regionale, 1951, pp. 173–4. For French knowledge of Axis aims, see Ernest Lagarde in *Procès Pétain*, p. 302, col. 1; Charles-Roux, pp. 186–96.

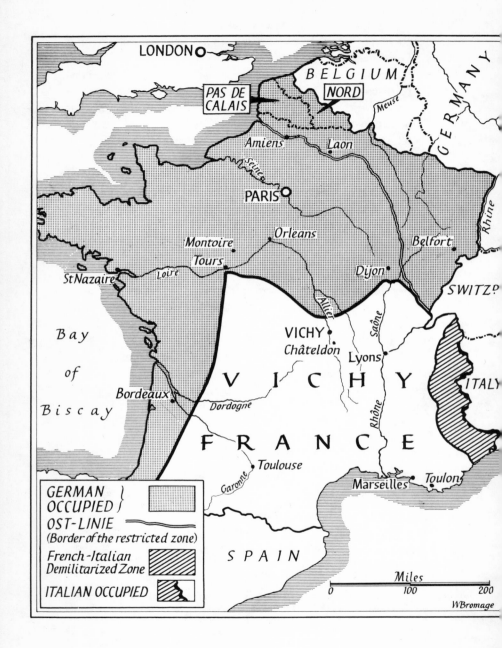

LONDON○

BELGIUM

PAS DE CALAIS

NORD

GERMANY

Meuse

Amiens   Laon

Seine

PARIS ○

Orleans   Belfort

Montoire
Tours

St Nazaire   Loire   Dijon

Allier   SWITZ.ᴰ

Bay   VICHY   Rhine
        Châteldon   Saône
of   Lyons
        ITALY
Biscay   Bordeaux
        Dordogne   Rhône

F R A N C E

Toulouse

Garonne   Marseilles   Toulon

GERMAN
OCCUPIED
OST-LINIE
(Border of the restricted zone)
French-Italian
Demilitarized Zone
ITALIAN OCCUPIED

S P A I N

Miles
0   100   200

WBromage

of the demarcation line between the occupied and unoccupied zones. Ostensibly little more than an administrative boundary, the Germans had in fact turned it into a kind of iron curtain across which the passage of persons and goods was virtually impossible. 'We had not envisaged such a rigorous demarcation line,' Baudouin noted in his diary on 13 July, and he reflected that, if it remained closed to traffic, the economic recovery of the country would be impossible and the nazification of the unoccupied zone could proceed unhindered. The Germans, of course, used the situation as a means of exerting pressure upon the French. 'That line is a bit we have put in the horse's mouth,' the chairman of the German delegation to the Franco-German armistice commission, General von Stülpnagel, told his French opposite number, General Huntziger. 'If France rears, we will tighten the curb. We will loosen it to the extent that France is amenable.' Von Stülpnagel's civilian colleague, Hans Hemmen, who was chairman of the economic committee of the armistice commission, was equally frank in a report to his superiors. Reviewing the first six months of his committee's activities, he wrote that 'the German delegation has realized that here [i.e. in the matter of the demarcation line] is the point of departure for the pursuit of German aims over and above the rights which accrue to us from the armistice, in order to obtain influence upon the whole of France's financial and economic life, especially in the unoccupied zone, in the direction of an alignment upon German interests'.[1]

Then there was the question of occupation costs. Under article 18 of the armistice agreement, France had contracted to pay the maintenance costs of the German occupation forces. When the Germans presented the bill on 8 August, however, the French found that they were expected to pay a fantastically inflated sum (20 million reichsmarks a day) at a fantastically inflated rate of exchange (20 francs to the reichsmark). The whole operation, in fact, was nothing more than legalized extortion. Repeated protests proved of no avail, however, and on 26 August the French were compelled to begin payments, backdated to 25 June.[2]

[1] Baudouin, pp. 245–6; Welck to Foreign Ministry, 17 July 1940, D.G.F.P., Series D, Vol. X, No. 184; Hemmen report, 15 January 1941, ND 1986–PS.
[2] For the notes on occupation costs exchanged between Hemmen and General Huntziger between 8 and 26 August 1940 and the record of a conversation between them on the 21st, see La Délégation Française, Vol. I, pp. 158–74. See also Yves Bouthillier, Le Drame de Vichy, Volume II, Les Finances sous la Contrainte, Paris, Plon, 1951 (hereafter cited as Bouthillier, Vol. II), pp. 36–48.

Indeed, the only limitations upon German demands were imposed by factors beyond French control, such as the threat of British counter-measures or the strength of Germany's own forces. Thus, when Hitler dropped his plan to establish German air bases in Morocco, which was presented to the French virtually in the form of an ultimatum on 15 July, this was not due to the French government's objections, but to his fear that any attempt to take over French territory in Africa might lead to a British intervention which he would be powerless to prevent.[1] Similarly, after discussing the French attitude to some German demands with von Stülpnagel, the chief-of-staff of the German army, General Franz Halder, noted in his diary on 22 August 1940, '. . . It is possible that military measures will have to be taken if France creates difficulties. But we are not ready for this in our present state of organization.'[2]

This, then, was the background against which Laval attempted to negotiate his Franco-German *rapprochement*. In the circumstances, it was small wonder that he achieved so little. Indeed, about the only success he managed to bring back from three visits to Paris during July and August was an agreement making postal traffic across the demarcation line more easy.[3] There was a similar lack of progress in the negotiations which took place at the level of the Franco-German armistice commission. Faced with this almost complete deadlock, Pétain decided to try a personal initiative and appeal to Hitler direct. He did so through a First World War air ace and personal friend, Colonel Fonck. The latter knew Goering well and, on 15 September, he was instructed by a coded message to approach the commander-in-chief of the *Luftwaffe* in order to try and arrange a meeting between Hitler and Pétain. Whether Fonck did in fact approach Goering is not

[1] For the German request for air bases in Morocco, see Welck to Foreign Ministry, 15 July 1940, D.G.F.P., Series D, Vol. X, No. 169; von Stülpnagel to Huntziger, 15 July 1940, *La Délégation Française*, Vol. I, pp. 463-4. For the French government's deliberations and refusal, see Baudouin, pp. 251-5; Bouthillier, Vol. I, pp. 167-8, 287-91 (texts of two draft replies to the German request); Weygand, pp. 320-21; Charles-Roux, pp. 172-5; Guérard, p. 31. For Hitler's change of mind, see the draft entry, dated 12 August 1940, in the *Kriegstagebuch des Oberkommandos der Wehrmacht* (*Wehrmachtführungsstab*). The *Kriegstagebuch* for this period is filmed on GFM/9936, but as, at the time of writing, it was due to be published in Germany, it will be cited hereafter as OKW/KTB, followed by the date, instead of by serial and frame number(s).

[2] Generaloberst Franz Halder, *Kriegstagebuch*, Volume II, Stuttgart, W. Kohlhammer Verlag, 1963 (hereafter cited as Halder), p. 73.

[3] Abetz to von Stülpnagel, 29 August 1940, *La Délégation Française*, Vol. I, p. 190, fn. 1.

known, but he certainly approached Abetz. The German ambassador told Hasso von Etzdorf, the foreign ministry representative with the army, that 'Fonck . . . asked in Marshal Pétain's name whether there was a possibility of Pétain's being received by Hitler. I replied that, in the light of the present state of the war, this did not seem likely, but that I would forward the matter to Berlin.' Although Abetz may have told Laval of Fonck's request, it was originally intended that neither he nor the rest of the cabinet should know anything about it.[1]

This secretiveness on the part of Pétain raises the whole question of his attitude towards Laval's German policy. According to Robert Aron, the Marshal opposed both Laval's policy of collaboration with Germany and Weygand's policy of 'open resistance', relying instead upon a policy of *attentisme*. Aron sees proof of this, not only in the Fonck mission, but also in two important governmental changes which took place in September 1940: the cabinet reshuffle of 6 September and the constitutional act of 24 September modifying the procedure for choosing the Marshal's successor. These are interpreted by Aron as successful attempts to reduce the influence of both Laval and Weygand.[2]

Even ignoring the somewhat dubious proposition that Weygand's policy was one of 'open resistance', Aron's thesis seems to be based on the account in Bouthillier's memoirs, in which the finance minister wrote that Abetz did not like the political complexion of the original Vichy government and sought, through Laval and his supporters, to make it more pro-German. 'There was only one way to ward off the evil blow which was being prepared,' wrote Bouthillier. 'This was to forestall it by reshaping the government without including a single minister who could be considered pro-German . . . or one of M. Laval's men.' The decision was pressed upon Pétain by 'two or three ministers' – subsequently identified as Alibert, Baudouin, and Bouthillier himself – on 4 September. The list of members of the new cabinet was drawn up on the 5th and published on the 6th. The elimination of General Weygand, who was sent as Pétain's special representative to French Africa, accords ill with Bouthillier's thesis and is unconvincingly explained away as the result of an ultimatum from Laval.[3]

---

[1] Fernet, pp. 34–5, 37; Abetz to von Etzdorf, 18 September 1940, GFM/364/206021–30 (the quotation is from frame 206022).
[2] Aron, pp. 282–3.
[3] Bouthillier, Vol. I, pp. 176–80; Bouthillier in C.E., *Témoignages*, Vol. VIII, pp. 2543–6.

One would hardly gather from Baudouin's account that he was involved in any plot, with Bouthillier or anyone else. On 26 August Pétain told him that 'he has had enough of parliamentarians and . . . he intends to get rid of them soon'. On 4 September he told Baudouin and Bouthillier that, before the week was out, he intended to reshape his government, excluding all members of parliament. The move was designed 'to permit more vigorous governmental action'. The following day Weygand told Baudouin that he too had been asked to leave the government to counterbalance the exclusion of the members of parliament.[1]

To judge from Baudouin's version, therefore, the initiative for the cabinet changes came from the Marshal himself and was inspired solely by a desire to get rid of ministers who had been members of parliament. This interpretation is confirmed by Pétain's remark to the head of his civilian secretariat on 6 September that 'the parliamentarians annoy me. . . . They make me waste valuable time and, what's more, they are unpopular. They are a heavy burden which I must get rid of.'[2]

This is not to say that Laval was unaffected by the ministerial changes. He had tried to use them to obtain a portfolio for himself and to ensure that the ministry of the interior was directly dependent upon him as deputy premier. He succeeded in his first aim, becoming minister of information, but failed in the second. Marcel Peyrouton, the new minister of the interior, was appointed to the government as a full minister in his own right. Laval also failed in his attempt to keep the former minister of the interior, his friend Adrien Marquet, in the government. This failure led to a bitter exchange between the two men, in which Marquet unjustly accused Laval of stabbing him in the back.[3] There is no evidence, however, to support the claim that any of these changes was inspired wholly or partly by Laval's foreign policy.

There is rather more substance in the claim that Pétain was trying to renege his commitment that Laval should be his successor. As early

---

[1] Baudouin, pp. 316, 332–44.

[2] Du Moulin, p. 35.

[3] Baudouin, pp. 333–5; Du Moulin, p. 37; Marcel Peyrouton, *Du Service Public à la Prison Commune*, Paris, Plon, 1950 (hereafter cited as Peyrouton), p. 105. Marquet had rather a nerve in accusing Laval of stabbing him in the back. He had caused some unflattering comments upon Laval to be conveyed to the Paris office of Heydrich's *Sicherheitsdienst* (the S.S. intelligence agency). See Enclosure, Heydrich to Ribbentrop, 27 July 1940, D.G.F.P., Series D, Vol. X, No. 247.

as 18 July he had told Baudouin he was worried by the deputy premier's pro-German attitude. 'Assuming the Germans give me enough
time,' he said, 'I must go back on the arrangement I've made to make
him my successor.' Nothing more was heard of this, however, until 9
September when Pétain's friend and adviser, Admiral Fernet, told
Baudouin and Bouthillier that the Marshal was planning to repeal the
fourth constitutional act and throw the choice of a successor into the
hands of the cabinet. Pétain discussed this suggestion with Laval himself, who not surprisingly hotly opposed it. 'Nevertheless, I shall continue along this path,' Pétain later told Baudouin and Bouthillier. 'It is
the beginning of the offensive.'[1]

Robert Aron is quite wrong, however, in implying that the constitutional act of 24 September 1940 marked an important stage in this
'offensive'. Thus, in stating that, in the event of Laval's being prevented from assuming the succession, the cabinet would elect a new
successor, the act did not 'implicitly limit Laval's prerogatives by
admitting that someone apart from himself could be "dauphin".'[2]
Exactly the same provision was contained in the original constitutional
act of 12 July 1940. The only difference between the two texts was that
the July act spoke of seven votes being needed to elect a successor,
whereas the September act did not mention a number, referring only
to a majority of votes. The difference was due quite simply to the fact
that the reshuffle of 6 September had altered the size of the cabinet.
There was no change in Laval's position as 'dauphin'.[3] Any plans that
Pétain had entertained about replacing him had evidently been
abandoned.

It is clear from Baudouin's diary that such plans existed, but were
they due to disagreements over foreign policy? Pétain's remark of
18 July would suggest that they were, but in the September discussions
foreign policy was not mentioned. Du Moulin de Labarthète suggested
that Pétain disliked Laval for the same reasons as he disliked other
parliamentarians. When he asked the Marshal on 6 September whether
Laval was going to be excluded from the government along with the
rest, he was told, 'No, it's different with Laval. I'm keeping him, for the
time being at any rate. He's no better than the others, but he's done me

---

[1] Baudouin, pp. 255, 339–40.
[2] Aron, p. 283.
[3] Compare the two texts in J.O., *Lois et Decrets*, 12 July 1940; 25 September 1940.

too many favours.'[1] It was thus partly out of a sense of obligation that Laval's position was preserved. But there was far more to it than this. In addition to services rendered in the past, Pétain also hoped that they would be rendered in the future, and nowhere more than in the field of Franco-German relations. Far from Laval's German policy being a possible cause of his demotion or dismissal, it may have been the reason for his continued political survival. 'I remain convinced,' wrote Jacques Guérard, the head of Baudouin's secretariat, 'that during the summer of 1940, Pétain . . . was Laval's most reliable and practically his sole support, and that it was the Franco-German negotiations . . . which protected Laval from an eviction which was on the cards from July onwards, and won him a respite until December.'[2]

The Fonck mission, then, should be seen more as an attempt to open a third channel of communication to the Germans – in addition to Laval and the armistice commission – then as an effort to implement a different policy. The need for secrecy is easily explained by the fear of offending Laval, who would have resented any attempt to by-pass him, and also by the need to preserve the Marshal's prestige in the event of a rebuff. As for the ministerial reshuffle of 6 September, with its anti-parliamentary overtones, this fits much more into the framework of the Marshal's 'National Revolution' – in which Laval displayed next to no interest – than into any designs in the field of foreign policy.[3]

There was no immediate reaction to the Fonck mission from the German side, and Franco-German relations might have continued along their unsatisfactory course had it not been for two developments which were largely beyond the control of the Vichy government: namely, the pro-Gaullist revolts in the French colonies, and the failure to bring Spain into the war on the side of the Axis.

General de Gaulle's escape to London on 17 June and his formation, with British backing, of the 'Free French' organization provided a focal point around which those Frenchmen who wished to continue the fight against Germany could gather. This desire for continued resistance was particularly strong in some parts of the Empire, where the administration and armed forces felt they had been betrayed by the metro-

---

[1] Du Moulin, p. 36.
[2] Guérard, p. 43.
[3] For the 'National Revolution', see Aron, pp. 196–251.

politan government. Chad was the first French colony in Africa to go over to the Free French, on 26 August 1940, and it was quickly followed by French Equatorial Africa and the Cameroons. In a memorandum of 31 August, which was not intended for the Germans but which was obtained by members of Heydrich's *Sicherheitsdienst*, General Huntziger described the consequences of the dissidence movements. 'At the present time,' he wrote, 'the French empire finds itself . . . threatened by disintegration of a more or less extensive nature. From now on, this situation presents an immediate danger, not only to French interests, but even to those of Germany and Italy. The seizure of French Equatorial Africa by England involves the risk of strengthening the economic potential of that power while, at the same time, giving her important strategic positions. . . . It goes without saying that the extension of the rebellion, if it reached French West Africa and the French territories bordering the Mediterranean, would increase the above-mentioned danger to a very considerable degree. . . . In any event, France, thereby reduced in her colonial power, would only appear as a much enfeebled element of co-operation in the continental European bloc in the future.'[1]

Huntziger's last point was not lost upon Laval. In November, he told an expert in colonial affairs, 'I don't want all our colonies to quit like that. What would I have left to negotiate with? As far as I'm concerned, our colonies are a means of pressure, an instrument. As long as they are there, I can talk with the Germans. That's because they are scared of seeing them go over to the other side. I use them to arrange things. If they disappear, what will they do with France?'[2] If the fleet was one of defeated France's few remaining assets, her colonies were undoubtedly another.

Laval was in Paris when the first African colonies joined de Gaulle, and it is in this context that we must interpret Baudouin's startling assertion that, during his visit, the deputy premier offered Field-Marshal von Brauchitsch, the commander-in-chief of the German army, France's full participation in the war against England. 'As we were leaving the cabinet meeting,' Baudouin noted in his diary on 30 August, 'Laval calmly told me . . . that he had offered the field-marshal France's entry into the war against England. Von Brauchitsch

---

[1] Huntziger memorandum, 31 August 1940, GFM/473/228858–60.
[2] Raoul Monmarson in *La Vie de la France*, Vol. III, p. 1234.

greeted this offer with contempt [and replied], "We don't need your help, which would be practically nil in any case." ' De Brinon, who was present at the meeting with von Brauchitsch, presents it in a rather different and much more plausible light. '. . . The first African rebellions were discussed,' de Brinon wrote later, '. . . and Laval asked for the military means to combat them. Brauchitsch replied coldly that he had no power to discuss political questions and that he would refer them to Hitler, upon whom the decision depended after examination.'[1]

In other words, according to de Brinon's account, Laval was merely trying to win concessions under the armistice agreement so that France could defend her colonies against subversion. This was precisely what General Huntziger was trying to do at the same time on the armistice commission. As he had written, 'Bearing in mind the gravity of the situation, it is not only opportune to maintain in the French colonies the forces at present stationed there and to continue to defer the implementation of the clauses of the armistice agreement relating to the disarmament of the air force and the fleet, but even to make provision for additional exemptions in the event of the situation worsening.' Huntziger also made much of the fact that, whereas Anglo-Gaullist propaganda had promised that the dissident colonies would remain French after the war, the Germans had given no similar guarantee in respect of the French empire. He repeated this point in a note which he handed to the German delegation on 31 August and in a conversation he had on the same day with one of its members, General Mieth.[2] As we shall see, this was a theme upon which Laval also placed considerable emphasis.

As the situation in Africa worsened, so the French became more insistent. A most important conversation took place on 21 September between General von Stülpnagel and General Doyen, who had replaced Huntziger as chairman of the French delegation to the armistice commission after the latter had been appointed war minister in the cabinet changes of 6 September. 'My government,' he said, 'has instructed me to inform you that it has decided to defend its colonies and its communications with them energetically, and to ask you to provide it with

[1] Baudouin, p. 325; de Brinon, p. 24.
[2] Huntziger memorandum, 31 August 1940, loc. cit.; Undated von Rintelen memorandum, GFM/121/120011-12. Neither Huntziger's memorandum of 31 August, his note to the German delegation, nor a record of his conversation with General Mieth is published in *La Délégation Française*.

the necessary means to confront the new situation.' If the Germans agreed to this, Doyen went on, 'our action will assume, in the eyes of French and foreign opinion, the character of real collaboration with you, with all the risks that it involves for us. If I add to this collaboration that which is requested of us by your sub-committee on war industries – namely, the participation of our industry in the free zone in the manufacture of war material for Germany – the collaboration between France and Germany will assume a much more extensive character.' This would involve 'a serious political problem' for France, both in respect of possible British reactions and of French public opinion. The government must be able to tell the latter that 'if we are giving our unreserved collaboration in the industrial field and in the defence of our colonies, we have obtained some compensations from Germany. For example, if our attitude results in hostilities with England, it is quite certain that the French people would not understand having to shed their blood to defend their colonies if they were not sure of keeping them.' What, in fact, was required was 'a political compensation in a form to be determined . . . in order that the collaboration provided by us will result in an improvement of the atmosphere between the two countries, make relations with the occupation authorities more easy and, I may add, permit our government to enter upon this road without serious repercussions for our country resulting from it.' Von Stülpnagel replied that Doyen's statements raised 'vast political questions and . . . problems of the highest importance', which he was unable to answer himself but which he would refer to his superiors in Berlin. He later told General Halder that he saw Doyen's remarks as 'clear allusions to the desire for a Franco-German alliance'.[1]

Hitler was certainly not ready for such a step at this stage. His military advisers had warned him of the dangers inherent in the African situation and he was prepared to grant the French limited concessions to meet them.[2] But he still did not trust the French and would have

[1] Unsigned memorandum, 23 September 1940, *La Délégation Française*, Vol. I, pp. 326–34; Halder, p. 109.

[2] For the views of Hitler's military advisers, see OKW/KTB, 2 September 1940; Woermann memorandum, 5 September 1940, D.G.F.P., Series D, Vol. XI, No. 20; Führer naval conference of 6 September 1940, published in *Brassey's Naval Annual 1948*, London, William Clowes & Sons Ltd., 1948 (hereafter cited as Führer Naval Conferences), p. 135. For Hitler's concessions, see Brinkmann to Attaché Group of Army General Staff, 8 September 1940, D.G.F.P., Series D, Vol. XI, No. 33; Von Stülpnagel to Huntziger, 11 September 1940, *La Délégation Française*, Vol. I, pp. 261–2.

preferred help from another quarter. Nowhere is this feeling expressed more clearly than in a letter he wrote to Mussolini on 17 September. 'France as such is finished,' he said. 'There is still danger of a secession movement in her northern colonies. There is no assurance that such secession might not even occur in secret agreement with the French government. If, however – whether with or without the knowledge or desire of the Vichy government – North Africa should join up with the British, this might give new impetus to the British cause, at least for a certain period. But as soon as there is a reliable bridge to North Africa via Spain I would no longer consider this danger to be very great. For Spain, too, a clear decision in this direction means increased security.'[1]

Spain had already offered to enter the war on 19 June 1940, when her rulers clearly thought that it was as good as over anyway, in exchange for large tracts of French territory. The Germans, who naturally shared the common belief in their imminent victory, saw no need to share it with the Spaniards and their reply to the Spanish offer was distinctly cool. By the beginning of August, however, their attitude had changed and Ribbentrop was telling the German ambassador in Spain that 'what we want to achieve now is Spain's early entry into the war'. But in the meantime, the Spanish government had lost a little of its own initial enthusiasm, a process which continued to develop as the long-expected German invasion of England failed to take place. By the middle of September the negotiations between Germany and Spain were virtually deadlocked, with both sides making unacceptable demands upon the other.[2]

It was precisely at the moment when Hitler and Ribbentrop were grappling with General Franco's special envoy, Serrano Suñer, that the decisive event which opened the way to a breakthrough in Franco-German relations took place. This was the Free French attack upon

[1] Hitler to Mussolini, 17 September 1940, D.G.F.P., Series D, Vol. XI, No. 68. The Italians, fearful of any repercussions Franco-German collaboration might have upon their position as Germany's senior partner, were even more awkward than the Germans about granting concessions to the French. See, for example, the unsigned memorandum of the von Stülpnagel–Huntziger conversation of 12 September 1940, *La Délégation Française*, Vol. I, pp. 273–84.

[2] Stohrer to Foreign Ministry, 19 June 1940, D.G.F.P., Series D, Vol. IX, No. 488; Weiszäcker memorandum, 25 June 1940, ibid., Vol. X, No. 15; Ribbentrop to Stohrer, 2 August 1940, ibid., No. 274. The question of Spain's entry into the war in 1940 is fully dealt with in Donald S. Detwiler, *Hitler, Franco and Gibraltar*, Wiesbaden, Franz Steiner Verlag GmbH, 1962 (hereafter cited as Detwiler).

the French West African port of Dakar. On the morning of 23 September 1940, an Anglo-Free French naval squadron appeared off Dakar. General de Gaulle himself was present in his flagship, the *Westerland*. Envoys were despatched to try and persuade the governor to throw in his lot with the Free French, but they were either interned or fired upon and forced to withdraw. The Vichy shore batteries and ships in the harbour opened fire on the Anglo-Free French squadron and the latter replied in kind. Attempts to land a small invading force were repulsed. The following day the British commander, Admiral Cunningham, issued an ultimatum to the effect that, if Dakar did not surrender, its fortifications would be razed to the ground and the town occupied. Governor Boisson replied defiantly, 'France has entrusted Dakar to me; I shall defend Dakar to the end.' Fighting resumed, ceased in the evening, and resumed again the following morning, after which the Anglo-Free French squadron, which had suffered considerable damage, withdrew on orders from London.[1]

The reaction in Vichy to events in Dakar was swift. It was decided to try and use the crisis to win further military concessions from the Germans and to obtain a guarantee that France's West African colonies would not be occupied by the Germans or Italians, either then or in any peace settlement. Laval, who was planning to go to Paris, anyway, was charged with conducting these negotiations. At the same time, Baudouin, who claimed that he feared the consequences of another Laval–von Brauchitsch meeting, suggested that General Huntziger should accompany Laval and that he rather than the deputy premier should talk to the German army commander. This suggestion was accepted, although in the event, the consequences of the Huntziger–von Brauchitsch meeting were very different from those Baudouin claimed he intended. It was also agreed that French aircraft based in Algeria should carry out a reprisal raid upon Gibraltar.[2]

Laval set out for Paris on the morning of 24 September and spoke

[1] There are numerous accounts of the Dakar expedition. On the Anglo-Free French side, see in particular Churchill, pp. 419–37; de Gaulle, Vol. I, pp. 95–111. On the Vichy side, see the report dated 7 October 1940 by Rear-Admiral Landriau, the commander of the defending naval forces, in Kammerer, *Flotte Française*, pp. 517–23; the various documents printed in *La Délégation Française*, Vol. I, pp. 384–95. The French government had got wind of a possible Gaullist attack on Dakar and had obtained authorization from the Germans and Italians to send naval reinforcements. Their arrival undoubtedly contributed to the Anglo-Free French defeat. See Bouthillier, Vol. I, pp. 162–3.

[2] Baudouin, pp. 355–7.

with Abetz the same evening. Apart from a gratuitous aside to the effect that 'he wished and hoped that France could contribute her modest share to the final overthrow of England' by defending Dakar, he stuck to his instructions, calling for 'further reinforcement of the French naval and air forces' and enquiring 'whether a German declaration would be possible to the effect that the peace treaty would leave France's West African colonial possessions untouched'.[1]

General Huntziger was due to leave Vichy the following day and Laval asked Abetz to arrange for him to see von Brauchitsch. The field-marshal agreed to see Huntziger on 26 September, but insisted that Laval should not be present. He had obviously taken as much of a dislike to Laval as the latter had to him.[2]

The Huntziger–von Brauchitsch conversation, in fact, created much more of an impression with the Germans than that between Laval and Abetz. In the first place, it covered more ground. Huntziger dealt with economic questions, such as the demarcation line and industrial production, as well as with the situation in the colonies. Even here, he did not confine himself to Dakar, but ranged across the whole field of North Africa, Syria, and Indochina. His main theme, however, was stated in his opening remarks. 'He stressed the fact,' runs the German record, 'that the French government was entirely serious in its fight against English encroachments, and against the former French general, M. de Gaulle, and he wished to emphasize this particularly in view of the fact that in Germany and Italy there had been doubts as to the loyalty of the French government. On the other hand, he did not want to conceal the fact that it was not easy for the French government to convince the French who were fighting down there of the necessity and usefulness of this fight. English propaganda, which made use of the argument that the French were defending their colonies only in the end to lose them to Germany or Italy anyway, was very effective and difficult to refute. France had a dark and uncertain future ahead of her. One might give her a gleam of hope and thus enable the French government to combat English propaganda and the doubts of the French effectively. It was the hard fact, however, that though France had concluded an armistice agreement with Germany she was actually fighting,

---

[1] Abetz to Foreign Ministry, 25 September 1940, D.G.F.P., Series D, Vol XI, No. 102.

[2] Mittelsten-Scheid memorandum, 24 September 1940, together with von Etzdorf's marginal comments of the 25th, GFM/364/206031-2. For Laval's attitude towards von Brauchitsch, see Paul Luquet in *La Vie de la France*, Vol. III, p. 1199.

and indeed fighting with Germany against England. This fact had to be taken into consideration.'[1]

Von Brauchitsch did not adopt any positive attitude towards Huntziger's statements, merely saying that 'he would transmit the various points and questions, in so far as it appeared to him proper, to the competent authorities,' and both the war minister and Laval returned to Vichy with the feeling that they had accomplished very little. But already Hitler's attitude was changing. On 25 September General Jodl, the head of the *Wehrmacht* operations staff, told one of his colleagues, General Warlimont, that 'while the Führer on the occasion of releasing French forces for defence against English attacks on Dakar followed the advice of the Reich foreign minister and excluded the French naval forces stationed at Toulon, thereby again expressing his distrust of French intentions, it nevertheless appears that a change is taking place in his views.' Jodl realized that Franco-German collaboration would raise difficulties in respect of Italian and Spanish claims on French colonies, but felt that there were countervailing advantages. 'What seemed of importance to him,' he concluded, 'is . . . the influencing of the Führer further in this direction.'[2]

Grand-Admiral Raeder, the commander-in-chief of the German navy, made similar points in a conference with Hitler on the following day. The question of North-West Africa was 'of decisive importance', he maintained. 'All indications are that Britain with the help of Gaullist France, and possibly also of the U.S.A., wants to make this region a centre of resistance and to set up air bases for attack against Italy.' 'In general,' he concluded, 'it appears important to co-operate with France in order to protect North-West Africa.' Hitler agreed with 'the general trend of [Raeder's] thought'. After completing the proposed alliance with Japan, he intended to confer with Mussolini 'and possibly also with France. He will have to decide whether co-operation with France or with Spain is more profitable; probably with France, since Spain demands a great deal (French Morocco) but offers little. France must guarantee beforehand to fulfil certain German and Italian demands; and agreement could then be reached regarding the African colonies.' The record of the conference noted that Hitler was 'obviously hesitant'

[1] Unsigned memorandum, 1 October 1940, D.G.F.P., Series D, Vol. XI, No. 112.
[2] Ibid.; Baudouin, pp. 362–3; OKW/KTB, 25 September 1940, printed in D.G.F.P., Series D, Vol. XI, pp. 181–2.

about allowing the French to use additional ships from Toulon. 'He feels himself bound by previous decisions. He wishes to discuss this matter with the Duce before deciding.'[1]

The meeting with Mussolini took place at the Brenner on 4 October. After assuring the Duce that 'Germany would never conclude peace with France without satisfaction of the Italian claims', Hitler went on to discuss the question of Spanish entry into the war and the possible consequences of her territorial demands upon France, which included Morocco and Oran. He feared that 'a pledge of territorial concessions of this kind to Spain might result in two reactions: first, British occupation of Spanish bases in the Canaries, and secondly, the adhesion of the French empire in North Africa to de Gaulle. This would be serious and would involve the Axis in extending its own operational front.' Spanish claims could only be entertained when it was absolutely certain that British landings in Africa were impossible – 'i.e. only when England was entirely beaten or when bases for dive bombers were assured in a circumference of 350 kilometres from the landing points of the English.'

'In these circumstances,' he continued, 'the question arose whether it was not possible to bring France and Spain to a common line and in this way bring about a continental coalition against England. The French knew that they had to cede some territory. The Italian claims had already been communicated to them before the war. If it were now made clear to them that they could compensate themselves with English Nigeria for a limited cession of Moroccan territory, then it might perhaps not be impossible to move them to accept modest Spanish claims. . . . In these circumstances the French would after all still retain the main parts of their colonial empire, for Germany intended to ask only to round off her territory in central Africa but nothing more.' Referring to Huntziger's conversation with von Brauchitsch Hitler 'stressed in particular the wish expressed by Huntziger that France recognized her defeat, to be sure, but did want to save the main part of her colonial empire'. Of course, Hitler felt that 'France should never again be permitted to become a strong power, since she would in no case forget the present defeat by Germany and Italy and would take the first opportunity for *revanche*. . . . In spite of the present England and France would sooner or later get together again.' Nevertheless, at the

[1] Führer Naval Conferences, pp. 141–42.

present time, 'the ideal solution consisted in creating a European coalition against England including France and Spain.' 'Fantastic though it may seem,' wrote Ciano in summing up this part of the conversation, 'Hitler does not exclude the possibility of having French forces at our side in a continental coalition against Great Britain.'

Mussolini seemed ready to accept Hitler's general thesis, always providing that he was assured of his pound of flesh in the shape of Nice, Corsica, Tunisia, and French Somaliland. At the conclusion of the conversation means of contacting the French were discussed, but Hitler did not at that stage mention the possibility of using Laval. Instead, he spoke of possible meetings with the former French ambassador in Berlin, André François-Poncet, who seems to have been acting as another of Pétain's confidential envoys, or with General Huntziger.[1]

Hitler was indeed walking a slippery tightrope. He hated France and the French and would infinitely have preferred to rely upon Italy, with the possible addition of Spain. At Dakar, however, the French had shown that they were willing to fight the English, whereas the Spaniards were showing a marked reluctance to do so. At the same time, Germany had made promises to Italy and half-promises to Spain about the eventual disposal of France's colonial empire which could throw the whole of that empire into the hands of de Gaulle if they became known. No wonder the Führer declared that 'the resolution of the conflicting interests of France, Italy, and Spain in Africa is only possible through a grandiose fraud'.[2]

Only a few days after the Brenner meeting, Hitler had come to the conclusion that nothing less than a personal meeting with Marshal Pétain would suffice to iron out his future policy towards France. This, at any rate, was the burden of what von Brauchitsch told General Halder on 11 October after a visit to Berlin.[3] That very same day, Pétain made a scarcely-veiled appeal to the German leader in a broadcast address to the French people. Referring to the need for international collaboration, the Marshal declared, 'France is ready to seek this collaboration in all fields and with all her neighbours. She is aware,

---

[1] Schmidt memorandum, 4 October 1940, D.G.F.P., Series D, Vol. XI, No. 149; Ciano memorandum, 4 October 1940, Ciano, *L'Europa*, pp. 594–9. Quotations are taken from both the German and Italian records. For François-Poncet's activities, see Baudouin, p. 370.

[2] Halder, p. 124.

[3] Ibid., p. 133.

moreover, that whatever the political map of Europe and the world may be, the problem of Franco-German relations, which were so criminally treated in the past, will continue to shape her future. No doubt Germany can choose on the morrow of her victory over our arms, between a traditional peace of oppression and an entirely new peace of collaboration. . . . The choice belongs first of all to the victor. It also depends upon the vanquished.' This message was drafted mainly by Gaston Bergery, after consultation with du Moulin, Belin, Bouthillier, Baudouin, and Peyrouton. It was not, therefore, inspired by Laval.[1]

About 20 October, Laval, who was on one of his visits to Paris, was informed by Abetz that he would shortly be meeting Ribbentrop. He was told to keep this information strictly to himself, but insisted that he must tell Pétain. He accordingly returned to Vichy and informed the Marshal, either on the evening of the 20th or some time the following day. He then returned to Paris, where he had been told to present himself with a suitcase at the German embassy[2] on the morning of the 22nd. De Brinon was with him and the two men were driven off in official cars in the direction of Tours. It was only in the evening, after driving on from Tours, that Abetz told Laval, 'I must warn you . . . that it's not only M. von Ribbentrop whom you are going to see, but also Chancellor Hitler.' '*Merde, alors!*' exclaimed the incredulous Frenchman.[3]

The meeting took place in the Führer's special train at the small country station of Montoire, and the conversation is recorded in one of the few extant contemporary documents written by Laval himself, as well as in an official German version. Hitler began by emphasizing that he had not come to discuss the details of Franco-German relations, but merely sought 'a clarification of fundamentals'. Militarily speaking, the outcome of the war was 'absolutely beyond doubt' and 'it should be obvious to Laval that someone had to take responsibility for the costs of the war and bear their consequences'. This question was 'decisive'

[1] Philippe Pétain, *Quatre Années au Pouvoir*, Paris, La Couronne Littéraire, 1949 (hereafter cited as Pétain), p. 62. Pétain was also continuing his efforts to arrange a meeting with Hitler through unofficial channels. See the telegram of the German minister in Geneva, Krauel, to the foreign ministry, 11 October 1940, GFM/121/120059-60.

[2] Strictly speaking, Abetz's office in Paris was not raised to the status of an embassy until November 1940, but it is convenient to use the term.

[3] Laval in *Procès Pétain*, p. 194, cols. 1-2; de Brinon, p. 25. The '*merde, alors!*' is toned down to '*sans blague!*' in some accounts.

for Germany. 'From the military point of view,' he went on, 'France was the first country conquered and consequently an enemy to be held primarily responsible.' But, he hinted, 'it was also conceivable that the destruction of England would offer him other opportunities as well.'

According to his own notes, Laval replied that he would have preferred to have talked with Hitler before the war, but that the problem was still the same: 'an end must be made to the rivalry dividing the two countries, which have continually clashed with one another, with varying fortunes, in the past . . . Only a peace which is honourable for France, which conforms with her past, her genius, and her interests, can put an end to this rivalry and settle her relations with Germany.'[1] Hitler retorted that there could be no question of a definitive settlement of Franco-German relations until the war was over. In the meantime, 'the question of who would pay the costs remained open, and if Germany should happen to find an opportunity at some later date to make a reasonable settlement elsewhere, no one could expect that she would fight on merely to spare France'. He intended to mobilize the entire continent against England, and Franco-German relations would largely depend upon the attitude France adopted towards this mobilization. '. . . The general extension of the front against England,' he warned, 'would obviously be determined or at least essentially affected by consideration of French interests or disregard of these interests, depending on the attitude France took. . . . It was conceivable . . . that France not only would not have to endure the suffering which she herself inflicted on Germany in 1918 and which she would, according to certain publications, inflict on Germany again in case of victory, but would receive consideration commensurate with her importance, both in Europe and in Africa. But if the war should last longer and Germany should find a settlement in another direction, the Reich would also be forced to indemnify itself in some other way.'

Referring to Africa, Laval stated (according to his notes) that 'collaboration . . . must not involve any derogation of the principle of our sovereignty. These territories, which are bathed in French blood, are as dear to France as her metropolitan provinces.' After pointing out that Germany's former colonies, which had been taken from her in

---

[1] The German record confirms the gist of these remarks, but spices them with ardent expressions of hope that England would be defeated and statements that the bulk of the French people would be prepared to support a policy of Franco-German collaboration.

1918, had also been bathed in German blood, Hitler replied that if peace were concluded at England's expense, France need not suffer 'any considerable diminution of her total holdings in Africa', even if Italian and Spanish as well as German claims were taken into account. 'A settlement would have to be found here,' the Führer concluded, 'that would give the most lasting protection to the interests of the continental European nations in this African continent and a territorial arrangement would have to be established that would do justice to the interests of all.'

Hitler had álready made it clear that he did not expect an immediate answer to the points he had raised. He explained that he was proposing to go on from Montoire to see General Franco and he suggested that he might meet Pétain on his return on 24 October. In the Marshal's name, Laval accepted the Führer's invitation with alacrity.[1]

Pétain had been informed of the Hitler–Laval meeting, and of Hitler's invitation, before Laval returned to Vichy. He is reported to have expressed concern at the prospect of meeting Hitler, which is rather surprising considering the effort he had expended during the previous month trying to arrange it. In any event, the whole cabinet were able to weigh the issue on the afternoon of 23 October, when Laval made his report on what had happened. His account, which Bouthillier reproduces in his memoirs, was an accurate one. His conclusions were just as clear-cut. It would be 'a crime against France,' he maintained, not to accept Hitler's invitation. 'We shall have to endure English reprisals, but we must take every risk in order to seize the magnificent opportunity which now presents itself to France'. 'France,' he declared, according to Baudouin's diary, 'is at the parting of the ways. Everyone must now assume his responsibilities. As far as he was concerned, his choice was already made and he would passionately defend his thesis when the matter was discussed in the cabinet.'[2]

Baudouin could be forgiven for thinking that Hitler was about to ask for France's entry into the war against England. In a private talk with Pétain, he endeavoured to convince the latter of the folly of such a step. The Marshal agreed. He was 'absolutely hostile,' he said, 'to a

---

[1] Schmidt memorandum, 22 October 1940, D.G.F.P., Series D, Vol. XI, No. 212; Laval's notes, published by Albert Kammerer in Part I, of 'Le Véritable Montoire', Une Semaine dans le Monde, 1 May 1948.

[2] Bouthillier, Vol. I., pp. 196–7; Baudouin, pp. 375–8.

declaration of war upon England,' and he asked the foreign minister to accompany him to Montoire so that they could discuss the points that were raised. At the same time, Laval was re-emphasizing his point of view to Bouthillier and Huntziger. 'Everything will rest,' he said, 'upon a double collaboration. We must give in in the economic sphere in order to obtain considerable military advantage. . . . May France . . . choose while there is still time.'[1]

When Laval heard that Pétain wanted to bring Baudouin with him, he interposed his vote, claiming that Abetz had refused to allow it. When the Marshal persisted, Laval replied that, if he insisted, he would refuse to come himself. Pétain thereupon gave in and asked Admiral Fernet to ask the foreign minister 'to put up even with this'. Baudouin, of course, had little choice in the matter, but he vowed that he would submit his resignation upon the Marshal's return. 'I can only remain,' he noted in his diary, 'if I am in complete agreement with my two superiors: the Marshal and the deputy premier, and if I am able to exercise my functions with the necessary freedom and authority. Since this evening, this is no longer the case.'[2]

While Pétain was settling the composition of his entourage, Hitler was meeting General Franco at Hendaye, trying to persuade him both of the need to bring Spain into his continental coalition and of the wisdom of including France as well. Although a protocol which provided for Spain's eventual entry into the war was agreed upon, it was so hedged about with conditions as to be virtually worthless. Hitler later told Mussolini and Ciano that he would prefer to have three or four teeth out rather than go through the ordeal of negotiating with Franco again. He was even more uncomplimentary to members of his own staff, referring to the Spanish leader as a 'Jesuit swine'. The Führer thus returned to Montoire with his 'grandiose fraud' no nearer realization.[3]

Pétain's party, which finally consisted of Laval, de Brinon, du Moulin, and his doctor, Ménétrel, left Vichy at seven o'clock on the morning of

---

[1] Baudouin, pp. 378–9; Bouthillier, Vol. I, p. 197.

[2] Laval in *Procès Pétain*, p. 203, col. 2; Baudouin, p. 379; Fernet, p. 60. Charles-Roux, the permanent head of the foreign office, also decided to resign after Montoire, but this was due to his fundamental disagreement with the policy being pursued rather than to the fact of his being by-passed. See Charles-Roux, pp. 357–83.

[3] On the Hendaye meeting, see Detwiler, pp. 56–62. Ciano memorandum, 28 October 1940, Ciano, *L'Europa*, p. 604; Halder, p. 158.

24 October. They reached Montoire in the early evening. Only Pétain and Laval were permitted to enter the Führer's coach, the others being directed to a nearby restaurant car complete with refreshments.[1]

In Hitler's coach, it was Pétain who, after the customary exchange of courtesies, got down to brass tacks. Referring to the possibilities of Franco-German co-operation, he regretted that it had not taken place before the war, but added that 'there was perhaps still time to regain what had been lost. The English were affording the best opportunity for that.' Speaking of Anglo-Gaullist attacks upon French colonies, the Marshal declared that 'in this respect, and since the Führer had done France the honour of speaking of co-operation, a field might be found where its realization between the two countries was a practical possibility. He did not wish to go into details, but he could give assurance for his own person that as far as matters depended on him everything would be done in order to secure these colonial territories for France.'

In his reply, Hitler went into considerable military detail for Pétain's benefit in order to show how the final outcome of the war was already settled. At the same time, he wanted to shorten the war by as much as possible, for 'prolongation . . . not only inflicted a burden primary on Germany but was to the disadvantage of all of Europe, and . . . it would increase exorbitantly the final reckoning that would have to be faced one day.' This reckoning would involve the satisfaction of 'the vital demands of some peoples in Europe, which had not been met or out of which they had been cheated in the past' and 'payment of the material costs of the war'. He believed that, as England was mainly responsible for the war, she should bear the major burden of the costs. 'He was acting at the present time,' he explained, 'to organize a European and in part extra-European community against Britain, the enemy of the continent. He had exchanged ideas with the French government with a view to ascertaining whether France was prepared to join and co-operate with this community. It was imperative to study the possibilities of ending this war that might result from such a co-operation between Germany and Italy, on the one side, and France on the other.'

Pétain replied that he was 'in no position at this time to define the exact limits of French co-operation with Germany. All he could do

---

[1] Baudouin, p. 380; du Moulin, pp. 47–51.

was to express himself in favour of the principle of such co-operation.'
He could not enter into any binding commitments without first consulting his government. At this point, Laval broke into the conversation to explain the French attitude more fully. 'In accepting the principle of co-operation with Germany,' he said, 'Marshal Pétain has
pointed to the larger military possibilities open to France in Africa.
. . . But generally, in taking further action, it would be necessary to
take account of the state of public opinion in France.' The very fact
that a Hitler–Pétain meeting had taken place would have 'a deep and
favourable impression on French public opinion. . . . But if France
were to commit herself today as to the conditions of that co-operation,
this would not advance the relationship to Germany but on the contrary
have a detrimental influence.' Going right to the heart of the matter he
thought Hitler had in mind, Laval pointed out that Pétain could not
declare war without a vote by parliament, which would probably be
refused. He suggested that there were 'other possibilities' by which
co-operation could be achieved. 'France could offer resistance . . .
and this could in the final account accomplish the same results as those
produced by actual co-operation.' France wanted to accept Germany's
generous offer, he concluded, but 'in the beginning . . . as Marshal
Pétain had pointed out, it was necessary to proceed slowly and with
caution'.

After some further less important exchanges, Hitler summed up the
conversation as follows: 'Marshal Pétain says that he is prepared in
principle to consider co-operation with Germany as outlined by the
Führer. The conditions of this co-operation would be established and
settled in detail from case to case. Marshal Pétain anticipates from this
a more advantageous outcome of the war for France. The Führer declares that he is in agreement.'[1]

Since the Liberation, thousands of words have been written attempting either to condemn or to justify the Montoire meetings. Unfortunately, the sheer volume of this polemic has tended to obscure the
basic historical issue: namely, the contemporary attitudes and expectations of the participants.

---

[1] Schmidt memorandum, 24 October 1940, D.G.F.P., Series D, Vol. XI, No. 227.
Laval's own notes, which are less full than those on his own meeting with Hitler, are
printed in Part II of Albert Kammerer, 'Le Véritable Montoire', Une Semaine dans le Monde,
8 May 1948.

There can be little doubt that, by and large, Hitler was satisfied with the outcome of his talks with the French leaders. Although he described Laval to Mussolini and Ciano as 'a dirty democratic cheap-jack politician who doesn't believe what he says', he seems to have been genuinely impressed by the personality of Marshal Pétain.[1] He did not seem particularly worried that the French had shown reluctance to declare outright war upon England. They had shown a determination to defend their colonial empire and he probably reasoned that this attitude would result in *de facto* hostilities. Such, at any rate, is the impression which emerges from a conference at O.K.W. headquarters on 1 November 1940 between Keitel, Jodl, and Warlimont, from the latter's memorandum for the *Luftwaffe* on the following day, and from Hitler's own war directive on 12 November. 'The aim of my policy toward France,' Hitler stated, 'is to co-operate with this country in the most effective way for the future prosecution of the war against England. For the time being France will have the role of a "non-belligerent power" which will have to tolerate German military measures on her territory, in the African colonies especially, and to give support, as far as possible, even by using her own means of defence. The most pressing task of the French is the defensive and offensive protection of their African possessions . . . against England and the de Gaulle movement. From this task the participation of France in the war against England can develop in full force.'[2]

At the same time, it seems that at one stage the Germans had hoped for something more from Montoire. The German foreign ministry archives contain two documents which were obviously drawn up in connection with the meetings, but which were never handed over to the French. The first is a draft letter from Ribbentrop to Laval, purporting to summarize the results of the conversations. Its most important passage reads, 'The French government . . . will publicly and formally declare itself to be in a state of war with England . . . and will take action accordingly.' The second document is the draft text of a German–French–Italian protocol, which sets out most of the

[1] Ciano memorandum, 28 October 1940, Ciano, *L'Europa*, p. 602; Halder, pp. 157–8; OKW/KTB, 29 October 1940.

[2] Ibid., 1 November 1940; Warlimont memorandum, 2 November 1940, GMR/T-77/781/5508406-7; Führer Directive, 12 November 1940, D.G.F.P., Series D, Vol. XI, No. 323. The description of France's role is practically identical in the *Kriegstagebuch*, Warlimont's memorandum, and the Führer directive.

1a. The village of Châteldon where Laval was born. In the middle distance is the castle which he bought in 1932

1b Pierre Laval as a Socialist Deputy during the First World War

2a. Laval's first cabinet, January 1931. In the front row, from left to right, are André Maginot (Minister of War), Aristide Briand (Foreign Minister), Laval, André Tardieu (Minister of Agriculture), and Paul Reynaud (Minister of Colonies). The man standing behind Briand is Pierre Etienne Flandin (Minister of Finance)

2b. Laval and Briand, with Chancellor Heinrich Brüning, in Berlin, September 1931

3. The Laval-Hoover conversation in the White House, October 1931. From left to right are Buisson (a civil servant acting as Laval's interpreter), Laval, Hoover, Undersecretary of State Ogden Mills, and Secretary of State Henry L. Stimson

4a. Laval signing the Franco-Italian Agreement in the presence of Mussolini in Rome, January 1935

4b. Laval and Stalin in Moscow, May 1935

5a. Laval and Anthony Eden during one of their discussions on the Abyssinian question, 1935

5b. Laval and the British foreign secretary, Sir Samuel Hoare, meeting in Paris to draw up the Hoare-Laval Plan, December 1935

6. Crisis talks as France falls, 1940. From left to right are General Maxime Weygand French Commander-in-Chief), Paul Baudouin (Undersecretary of State to the Prime Minister), Prime Minister Paul Reynaud, and Marshal Pétain (deputy Prime Minister)

7. The Juggler

A Frog He Would A-Wooing Go!

OH, YEAH ?

9a. Montoire, 22 October 1940. From left to right are Hitler, Laval, Ribbentrop, and Hitler's interpreter, Paul Schmidt

9b. The French cabinet meets to discuss the Montoire meetings, October 1940. From left to right around the table are General Huntziger (War Minister), Raphaël Alibert (Minister of Justice), Marshal Pétain, Paul Baudouin (Foreign Minister), Admiral Darlan (Minister of Marine), M. Caziot (Minister of Agriculture), Marcel Peyrouton (Minister of the Interior), Laval, Yves Bouthillier (Minister of Finance), and René Belin (Minister of Industrial Production and Labour)

10a. Otto Abetz, German Ambassador to Vichy France, at his trial in Paris in 1949

10b. The Demarcation Line between the Occupied and Unoccupied Zones of France

11a. Laval being helped to his car after the attempt on his life, 27 August 1941

11b. Marshal Pétain and his 'successor' Admiral Darlan taking a stroll in Vichy, 1941

12. Laval greets the first French prisoners-of-war paroled under the Relève Scheme, August 1942

13. Franco–German–Italian meeting at Hitler's headquarters, December 1942. From left to right, around the table, are Ribbentrop, the interpreter Schmidt, Laval, Hitler, Italian Foreign Minister Ciano, and Goering

14a. Jacques Doriot, leader of the Parti Populaire Français

14b. Marcel Déat, leader of Rassemblement National Populaire (appointed Minister of Labour and National Solidarity, March 1944)

FOUR ULTRA-COLLABORATIONISTS

14c. Joseph Darnand, leader of the *Milice* (appointed Secretary-General for the Maintenance of Order, December 1943)

14d. Fernand de Brinon, Vichy Ambassador to the German Authorities in Paris, 1940–44

15. The Castle of Sigmaringen, where Laval and other members of the Vichy government were interned by the Germans in 1944–5

16a. Laval angrily protesting at his trial, October 1945

16b. Laval's execution, 15 October 1945

points contained in the draft letter with the curious exception of the French declaration of war. On this point the protocol merely states that 'the Axis powers and the French government have a common interest in seeing England defeated within the shortest time. The French government will therefore support the measures of the Axis powers to this end within the framework of its resources.' Other points in the protocol include a recognition of France's 'rightful place in a reorganized Europe', the promise of further derogations from the armistice agreements to enable her to defend her colonies, and a pledge that, in any territorial readjustment which followed the war, she would be compensated for any territory she had to cede to Germany, Italy, and Spain so that 'in the final outcome France shall have a colonial domain in Africa substantially equivalent to her possessions today'. An equally important 'annex' to the protocol promises the attachment of the *départements* of the Nord and Pas-de-Calais to the German military commander in France, the waiving of German insistence upon policing French frontiers, an unspecified reduction in occupation costs and consideration of French labour needs when making requisitions and releasing prisoners-of-war.[1]

It is a complete mystery why these documents were not handed over to the French. Abetz offers an ingenious explanation in his memoirs. He states that the protocol was drawn up after the Montoire meetings for submission to the Italian government and that detailed discussions between Ribbentrop and Laval on the basis of the agreement reached in principle at Montoire were scheduled to begin in Paris immediately. However, the unexpected news of the imminent Italian invasion of Greece resulted in a sudden change of plan and both Ribbentrop and Hitler went instead to Florence to see Mussolini. 'As the Italian attack had far-reaching consequences for Axis policy through the Balkans,' Abetz writes, 'Ribbentrop's attention was completely diverted from France by this question in the following weeks. The conversation between the foreign minister and the French leader was therefore repeatedly postponed.' However, there is evidence that the protocol was drafted before the Montoire meetings, which suggests that a decision not to show it to the French was made before the news of the Italian

[1] Unsigned memorandum, D.G.F.P., Series D, Vol. XI, No. 207; Draft Protocol, ibid., No. 208.

invasion of Greece was received.[1] This may have been because Hitler did not obtain what he considered to be a firm enough commitment from Pétain and Laval. More likely, it may have been due to the disappointing results of the Hendaye meeting with Franco, for as far as Hitler was concerned, collaboration with France was always intended to be part of a much wider design.

A good starting-point for an examination of the French attitude to Montoire is Marshal Pétain's broadcast address to the French people on 30 October. 'I responded freely to the Führer's invitation,' he said. 'I underwent no *diktat*, no pressure from him. A collaboration was envisaged between our two countries. I accepted the principle. The details will be discussed later.' He explained that it was in order to preserve French unity that he had entered upon the path of collaboration. He hoped that the sufferings of France could be reduced thereby, and he specifically mentioned the questions of prisoners-of-war, occupation costs, the demarcation line and the administration and feeding of the country. 'This collaboration must be sincere,' he went on. 'It must exclude any thought of aggression and must involve a patient and confident effort.' France had many obligations towards Germany under the armistice agreement, but at any rate she remained sovereign. 'This sovereignty compels her to defend her soil, to extinguish differences of opinion and to suppress the dissident movements in her colonies.' This policy, the Marshal concluded, was his own. 'The members of the government are responsible only to me. It is I alone whom history will judge.'[2]

Words were followed by deeds. On 31 October, the day after Pétain's address, a conference was held at the German embassy in Paris. It was attended by Laval, Bouthillier, and Huntziger, as well as by German representatives. Referring to Hitler's 'generous gesture' in offering collaboration to a defeated France and the French government's unreserved acceptance of it, Laval spoke of 'the necessity of a stronger military effort to reconquer France's rebellious colonies and the granting of economic concessions which could be held up propagandistically to the masses of the population as resulting from the policy decided on at Montoire'. General Huntziger had brought a memorandum setting out

---

[1] Abetz, pp. 157–9; Kordt note, 8 November 1940, D.G.F.P., Series D, Vol. XI, No. 207, fn. 1.
[2] Pétain, pp. 69–71.

French requests designed to fulfil the first part of this programme and, in connection with the second, Laval wondered 'whether direct conversations could not be started in Paris next week between minister Hemmen and finance minister Bouthillier on the possibility of a reduction in occupation costs, a relaxation of the demarcation line, and a changed ratio between the value of the franc and that of the reichsmark'. He also thought it important that the *départements* of the Nord and Pas-de-Calais should be placed under the military commander in France. The Montoire meeting, Laval concluded, had given rise to 'tremendous excitement' in his country. 'The danger existed that the exaggerated pessimism would be followed by an exaggerated optimism, which could all too easily change into a feeling of disappointment.' France realized that the effects of the war could not be removed in a hurry, 'but precisely for this reason it was necessary to give public opinion the impression that the policy of Montoire represented a beginning in the recovery of France.'[1]

The Paris conference was clearly a carefully co-ordinated follow-up to Pétain's broadcast declarations. General Huntziger handed his lengthy memorandum to the armistice commission and told Lieutenant-Colonel Speidel, the chief-of-staff to the German military commander in France, that the French were resolved, not only to defend their colonies against future English attacks, 'but also, wherever necessary, to attack the English in order to recover lost territory.' Bouthillier, armed with another long memorandum on administrative and economic questions, began negotiations with Hemmen. A few days later, the French delegate in charge of prisoner-of-war questions, M. Scapini, wrote a long letter to Abetz requesting the release of more men in order to increase the efficiency of the French economy and thereby step up its contribution to the German war effort. On 5 November General Doyen wrote to General von Stülpnagel envisaging the possibility of an attack on the dissident Chad colony in January 1941.[2]

The cumulative effect of this evidence is overwhelming. The French

[1] Abetz to Foreign Ministry, 1 November 1940, D.G.F.P., Series D, Vol. XI, No. 272. See also Hemmen memorandum, 31 October 1940, in Bouthillier, Vol. I, pp. 293–6.

[2] Huntziger memorandum, 31 October 1940, *La Délégation Française*, Vol II, pp. 392–418; Speidel memorandum, 31 October 1940, GMR/T–77/782/5509125–6; Bouthillier memorandum, 30 October 1940, in Bouthillier, Vol. II, pp. 499–503; Ibid., Vol. I, pp. 205–6; Scapini to Abetz, 4 November 1940, *La Délégation Française*, Vol. II, pp. 326–31; Doyen to von Stülpnagel, 5 November 1940, ibid., pp. 321–5.

government clearly saw the Mon'oire meetings as a potential break-through in Franco-German relations. They planned to exploit them to the utmost in order to gain concessions in the military, economic, and administrative fields, even at the recognized risk of *de facto* hostilities with Britain in Africa.

In these circumstances, it is hard to represent Laval as virtually the sole apostle of collaboration with Germany, while Pétain and other leading ministers were playing a subtle 'double game' behind his back. Pétain's alleged comment on Montoire – 'it will take six months to discuss it and six months to forget it'[1] – sounds suspiciously like a clever phrase dreamed up after the Liberation and bears no relation to the policy the French government sought to pursue at the time. 'Revisionist' historians have made much of the so-called 'secret agreement' which is alleged to have been reached between Pétain and Churchill at the time of Montoire and which, according to them, gave the meeting its real significance. While Pétain was talking generalities with Hitler, they argue, his representative, Professor Louis Rougier, was making precise arrangements with the British government concerning the easing of the blockade of French ports, the preservation of the *status quo* in the French empire, the ending of radio attacks upon the Vichy government, and the possibility of France re-entering the war on Britain's side. Recent research, however, has proved quite conclusively that this thesis is untenable. Professor Rougier was certainly in London at the time of the Montoire meeting, but this was pure coincidence. There is no evidence that he enjoyed Pétain's special confidence or that he was empowered to negotiate any kind of agreement. In fact, no agreement was ever concluded.[2]

This is not to say that there was a complete identity of views between the members of the Vichy government. Laval knew what he wanted: full French participation in a European new order at Britain's expense To judge by their statements and their actions, men like Huntziger

---

[1] Paul Estèbe in *Procès Pétain*, p. 313, col. 1.
[2] The fullest exposition of the 'revisionist' thesis of Montoire is L. D. Girard, *Montoire, Verdun diplomatique*, Paris, André Bonne, 1948. It is echoed, albeit with reservations, in Aron, pp. 299–310. The literature on the 'secret agreement' is considerable and has been ably summarized and dissected in two independent studies which effectively dispose of the myth: General G. Schmitt, *Les Accords Secrets Franco-Britanniques de Novembre–Décembre 1940*, Paris, Presses Universitaires de France, 1957 (hereafter cited as Schmitt); P. M. H. Bell, *Anglo-French Relations, May–December 1940*, unpublished M. Litt. thesis, deposited in the Bodleian Library, Oxford, October 1957.

and Admiral Darlan largely shared his point of view, even if they did not always agree with his methods.[1] On the other hand, Pétain, Baudouin, and certainly Bouthillier were much less sure. 'I have no love for the British,' confessed the Marshal to the American *chargé d'affaires* on 16 November, 'and I shall defend French territory against them. But their victory is much better for France than that of Germany.'[2] However, the Germans were on French soil and the French empire was under attack. In the circumstances, the government felt it had no alternative but to collaborate, and there is every reason to believe that it did so loyally and with its eyes wide open.

The results of Montoire were a disappointment to both sides. They did not lead to Anglo-French hostilities in Africa, let alone to a French declaration of war upon England, as the Germans had hoped. Still less did they bring any significant improvement in France's relations with her conqueror, as the French had hoped. Once again, it is necessary to turn to factors beyond the control of the French government to discover the reasons.

In a lengthy account of his first term as German ambassador in Paris, written in July 1943, Abetz declared that English, Italians, Frenchmen, and Germans had vied with each other in sabotaging Montoire from the very beginning.[3] Whether English propaganda and French opposition to collaboration had quite the influence Abetz assigned to them is open to dispute, but there is no doubt about the importance of Italian and German actions.

The Italians were suspicious of Hitler's Montoire policy from the start. When they were first informed of the meeting, Ciano noted in his diary that 'a *rapprochement* between Berlin and Paris could only operate at our expense in the long run', and when Ribbentrop telephoned him on 24 October after the conversations had actually taken place, he commented, 'I do not hide my mistrust and my suspicions: we must ensure that the insinuation of France into the Axis does not take place to our detriment.' In a letter to Hitler, which was written on 19 October but not received until after Montoire, Mussolini himself was severely

---

[1] Huntziger's views have already been quoted frequently. For Darlan's, see his note of 8 November 1940 in Bouthillier, Vol. I, pp. 301–4.

[2] Matthews to Hull, 16 November 1940, F.R.U.S., 1940, Vol. II, pp. 411–14.

[3] Abetz Papers, GFM/P3/00037. A French translation of these papers was published as *Pétain et les Allemands*, Paris, Editions Gaucher, 1948.

critical of a policy of collaboration with France, and during the remainder of 1940 the Italians lost no opportunity to make matters awkward for the French, particularly in respect of obtaining derogations from the armistice agreement.[1]

The Germans' initial response to Montoire seemed to be the announcement on 3 November by Gauleiter Bürckel that large-scale deportations of pro-French Lorrainers would shortly be carried out, as the *département* 'will have to be truly German for evermore'. Abetz, who knew of the proposed expulsions in advance, protested against the psychological blunder of carrying them out immediately after Montoire. He suggested postponement until such a time as 'the operation may find its natural place within the framework of a general settlement between Germany and France'. But Hitler had already decided that the operation must be pushed through as quickly as possible so that it would already be completed by the time negotiations with the French began. By approaching Bürckel directly, Laval managed to obtain a week's delay before the deportations were begun, but nothing more. A French protest to the armistice commission was returned as 'unreceivable'. At the time it was written, 41 trainloads of Lorrainers had already been expelled.[2]

Then there was considerable delay in arranging the Laval–Ribbentrop meeting which was intended to negotiate the details of the agreement reached in principle at Montoire. On 4 November Abetz was informed that this meeting would take place 'in the very near future', but on 16 November von Etzdorf told General Halder that it had been 'postponed'. On 25 November (a Monday), Abetz told Halder that it would take place 'at the end of this week'. Then it was apparently postponed again until 'the first thing after Christmas' before being brought forward to coincide with Hitler's theatrical gesture of transporting the ashes of Napoleon's son to Paris in mid-December.[3] By the time this took place, however, Laval had been dismissed from power. The Germans had plenty of excuses for delaying the meeting, including the

---

[1] Ciano, *Diario*, 20, 24 October 1940; Mussolini to Hitler, 19 October 1940, D.G.F.P., Series D, Vol. XI, No. 199. See also OKW/KTB, 14 November 1940.

[2] Bürckel proclamation, *La Délégation Française*, Vol. II, pp. 385–6; Abetz to Foreign Ministry, 31 October 1940, D.G.F.P., Series D, Vol. XI, No. 271; Bürckel to Ribbentrop, 15 November 1940, ibid., No. 337; OKW/KTB, 1 November 1940; Doyen to Stülpnagel, 18 November 1940, *La Délégation Française*, Vol. II, pp. 383–4, 386.

[3] See below, pp. 253–54.

Italian involvement in Greece and growing evidence of Soviet expansionism, but inevitably the impression was created in Vichy of a lack of interest in French problems.[1]

There was a similar delay in dealing with the French requests for derogations from the armistice agreement in order to permit them to defend their colonies. On 2 November, General von Stülpnagel asked the French for further details of their needs, and a revised version of Huntziger's memorandum of 31 October was given to the Germans on 12 November. Two days later Hitler authorized a few concessions, but it was not until 26 November that Field-Marshal Keitel went through the revised memorandum in detail. Even then a large number of questions were left in suspension and one of the keenest advocates of Franco-German collaboration in the German military establishment, General Warlimont, wrote a memorandum on 3 December urging rapid decisions on the points that were still outstanding.[2] Once again, however, no final decisions had been taken by the time of Laval's dismissal.

Virtually, the only concession the French obtained was the so-called 'Berlin protocol' of 16 November, which provided for the provisional release of certain categories of French prisoners-of-war. Laval described this agreement as 'a first and happy consequence of the historic meetings at Montoire', but it did not amount to much. Its main provision was for the release of prisoners-of-war who had four or more children or elder brothers who had four or more children to support. This was an even more restricted category than might appear at first sight, for as General Doyen told his German counterpart on 26 November, all 'other ranks' who had four or more children had already been demobilized before the collapse. The concession therefore applied

---

[1] Ritter to Abetz, 4 November 1940, D.G.F.P., Series D, Vol. XI, No. 285; Halder, pp. 184, 192, 224; OKW/KTB, 14 November 1940.

[2] Michelier to Huntziger, 2 November 1940, *La Délégation Française*, Vol. II, pp. 389–90; aide-mémoire of 12 November 1940, ibid., pp. 392–418; Welck to Foreign Ministry, 14 November 1940, D.G.F.P., Series D, Vol. XI, No. 321, fn. 4; a summary of the French requests with Keitel's handwritten comments of 26 November can be found on GMR/T-77/782/5509079–92. His decisions, together with other derogations from the armistice agreement, are summarized in the appendix to a memorandum for Warlimont, dated 27 November 1940, on ibid., 5509050–55. Warlimont's memorandum of 3 December 1940, which includes an appendix summarizing all French requests upon which decisions were still pending, is on ibid., 781/5508394–403.

9*

only to officers and N.C.Os. Still, as Pétain remarked to the American *chargé d'affaires*, 'that at least was something'.[1]

Laval seemed quite undaunted by the transparent failure of his policy to produce results. After Montoire, he had taken over the portfolio of foreign minister when Baudouin carried out his threat to resign.[2] This gave him titular as well as practical control over Franco-German relations and he was even less inclined to brook interference than before. On one occasion he turned on Bouthillier, who had criticized him, with the remark, 'France has already lost the war. I shall prevent you and the others from losing her the peace.' 'In M. Laval's eyes,' wrote Marcel Peyrouton, the minister of the interior, 'we were innocents. We could be valuable technicians, but we would never be politicians – the Marshal least of all.'[3]

This attitude led Laval into taking decisions on his own initiative without consulting his colleagues. The most notorious examples of this concerned the Bor copper mines and the Belgian gold reserves. The Bor mines, which were French-owned, were situated in Yugoslavia. The Germans had expressed an interest in acquiring control over them as early as September 1940, but had run into opposition from the French government. Then, shortly after Montoire, Laval took it upon himself to instruct the directors of the company to sell out to the Germans, thus presenting his cabinet colleagues with a *fait accompli*. His post-war justification – apart from a denial that he had acted unilaterally – was that the French were powerless to prevent the Germans from gaining something they were clearly so anxious to obtain. It is quite evident, however, that he considered the matter of secondary importance, and he freely admitted that, when Abetz first told him about the mines, he did not even know where they were.[4]

The Belgian gold reserves – just under 200 metric tons – had been

---

[1] Albrecht to Scapini, 16 November 1940, *La Délégation Française*, Vol. II, pp. 470–71, Laval to Huntziger, 19 November 1940, ibid., pp. 471–2; memorandum of Doyen-von Stülpnagel conversation, 26 November 1940, ibid., Vol. III, pp. 30–38; Matthews to Hull, 16 November 1940, F.R.U.S., 1940, Vol. II, p. 412.

[2] Laval did not want to become foreign minister. He would have preferred the ministry of the interior 'in order to keep firm control over the country on behalf of the policy decided upon [at Montoire]'. See Baudouin, pp. 382–8; Abetz to Foreign Ministry, 26 October 1940, D.G.F.P., Series D, Vol. XI, No. 234.

[3] Bouthillier, Vol. I, p. 210; Peyrouton, p. 145.

[4] Bouthillier, Vol. I, pp. 229–32, Vol. II pp. 115–21; *Laval Parle*, pp. 171–9.

handed over to the Bank of France for safe keeping by the Belgian government before the fall of France. They had subsequently been transferred to French West Africa to keep them out of German hands. The Germans asked that they should be returned to France so that they would not fall into British hands and the French agreed, on condition that they would be handed over to representatives of the Belgian National Bank. An agreement to this effect was signed in Paris on 29 October. The Germans, however, then began to insist that, as occupying power, they enjoyed all the rights of the Belgian National Bank and demanded that the gold be handed over to them. The French dug their heels in until Hemmen approached Laval on 29 November. The latter, who was in Paris for top-level military-political talks, obviously thought that this was yet another secondary issue upon which it was not worth taking a stand and accepted the German thesis on behalf of the French government.[1]

These gratuitous actions of Laval's were a key factor in his eventual dismissal. The clearest proof lies in that it was Bouthillier, whose position as finance minister had been undercut in both these affairs, who took the lead in pressing for his removal. On 10 November, two days after he had first heard of the cession of the Bor mines, Bouthillier tried to warn Pétain that 'the question from now on was to know which one – [the Marshal] or Laval – would have to quit his post in the near future'. Writing after the war, Bouthillier was at great pains to emphasize that it was his opposition to Laval's policy of collaboration which prompted him to seek the latter's removal. In support, he cites the deputy premier's account to the cabinet of a conversation with Gœring on 9 November. But in promising the *Reichsmarschall* that the Gaullists would be driven out of French Africa – without German aid, it should be emphasized – Laval had done no more than repeat what Huntziger, Doyen, and Pétain himself had said before and were to go on saying in future. What was really disturbing about the Laval–Gœring conversation – and this gives added point to Bouthillier's warning that either Laval or Pétain would have to be replaced – was the obvious relish with which the deputy premier pointed out to Gœring that, if anything happened to the Marshal, he would become head of state. There were many

---

[1] Bouthillier, Vol. I, pp. 232–5; Vol. II, pp. 135–50; Debray memorandum, April 1944; *La Délégation Française*, Vol. III, pp. 163–6; Hemmen and Abetz to Foreign Ministry, 30 November 1940, GFM/1002/306351–2.

ministers who, while serving gladly under Pétain, would never agree to serve under Laval.[1]

It was a group of such ministers, including Baudouin (now secretary of state to Pétain) and Peyrouton, that Bouthillier gathered round him after 10 November. On 23 November he saw Pétain again and told him that these men shared his view that 'this situation could not go on for very long'. The affair of the Belgian gold reserves further strengthened Bouthillier's resolve. 'I will never work with that man again,' he exclaimed angrily and told Pétain outright on 2 December that unless Laval were dismissed he would resign himself. At first the Marshal demurred, accusing Bouthillier of impetuosity, but he eventually came round. 'Do not leave,' he said. 'He is the one who shall leave.'[2]

On 3 and 4 December, Pétain went on an official visit to Marseilles and Toulon. He was accompanied by Peyrouton and Bouthillier, who had agreed beforehand to keep up the pressure to get rid of Laval. Bouthillier also discussed the question with Admiral Darlan who assured him, 'On a nod from you, *vieil ami*, I'm with you to the end.'[3]

There was also talk of Laval's successor. Bouthillier had met Pierre-Etienne Flandin on a visit to Paris on 21 November and considered him a suitable candidate. Pétain's own initial choice was François-Poncet, but Bouthillier felt that he would be unacceptable to the Germans. Pétain was none too keen on Flandin – 'another parliamentarian', he complained – but he finally agreed that he should be invited to Vichy for consultation. Bouthillier had already taken the precaution of issuing the invitation.[4]

Laval was not unaware of these intrigues against him, but his supreme self-confidence blinded him to the real danger to his position. 'They won't dare,' he boasted to his friends. 'They know what I'm going to get out of the Germans. If necessary, I'll bang on the table and they'll

[1] Bouthillier, Vol. I, pp. 214–17; Ribbentrop to Abetz, 9 November 1940, D.G.F.P. Series D, Vol. XI, No. 306.

[2] Bouthillier, Vol. I, pp. 218, 227, 242–3. See also Baudouin, pp. 401–2. Peyrouton's account (Peyrouton, pp. 176–8) confirms the general outline of Bouthillier's, but gives no precise dates.

[3] Bouthillier, Vol. I, pp. 244–5; Baudouin, p. 402. Darlan's motives in wanting to get rid of Laval are obscure. He may, of course, have wanted to replace him, which he eventually did.

[4] Bouthillier, Vol. I, pp. 220, 245–8. Du Moulin claims (du Moulin, p. 61) that Pétain's friend and adviser, General Laure, suggested Flandin's name.

scuttle off like rabbits into their burrows. I will save my country in spite of them – in spite of everybody.'[1]

The deputy premier may have had some justification for his self-assurance. After all, Baudouin admitted that no one would have spoken a word of criticism of Laval at the cabinet meeting of 2 December had he actually been present. What was more, he must have felt that at long last his policy was beginning to bear fruit. On 23 November he had told Abetz that the service ministers 'had drafted a plan of operations for an intended action against the rebellious territories in Africa and that this plan was now completed'. He wanted to know whether it should be discussed at his forthcoming meeting with Ribbentrop or separately with the German military authoritie's. When he left Vichy again for Paris on 26 November, he evidently thought he was going on to Berlin to see Ribbentrop, but Hitler had already decided that the military conversations should be held first. General Warlimont was sent to Paris and, soon after his own arrival, Laval sent for Darlan and Huntziger to join him.[2]

The conference with General Warlimont took place on 29 November. In addition to Laval, Huntziger, and Darlan, it was attended by Abetz, de Brinon, and Major Stehlin of the French air force, together with a number of lesser civilian and military officials. After a brief word of welcome from Abetz, Huntziger explained the French plans. There were, he said, two ways of recovering the Chad colony from the Free French. The first was to attack through Nigeria, which was impossible because the British colony was too strong. The second was to attack from the north, thus avoiding British territory. This would be 'difficult, but . . . not impossible'. Speaking from the naval point of view, Admiral Darlan declared that the main task was to keep open the supply lines between metropolitan France and the colonies. The French navy could do this provided part of the English fleet remained tied down in the North Sea and the Mediterranean. The English presence at Gibraltar did present difficulties, but they could be overcome by the use of bombers based in Morocco and Oran. On the air side, Major Stehlin said that the main problem was one of aircraft

---

[1] Jaffré, p. 160; Mallet, Vol. I, p. 295.
[2] Baudouin, pp. 398, 400–401; Abetz to Foreign Ministry, 23 November 1940, D.G.F.P., Series D, Vol. XI, No. 385; Schwarzmann to Abetz, 27 November 1940, ibid., No. 410. The situation in the French empire was deteriorating. Gabon had gone over to the Free French in November.

construction as France would soon have no more 'planes left in reserve. All three military men stressed, with particulars, the difficulties which the Italians were creating.

Warlimont asked whether the requests which the French had already made in their October and November memoranda would suffice for carrying out the operations they had outlined. Huntziger replied that preparations would be completed by April 1941, but, because of the rainy season, it would not be possible to launch an attack until the following November. Obviously somewhat concerned by the delay, Warlimont asked whether it would not be possible instead to launch a direct attack upon the British ports of Freetown and Bathurst in order to give the French fleet operational freedom off the African coast. Huntziger replied that this would be difficult because of British strength in the area. If such an operation were undertaken, the French would certainly require increased reinforcements, but he expressed readiness to examine the problem further.

Huntziger's main objection, however, seemed to be that it would be difficult to attack a British colony directly without further provocation. At this point Laval intervened to point out that Sir Samuel Hoare, the British ambassador in Madrid, had recently told his French counterpart that, if the French fleet attempted to set sail from its present bases, the British would open fire on it and that any attack upon de Gaulle would 'almost inevitably involve a conflict between Great Britain and France'. Laval indicated that this would create 'a completely new strategic situation, which would remove the restrictions upon a direct attack against British territory . . .'[1]

This first meeting was inconclusive. Abetz later complained to Huntziger, Darlan, and Laval of the long delays which seemed to be involved in the French plans and of their essentially defensive nature. Huntziger accepted Abetz's criticisms, but said that 'he could not justify it to his military conscience to present Germany with the prospect of more extensive and quicker operations than were possible'. The German ambassador found Darlan more inclined towards an offensive operation against de Gaulle and the British. He felt that the French naval moves he contemplated would in any case 'result in a state of open warfare at sea'. Laval shared Abetz's disappointment and resolved to do something about it. On 4 December, he told Lieutenant-

[1] Achenbach memorandum, 29 November 1940, GMR/T–77/782/5509061–78.

Colonel Speidel, the chief-of-staff to the German military commander in France, that he would put it to the cabinet the following day that 'the question at issue was not whether to draft a plan to retain the colonies which would be practical six or twelve months from now, but rather whether to attack de Gaulle and thus Great Britain in order to reconquer the lost territories'.[1]

There is no record in available French sources of a discussion of these plans by the French government on 5 December. But Baudouin and Bouthillier refer to discussions which took place on the 7th and 9th, when it was known that General Warlimont would be returning to Paris on the 10th. Their accounts would lead one to believe that Laval alone was eager for an offensive operation against the British and Free French and that Pétain sought to restrain him, instructing Huntziger to stick to his original plan and avoid discussion of a direct attack upon a British colony.[2]

Unfortunately, the German record of the meeting on 10 December exposes the falsity of these assertions. In the event of hostile British action, General Huntziger now proposed an air attack upon Kano in northern Nigeria, the seizure of Bathurst, and an air attack upon Freetown, in addition to the operations against the Free French in Chad. Admiral Darlan added that the air attack upon Freetown could be combined with a submarine attack upon any ships that were in the harbour. The date for launching the Chad operation was advanced to the end of February 1941. In order to create the right psychological atmosphere for these military measures, Laval repeatedly stressed the need for a declaration that Germany had no designs upon French colonial territory. This would take the wind right out of de Gaulle's sails and expose him for what he was, 'a common English agent'. He also appealed to the Germans to help dissipate Italian fears. 'If you help us, we are ready to act,' the deputy premier concluded. 'France is ready to act and to act at once.'[3]

Warlimont was tremendously impressed by this display of French

[1] Abetz to Foreign Ministry, 1 December 1940, D.G.F.P., Series D, Vol. XI, No. 434; OKW/KTB, 7 December 1940, ibid., fn. 2.

[2] Baudouin, pp. 404–5; Bouthillier, Vol. I, p. 250.

[3] Achenbach memorandum, 10 December 1940, GMR/T–77/782/5508979–96. There is also a copy in the German foreign ministry archives, GFM/471/228340–57, and a French version which follows the German practically word for word, La Délégation Française, Vol. V, pp. 449–62.

energy. 'Total impression of the German ambassador in Paris and the representative of O.K.W.,' he wrote in a minute on 12 December, 'is that French willingness has received a decisive impetus since the first conference, and that there can be no doubt about the sincerity of the military intentions of the Pétain government.' With Keitel's approval, a note from Jodl accompanied Warlimont's written report to Hitler. It read, 'We must strike while the iron is hot. Further setbacks on the part of our allies[1] can all too easily bring about a stiffening of the French attitude.'[2]

It is clear then that the French and General Warlimont took these military conversations seriously. But how seriously did Hitler take them? Warlimont himself subsequently came to believe that he was chosen to take part in these talks, less on account of his knowledge of France and the French language, than because his rank and the status of his department would make it easier to disavow him.[3] In fact, it seems that Hitler's mind was going through a period of even more than usually rapid oscillation.

In spite of the rebuff at Hendaye, he was still trying to get Spain into the war and had drawn up a plan – with the code-name of 'Felix' – for the seizure of Gibraltar with Spanish assistance. It was clear from a conference he had with von Brauchitsch and Halder on 5 December that the plan was inspired as much by suspicion of France as by a desire to collaborate with her. He felt that it was not impossible that the French colonies were in league against Vichy and that, if French North Africa declared itself independent, the situation would become more difficult, as the French government might declare itself unable to take energetic counter-measures. The situation would be quite different, however, if there were German troops in Morocco. Invasion of Morocco and the control of the Straits of Gibraltar would enable Germany to deal with the British and French at the same time. 'With the straits in our hands and German troops in Morocco,' he continued, 'we can certainly negotiate with the Vichy government. Then they can't dodge the issue any more.'[4]

[1] The Italians were in considerable difficulties at this time.
[2] Warlimont minute, 12 December 1940, D.G.F.P., Series D, Vol. XI, No. 506; OKW/KTB, 12 December 1940.
[3] Walter Warlimont, *Im Hauptquartier der deutschen Wehrmacht, 1939–45*, Frankfurt-am-Main, Bernard & Graefe Verlag für Wehrwesen, 1962, p. 138, fn. 37.
[4] Halder, p. 212. For German military planning with regard to Spain in the autumn and winter of 1940, see Detwiler, chapters VI and VII.

Hitler's fears for North Africa were largely the result of an influx of reports of the unreliability of Pétain's delegate there, General Weygand. He was so concerned by these reports that on 8 December he ordered plans to be drawn up for the occupation of the rest of metropolitan France. By the 10th the O.K.W. had produced a draft plan for Operation 'Attila', as it was known, and the Führer had signed it. On the 11th it was circulated to the three services and preparations put in hand.[1]

At about the same time, however, Hitler received yet another rebuff from General Franco. On 7 December the latter told Admiral Canaris, the head of German intelligence, that it would be quite impossible for Spain to enter the war on 10 January 1941, which was the date laid down in the 'Felix' plan. Hitler, therefore, had no alternative but to cancel the operation 'since the necessary political pre-requisites no longer exist'. On 9 December, while his planners were working on Operation 'Attila', Hitler told General Halder that Spain's refusal had rendered all previous arrangements null and void and that he was thinking of using the free hand thereby acquired 'to bring [the French] into his policy through the promise of preserving their African possessions'. In this connection, he felt that 'no particular respect' needed any longer to be paid to Italian wishes.[2]

It is impossible to say what Hitler's final decision would have been, for the situation was changed completely by Laval's sudden dismissal on 13 December. Pétain had seen Flandin on 7 December and again on the 8th. He seems to have made up his mind to dismiss Laval on the 9th and he wrote a letter to Hitler that evening in which he announced his decision and asked the Führer to agree to the appointment of Flandin as Laval's successor. For reasons which remain obscure, however, this letter was not delivered.[3]

Two days later, on 12 December, a fantastic report reached Vichy

[1] Stohrer to Foreign Ministry, 29 November 1940, GFM/121/120200; OKW/KTB, 8, 9, 10 December 1940; Führer Directive ('Operation Attila'), 10 December 1940, D.G.F.P., Series D, Vol. XI, No. 488. See also Hitler to Mussolini, 5 December 1940, ibid., No. 452.

[2] Stohrer to Foreign Ministry, 12 December 1940, ibid., No. 500; OKW/KTB, 8, 10 December 1940, ibid., No. 476, fn. 2; Halder, p. 219.

[3] Flandin's evidence in *Procès Flandin*, pp. 162-4; Bouthillier, Vol. I, pp. 249-51; Noguères, p. 269 (text of the letter to Hitler). According to Bouthillier and Baudouin (who obtained his version from du Moulin), Pétain simply changed his mind about having the letter delivered. According to Noguères, however, who presumably based his account upon material in the Pétain trial dossiers, the bearer of the letter did not deliver it after he was told upon his arrival in Paris of Hitler's proposal concerning the Duc de Reichstadt's ashes (see below). Cf. Bouthillier, Vol. I, p. 251; Baudouin, pp. 413-14; Noguères, p. 269.

from Paris. Hitler was sending Pétain an invitation to come to the capital on 15 December, the anniversary of the return of Napoleon's remains from Saint Helena, to attend a similar theatrical ceremony: the return of the ashes of Napoleon's son, the Duc de Reichstadt, from Vienna. Laval, telephoning Vichy from Paris, stressed the need for the Marshal to accept the Führer's invitation.[1]

Laval later described Hitler's proposal as 'one of those sentimental gestures to which he was occasionally prone alongside less sentimental initiatives', and although he was concerned that the Marshal might not wish to make the journey on account of his age and the bitterly cold weather, he had no intention of seeing his more important tasks compromised by a refusal. When du Moulin rudely informed him that Pétain would not come, he resolved to go to Vichy and fetch him. The proposal was seen quite differently in Vichy. There, the Marshal's advisers viewed it as a trap to get him to Paris alone, where he would be forced to sign a decree delegating his powers as head of the government to Laval. The latter would then form a new government, including 'numerous undesirable elements', the most notable of whom would probably be Marcel Déat, editor of the Paris newspaper L'Œuvre and author of a recent series of virulently anti-Pétainist articles.[2]

Accompanied by de Brinon, who had been instructed to deliver Hitler's invitation to Pétain personally, Laval arrived in Vichy around midday on Friday 13 December. At first, Pétain persisted in his refusal to come to Paris, but eventually gave in under the combined pressure of Laval and de Brinon. He even resolved to make a virtue out of necessity by visiting other towns north of the demarcation line, thereby turning the journey into a triumphal tour of the occupied zone.

The news of the Marshal's change of mind leaked out soon after lunch. Peyrouton, who had just received fresh confirmation that the German embassy was planning to set up a 'more docile' French government, told Bouthillier, 'We've had it . . . if we don't take action.' 'It will have to be tonight,' replied Bouthillier. 'I'll arrest him,' said Peyrouton. 'He mustn't gather together Abetz and his crowd.' While

---

[1] Bouthillier, Vol. I, pp. 252–3; du Moulin, pp. 62–3; de Brinon, pp. 49–50. Baudouin states (Baudouin, p. 407) that news of Hitler's proposal reached Vichy on the 11th. All other sources are agreed, however, in saying that it was 12 December.

[2] Laval in Procès Pétain, p. 197, cols. 2–3; Laval Parle, pp. 73–5; du Moulin, pp. 62–3; Baudouin, p. 408. Extracts from Marcel Déat's articles are printed in Bouthillier, Vol. I, p. 307.

Bouthillier telephoned Darlan, Huntziger, and Baudouin, Peyrouton went to tell the Marshal that he would shortly be receiving a delegation of his ministers demanding Laval's removal and that there was no need to worry about his reaction as he would be arrested.

It was shortly before 4 p.m. that the 'plotters' – Bouthillier, Peyrouton, Darlan, and Huntziger – met in du Moulin's office. Baudouin joined them later. Only Huntziger expressed some uneasiness, but he did not press the point. Just as they were about to leave to see Pétain, Raphaël Alibert, the minister of justice, turned up unexpectedly. He could tell by their sudden silence that something was up. Then they told him and he, too, joined the delegation.

The meeting with Pétain was brief. Darlan explained why it was necessary to get rid of Laval. Peyrouton outlined the plans for the deputy premier's arrest. It was agreed that a ministerial meeting under Laval's chairmanship, which was due to begin at 5 p.m., would take place as planned in order to avoid arousing his suspicions. This would be followed by a full cabinet meeting at 8 p.m. at which he would be forced to resign.

Laval certainly walked right into the trap. When Pétain asked all the ministers to sign a collective letter of resignation, he did so without a qualm, thinking it was a device to get rid of M. Belin, the minister of labour, with whom he had recently been in disagreement. He was therefore stunned when, after retiring for a few moments, the Marshal returned to announce, 'The resignations of MM. Laval and Ripert[1] are accepted.' Laval rose to his feet. 'Why, *Monsieur le Maréchal?*' he asked. 'I saw you not so long ago. We had a pleasant chat and you didn't blame me for anything. Why are you taking this step?' 'For not keeping me informed and for never giving me notes in writing,' Pétain replied. 'I have my methods of working,' Laval snapped back. 'It's only the results that count. I've never refused *you* an explanation, but I don't trust some of your ministers!' 'You've lost my confidence,' retorted Pétain quite simply. Sensing the Marshal's determination, Laval had no option but to acquiesce. 'I hope, *Monsieur le Maréchal,*' he concluded bitterly, 'that your successive contradictory decisions do not

[1] Ripert was minister of education. Baudouin, Bouthillier, and Peyrouton state that his resignation was accepted in order to make way for Jacques Chevalier, negotiator of the second 'secret agreement' with England. Laval, however, maintained that Ripert had wanted to resign anyway. He was not present at the cabinet meeting.

cause too much harm to our country.' After a formal handshake, he turned and left the room.

It was Laval's intention to return to Paris that night with his wife and daughter and he returned to his office to sort out his papers. He dined with de Brinon and then resumed packing. Suddenly Ralph Heinzen, the American journalist representing United Press International in Vichy, appeared to tell him that his chauffeur had been arrested and his car taken away. Laval immediately telephoned Peyrouton's office and gave the unfortunate official on duty a piece of his mind. He then got on to du Moulin and told him to ask the Marshal for an explanation. Du Moulin replied that Pétain was asleep. 'All right then, wake him up!' replied Laval. In fact, Pétain was far from asleep, but he told du Moulin and his doctor, Ménétrel, to continue to pretend that he was and to try and keep Laval occupied. The two men found the sacked minister in a state of considerable agitation. The building was surrounded not only by regular policemen but by leather-jacketed steel-helmeted members of the *Groupes de Protection* (G.P.), Pétain's personal bodyguard recruited mainly from among ex-*Cagoulards*. 'I tell you they're out to get me,' exclaimed Laval, taking a pen-knife out of his pocket. 'And I've got nothing to defend myself with. . . . What swine! . . . And it's Friday the 13th as well!'

He was soon to be relieved of his anxieties. Commissioner Mondanel of the Sûreté Nationale arrived to tell Laval that he had orders to take him to Châteldon. 'Have you got this order on you?' asked Laval. 'Yes, *Monsieur le Président*,' Mondanel replied. 'Alright,' said Laval, 'I believe you. I don't need to read your paper. Just give me five minutes.' They did so and at about 11 p.m. Laval drove off to Châteldon in a police car. He had wisely obtained an assurance from Mondanel that his escort would consist of regular policemen and not members of the G.P.[1]

At 7.30 p.m. on the following day, Pétain announced his decision to the nation. 'People of France,' he said, 'I have just taken a decision which I judge to be in the country's interest. M. Pierre Laval is no

---

[1] My account of the events of 13 December is based upon the following sources: Laval in *Procès Pétain*, pp. 197, col. 3, 198, cols. 1–2; *Laval Parle*, pp. 75–7; de Brinon, pp. 51–4; Bouthillier, Vol. I, pp. 253–8; Baudouin, pp. 408–13; Peyrouton, pp. 179–83; du Moulin, pp. 63–72; Charles Rochat in *La Vie de la France*, Vol. III, p. 1108. Naturally enough, there are occasional divergences between the various accounts, particularly in respect of times, but they still coincide to a considerable degree.

longer a member of the government. M. Pierre-Etienne Flandin receives the portfolio of foreign affairs. Constitutional act number 4, which designates my successor, is repealed. It is for important reasons of internal policy that I resolved to proceed with this step. It does not affect our relations with Germany in any way. I remain at the helm. The National Revolution continues.'[1]

What was the reason for Laval's dismissal? Baudouin, Bouthillier, and Peyrouton find it in the deputy premier's excessive zeal for collaboration with Germany as exemplified in the military conversations with General Warlimont and the plans for the reconquest of the Chad. But this is a post-war explanation, belied by contemporary documents. At the military conferences of 29 November and 10 December, General Huntziger and Admiral Darlan made the running as much as Laval and, if the latter may be accused of acting as a lone wolf, it is inconceivable that the other two could have said what they did without the full backing of Marshal Pétain and the majority at any rate of the rest of the government. Indeed, Pétain's determination to recover the dissident colonies was emphasized in a conversation he had on 12 December – the day before Laval's dismissal – with Robert Murphy, the American *chargé d'affaires* in Vichy. The Marshal went out of his way to tell Murphy that Weygand was 'now organizing an expeditionary force to defend the Chad against any expedition, British or de Gaulle, which may be operating in that territory'.[2]

A similar interpretation links Laval's dismissal with yet another 'secret agreement' with the British, allegedly concluded on 6 December and 'ratified' on the 9th. There had certainly been contacts through the Canadian minister in Vichy between the British foreign secretary, Lord Halifax, and one of his old French friends, M. Jacques Chevalier, an official in the Vichy ministry of education. But, as in the case of the 'Rougier mission' of October, no agreement was ever reached.[3]

The real reason for Laval's dismissal lies in the fundamental incompatibility between him and Pétain. The latter's remark to du Moulin at the time of the cabinet changes of September 1940 – 'He's no better than the other [parliamentarians] but he's done me too many favours' – is significant in this respect. Laval was a parliamentarian.

[1] Aron, p. 335.
[2] Murphy to Hull, 12 December 1940, F.R.U.S., 1940, Vol. II, pp. 418–20.
[3] See Schmitt, chapter IX.

His methods of working appeared slovenly to the Marshal's precise military mind and he showed a marked lack of deference, instanced by his habit of blowing cigarette smoke in Pétain's face.[1] But above all, perhaps, he tended to take too much upon himself, and in so doing he aroused not only Pétain's anger, but that of his cabinet colleagues as well. Baudouin's frustration at being excluded from Franco-German negotiations while he was still foreign minister and Bouthillier's fury at being undercut in the Bor mines and Belgian gold negotiations, when combined with these technocrats' traditional suspicion of the wily politician, were enough to store up a tremendous reservoir of ill-will towards Laval.

Then, early in December, rumours began spreading that Laval was planning to assume even greater powers. On 6 December he complained to Baudouin that he was not able to govern. 'He wants to be head of the government,' Baudouin noted in his diary, 'with the Marshal remaining as head of state only. He says that negotiations with the Germans are being held back because the Germans feel that he hasn't the necessary powers . . .' The following day, Flandin told Bouthillier that Laval 'was determined to force matters. He would go as far as provoking the formation of an entirely new government consisting solely of his stooges.' The ministry of the interior, Bouthillier noted subsequently, was to receive many similar reports in the next few days. Baudouin told Pétain what he had heard and no doubt Bouthillier and Peyrouton did the same. These rumours would almost certainly be enough to account for Pétain's undelivered letter to Hitler of 9 December in which he alluded to 'certain intrigues by my foreign minister which, together with other serious reasons, lead me to lose confidence in him'.[2]

Hitler's invitation to Pétain to attend the Duc de Reichstadt ceremony in Paris was interpreted as a trap to force him to sign away his powers to Laval, and it was precisely when Peyrouton and Bouthillier learned that the Marshal had changed his mind and was going after all that they resolved to act 'tonight'. There can be no other explanation for the suddenness of Laval's dismissal than the determination that he must not be allowed to take Pétain to Paris for fear of what would happen when they arrived there. Baudouin admitted as much to Robert Murphy on 16 December. Baudouin told the American diplomat

---

[1] De Brinon, p. 44; Jaffré, p. 162.
[2] Baudouin, pp. 402–5; Bouthillier, Vol. I, pp. 249–50; Noguères, p. 269.

'in the strictest confidence' that 'the immediate reason for Pétain's dismissal of Laval is the evidence adduced by Peyrouton . . . and others in the cabinet that Laval planned, after Marshal Pétain's arrival in Versailles, to effect his *de facto* sequestration and obtain from the Marshal his signature to documents which would constitute Laval head of the French state. When the evidence of this conspiracy on the part of Laval was brought to the Marshal's attention he decided it was time for Laval to leave.'[1]

Laval himself offered an interesting gloss on this interpretation at his meeting with Hitler in Munich on 10 November 1942. When the British learned of the military conversations in Paris, he said, they 'had made use of the many varied and effective means at their disposal in Vichy in order to present Marshal Pétain with the hypothesis, which was so insulting to the Führer and by the same token so shocking to him and Laval, that Pétain's participation in the burial of the Duc de Reichstadt's remains would be used as an opportunity to arrest him.' Upbraiding Pétain with the memory of the incident in 1944, Laval claimed that a British agent had boasted that 13 December 1940 was 'the Intelligence Service's finest stroke in ten years'.[2]

The British may have had a hand in spreading the rumours. After all, Marcel Peyrouton wrote in his memoirs of two unidentified 'informants' who, together with Jacques Chevalier, came to see him on 13 December. One of them, from Paris, told him that the Germans were planning to set up a 'more docile' French government.[3] Chevalier was in touch with the British and these mysterious 'informants' may have been British themselves, or Frenchmen working for the British. This version provides the only feasible connection between Laval's dismissal and the Chad expedition, but it does not alter the basic fact. Whoever was responsible for spreading the rumours that Laval was preparing to usurp Pétain's position, it was these rumours that led to his downfall.

Of course, if Laval's methods – however unpopular – had paid off in terms of important concessions from the Germans, he would almost certainly never have been dismissed. He claimed subsequently that he

[1] Murphy to Hull, 16 December 1940, F.R.U.S., 1940, Vol. II, p. 423.
[2] Schmidt, memorandum, 12 November 1942, GFM/F1/0126–55 (the quotation is from frame 0138); Jean Tracou, *Le Maréchal aux Liens*, Paris, André Bonne, 1948, p. 93.
[3] Peyrouton, p. 179.

was due to meet Ribbentrop on 22 December and that the German foreign minister was going to announce the release of a first batch of 150,000 prisoners-of-war, the attachment of the *départements* of the Nord and Pas-de-Calais to the administration in Paris, a considerable relaxation of conditions at the demarcation line, and a reduction on occupation costs from 400 million francs a day to 180 million.[1] Unfortunately, there is no evidence of these alleged concessions in the German foreign ministry archives. The most that can be said is that the Germans would probably have agreed to transfer the Nord and Pas-de-Calais to their military administration in Paris and would have been prepared to discuss the demarcation line and occupation costs. On the other hand, they would almost certainly have refused any further liberation of prisoners-of-war.[2]

13 December 1940 marked the end of Laval's fruitless quest for a Franco-German partnership in the new Europe of Adolf Hitler. True, he renewed his efforts when he returned to power in April 1942, but he soon found that the situation had changed so much by then as to present him with what amounted to a different problem. Gradually he came to realize what the less prejudiced had realized long before: that it was not a question of partnership, but of survival.

---

[1] *Laval Parle*, p. 85. These concessions were not simply a post-war invention of Laval's as can be seen from his conversation with Darlan on 4 February 1941. (See the latter's note in Darlan, pp. 279–80.) The source was Abetz.

[2] Woermann memorandum, 25 November 1940, D.G.F.P., Series D, Vol. XI, No. 401; Unsigned memorandum, 25 November 1940, GFM/121/120186–7. For Abetz's own suggestions on the concessions to be given the French, see his report dated 19 November 1940 in the Abetz papers, GFM/P3/00050–53. Ribbentrop's comment to Ciano was that, when he saw Laval, he intended to put 'plenty of water in his wine'. See Ciano memorandum, 4 November 1940, Ciano, *L'Europa*, p. 611.

8

Interlude

December 1940 – April 1942

If anyone felt his dismissal more keenly than Laval himself, it was Otto Abetz, the German ambassador in Paris. Collaboration with France was advocated at different times by various German personalities, but none of them seems to have attached special importance to Laval's presence in the government. Indeed, the German military authorities in France, according to de Brinon, 'considered that the aged Marshal was free to choose his colleagues. They trusted him – all the more so as Laval was replaced by Flandin.'[1] But Abetz's whole policy had been based upon a close personal relationship with Laval and he saw the latter's dismissal as a threat to both the policy and his own position. In the weeks that followed 13 December 1940, it was Abetz who, together with like-minded Frenchmen, made the running in the various attempts to have Laval reinstated.

His reaction to Laval's dismissal was certainly swift. At 10.30 p.m. on 14 December, the foreign ministry representative on the armistice commission informed the French that 'the Reich government expects that no changes of any kind will be made in the French government before ambassador Abetz has talked with Marshal Pétain' and that 'nothing whatever will be published about changes in the French government which have taken place or are being planned.'[2] Swift though it was, the reaction was in one sense already too late, for Pétain had already broadcast the news of Laval's dismissal to France and the world before the German *démarche* took place.

The following day, 15 December, was the occasion of the postponed

---

[1] De Brinon, p. 58. Ever since he sent a telegram of congratulation to Hitler at the time of the Munich agreement, Flandin had been regarded as extremely pro-German.

[2] Hencke to Foreign Ministry, 14 December 1940, D.G.F.P., Series D, Vol. XI, No. 517.

ceremony to mark the transfer of the Duc de Reichstadt's ashes to Paris. In the circumstances, it was not surprising that Pétain failed to attend, but he did send Admiral Darlan and General Laure as his personal representatives. This gave Abetz an opportunity to present his views to two leading figures in the French government, and he made the most of it. In his speech at the ceremony, he referred to Laval by name as 'the guarantor of collaboration',[1] and in private conversation with Darlan and Laure was violently critical of the French government's action, even going so far as to accuse some ministers of being in British pay![2] General Laure, who returned to Vichy later the same day, told a cabinet meeting that the German attitude seemed to be: 'France is free to have the government she desires. Marshal Pétain is therefore at liberty to change his ministry. But Pierre Laval's absence puts an end to the policy of collaboration.'[3]

Ignoring Darlan's objection that the Marshal would rather resign than reinstate Laval, Abetz set off for Vichy on 16 December, accompanied by ten heavily-armed members of the S.S. He explained the escort to the French – not very tactfully – on the grounds that 'the band of criminals which the French minister of the interior had provided for himself as special police and on which the French government was trying to shift the responsibility for the arrests of 13 December justified these security measures'.[4]

Abetz had his first audience with Pétain at 10 a.m. on 17 December. Darlan was also present, but seems to have taken little part in the proceedings. 'In accordance with instructions,' the German ambassador subsequently wrote in his report to Berlin, 'I presented . . . our demands for a reconstruction of the French government. . . .' According to the Marshal's official reply,[5] these were fourfold. First of all, Laval was to be reinstated as minister of the interior, Flandin remaining foreign minister. Secondly, M. Caziot, the minister of agriculture, and M. Belin, the minister of labour, who were considered anti-German, were to be dismissed. Thirdly, a four-man directorate, consisting of Darlan, General Huntziger, Flandin, and Laval, was to be set up in

[1] *Manchester Guardian*, 17 December 1940.
[2] Darlan, pp. 261–2.
[3] Baudouin, pp. 416–17.
[4] Abetz to Foreign Ministry, 18 December 1940, D.G.F.P., Series D, Vol. XI, No. 531.
[5] Abetz to Foreign Ministry, 18 December 1940, ibid., No. 530.

place of the post of deputy premier. Finally, General de la Laurencie, the French government's delegate in the occupied zone, was to be replaced by the more amenable de Brinon. French sources state that Abetz also requested the dismissal of Peyrouton and Alibert, the two ministers held responsible for Laval's arrest.[1] The German ambassador explained that 'the Führer considered the conduct of the French government towards Laval a personal affront' and warned that while 'Germany did not want to impair the French government's freedom of action in any way . . . in case of a French refusal [she] would not continue the policy of co-operation which had been made possible [at] . . . Montoire.'

When Pétain replied that his decision to part with Laval was 'irrevocable', Abetz claimed that he stood up as if to leave, whereupon 'Pétain . . . urged me to discuss the German demands with him . . . once more, most of which were, after all, acceptable to him'. This performance, Abetz alleged, was repeated no less than five times during the course of the meeting.

The German ambassador also expressed astonishment that Laval was still under arrest. The Marshal professed to know nothing about this and ordered his immediate release. He added that Laval would have to be brought into any discussions concerning his reinstatement to the government and, when Abetz agreed, he instructed du Moulin to fetch him from his home at Châteldon.

'Only once in my life did I show a lack of respect towards the Marshal,' Laval stated at the Pétain trial in 1945. 'It was on that day.' 'I thank you on my own account and I have been asked by my wife and daughter . . . to thank you for the consideration you have shown to us,' he began ironically. Pétain simply denied all knowledge of what had happened and then, adding insult to injury, offered Laval the choice between the ministries of agriculture and labour. Abetz immediately interjected that this was 'tantamount to a rejection of our demand' and threatened, once again, to walk out. Laval lost his temper. Indignantly rejecting any suggestion of a subordinate post, he accused Pétain, according to Abetz, of 'insincerity and double-dealing with England', while du Moulin, who was outside the door, claimed he heard him call the Marshal 'a puppet, a windbag and a weathercock,

[1] Baudouin, p. 419; Bouthillier, Vol. I, p. 264.

twirling in every breeze'. Upon this somewhat inauspicious note, the meeting broke up for lunch.[1]

Immediately after the meal, the cabinet met to consider its reply to Abetz's demands. The consensus was that the violence of Laval's outburst had shocked even the German ambassador, and it was decided to take advantage of this and play for time. Pétain's reply, couched in the form of a letter to Hitler, accordingly promised 'a thorough investigation into the actual merit of the complaints which led me to part with M. Pierre Laval' and into 'the intrigues with which M. Peyrouton, M. Caziot and M. Belin are charged by ambassador Abetz'. In the meantime, the principle of a directorate was accepted and General de la Laurencie was duly replaced by de Brinon.[2]

It was Abetz's contention that Pétain had proposed the investigations 'merely for the purpose of being able to make it appear to his cabinet and to the public that in reappointing Laval and dismissing the ministers objected to he was acting on his own initiative'. If the Marshal did say this, he soon changed his mind. In the meantime, however, Abetz was able to return to Paris that same evening, well satisfied with the results of his trip to Vichy. Laval, who feared assassination,[3] went with him.[4]

Laval's successor, Flandin, had been confined to bed with a throat infection during Abetz's visit and had not played much part in the negotiations concerning Laval's reinstatement. After the ambassador's departure, however, he threw himself into a hard-fought struggle, which was to end in the Pyrrhic victory of Laval's continued exclusion at the price of his own resignation.

Flandin's view seems to have been that the Germans would simply have to get used to the absence of Laval and, after threatening the

[1] Abetz to Foreign Ministry, 18 December 1940, D.G.F.P., Series D, Vol. XI, No. 531; Laval in *Procès Pétain*, pp. 198, col. 3–199, col. 2; *Laval Parle*, pp. 78–9; du Moulin, pp. 80–82.

[2] Baudouin, pp. 419–20; Bouthillier, Vol. I, p. 264; Abetz to Foreign Ministry, 18 December 1940; D.G.F.P., Series D, Vol. XI, No. 530.

[3] Laval subsequently wrote: 'I heard later from the French police that on Thursday the 19th, my guard was to be replaced by the G.P. and that a man called Norey was to shoot me down on the pretext that I was trying to escape' (*Laval Parle*, p. 79). Abetz stated that, after Laval's meeting with Pétain, he provided the former minister with two S.S. bodyguards, 'since after the *gardes mobiles* guarding him had been withdrawn there was reason to fear an attempt at assassination' (Abetz to Foreign Ministry, 18 December 1940, D.G.F.P., Series D, Vol. IX, No. 531, p. 859).

[4] Abetz to Foreign Ministry, 18 December 1940, D.G.F.P., Series D, Vol. XI, No. 531.

ditherers – who included the Marshal – with his own resignation, he obtained cabinet backing on 20 December for instructions to de Brinon which stated that, while Pétain was prepared to dissolve the *Groupes de Protection* and dismiss Alibert, he 'persisted in his irrevocable decision to deprive himself for an indeterminate period of the co-operation of M. Laval'. Further insistence upon the latter's reinstatement, the instructions continued, could only 'inflame to no purpose the relations which exist between the occupation authorities and the chief of state . . .' At the same time, it was emphasized that Pétain's decision 'in no way signifies a difference of opinion over the policy of collaboration as it was defined by M. Hitler and the Marshal at Montoire, a policy to which the Marshal remains completely wedded and which he intends, in the future as in the past, to make compulsory for all members of his government.'[1]

Curiously enough, in spite of the flat refusal to reinstate Laval, Abetz seemed prepared to accept the French proposals, if only as a temporary solution. 'In the present situation,' he telegraphed to Berlin, 'Laval, by his presence in Paris, constitutes an effective means of internal political pressure against the Vichy government. Within the framework of the Vichy government, however, Laval would only meet with opposition because of the attitude of the Marshal and for the time being would not be able to exert much influence.' Moreover, he added, Pétain's refusal to reinstate Laval would deprive the French of the right to ask for German concessions in return for collaboration. Abetz was especially pleased by the news, contained in de Brinon's instructions, that Admiral Darlan was to preside over the directorate which, below the Marshal, was to be at the apex of the French government. This step, which he claimed was taken at his suggestion, was 'in a positive sense the most important of the decisions taken by Pétain, since in this way a man who is a proven enemy of England and personally very well disposed toward Laval moves into the second most important position in the state.' 'I propose,' Abetz concluded, 'that for the moment we content ourselves with the results achieved and not force the reinstatement of Laval until the moment is more favourable and after Darlan's personal position of power has been strengthened.'[2]

---

[1] *Procès Flandin*, pp. 171–2; Baudouin, pp. 422–3; Bouthillier, Vol. I, p. 267. The full text of de Brinon's instructions is printed in de Brinon, pp. 62–4.
[2] Abetz to Foreign Ministry, 21 December 1940, D.G.F.P., Series D, Vol. XI, No. 543.

In his reply, Ribbentrop instructed Abetz to inform de Brinon that 'the government of the Reich is compelled to note with the utmost astonishment that Marshal Pétain has not lived up to the agreement reached in the conversation of 18 December. M. Laval has thus far not been appointed to the cabinet.' Nevertheless, Abetz was permitted to receive the French government's communication officially, Ribbentrop taking refuge behind the promise, also contained in de Brinon's instructions, of a further letter from Pétain to Hitler. 'The government of the Reich,' Ribbentrop wrote, '. . . will not take a definite stand on the matter as a whole until after it has learned of the contents.' In the meantime, it was expected that nothing more would be done about the government reorganization and that no information about it would be published.[1]

Pétain's letter to Hitler – the third[2] in a fortnight – was handed over to the Führer in person by Admiral Darlan in a meeting at Beauvais on Christmas Day. While expressing his wholehearted desire to continue collaboration, the Marshal explained, 'My grievances against M. Laval are well-founded. The attitude which he took toward me in the presence of Herr Abetz . . . renders impossible henceforth and for an indeterminate period the participation of M. Laval in the government which I lead. Even if I wished it, the improper conduct of M. Laval now being largely a matter of common knowledge, I would risk inflicting a dangerous blow to the unity of the empire.'[3]

In his conversation with Darlan, Hitler stated that 'fundamentally it could be a matter of indifference to Germany what persons were in the French government,' but 'if Laval's person was represented as an intolerable element in the government . . . he (the Führer) found it rather tactless that a meeting between him and Laval had been permitted to come about at all.' He seized upon Pétain's remark that Laval's reinstatement would endanger the unity of the empire as evidence of blackmail by General Weygand, which he clearly believed to be the real reason for the French deputy premier's dismissal.[4]

---

[1] Ribbentrop to Abetz, 21 December 1940, ibid., No. 546.

[2] The fourth if one counts the message which de la Laurencie failed to deliver before 13 December.

[3] The text of the letter is contained in Abetz to Foreign Ministry, 25 December 1940, D.G.F.P., Series D, Vol. XI, No. 566.

[4] Cf. OKW/KTB, 20 December 1940, quoted in D.G.F.P., Series D, Vol. XI, p. 918, and Hitler to Mussolini, 31 December 1940, ibid., No. 586, p. 991.

Darlan attempted to counter Hitler's arguments by extolling his own virtues. 'Personally,' he said, 'he had always, since playing a role in the public life of France, been a supporter of German–French co-opera-tion. Since the Führer had spoken of certain mistakes of French foreign policy before the war, he wished to state in this connection that, during all the twenty years that had elapsed since the last war, no naval chief in France had ever been consulted on foreign policy. If this had been done, events would have taken a different turn.' There was much more in the same vein.[1]

Darlan was evidently seeking to convince Hitler that he was a satis-factory alternative to Laval. This emerges clearly from the recollections of Major Paul Stehlin, an air force officer who accompanied Darlan to Beauvais. After the meeting with the Führer, Darlan told him that he wanted to see Abetz 'in order to tell him what I didn't get the chance to tell Hitler'. This was to the effect that 'he possessed assets which Laval didn't have. He had the prestige of a military leader who had not been defeated. He could get France to participate in a rapid German victory over Great Britain. In order to do this it was necessary that he be-come, in practice, head of the government and take over responsibility for defence and foreign affairs. One of his first decisions then would be to recall Weygand from Algiers and replace him by a military leader in whom he had complete confidence because directly subordinate to himself.'[2]

If Abetz was told all this, he was clearly unimpressed, for he had now reverted to his original belief that Laval's presence in the French government was essential and telegraphed Berlin on 26 December that 'the question of Laval has assumed the character of a test of strength' between Vichy and the German government. Although Darlan did not discuss the matter with Abetz, he was said to have told de Brinon that 'he had the impression that a great wrong had been done to Laval. If he were given a little time, he would be determined as president of the directorate to work for a return of Laval to the government.'[3]

Abetz and his French allies did everything within their power to strengthen this alleged resolve of Darlan's. During the first half of

[1] Schmidt memorandum, 24 (sic) December 1940, ibid, No. 564. Darlan's own notes of the meeting are printed in Darlan, pp. 263–7.
[2] Paul Stehlin, Témoignage pour l'Histoire, Paris, Robert Laffont, 1964, pp. 307–8.
[3] Abetz to Foreign Ministry, 26 December 1940, D.G.F.P., Series D, Vol. XI, No. 569.

January 1941, wrote Bouthillier, the French government was subjected 'to pressure which was constant in strength and varied in approach. M. de Brinon, by means of official notes, and writers, by means of unexpected visits, threatened the Marshal with frightful disasters and innumerable calamities if . . . Laval did not resume his place in the government. The Paris press was not the least of the instruments which the German embassy used to intimidate the French government and overcome its resistance.'[1]

Nevertheless, it seems that Abetz was acting largely on his own initiative. Hitler's attitude, for example, was one of callous indifference, tempered only by fears of the possible consequences on any attempt to force the issue. Thus, on 18 December, he was reported to be 'uncertain as to whether he still needed France. The conclusion of peace with England at France's expense continues to tantalize him.'[2] On the 25th, he told Darlan that 'fundamentally it could be a matter of indifference to Germany what persons were in the French government' and, on 9 January 1941, he stated at a conference of his military chiefs that 'after the dismissal of Laval Germany has no longer any obligations [towards France], and this is just as well.'[3] His only fear, as always, was that French North Africa might go over to de Gaulle or the British.[4] It may well have been this fear which prevented him from ordering the occupation of the rest of France.[5]

In a conversation on 8 January 1941 with Baron Jacques Benoist-Méchin, the Germanophile French intellectual and Berlin representative of the French delegation for prisoners-of-war, Abetz admitted that he risked incurring the displeasure of his superiors by his continued support for Laval. 'If I desire Laval's return with all my heart,' he explained, 'it's because I love France and I would not like to see her

[1] Bouthillier, Vol. I, p. 271. Cf. de Brinon's message of 11 January 1941, ibid., pp. 272-3 and extracts from the Paris press, ibid., pp. 307-10.

[2] Halder, p. 236.

[3] OKW/KTB, 9 January 1941, cited in D.G.F.P., Series D, Vol. XI, p. 1058.

[4] Cf. Hitler's remarks to Mussolini at their meeting on 19 January 1941, Schmidt memorandum, 21 January 1941, ibid., No. 672. The Italian record of this conversation is printed in Ciano, L'Europa, pp. 628-9.

[5] This, in fact, was what Goering's chief-of-staff, General Bodenschatz, allegedly told Major Stehlin in Berlin on 20 December (Stehlin, op. cit., pp. 290-92). Such frankness on the part of a high-ranking German officer to a Frenchman may seem unusual, but it must be remembered that Stehlin knew Bodenschatz well when he was assistant air attaché in Berlin before the war, which was, of course, the very reason he was sent on this special mission to the German capital. In any case, Bodenschatz's remarks make military sense.

crushed. . . . I would like to arrive at a reasonable and freely-negotiated peace which would ensure the existence of future generations. Only Laval can obtain that peace.'[1]

With the equally fervent support of de Brinon, Benoist-Méchin was persuaded by Abetz to go on a special mission to Vichy in an effort to convince the Marshal and his entourage of the dire consequences of a failure to reinstate Laval. One piece of ammunition which de Brinon provided for Benoist-Méchin's armoury was the news that the German military authorities were planning to conduct a census in the occupied zone of all males between the ages of 18 and 45. This could easily be interpreted as a prelude to some form of compulsory labour service.[2]

While Pétain was 'visibly moved' by what Benoist-Méchin had to say, both he and his advisers wanted to know two things before they would reconsider their refusal to reappoint Laval. Firstly, was Laval's return to the government a *sine qua non* of continued collaboration? Secondly, how far did Abetz have the backing of Berlin? Benoist-Méchin was instructed to ask the German ambassador the first question point-blank and, if the reply was in the affirmative, to propose a complicated procedure whereby Laval would be reinstated. It involved the following steps: 1). Laval was to write a personal letter to the Marshal, apologizing for the way he had behaved at their last meeting. 2). If the letter was satisfactory, there would be a meeting between the two men. 3). Pétain requested permission to visit Versailles and other towns in the occupied zone from time to time, in order to compensate for the loss of prestige involved in reinstating Laval. 4). He also proposed the appointment of a French press censor to the German military authorities, who would be empowered to prevent attacks upon him and his government by the press in the occupied zone. 5). When these two requests were granted, Laval would be appointed a minister of state and a member of the directorate. These proposals, Pétain told Benoist-Méchin, were designed 'to make the Germans come clean'. Either Hitler did not really want Laval, in which case no more would be heard of him, or he did, in which case

---

[1] Benoist-Méchin's diary for the period 11 December 1940 to 18 January 1941 is printed in *La Vie de la France*, Vol. III, pp. 1703–24. The quotation is from pp. 1708–9.

[2] Ibid., p. 1709. I have found no reference to a proposed census in any of the German records I have consulted.

he should give him 'a dowry' of such important concessions that 'the whole of France understands why I re-appointed him'.[1]

Abetz telegraphed a version of Pétain's proposals to the foreign ministry on 13 January.[2] No reply has been found in the available German records, but Scapini, Benoist-Méchin's superior, told him on the 14th that 'Hitler and Ribbentrop seem to have no interest in the matter. According to M. de Brinon, ambassador Abetz has even been asked to exert no pressure in favour of M. Laval's return.'[3] If this was true, it made little difference, for there were Frenchmen ready to exert that pressure in the ambassador's place. Scapini had already told Benoist-Méchin not to wait for a German reply. 'The question of Laval's return must be settled by Frenchmen,' he said. 'If concessions are to be asked of the Germans, they can only be obtained afterwards.'[4]

The major obstacle to further progress, in fact, was not the attitude of the German government, but that of Laval himself. Since his arrival in Paris on 18 December he had done little except write an effusive letter to Hitler, thanking him for his 'liberation' and expressing the hope that France would not be made to suffer for the mistake of her government.[5] He had told Benoist-Méchin, before the latter set out for Vichy, that he had no desire whatever to re-enter the government, and when it was suggested that he should write a letter of apology to the Marshal, he exploded with indignation. 'Me, apologize to the Marshal!' he exclaimed. 'I reckon he ought to apologize to me.'[6]

In the face of Benoist-Méchin's insistence, however, Laval eventually agreed to reconsider and, after much drafting and re-drafting, a letter was ready by the evening of 15 January.[7] It was a curious document, hardly calculated one would have thought to serve the purpose for which it was supposedly intended. He had remained silent for a month, Laval explained, in order to give the Marshal time to investigate 'the slanderous accusations' which had been made against him. 'I rely upon

---

[1] A full account of Benoist-Méchin's mission can be found in his diary, loc. cit., pp. 1710–16.

[2] Abetz to Foreign Ministry, 13 January 1941, D.G.F.P., Series D. Vol. XI, No. 645.

[3] Benoist-Méchin's diary, loc, cit., p. 1718.

[4] Ibid., p. 1717.

[5] The letter was dated 20 December 1940. For the full text (in German translation), see Abetz Papers, GFM/P3/00071–2.

[6] Benoist-Méchin's diary, loc. cit., p. 1717.

[7] Ibid., pp. 1717–19. See also Laval in *Procès Pétain*, p. 200, col. 1.

your uprightness,' he went on, 'to delay no longer in making known the truth. If you were misled, you must say so. If I acted dishonourably, you cannot remain silent. Every charge must be detailed, proved, or rejected.' What he termed 'the perfectly natural vehemence of my language' on 17 December had been directed, not at Pétain, but at those who were behind the 'unbelievable and abominable plot' against himself. 'Circumstances are such,' he concluded, 'that no one must resign himself to a mistake. Each of us must think only of the fate of France. This sole consideration inspired me when I pursued the policy of far-reaching and loyal collaboration with Germany. With the same consideration in mind, I am sending you this letter in the present situation, in the certainty that you will appreciate its complete sincerity.'[1]

In spite of the uncompromising tone of this communication, Pétain agreed to meet Laval and the confrontation took place on Saturday, 18 January, at the tiny railway station of la Ferté-Hauterive on the line between Vichy and Moulins. Afterwards, a communiqué was issued to the press which stated laconically that the two men had met and that, during the course of a long conversation, 'the misunderstandings which had led to the events of 13 December had been removed.'[2]

This communiqué, Abetz reported to Berlin on 19 January, 'permits Germany to express the hope . . . that Laval will be reappointed to the government as minister of the interior and member of the directorate, and that the elements responsible for 13 December 1940 will be punished and removed.'[3] A closer examination of the evidence, however, shows that Abetz was indulging in wishful thinking. In the first place, there is nothing to suggest that Pétain was seriously considering the reappointment of Laval when he agreed to meet him. Indeed, he described the proposed meeting to some of his ministers as 'a gesture and nothing more'.[4] Secondly, there is no evidence that Laval was really interested in rejoining the government at this stage. The nature of his remarks to Benoist-Méchin and the tone of his letter to Pétain suggest that he was chiefly concerned to clear his name of the charges which had been made against him and which he deeply

[1] The full text of the letter (in German translation) may be found in Abetz to Foreign Ministry, 18 January 1941, GFM/221/149648–50.
[2] Le Temps, 22 January 1941.
[3] Abetz to Foreign Ministry, 19 January 1941, D.G.F.P., Series D, Vol. XI, No. 674.
[4] Bouthillier, Vol. I, p. 276. See also his remarks to du Moulin, du Moulin, p. 129.

resented. This impression is confirmed by the post-war accounts of the meeting by both Laval and du Moulin, who was also present. They show quite clearly that the main topic of conversation was the criticism of Laval's conduct prior to his dismissal. When the possibility of his re-entry into the government was mentioned, it seems to have been vehemently ruled out by both parties.[1]

But Abetz was not the only one who misinterpreted the la Ferté meeting. Laval's successor Flandin, who had been kept completely in the dark, also jumped to the conclusion that it was the prelude to Laval's re-entry into the government. 'Burning his boats' as he described it after the war, he summoned a conference of all the German press representatives in Vichy to tell them that 'the communiqué is not what Laval wanted' and that 'the conversation did not correspond with the Marshal's expectations'. It was the latter's 'ardent desire', he explained, 'not to reinstate Laval to the government', but, 'at the same time [he] wanted to make it clear to the German authorities that not to reappoint Laval did not signify the abandonment of collaboration'. If they insisted that it was a necessary precondition for collaboration, Pétain would bow to their wishes because he wished to continue the policy, but it would be a deep disappointment to him and 'would greatly affect his prestige'.[2]

Flandin claimed at his trial in 1947 that the Germans instantly retaliated against his statement by closing the demarcation line to all men between the ages of 18 and 45.[3] There is no allusion to such a decision in either the foreign ministry files or the available records of the German and French delegations to the armistice commission. What is certain, however, is that Abetz thereafter added Flandin's name to his already long list of *personae non gratae* in the Vichy government. As the unfortunate foreign minister was soon to discover, this did not unduly upset those who, like Admiral Darlan, already had their eye on the main chance.

Indeed, the star of the man who had earlier been described by General von Stülpnagel as a 'straightforward, honest old salt',[4] was in the ascendant. Shortly before 27 January, Hitler had informed Abetz

---

[1] Ibid., pp. 129–32; Laval in *Procès Pétain*, p. 200, cols. 1–2; *Laval Parle*, pp. 83–4.
[2] Rahn to Foreign Ministry, 22 January 1941, GFM/221/149060–63.
[3] *Procès Flandin*, p. 193.
[4] Halder, p. 236.

personally that 'he did not want to have Laval in the French government. He must remain in Paris and be available as an opponent of
Pétain. . . . [He] will be kept ready for the future formation of a
government in France in the event of Weygand throwing in his lot with
the English or de Gaulle. Darlan is at present the crown prince. . . .
He must be supported.'[1]

Abetz clearly found it difficult to keep to these instructions. In a
conversation with de Brinon on 29 January, he painted an alarmist
picture of Hitler's intentions towards France, allegedly based upon his
recent conversation with him. 'The Führer has waited for more than a
month for the French government to remedy its mistakes of its own
accord,' he said. 'Nothing useful has been accomplished. He therefore
considers that the policy undertaken at Montoire must be stopped.' He
was envisaging *inter alia*, Abetz claimed, a more rigorous sealing of the
demarcation line and had decided 'to hold the French government
responsible for any extension of dissidence [in the colonies] and to
consider it as a breach of the armistice agreement'.[2]

This was a considerable extension of what Abetz had told von
Brauchitsch, the German army commander, of his conversation with
Hitler[3] and one must assume that he was exaggerating for a purpose.
The French government certainly interpreted his reference to its
failure to 'remedy its mistakes of its own accord' as an allusion to the
refusal to reappoint Laval. Darlan was prepared to accept his reinstatement – always providing he did not become deputy premier, a
post he had earmarked for himself[4] – but not all members of the
government agreed with him. At a meeting of the directorate on either
30 or 31 January, which was also attended by Peyrouton and Bouthillier, there was said to have been 'a violent argument' between the
military and civilian members in which the former supported Laval's
reinstatement and the latter opposed it. Reporting this news from de
Brinon, Abetz added, 'Darlan enquires every day . . . whether he
could not come to Paris and bring to Laval proposals for his return

---

[1] Ibid., pp. 261–2.

[2] De Brinon to Pétain, 30 January 1941, printed in Darlan, pp. 271–4.

[3] According to the Halder diary, Abetz had simply told von Brauchitsch, 'Collaboration
is at present considered no longer in existence. The Führer will inform Pétain and will fall
back upon the armistice' (Halder, pp. 261–2).

[4] See Darlan's note of 30 January 1941 in Darlan, p. 270, and his handwritten comment
on de Brinon's letter to Pétain of the same date, ibid., p. 274.

to the government.' The German ambassador thus covered himself by making out that the initiative had come from the French and, for good measure, he added that 'in order to gain time and to exclude any possibility of a compromise settlement,' he had told Laval, 'to demand as a minimum requirement the posts of foreign minister, minister of interior, and of premier in a cabinet purged of the former civilian elements.'[1]

On 1 February, Abetz reported that de Brinon had brought a message from Pétain which stated that he intended to recall Laval to the government, but wanted Darlan to have a discussion with Laval and Abetz before announcing the decision. Probably fearing that his superiors would not allow Darlan to come to Paris simply in order to discuss Laval's return to the government, Abetz hastened to add that there were 'a number of technical reasons in favour of Darlan's trip which are in the interest of the military administration of occupied France. . . . A number of urgent administrative and economic measures that can be taken only in agreement with the French government have been postponed, and these could be decided in a discussion with Darlan.'[2] The decision to include a separate justification for Darlan's visit was a wise one. The following day Ribbentrop replied that the admiral could come to Paris to discuss administrative questions, but that, as far as Laval was concerned, Abetz was to keep to the instructions he had been given in Germany and not permit the former deputy premier to return to the unoccupied zone.[3]

'Administrative questions' were, however, neither Darlan's nor Abetz's chief concern. When the former arrived in Paris, on 3 February, his first task was to offer Laval, in Pétain's name, a post in and membership of the directorate of a government of which he himself would be deputy premier. He found Laval, who was evidently sticking closely to Abetz's advice, in an uncompromising mood. 'He could not agree to enter a government functioning in that way,' he told Darlan. '. . . What was more, he could not accept certain members of the government as colleagues and . . . with the exception of Admiral Darlan and General Huntziger, everyone must go.' While he was prepared to allow Darlan to become the Marshal's successor, he wanted to

[1] Abetz to Foreign Ministry, 31 January 1941, D.G.F.P., Series D, Vol. XI, No. 736.
[2] Abetz to Foreign Ministry, 1 February 1941, Ibid., Vol. XII, No. 1.
[3] Ribbentrop to Abetz, 2 February 1941, Abetz Papers, GFM/P3/00099.

become prime minister, a post which would henceforth be separate from that of head of state and whose occupant would enjoy virtually autocratic powers.[1]

According to Abetz, Darlan did not discuss these matters with him, confining himself to the 'administrative questions' already mentioned. But he was reported to have told de Brinon that 'he personally agreed to these demands of Laval's,' although he 'did not believe he would succeed with the Marshal all at once.'[2] Darlan, however, tells quite a different story. According to his account, the governmental question was discussed in considerable detail with Abetz and his principal counsellor, Ernst Achenbach. The German ambassador was stated to have reaffirmed Hitler's determination not to deal with the existing French government, to have attacked Flandin as 'one of the principal opponents of the resumption of collaboration', and, like Laval, to have criticized Pétain's combination of the functions of head of state and head of the government. But when Darlan asked Abetz and Achenbach point-blank whether the Germans would only resume collaboration if Laval became deputy premier, they replied 'evasively', giving him to understand that 'they did not adhere rigidly to the deputy premiership, but that M. Laval must be certain that his freedom and his safety would not be threatened'.[3]

Before returning to Vichy on the following day, Darlan saw Laval once more, and, after explaining that he did not think the Marshal would accept Laval's proposals, suggested a compromise solution. This entailed Pétain's continuance as prime minister, a directorate of Darlan, Huntziger, and Laval, and the participation of Darlan and Laval in the choice of the remaining members of the government. 'He neither accepted nor refused,' Darlan noted, 'but told me that, having been scalded once, he did not want to be again and that, in any case, he insisted upon [the ministry of] the interior.' 'Tell the Marshal,' he said, '. . . that I consider that his prestige and authority must be preserved and that the best way to do it is to place him above the day-to-day struggle.'[4]

In the absence of more precise evidence, it is impossible to tell

[1] See Darlan's record of the conversation in Darlan, pp. 275–6.
[2] Abetz to Foreign Ministry, 4 February 1941, D.G.F.P., Series D, Vol. XII, No. 11.
[3] Darlan, pp. 277–8.
[4] Ibid., pp. 279–80.

whether Laval was any more prepared to re-enter the government at the beginning of February than he had been at the time of the la Ferté meeting. His conditions were so outrageous as to invite repudiation, but, at the same time, he was acting under the advice of Abetz who believed that 'Pétain might be tempted, in the hope of exerting some influence on the text of the Führer's [reply to his letter of 23 December 1940], even at the last moment to comply with Laval's conditions to a large extent.'[1] What was more, Darlan had not rejected these conditions out of hand, but had suggested a compromise which Laval 'neither accepted nor refused', apparently leaving the door open for further negotiations.

Obviously exasperated by Abetz's continued defiance of his instructions, however, Ribbentrop sent him a curt telegram on 5 February, which read, 'Please act according to the instructions you received in Fuschl so that Laval remains in the occupied zone and that, for the moment, no agreement comes about between Laval and Vichy.'[2] Even Abetz could not ignore such a peremptory order and, only two days later, Darlan was able to write that the German embassy was now prepared to forgo Laval's immediate reinstatement to the government, provided certain conditions were fulfilled. These included Darlan's nomination as Pétain's successor, the delegation of prime ministerial powers to him, and the dismissal of certain ministers, notably Flandin, Bouthillier, Berthelot, and Caziot.[3]

Darlan and Pétain still seem to have been prepared to offer Laval the post of minister of state and a seat on the directory, but, according to Darlan, who saw him on 7 February, 'he had recovered all his intransigence'. The admiral advised Laval to 'be patient and not to oppose the action of the Marshal and the new government', as Pétain's final decision about his future would depend upon his attitude. 'I hope,' Darlan noted, 'that I have convinced him – with the help of the German embassy moreover – that it was preferable, not only for collaboration but for himself, if he did not return immediately. . . .' Abetz claimed that 'Darlan and Laval have agreed confidentially that at a time to be agreed upon with the embassy, Laval will move into Darlan's functions as premier, foreign minister, minister of interior, and

---

[1] Abetz to Foreign Ministry, 4 February 1941, D.G.F.P., Series D, Vol. XII, No. 11.
[2] Ribbentrop to Abetz, 5 February 1941, Abetz Papers GFM/P3/00102.
[3] Darlan note, 7 February 1941, Darlan, pp. 281–6.

minister of information, and Darlan will limit himself to the functions of deputy chief of state and later chief of state.' Needless to say, perhaps, there is no confirmation of this in Darlan's version of events, although he did agree that 'in the coming weeks, it will be one of my essential tasks to settle, in agreement with the embassy, the methods of [Laval's] return'.[1]

The *dénouement* of the two-month-old governmental crisis thereafter moved rapidly towards its climax. On 9 February, Pétain appointed Darlan deputy premier and minister of foreign affairs, which he combined with his existing posts of navy minister and commander-in-chief of the navy. The next day he was nominated the Marshal's successor and a week later he became minister of the interior as well. What was left of the government was appointed on 24 February. Of the long list of ministers whose dismissal Abetz had from time to time demanded since 13 December 1940, only Flandin, Peyrouton, and Alibert were missing from the new government.[2] Virtually the sole achievement of the German ambassador's long campaign in favour of the reinstatement of Laval was the creation of a rival 'strong man' in the French government, whose position was to remain practically unassailable for the next twelve months.

Writing in 1945, Laval claimed that, between February 1941 and March 1942, he had had 'no contact with the Marshal or with Darlan'. He had lived in Paris and had frequently made 'fairly lengthy stays at Châteldon', but had never visited Vichy. 'I received no visits,' he wrote, 'and I indulged in no activity which would have facilitated my return to power.'[3] While Laval's post-war statements were often disingenuous, few were quite so disingenuous as this.

At the end of May 1941, the world's press carried reports of a lengthy interview which Laval had given to an American journalist friend, Ralph Heinzen, the Vichy correspondent of the United Press. The interview was, at one and the same time, an appeal to the United States not to enter the war and a justification of French collaboration

---

[1] Darlan note, 7 February 1941, Darlan, pp. 281–6 (the quotations are from pp. 284–5); Abetz to Foreign Ministry, 8 February 1941, D.G.F.P., Series D, Vol. XII, No. 29.

[2] Darlan note, 25 February 1941, Darlan, p. 289. Paul Baudouin had already resigned of his own accord on 2 January 1941 (Baudouin, pp. 428–9).

[3] *Laval Parle*, p. 94.

with Germany. Laval told Heinzen that he could not accept that the Franco-German peace in which he had believed since his meeting with Hitler at Montoire was incompatible with the idea America had of France. 'Would the United States want to push France,' he asked, 'into a contrary peace, a peace of destruction and division, by urging her to spurn the extended hand of Hitler – a hand extended in a gesture quite unique in history?' Americans did not seem to realize, he went on, that 'this is not a war like other wars; it is a revolution from which a new Europe – rejuvenated, reorganized, and prosperous – must come'. Liberty would remain in the country of its birth and so would democracy, but not 'the democracy that caused us so much trouble and to which we owe our present collapse'. Looking forward beyond the war to an era of peace and the creation of 'a new social system', Laval asked, 'Does the United States really want to paralyse our nation on the road to national recovery? Is the United States going to delay the hour when France can step forward boldly to the future by cruel, bloody intervention?' The Americans, he concluded, could play 'a magnificent role' in the rebuilding of Europe, but they could only do so in peace. As for France, she might 'some day become the link between your continent and ours. . . . But you must understand that France cannot fulfil [this] role . . . unless she agrees to practise the policy of total collaboration with Germany.'[1]

There appear to have been three main reasons behind this interview, which was given with the knowledge of the German embassy. In the first place, the prospect of active military collaboration between France and Germany had come a lot nearer reality than at any time since November-December 1940 as a result of the Rashid Ali revolt in Iraq and the Hitler–Darlan meeting of 11 May. Four days after the Laval–Heinzen interview, in fact, the so-called 'Paris protocols' were signed, which foreshadowed the transfer of French war *matériel* in Syria to the Iraqi rebels, the granting of overflight and through transport facilities to the Germans, together with an air base at Aleppo, and the use of the ports of Bizerta and Dakar.[2] Although they were not of course aware of

---

[1] The quotations from the Laval–Heinzen interview are taken from the fullest printed version I have seen, in the *New York Times*, 26, 27 May 1941. The interview actually took place on the 24th. A complete text of Laval's remarks in German translation may be found in Schleier to Foreign Ministry, 27 May 1941, GFM/221/149358–67.

[2] For the Hitler–Darlan meeting, see undated Schmidt memorandum, D.G.F.P., Series D, Vol. XII, No. 491. The 'Paris protocols' are printed in ibid., No. 559.

all the details of the negotiations, the British and Americans sharply attacked Darlan's policies. Laval's interview, said Abetz, was designed 'to remove any doubts that unanimity reigns, both in the Vichy government and in public opinion in the occupied zone, in respect of any American or Anglo-Saxon attempt at interference'.

Secondly, President Roosevelt was due to make an important broadcast speech on 27 May. One of the major themes of British propaganda in the United States was that France could be liberated from the German yoke, and Laval thought it 'important' to inform American public opinion before the president's speech that 'France did not want to be "liberated", but to settle her future fate herself in collaboration with Germany'.

Finally, Abetz commented, it was desirable from the point of view of French internal politics to remove the impression which Laval's re-emergence into public view might create among the out-and-out collaborationists that, once agreement had been reached with Vichy, they would be dropped. 'By means of the Laval interview,' Abetz maintained, 'this purpose will be attained in a way which cannot offend the Vichy government in the slightest, but, on the contrary, in a way which is suitable for the preparation of the ground for a reconciliation between the Marshal and Laval.'[1] In view of the negligible influence which any pronouncement of Laval's was likely to have upon British or American public opinion – let alone their governments – one may be forgiven for thinking that, for both Abetz and Laval, the main reason for the interview was precisely 'the preparation of the ground for a reconciliation' between the latter and Pétain.

Nothing came of this attempt, and a couple of months later Laval resorted to a more direct approach. Rumours were circulating concerning a reshuffle of the Vichy government and he tried to take advantage of it. In a conversation which must have taken place towards the end of July or the beginning of August, he told Jacques Guérard that 'he wished to return to the government before the events of the summer, which could have crucial political repercussions'.[2] In order to do so, he was prepared to sacrifice his pride and make do with the ministry of

[1] Abetz to Foreign Ministry, 27 May 1941, GFM/221/149355–6.
[2] 'The events of the summer' to which Laval alluded are obscure. They may have been developments in Franco-German relations or perhaps the expected German defeat of the Soviet Union.

the interior. Darlan had held the post since February, but there was talk of transferring it to Pierre Pucheu, who was then secretary of state for industrial production. Laval asked Guérard, who knew Pucheu, to approach the latter and persuade him not to accept the offer. Guérard set off for Vichy with a friend, who knew Pucheu much better than he did, but Laval's opponents had got wind of his plans, and when they arrived they found that the decree appointing Pucheu had already been signed.[1]

If we are to believe a report which came into German hands in September, the Vichy government performed an astonishing *volte-face* towards Laval only a matter of weeks after the incident described above. On 27 August, Laval was reported to have told a German agent that 'on 25 August, Pétain had asked him, Laval, to take over the foreign ministry and the supervision of relations with Germany.' But, Laval added, 'he had refused, because he would only be the front man for those existing ministers who did not want sincere collaboration with Germany.' Only the day before, he claimed, Pucheu had personally tried to persuade him to change his mind, but to no avail.[2]

It is hard to credit this story. The French government was undoubtedly experiencing difficulties in negotiating with the Germans at the end of August, but it was experiencing them at the beginning of the month as well, when Laval's approaches were rebuffed. If there was any truth in it, however, further developments were effectively prevented. Only a few hours after his conversation with Hagedorn, Laval was the victim of an assassination attempt which almost cost him his life.

After the German invasion of Russia in June 1941, the ultra-collaborationist groups in Paris had proposed the formation of a volunteer unit to fight on the eastern front. With the blessing of the Germans and the support of the French government, the unit was formed as the *Légion des Volontaires Français contre le Bolchevisme* (L.V.F.) in July.[3] On the occasion of the despatch of the first men to the east, a special ceremonial parade was held at the Borgnies-Desbordes barracks at Versailles on 27 August. Among those present were de Brinon, Marcel

---

[1] Guérard, pp. 68–9. The story is confirmed by Pucheu himself. See Pierre Pucheu, *Ma Vie*, Paris, Amiot Dumont, 1948 (hereafter cited as Pucheu), p. 204.

[2] Undated Hagedorn memorandum, GFM/386/211413–17. See also the covering Woermann memorandum, 20 September 1941, ibid., 211412.

[3] For the L.V.F., see Noguères, pp. 354–9.

Déat, and Laval. As they reviewed the ranks of *légionnaires*, a volley of shots suddenly rang out. Five people, including Laval and Déat, were wounded.[1]

They were rushed to the nearest hospital, where an examination revealed that Laval had been hit in the shoulder and the chest. The chest wound was causing him to cough up large quantities of blood and X-ray photographs showed that a 6.35 mm. bullet had come to a stop barely a quarter of an inch from his heart. Deciding that it was too risky to remove it, the chief surgeon, Dr Pierre Barragué, confined himself to repairing the damage it had done. His surgery was successful, but Laval contracted a post-operative lung infection and for several days his temperature rose above 104 degrees. A less robust individual would almost certainly have died.[2]

Laval's would-be assassin was a 21-year-old ex-sailor from Caen, called Paul Collette. According to his own account, written after the war, he had deliberately enlisted in the L.V.F. in the hope that he would see and be able to kill one or more of the leading French collaborationists. He had written to Eugène Deloncle, the former *Cagoulard* leader and one of the Legion's organizers, on 16 August and had received a reply on the 26th inviting him to report to Versailles on the following day. He did not know that the ceremony was due to take place on the 27th or who would be attending it, and simply seized the opportunity which was presented to him.[3] Laval, however, did not believe that the incident was quite so fortuitous. 'I did not even want . . . to go to Versailles,' he told one of his examining magistrates in September 1945. '. . . It was one of Eugène Deloncle's collaborators, a certain Vanor, who insisted in a particularly pressing fashion. And today I am convinced that Doriot and Deloncle wanted to have me murdered on that occasion because they wanted me out of the way.'[4]

The Germans, it seems, wished to execute Collette immediately, but Laval begged them not to do so. 'It would be a grave mistake,' he said,

---

[1] For contemporary reports of the assassination attempt, see Schleier to Foreign Ministry, 27 August 1941, GFM/386/211386–7, and the press.

[2] Dr Pierre Barragué in *La Vie de la France*, Vol. III, pp. 1384–5.

[3] Paul Collette, *J'ai tiré sur Laval*, Caen, Ozanne, 1946, pp. 11–27. See Abetz to Foreign Ministry, 28 August 1941, GFM/386/211388–9; S.S. report, 29 August 1941, ND, NO–2837.

[4] *Le Monde*, 11 September 1945. It is perhaps interesting to note in this connection that Collette was active in right-wing politics before the war.

'you don't understand the reactions of the French public as I do.'[1] When Collette was sentenced to death by a French court on 1 October 1941, both Laval and Déat petitioned Marshal Pétain for mercy and a reprieve was granted two days later.[2]

Although Laval was well enough to leave hospital in mid-September, the completion of his convalescence seems to have kept him out of politics for some time. By December, however, he was engaged in 'tactical conversations' about his return to power with key members of Jacques Doriot's *Parti Populaire Français* (P.P.F.), another of the Paris collaborationist groups. Living in Paris as he did, it was natural enough that Laval should deal with men like Doriot, but the evidence suggests that, while he was eager to enlist the support of their propaganda machinery to help him return to power, he was by no means anxious to provide the desired *quid pro quo*: a promise to take them into his government. His reluctance to give the necessary assurances to Doriot, for example, meant that it was not until 30 March 1942, only a fortnight before his return to power, that he obtained the P.P.F. leader's agreement to launch a propaganda campaign in favour of a Laval government. Even then, the assurances were couched in the most general terms, in the form of a promise 'to grant the P.P.F. every facility'.[3]

Laval was able to keep Doriot and the other extremists at bay because he knew that he had the support of more powerful allies. These were headed, as usual, by Abetz and his colleagues at the German embassy in Paris. From the end of January 1942, Darlan subsequently noted, 'it became clear that the Germans wanted to see a more pliable man than [myself] at the head of the French government. They let it be known "that no conversation would be possible with the existing government." They let it be understood that the S.S. were going to take over the control of German policy in France and that the occupation would be much harsher.' In February, Ernst Achenbach paid a private visit to Vichy, during the course of which he warned Pétain that if Laval did not rejoin the government, a *Gauleiter* would be appointed for France. In mid-March, another member of the embassy

---

[1] Dr Pierre Barragué, loc. cit. See also Paul Luquet in *La Vie de la France*, Vol. III, p. 1200. General Chambrun, ibid., p. 1689.

[2] *New York Times*, 2 and 4 October 1941. In his memoirs (op. cit., p. 50), Collette denies that Laval and Déat appealed for mercy on his behalf, but the press reports – from a not unsympathetic source – are quite categorical.

[3] Unsigned *Abwehr* report, 21 October [1942], GMR/T–501/189/001068–76.

staff, Professor Grimm, also took the opportunity of a trip to Vichy to stress the need for Laval's reappointment to the government.[1]

Darlan might have been more able to resist this insidious German pressure if he could have counted upon the full support of his own government, but an influential group of ministers, headed by Benoist-Méchin, were also working for Laval's return. What was more, they had succeeded in winning over such influential people as Madame Pétain and the Marshal's doctor/confidant, Bernard Ménétrel.[2] In support of their views, the group could cite the admiral's failure, despite repeated attempts, to restart fruitful negotiations with Germany following the original French refusal in June 1941 to implement the Paris protocols without substantial German counter-concessions. Of course, the Germans were as much if not more to blame for this than Darlan, but it was easy to create the impression that someone else might be more successful.[3] The fiasco of the Riom trial, in which members of the *Front Populaire* governments charged with negligence in preparing France's defences succeeded in turning the tables on their accusers, only added to Darlan's discomfiture.[4] Finally, the news of Hitler's decision of 9 March 1942 to appoint a top-ranking S.S. officer to take over police functions in the occupied zone seemed to confirm the gloomiest prognostications of the pessimists.[5]

Laval was undoubtedly well aware of the intrigues which were being conducted on his behalf,[6] and in the middle of March he entered the field himself. In a conversation with Helmuth Knochen, one of the S.S. representatives in Paris, he complained of the deterioration in Franco-German relations and expressed the hope that he might discuss the matter with a leading German personality. Knochen told him that *Reichsmarschall* Goering was expected shortly in Paris and that he would arrange for Laval to meet him.[7]

Exactly what Laval hoped to gain by his meeting with Goering is

[1] Undated Darlan note, Darlan, pp. 91–2; Aron, pp. 479–80.
[2] Undated Darlan note, loc. cit.; du Moulin, pp. 394–5; de Brinon, p. 98.
[3] For details of Franco-German relations during the period June 1941 to March 1942, see Aron, pp. 449–79; Adrienne Doris Hytier, *Two Years of French Foreign Policy, Vichy 1940–1942*, Paris–Geneva, Librairie E. Droz, 1958, chapter X; and the documents printed in D.G.F.P., Series D, Vol. XIII.
[4] For the Riom trial, see Hytier, op. cit., pp. 329–30.
[5] The full text of Hitler's order of 9 March 1942 may be found on GFM/4644/E209341–2.
[6] Cf. de Brinon, p. 98.
[7] *Laval Parle*, p. 94; Helmuth Knochen in *La Vie de la France*, Vol. III, p. 1776.

uncertain, but if he wanted encouragement for his bid to re-enter the government, he was to be disappointed. In what Laval subsequently described as 'virtually a monologue', Goering delivered a long and violent attack upon France and French policy, declaring that both he and the Führer 'now knew the real feelings which the French had towards Germany and that henceforth the Germans would act in accordance with these feelings of hostility towards them'. Although he did not specifically mention Poland, Laval gained the impression from the tone of his remarks that a similar fate was in store for France. In the circumstances, Goering strongly advised Laval, whom he described as 'an honest enemy', *not* to accept an invitation to re-enter the government. 'One day perhaps, when peace has returned, we will collaborate with you,' he said, 'but not now.'[1]

The outcome of Goering's advice, which was reinforced from other sources,[2] was the reverse of that which might have been expected. Instead of abandoning his efforts to return to power, Laval redoubled them. De Brinon believed that 'ambition and the taste for power were to be . . . stronger than instinct',[3] but this is altogether too simple an explanation. Laval was animated by a blinding faith in his own capabilities and there is no reason to doubt that he was at least partially motivated by the conviction that he alone could prevent the awful fate which faced his country. In spite of unanimous opposition from his family, he pressed on with his plans. 'I considered it most blameworthy to refuse,' he wrote in 1945, 'if, as a result of my presence, my actions, and my words, I could reduce to some extent the misery of France and the French people.'[4]

Goering had told Laval that his conversation with him must remain confidential, but the latter lost no time in sending his son-in-law, René de Chambrun, to Vichy to arrange a meeting with Marshal Pétain so that he could pass on what the German leader had said.[5] The meeting

---

[1] Laval in *Procès Pétain*, p. 200, cols. 2–3: *Laval Parle*, pp. 94–95; Abetz to Foreign Ministry, 8 April 1942, Abetz Papers, GFM/P3/00215–17. This latter account was also derived from Laval. Unfortunately, no German record of the conversation seems to have survived.

[2] Cf. the remarks of Colonel Speidel, chief-of-staff to the German military commander in France, to de Brinon (de Brinon, p. 98).

[3] Ibid., p. 99.

[4] *Laval Parle*, p. 96.

[5] De Brinon, p. 99; du Moulin, pp. 392–3; Leahy to Hull, 27 March 1942, F.R.U.S., 1942, Vol. II, p. 156.

took place on 26 March in the forest of Randan near Vichy. Laval did not actually suggest that he should return to power, but he warned the Marshal that 'through the weakness of his present government he had now lost 90 per cent of his popularity and that the moment had come for a "strong government".' 'If you do not consent to establishing a strong government,' he told Pétain, 'you risk the setting up by Germany of a separate government in Paris. I do not want to be your successor but the people around you must be eliminated. They are too weak.'[1] In view of the 'frequently uncertain attitude of many government agencies,' he added, 'France would find herself in an extremely difficult position morally after the inevitable German victory. It was in France's interest now, therefore, to seek close collaboration with Germany in every matter.'[2]

Pétain promised to consult Darlan, who had not been informed of the Randan meeting beforehand. The admiral was naturally extremely irritated, but was persuaded to see Laval and offer him a post in the government. Laval refused, not, as he implied later, because he was still undecided whether or not to accept Goering's advice, but because he was holding out, as he had done a year earlier, for full powers.[3]

The possibility of Laval's return to power greatly disturbed the United States government which, although now at war with Germany, retained diplomatic representation at Vichy and was continuing its earlier policy of trying to restrain the French government from the worst excesses of collaboration. Upon hearing the news of the Randan meeting, the under-secretary of state Sumner Welles telegraphed the American ambassador in Vichy, Admiral Leahy, 'by direction of the president', instructing him to deliver a message to Marshal Pétain 'at any moment at which in your judgment it appears probable that Laval is to return to the French government' which warned that '. . . were M. Laval or any individual identified with his policy to be called upon to enter the French government in any controlling position, the United States government would be obliged to discontinue its existing rela-

---

[1] Ibid., p. 157. The source of Leahy's information was Ralph Heinzen, who obtained his account directly from Laval. Cf. William L. Langer, *Our Vichy Gamble*, New York, Alfred A. Knopf, 1947, p. 246, fn. 83.

[2] Abetz to Foreign Ministry, 27 March 1942, GFM/112/116480–81.

[3] Undated Darlan note, Darlan, p. 92; Laval in *Procès Pétain*, pp. 200, col. 3, 201, col 1; *Laval Parle*, pp. 95–6; Pucheu, pp. 210–11; Abetz to Foreign Ministry, 27 March 1942, GFM/112/116480–81; Leahy to Hull, 27 March 1942, F.R.U.S., 1942, Vol. II, pp. 156–7.

tions of confidence . . . with the French government at Vichy.'[1]
Admiral Leahy gave this message to Pétain on 30 March. He added
that, in his personal opinion, the threat contained in his government's
communication signified nothing less than the breaking off of diplomatic relations.[2]

This threat seems to have had its effect. Whether Pétain actually told
Laval at their next meeting on 2 April that he had given up the idea of
recalling him to the government is uncertain – accounts of the meeting
vary[3] – but the Marshal certainly acted as though he had. On 4 April, he
gave his old friend Colonel Fonck instructions to go to the Paris office
of the *Sicherheitsdienst* (S.D.) with a list of ministers to be transmitted
to Germany for Hitler's approval. The list did not include Laval's
name. Indeed, it contained such notorious opponents of Franco-
German collaboration as François Charles-Roux, the erstwhile permanent head of the Quai d'Orsay who had resigned at the time of Montoire, and General Picquendar. The S.D. was deliberately chosen as the
channel for transmittal because of doubts as to the reliability of the
embassy. If necessary, Fonck was empowered to go to Berlin to continue negotiations. Needless to say, the S.D. informed the foreign
ministry, and Abetz, who was in Germany at the time, instructed his
colleagues to pass on the news to 'our political friends, especially
Darlan, Laval, and Benoist-Méchin'.[4]

In the meantime, Benoist-Méchin had informed Rudolf Schleier,
who was in charge of the German embassy in Abetz's absence, of the
American 'ultimatum'. This item of information was immediately
relayed to the foreign ministry and Abetz[5] and played a significant,
though by no means clear, part in the subsequent course of events.
French sources – and this includes Laval – are unanimous in declaring
that, when he heard of Roosevelt's threat, Hitler issued an ultimatum

[1] Welles to Leahy 27, March 1942, ibid., pp. 160–61.

[2] Leahy to Hull, 30 March 1942, ibid., p. 161. In fact, Leahy was opposed to the idea of a
break in diplomatic relations, which was indeed the United States government's intended
riposte to Laval's reappointment. In a private letter to Welles, he urged his own recall as an
alternative (William D. Leahy, *I Was There*, London, Gollancz, 1950, pp. 109–10).

[3] Undated Darlan note, Darlan, p. 92; Pucheu, p. 211; du Moulin, p. 396; Captaine de
Vaisseau Féat in *La Vie de la France*, Vol. III, pp. 1696–7.

[4] Abetz to Paris embassy, 9 April 1942, GFM/112/116507–8. Du Moulin tried his hand
at the construction of yet another list of ministers (du Moulin, pp. 396–8). Pétain subsequently apologized to Darlan for the Fonck mission. See Pétain to Darlan, 12 April 1942, in
Darlan, p. 296.

[5] Schleier to Foreign Ministry, 4 April 1942, GFM/112/116499–501.

of his own to the effect that he would judge France's willingness to collaborate with Germany by the presence or absence of Laval in the French government. Thenceforth, they argue, his return to power was inevitable.[1]

German sources, however, are equally unanimous in declaring that there was no German pressure. Affirmations to this effect to the Italians[2] and the Japanese[3] can be written off as manifestions of a desire not to offend the susceptibilities of difficult allies who might fear that Laval's return to power heralded German backing for French opposition to their annexationist plans. But what are we to make of Abetz's 'confidential remarks' to an army officer that 'the German government played no part in the transformation of the French government'?[4] In his memoirs, moreover, Abetz recalled that he was at Hitler's headquarters when news of the change was received and 'was thus an on the spot witness of the displeasure at the decision reached in Vichy'.[5] When Laval subsequently described Hitler's alleged reaction to the American ultimatum in an off-the-record speech, Ribbentrop commented that he 'knew nothing of such a remark by the Führer'.[6]

Some light is thrown on the matter by a letter which Lieutenant-General Hanesse, Goering's representative in Paris, wrote to the *Reichsmarschall* in the middle of April. Hanesse reported that René de Chambrun had told him that, shortly after Easter (which was on 5 April), he had received an urgent message from Achenbach of the German embassy just as he was about to leave for Vichy to see his father-in-law. Achenbach informed him that Hitler had told Abetz that he agreed with the sentiments expressed in a recent article by the collaborationist journalist Jean Luchaire, to which Abetz had drawn his attention, and that he now considered Laval's return to power

---

[1] Laval speech to teachers' dinner, 3 September 1942 (unpublished text kindly communicated to me by M. René de Chambrun); undated Darlan note, Darlan, p. 93; Darlan to Pétain, 5 October 1942, in Admiral Docteur, *La Grande Enigme de la Guerre: Darlan, Amiral de la Flotte*, Paris, Editions de la Couronne, 1949, p. 232; de Brinon, p. 103; Pucheu, pp. 211–12.
[2] Ciano memorandum, 29–30 April 1942, in Ciano, *L'Europa*, p. 717.
[3] Ribbentrop to Ott, 19 April 1942, GFM/112/116566.
[4] Brandts to Armistice Commission Armaments Section, 22 April 1942, GMR/T–77/ 638/1833344–5. Cf. also Woermann's briefing, ibid., 30 April 1942, ibid., 1833342–3.
[5] Abetz, p. 234.
[6] Ribbentrop to Abetz, 17 June 1942, GFM/422/217227–9. Abetz had telegraphed a report of Laval's speech, which had been made on 13 June, to the foreign ministry (Abetz to Foreign Ministry, 14 June 1942, ibid., 217202–5).

'desirable'. 'Encouraged by this cordial and spontaneous message from the chancellor,' Hanesse concluded, Laval had 'intensified his negotiations with Pétain.'[1]

Luchaire's article, which was almost certainly inspired by the German embassy and which appeared in *Le Nouveau Temps* on 5 April, stated that France could not afford to lose a single day in remedying the tragic situation in which she found herself. She had, however, to put a stop to 'United States blackmail' which was being exercised by the American radio and the American embassy in Vichy. 'By asking Vichy not to compose a collaborationist government,' Luchaire concluded, 'the U.S.A. has forced Vichy to choose between Washington and Berlin. It has therefore struck a deadly blow to the wait-and-see policy.'[2] It is easy to see how these remarks, which did not mention Laval by name, could have received a general endorsement from Hitler. It is equally easy to see how this endorsement could have been deliberately twisted by Abetz and his colleagues into an ultimatum to the French government to bring back Laval.

On the same day that Benoist-Méchin informed the Germans of the United States government's warning – 3 April – he also told them that Darlan, whose irritation at the way he had been treated over the Randan meeting had given way to his customary instinct for self-preservation, had suggested three alternative solutions to the governmental problem. In the first he would become commander-in-chief of all the armed forces while Laval was appointed deputy premier. In the second, he would share the deputy premiership with Laval, and, in the third, he would remain deputy premier himself with Laval in a subordinate post. Both he and Laval were said to favour the first solution and Pétain was to be asked to make up his mind in the near future.

At this stage, however, the Marshal was still under the influence of the American warning and was also on the point of sending Colonel Fonck to sound out the *Sicherheitsdienst* in Paris. In other words, he was not interested in Darlan's proposals. It was not until some time later, when Fonck's mission had clearly failed and when the German

---

[1] Enclosure in Goering to Ribbentrop, 16 April 1942, ibid., 112/116549-50. De Brinon was also informed by Achenbach of Hitler's approval of Luchaire's article (de Brinon, p. 103).

[2] B.B.C., *Daily Digest of Foreign Broadcasts*, 8 April 1942, Part I, Section 1C, pp. iv–v. The article was broadcast over Paris radio on 7 April.

embassy had begun to bombard Vichy with its fabricated threats, that he changed his mind. On 13 April, de Brinon flew to Vichy to impress upon him the need to make a quick decision.[1] With the admiral's support, de Brinon urged the adoption of Darlan's first solution. 'I've long held the same opinion,' Pétain blandly replied and asked the two men to consult Laval at once.[2]

By prior arrangement no doubt, Laval was staying nearby at Châteldon. When Darlan and de Brinon arrived at his home, they found him apparently less interested in the offer they had brought than in the elucidation of Darlan's rôle in the events of 13 December 1940. In fact, the two were linked, for Laval made it quite clear that he was not prepared to work with any of the ministers who had been responsible for his dismissal sixteen months previously. Darlan's rather lame explanation seemed to satisfy him, however, and agreement was reached in principle on the basis of the admiral's proposal. This agreement was confirmed the following day at a meeting between Laval and Pétain.[3]

Now it was only a matter of choosing a government and of defining Laval's powers more precisely. The list of ministers was ready on 18 April and was published in the *Journal Officiel* on the following day. As was to be expected, the 'men of 13 December' – Bouthillier (finance), Belin (labour), and Caziot (agriculture) – were dropped. They were replaced by Laval's friend and former colleague, Pierre Cathala, an ex-syndicalist and friend of Mussolini's, Hubert Lagardelle, and a 'technician', Jacques Leroy-Ladurie. There were many other changes and, of the senior members of Darlan's government, only Joseph Barthélemy, Pétain's confidant Lucien Romier, Admiral Platon, and Benoist-Méchin survived.[4] Laval had tried to include a number of members of parliament – among them his friend Adrien Marquet – but they had either asked for posts he was not prepared to give them or had simply refused any post at all. He was more successful in excluding the ultra-collaborationists, whose propaganda he had been using to accelerate his return to power. He told Marcel Déat on 15 April that it

---

[1] Schleier to Foreign Ministry, 4 April 1942, GFM/112/116499–501; de Brinon, p. 102.
[2] Ibid., pp. 104–5.
[3] Ibid., pp. 105–8; Schleier to Foreign Ministry, 13, 14 April 1942, GFM/112/116525–6, 116527.
[4] For the composition of Laval's government, see J.O., *Lois et Décrets*, 19 April 1942, p. 1494, cols. 2–3.

was impossible to appoint him without appointing Doriot as well, 'and that wouldn't do you, the Marshal, or me any good'.[1]

While Darlan remained Pétain's successor, Laval, in addition to combining the portfolios of foreign affairs, the interior, and information, was designated 'head of the government', a new position which was described in a constitutional act as disposing of 'effective control of the internal and external policy of France'. He was responsible only to Pétain, as head of state.[2]

The terms on which Laval returned to power in April 1942 were strikingly similar to those which he had demanded in February 1941. He now had all the guarantees he wanted against a repetition of 13 December. But his real enemies were not in Vichy; they were in Berlin.

[1] For details of the formation of Laval's government, see de Brinon, pp. 108–13; Guérard, pp. 71–3; Pierre Cathala in La Vie de la France, Vol. I, pp. 96–7; Adrien Marquet in ibid., Vol. III, pp. 1497–8; René Bousquet in ibid., pp. 1558–9.
[2] For the text of the constitutional act, see J.O., Lois et Décrets, 19 April 1942, p. 1494, col. 2.

9

The Collaboration: The Second Round

April – November 1942

When Laval was dismissed in December 1940, the Second World War was still essentially a European conflict. By the time he returned to power in April 1942, however, it had assumed global proportions. On 22 June 1941, the Germans invaded the Soviet Union. On 7 December, the Japanese struck at the United States naval base at Pearl Harbour and attacked British possessions in the Far East. Four days later, Hitler and Mussolini gratuitously linked their fate to that of the land of the rising sun by declaring war upon the United States.

Germany's attack upon the Soviet Union, and even more the entry of the United States into the war, marked the beginning of the end for the Axis powers. But in April 1942, the situation did not look anything like as clear-cut as this; Hitler's armies were deep inside Russia and on 5 April he signed the directive which was to take them into the Caucasus later in the year. Although there had been stalemate in North Africa since January, it was to be broken on 27 May, when Rommel launched an offensive which was to carry his combined Italo-German forces nearly all the way to Cairo. In the Far East, the Japanese had conquered Malaya, the Dutch East Indies, and all but the tiny island of Corregidor in the Philippines. Their forces had also landed in New Guinea and were making considerable headway in Burma. 'I wish I could see more daylight as to how we are to keep going through 1942,' Churchill's principal military adviser noted in his diary on 7 April.[1]

In the circumstances, Laval need not be blamed for continuing to believe, as he had done in 1940, in the probability of an Axis victory. But, just as in 1940, it was not merely a matter of belief, but of desire.

---

[1] Arthur Bryant, *The Turn of the Tide*, London, Collins, 1957, p. 350.

The German invasion of Russia, he told the French people in a broad-cast on 20 April 1942, had 'revealed the purpose' of the war. Did they really believe that if the Soviets won, they would stop at the French frontier? No, France was faced with a choice: 'either to be integrated, with our honour and vital interests respected, in a new, pacified Europe which will emerge tomorrow from the epic which is unfolding before our eyes, or resign ourselves to seeing the disappearance of our civilization.' His own mind was made up. 'No threat will prevent me from pursuing agreement and reconciliation with Germany, because this policy is prompted solely by a concern for France, whose overriding interest has been, is, and always will be, my only guide.' There was no other policy, he concluded, which could defend the interests of French prisoners-of-war, alleviate the country's burdens, loosen its shackles and 'ensure the future of our children, the grandeur of France, and the fate of our empire'.[1]

In private, Laval was less lyrical but equally categorical. He told the American ambassador, Admiral Leahy, on 27 April that 'in the event of a victory over Germany by Soviet Russia and England, Bolshevism in Europe would inevitably follow. Under such circumstances he would prefer to see Germany win the war. . . . He felt that an under-standing could be reached [with Germany] which would result in a lasting peace in Europe and he believed that a German victory (or possibly a negotiated peace) is preferable to a British and Soviet victory.'[2]

But if 'he was vehement in his attack on Great Britain, claiming that she is basically responsible for the plight in which France finds herself today', he insisted that he wished to maintain good relations with the United States. 'He repeated on two occasions,' Leahy reported, 'that neither by word nor act would his government make any unfriendly gesture to the United States.'[3] Ten days earlier, he had given a similar assurance to Jacques Lemaigre-Dubreuil, a French industrialist whom he knew to be in touch with Robert Murphy, President Roosevelt's special representative in French North Africa. 'Tell him,' he said, 'that President Roosevelt and the Americans . . . can insult me and

---

[1] *Le Temps*, 22 April 1942.
[2] Leahy to Hull, 27 April 1942, F.R.U.S., 1942, Vol. II, pp. 181-2. Two close advisers of Laval have emphasized the importance of this conversation as an indication of Laval's policy. See Charles Rochat in *La Vie de la France*, Vol. III, p. 1109; Guérard, p. 86.
[3] Ibid.

drag me in the mud, but I will never utter a word and never commit an act which can be unfavourably interpreted by America, whose friendship is vital for France.'[1]

Unfortunately, the Americans were in no need to respond to overtures from a man for whom they had lost all political consideration. After Laval's return to power, in fact, there was a distinct deterioration in the never very cordial relations between the United States and Vichy.

First of all, Admiral Leahy was recalled 'for consultation', leaving Mr Pinkney Tuck in charge of the United States mission.[2] Then, on 4 May, the United States government issued a statement to the press giving its full support to the British invasion of Madagascar, which was designed to forestall the possible occupation of the island by the Japanese.[3] The following day, Laval handed a stiff note of protest to Mr Tuck and referred to his conversation with Admiral Leahy. He 'repeated that he desired to commit no unfriendly act against us', Tuck informed Washington. 'This sentiment he thought represented the true feeling of the people of both countries.'[4]

More serious were developments in the French West Indies. After the French collapse of 1940, the Americans had concluded an informal agreement with Admiral Georges Robert, the French high commissioner, as part of their policy of maintaining the neutrality of the western hemisphere. Under the terms of this agreement, Robert continued to act as Vichy's representative, but undertook not to allow the warships under his command to leave the area without prior consultation with the United States, and accepted the appointment of an American naval officer to keep an eye on the situation. This arrangement was confirmed after the United States entered the war in December 1941.[5]

But on 9 May 1942, Admiral Hoover, the American naval commander in the Caribbean, presented Robert with a memorandum which

---

[1] Jacques Lemaigre-Dubreuil in *La Vie de la France*, Vol. III, p. 1181.
[2] Welles to Leahy, 15, 16 April 1942, F.R.U.S., 1942, Vol. II, pp. 170, 171.
[3] Hull to Tuck, 4 May 1942, ibid., pp. 698–9. It is uncertain whether, in fact, the Japanese did intend to occupy Madagascar. Laval told the Germans that he intended to ask them to do so. Cf. Schleier to Foreign Ministry, 27 April 1942, GFM/112/116617–18.
[4] Tuck to Hull, 5 May 1942, F.R.U.S., 1942, Vol. II, p. 700.
[5] For details, see Blocker to Hull, 7 August 1940, ibid., 1940, Vol. II, pp. 513–16; Admiral Georges Robert, *La France aux Antilles de 1939 à 1943*, Paris, Plon, 1950, pp. 79–83, 109–15.

stated that 'in the light of the announced policy of the present chief of
the French government at Vichy [i.e. Laval], looking toward further
collaboration with Germany, it is no longer possible for the government of the United States to maintain the present arrangements. . . .'
Among other things the memorandum called for the immediate immobilization of the French warships and American control of all communications. But what was probably most important of all, from the
point-of-view of Vichy, was the American invitation to Robert to disassociate himself completely from the French government and negotiate with the United States direct.[1]

When the French ambassador in Washington, Henry Haye, protested about this and suggested that the Americans should negotiate
with his government, Cordell Hull, the United States secretary of
state, replied in the most self-righteous tones. 'I . . . said with some
emphasis,' runs his record of the conversation, 'that with Laval bound
by ties of friendship and loyalty to Hitler in this unspeakable movement
of utter destruction of everything that is worthwhile to humanity . . .
it would be incomprehensible that this government would even re-
motely consider sitting down and negotiating in the instant [sic] situation with Laval.'[2]

Robert, however, had already obtained authorization from the
American representative on the spot to cable Vichy for instructions
and, in response to his own suggestion, he was empowered to accept
the principle of immobilization and to negotiate on the other points in
the American memorandum. These negotiations, which took six
months to complete, resulted in some concessions by the Americans
and preserved at least a semblance of Vichy sovereignty over the
French West Indies.[3] The Germans were indignant at Robert's being
permitted to negotiate and repeatedly insisted that the immobilization
of his ships was a breach of the armistice agreement and that he should
scuttle them forthwith. Laval replied that he was seeking to compromise the United States government in the eyes of prudent Americans
and Latin American governments, an endeavour in which he claimed
some success. He assured the Germans that the ships would be scuttled

---

[1] Hoover to Robert, 9 May 1942, F.R.U.S., 1942, Vol. II, pp. 625–7.
[2] Hull memorandum, 11 May 1942, ibid., pp. 627–9.
[3] Robert, op. cit., pp. 121–34. As the result of an American blockade in May 1943,
Admiral Robert finally severed his connection with Vichy in July of the same year.

'at the slightest sign of an attempt at a surprise attack'. The Germans were not convinced, but let the matter drop.[1]

Laval's negotiations with the Germans over the French West Indies show a slight but important shift in his tactics from those he had employed in 1940. Then he had made gratuitous concessions – over the Bor mines and the Belgian gold for example[2] – in the hope that they would help produce an atmosphere of goodwill. Now, it seemed, he had learned that this approach did not pay and one can detect increasing evidence of tactical hard-bargaining within the strategic framework of his policy of Franco-German collaboration. But the strategic framework remained. 'The policy of agreement and reconciliation with Germany,' he told the French people on 20 April, 'must be carried out loyally. . . . It must exclude all equivocation and it is only upon sincerity of word and deed that lasting agreement and reconciliation can be based.'[3] By and large, Laval continued to live up to his own precept.

He would have strenuously denied any charge of *naïveté*. 'I am sometimes asked, "Do you have confidence in Germany?" ' he told a private meeting of prefects in September 1942. 'It's not a question of confidence. I have no means of finding out whether the person I'm talking to, whoever he may be, is sincere. But . . . I can tell the difference between intelligence and stupidity. Clearly, for France in her present position, intelligence consists of practising a policy of *entente* with Germany in order to survive. But the same intelligence compels Germany to practise the same policy. . . . I defy anyone – and I've said this to the Germans – to build a solid, articulated, and viable Europe without France's consent. France cannot be destroyed. She is an old country who, despite her misfortunes, has, and always will have, thanks to her past, a tremendous prestige in the world, whatever the fate inflicted upon her.'[4]

Unfortunately, the Germans did not share Laval's conception of what was intelligent and what was stupid. On 31 January 1942, Hitler told a group of his intimates that 'France remains hostile to us. She

[1] Ribbentrop to Abetz, 12, 15 May 1942, GFM/422/216982-3, 217021-4; Abetz to Foreign Ministry, 17 May 1942, ibid., 217048-50, 217051-4; Ribbentrop to Abetz, 17 May 1942, ibid., 217055-6; Rintelen to Abetz, 20 May 1942, ibid., 217072.

[2] See above, pp. 246-47.

[3] *Le Temps*, 22 April 1942.

[4] Speech to prefects of the unoccupied zone, 25 September 1942 (unpublished text kindly communicated to me by M. René de Chambrun).

contains, in addition to her Nordic blood, a blood that will always be foreign to us. . . . In imitation of Talleyrand in 1815, the French try to profit by our moments of weakness to get the greatest possible advantage from the situation. But with me they won't succeed in their plans. There's no possibility of our making any pact with the French before we've definitely ensured our power. Our policy, at this moment, must consist in cleverly playing off one lot against the other. There must be two Frances. Thus, the French who have compromised themselves with us will find it to their own interests that we should remain in Paris as long as possible. But our best protection against France will be for us to maintain a strong friendship, lasting for centuries, with Italy. Unlike France, Italy is inspired by political notions that are close to ours.'[1]

Laval's accession to power did nothing to alter the Führer's views. No one in France, he said on 13 May, had sufficient calibre to take the necessary decisions – certainly not Laval, whom he described as 'nothing but a parliamentary hack'.[2] In August, he went even further in his disparagement of the French prime minister. There was a common thread which linked de Gaulle and Laval, he told the Italian ambassador. 'Basically,' he explained, 'the former is simply trying to obtain by force what Laval seeks to get by cunning.'[3] But perhaps the best indication of his feelings was his signing, on 29 May 1942, of an updated order for the occupation of the rest of France (Operation 'Anton'). The requirements of the eastern front meant that sufficient numbers of troops could not be kept permanently on stand-by, as for Operation 'Attila', but the possibility of invading the unoccupied zone was always in Hitler's mind.[4]

The Führer's anti-French views were shared by other senior members of the Nazi hierarchy. Goebbels noted in his diary on 2 April 1942 that 'we must not hold out any great hopes in respect of the French situation. I consider the French people to be sick and rotten. Something worthwhile in the way of positive contributions to the resurrection of Europe is hardly to be expected from them. This proves that

[1] *Hitler's Secret Conversations, 1941–44*, New York, Signet Books, 1961, pp. 264–5.
[2] Ibid., pp. 449–50.
[3] Alfieri to Ciano, 5 August 1942, in Dino Alfieri, *Due Dittatori di Fronte*, Milan, Rizzoli, 1948, p. 258.
[4] Führer directive No. 42, 29 May 1942, in Walther Hubatsch (ed.), *Hitlers Weisungen für die Kriegführung, 1939–45*, Frankfurt-am-Main, Bernard und Graefe Verlag für Wehrwesen, 1962, pp. 189–91.

the Führer's policy towards France has been absolutely correct. The French must be put on ice. As soon as they are flattered, they treat it as pseudo-revenge. The more they are left in suspense, the quicker they will be inclined to stay in their place.'[1]

In a speech to senior officials on the food situation in August 1942, Goering provided a definition of Franco-German collaboration which could have been extended to fields other than the economic. 'If they hand over until they can't hand over any more,' he declared, 'and if they do it of their own free will, then I'll say that I'm collaborating. But if they bolt everything down themselves, then they're not collaborating, and that must be made clear to the French.' As for Laval, Goering jokingly observed that he served the purpose of soothing Abetz[2] and that, as a consolation, he might be allowed to eat in Maxim's, which should be closed to all other Frenchmen.[3]

An incident which occurred at the beginning of Laval's second period of office and which served to confirm German suspicion of France was the escape of General Giraud. Commander of the 9th army, Giraud had been captured by the Germans in May 1940 and was interned in the castle of Königstein on the River Elbe. Having already escaped once from German captivity, during the First World War, Giraud was determined on a repeat performance and after lengthy preparations, which included learning German, he went over the wall on 17 April 1942. After a series of adventures, he crossed the Swiss frontier on 22 April and arrived in the unoccupied zone of France on the 25th.[4]

Hitler was extremely concerned at Giraud's escape. 'We must do everything possible to recapture this man,' he declared on 25 April. 'As far as I know, he is a general of great ability and energy, who might well join the opposition forces of de Gaulle and even take command of them.'[5] 'For my part,' he added ominously, 'I see in the escape of this general, to whom every possible facility has been granted to alleviate the burden of his captivity, a significant pointer to the real attitude of the French toward us. We must therefore keep a very cool head in our

[1] Louis P. Lochner (ed.), *Goebbels Tagebücher*, Zurich, Atlantis Verlag, 1948, pp. 150–51.
[2] Goering was only slightly exaggerating when he said that Abetz was the only man who believed in collaboration. Hitler was already suspicious of his ambassador for this very reason. See *Goebbels Tagebücher*, op. cit., p. 46; *Hitler's Secret Conversations*, op. cit., p. 332.
[3] Goering speech, 6 August 1942, ND USSR–170.
[4] General Henri Giraud, *Mes Evasions*, Paris, Julliard, 1946, pp. 73–129.
[5] According to Abetz, Hitler believed that Giraud was the author of de Gaulle's *Vers l'Armée du Métier* (Abetz, p. 236).

dealings with them, both now during the armistice period and later when the peace treaty is formulated; and we must bear in mind all historical precedents and take decisions in which sentiment plays no part.'[1]

What made matters worse was that, initially at any rate, Giraud received something of a hero's welcome from the French government and was invited to lunch with Pétain.[2] Only Laval was unhappy. He bluntly told Giraud that his escape had damaged his policy of Franco-German collaboration. Of course every prisoner-of-war had a theoretical right to escape, but Giraud was a special case. Laval suggested that he should return to Germany voluntarily.[3]

But Giraud turned a deaf ear to all such appeals, even when spiced with the offer of a government post to help look after the interests of French prisoners-of-war. He failed to respond to the arguments of Abetz, whom he met at Moulins on 2 May,[4] and even to those of the Marshal, who, under considerable pressure, had begun to side with Laval. When the latter drew his attention on one occasion to the fact that the Germans would probably take their revenge for his escape by inflicting hardships upon other French prisoners, Giraud unrealistically asked the prime minister to show him the paragraph of the Geneva Convention which would permit such a violation of the law. Laval became increasingly exasperated. 'The ——!' he was reported to have exclaimed. 'He gives me the ——! Why didn't he go to England in the first place?'[5]

The most that Laval was able to extract from Giraud was his signature to a letter to Pétain in which he gave 'his word of honour as an officer' to do 'nothing which can in any way harm your relations with the German government or hinder the work which you have charged Admiral Darlan and President Pierre Laval to carry out under your high authority.'[6] But, as Giraud himself admitted, he did not consider

---

[1] *Hitler's Secret Conversations*, op. cit., pp. 417–18. See also *Goebbels Tagebücher*, op. cit., pp. 175–6.

[2] Giraud, op. cit., p. 131.

[3] Ibid., pp. 133–4.

[4] For two very different accounts of the meeting, see ibid., pp. 137–9; and Abetz to Foreign Ministry, 3 May 1942, GFM/422/216899–908.

[5] Giraud, op. cit., pp. 135–7, 139–44.

[6] For the text of the letter, which is dated 4 May 1942, see Albert Kammerer, *Du Débarquement Africain au Meurtre de Darlan*, Paris, Flammarion, 1949 (hereafter cited as Kammerer, *Débarquement*), p. 106.

himself in any way bound by this pledge and, as early as June 1942, he was in touch with the Americans as a preliminary to the long negotiations which led to his participation in the Allied landings in North Africa the following November.[1] In the long run, Giraud's attitude may have been the correct one. But he was almost completely devoid of political sense and his conduct was unnecessarily provocative. The Germans did retaliate by clamping down on concessions to French prisoners-of-war,[2] and the whole affair succeeded in making Laval's task a great deal more difficult than it was already.

It was partly no doubt as a result of the Giraud affair that Laval decided to write a personal letter to Ribbentrop, the German foreign minister. Dated 12 May 1942, it began by affirming that Laval's determination to do all he could in the interests of Franco-German collaboration was known by everyone. Moreover, the prime minister went on, 'Frenchmen know that future peace is assured as a result of our understanding and I am certain that, in these conditions, France will find a place in the new Europe worthy of her past.' Germany was waging 'a gigantic struggle' against bolshevism and he wanted Ribbentrop to know that France was ready and willing to play a part in it. 'For this greatest battle in history, Germany has mobilized the youngest and most active elements of her population and is therefore short of manpower. I am aware of these needs and am prepared to place my support at your disposal. I therefore desire that Frenchmen will, in as large numbers as possible, take the place in your factories of those who go to the eastern front. The Frenchman is attached to his native soil, but I know he would be prepared to leave it for a purpose whose national and historical importance had been made clear to him.'[3]

The Germans were indeed short of labour[4] and, on 21 March 1942, Hitler had appointed Fritz Sauckel as special plenipotentiary for labour to fill the gaps.[5] The Germans had recruited labour in France before March 1942, sometimes using force, but Sauckel's appointment gave the matter fresh impetus. He proposed to obtain 350,000 workers from

---

[1] Giraud, op. cit., pp. 151–82.
[2] See Keitel's order of 6 May 1942 on GFM/422/216938.
[3] The letter (in German translation) is contained in Abetz to Foreign Ministry, 12 May 1942, ibid., 216982–3. Ribbentrop's reply, dated 26 May, was a frigid document which called for acts rather than hopes and assurances from the French government (ibid., 899/292349–50).
[4] See Goebbels Tagebücher, op. cit., pp. 76, 107.
[5] The decree appointing Sauckel is ND RF–0009.

both zones during the period 15 May–15 June. Of these, 150,000 were to be skilled workers, mainly in the metal industries.[1] Laval was almost certainly aware of these proposals at the time he wrote his letter to Ribbentrop. The purpose of his offer to co-operate was undoubtedly to try and get the Franco-German dialogue going on a more general plane. This is confirmed by the fact that he repeatedly used the occasion of what were supposed to be technical talks about the labour question to press for early discussions with Ribbentrop on wider political issues.[2]

On the technical level itself, the discussions dragged on until Sauckel's original deadline had been passed. The main difficulty was in obtaining a *quid pro quo* from the Germans. As the French negotiators pointed out, however willing their government was to help, 'it would be impossible for it to envisage these departures if the psychological conditions were not created by measures taken on the German side, particularly in respect of prisoners-of-war.' The French were pressing for the paroling of one prisoner-of-war for every worker who went to Germany, but the Germans would not accept this. All that they were able to obtain in the end was the paroling of one prisoner for three skilled workers. All the prisoners were to come from farming families because of the shortage of agricultural labour in France. At a meeting with Sauckel on 16 June, when agreement was finally reached, Laval said that both he and Pétain were 'sincerely grateful' for Hitler's generous gesture.[3]

On 22 June 1942, Laval made a broadcast speech in which he launched the so-called *relève*, or exchange-scheme. When he had returned to power, he explained, his first thoughts had been for the French prisoners-of-war. Alluding to the Giraud affair, he said that, although he had not expected 'massive liberations', he had reason to believe that concessions would have been made but for a 'notorious escape'. Now, however, there was fresh hope for the prisoners. Germany was short of labour and Hitler had agreed to release 'an important

[1] Schleier to von Stülpnagel, 27 April 1942, GFM/3821/E043521–2; Luther to Abetz, 2, 8 May 1942, ibid., E043526–7, E043528; Situation report of the military commander in France for April/May 1942, GMR/T–501/144/000211.

[2] Cf. Hemmen to Foreign Ministry, 12 May 1942, GFM/422/216996–9; Abetz to Foreign Ministry, 16 June 1942, ibid., 217212–17.

[3] 'Collaborators of Bichelonne [minister of industrial production]' in *La Vie de la France*, Vol. I, pp. 41–2; Jacques Barnaud in C.E. *Témoignages*, Vol. VIII, pp. 2322–3; Abetz to Foreign Ministry, 16 June 1942, GFM/422/217212–17.

number' of prisoners in exchange for French workers. Moreover, France could 'not remain passive and indifferent in the face of the huge sacrifices Germany is making to construct a Europe in which we must assume our place.' 'Workers of France,' he declared, 'it is for the freedom of the prisoners that you will go to work in Germany! It is for our country that you will go in large numbers! It is in order that France may find her place in the new Europe that you will respond to my appeal!'[1]

The speech also contained a sentence which might almost be described as Laval's epitaph: 'I desire the victory of Germany, for without it, bolshevism would tomorrow install itself everywhere.' There was nothing unusual about such a sentiment on Laval's part. He had said much the same sort of thing before and would go on saying it in the future, but for some reason this particular ùtterance stuck in the collective consciousness of the French people. It became indissolubly associated with Laval, so much so in fact that he complained to one of his lawyers in 1945 that it threatened to become the pivot of his entire trial.[2]

It was certainly considered sufficiently damning by Pétain (or his defence) to impel him to try and disassociate himself from it when he was accused of having done nothing to protest about it. At his pre-trial hearings, the Marshal claimed that not only had he 'protested violently' against the passage in question when the speech was discussed at a cabinet meeting after its delivery, but that it had been 'disapproved of by everyone'. However, the evidence bears out neither of these contentions. The minutes of the cabinet meeting of 26 June, when the speech was discussed, contain no hint of disapprobation, nor of a protest by the Marshal. This is confirmed by the diary of General Bridoux, the minister of war. On the other hand, Admiral Darlan did write a note to Laval in which he congratulated him on his 'moving and courageous speech'.[3]

In addition, Laval claimed that he had discussed the speech with Pétain *before* it was broadcast and that while the latter had taken objection to the passage, it was not in the way he was trying to make out in

[1] *Le Temps*, 24 June 1942.
[2] Jaffré, p. 176. The phrase figured prominently in the charges against him. See *Procès Laval*, p. 29.
[3] The evidence is set out in Noguères, pp. 397–400.

1945. The original draft, Laval explained, read, 'I believe in the victory of Germany and I desire it. . . .' Charles Rochat, the permanent head of the foreign ministry, expressed his doubts about the wisdom of using such language and, after some discussion, Laval took the text to Pétain for arbitration. The Marshal's attitude was one that would appear strange had it been expressed by anyone other than an octogenarian soldier. 'You are not a soldier,' he told Laval, 'and you have no right to say, "I believe in". You know nothing about it. . . . In your place I would cut out "I believe in the victory of Germany".' Laval did so and maintained that Pétain raised no objection to the version which remained and which was broadcast.[1]

No sooner had Laval left the witness box, however, than the Marshal made one of his rare interventions in open court.[2] 'I reacted very violently,' he declared, 'when I heard that passage of M. Laval's – "I desire the victory of Germany" – in the speech. He has just said that he came to see me with M. Rochat . . . to show me this passage. Well, M. Rochat would never have agreed to the retention of this passage and I agreed with him. And then, when I heard it on the radio . . . when I heard this passage repeated on the radio, I leaped to my feet. I did not understand. I thought it had been cut out and I was deeply distressed that it had remained.'[3] Taxed with this statement the following day, Laval replied, 'I have nothing to add to what I have said. I will only repeat what you have already heard. The Marshal displayed no indignation. He made me cut out the words "I believe in" and leave the word "desire".'[4] The issue was finally settled during the prosecution's closing speech, when a written statement from Rochat, who had sought asylum in Switzerland, was read out to the court. It confirmed Laval's version of what took place.[5]

Laval freely admitted that he knew his words would be 'like a drop of sulphuric acid . . . on the skin of suffering people', but he maintained that he had included them in order to convince the Germans of his sincerity, so that he could obtain more concessions from them.[6] But the words, and indeed the entire speech, were also designed for

[1] Laval in *Procès Pétain*, p. 201, cols. 2–3.
[2] He had refused to take part in the proceedings on the grounds that the court had no competence to try him.
[3] *Procès Pétain*, p. 202, col. 3.
[4] Ibid., p. 205, col. 1.
[5] Ibid., pp. 336, col. 3 – p. 337.
[6] Ibid., p. 201.

another purpose: to spike the guns of the ultra-collaborationists in Paris, who were causing more and more trouble for Laval.

Jacques Doriot, leader of the *Parti Populaire Français* (P.P.F.), was the most dangerous of the ultras. He had a disciplined paramilitary organization behind him and was thought to enjoy the support of the S.S. who, since the installation of *Brigadeführer* Oberg as Higher S.S. and Police Leader in May, were becoming an increasingly powerful force to be reckoned with in the German administration, alongside the army and the embassy. Moreover, Doriot had a personal grievance against Laval, for it will be recalled that, despite his party's support for the latter's return to power, he had been deliberately excluded from the government.[1] Since then, relations between the two men had deteriorated rapidly and, just over a fortnight before Laval's speech, Doriot had been summoned to his presence and told that he would not be allowed to carry out a propaganda tour of the unoccupied zone and North Africa for 'political reasons'.[2]

This may have been the last straw. At any rate, a German army report for the month of July stated that 'in recent months, the P.P.F. has been showing increased activity. While it still supports the overall direction of the government, it is to some extent becoming more sharply critical of Laval, on the grounds that he is not solving urgent problems quickly enough. The party therefore wants to take part in the government. Its enemies accuse Doriot of aiming to replace Laval as head of the government shortly thereafter.'[3] These 'enemies' certainly included Laval himself. Jean Jardin, who was chief secretary in his political office in 1942, has written that, at the time of his 22 June speech, Laval feared the formation of a Doriot government at any moment.[4]

There can be little doubt that the Germans did not seriously intend to try and replace Laval by Doriot. Oberg personally assured the prime minister that there was no truth in the rumours that Doriot enjoyed S.S. support. They had, he claimed, been put about by Doriot himself.[5] In September, moreover, Ribbentrop instructed Abetz on Hitler's behalf to deny all stories that the Germans wanted

---

[1] See above, pp. 289–90.

[2] *Abwehr* report, 21 October [1942], GMR/T–501/189/001068–76; Mayer notes, 14 October 1942, ibid., 001051–63.

[3] Armaments control section report, 24 August 1942, ibid., T–77/638/1833432–9.

[4] Jean Jardin in *La Vie de la France*, Vol. II, p. 1099.

[5] *Abwehr* report, 21 October [1942], GMR/T–501/189/001068–76.

to see Doriot replace Laval.[1] On 22 October, Doriot himself, perhaps at German instigation, promised Laval that 'in future he would drop all activities against [his] government and would see that his followers did likewise'.[2] However, the Germans may have found it expedient from time to time to use the Doriot bogey to play upon Laval's very real fears of another 13 December. The P.P.F. leader, however, was not the type to see through such a stratagem and took himself very seriously. He did not keep his promise of 22 October for long.

In the meantime, the situation in which Laval was governing grew more and more difficult. When he had been in power in 1940, for example, there had been no organized resistance movements. By 1942, however, the number of hostile acts against the occupation forces was continually on the increase.[3] The Germans reacted with Draconian measures. On 21 August 1941, the military command decreed that all Frenchmen held by the Germans were to be considered as hostages, liable to be shot in reprisal for attacks upon German personnel.[4] On 10 July 1942, Oberg, whose S.S. had taken over the function of protecting German interests, issued an order extending the penalties for 'assassins, saboteurs, and agitators' in the occupied zone – which included shooting and deportation – to their families if they failed to give themselves up within ten days.[5] The French authorities could boast that skilful negotiations prevented the police forces from falling completely under German control,[6] but they paid a price for it. In October, both Oberg and the military commander told Abetz of the 'exemplary assistance' they had received from the French police in catching those to whom they referred as terrorists.[7]

The French police, and the French government, also co-operated with the Germans in an even more odious enterprise: the deportation of Jews to the Nazi extermination camps in eastern Europe. Vichy had enacted anti-Semitic legislation, as much from its own inclinations as from German pressure, as early as October 1940, and, although Laval had opposed it, his signature eventually appeared on the text of

[1] Ribbentrop to Abetz, 21 September 1942, GFM/434/220463.
[2] *Abwehr* report, 28 October 1942, GMR/T-501/189/001047.
[3] For a history of the resistance, see Henri Michel, *Histoire de la Résistance en France*, Paris, Presses Universitaires de France, 3rd edition, 1962.
[4] Noguères, p. 334.
[5] Schwendemann to Foreign Ministry, 22 July 1942, GFM/434/220174-5.
[6] Cf. Amédée Bussière (Paris prefect of police) in *La Vie de la France*, Vol. I, pp. 576-7.
[7] Abetz to Foreign Ministry, 28 October 1942, GFM/443/221490-91.

the law itself.[1] Among other things, it empowered the government to intern foreign and stateless Jews, and, by the end of 1940, no less than 20,000 of these unfortunates – most of whom had fled to France precisely to escape Nazi persecution – were said to be in internment camps in the unoccupied zone.[2] More anti-Semitic legislation was enacted while Laval was out of office during 1941,[3] and when he returned to power the Germans had already decided upon what was euphemistically known as the 'final solution' of the Jewish problem. At the beginning of March 1942, the first plans for the deportation of Jews from the occupied zone were approved.[4]

Originally, the number of Jews to be deported from France was set at 5,000. On 11 June 1942, this figure was raised to 100,000, the total to come from both zones. On the 23rd, however, Himmler gave orders that all Jews in France were to be deported.[5] Laval was informed of this at the beginning of July, and he and his colleagues quickly decided that the only thing they could do was to sacrifice the foreign and stateless Jews in the hope of saving the French ones. But whereas their original demands referred only to Jews between the ages of 16 and 45, he suggested that children under 16 should not be separated from their parents. The first train-loads of Jews from the camps in the unoccupied zone crossed the demarcation line in August. Further round-ups by the French police in the unoccupied zone more than replaced those who had gone. In addition, the French authorities carried out a particularly effective round-up in the Paris area on their own initiative, which resulted in the internment of nearly 13,000 foreign and stateless Jews. By the beginning of September, 27,000 Jews had been deported from France; 18,000 from the occupied zone and 9,000 from the unoccupied zone.[6]

---

[1] Aron, pp. 227–33; Noguères, pp. 273–5; Baudouin, p. 341; law of 3 October 1940, J.O. Lois et Décrets, 18 October 1940, p. 5323.
[2] Schleier to Foreign Ministry, 11 September 1942, GFM/5549/E387802–3.
[3] Aron, pp. 419–20; Noguères, pp. 275–9.
[4] Dannecker memorandum, 10 March 1942, ND RF–1216.
[5] Dannecker memorandum, 15 June 1942, ibid., RF–1217; Dannecker–Eichmann memorandum, 1 July 1942, ibid., RF–1223.
[6] Dannecker memorandum, 6 July 1942, ibid., RF–1225; Dannecker to RSHA–IVB4 (the S.S. Jewish office in Berlin), 6 July 1942, in Henri Monneray (ed.), La Persecution des Juifs en France et dans les Autres Pays de l'Ouest, Paris, Centre de Documentation Juive Contemporaine, 1947, photostat between pp. 128–9; Röthke memorandum 13 August 1942, ND RF–1234; Ahnert memorandum, 3 September 1942, ibid., RF–1227; Schleier to Foreign Ministry, 11 September 1942, GFM/5549/E387802–3.

Laval's attitude towards the foreign Jews was remarkably callous for a man of his basically non-violent temperament. He told an American Quaker who had come to protest about the deportations that 'these foreign Jews had always been a problem in France and the French government was glad that a change in the German attitude towards them gave France an opportunity to get rid of them'.[1] When the Catholic church added its voice to those of the protesters, Laval told Abetz that the government would not tolerate such interference and said that, if the clergy attempted to shelter Jews in religious buildings, he would not hesitate to send in police to drag them out. At least one Jesuit elder was arrested – for trying to hide 80 Jewish children.[2]

After the war, Laval claimed that Oberg had told him that it was the German government's intention 'to set up a Jewish state . . . in Poland'.[3] His private secretary, André Guénier, has written that 'President Laval . . . never suspected the inhuman system and the atrocities to which the people who were arrested and deported to the east were subjected. . . . If he had known, none of the considerations which compelled him to hang on to the government of the country, however serious, would have retained their validity. He would have denounced the fact before the civilized world and would have refused any contact with the representatives of a government indulging in such acts of barbarism.'[4] This is hard to credit, but it may just be possible that Laval did succeed in convincing himself that no harm would come to those Jews he handed over to the Germans.

On the other hand, it cannot be denied that Laval fought very hard for the French Jews. This, of course, was the whole aim of his policy. 'Every time a foreign Jew leaves our territory,' he told a private meeting of prefects in September 1942, 'it's one more gained for France.'[5] The Germans warned him that, eventually, the deportations would have to be extended to French Jews and they suggested that one way in which a start could be made would be to enact legislation depriving

---

[1] Thompson to Hull, 7 August 1942, F.R.U.S., 1942, Vol. I, pp. 463–4.
[2] Abetz to Foreign Ministry, 28 August, 1 September 1942, GFM/434/220323-4, 230345.
[3] *Laval Parle*, p. 105.
[4] André Guénier in *La Vie de la France*, Vol. III, p. 1359.
[5] Speech to prefects of the unoccupied zone, 25 September 1942 (unpublished text kindly communicated to me by M. René de Chambrun.

certain naturalized Jews of their French nationality, thus rendering them liable for deportation. But Laval refused to accept this and, on 26 September 1942, the S.S. Jewish office in Berlin was informed that, in view of Laval's and Pétain's attitude, Oberg had sent a message to Himmler saying that the extension of the deportations to French Jews would have the 'gravest consequences'.[1] Even in the case of foreign Jews, Laval seems to have done something to slow down the rate of deportation[2] and he did suggest that the United States might care to admit some of the foreign Jewish children as refugees.[3]

The plans for labour recruitment did not run smoothly either, in spite of a much-publicized ceremony at Compiègne on 11 August when the first train-load of paroled prisoners-of-war arrived from Germany.[4] Recruits soon found that conditions in Germany were not nearly as rosy as Laval had tried to paint them in his 22 June speech, and the German army liaison officer with the economic delegation of the armistice commission reported on 19 August that 'the results of the labour recruiting drive are becomingly increasingly meagre. In recent weeks, the numbers are even less than those in the period before the Sauckel campaign.'[5] This was a slight exaggeration. The actual figures show that, prior to 1 June, 10,000 workers a month were leaving for Germany, whereas during the period 1 June to 15 August, in spite of the French government's intensive propaganda, only 40,000 did so. The unoccupied zone's contribution – 12,000 – was particularly disappointing and, most important of all, by the beginning of September only 17,000 of the planned 150,000 skilled workers had been recruited.[6]

[1] Röthke memoranda, 13 August, 1 September 1942, ND RF-1234, 1228; Anhert memorandum, 3 September 1942, ibid., RF-1227; Knochen to RSHA-IVB-4, 26 September 1942, ibid., NG-1971.

[2] Notably by persuading certain neutral and pro-Axis governments whose nationals were affected to protest. See Laval Parle, p. 105; Rochat in La Vie de la France, Vol. II, p. 1110; Bousquet in ibid., Vol. III, p. 1571.

[3] Tuck to Hull, 11 September 1942, F.R.U.S., 1942, Vol. II, pp. 712–13. Agreement was reached for the evacuation of 5,000 children, but the rupture in diplomatic relations between the two countries in November (see below, p. 325) prevented its execution. See the documents printed in ibid., pp. 713–16.

[4] Le Temps, 13 August 1942.

[5] Brandts to Armistice Commission Armaments Section, 19 August 1942, GMR/T-77/638/1833312–13.

[6] Armaments Control Section report, 15 September 1942, ibid., 1833404–12; 'Collaborators of Bichelonne' in La Vie de la France, Vol. I, p. 42.

Faced with this situation, the Germans decided to resort to compulsion and on 30 August, Sauckel published in Paris a decree rendering all men and women in countries occupied and administered by the Germans liable for labour service.[1] The following day, Laval made an energetic protest to Abetz. Under the armistice agreement, he maintained, neither the occupied nor the unoccupied zones were German-administered territory. 'If this decree were to be implemented, even in the occupied zone,' he warned, 'he would be compelled to resign.'[2]

Nevertheless, he had already recognized the need for 'very energetic measures',[3] and at a meeting at the German embassy on 1 September Dr Michel of the military commander's labour department put forward a compromise proposal. Laval might find it 'easier and more profitable from the domestic political point-of-view,' he suggested, 'if the problems of the relève were tackled within the overall framework of labour mobilization for the public sector. Then it would not be a case of compulsory measures being taken for the despatch of workers to Germany, but results would flow from the compulsory measures taken for the whole of the French economy which would include the requirements of the relève as a secondary effect.'[4] Laval accepted this solution and, after a 'stormy' debate in the French cabinet, a law was promulgated on 4 September which made every Frenchman between the ages of 18 and 50 and every unmarried Frenchwoman between the ages of 21 and 35 liable 'to carry out any work which the government judges useful in the higher interest of the nation'.[5]

At the same time as the new labour law was published, the global target figure for recruitment was revised downwards. It was now agreed that only 250,000 workers should go to Germany; the other 100,000 were to work for the Germans in France under the auspices of the so-called Todt organization. But the target figure for skilled

---

[1] The law, which was actually signed on 22 August 1942, was cited at Nuremberg as ND RF-0017 and was read in full to the court by M. Herzog, one of the French prosecutors. See International Military Tribunal, *Trial of the Major War Criminals*, Vol. V, Nuremberg, 1947, pp. 446–7.
[2] Unsigned memorandum, 2 September 1942, GFM/3821/E043534-48; *Laval Parle*, pp. 122–3.
[3] Noehring to Foreign Ministry, 24 August 1942, GFM/434/220305-7.
[4] Unsigned memorandum, 2 September 1942, ibid., 3821/E043534-48.
[5] Krug to Abetz, 4 September 1942 (twice), ibid., E04359-60, E04361-2; J.O. *Lois et Décrets*, 13 September 1942, p. 3122, cols. 1-2.

workers – 150,000 – was to remain the same, and a deadline of 15 October was set for its fulfilment.[1]

But there was little improvement in the weeks that followed. 'The whole outcome of the operation,' wrote the liaison officer with the economic delegation of the armistice commission at the beginning of October, 'proves that the more rigorously compulsion is applied, the more meagre the results of the recruiting authorities are.'[2] Yet when they were told on 7 and 8 October that the 150,000 target for skilled workers could not be reached before the end of November, the Germans insisted that something be done to speed up recruitment. Laval and his colleagues, Abetz reported, were prepared to allow the military commander to use force in the occupied zone, provided it was done locally through the area commanders and not published and enacted as a general principle. If the military commander introduced generalized compulsion, it would 'produce a government crisis of the first magnitude and would also put a stop to the principle of collaboration in other fields as well'. Hitler, Ribbentrop, and Sauckel accepted this argument and the military commander was instructed accordingly.[3]

Exhortation, however, continued to be employed, particularly for the benefit of the unoccupied zone. 'I am not sure,' said Laval in another major broadcast appeal on 20 October, 'that you fully appreciate the historical importance of the time in which we are living. Some Frenchmen, in fact, seem to have forgotten and believe that salvation will come to us from abroad. . . . As head of the government, I cannot give way to these dangerous illusions.' France had to rely upon her own resources and she had to collaborate with Germany. 'I am certain – and do not doubt for one moment that I am speaking the truth – that if Germany were beaten, the Soviets would call the tune in Europe tomorrow. This would mean the end of the independence and the patriotism of nations. It would also mean the end of that human and generous policy . . . of real socialism which, based upon the ruins of a capitalism which has abused its power, will impose itself upon Europe tomorrow, while at the same time respecting the individual geniuses of each people.'

[1] Abetz to Foreign Ministry, 18 September 1942, GFM/434/220433.
[2] Brandts to Armistice Commission Armaments Section, 7 October 1942, GMR/T–77/638/1833291–3.
[3] Abetz to Foreign Ministry, 7 October 1942, GFM/443/221423–6; Ribbentrop to Abetz 10 October 1942, ibid., 221434–5.

Their sacrifice would not be in vain, he told his audience. Only the previous day he had been informed that if a little more than 100,000 skilled workers agreed to go to Germany, the wives of prisoners-of-war would be allowed to join their husbands. 'In 1939, millions of others received the order to leave. They were not given the chance to discuss this order. They carried it out. They went. Why should you discuss the appeal which the government is addressing to you today?' He warned them that, if they did not go voluntarily, the Germans might resort to compulsion. 'This test is decisive,' he concluded. 'Overcome your selfishness. You have the chance to recover with your tools what France has lost by arms. For yourselves, for the prisoners, for France, you must obey the government's orders.'[1]

The deadline for the skilled workers was postponed for a further four weeks, which would have meant 7,000 men a day leaving France. Even with the aid of forced recruitment in individual factories, however, the daily total never rose above 3,000 before the beginning of November.[2] What was the reason for this? Some have put it down to the procrastination of the French authorities, including Laval himself. 'Sauckel wants men,' he is reported to have told his friend and finance minister, Pierre Cathala. 'I shall give him legal texts.'[3] According to Jacques Barnaud, who took part in many of the labour negotiations, the French officials 'put as many spokes in the wheel as possible . . . Laval . . . was well aware of the fact that we were using delaying tactics, but he never asked us to change our methods and accept the views of the enemy.'[4]

This may indeed be part of the explanation, although the profound hostility of the French working man was almost certainly a much more important factor. But as in the case of the Jews, Laval had compromised himself by going as far as he had. 'While a gradually increasing consolidation of the Laval government's authority could be observed in recent months,' a Germany army report noted at the end of October, '. . . the favourable development came to a standstill during the course of September. . . . The enactment of the compulsory labour law and the anti-Jewish campaign, which is incomprehensible

[1] *Le Temps*, 22 October 1942.
[2] Brandts to Armistice Commission Armaments Section 21 October, 4 November 1942, GMR/T-77/638/1833284-6, 1833277-80.
[3] Cathala in *La Vie de la France*, Vol I, p. 106.
[4] C.E. *Témoignages*, Vol. VIII, pp. 2321-2.

to the French mind . . . seem to be the major causes of the fall in Laval's prestige. In contrast with this, Laval could not show the people clear new successes for his policy, so that the opposition to the line he is pursuing intensified.'[1]

The deportation of foreign Jews and the despatch of French workers to Germany, however, illustrate but one facet of Laval's policy towards Germany. They were concessions which had to be made as proof of his willingness to collaborate, and, the *relève* notwithstanding, no real advantages were obtained in return. Laval had much higher hopes in respect of the military negotiations which were conducted throughout the period from May to November 1942.

As in 1940, France possessed three assets which made her 'alliance-worthy' – to use one of Hitler's favourite expressions – as distinct from exploitable. These were her empire, her fleet, and her armistice army. Unfortunately, the first of these was rapidly depreciating. By May 1942, French Equatorial Africa and Syria had gone over to the Gaullists; Indochina was to all intents and purposes controlled by the Japanese; Madagascar had been invaded by the British; and the French West Indies preserved only the most tenuous links with Vichy. Only North Africa (Morocco, Algeria, and Tunisia) and French West Africa remained, but there was a growing danger that these too would be attacked, particularly now that the United States had entered the war. In his conversation with Admiral Leahy in April, Laval had emphasized that 'he was prepared to defend France and her empire against all comers and he stated specifically that if the British or Americans were to attempt to effect a landing either on the soil of metropolitan France or on French North African territory, he would resist them to the best of his ability.'[2] Stronger armed forces would not only enable him to do this; they would increase France's 'alliance worthiness' still further and make her a power to be reckoned with at the time of a peace treaty. Laval hoped, and believed, that the Germans would consent to the necessary reinforcements.[3]

That Marshal Pétain fully shared Laval's desire for military collaboration in this sense is shown by two conversations which he had with Rudolf Rahn of the German embassy at the end of May. According to

---

[1] Armaments Control Section report, 24 October 1942, GMR/T–77/638/1833414–22.
[2] Leahy to Hull, 27 April 1942, F.R.U.S., 1942, Vol. II, pp. 181–2.
[3] Jacques Lemaigre-Dubreuil in *La Vie de la France*, Vol. III, p. 1180.

Abetz's report, 'on both occasions [Pétain] told [Rahn] with an extraordinary display of apprehension that he considered Anglo-American attacks upon French coastal areas and upon French North and West Africa as inevitable.' In the circumstances, he thought it desirable that there should be co-operation between the French and German armies to meet such attacks, and he even went so far as to suggest discussions at general staff level about North and West Africa.[1] Laval made similar proposals and apparently also raised the question of reinforcements for French forces in Africa. After top-level discussions between Hitler, Ribbentrop, and Keitel, the Germans decided that, while they would ignore the request for staff talks, they were prepared to consider reinforcements for *West* Africa. In order to avoid the impression that this was a unilateral concession, however, the French were to be told to send a formal request through the armistice commission.[2]

The Germans also wanted a *quid pro quo*. Negotiations had been in progress for some time with the French concerning the handing over of neutral shipping – mainly Greek, Norwegian, and Danish – which had taken refuge in French ports when their countries were invaded by the Axis. Although the German armistice delegation was instructed in the last resort to treat the requests for reinforcements independently, an attempt was to be made to link the two questions.[3]

At first, Laval displayed considerable reluctance to fall in with German wishes. In spite of an earlier promise to Abetz, he told Hemmen, the head of the German economic delegation to the armistice commission, that 'it was quite impossible to hand these ships over to Germany'. There were, he explained, too many French ships in British-controlled ports which would be seized the moment this happened, and France needed all the tonnage she could muster. 'He stressed,' Hemmen noted, 'that this question ought not to be confused with the joint defence of Africa, as had happened on the German side.'[4] Largely, no doubt, as a result of this attitude, the negotiations dragged on until mid-August, when they were taken out of the hands of the

---

[1] Abetz to Foreign Ministry, 1 June 1942, Abetz Papers, GFM/P3/00247-8.
[2] Ritter memorandum, 8 June 1942, ibid., 899/292337-9.
[3] Ibid.; Enclosure in Welck to Foreign Ministry, 14 August 1942, ibid., 434/220274-5.
[4] Hemmen memorandum, 23 June 1942, ibid., 899/293201-2. Cf. Abetz to Foreign Ministry, 19 June 1942, ibid., 422/217235-6.

armistice commission and entrusted to *Reichsstatthalter* Kaufmann, a special plenipotentiary for shipping questions.[1]

An incident which may have induced Laval to accept the link between the neutral shipping negotiations and the reinforcement of the French armed forces was the Anglo-Canadian raid on Dieppe on 19 August, which underlined the threat to France herself. It was certainly the occasion for a renewed request by Marshal Pétain that France be allowed to co-operate with Germany in her own defence. In a personal message to Hitler on 21 August, the Marshal declared, 'After a conversation which I have just had with President Laval, and on account of the most recent British act of aggression which this time has taken place on our soil, I propose that you envisage France's participation in her own defence. I am ready to examine the methods of this participation as the sincere expression of my desire to have France contribute to the safeguarding of Europe.'[2]

There was considerable debate at the Pétain trial concerning the authenticity of this message. Laval denied all knowledge of it; de Brinon could not swear that it came from Pétain personally; Pétain himself stubbornly refused all comment. On the basis of his study of all the material in the trial dossiers, Louis Noguères concluded that 'in all fairness, it must be said that there is no proof that Marshal Pétain was the author of the message of 21 August 1942'.[3] The source of the confusion was that the only text of the message available to the court was a teleprint received by Benoist-Méchin's office in Paris.[4] There was, therefore, nothing in Pétain's handwriting to authenticate it. The German foreign ministry archives, however, contain a telegram from Abetz giving a German translation of the message and stating that the original, in the form of a letter, had been brought by courier from Vichy and would be forwarded to Berlin in the next diplomatic bag.[5] Although the actual letter has not been found, this telegram shows that it existed and is reasonable proof of its authenticity. The teleprint which found its way into the files of the French high court was clearly only intended for purposes of information.

[1] Wiehl memorandum, 13 August 1942, ibid., 434/22069–71.
[2] Noguères, p. 561.
[3] Noguères, pp. 560–66; *Procès Pétain*, pp. 40, col. 3–41, cols. 1–2; 207–8 (Laval); 287, col. 3 (de Brinon).
[4] See the photocopy at the back of Noguères' book.
[5] Abetz to Foreign Ministry, 22 August 1942, GFM/434/220294.

Rather more doubt attaches to the authenticity of the message, conveyed to the German commander-in-chief in the west by de Brinon on behalf of both Laval and Pétain, congratulating the Germans for their success in effecting the 'prompt cleansing of French soil' of the invaders. At his pre-trial hearings, Pétain consistently denied having had anything to do with this message and, at the trial itself, a witness testified that the Marshal had described it as 'another fake by that dungheap de Brinon'.[1] The German foreign ministry archives contain a telegram from Abetz relaying de Brinon's congratulations, on behalf of Laval alone, for the 'prompt expulsion of the English from Dieppe', but otherwise throw no direct light on the episode.[2] They do, however, contain a report from the new German representative in Vichy, Krug von Nidda, which describes French government reactions to the Dieppe raid. Pétain told Krug that 'yesterday [19 August] was a happy day, with whose outcome all Frenchmen are satisfied' and Laval told him that 'your success is ours also'.[3] The message to the German commander-in-chief may therefore be accepted as a fair representation of the views which both Pétain and Laval, for whatever reasons, thought it desirable to convey to the Germans.

It was just over a week after the Dieppe raid that Kaufmann reached an agreement in principle with Laval and the French navy minister, Admiral Auphan, as a result of which about 130,000 tons of shipping was made available to the Germans.[4] On 9 September, the French were duly informed of concessions allowed them in respect of reinforcements for West Africa. These included the release of nearly 3,000 prisoners-of-war, as well as permission to transfer some weapons and munitions from stocks.[5] During the course of one of his conversations with Sauckel on 17 September, Laval made another general request for reinforcements, and the labour plenipotentiary took it up with Hitler. After being told that the latter had agreed in principle, the French sent another note to Wiesbaden in which they asked for the fulfilment of all earlier requests which had been refused. It subsequently transpired,

---

[1] Noguères, pp. 556–60; Charles Donati in *Procès Pétain*, p. 291, col. 3.
[2] Abetz to Foreign Ministry, 19 August 1942, GFM/434/220283.
[3] Schleier to Foreign Ministry, 20 August 1942, ibid., 220287–91.
[4] Abetz to Foreign Ministry, 28 August 1942, ibid., 220325–7; Wiehl to von Rintelen, 2 September 1942, ibid., 220346–7.
[5] *O.K.W. Wehrmachtführungsstab* to Foreign Ministry, 5 September 1942, ibid., 220376–7. 'Dossier Vignol' in *La Délégation Française*, Vol. V, p. 419.

however, that the Führer had thought his remarks to Sauckel did not go beyond the concessions already granted and the German delegation was instructed to handle the new request 'in a dilatory manner'. Nevertheless, the French did eventually get their two fighter squadrons.[1]

Laval did not confine his attentions to the regular armed forces; he also tried to strengthen the anti-Bolshevik Legion (L.V.F.)[2] and bring it under direct government control. The idea originated with Jacques Benoist-Méchin, one of the secretaries of state to the prime minister. When still a member of the Darlan government, Benoist-Méchin had written a memorandum calling for the takeover of the L.V.F. '(a) to integrate us into the common struggle; (b) to bridge the gap which separates us from our conquerors; (c) to ensure, in the final analysis, that the substantial sacrifices we are making without any worthwhile return in the economic field produce beneficial results in the political sphere.' He envisaged a state of 'belligerency' between France and the Soviet Union and the eventual reconquest of the dissident portions of the French empire. A government which was capable of decisive action, he concluded, would win Hitler's confidence and would 'obtain the weapons and the material equipment essential for the pursuit of its policy and the reconquest of our African empire'.[3]

Not only did Laval accept Benoist-Méchin's views, but he also had a private reason for wanting to do something about the L.V.F.: it was dominated by the ultra-collaborationists in Paris. 'I don't trust that organization,' he told the man whom he wanted to command the new government-controlled formation, 'because it has ulterior motives and domestic political ambitions. I can't suppress it without offending the Germans, but you will absorb it. . . . It will be drowned in your splendid division.'[4]

With Laval's blessing, therefore, Benoist-Méchin set about the task he had outlined in his memorandum. At a meeting of the L.V.F.'s central committee on 22 June, he persuaded its members to dissolve their own organization and merge with the proposed new formation.

[1] Welck to Foreign Ministry, 2, 10 October 1942, GFM/443/221401-3, 221436; 'Dossier Vignol', loc. cit., p. 420.

[2] For the L.V.F., see above, p. 280.

[3] Benoist-Méchin memorandum, 28 March 1942, cited in Jean-Louis Aujol (ed.), Le Procès Benoist-Méchin, Paris, Albin Michel, 1948, pp. 409-10.

[4] General Jean Perré in La Vie de la France, Vol. III, pp. 1665-7. General Perré did not accept Laval's invitation.

The latter, which was officially established on 18 July, was known as the *Légion Tricolore*. Unlike the L.V.F., it was to be financed by the French government and its members were to wear French uniforms and be entitled to receive French decorations. Most important of all, perhaps, it was no longer to be confined solely to the eastern front, but could be used 'on any front where the national interest is at stake'.[1]

From Benoist-Méchin's evidence at his trial in 1947,[2] one would gather that the Germans were uniformly opposed to the *Légion Tricolore*, but this would be a false impression. Abetz strongly recommended the idea to his superiors and both the O.K.W. and the army high command thought it generally acceptable on military grounds, although they did not accept a French proposal that the new legion should be allowed to recruit some of its cadres from the regular armistice army.[3] The veto came from Hitler himself. While he was prepared to allow some expansion of the L.V.F., he refused to consider its merger with the *Légion Tricolore* and he insisted that it be retained on the eastern front.[4] The reason for his attitude may be deduced from a remark he made to Mussolini in April, when he first got wind of Benoist-Méchin's plan. One of the latter's memoranda – probably the one previously quoted – had fallen into German hands and Hitler had read it. 'It had been quite clearly stated,' Hitler told the Duce, 'that if France wanted to become powerful again, she must have weapons and that the only way to achieve this was through Laval and collaboration.'[5] The Führer would have been suspicious of the *Légion Tricolore* in any case; when he knew its architect's real intentions as well, its rejection was inevitable.

The rejection was followed by Benoist-Méchin's resignation from the government. Of course, it suited the latter's book after the war to suggest that this was a simple case of cause and effect. Growing friction with the Germans and opposition to Laval's policies, he claimed, led to his decision to depart.[6] In fact, the truth was more complicated.

[1] Noguères, pp. 359–61; Benoist-Méchin's evidence in *Procès Benoist-Méchin*, op. cit., pp. 416–19; General Bridoux's undated letter, ibid., pp. 554–6; Abetz to Foreign Ministry, 23 July 1942, GFM/434/220190–95; Law of 18 July 1942, J.O. *Lois et Décrets*, 8 August 1942, p. 2722.
[2] *Procès Benoist-Méchin*, op. cit., pp. 420–23.
[3] Abetz to Foreign Ministry, 23 July 1942, GFM/434/220190–95; Ritter memorandum, 7 August 1942, ibid., 926/297239–40.
[4] Warlimont to Army General Staff, Quartermaster Section IV [western Europe], 19 September 1942, ibid., 297170–71.
[5] Schmidt memorandum, 2 May 1942, GFM/F18/319.
[6] *Procès Benoist-Méchin*, op. cit., pp. 423, 430–31.

Unable to believe that Laval's foreign policy was responsible for German coolness towards his plans, he apparently began to think that the prime minister's domestic policy was to blame: it was not sufficiently aligned upon those of Nazi Germany and Fascist Italy. Laval, who was concerned at the potential threat to his position from Doriot and the other Paris ultras, took what Abetz later described as Benoist-Méchin's 'purely theoretical train of thought' as evidence that his secretary of state had gone over to the extremists, accused him of plotting against him, and fired him.[1]

The failure of the *Légion Tricolore* did not cause Laval to abandon all hope of strengthening the French army with some form of volunteer force. During October 1942, Admiral de Laborde, the commander of the French Fleet at Toulon, revived an old idea by proposing that a volunteer force be recruited to recapture the Chad colony from the Gaullists. This plan received the endorsement of both Pétain and Laval and was discussed in some detail by de Laborde and Colonel Böhme of the armistice commission in Paris on 6 November.[2] It is impossible to say what results these discussions might have produced, for the Allied landings in North Africa two days later completely revolutionized the entire strategic situation in the Mediterranean and Africa. The Chad project was consigned to oblivion, to join the many other schemes which the French government had sponsored in its vain attempt to secure a place in the sun in Hitler's new order.

---

[1] Abetz to Foreign Ministry, 30 September 1942, GFM/434/220500–502. See also de Brinon, pp. 126–8; Amédée Bussière in *La Vie de la France*, Vol. I, p. 582.

[2] Welck to Foreign Ministry, 29 October 1942, GFM/443/221495; Schnurre memorandum, 31 October 1942, ibid., 926/297124; Abetz to Foreign Ministry, 7 November 1942, ibid., 443/221520–22; de Laborde's report, 9 November 1942, in Kammerer, *Flotte Française*, pp. 535–8.

10

Twenty Crucial Days

8th – 27th November 1942

At the beginning of November 1942, the Germans detected a sizeable concentration of Allied shipping at Gibraltar. At first they interpreted it as a supply convoy bound for Malta. On 6 November, however, as the fleet steamed eastwards, the large number of transports led them to revise their earlier opinion. It was, they decided, an invasion force and the possible destinations canvassed included Sicily, Sardinia, and Crete. The most likely one, however, was held to be Libya, where the invaders would take Rommel's combined Italo-German army, already reeling from the effects of Montgomery's offensive at El Alamein, in the rear. Although French North Africa had also been mentioned as a possibility, it was dismissed in most estimates as the least likely of all. The surprise, therefore, when Anglo-American forces landed in the vicinity of Algiers and Oran and along the Atlantic coast of Morocco in the small hours of Sunday 8 November was almost total.[1]

But was it a total surprise to the French? Hitler did not think so. 'There is certainly a plot here,' he told Ciano on 9 November.[2] The reason for his suspicion was that on 23 October Laval had informed the Germans of Pétain's proposal to make a tour of North and West Africa 'in order to show the unity of the motherland and the empire and to strengthen the population, the administration, and the armed forces in their loyalty to the government and their preparations against possible Anglo-Saxon attacks.' Ribbentrop told Abetz, 'that [Pétain] would thereby fall strongly under the influence of an atmosphere inimical to

---

[1] *Luftwaffe* report, 3 November 1942, in Al. Hillgruber (ed.), *Kriegstagebuch des Ober-kommandos der Wehrmacht, 1940–45*, Vol. II (1942), Part II, Frankfurt-am-Main, Bernard und Graefe Verlag für Wehrwesen, 1963 (hereafter cited as Kriegstagebuch 1942), p. 901; German Navy report on Relations with France, ibid., pp. 902, 912; Greiner notes, 4, 6, 7 November 1942, ibid., pp. 902, 912, 916; Warlimont commentary, ibid., p. 918.

[2] Schmidt memorandum, 12 November 1942, GFM/F1/0110-22.

Laval's intentions.'[1] If the Germans had not withheld their consent, Hitler told Ciano, Pétain would have been in Africa when the Allies landed.

It would be easy to dismiss Hitler's attitude as the result of a combination of coincidence and inveterate suspicion, were it not that we now know that shortly before the Allied landings two former Vichy ministers advised Pétain to go to Africa immediately prior to their taking place. One of these ex-ministers, Pierre Pucheu, was speaking in general terms and did not know that the landings were imminent, but the other, General Bergeret, did know and testified that he told Pétain as much. The curious thing is that both men stated categorically that Pétain refused to consider the idea. In the one case he referred to the possible fate of the forty million French people he would leave behind; in the other to that of the one-and-a-half million prisoners-of-war.[2] Did the Marshal perhaps change his mind? His conduct after the Allied landings, as well as the fact that it was Laval who approached the Germans with the proposal that he should go to Africa, suggest that he did not and that the whole affair was indeed a coincidence. But one cannot be sure.

There is no doubt, however, that Admiral Darlan's presence in Algiers at the time of the landings was purely fortuitous. The Marshal's heir and commander-in-chief of the armed forces had secretly been in touch with the Americans to offer his support in the event of a landing, but he received no forewarning of Allied intentions. As Roosevelt's special representative in North Africa, Robert Murphy, subsequently wrote, 'There were two main reasons why no understanding with him had been reached up to the twelfth hour. For one thing, none of the Allies really trusted Darlan, especially in view of his intense dislike of the British. The second reason was that a firm agreement had been made two weeks before the landings to include . . . Giraud in the Allied strategy, and it was thought impossible on such short notice to induce the two Frenchmen to accept joint operations.'[3]

Nevertheless, at the end of October, Darlan turned up in Algiers. He came on the last leg of a tour of inspection of French Africa, and also

[1] Abetz to Foreign Ministry, 23 October 1942, ibid., 443/221466; Ribbentop to Abetz, 4 November 1942, ibid., 221517; Abetz to Foreign Ministry, 5 November 1942, ibid., 221519.
[2] Pucheu, pp. 41–44; General Bergeret in *Procès Pétain*, p. 261, col. 2.
[3] Robert Murphy, *Diplomat Among Warriors*, New York, Doubleday, 1964, pp. 112–15.

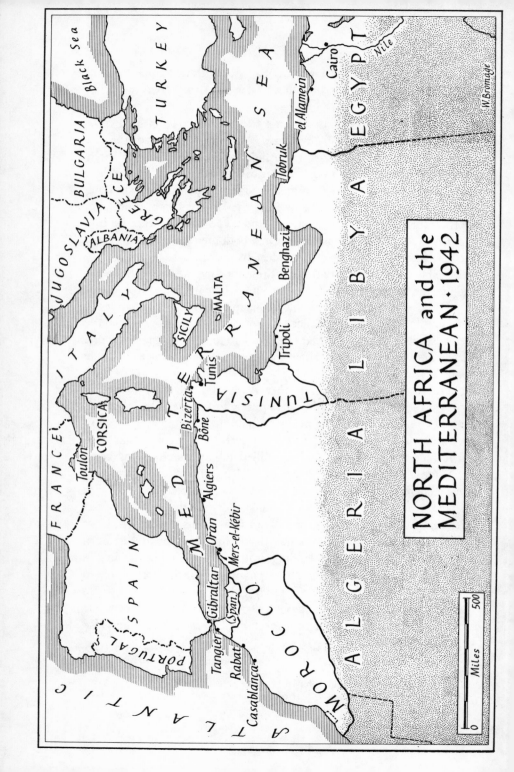

NORTH AFRICA and the
MEDITERRANEAN · 1942

W.Bromage

Black Sea

TURKEY

BULGARIA

JUGOSLAVIA

GREECE

ALBANIA

Nile

Cairo

EGYPT

el Alamein

Tobruk

Benghazi

LIBYA

Tripoli

MALTA

SICILY

Tunis

Bizerta

Bône

TUNISIA

MEDITERRANEAN SEA

ITALY

CORSICA

Toulon

FRANCE

SPAIN

ALGERIA

Algiers

Oran

Mers-el-Kébir

Gibraltar

Tangier

(Span.)

Rabat

Casablanca

MOROCCO

PORTUGAL

ATLANTIC

0

500

Miles

to see his son, who had recently been taken ill with poliomyelitis. He returned to Vichy on 30 October, but news of a sudden deterioration in his son's condition brought him back to Algiers on 5 November. 'Darlan's presence here on D-Day might be embarrassing,' Murphy cabled Roosevelt's chief-of-staff, 'but it is believed he will depart before then.'[1] But although the crisis passed, Darlan decided to stay on for a few days to see that the improvement in his son's health was permanent. It was thus that he was in Algiers on 'D-Day'.[2]

News of the Allied landings began to come in to Vichy at about 3 a.m.[3] At 4, a message from President Roosevelt arrived for Marshal Pétain. 'When your government concluded the armistice convention in 1940,' it began, 'it was impossible for any of us to foresee the programme of systematic plunder which the German *Reich* would inflict on the French people.' Now, Germany and Italy were planning to invade North Africa and this would be a threat to the security of the United States and Latin America as well as sounding 'the death knell of the French empire'. The president had therefore decided to send 'powerful American armed forces to co-operate with the governing agencies of Algeria, Tunisia, and Morocco in repelling this latest act in the long litany of German and Italian international crime'. Their 'immediate aim' was 'to support and aid the French authorities and their administrations'; their 'ultimate and greater aim' was 'the liberation of France and its empire from the Axis yoke'. '. . . The United States seeks no territories and remembers always the historic friendship and mutual aid which we have so greatly given to each other,' the president concluded. 'I send to you, and through you, to the people of France my deep hope and belief that we are all of us soon to enter into happier days.'[4]

When Laval arrived in Vichy at 4.15 a.m., hot-foot from his home at Châteldon, his first task was to draft a reply to this message in conjunction with some of his and the Marshal's closest advisers. It was an uncompromising document which reflected their bitter indignation at

[1] Murphy to Leahy, 5 November 1942, F.R.U.S., 1942, Vol. II, p. 425.
[2] Darlan, pp. 183–7. The evidence set out in these pages is quite conclusive.
[3] All times in this chapter are expressed in Vichy time, which was the same as German time. This was one hour in advance of North African time and two hours in advance of G.M.T. French navy telegrams, which formed one of the main channels of communication between Vichy and North Africa, were dated in G.M.T. See C.E. *Rapport*, Vol. II, p. 511.
[4] *Department of State Bulletin*, 14 November 1942, pp. 904–5.

what had happened. 'It is with stupor and grief that I learned during the night of the aggression of your troops against North Africa,' it began. '. . . You invoke pretexts which nothing justifies. . . . I have always declared that we would defend our empire if it were attacked, you knew that we would defend it against any aggressor whoever he might be. You knew that I would keep my word. . . . France and her honour are at stake. We are attacked. We shall defend ourselves. This is the order I am giving.'[1]

Laval also had to consider a German offer of air support, made initially through the armistice commission at Wiesbaden and apparently repeated by Krug von Nidda, the foreign ministry representative at Vichy. Admittedly the offer had been made at a time when the Germans still thought the Allied landings would take place further to the east, but it had not been withdrawn. After some discussion, it was evidently decided that the best thing to do would be to consult the senior government representative on the spot. At 7 a.m. the navy minister, Admiral Auphan, cabled the following request to Admiral Darlan: 'O.K.W. proposes Axis air support based on Sicily–Sardinia. In what form and in what area would you welcome this support?'[2]

From the very beginning, however, Laval's fertile mind was reaching out beyond the immediate situation. In a conversation with Krug von Nidda at 5.30 a.m., he told the German that he would urge Pétain, who was being allowed to sleep on undisturbed for the moment, to 'address himself to the German government with the request for a declaration guaranteeing the integrity of France's metropolitan territory and empire, with the exception of Alsace-Lorraine. . . . The declaration . . . would serve the purpose of preventing a possible dissidence movement in Africa.'[3] As we have seen, Laval tried to obtain such a pledge from Germany in 1940. The Allies had repeatedly given it and Roosevelt's message to Pétain seemed to contain a reaffirmation, but the Germans had always held back. Laval instantly saw and seized the opportunity to reopen the question, but unfortunately events were to move too swiftly for him.

At 7 a.m. Pétain was awakened and told of the landings. He soon approved of the proposed reply to Roosevelt and, shortly before

[1] Noguères, p. 412; Tuck to Hull, 8 November 1942, F.R.U.S., 1942, Vol. II, p. 431.
[2] Noguères, p. 412; Auphan to Darlan, 8 November 1942, C.E. *Rapport*, Vol. II, p. 535.
[3] Abetz to Foreign Ministry, 8 November 1942, GFM/443/221529–30.

8 o'clock, it was cabled to the French government representatives in North Africa, together with instructions to resist the invaders.[1] Just after 9, the American *chargé d'affaires* called upon the Marshal. He was handed a text of the reply and Pétain reminded him that 'he had told Admiral Leahy that France would resist any attack on her empire, by whomsoever and that there was no other course of action open to him than to order measures of defence'. As the *chargé* rose to take his leave, the Marshal grasped him by the hands and looked at him 'steadfastly and smiling'. He escorted the diplomat to the ante-room and then 'turned briskly back to his office humming a little tune'.[2]

The French cabinet was given a full situation report at a meeting at 11 a.m. In addition to the landings, they were told, there had been an attempted Gaullist *coup* in Morocco, and General Giraud had broadcast an appeal to all French forces in North Africa to go over to the Allies. The cabinet was unanimous in its approval of Pétain's order to resist the invaders and of Laval's appeal to the Germans for a guarantee to France's territorial integrity. The major question which it still had to decide was to what extent it should accept the German offer of Axis air support. Admiral Darlan's reply to the request which had been sent to him earlier that morning had been received shortly before the cabinet meeting. It called for air attacks upon the Allied shipping off Algiers.[3] Laval was hesitant about accepting the German offer on the grounds that it would, as he put it, 'call down the thunderbolt', but felt that to refuse it would create the impression that the government favoured dissidence. He therefore urged acceptance of Darlan's proposal and the cabinet backed him up.[4]

In the meantime, Laval's appeal for a German guarantee had arrived at Hitler's headquarters in Munich.[5] Hitler was no keener on collaboration with the French than he had ever been, but the situation was pressing and he asked for Mussolini's opinion. At noon the Duce informed the German military attaché in Rome, General von Rintelen, as follows: 'If the French government is really prepared to fight, together with us, against the British and Americans, then I am ready to

---

[1] Noguères, pp. 412, 417–18; Kammerer, *Débarquement*, p. 293.
[2] Tuck to Hull, 8 November 1942, F.R.U.S., 1942, Vol. II, pp. 430–32.
[3] Darlan to Admiralty, 8 November 1942, C.E. *Rapport*, Vol. II, p. 535.
[4] The minutes of the cabinet meeting are printed in Kammerer, *Débarquement*, pp. 661–4.
[5] Unsigned memorandum, 8 November 1942, GFM/443/221539. Hitler was in Munich for the anniversary of the abortive *putsch* of 1924.

agree. In order to clarify the situation, it seems to me imperative that France should not only break off diplomatic relations with America, but declare war upon England and the U.S.A. . . . In order to resist aggression against North African territory, an agreement with respect to the landing of [Axis] ground forces in Tunisia is absolutely vital.' If the French government was not prepared to play ball, Mussolini went on, then the rest of France should be occupied immediately, together with the island of Corsica. He would, however, prefer collaboration.[1]

The upshot of this was an urgent telephone message instructing Abetz to approach the French government with the request to declare war upon Britain and the United States. 'If the French government takes such an unequivocal stand,' the message concluded, 'we would be ready to accompany it through thick and thin.'[2]

There is no German record of the reception of this proposal. Writing in 1945 Laval stated that it was 2.50 p.m. when Krug came to see him. The German asked him to preserve the utmost discretion concerning the proposal, while at the same time strongly urging him to accept it. He 'seemed very disappointed by my extremely reserved attitude,' Laval wrote. 'I confined myself to polite remarks and there could be no doubt about my refusal . . . I informed [the Marshal], saying spontaneously that the proposal must be rejected in a way that was as emphatic as it was polite and that I saw no need to inform the cabinet. This was also the Marshal's opinion.'[3] Laval's near-contemporary account is not nearly as clear-cut. Informing the French cabinet of the German offer on 11 November, Laval went on, 'Since it was impossible to reply in the negative or in the affirmative, a conversation was begun.'[4] The point was, of course, that while the Germans had indicated their readiness to accompany France 'through thick and thin', they had made no mention of the proposed guarantee of her territorial integrity. By this stage, Laval had learned not to make concessions of this nature without receiving something substantial in return.

Laval's real feelings were shown in a conversation he had later that

---

[1] Bismarck to Foreign Ministry, 9 November 1942, ibid., 221562–4. Rintelen was an O.K.W. representative and the original message would have been sent through military channels. Bismarck was merely relaying a copy for the information of the foreign ministry which accounts for the date of the 9th.

[2] Weizsäcker to Ribbentrop, 8 November 1942, ibid., 221550–51.

[3] *Laval Parle*, p. 134.

[4] See the minutes printed in Kammerer, *Débarquement*, p. 670.

afternoon with General Weygand, whom Pétain had summoned from his seaside retreat to advise him. 'I detest communism,' he told the general. 'I've never been wrong and if we don't fight I'm sure that communism will extend over Europe. But I do not conceive of an *entente* with Germany without complete spiritual freedom for our country.' Weygand, who had always had little patience with Laval's views, retorted, 'Look at what's happening with the *relève*! Anti-German workers are becoming communists so as not to go and work in Germany. As far as America is concerned, we should do the minimum to satisfy the Germans.' 'We shall take note that the Americans have broken off relations with us,' Laval replied. 'In order to fight, we must combine moral and material pre-requisites. We have neither. The Germans will ask us to choose. . . . I shall reply that I can do no more because I don't have anything. If Hitler pledged himself to maintain the integrity of the empire, that would be something gained.' But, he concluded with resignation, 'he won't make that declaration.'[1]

The cabinet met for the second time at 6.15 p.m. Laval explained that the Germans were pressing for a break in diplomatic relations between France and the United States, but he made no mention of the request for a declaration of war. He added that, if there was no break, strong German reactions were to be feared, and the cabinet accordingly agreed to a communiqué which simply stated that, by their action in invading North Africa, the Americans had broken off relations.[2] There was a further discussion of Axis air support. Shortly after the previous cabinet meeting, the government had informed both the German and Italian armistice delegations that it was prepared to accept air support on condition that the 'planes used their own bases'.[3] Now the Germans were calling for overflight facilities and the use of French bases in North Africa. The cabinet agreed to the granting of overflight facilities, but postponed a decision on the use of French bases pending further consultation with the area commanders concerned.[4]

[1] Ménétrel notes in Noguères, p. 483. Both Ménétrel and Noguères misdated these notes as referring to a conversation on 12 November, but M. P. Dhers in his book *Regards Nouveaux sur les Années Quarante*, Paris, Flammarion, 1958, pp. 120–21, has shown conclusively that they belong to the 8th.

[2] The French decision was communicated to the American *chargé* immediately after the cabinet meeting. See Tuck to Hull, 8 November 1942, F.R.U.S., 1942, Vol. II, pp. 201–2.

[3] See the Admiralty telegram in C.E. *Rapport*, Vol. II, p. 535; Welck to Foreign Ministry, 8 November 1942, GFM/443/221547–8.

[4] The minutes of the cabinet meeting are printed in Kammerer, *Débarquement*, pp. 664–5.

Soon after the cabinet meeting, Laval had another conversation with Krug. While he was personally in favour of a declaration of war upon Britain and the United States, he explained, Marshal Pétain had not been in a position to take a definite decision at the cabinet meeting 'because he had been so exhausted on account of his advanced age after the discussion about the breaking-off of diplomatic relations with the United States that he was no longer receptive'. However, Laval went on, he would obtain the Marshal's consent first thing in the morning. After this somewhat less than frank account of what had taken place, he came to the real point. He 'requested an audience with the Führer in order to examine in detail the latter's standpoint in respect of the declaration of war . . . and the related development of Franco-German relations'.[1]

In one way, Laval was right to delay. At about the same time he was speaking to Krug, Mussolini was telling von Rintelen that he felt that Germany and Italy should not enter into any territorial commitments with regard to France at this stage. 'We are fighting a war of survival,' he maintained. 'The first priority is to win and we should postpone all territorial questions until later. When we have won, there will be sufficient points of compensation for the French.'[2]

On the other hand, the longer Laval delayed, the more hesitant Hitler became. Already French resistance in North Africa was weakening and Admiral Darlan cabled Vichy at 7 p.m. that he had authorized General Juin to negotiate a cease-fire for the city of Algiers itself.[3] The French insistence upon the Axis aircraft using their own bases probably also helped to arouse Hitler's barely-concealed suspicion of French motives,[4] and, at 6 p.m., he had already sent a distinctly cool rejoinder to the navy's enthusiastic call for Franco-German collaboration. While he agreed that such collaboration was desirable, it ran, 'it was not yet clear whether the preconditions . . . existed. The fact that Darlan

[1] Abetz to Foreign Ministry, 8 November 1942, GFM/443/221545.
[2] Bismarck to Foreign Ministry, 9 November 1942, GFM/443/221562-4.
[3] Darlan to Admiralty, 8 November 1942, C.E. *Rapport*, Vol. II, p. 518. This text is slightly corrupt, however, and a better one may be found in Kammerer, *Débarquement*, p. 275.
[4] In a telegram to the foreign ministry from Wiesbaden, which was sent at 5.20 p.m., Welck reported that 'among the German delegation, the impression remains that there is no readiness on the part of the French government for unconditional military collaboration with the Axis. Strong political pressure is held to be essential to secure this readiness . . .' (GFM/443/221547-8).

and Juin – about whom it was not clear whether they were prisoners in Algiers or could fight their way out – were unavailable must give rise to scepticism. The suspicion remained that Giraud's escape had been master-minded by the Americans. It must also be reckoned that powerful forces are active on the enemy side in metropolitan France. The question was, therefore, whether military collaboration with France was not tantamount to the filling of a bottomless cask, whereby we had to expend resources whose use for our benefit was not guaranteed.'[1] Already, on the previous day, Hitler had ordered the units earmarked for the occupation of the rest of France (Operation 'Anton') to be placed on standby. Now he ordered them to move up to the demarcation line. The Italians were taking similar precautions.[2]

Further evidence of a hardening of Hitler's attitude was provided by the ultimatum handed over to the French delegation at Wiesbaden at 12.15 a.m. on 9 November. This gave the French government one hour in which to agree to Axis aircraft using bases in Tunisia and eastern Algeria, failing which 'the O.K.W. would take the measures which it deems appropriate of its own accord'. The French had no alternative but to accept and the commanders in Tunisia were duly informed.[3]

That same night, Ribbentrop telephoned Ciano with an urgent request that Mussolini should meet Hitler in Munich as soon as possible. 'The moment has come,' he said, 'to formulate our line of conduct with respect to France.' The Duce, who claimed to be unwell, was unwilling to make the journey and delegated Ciano to take his place. His instructions were virtually identical to the message he had already sent to Hitler through von Rintelen: if France was really prepared to collaborate, she should be given every assistance; if not, both the unoccupied zone and Corsica should be occupied.[4] In order to find out exactly what the French attitude was, the Germans also summoned Laval to the meeting.[5]

His departure, however, was overshadowed by the receipt of another telegram from Admiral Darlan, in which the latter stated that General

[1] Germany Navy report on Relations with France, Kriegstagebuch 1942, p. 923.
[2] Greiner notes, 7, 8 November 1942, ibid., pp. 916, 922.
[3] Welck to Foreign Ministry, 9 November 1942, GFM/443/221555, 221559; Admiralty to Admiral Derrien (naval commander, Bizerta), 9 November 1942, C.E. *Rapport*, Vol. II, p. 528.
[4] Ciano, *Diario*, 9 November 1942.
[5] Laval's statement to French cabinet, 11 November 1942, in Kammerer, *Débarquement*, p. 670; Guérard, p. 99.

Juin had signed an armistice for the city of Algiers with the American General Ryder. But this was not all. Darlan had also seen Ryder and the latter had expressed a desire to negotiate a cease-fire agreement for the whole of Algeria and Tunisia. Darlan had not rejected this possibility, merely enquiring whether Ryder's promise that the French government's civil administration would be allowed to continue to function applied to the Marshal's government. He was told that this question would be answered the following day (the 9th). As soon as he knew the precise proposals, Darlan concluded, he would inform Pétain and await his instructions.[1]

This telegram threatened to create a grave embarrassment for Laval. How could he negotiate a guarantee of the French empire with Hitler when Darlan might pull the ground from under his feet at any moment by concluding a separate agreement with the Americans? At 9 a.m. on the 9th, shortly before his departure for Munich, he persuaded Pétain to send Darlan the following order: 'As the head of government is at present away, no negotiations must take place before his return.'[2] As he journeyed towards his crucial meeting with the Nazi leader, he must have prayed that his colleague and former rival would obey.

Certainly, at this stage, Darlan had by no means made up his mind to do a deal with the Americans. He replied to the Laval–Pétain telegram by saying that, apart from the special case of Algiers, he had no intention of negotiating, but only of listening and reporting back.[3] In a later telegram in reply to a request for his views on the situation, he seemed unable to make up his mind whether it would be better to negotiate with the Americans or call upon the Germans for help. The former course might well precipitate the occupation of the rest of metropolitan France and was, in any case becoming increasingly difficult with every hour resistance lasted. On the other hand, Germany would turn North Africa into a battlefield and thus divide it into two parts which France might not be able to reunite. Moreover, Germany's ultimate intentions were unknown. 'If Germany does help us,' he concluded, 'it is essential that she alters the armistice arrangements, replacing them with another political formula which will enable us to

---

[1] Darlan to Admiralty (for Pétain), 8 November 1942, C.E. *Rapport*, Vol. II, p. 519.

[2] Admiral G. Auphan, '*Histoire de mes "Trahisons"* ', in *Les Grimaces de l'Histoire*, Paris, Les Iles d'Or, 1951 (hereafter cited as Auphan), pp. 279–80; Admiralty to Darlan, 9 November 1942, C.E. *Rapport*, Vol. II, p. 519.

[3] Darlan to Admiralty (for Pétain), 9 November 1942, ibid., p. 520.

recover our capabilities.'[1] This, of course, was exactly what Laval was trying to obtain.

Laval was due to meet Hitler at 11 p.m. on the evening of the 9th, but fog delayed his car and he did not arrive in Munich until 4 a.m. the following morning.[2] In the meantime, Ciano had already had one conversation with Hitler. The Führer, the Italian foreign minister noted in his diary, 'entertains no great illusions regarding the French willingness to fight. . . . He will listen to Laval, but nothing the latter says can alter the point of view which he has already adopted: total occupation of France, landing in Corsica, and [establishment of] a bridgehead in Tunisia.'[3] The German record is not so categorical about the decisions already taken as Ciano's diary entry, but it abundantly confirms Hitler's scepticism concerning French readiness to collaborate.[4]

It is not clear to what extent Hitler was in possession of up-to-the-minute information about developments in North Africa, but events which took place there during the evening of the 9th would certainly have reinforced this scepticism. At 6.45 p.m., General Ryder and Robert Murphy handed Darlan the text of the American proposals for a cease-fire throughout North Africa, including Morocco as well as Algeria and Tunisia. At 8 p.m., the Admiral cabled a summary to Pétain. In a separate telegram, his military advisers urged that, from a military point of view, there was no alternative but to cease resistance, but they carefully refrained from commenting upon the political implications. As for Darlan himself, he continued to sit on the fence. 'In the present overall situation,' he cabled Vichy, 'acceptance [of the American proposals] would place us in a delicate position and would risk leading to the rupture of the armistice. At the same time, it may be wondered whether the occupation of the [French] Mediterranean coast will not take place in any case.' In conclusion, he could only lob the ball into the Marshal's court, with the assurance that any order the latter gave would be obeyed.[5]

---

[1] Darlan to Admiralty, 9 November 1942, in Kammerer, *Débarquement*, p. 371, fn. 2.

[2] *Laval Parle*, p. 135; Abetz, p. 257; Noguères, p. 441.

[3] Ciano, *Diario*, 9 November 1942.

[4] Schmidt memorandum, 12 November 1942, GFM/F1/0110–22.

[5] The French minutes of the Ryder–Murphy–Darlan meeting are printed in Darlan, pp. 303–5. The telegram summarizing the American proposals which Darlan sent to Vichy is printed in C.E. *Rapport*, Vol. II, p. 521. The views of Darlan's military advisers are set out in Kammerer, *Débarquement*, pp. 375–6, and those of Darlan himself in ibid., p. 376.

Before any orders arrived, however, he had already given in to the Americans. Another meeting had been arranged for 11 a.m. the following morning (10 November) and, when it took place, Darlan found himself confronted, not by General Ryder, but by Eisenhower's brash, table-pounding chief-of-staff, General Mark Clark, who had flown into Algiers the previous evening. Clark made it clear that he had no intention of hanging about waiting for instructions from Vichy. 'If the admiral will not issue instructions for the cessation of hostilities,' he declared, 'I will go to General Giraud [who had also arrived in Algiers]. He will sign the terms and issue the necessary orders.' Even more than the military situation, this threat was decisive. In order to preserve both the vestiges of Vichy sovereignty over North Africa and his own position, Darlan issued an order to all area commanders, instructing them to cease fire. At the same time, he announced that he had assumed full authority in North Africa in Pétain's name.[1]

When the news of Darlan's surrender arrived in Vichy at about 1.30 p.m., the Marshal and his advisers were already discussing the terms of a reply to his earlier request for instructions. General Weygand had been in favour of empowering Darlan to sign an armistice in North Africa and, when he learned that he had in fact done so, he strongly urged that he should be backed up by the government. 'I have never been in agreement with Admiral Darlan,' he told Pétain, 'but as he's acting in France's interests, we must support him with all our might.' Others were less sure, however. Rochat took the view that nothing should be done until Laval returned from Munich and he was supported by a frantic telephone call from the prime minister himself. 'I'm just about to be received by Hitler,' said Laval, 'so don't do anything for the moment. If you negotiate with the Americans before I've returned and had a chance to discuss it with you, everything is wrecked and I shall resign.' This intervention seems to have been decisive. At about 3 p.m., Pétain sent the following telegram to Darlan and the other commanders in North Africa: 'I issued the order to resist the aggressor. That order still stands.' 'Tell the Marshal that he has once

[1] The French minutes of the Darlan–Clark meeting are printed in Darlan, pp. 197–202. For Clark's own account, from which the quotation is taken, see Mark W. Clark, *Calculated Risk*, New York, Harper, 1950 (hereafter cited as Clark), pp. 106–12. Darlan's cease-fire order is printed in Darlan, pp. 202–3. His telegram to Pétain in which he sought to justify his decision is printed in ibid., p. 203.

again saved France,' said Laval when the news was 'phoned through to him.[1]

Of the many myths that surround the history of Vichy France, one of the most persistent is that, in spite of his public statements to the contrary, Pétain secretly gave Darlan to understand that he approved of his action in negotiating with the Americans and reaching a cease-fire agreement. This approval is said to have been conveyed by the so-called 'secret telegrams', sent by Admiral Auphan in a naval code which the Germans did not know. The first of these 'secret telegrams' is alleged to have been sent as a commentary upon the telegram quoted in the previous paragraph and, according to Dr Ménétrel's notes, told Darlan to take no notice of messages and orders sent under compulsion and that the Marshal was 'in complete agreement' with him.[2]

Unfortunately, there are two drawbacks to accepting Ménétrel's account. In the first place, it does not come from his contemporary notes, but from a post-war commentary upon a cryptic passage in them. Secondly, and more important, his version of the message is quite different from that given by Admiral Auphan, the man who actually sent it. Auphan's text simply says, 'Understand that this order' – i.e. for the continuation of resistance – 'was necessary for negotiations in progress'. This was merely a justification of Pétain's earlier telegram, designed perhaps to soothe Darlan's injured pride at having been disowned by his government. At most, it was an indication that there might be a change in policy after Laval's return from Munich. It in no way sanctioned the action Darlan had already taken, let alone gave him *carte blanche* for the future. Moreover, after Darlan had replied that he had 'received and understood' the secret telegram, he countermanded his cease-fire order and told the Americans that he was henceforth their prisoner. This was hardly the action of a man who had just received his government's full, if confidential, support. Fortunately for the Americans, the original cease-fire order continued to be generally

[1] Sources for the discussions at Vichy are Ménétrel's notes, 10 November 1942, in Noguères, pp. 446–8; Weygand, p. 548; Auphan, pp. 280–81; and Guérard, pp. 100–101. For Laval's telephone conversations, see Mallet, Vol. II, p. 108 and Guérard, loc. cit. For Pétain's telegram to Darlan, see Kammerer, *Débarquement*, p. 408. Kammerer gives the time of despatch as 2.50 p.m., but Ménétrel states that it was 3.14.

[2] Ménétrel's notes, 10 November 1942, in Noguères, pp. 448–9. His version is accepted by Kammerer (*Débarquement*, pp. 408–11) and by Aron (p. 560), who quotes, however another version of the text of the 'secret telegram'.

observed, but there is no evidence that this was due to any intervention of Darlan's.[1]

At about the time Darlan informed Vichy of his decision to countermand his cease-fire order and place himself in the hands of the Americans (5.35 p.m.), Laval began his long-awaited conversation with Hitler. The latter came straight to the point. 'There were only two choices for France,' he declared: 'either clear and definite alignment with the Axis or the loss of her entire colonial empire.' What was more, the French could not hold out in North Africa without strong Axis support. He wanted to know whether France was prepared to accept it, and asked Laval to give him a report on the situation.

Laval admitted that the situation in North Africa was 'serious'. Fortunately, he had been able to neutralize Darlan's negotiations with the Allies by persuading Pétain to issue his order for continued resistance. He had considerable faith in General Noguès and Admiral Estéva, the governor-generals of Morocco and Tunisia respectively, and thought that even though Algiers itself had fallen, the governor-general, General Chatel, could carry on the fight in the south. He carefully refrained from alluding to Hitler's insistence upon the need for Axis support, even after the Führer had seized upon a remark of his calling for 'urgent countermeasures' to put the demand that Tunis and Bizerta be placed at Germany's and Italy's disposal in order to prepare a counter-attack. Instead, he sought to guide the conversation into more general channels. 'France's position was difficult,' he complained, 'to the extent that in many spheres – particularly the economic – she had to behave like an ally of the Axis, whereas in others she was treated as a defeated country without being offered the slightest hope concerning her future fate.'

Ignoring Hitler's interjection that France's fate lay in her own hands, he went on to expand upon his favourite theme: a European new order. In terms almost identical to those he had used when speaking to Curtius eleven years previously,[2] he said that 'whereas in the

---

[1] For Auphan's text, see Auphan, p. 282. It is confirmed by his adjutant, Commodore Archambaud, in *Procès Pétain*, p. 280, col. 2. Both sources also give Darlan's reply. For Darlan's subsequent action, see his own undated note in Darlan, p. 217; Darlan to Pétain, 10 November 1942, in Kammerer, *Débarquement*, p. 415; and Clark, p. 113. My whole interpretation of the 'secret telegrams' is based upon Schmitt, Chapter XVII, although I do not accept all the author's conclusions.

[2] See above, p. 24.

past wars had been fought between village and village, and later between country and country, an entire continent must now be organized for peace. But this was not possible if each country insisted on putting forward certain demands for the satisfaction of its natural greed. . . . He did not want certain egoisms to hinder the erection of the structure desired by the peoples of Europe. . . . This conversation showed . . . that he wanted to do everything to facilitate Germany's victory. But in order to carry out this aim, he required certain moral and political preconditions, i.e. the victors must help him by creating a suitable atmosphere.'

Hitler was getting increasingly tired of this philosophical discourse. He interrupted once again to say that 'time was pressing and, at the moment, it was a question of whether it was possible to provide safe ports for disembarkation for the Axis in Tunis and Bizerta and air force bases in Tunis. . . . If it was not possible, collaboration was over.' Laval replied that, while he personally would support Hitler's demand, he could not commit Pétain. He took advantage of Ciano's presence, however, to link the question with Italy's territorial demands, which he doubtless considered one of the 'egoisms' which were hindering the establishment of the new Europe. It was true that Italy had never demanded Tunisia officially, he said, but she had inspired press and radio campaigns for its annexation, together with that of Corsica and Nice. He wanted to make it quite clear that France would never accept such a demand. In this context, he could not predict the attitude of the French government to the admission of Italian, as well as German, troops to Tunisia. He feared that, by inviting Italian participation, he would be accused of acquiescing in Italian demands.

But when it was clear that there was no possibility of driving a wedge between the two Axis powers over this issue, Laval was forced to give in. He advised the Germans to send another ultimatum. Pétain would have to protest, 'but the form of this protest could be agreed beforehand with Germany.' Nevertheless, Laval continued to plead for a greater understanding of France's position. 'The present state of Franco-German relations,' he said, 'was described by many Frenchmen' – not himself, he hastened to add – 'as a kind of one-way street.' He wanted more contacts with the Germans and concluded that it would be desirable if 'Germany made some gesture or declaration which would render his task in France more easy'. He emphasized his

' "fanatical determination" to do all he could to help Germany in her struggle against Bolshevism'.[1]

At no time during the course of the conversation did Hitler mention his earlier offer of an alliance 'through thick and thin'. In 1945, Laval explained this by saying that Abetz had already told Hitler that he had rejected the offer.[2] In his contemporary account to the French cabinet, however, Laval never mentioned a specific rejection[3] and left Hitler's omission unexplained.[4] A possible explanation is that Laval was still playing for time, waiting to see what he could extract from the Germans before committing himself. In this context, it is significant that, in addition to his more general pleas for better understanding, he repeated his earlier proposal for a guarantee of the French empire. Unknown to him, the Germans had actually drafted such a guarantee[5] but it was not handed over. This was probably due, in the first place, to the uncertain nature of French resistance in North Africa, and, secondly, to Laval's evasive attitude during the conversation, which would merely have confirmed Hitler in his suspicion of everything French. At 8.30 that same evening, the Führer issued the order for the occupation of the rest of France to take effect from 7 a.m. the following morning.[6]

This was, of course, unknown to the French government and Laval.[7] Their immediate problem was the German demand that Axis troops be permitted to land in Tunisia. Laval, as we have seen, had been unable to win any concessions on this point and had finally advised the Germans to confront Vichy with an ultimatum, which they duly did.[8] There was some debate among Pétain's advisers as to whether the ultimatum should be accepted, Admiral Auphan in particular arguing that its acceptance would deprive those French forces which were still

[1] Schmidt memorandum, 12 November 1942, GFM/F1/0126-55.
[2] *Laval Parle*, p. 136.
[3] He did however refer to a separate conversation with Ribbentrop, of which there seems to be no surviving record in the German Foreign Ministry files.
[4] French cabinet minutes of 11 November 1942 in Kammerer, *Débarquement*, p. 670.
[5] This unsigned, undated document (GFM/F9/0006-7) pledged the German and Italian governments to preserve metropolitan France within her 1914 frontiers (i.e. minus Alsace-Lorraine) and to allow her to keep the equivalent of her colonial empire in Africa.
[6] Greiner notes, 11, 14 November 1942, Kriegstagebuch 1942, pp. 936, 954.
[7] Ribbentrop told Ciano that Laval would not be informed until the following morning (Ciano, *Diario*, 10-11 November 1942).
[8] Noguères, pp. 444-5. According to this source, the ultimatum was not handed over until 11.50 p.m. But its tenor was certainly known beforehand.

TWENTY CRUCIAL DAYS · 335

resisting of any incentive to continue the fight.[1] But it was he who finally sent the telegram ordering the French naval commander at Bizerta not to resist the Axis landings. 'I am well aware of the possible repercussions of this operation,' he concluded, 'but please believe that I am only thinking of France's ultimate benefit.'[2] At dinner that evening, Pétain told Auphan and Weygand that he thought Laval had given in too easily over Tunisia and that he was thinking of repeating 'the 13 December *coup*' on his return.[3] The turn of events, as well as his own apparently total loss of control of the situation, rendered this an empty threat however.

During the night of 10–11 November, resistance to the Allied landings ceased in Morocco. (The cease-fire in Algeria, it will be recalled, had taken place on the 10th.) In a telegram to Pétain on the 11th, General Noguès the governor-general explained that he had received Darlan's original cease-fire order on the afternoon of the 10th and that by the time he had heard to the contrary from Vichy at about midnight, he had already complied. He was meeting the American commander at 4 p.m. on the 11th to discuss the conditions of the cease-fire and would report on the results of these discussions.[4] For some unexplained reason, Noguès' telegram did not reach Vichy until the following morning, the 12th and, as we shall see, this may have had at least one important consequence.[5]

Meanwhile, the naval commander at Casablanca, Admiral Michelier, had sent two urgent telegrams to the French admiralty asking for verification of Darlan's and Noguès' orders. At 10.40 p.m. the admiralty replied that Pétain's orders were 'to continue hostilities for as long as possible'.[6] Admiral Auphan subsequently claimed that he had deliberately inserted the phrase 'for as long as possible' on his own initiative, in order to enable Michelier to negotiate with the Americans.[7] It certainly gave the Casablanca commander the loophole he needed in the light of the desperate situation his forces found themselves in after their terrific pounding. At 4.45 a.m. on the morning of the 11th, he

[1] Ménétrel's notes, 10 November 1942, ibid., pp. 450–51.
[2] Auphan to Derrien, 10 November 1942, in Kammerer, *Débarquement*, p. 423.
[3] Auphan, p. 297.
[4] Noguès to Pétain, 11 November 1942, C.E. *Rapport*, Vol. II, p. 539.
[5] See below, pp. 337–38.
[6] Michelier to Admiralty, 10 November 1942, C.E. *Rapport*, Vol. II, pp. 523, 524; Admiralty to Michelier, 10 November 1942, ibid., p. 524.
[7] Auphan, p. 281.

telegraphed the admiralty that he had ordered a cease-fire that morning, 'thereby executing the orders of the governor-general . . . and acting in conformity with those you sent me on 10 November.'[1]

At about 4 a.m. on the morning of 11 November, the twenty-fourth anniversary of the armistice of 1918, Laval was awakened by Abetz to be told that the Axis were going to occupy the rest of France. He wrote later that he protested vociferously, particularly against the entry of Italian troops, but that Abetz replied, 'It's a decision of the Führer's; there's nothing to be done.'[2]

At 5.30 a.m., Krug von Nidda delivered Hitler's letter to Pétain announcing the decision to Rochat. It was a characteristically long-winded document which sought to justify the German action by referring to the alleged intention of the British and Americans to invade Corsica and southern France. It went on to assure the Marshal that the action was not directed against him personally, or against the French administration. The German troops would withdraw to the old demarcation line as soon as the situation allowed and, in the meantime, the Marshal and his ministers could move about France at their will. They could even transfer the seat of government from Vichy to Versailles if they desired. 'Germany has . . . decided to defend the frontiers of your country side by side with the French soldiers,' Hitler concluded, 'and at the same time the frontiers of culture and European civilization. As far as the German troops are concerned, they will do what is necessary to attain this aim in their own way, which is the way of friendship towards the French people. I should like to ask you, *Monsieur le Maréchal*, to see that the government takes the necessary measures for the elimination of all tension and to guarantee the putting into force of this necessary measure, also in the interest of France.'[3]

Hitler was doubtless concerned at the possibility of armed resistance to the entry of the Axis forces. Contingency plans had indeed been drawn up,[4] but immediately after Krug's *démarche* and without even consulting Pétain, who was still asleep, the three service ministers and Bousquet issued orders to all military and police units not to oppose

---

[1] Michelier to Admiralty, 11 November 1942, C.E. *Rapport*, Vol. II, pp. 538–9.
[2] *Laval Parle*, p. 137.
[3] For the full text of Hitler's letter, which was made public at the time, see *The Times*, 12 November 1942. The German text is on GFM/443/221578–85.
[4] Weygand, p. 548.

the Axis forces.[1] Only General de Lattre de Tassigny, the commanding officer of the 16th infantry division at Montpellier, carried out an earlier order to pull all his troops out of their barracks and deploy them in positions from which they could resist the Germans. He was relieved of his command and placed under arrest.[2] Apart from this, the occupation of the rest of metropolitan France and Corsica proceeded largely without incident.[3]

Nevertheless, there was fierce debate at Vichy about the French government's next steps. Admiral Auphan and General Weygand argued strongly that a telegram should be sent to Darlan, instructing him to cease fire. In view of the German action, they maintained, it was madness to continue fighting in North Africa. They also argued that the fleet at Toulon should be ordered to sail for North Africa to prevent it from falling into German hands. Once again, however, Rochat carried the day with his insistence that nothing should be done until Laval returned from Munich.[4] One of the few things upon which everyone could agree was the appointment of General Noguès as Marshal Pétain's sole representative in North Africa, and a telegram announcing this was sent to all area commanders at 10 a.m.[5] It was followed by a second 'secret telegram' to Darlan, explaining that the only reason why the appointment had been made was because he was thought to be a prisoner.[6] No more than the first did this second 'secret telegram' condone Darlan's original cease-fire order or empower him to negotiate with the Americans.

The choice of Noguès as Darlan's successor was probably influenced by the arrival of his special envoy, Major Bataille, bearing a personal letter assuring Pétain that, as long as he (Noguès) remained in command, all Pétain's orders would be obeyed.[7] But this letter had been written on the morning of 10 November, before Darlan's cease-fire order and Noguès' acceptance of it. News of Michelier's surrender at

---

[1] Schleier to Foreign Ministry, 11 November 1942, GFM/443/221573.
[2] Kammerer, *Débarquement*, pp. 440–41.
[3] The Italians were slightly delayed in reaching Corsica because of rough weather. See Marshal Ugo Cavallero, *Comando Supremo, Diario 1940–43*, Bologna, Cappelli, 1948, p. 383.
[4] Ménétrel notes, 11 November 1942, in Noguères, pp. 467–9; Auphan, pp. 285–6.
[5] Admiralty to Admirals Michelier, Rioult (Oran), Moreau (Algiers) and Derrien, 11 November 1942, C.E. *Rapport*, Vol. II, p. 539.
[6] Auphan, p. 28; Archambaud in *Procès Pétain* p. 280, col. 2.
[7] For the text of the letter, see Noguères, p. 454.

Casablanca had by now arrived in Vichy, but Pétain and his advisers still did not know of Noguès' rendezvous with the Americans that afternoon because the telegram announcing it had not yet arrived. If it had, some of the Marshal's ministers might have thought twice about giving Noguès such extensive powers. Admiral Auphan, on the other hand, has argued that the powers were granted to Noguès precisely to enable him to negotiate, and he has even suggested that Major Bataille, who returned to Morocco on the morning of 11 November, was given a verbal message to this effect to take back to his superior. There is, however, no reliable evidence to support these contentions.[1]

After the telegram announcing Noguès' appointment had been sent, Weygand suggested to Pétain that he make a formal protest to the Germans about their decision to occupy the whole of France. He had even taken the liberty of preparing a draft for the purpose and, at 10.40 a.m., the Marshal read it to Field-Marshal von Rundstedt, the German army commander in western Europe. It was also broadcast repeatedly over the French radio, but Pétain largely destroyed its value as far as the Germans were concerned by explaining to von Rundstedt that he had to make the protest 'on account of public opinion in France'.[2] We shall see what effect it had upon Admiral Darlan in Algiers.

As well as his protest, Pétain made two requests to von Rundstedt. The first, which aimed at excluding Italian troops from the occupation of Nice, came to nothing, but the second, which concerned the fleet at Toulon, had very important consequences. Pétain asked that Toulon should remain unoccupied. This was obviously part of a co-ordinated programme, for while he was speaking to von Rundstedt, Admiral Marquis, the commander of the Toulon naval base, put the same request to Admiral de Feo of the Italian armistice commission and Admiral Auphan wrote a personal letter to the commander-in-chief of the German navy, Grand-Admiral Raeder, asking that the French navy as well as the Marshal's independence be respected.[3] The purpose of all these moves was quite obviously to prevent the fleet from falling

[1] Auphan, p. 286. The last part of this paragraph relies heavily upon General G. Schmitt, 'La Matinée du 11 novembre 1942 à Vichy', Revue d'Histoire de la 2ème Guerre Mondiale, October 1962, pp. 77–80.

[2] Ménétrel notes, 11 November 1942, Noguères, pp. 469–70; Schleier to Foreign Ministry, 11 November 1942, GFM/443/221596–8.

[3] Ibid.; Welck to Foreign Ministry, 11 November 1942, ibid., 221606–7; Auphan letter to Raeder, 11 November 1942, in Kammerer, Flotte Française, p. 539.

into Axis hands and thereby give the French government at least some room for manœuvre.

Fortunately for the French, their request coincided with the views of the German naval staff. The latter had already informed Hitler that, in its opinion, only 'co-operation with the French promised success in combating further enemy plans' and proposed that the defence of Toulon at any rate should be entrusted to them. Hitler and Mussolini agreed on condition that the base and fleet commanders at Toulon gave a solemn pledge not to undertake any action against the Axis and to defend Toulon against any Allied or dissident French attack. This presented no great problem to Admirals Marquis and de Laborde. After all, their orders were to scuttle if necessary to prevent the fleet from falling into foreign hands, but not to take any offensive action. When the matter was put to them at about 11 p.m. that evening, Marquis accepted straightaway and de Laborde merely requested that he be given a categorical assurance that no German or Italian would set foot on one of his ships and that he be allowed to consult his officers before committing them as individuals. The Germans agreed. The following morning, only two officers jibbed at what de Laborde had done and were immediately replaced. For the moment, at any rate, the fleet was safe.[1]

The same, alas, could not be said of the empire. In Morocco, General Noguès had his meeting with the American commander, General Patton, and was shocked at the armistice terms communicated to him. He told Pétain that they were 'even more harsh than those in the Franco-German conventions' and Patton that they did not correspond with what he knew of the agreement reached in Algiers. He proposed that, for the moment, they should confine themselves to what was immediately necessary. Patton agreed, and Noguès reported to Pétain that 'it was conceded that the military, political, and administrative structure of the country would be strictly maintained'.[2] It was probably the inconclusive nature of this settlement as much as his appointment as Pétain's plenipotentiary and Darlan's invitation which prompted him to go to Algiers the following day.[3]

In Algeria, the decisive event was receipt of the news of the German

[1] Germany Navy report on Franco-German relations, Kriegstagebuch 1942, p. 937; Welck to Foreign Ministry, 11 November 1942, GFM/443/221606-7; Auphan, pp. 286, 290-91; De Laborde report to Pétain, 12 November 1942, Noguères, pp. 526-9.

[2] Noguès to Pétain, 11 November 1942, in Kammerer, Débarquement, p. 458.

[3] Ibid.

invasion of the unoccupied zone and Marshal Pétain's protest. In the morning, General Clark had asked Darlan to summon the French fleet to North Africa and to order Admiral Estéva, the governor-general of Tunisia, to resist the imminent Axis troop landings. Darlan refused and the reasons he gave show quite clearly that he had not interpreted the 'secret telegrams' as conveying government approval of his earlier actions. 'I have no authority to summon the fleet,' he told Clark, 'and in view of my dismissal by Pétain I am not certain that any orders given by me will be obeyed.' Clark was furious and stormed out saying, 'There is no indication of any desire on your part to assist the allied cause.'[1]

By early afternoon, however, Darlan had changed his mind – 'a fact which,' Clark subsequently commented, 'he tried to attribute to the receipt of information that . . . von Rundstedt and Marshal Pétain were at odds concerning the occupation of southern France.' Clark may have been too cynical, for this was precisely the reason which Darlan gave in a private note which he wrote for his own use at the beginning of December. 'On 11 November,' the relevant passage ran, 'the Germans broke the armistice and, in conjunction with the Italians, invaded the whole of metropolitan France with the exception of the fortress at Toulon, which was reserved for the French fleet. The Marshal made a solemn protest against this violation of the armistice. Admiral [Darlan] then took the view that, while remaining loyal to the Marshal's person, he could resume his freedom of action.'[2] There is, it should be noted, no reference to 'secret telegrams'.

Whatever his motives, Darlan acted with the zeal of the recent convert. In Clark's presence, he telephoned Admiral Estéva and ordered him to resist the Axis landings. At 5.47 p.m., he appealed to the French fleet at Toulon to sail for Africa. General Juin, the commander of French ground forces in North Africa, was no less enthusiastic. He issued orders to all his subordinates that 'any attempt at intervention by Axis forces in North Africa must be repulsed by force', and personally telephoned detailed instructions to General Barré, the ground commander in Tunisia and eastern Algeria.[3]

---

[1] Clark, pp. 114–15.
[2] Ibid., pp. 115–16; undated Darlan note in Darlan, p. 217.
[3] Clark, p. 116; Darlan to Admiralty, 11 November 1942, in Kammerer, *Débarquement*, p. 447; Marshal Alphonse Juin, *Mémoires*, Vol. I, *Alger–Tunis–Rome*, Paris, Fayard, 1959 (hereafter cited as Juin), pp. 100–101; General Georges Barré, *Tunisie, 1942–43*, Paris, Éditions Berger-Levrault, 1950, p. 119.

Unfortunately, none of these measures met with the hoped-for success. Admiral de Laborde replied to Darlan's appeal to sail to Africa with the expression made famous by General Cambronne at Waterloo, while in Algiers itself, two of Juin's subordinates, Generals Koeltz and Mendigal, told him that they could not obey his order to resist the Axis until they had received confirmation from General Noguès.[1]

But this was nothing to the confusion in Tunisia. Already, at 10.45 that morning, Admiral Derrien had telegraphed the admiralty from Bizerta requesting guidance. 'The struggle is continuing against the Anglo-Saxons,' he said. 'After having telephoned General Juin, General Barré believes that the line to follow is strict neutrality towards all belligerents. Request you to take all measures to put an end to such confusion as soon as possible because it is creating a dangerous uneasiness in men's minds.'[2] It was six hours before Admiral Auphan, acting as lone-wolf again, replied to Derrien's urgent appeal. 'Since last night's events,' he said, 'my personal opinion is a passive attitude towards everyone. But the government's position will not be decided until this evening.'[3] By then, however, Derrien had already received Juin's orders to resist the Axis and at 5.22 p.m. – almost certainly before Auphan's telegram had been decoded and read by him – he issued his own orders to resist any Axis attempt to land troops, to open fire on any Axis ship approaching the shore, and not to engage in any hostile action against Allied ships, troops, or 'planes. Because of Axis air superiority, however, he forbade any attacks upon German and Italian aircraft except in self-defence.[4]

All this, of course, was unknown in Vichy, where Laval had returned by air from Munich at 2 p.m. 'I had a rough time,' he explained, although he blamed it on to the Italians.[5] At 5.30 there was a cabinet meeting. Laval gave a long account of the events of the previous three days, including Hitler's offer of an alliance 'through thick and thin'. As we have already seen, he gave no explanation of what had happened to

[1] Kammerer, *Débarquement*, pp. 447–8; Juin, p. 102.
[2] Derrien to Admiralty, 11 November 1942, C.E. *Rapport*, Vol. II, p. 540.
[3] Auphan to Derrien, 11 November 1942, C.E. *Rapport*, Vol. II, p. 541.
[4] For the text of Derrien's order, see Kammerer, *Débarquement*, pp. 463–4. For the explanation of the passage concerning Axis aircraft, see General Barré, op. cit., pp. 119–20.
[5] Ménétrel notes, 11 November 1942, in Noguères, pp. 470–71.

it, although he did say that he thought the Italians had blackmailed their allies. 'They are petrified of a Franco-German *entente*,' he maintained. The discussion turned to the situation in North Africa. Admiral Auphan recommended a cease-fire. General Brévié, the minister for the colonies, said that, if the Germans recaptured North Africa, they would never return it to France. He thought the fight should continue. Laval agreed. 'To give the order to cease fire in Africa would mean opening fire in France,' he declared. He proposed, and the cabinet accepted, the following announcement: 'The Marshal and the government pay homage to the loyalty and bravery of the African army and rely upon it to continue the struggle to the limit of its resources in the interest of France and the empire.'[1]

At 9.47 p.m., the admiralty telegraphed Derrien, 'You will read in the cabinet communiqué that the Marshal has decided to continue the struggle against Anglo-Saxon aggression within the limits of material means and possibilities. You must also allow Italo-German forces landing in Tunisia to pass without interference. Obey the Marshal's order.'[2] Shortly before 1 a.m. on 12 November, the unfortunate and greatly confused Derrien countermanded his previous order to resist the Axis and ordered 'strict neutrality towards all foreign forces . . .'[3] This was not quite what the government had asked for, but it had the advantage of being fifty per cent acceptable to both sides.

The following morning, the French government had a fresh problem on its hands. Bousquet informed Laval and Weygand that he had received an order from Himmler, presumably through Oberg, to place Weygand under surveillance. The Germans, with reason, were highly suspicious of his attitude.[4] Bousquet said that he had told the Germans that Weygand was the Marshal's guest and that he (Bousquet) would answer for him personally. Laval associated himself with Bousquet's statement, but this did not prevent him from having a fierce argument over policy with Weygand after the police chief had left. 'I tell you in all seriousness,' the general declared, 'that the policy the government is pursuing is dividing the country from the Marshal.' 'What do you

---

[1] The minutes of the cabinet meeting are printed in Kammerer *Débarquement*, pp. 669–71.
[2] Admiralty to Derrien, 11 November 1942, C.E. *Rapport*, Vol. II, pp. 541–2.
[3] For the text of Derrien's order, see Kammerer, *Débarquement*, p. 465.
[4] See Schleier to Foreign Ministry, 11 November 1942, GFM/443/221570, 221571–2. According to the second of these telegrams, Bousquet, far from discouraging German suspicions, encouraged them by relating some of the things Weygand had said to Pétain.

expect me to do?' asked Laval. 'I'm certain that if the Anglo-Saxons are the winners in this war, it will mean bolshevism.' Weygand replied that, thanks to its policy, the government was acting as 'the accomplice of communism'. He told the prime minister that his actions were opposed by 95 per cent of the French people. 'The figure is probably 98 per cent,' Laval retorted, expressing his determination 'to make the French people happy in spite of themselves'.[1]

Later that day, Weygand left Vichy. Pétain had advised him against returning to his home on the Mediterranean and it was arranged that he should spend a few days at the prefecture at Guéret in the Creuse until a new residence was found for him in that area. But Weygand never reached Guéret. About a quarter of an hour out of Vichy, his car ran into a German road block. The S.S., who had been watching his every move since the previous day, arrested him and he was taken to Germany.[2]

Meanwhile, in Algiers, General Clark had been awakened to be told that the orders to resist the Axis had been revoked. Both Darlan and Juin told him that they must wait for Noguès, who was now on his way to Algiers. Clark's short temper flared again as he insisted that the orders be reinstated. 'Your future depends on whether you do this or not,' he threatened, and the two men reluctantly complied. When Noguès arrived, Clark told him bluntly, 'I do not recognize either you or Pétain,' and he insisted that Giraud, whom Noguès regarded as a traitor, be brought into any settlement which was reached.[3]

But the long negotiations which took place that evening were inconclusive. Noguès sent a progress report to Vichy in the form of a crucial telegram (No. 50803), which was despatched at 3.24 a.m. on the morning of 13 November. 'After very difficult discussions,' it ran, 'Admiral Darlan and I . . . have reached an agreement in principle which preserves the existing military, political, and administrative framework and which does not give General Giraud the post of commander-in-chief which had been formally promised him by the Americans. This solution was difficult to obtain and provoked a violent reaction from the interested party, who undertook to chase the Germans out of Tunisia with a few battalions of the Constantine division. It will certainly not

[1] Ménétrel notes, 12 November 1942, in Noguères, pp. 478–9; Weygand, p. 551.
[2] Ibid., pp. 550–52; Schleier to Foreign Ministry, 11 November 1942, GFM/443/221570.
[3] Clark, pp. 117–19; Juin, pp. 103–4.

be maintained unless you reappoint Admiral Darlan to represent you in Africa. . . . It is vital to take this decision with the utmost expedition, given the uneasiness which is prevalent. . . .'[1]

This telegram does not contain the slightest hint that North Africa should re-enter the war on the side of the Allies. If anything, it implies an attitude of neutrality. Whether Noguès was still hoping for a solution along these lines is not clear, but what is certain is that the French government was called upon to pronounce upon a proposal which was to become out-of-date almost as soon as it was received.

In any case, neutrality was hardly the policy the French government was pursuing. At 3.5 p.m., Admiral Derrien, who was obviously being careful not to take any more independent initiatives, telegraphed the admiralty to say that the Italian and German ships which were expected to arrive at Bizerta would need French naval help in unloading. Should he give it? 'Answer in the affirmative,' replied the admiralty in record time. Later that evening, Pétain instructed General Barré through Admiral Derrien that 'his mission still consists of defending the territory of Tunisia against any Anglo-Saxon action'.[2]

If we assume that General Noguès' telegram requesting Darlan's reinstatement was received and decoded by about 4 a.m. on the morning of 13 November, it was no less than nine hours before an acknowledgement was sent and twelve hours before a reply. Even then the latter was the last and most significant of Admiral Auphan's personal initiatives and not an official answer at all. 'The Marshal approved the reinstatement of Admiral Darlan,' Auphan wrote subsequently, 'and instructed me to draft a reply in his presence which I showed to M. Laval before sending it. But M. Laval, although he said that he was basically in agreement, did not want to reply before obtaining advance assurance of German agreement. This made the whole thing impossible. As I could not get his counter-signature for the despatch of the telegram, I took it upon myself to send Admiral Darlan, via my secret link, the following telegram referring to Noguès' message: "Private agreement of Marshal and President Laval, but before replying to you, the occupation authorities are being consulted." ' It was sent at 4 p.m.

---

[1] Noguès to Pétain, 13 November 1942, C.E. *Rapport*, Vol. II, pp. 542–3.
[2] Derrien to Admiralty, 12 November 1942, C.E. *Rapport*, Vol. II, p. 540; Admiralty to Derrien, 12 November 1942, ibid.; Pétain to Derrien for Barré, 12 November 1942, ibid., p. 542.

and was followed by another, this time sent through normal channels, promising a quick reply.[1]

By this time, however, the crucial decisions had already been taken in Algiers. Clark had seen Noguès, Darlan, and the others in the morning and 'minced no words in telling them that they would have to agree or [he] would put them in immediate custody and establish military government'. He then went off to meet General Eisenhower and Admiral Cunningham, who were flying in from Gibraltar to set the seal upon whatever agreement was reached, and while the Allied party was lunching, they were told that the French had worked out a compromise. The meeting which took place between Eisenhower, Cunningham, and the French at 3 p.m. that afternoon was therefore a formality. 'In outline,' Clark wrote later, 'the agreement was that Darlan would head the civil and political government of all French North Africa; the present governors . . . would remain at their posts; Giraud would head the French armed forces, organizing a reinforced army to fight at our side . . . but, for the time being, [his] appointment would be kept quiet for political amity.'[2]

Auphan's telegram therefore – the third of the famous 'secret telegrams' – had no influence whatever upon the decisions reached. Nor should it be interpreted as implying some kind of retrospective endorsement of them.[3] In the first place, it was sent entirely upon Auphan's own initiative and we only have his word for the 'private agreement' of Pétain and Laval. There is no evidence that either of them saw the text of the telegram before it was sent. Secondly, even if we assume that the 'private agreement' existed, and of course neither Noguès nor Darlan had any reason to doubt this, then it was agreement to the terms set out in Noguès' telegram number 50803, including neutrality and the exclusion of Giraud, and not to those which were actually agreed upon in Algiers.

[1] For the acknowledgement, see Auphan to Noguès, 13 November 1942, ibid., p. 543. For Auphan's account of the drafting of the reply, see Auphan, p. 293. The text he quotes is, in fact, slightly inaccurate. For the correct text, and the time of despatch, see Darlan, p. 207. For Laval's attempt to obtain German agreement for the reinstatement of Darlan, see Abetz to Foreign Ministry, 13 November 1942, GFM/443/221630. For the regular telegram promising an early reply, see C.E. *Rapport*, Vol. II, p. 543.

[2] Clark, pp. 121–2; Juin, pp. 107–8; Captain Harry C. Butcher, *Three Years with Eisenhower*, London, Heinemann, 1946, pp. 163–5.

[3] Of course, Darlan and Noguès subsequently tried to use it as such. See Juin, pp. 108–9; Darlan's letter to Admiral Leahy, 27 November 1942, in Darlan, pp. 223–5.

Later in the day, both Noguès and Darlan issued proclamations. Noguès announced that he was handing over his powers to Darlan, while the latter declared that he had 'assumed responsibility in Africa on behalf of the government [and] with the assent of the American authorities, with whom I have agreed to defend North Africa'.[1] When this text became known in Vichy, Laval immediately cabled Darlan for confirmation, pointing out that 'the terms communicated by [the news agency] are, in fact, inadmissible and incompatible with the government's instructions'.[2]

Important though they were, events in North Africa were not Laval's sole concern on 13 November. There was the matter of General Weygand, concerning whose whereabouts the French government had only the vaguest idea. At 12.50 p.m., acting on instructions from Ribbentrop, Krug von Nidda explained to the prime minister that Weygand had been taken to Germany, where he would be treated as a prisoner-of-war in accordance with his rank. His arrest was justified on the grounds of his dealings with Murphy when he had been the government's representative in North Africa and his recent anti-German attitude. If he were not taken into custody, it was claimed, he might try to emulate General Giraud. Laval replied that Pétain had just sent a letter to Abetz in which he guaranteed Weygand's loyalty with his own word of honour.[3] That evening, Laval, Bousquet, Dr Ménétrel, and Jean Jardel of Pétain's secretariat saw Krug again and expressed the hope that the Marshal's letter would lead to a satisfactory solution of the problem. Otherwise they feared that news of Weygand's arrest would lead to further dissidence in North Africa and 'repercussions' in the army in metropolitan France.[4] At 2.20 a.m. on 14 November, however, Ribbentrop telegraphed Abetz rejecting Pétain's letter.[5] Vichy protested no more.

During the night, also, Darlan sent Laval the official text of his proclamation. It was exactly the same as the text supplied by the news agency, and the best part of the following day was taken up with a

---

[1] For the full texts of Noguès and Darlan's proclamation, see Noguères, pp. 484–5.
[2] Laval to Darlan, 13 November 1942, C.E. *Rapport*, Vol. II, p. 543.
[3] Ribbentrop to Abetz, 13 November 1942, GFM/443/221627–8; Abetz to Foreign Ministry 13 November 1942, ibid., 221636. For the text of Pétain's letter, see Noguères, pp. 486–7.
[4] Abetz to Foreign Ministry, 13 November 1942, GFM/443/221644–5.
[5] Ribbentrop to Abetz, 14 November, ibid., 221651–3.

discussion of the reply. It was finally sent at 6.5 p.m. on the 14th in the form of a telegram from Pétain to the admiral. 'You should defend North Africa against American aggression,' it ran. 'The decision you have taken in violation of my orders is contrary to the mission with which you were entrusted. I order the army of Africa not to undertake any action in any circumstances against the Axis forces and not to add to the misfortunes of the country.'[1]

Another problem which was raised by Darlan's conduct was the question of the Marshal's succession. It was clearly impossible for a rebel to remain heir-apparent. Laval raised the point on the morning of 14 November, saying that Krug had insisted the succession law be changed. 'It is impossible for you to hand over your powers to anybody,' he told the Marshal, and suggested that, in the event of the latter's incapacity, they should be entrusted to himself for a month pending a final decision by the cabinet.[2] There is no evidence in the German foreign ministry files that Krug did in fact raise this question, and, although the German embassy staff were only too capable of taking personal initiatives, this does not seem to be one of them. It was more likely a case of Laval seizing the opportunity to extend his already considerable powers.

Darlan's defection certainly seemed to have produced another crisis which would require exceptional powers for its solution. At 6 p.m., de Brinon arrived from Paris with the shattering news that Ribbentrop had demanded a declaration of war upon the United States within 24 hours. Laval was said to be 'staggered' by this information and neither he, the Marshal, nor any of the senior ministers consulted could make up their minds what to do beyond taking the apparently not very relevant decision to send Admiral Platon, one of the secretaries of state to the prime minister and an ardent collaborationist, on a mission to Tunisia. Had his colleagues any idea of the problems he would be called upon to deal with, Platon wanted to know. 'No,' was the answer, 'play it by ear!' 'There are signs that we are on the eve of serious steps by Germany,' Laval declared solemnly, 'very serious steps. We are

---

[1] Ménétrel notes, 14 November 1942, in Noguères, pp. 496–8; cabinet minutes in Kammerer, *Débarquement*, pp. 674–5; Pétain to Darlan, 14 November 1942, C.E. *Rapport*, Vol. II, p. 544.

[2] Ménétrel notes, 14 November 1942, in Noguères, p. 496. Laval also raised the matter at the cabinet meeting, but did not mention his own intended rôle. See Kammerer, *Débarquement*, p. 674.

really up against it. We run the risk of experiencing the fate of Poland.
. . . I think that Europe will become a veritable fortress. We must do
everything to preserve a semblance of government. We must not throw
everything away.'[1]

By the following morning (15 November), the situation, although
still serious, did not look quite so desperate. A long telegram had been
received from General Noguès in which he attempted to explain the
events of 13 November and put them in as favourable a light as possible. The upshot of his argument was that General Giraud had agreed
to take orders from Darlan, that everyone – including the Americans –
was opposed to the arrival of de Gaulle, and that General Eisenhower
had promised to respect the territorial integrity of the French empire.
Noguès explained that the passage in Darlan's proclamation about the
joint defence of North Africa had been inserted as the result of an ultimatum by General Clark. 'We had promised to defend the Spanish
frontier and the Algeria–Tunisia frontier,' he admitted, 'but it was
understood that this would not be made public.' In fact, he added, they
had been powerless against what amounted to a full-scale occupation.
Moreover, there was considerable pro-American feeling in the army
and among the civilian population. 'It was more worthwhile to canalize
it,' he concluded. 'The main point was to preserve a united French
North Africa around the name of the Marshal and not in the name of
the dissident movement and, in addition, to preserve the existing
framework in order not to upset the natives and to impel them to seek
protection from other quarters.'[2]

On top of this telegram, with its emphasis upon the preservation of
the *status quo*, came a more detailed explanation of German demands
by de Brinon. It appeared that what the Germans were asking for was
not so much a declaration of war as some form of 'recognition' that a
state of war existed already. 'This commits us to nothing,' de Brinon
told Pétain and Laval, 'but it makes it impossible for hostilities to begin
again between Germany and ourselves. . . . It is the only way to
preserve what we have.' He also suggested the formation of an 'Imperial Legion', consisting of volunteers, to help recover the empire.
Most important of all, however, de Brinon disclosed that the German

---

[1] Ménétrel notes, 14 November 1942, in Noguères, pp. 498–9. See also de Brinon, p. 133.
[2] Noguès to Pétain, 14–15 November 1942, in Noguères, pp. 494–5. Kammerer also
prints the full text (Kammerer, *Débarquement*, pp. 673–4) but misdates it 13–14 November.

demands did not come from Berlin at all, but were merely Abetz's personal suggestions. There is no direct evidence that this crucial fact registered with Laval, but it seems almost incredible that it did not and it may go some way towards accounting for his new insistence upon seeing Hitler again before committing himself. But there was no immediate reaction and, after some resistance, Pétain was prevailed upon to agree to the preparation of a communiqué 'recognizing' the existence of a state of war, which would be presented to the cabinet for approval. After drafting the document, de Brinon flew back to Paris.[1]

The cabinet meeting began at 3 p.m., but no sooner had the ministers begun discussing the terms of the proposed communiqué than they were informed of a proclamation which General Giraud had just made in which he expressed his desire to free both North Africa and metropolitan France from Axis control in the Marshal's name. This, it was decided, created an entirely new situation, and the original draft communiqué was abandoned for a thorough re-examination of the whole issue. Quite why Giraud's proclamation was considered so important is unclear, unless it was because its call for an offensive against the Axis contrasted so sharply with the tone of Noguès' telegram. At any rate, after what the minutes describe as 'a discussion of a very high order', Laval summarized the two main currents of opinion within the government. The first, basing itself upon public opinion and the morale of the armed forces, opposed a policy which it was felt would lead to 'widespread dissidence within the home army itself and a schism among Frenchmen which was capable of resulting in civil war'. The other and majority view, however, was that 'the time had come to make a clear choice over policy and go back to Hitler's communication of 8 November resulting in a political alliance'. Laval was to resume negotiations with the Führer, accepting the latter's offer on condition that French sovereignty was formally recognized and that the Axis powers agreed to maintain the power of France both in Europe and in the empire. 'To put it in general terms,' the minutes stated, 'France ought no longer to be treated as a defeated nation, but as an ally.'[2]

Many of those in the minority felt that they had now come to the

---

[1] Ménétrel notes, 15 November 1942, in Noguères, pp. 504–5; de Brinon, pp. 134–6. De Brinon misdates the conversation as taking place on the 16th.

[2] The cabinet minutes are printed in Kammerer, *Débarquement*, pp. 675–6.

end of the road. Admiral Auphan offered his resignation on the spot. He was followed by M. Gibrat, the transport minister, and M. Barnaud, the secretary of state for Franco-German economic relations. At this point, Laval intervened to say that if one more minister resigned, he would find it impossible to carry on himself. M. Barthélemy, the minister of justice, said that while he shared the minority view, he would not resign and thereby become, as he put it, 'the old plant which, when it's torn out, brings down the old wall.' For the moment, the government was safe.[1]

But Laval was badly shaken. He had already been thinking of strengthening his position, as his proposal to make himself the Marshal's interim successor indicates. Now he decided that something far more drastic was required. As he told Krug von Nidda on 16 November, he had resolved 'to demand completely dictatorial powers from the head of state. . . . With the situation as it was, when he had to deal with the Führer and the Duce, he was no longer in a position to keep on asking Marshal Pétain for his agreement when important political decisions had to be taken, or to have to convince him and any ministers who happened to be reluctant of [the wisdom of] his policy by means of hour-long debates.'[2]

16 and 17 November, in fact, were largely taken up in extracting two new constitutional acts from Pétain. The first appointed Laval his successor for a period of one month should he be prevented from exercising his functions. At the end of this period, the cabinet would designate the definitive successor. The second gave Laval full powers to promulgate laws and decrees under his own signature. 'I accept all the responsibilities, whatever they may be,' Laval declared, 'and I accept that you, *Monsieur le Maréchal*, be relieved of them.' But the old soldier was deeply suspicious of the wily politician's eagerness to shoulder every burden and, with the support of his wife and his minister of justice, he held out until Laval agreed to bide by the terms of a secret letter which placed considerable limitations upon the powers he was seeking. The letter stated that Laval was not to declare war, although he could order measures of self-defence if the country were attacked. He was to respect 'the spiritual traditions of France' and was to guarantee 'the absolute personal and material security of the

---

[1] Jacques Barnaud in C.E. *Témoignages*, Vol. VIII, p. 2310. See also Auphan, pp. 295-6.
[2] Abetz to Foreign Ministry, 16 November 1942, GFM/443/221693-4.

Alsatians and Lorrainers, the political detainees and all those who . . . have found refuge in our country'. Pétain would continue to take an interest in domestic policy, and no member of the government was to be appointed without his consent. Finally, Laval could not promulgate constitutional acts under his own signature.[1]

Although signed on 17 November, the new acts were not published in the *Journal Officiel* until the 19th. That evening, the Marshal gave a short broadcast speech. 'Generals in the service of a foreign power,' he began, 'have refused to obey my orders.' The armed forces in Africa were to refuse to obey them and continue to resist 'Anglo-Saxon aggression'. The situation was difficult and he had decided to increase Laval's powers to enable him to deal with it. 'Unity is more indispensable than ever,' he concluded. 'I remain your guide. You have only one duty: to obey. You have only one government: that which I direct. You have only one country which I embody: France.'[2]

He was followed on 20 November by Laval. The result of five hours of careful drafting, the speech was a sustained attack upon the United States and a defence of Franco-German collaboration, but which still managed to avoid any dangerous commitments. France could not survive without her empire, Laval explained. The Anglo-Saxons had taken it away piece by piece and they would never give it back. He described his conversation with Admiral Leahy in April 1942 at great length in order to show his peaceful intentions. 'By attacking North Africa, which is the natural extension of France,' he declared, 'it is Roosevelt who . . . has created the irreparable [breach] between us which we have done everything to avoid.'[3] By their actions in North Africa, the American authorities had shown what would happen if they won the war. 'We would have to submit to the domination of communists and Jews,' he claimed. 'We do not want universal bolshevism to come in the wake of its Anglo-Saxon accomplices and extinguish the light of French civilization for ever.' Montoire had shown the way

[1] For the discussions with Pétain, see Ménétrel notes, 16, 17 November 1942, in Noguères, pp. 507–17. See also Barthélemy's note, 16 November 1942, printed in Kammerer, *Débarquement*, pp. 677–8. The full text of Pétain's secret letter to Laval, which is dated 17 November 1942, is printed in Pétain, pp. 133–4.

[2] For the texts of the constitutional acts, see J.O., *Lois et Décrets*, 19 November 1942, p. 3834. For the text of Pétain's broadcast speech, see Noguères, p. 520.

[3] This sentence was the closest Laval would go to 'recognizing' the existence of a state of war, and he was reluctant to include even this. See de Brinon, p. 144.

for the preservation of France and her empire. The policy envisaged then could still be implemented and upon it depended the fate of 1,200,000 French prisoners-of-war. 'Once I spoke in the name of a strong France,' he concluded. 'Today she is wounded, but she has remained great. There can be no Europe without France and her empire.'[1]

The three ministers who had offered their resignations on 15 November confirmed them on the 17th when the new constitutional acts were signed. Except for Auphan, who he realized was his most implacable enemy in the cabinet, Laval was sorry to see them go. He spent an hour and a half trying to persuade Jacques Barnaud to change his mind and stay in the government. 'I know why you're going,' he told Barnaud in a revealing attempt to justify his policy, 'but I don't altogether understand it . . . I'm acting as though the Germans must win the war. Will the Germans win the war? I haven't a clue; I'm no fortune-teller. The longer it lasts, the less I believe it, but I think that a two-faced policy is worthless. There are two men who can render service to their country: General de Gaulle and myself. If the Germans win the war or manage to arrive at a compromise peace, let us practise a policy of loyalty with them and not one of haggling. Perhaps I can still be of service to my country and discuss an honourable peace treaty with the Germans. If the Germans are beaten, General de Gaulle will return. He will be supported, and I have no illusions about this, by 80 or 90 per cent of the French people and I shall be hanged. So what? There are two men who can save our country at the present time, and if I weren't Laval, I would like to be General de Gaulle.'[2]

He certainly continued to 'practise a policy of loyalty' towards the Germans. Co-belligerence was out of the question as a result of his secret pledge to Pétain, but in his speech of 20 November he gave his blessing to the imperial legion, or 'African Phalanx' as it was to be called. On 23 November, he told Field Marshal von Rundstedt that he hoped the Phalanx would soon be ready 'in order to take up the struggle in North Africa for the expulsion of the Anglo-Saxon intruders side by side with the forces of the Axis'.[3] The day before, he had reached an agreement with Kaufmann for the handing over of French merchant

[1] *Le Temps*, 23 November 1942. For the drafting of the speech, see de Brinon, loc. cit.
[2] Jacques Barnaud in C.E. *Témoignages*, Vol. VIII, pp. 2311–12.
[3] Schleier to Foreign Ministry, 23 November 1942, GFM/110/115153–5.

shipping in the Mediterranean to the Germans. 'In so doing,' he wrote in a letter to Hitler, 'the French government finds the opportunity to express through this first action its desire to take both sides in the gigantic struggle which you are waging.'[1]

The central theme of all his dealings with the Germans remained the urgent need for a new meeting with Hitler. On 17 November, when the constitutional acts were signed, he asked Krug for 'a new meeting with the Führer in order to arrive at practical solutions in Franco-German collaboration. . . . He counted on the Führer's understanding in this matter.'[2] On 22 November, in his personal letter to Hitler, he wrote, 'I hope that the time is near when I could determine with you, Herr Chancellor, the bases of the action which France intends to carry out alongside you for the reconquest of North Africa. I am determined to do everything within the capabilities of France to help you to destroy bolshevism and to prevent the influence of America upon Europe and its African extension. Moral and political conditions must be created in France with a view to this action. I am sure they will result from the conversation which I am requesting of you and which I hope is imminent.'[3] On 24 November, he told Sauckel, who had come to warn him of fresh demands for French labour in the new year, that 'France was worth more than a simple reservoir of labour. It was essential in the interests of both countries to hold political discussions in the near future, not least in respect of the reconquest of North Africa. . . . The moment had come when people had to say what they wanted, what aims they had, and how they wanted to attain them. He was prepared to answer all these questions.'[4] In a conversation with Achenbach of the German embassy on the same day, he reverted to the need for a guarantee of 'France's territory and colonial potential'.[5]

If Laval really thought anything worthwhile would come out of a meeting with Hitler, he was living in a fool's paradise. On 17 November, the German navy high command was informed that 'Hitler's deep suspicion of France was not to be shaken and dominated all measures

[1] Laval letter to Hitler, 22 November 1942, cited by *Procureur Général* Mornet in *Procès Laval*, p. 295.
[2] Abetz to Foreign Ministry, 17 November 1942, GFM/443/221712–14.
[3] Laval letter to Hitler, 22 November 1942, *Procès Laval*, p. 295.
[4] Schleier to Foreign Ministry, 24 November 1942, GFM/110/115163–5.
[5] Schleier to Foreign Ministry, 24 November 1942, ibid., 115173–4.

up for discussion. The first attempt at practical collaboration with France in common opposition to the Anglo-Saxon attacks in North Africa was wrecked. Matters ought now to be regarded, therefore, solely "in their harsh reality and from the point of view of our own interest".' The Führer was not even sure of the reliability of the French fleet and, following fears expressed by German military representatives in France that Toulon might become the bridgehead for an Allied invasion, he ordered plans to be drawn up for the seizure of the town and the fleet (Operation 'Lila').[1] His suspicions could only have been strengthened by the defection of General Barré in Tunisia on 19 November and the rallying of French West Africa to Darlan on the 23rd.[2]

As for the staunchest German advocate of collaboration, ambassador Abetz, he was in disgrace. Although the embassy faithfully transmitted Laval's requests for a meeting with Hitler to Berlin, Abetz was privately in despair. 'Those people are mad,' he told de Brinon on 15 November, referring to the Vichy government. '. . . They are ruining France. The first essential is to have a clear-cut attitude. Laval is asking for a new conversation with the Führer, who will certainly refuse. There's not the slightest point in it for him. . . . I'm not speaking to you as ambassador, but as an advocate of an agreement which will prevent war between France and Germany for generations and which will, in any case, prevent the dismemberment of the country. . . .'[3] His agitation was understandable. He had been acting entirely on his own initiative and had clearly hoped to present his superiors with the *fait accompli* of a co-belligerent France, not recommend the opening of negotiations on the subject. The telegrams announcing Laval's plans, reporting the constitutional changes, and relaying accounts of French governmental discussions remained unanswered until the evening of 19 November, when a curt message from Ribbentrop requested Abetz 'to abstain from any activity . . . in matters affecting future political development in France and to take no individual initiatives whatever'. Krug von Nidda in Vichy was to be told likewise.[4] Shortly afterwards,

---

[1] Germany Navy report on Franco-German relations, Kriegstagebuch 1942, pp. 975, 983, 988.

[2] For the opening of hostilities between Barré's forces and the Germans, see General Georges Barré, *Tunisie, 1942–43*, Paris, Editions Berger-Levrault, 1950, pp. 175–81. For developments in French West Africa, see Kammerer, *Débarquement*, pp. 591–602.

[3] De Brinon, p. 139.

[4] Ribbentrop to Abetz, 19 November 1942, GFM/443/221750.

Abetz was recalled to Germany.[1] There could be no other solution to the problem of an ambassador whose conduct was so at variance with the policy of his government.

Hitler gave the order to implement Operation 'Lila' on 25 November.[2] In another long letter to Marshal Pétain, he explained that '. . . after learning that the French generals and admirals have broken their word of honour by their now proved intention to open to the Anglo-Jewish warmongers metropolitan France as well as North Africa, I have given the order to occupy Toulon at once, and to prevent the ships from leaving port or to destroy them. . . . I have [also] given the order to demobilize all those units of the French armed forces which, contrary to the orders of their own government, are being instigated by their officers to resist Germany actively.' This did not mean that Germany did not want to collaborate with France. On the contrary, it would 'help towards a realization of this policy'. He concluded with the hope that 'a collaboration – in which we expect from France nothing but loyalty and the understanding of the common fate of Europe – will now begin'.[3] The letter was accompanied by two aides-mémoire, which detailed the Führer's charges against 'the French generals and admirals'.[4]

Krug von Nidda was instructed to deliver a copy of the letter to Pétain and the accompanying aides-mémoire to Laval at 4.30 a.m. precisely on 27 November, by which time the operation would be well under way. He was also to deliver a personal letter from Ribbentrop to the French prime minister, which was essentially a commentary upon the Führer's letter to Pétain but which also contained the long-awaited promise of an early meeting between the former and Laval. The Germans could not have chosen a better coating with which to sweeten their latest, extremely bitter pill.[5]

Aroused from his sleep at his home at Châteldon, Laval, according to a French eye-witness, 'immediately protested in vehement terms' at

[1] Abetz, pp. 258-9.
[2] Greiner notes, 25 November 1942, Kriegstagebuch 1942, pp. 1019-20. Some of the information which impelled him to act evidently came from the Italians. See his letter to Mussolini, 26 November 1942, GFM/F10/268-71.
[3] The Times, 28 November 1942. The German text is on GFM/110/115212-24.
[4] The texts of the two aides-mémoire are on ibid., 115225-32 and 115233-7. They were not made public at the time.
[5] Ribbentrop to Schleier, 26 November 1942, ibid., 115244-5. The text of Ribbentrop's letter to Laval is on ibid., 115239-43.

the German decisions.[1] Krug's account, however, is very different. 'Laval displayed marked self-possession,' he reported, 'and was hardly surprised at the announcement of the occupation of Toulon and the French fleet or of the eventual disarmament of specific units of the French armed forces.' He immediately agreed to take steps to issue orders that the German forces were not to be resisted and asked Rochat to call a meeting of the service ministers and a few others at Vichy.[2]

Hitler seems to have been resigned to the loss of the French fleet. 'As for the French navy,' he wrote in his letter to Mussolini, 'I fear that it will not come to us intact, but if this does happen, Italy is the only lawful possessor.'[3] His hopes must have been slim indeed to promise it to the Italians. At any rate, at 4.45 a.m., Admiral de Laborde was awakened on his flagship the *Strasbourg* to be told that the Germans had invaded the naval base and that the chief-of-staff to the base commander advised scuttling. Hardly able to credit the news, Admiral de Laborde tried to contact the shore. He finally obtained the base commander's chief-of-staff, who told him that 'someone' was in his office and promptly hung up. De Laborde ordered an immediate alert, but waited for more information before giving the final order to scuttle at 5.30.[4]

Meanwhile, the ministerial meeting was taking place at the Hôtel du Parc in Vichy. Admiral Le Luc, the naval chief-of-staff, was summoned to attend, and he subsequently testified that, when he arrived, he quickly gained the impression that 'the government had already taken the decision to negotiate with Germany over her ultimatum letter and to try and prevent the scuttling of the fleet or the commencement of firing while the negotiations were in progress'. Accordingly, Le Luc was asked to contact the naval base by telephone and rescind the standing order to scuttle in the event of hostile action. By the time he got through, however, the order had already been given and the first charges were already going off. Repeated breaks in the connection and requests for verification meant that, by the time the order was finally

---

[1] Charles Rochat in *La Vie de la France*, Vol. II, p. 1110. Laval's account (*Procès Pétain*, p. 209, col. 3 – 210, col. 1) is virtually identical.

[2] Schleier to Foreign Ministry, 27 November 1942, GFM/110/115249–50.

[3] Hitler's letter to Mussolini, 26 November 1942, ibid., F10/268–71.

[4] Undated de Laborde report in *La Vie de la France*, Vol. II, pp. 845–6.

received, understood, and transmitted, it was already too late.[1] Within a few hours, 250,000 tons of shipping was at the bottom of the harbour, including three battleships, seven cruisers, and one aircraft carrier.[2]

Of course, it can be argued that Laval did not seriously believe that he could stop the scuttling, that he knew it would be too late to do anything about it, and that he was merely putting on an act for the benefit of the Germans. This may have been the case, but it seems unlikely. Le Luc's reference to a government decision to negotiate rings true; Laval was always one for negotiation. But in order to negotiate, you must possess certain assets. On 8 November 1942, Laval's government had a large area of metropolitan territory free from Axis troops, an empire, an army and air force of sorts, and a fleet. By 27 November, it had none of these things. Henceforth it would have to rely solely upon the skill of its leaders and the determination of the French people.

---

[1] Henri Noguères, *Le Suicide de la Flotte Française à Toulon*, Paris, Robert Laffont, 1963, pp. 141–51. This book gives a thrilling step-by-step account of the German attack upon Toulon and the scuttling of the fleet. Laval told the Germans that he had tried to prevent the scuttling. See German Navy report on Franco-German relations, Kriegstagebuch 1942, p. 1031, and Laval's letter to Hitler, 28 November 1942, in Henri Noguères, op. cit., pp. 299–300.

[2] Ibid., p. 314.

II

Total Occupation

December 1942 – August 1944

Something of Laval's view on the new situation which confronted his government after the success of the Allied landings in North Africa, the occupation of southern France, and the loss of the French fleet may be gleaned from an account of a conversation which he had at the beginning of December 1942 with a friendly Yugoslav industrialist and which found its way into the files of the *Abwehr*. He admitted that, immediately after the Allied landings, he thought that Germany would be defeated, but he now gave her 'a chance, albeit a small one'. Her best strategy, he thought, would be to seize Gibraltar and compel Spain to enter the war on the side of the Axis, thus cutting off the Allied forces in North Africa and threatening them from the rear. If this happened, he thought that 'his old idea of a compromise peace between Germany and America could again become valid'. But, in any case, he felt that he had no other choice but to put his money on Germany, at any rate until the final outcome of the fighting in the western Mediterranean. He therefore intended to continue with his policy of collaboration and would propose to the German government that France be treated 'not simply as a German satellite, but as a partner to be taken seriously in negotiations', that the French administration be given full executive powers, confining the German authorities to the purely military sphere, and that a stronger militia should be formed, which was capable both of maintaining order at home and of assisting the Germans in the reconquest of North Africa. If these proposals were accepted, France 'would be politically and economically at Germany's side'. But even if the fighting in the western Mediterranean went against Germany, France would still be able to draw advantages from the concessions. '. . . The policy of collaboration would still be in its beginnings and could easily be slowed down. Moreover, as a result of the . . . Ger-

358

man concessions, the French authorities would be more masters in their own house than at present, and could therefore offer the victorious Anglo-Saxons something, if only a little, in exchange for an understanding.'[1]

The significance of this conversation, in which Laval not only admitted the possibility of a German defeat but sketched a policy which made sense in that eventuality can hardly be exaggerated in the light of his previous attitude. The change of mood is reflected in the steps which he took to maintain contacts with the members of the American embassy staff who, following the break in diplomatic relations, were interned at Lourdes pending repatriation. Ralph Heinzen, the former Vichy representative of the United Press and a close friend of Laval's, told an *Abwehr* agent that 'about 10 December 1942 a secret representative of President Laval appeared in the Hôtel des Ambassadeurs in Lourdes in order to resume in secret the officially broken-off relations [with the United States]. This middleman is a certain Monohan, a lawyer who lives in Vichy, an American who has become a naturalized Frenchman and a partner of Count de Chambrun.'[2] Another *Abwehr* report stated that '. . . Laval had already taken steps through . . . Chambrun to get in touch with the American government via the American *chargé* in Lourdes. In this connection, the name of Bedaux was also mentioned. He was described as a useful contact, who would be admirably suited to negotiate Laval's proposals to Roosevelt via the American representative in Africa, Murphy.'[3]

If these contacts were in any way designed to sound out the possibilities of a compromise peace as mentioned above, President Roosevelt's public announcement of the policy of 'unconditional surrender' at the Casablanca conference on 24 January 1943 must have been a bitter blow to Laval. René de Chambrun has written, 'Generally speaking, my father-in-law directly and also through me always tried to keep the door as wide open as possible with the United States. He was not in agreement . . . with Roosevelt's plan ending in the complete destruction of Germany and his building up of Sovietic [sic]

---

[1] Unsigned memorandum, 18 December 1942, GMR/T–77/896/5647058–61.

[2] Rudolph to *Militärbefehlshaber Frankreich, Kommandostab Ic*, 31 December 1942, ibid., T–501/189/001085–6.

[3] Pfeiffer, to *Militärbefehlshaber Frankreich, Kommandostab Ic* and others, 5 January 1943, GMR/T–501/189/001087–8. It is, of course, possible that both reports quoted were 'plants' designed to discredit Laval, but on balance I do not think so.

Russia and until the end he always hoped . . . that Roosevelt would not be blind enough to refuse a negotiated peace which would have had as consequence the end of the Nazi régime'.[1] Contemporary confirmation of M. de Chambrun's letter comes from yet another *Abwehr* report, written in February 1943 and based upon conversations with Laval supporters. Laval 'wants the victory of the German army over the Russians', the report stated, 'but not the victory of National Socialism and Chancellor Hitler. . . . He is in favour of Franco-German collaboration, but with a Germany which is neither Marxist nor fascist. He believes that, sooner or later, the Nazi régime will collapse and give way to a "Fourth *Reich*" which will be neither Marxist nor Hitlerite'. He was in favour of 'a real European co-operation' and desired a Europe which, though resting upon strong, authoritarian governments, would be 'social and liberal' rather than communist or fascist. Britain was finished, and this suited him, but he envisaged 'co-operation between America and Europe in which France is to be the connecting link'.[2] The similarity between this last idea and the sentiments which he expressed, in entirely different circumstances, to ambassador Edge in 1931[3] is quite remarkable and indicates the basic continuity which underlay Laval's foreign policy.

While awaiting the advent of the Fourth *Reich*, however, Laval had perforce to deal with the leaders of the Third. In his letter to Laval of 26 November 1942, Ribbentrop had promised the French prime minister another audience with Hitler. It took place at the Führer's military headquarters in east Prussia on 19 December. Laval brought a whole series of requests with him, which he outlined to Ribbentrop beforehand. They included the abolition of the now superfluous demarcation line between the northern and southern zones of France, more concessions regarding prisoners-of-war, and the reconstitution of a small army and navy. On the domestic political front, the tergiversations of the government during November had led to increased hostility on the part of the ultra-collaborationist groups – especially Doriot's – and Laval asked for permission to dissolve what he called the 'sprinkling of parties' and replace then by a new *parti unique* under his own leadership. In the economic sphere, he had already been presented

---

[1] Letter, dated 13 September 1965, from M. de Chambrun to the author.
[2] *Abwehr* report, 23 February 1943, GMR/T-501/189/001042-3.
[3] See above, pp. 23-24.

with, and accepted, a German demand to increase the daily occupation costs from 15 to 25 million *Reichsmarks* as a result of the total occupation of France, but he warned that the country was nearing the limit of her financial capacity as a result of inflation. As for labour recruitment, there were 320,000 French workers in Germany and a further 550,000 working for German interests in France. It was hoped to increase the latter figure, but the French government could not go on sending workers to Germany as well. 100,000 would be the ceiling for 1943.[1]

When Laval went over these economic points again in Hitler's presence, he got short shrift from the latter and the other German leaders present. Goering repeatedly interrupted his exposition and blamed the inflation upon the black market, which he claimed was patronized exclusively by Frenchmen. Ribbentrop, too, produced figures to show that France was not nearly as badly off as Laval maintained, and when the discussion turned to labour recruitment, Hitler butted in to point out that, at least, the French workers in Germany were being paid and that Germany had been 'most generous' in releasing prisoners-of-war compared with France, who had waited two years after 1918 before releasing any. In reply to Laval's repeated requests for trust and for freedom to act in the interests of Franco-German collaboration, he concluded that while 'Laval personally enjoyed his complete trust', it remained to be seen whether the French prime minister could implement his policy. As long as there was no proof that he could, 'Laval could not expect that France would be trusted. The amount of freedom which could be accorded the French government depended upon two conditions: 1. the trust which Laval personally enjoyed, and 2. the need to safeguard the occupation army and the positions for the continued waging of the war.'[2]

Decisions concerning concessions to the French were taken at a top-level meeting at the Führer's headquarters on 22 December and were relayed to Paris, with Italian approval, on the 30th. Laval was to be told that proposals for the reconstitution of the French army should be channelled through the German commander-in-chief in the west, Field-Marshal von Rundstedt. The Germans were particularly in-

[1] Schmidt memorandum, 23 December 1942, GFM/F7/0222–203. For the mood of the ultra-collaborationists, see Schleier to Foreign Ministry, 3 December 1942, ibid., 110/115345–5. On the question of occupation costs, see undated Wiehl memorandum, ibid., 115301–5 and Hemmen to Foreign Ministry, 16 December 1942, ibid., 118437–8.

[2] Schmidt memorandum, 24 December 1942, ibid., F7/0202–193; F20/266–55.

terested in the formation of anti-aircraft and railway protection units. In addition, the French government could make proposals for the establishment of a *Phalange Africaine* of between 15 and 20,000 men. As far as the French navy was concerned, Laval was to be reminded that this was a matter which concerned both Axis powers. There was to be no change in the demarcation line between northern and southern France, and the two *départements* of the Nord and the Pas-de-Calais were to remain under the jurisdiction of the German military commander in Belgium. A change in the status of French prisoners-of-war, transforming them into civilian workers, was unacceptable, but the O.K.W. would examine the possibility of allowing them to spend short periods at home. The Germans had nothing against Laval forming a new political movement under his own leadership, provided it did not turn into an anti-German front. On the other hand, they opposed the dissolution of existing groups such as Doriot's on the grounds that, in the last resort, this would have to be carried out by the occupation authorities themselves.[1]

It was this final point which Laval seized upon when the decisions were communicated to him on 31 December, which shows how important he felt the rivalry of the ultra-collaborationists to be. The decision 'signified a political defeat for him', he claimed. '. . . To some extent, it put him on the same level as M. Doriot, and the French government's authority would be thereby endangered.' He did not agree that German forces would be needed to dissolve these movements and 'he earnestly hoped that the German government had not said the last word in this matter, for he was not sure how he could maintain the government's authority in these circumstances'. He even went so far as to suggest that some of the so-called collaborationist groups were being backed by the enemy, 'for the Anglo-Saxons must obviously have the greatest interest in creating the greatest difficulties in every possible way for a government which, like his own, was ready to put all French resources freely at Germany's disposal.'[2]

[1] Abetz to Ritter, 23 December 1942, ibid., 117/118512–14; Grote memorandum, 23 December 1942, ibid., 118517–24; Ribbentrop to Mackensen, 26 December 1942, ibid., 118557–60; Mackensen to Foreign Ministry, 29 December 1942, ibid., 118585; Bruns memorandum, 30 December 1942, ibid., 118592.
[2] Laval subsequently found his own way of curbing the ultra-collaborationists. According to an *Abwehr* report, he drew up the compulsory labour service lists in such a way as to conscript supporters of Doriot and Déat for work in Germany (*Abwehr* report, 10 February 1943, GMR/T–501/189/001050).

But Laval was clearly disappointed at everything the Germans had to offer. '. . . He could not believe,' he said, 'that this was the total outcome of his conversation with the Führer, who had assured him that he, Laval, personally enjoyed German trust. . . . He was sorry that Germany had not taken greater advantage of his good will and that she had not supported him in matters which did not affect German war potential.' Enemy propaganda continually harped on the theme of liberating France and returning her colonies to her. He retorted that 'the Americans would not do this, but, at the same time, he could not say that the Axis powers had told him that France would keep these territories'. If he was not to become completely isolated and then forced out of the government, Germany would have to meet him half-way.[1]

He soon found out, however, that the Germans were not prepared to do so. Indeed, when it came to the reconstitution of the French armed forces, they would not even go as far as they had led him to believe. On 12 January 1943, he sent a letter to Field-Marshal von Rundstedt in which he proposed that the *Garde Mobile* should be increased from 6,000 to 25,000 men and should form the nucleus of a new army, and that a *Phalange Africaine* of 18,000 men should be recruited 'to form the initial French participation in the reconquest of North Africa'. He also proposed the formation of anti-aircraft units and the strengthening of the transport police.[2] While these last two requests were agreed, Keitel told Colonel Böhme of the armistice commission that Hitler wanted negotiations concerning the establishment of the *Phalange Africaine* handled 'in a dilatory fashion'. On Rundstedt's suggestion, however, he eventually agreed to the formation of a much smaller force of 2,700 men, which was subsequently given the somewhat grandiose title of 'the first regiment of France'.[3] As for the *Garde Mobile*, Hitler was prepared to permit its reinforcement, but only on condition that it was administered as part of the police and did not become the nucleus of a new army.[4] There was a reason for this. The police were involved in some highly unpopular activities, including the

[1] Schleier to Foreign Ministry, 31 December 1942, GFM/117/118622-9.
[2] Laval to von Rundstedt, 12 January 1943, GMR/T-77/842/5585313-20.
[3] *Oberbefehlshaber West Ic* memorandum, 2 March 1943, ibid., 5585245-57; von Rundstedt to O.K.W. *Wehrmachtführungsstab*, 6 March 1943, ibid., 5585238-41; von Rundstedt to French government 10 April 1943, ibid., 5585228-32.
[4] Von Rundstedt to French government, 16 March 1943, ibid., 829/5567407-8.

suppression of the Resistance, and, as Hitler told Ciano on 18 December 1942, they would eventually become so compromised that 'nothing would be more unpleasant for them than that the Germans should one day leave the country, for they would then be exposed to the vengeance of their fellow-countrymen'.[1]

While they were paring down Laval's requests for the reconstitution of the French armed forces, the Germans increased their demands for French labour. As early as 30 December 1942, Laval had been told to expect a further demand for 250,000 workers to be sent to Germany during the next few months and, in spite of his insistence only a few days before that France could provide no more than 100,000 for the whole of 1943, he acquiesced. He did try to obtain an improvement in the *relève* system, whereby two prisoners-of-war would be released and a third permitted to become a civilian worker in Germany for every three workers sent from France, but Sauckel told him on 13 January 1943 that this was not possible. The most the Germans would agree to was the continuation of the existing system of one release for every three workers, plus permission for another 250,000 to become civilian workers after an equal number of workers had been sent from France.[2]

In order to recruit this number, the French government was forced to modify its labour law of September 1942 to provide for the calling-up of young men by age-groups, as if for military service. The new labour law, instituting the so-called *Service du Travail Obligatoire* (S.T.O.), was promulgated on 16 February 1943.[3] As a result, Sauckel was subsequently able to declare that 'only France had fulfilled the labour recruitment programme 100 per cent'.[4] But this was achieved at the cost of an even greater decline in the Vichy government's popularity with the French people, especially as there was no sign of any end to the German demands. After congratulating the French government on its success in fulfilling his second programme, Sauckel told Laval on 5 March that, after a month's pause in April, he wanted to examine the possibility of sending 100,000 men a month to Germany. The

[1] Schmidt memorandum, 21 December 1942, GFM/F20/623.
[2] Schleier to Foreign Ministry, 31 December 1942, GFM/117/118612–14; Schleier to Foreign Ministry, 13 January 1943, ibid., 128/70183–6.
[3] J.O., *Lois et Décrets*, 17 February 1943, p. 461.
[4] Schleier to Foreign Ministry, 24 April 1943, GFM/170/83679–92. See also Sauckel to Hitler, 6 April 1943, ND 407 (viii) – PS.

French prime minister replied that 'the new demands must bear a proper relationship to French capabilities. . . . One mustn't promote a policy which, while combating communism in the east, created it in the west.'[1]

Laval told Sauckel that he proposed to make use of the month's pause in labour recruitment to try and settle outstanding political questions with the German government which would strengthen his position *vis-à-vis* public opinion. Four days later, he addressed a passionate appeal to Hitler. 'My task is made all the more difficult,' he wrote, 'by the uncertainty in which France is held concerning the fate in store for her. Enemy propaganda has cheap but effective arguments. Daily it proclaims that one of the Allies' war aims is to restore France's territorial integrity, her empire, and her sovereignty. I am fighting with unequal weapons. What will become of France? As head of the government, I cannot answer this question which is put to me with increasing urgency every day as France's contribution to the European cause grows in size. How can I get the French people to join in Germany's struggles with a happy heart if they do not know what fate is in store for their country once the bolshevist peril is finally overcome? How can I get the French people to become true friends of the German people . . . if they are able to fear that, one day, they will be treated as conquered people? I know what an echo a generous declaration concerning France which emanated from you would find in the world. Such a declaration would constitute a real act of war on the moral and political level which would produce chaos in your enemies' camp. In France it would permit me to act.'[2]

Returning to the charge in a series of conversations with the German minister in Paris at the end of March, Laval said that his opponents were arguing that Germany could no longer win the war because her effort in the east would not leave her with enough strength to cope with the Anglo-Saxons in the west. He did not believe this, but the fact remained that, given the military situation, 'Germany would not march into Washington, London, and Moscow simultaneously in the foreseeable future'. Indeed, she would never march into Washington and, that being the case, 'a *modus vivendi* must be found, at any rate between Germany and America'. The American people, whom he

[1] Schleier to Foreign Ministry, 6 March 1943, GFM/170/83210–16.
[2] Schleier to Foreign Ministry, 11 March 1943, ibid., 83240–49.

described as 'moody' and prone to isolationism, had to be made to feel that the war was 'pointless'. 'He . . . was convinced that morally they would not be able to hold out for long against a really satisfied Europe, that is to say in the first instance against a Franco-German under-standing – even less so when they had to take account of the fact that the European continent could only be attacked effectively at the cost of unprecedented sacrifices, if at all.'

He saw his proposed declaration on the future of Europe as a means of convincing the Americans and envisaged something along the following lines: 'Peace in Europe will be realized according to the principles of justice. On the moral, cultural, and political plane, the independence of the peoples will be respected; on the material plane, the nations must support one another and so combine their economic interests that the needs of each nation can be satisfied other than by competition and force, which has been the way for too long in the past. On the basis of these principles, the new Europe will form a real federation from which the seeds of revenge will be for ever banished. The organization of all the countries which form our continent must be such that neither the victorious nor the defeated peoples are ever again tempted to turn against one another and to wage war. For one year, the French government . . . has obtained the collaboration of an ever-increasing number in the defence of the European cause. In this way, France has aligned herself on the side of those who are fighting against bolshevism. The understanding between the Axis powers and France is necessary within the framework of the principles which must determine the new Europe and ensure its peace. In recognition of the role which France has played in the world and which she must also play in the future, both in her own interest and in that of Europe, the Axis powers declare their readiness to secure for her a future in the new Europe which corresponds to her continental and imperial past.'[1]

The German reply to Laval's appeal was a polite brush-off. The French prime minister was to be told that his remarks had been noted with interest and brought to Hitler's attention, but that, in view of the military situation, the time was not ripe for their detailed considera-tion.[2] The Führer was more truthful in private. 'He had no interest,' he

[1] Schleier to Foreign Ministry, 4 April 1943, GFM/170/83514–22.
[2] Ribbentrop to Schleier, 11 April 1943, ibid., 83598–9.

told his advisers, ' "in organizing these countries which are merely our potential enemies".'[1]

But a chance to take the matter further came much sooner than might have been expected from the tone of Hitler's remark. It arose from rumours that Marshal Pétain was once again plotting to dismiss Laval. On 24 April, Walter Schellenberg, the head of the *Sicherheitsdienst*, informed the foreign ministry that an emissary from Pétain had informed the S.S. in Paris that 'the Laval government did not meet the needs of the situation', either externally or internally. The Marshal, the report went on, 'does not want to bear the responsibility for this government any longer under any circumstances. *He lets it be understood that he will quit his post as head of state* if Germany does not help him to get rid of Laval.' According to Schellenberg, this move arose from a recent visit to Vichy by a representative of the Portuguese dictator, Dr Salazar, who had convinced Pétain that Germany could no longer win the war and that, if he got rid of Laval, he would be in a position to take the initiative in respect of negotiations between the Axis, the neutrals, and the United States.[2]

When Schleier, the German minister, saw Laval on 23 April to give him the reply to his letter to Hitler, he found the French prime minister similarly preoccupied with rumours of a plot against him. There was, however, no mention of peace feelers in the lengthy account of the evidence which Laval gave him. Instead, Laval hinted at a much more likely explanation of Pétain's motives: namely, that the Marshal felt that he gave in too readily to German demands. Whatever the reason, Laval did not intend to be dismissed a second time. There were two courses open to him, he said. He could either resign or he could tell Pétain that 'he would remain under all circumstances, i.e. . . . against the Marshal's will and by force if necessary'. But in order to do the latter, he needed German support, and he told Schleier that 'in the interests of the continuation of the policy of Franco-German collaboration which he represented, and which was the only correct policy for France, he would be grateful if the Germans would enable him to take steps against this threatened conflict'.[3] Whether in answer

[1] Von Etzdorf notes, 13 April 1943, ibid., 1247/337908.
[2] Schellenberg to Foreign Ministry, 24 April 1943, GFM/170/84671-3 (emphasis in original).
[3] Schleier to Foreign Ministry, 24 April 1943, ibid., 83679-92.

to this appeal or on his own initiative, Hitler sent a stern letter to Pétain in which he warned the Marshal that, if the rumours were true, 'the German government is not in a position, and does not intend, to permit the continuity of the political evolution between France and the Axis powers to be called into question again by a possible repetition of events such as those of 13 December 1940.'[1] At the same time, Laval was summoned to Germany at once to meet the Führer.

Ciano's successor at the Italian Foreign Ministry, Bastianini, was also invited to the meeting, and Ribbentrop gave him a preliminary briefing on the situation which showed, among other things, the total cynicism of the Nazi leaders with respect to France and the well-nigh impossible position into which Laval had got himself as a result of dealing with them. 'There was no better man in France than [Laval] for the purposes of the Axis,' Ribbentrop claimed. 'Laval was smart and it was always possible to work well with smart people. He was convinced that only Axis victory could preserve France from bolshevism. To what extent Laval had had knowledge of events in Africa – and he certainly knew something – must remain uncertain. The decisive factor was, however, that he was tied to the Axis for better or for worse and could no longer pull out. He was a man who, with the aid of a French police force which was already seriously compromised in favour of the Axis, would maintain order in the country until the final victory. Germany and Italy must see to it that there was no basic change in this relatively satisfactory situation in France and that France made the greatest imaginable contribution to the war economy in respect of labour and industrial output. There was no better man than Laval to take care of this. From a purely French point of view, there might be better patriots who could arouse more sympathy. But even from a personal point of view, the only people who were sympathetic to him [Ribbentrop] were those who were useful to Germany and Italy.'[2]

Unaware of these remarks, Laval sought to use his unexpected invitation to Germany to extract from the Nazi leaders the declaration on

[1] Sonnleithner to Schleier, 29 April 1943, ibid., 83733–6. Hitler's letter is dated 28 April. In his reply, Pétain stated that he had no intention of deviating from the policy of collaboration with the Axis. He did not say in so many words that Laval would remain, but Dr Ménétrel assured Struwe, the German diplomatic representative in Vichy, that the prime minister still enjoyed the Marshal's full confidence (Quiring to Foreign Ministry, 29 April 1943, ibid., 83738–41).
[2] Schmidt memorandum, 30 April 1943, GFM/68/49189–206.

France's future which he had been trying to obtain during the previous few weeks. He got nowhere in his meeting with Ribbentrop,[1] and, when what was to prove his last meeting with Hitler began, the latter seemed hardly more accommodating. 'It could not be permitted,' the Führer told Laval, 'that France . . . should now calmly await the outcome of the struggle and even before its end request Germany and Italy to make a declaration which would give her complete security for the future in case of the victory of the Axis powers, but in the case of their defeat would allow France a free hand. Such an unreasonable request was unbearable.' In the past, he went on, there had been no question of compensation for co-operation; the victor had simply taken what he wanted. Germany had acted otherwise, but this 'was possible only so long as the French government comprehended the fateful character of the present struggle and gave assistance to the best of its ability. They must not always be presenting a demand for counter-payment and, if they received that, presenting a new one.' Hitler claimed that 'France had up to this time been handled with kid gloves' and that, while Germany and Italy had no intention of creating unnecessary difficulties for Laval, 'the situation . . . was not one in which the French government could take the position that, if certain requests which they had expressed were not fulfilled, the contributions need not be made. For these demands would be exacted by Germany under any circumstances.' It was Germany and Italy who were steering the European ship, he concluded, 'but the other European passengers could not get off without stepping into the void and perishing.' That being the case, he 'declared categorically (and he asked M. Laval to bring this to the attention of the Marshal) that under no circumstances could a repetition of 13 December 1940 be tolerated. That would involve serious consequences and would be regarded by Germany as an act directed against collaboration.'

In reply, Laval put his view that 'the war must end not only with the satisfaction of petty nationalistic desires, but something new and great in the shape of a United States of Europe must come from the present drama'. His purpose in requesting a declaration on France's future 'had not been one of pure diplomatic expediency but simply a desire to be able to make clearer to the French people that any effort which they made for the benefit of the common cause would be answered by an

[1] Schmidt memorandum, 2 May 1943, ibid., 49207–31.

alleviation of the demands made upon their country.' In France, as in Germany and Italy, 'there existed . . . a national sentiment which could not be left out of account. . . . The war could not be conducted by military means alone . . . but it must be waged also in the moral and political fields.' Hence his desire for a declaration. 'Of course,' he concluded, 'the French could also be compelled by force to make contributions. It would, however, be much better to obtain their voluntary collaboration. . . . The sentiment for collaboration was not compatible with measures of compulsion, which would produce results for Germany which were not to be compared with those which could be obtained voluntarily.'

The conversation continued along the same lines, with Bastianini taking up the cudgels where Hitler had left off. Finally, in reply to a remark from Ribbentrop that a written declaration would have no effect upon the French attitude anyway, Laval replied 'with a smile' – it must have been a grim one – 'that the purpose of his trip to Berchtesgaden had not been to receive a lesson in how to deal with the French people'. To which Hitler replied with a biting sarcasm that comes through the formal written record 'that Frenchmen had not always been able to discover the right way in which to address their fellow-countrymen. Perhaps it would have been better to have first talked to Daladier or Reynaud at Berchtesgaden before they plunged their people into disaster.'[1] Nevertheless, the Führer did say that he was prepared to agree to the publication of a communiqué, provided that it was agreed by Ribbentrop and Bastianini. This completely anodyne document, which stated that the share which France had to contribute to 'the efforts and sacrifices' of the Axis and the advantages which would accrue to her from such participation had been examined 'in complete objectivity', was the only positive outcome of the meeting.[2]

Although Laval spoke eloquently and at length about his vision of a new Europe in a broadcast speech on 5 June,[3] there seems little doubt that his meeting with Hitler put an end to any hopes he may still have entertained about the possibility of a real accommodation with Nazi

[1] Schmidt memorandum, 3 May 1943, GFM/68/49232–54. I have used the translation which appears in the United States *Department of State Bulletin*, 4 August 1946, pp. 197–201, 236.

[2] The text of the communiqué is printed in Max Domarus, *Hitler, Reden und Proklamationen 1932–45*, Vol. II, Munich, Süddetscher Verlag, 1965, p. 2008.

[3] The text is printed in the *Petit Parisien*, 7 June 1943.

Germany. Over the next six months, moreover, various events took place which must have strengthened his doubts as to the wisdom of anything beyond the necessary minimum of collaboration designed to avoid direct German rule over his country.

On the international front, the most important event as far as France was concerned was the elimination of fascist Italy from the war. On 12 May all organized resistance to the Anglo-American forces in Tunisia ceased. On 10 July Sicily was invaded and on the 25th Mussolini was forced to resign. On 3 September the Allies landed on the Italian mainland and an armistice was signed which came into force on the 8th. Just over a month later, on 13 October, the Italian government declared war on Germany. Although there was to be another 18 months of bitter fighting before the German forces in Italy finally surrendered, the fate of the western Mediterranean, to which Laval had referred in the conversation quoted at the beginning of this chapter, was as good as settled – in favour of the Allies.

This and other external events inevitably had their repercussions inside France. As it became increasingly clear that Germany was not going to win the war, so both active and passive opposition to the Germans increased. Active opposition – the 'Resistance' proper – became a serious threat in 1943 with the increase in numbers and the unification of the various networks.[1] According to German statistics, there were 534 killings and 3,802 acts of sabotage attributable to the Resistance between January and September 1943. In January 1,097 suspects were arrested; by September the number had risen to 3,759. Passive opposition, particularly among the police and administration, was no less serious. There were a thousand different ways in which officials could put their individual spokes in the German wheel and more and more availed themselves of the opportunity to do so. They had an added incentive in that nearly half of the killings attributed to the Resistance – 253 to be precise – were of Frenchmen. There was not much point in going out of one's way to help the Germans if they were going to lose the war in any case. There was even less if, by so doing, one became a target for Resistance reprisals.[2]

---

[1] For the growth and co-ordination of the resistance, see Henri Michel, *Histoire de la Résistance*, Paris, Presses Universitaires de France ('Que Sais-Je?' series No. 429), 1962, Chapters V, VII, VIII, X and XI.

[2] The figures are taken from Abetz, pp. 280–81.

Just how bad the situation had become by the middle of 1943 is evident from a top-secret report on the French police by Helmuth Knochen, the number two S.S. man in France. 'The experience of our offices clearly . . . shows,' he wrote, 'that the will to fight against the national Resistance movement is, in the main, lacking among the French police.' The Germans, Knochen continued, could probably still count upon their support for operations in which French and German interests coincided – against communists, for example – but 'an effective action against national Resistance movements and intelligence organizations working for the enemy is not to be expected as long as the military situation has not taken a decisive turn in our favour.' In the event of an Allied invasion, the best that could be hoped for was a neutral attitude on the part of the police. At worst, as he emphasized in a covering letter, they might attack the Germans in the rear.[1]

Laval was well aware of the turn events were taking. In April Sauckel had demanded a third recruitment programme of 220,000 workers to be sent to Germany in May and June. Laval accepted, but, by the beginning of July, only 130,000 had in fact been sent. The reason was, as he admitted to Schleier, that 'he could not rely upon the co-operation of the police and the lower ranks of the administration as much as he wished'.[2] From a purely personal point of view, the deteriorating situation was brought home to him on 17 September 1943 when a plot to blow up his car on the road from Châteldon to Vichy was discovered.[3] In the circumstances, he displayed a much tougher attitude in resisting the more outrageous German demands which were put to him during the summer of 1943.

One such demand was Sauckel's for yet another 500,000 workers by the end of the year, together with the transfer of one million more from civilian industry to war work inside France. For the first time, too, Sauckel insisted that women should be among those sent to Germany.[4]

[1] Knochen report, 19 August 1943, GMR/T–501/21/000169–88; Knochen to recipients of the report, 19 August 1943, ibid., 000167–8.
[2] Schleier to Foreign Ministry, 10 April, 14, 23 July 1943, GFM/170/83556–69, 242/158328–9, 158402–7.
[3] Reichel to *Oberbefehlshaber West*, *Abteilung Ic*, 19 September 1943, GMR/T–501/121/000043.
[4] Sauckel to Hitler, 27 June 1943, ND 556 (39)–PS. Hitler approved the programme a month later. See Stothfang memorandum 28 July 1943, ibid., 556(41)–PS.

On 6 August these inordinate demands were discussed during the course of a six-hour meeting with Laval, which the latter subsequently described as 'the toughest and most painful in which I have ever taken part'. While agreeing to the transfer of the million workers inside France and promising to try and complete the still unfulfilled third programme of 220,000 workers for Germany in May and June, Laval refused point-blank to agree to any further figure for the despatch of workers. 'After calm and cool reflection,' Sauckel wrote to Schleier at the conclusion of this meeting, 'I must tell you that I have lost all faith in the honesty and goodwill of the French prime minister Laval. His refusal constitutes an outright sabotage of Germany's life-and-death struggle against bolshevism.'[1] Nevertheless, Sauckel seems to have modified his demands as a result of the French government's opposition and to have agreed that the fulfilment of the third programme should have priority. Finally, on 16 October, he told Laval that 'the Führer had abandoned all claim to the recruitment of fresh workers until the end of the year . . . because Italian workers were available up to this date.' This may have been one reason, but an equally powerful one was Oberg's admission to Sauckel the previous day that 'there were totally insufficient [German] police and military available to carry out any large-scale actions against labour draft-dodgers'.[2]

It has been argued that the failure of Sauckel's demands was due less to any action on the part of Laval and the French government than to the flocking of eligible young men to join the Resistance.[3] This was undoubtedly a factor, but we have also noted the extent to which it was due to the lack of co-operation on the part of the French police and administration. To what extent Laval and his colleagues gave their tacit encouragement to this lack of co-operation is a moot point, although one official subsequently testified that Laval 'seemed to find the non-execution of his orders perfectly normal'.[4] What is certain is

---

[1] *Laval Parle*, pp. 125–6; Sauckel to Hitler, 9 August 1943, ibid., pp. 265–70. I have been unable to find a full German text of this document, although a page of it is reproduced in ibid., opposite page 265.

[2] Schleier to Foreign Ministry, 26 August, 17 October 1943, GFM/242/158607–8, 158930–33. The relevant files of the legal department of the German Foreign Ministry, which apparently contained more details of these negotiations, are missing.

[3] André Scherer in P. Arnoult et al., *La France sous l'Occupation*, Paris, Presses Universitaires de France, 1959, pp. 35–6.

[4] Marius Sarraz-Bournet in *La Vie de la France*, Vol. III, p. 1240. See also Paul Brun in ibid., Vol. I, pp. 462–3.

that the French government sought to play off one German authority against another in order to protect its labour force. Thus, in September 1943, before the decision to suspend the departure of workers to Germany became known, the French minister for industrial production, Jean Bichelonne, reached an agreement with Albert Speer, the German armaments minister, that French factories engaged in production for the latter would be protected from Sauckel's demands for labour. 'The last Sauckel programme of 500,000 will be correspondingly reduced,' ran the German record of the conversation.[1] The establishment of these *Sperrbetriebe* (or 'protected enterprises') subsequently became a sizeable bone of contention between Speer and Sauckel.[2]

Sauckel's efforts to obtain more workers were paralleled by those of the S.S. to secure the deportation of more Jews to the extermination camps in the east. There had been a lull in deportations between 11 November 1942 and 9 February 1943 for lack of transport[3] and the S.S. clearly wanted to make up for lost time. One report at the beginning of March estimated that there were still 270,000 Jews in France (70,000 in the northern zone and 200,000 in the south) and proposed their rounding-up and deportation at the rate of 8 to 10,000 a week from April. But the majority of these Jews were French and the problem remained how to overcome the French government's opposition to the deportation of Jews of French nationality. It was suggested that a start could be made by persuading the French authorities to denaturalize Jews of foreign origin who had acquired French nationality comparatively recently. These unfortunates would then become stateless and so liable to deportation.[4] The French government, it appears, originally agreed to this suggestion and proposed to make 1 January 1932 the date after which naturalization would be revoked. But it was soon pointed out that this would only affect 20,000 Jews and that a much better date would be 1 January 1927, because the French naturalization law of August 1927 had reduced the residence qualification period from ten to three years and, as a result of this liberalization,

[1] Schnurre memorandum, 22 September 1943, GFM/242/158740–43; *Laval Parle*, pp. 126–7.
[2] See below, pp. 390–91.
[3] Lucien Steinberg, *Les Autorités Allemandes en France Occupée: Inventaire commentée de la Collection de Documents conservés au Centre de Documentation Juive Contemporaine, Paris*, C.D.J.C., 1966, p. 171.
[4] Röthke report, 6 March 1943, ND 1230–RF.

no less than 50,000 Jews had been naturalized between 1927 and 1932. The Germans, therefore, insisted upon 1927 as the cut-off date.[1]

Although at least two drafts were prepared, Laval obviously changed his mind and decided to try and block the proposal. Pretending that he had hitherto been ignorant of the purpose of the law, he told Knochen on 7 August that 'the deportation of the de-naturalized Jews, as seemed to be intended by our [i.e. German] preparations in Paris, jeopardized the promulgation of the law. He could not lay himself open to the charge that he was promulgating the law in order to drive Jews into our hands. The measures we had in mind were so serious that he would have to discuss the matter with the Marshal once again.'[2] A week later, in the course of an hour-long conversation with two more S.S. officials, Laval reproduced this and a good many other reasons why it was impossible for the French government to promulgate the law at that particular time. '. . . It must be stated,' ran the German report of the conversation, 'that the French government no longer wishes to co-operate over the Jewish question.' The author reckoned that Pétain's alleged opposition to the law was 'by no means unwelcome' to Laval, who found it 'very convenient to shelter behind Pétain'. His insistence that the draft law had to be re-submitted to the cabinet was part of the same obstructionist tactic. 'The impression remains that Laval is using all means to find any opportunity of preventing the publications of the law, or at any rate of delaying it.' The report concluded with a plea for an additional company of German police to be sent to France, 'for whether the de-naturalization law is promulgated or not, large-scale help from the French police in the arrest of Jews can no longer be relied upon unless Germany's military situation radically improves in the next few days or weeks'.[3]

After the cabinet had met, and after further conversations between the French and German authorities, Marshal Pétain informed de

---

[1] Knochen to Oberg, 21 May 1943, document from the collection of the Centre de Documentation Juive Contemporaine in Paris, No. XXVI–74. Documents from this collection, which were kindly made available to me in photocopy by M. Mazor, the chief archivist at the Centre, will hereafter be cited as C.D.J.C., followed by the document number.

[2] Hagen memorandum, 11 August 1943, C.D.J.C. XXVII–35.

[3] Röthke memorandum, 14 August 1943, ibid., XXVII–36. One of the excuses which Laval gave for his own inaction was the non-co-operation of the Italian authorities in their zone of occupation. For further details of Italian protection of Jews in their zone, see Raul Hilberg, *The Destruction of the European Jews*, London, W. H. Allen, 1961, pp. 413–16.

376 · PIERRE LAVAL

Brinon on 24 August that he could not agree to the law. In the first
place, he wrote, it did not enable him to 'discriminate between individuals, some of whom had been able to render services to France'. In
the second place, the enforcement of such a law would vastly compli-
cate the task of the French police at the very time when the Germans
were insisting upon the maintenance of order in France. He went on
to point out, however, that he was prepared to revoke 'naturalizations
which were carried out in a hasty fashion' and that he had already set
up a commission for this purpose. He would instruct the minister of
justice to speed up the commission's work.[1] This was less of a concession than it seemed, for, as de Brinon explained to the Germans,
the commission was staffed with opponents of the government and the
de-naturalization policy.[2] What was more, it seemed that less than 500
Jews were likely to be affected by the commission's activities, compared with the 'many hundreds' which the minister of justice had
promised.[3] The de-naturalization policy was, in short, a complete
failure, and shortly before the Germans were driven out of France,
Röthke was forced to admit that 'nothing has come out of the [de-
naturalization] law because the French government wanted nothing to
come out of it'.[4]

There is evidence that Laval did his best to sabotage other anti-
Jewish measures. In May or June 1943 Darquier de Pellepoix, the
Vichy commissioner for Jewish affairs and one of the most virulent of
the French anti-Semites, complained bitterly to an *Abwehr* agent that
Laval had delayed signing a number of anti-Jewish decrees for no less
than nine months. These included prohibition of travel by Jews without the special permission of the secretariat for Jewish affairs, the ban-
ning of Jews from participation in business, and the compulsory wearing
of the yellow star.[5] In October the military authorities wrote to the
S.S. informing them that one of their agencies had picked up a report
that Laval had issued secret instructions that anti-Jewish legislation
was no longer to be applied. They asked for confirmation. Röthke
replied that the S.S. knew nothing about any secret instructions, but

[1] Noguères, pp. 288–9.
[2] Hagen memorandum, 26 August 1943, C.D.J.C., XXVII–41.
[3] Unsigned, undated memorandum (in French), ibid., XXVII–50.
[4] Röthke note, 4 July 1944, ibid.
[5] *Abwehr* report, 12 June 1943, GMR/T–501/189/001009. See also Paul Morand in *La
Vie de la France*, Vol. III, p. 1433.

confirmed that 'it is certainly the case that the attitude of the French government and the French authorities towards the Jewish question has hardened in recent months'.[1] The Germans finally lost patience with French procrastination and, on 14 April 1944, Knochen issued lengthy instructions for the arrest and deportation of all Jews in France, whether they were of French nationality or not.[2] To judge from the published figures of deportations, these instructions had no great effect upon the numbers of Jews deported,[3] partly, perhaps, because the S.S. found it increasingly difficult to secure army co-operation in the face of the anticipated Allied invasion.[4] As a result of Laval's and the Vichy government's policy, therefore, French Jews received a considerable degree of protection. But this was deliberately achieved at the expense of the foreign Jews living in France, many of whom had fled from Nazi persecution before the outbreak of war.

Laval was undoubtedly handicapped in his efforts to stand up to the Germans by the plots and intrigues which surrounded him during the summer and autumn of 1943. Hitler's letter to Pétain on 28 April had nipped one plot in the bud, but it provided only a temporary respite. The air continued to buzz with rumours of government changes as the ultra-collaborationists on the one hand and Marshal Pétain and some of his advisers on the other sought to undermine the prime minister's position in order to gain their respective ends. Indeed, it seemed that the more impotent the Vichy government became, the more eager were opposing factions to control it.

One of the key figures in the ultra-collaborationist intrigues was none other than Fernand de Brinon, Laval's own choice as French ambassador to the German authorities in Paris. In May 1943, de Brinon sent a lengthy report on the situation in France to Goebbels through the intermediary of a Baron von dem Bongart, an official in the propaganda ministry. Goebbels, in turn, forwarded it to Hitler. The report was critical of the Vichy government, and of Laval, but made no specific suggestions for government changes.[5] By August, however, he was

---

[1] *Militärbefehlshaber Frankreich, Abteilung Ic* to Knochen, 4 October 1943; Röthke to *Militärbefehlshaber Frankreich, Abteilung Ic*, 18 October 1943, C.D.J.C. XLVI-*chemise G.*

[2] Knochen order, 14 April 1944, ibid., CDXXXIV-10.

[3] Lucien Steinberg, *Les Autorités Allemandes en France Occupée: Inventaire commentée de la Collection de Documents conservés au Centre de Documentation Juive Contemporaine,* Paris C.D.J.C., 1966, p. 171.

[4] Röthke memorandum, 17 May 1944, C.D.J.C. XLVI-*chemise M.*

[5] Goebbels to Hitler, 7 June 1943, and Enclosures, GFM/1107/319513–28.

involved in some sort of conspiracy designed to exploit the rift between Laval and Sauckel and possibly replace the former as prime minister.[1] This manœuvre came to nothing, in spite of the rumoured support of the S.S., but de Brinon remained undaunted. In September he accompanied Baron von dem Bongart to Vichy, where the latter, who was allegedly on a fact-finding mission for the S.S., gave vent to anti-Lavalist sentiments and openly expressed surprise that the French government could find no room for 'so gifted a politician as Admiral Platon', whom Laval had dismissed from his post as secretary of state in March on account of his intrigues.[2]

It was also probably more than a coincidence that, while Bongart was in France, he was handed a lengthy manifesto drawn up by five ultra-collaborationist leaders in which they diagnosed the ills from which France was suffering and offered their remedies. Resistance 'terrorism', the manifesto maintained, was resulting in the increasing impotence of the government. This tendency was aggravated by the disintegration of the collaborationists, which was due to three main factors: the attacks upon them by the Resistance, the disagreements of their leaders, and the pusillanimous attitude of the Vichy government towards a thorough-going transformation of the country along national socialist lines. After excluding a number of possible solutions, the manifesto concluded that the only effective remedy would be to surround Laval – who was still deemed indispensable – by a government consisting of as many of the collaborationist leaders as possible, which, after a thorough purge of the police and administration, and the establishment of a unified militia and a single party, would carry out the national socialist revolution and negotiate a completely new agreement with Germany, in which the latter would guarantee French territory (apart from Alsace-Lorraine), place no obstacle in the way of France's political and social transformation, and work out a new basis for collaboration in the political, economic, and military fields.[3]

Laval cleverly countered the manifesto by insisting that, while he had no objection in principle to taking the ultra-collaborationist leaders

---

[1] Félix Olivier-Martin in *La Vie de la France*, Vol. II, p. 1049; Schleier to Foreign Ministry, 13 August 1943, GFM/242/158552–7.

[2] Schleier to Foreign Ministry, 2 October 1943, ibid., 158221–4. For Platon's dismissal, see Schleier to Foreign Ministry, 25 March 1943, ibid., 170/83,517–18.

[3] The full text of the manifesto is printed in Gabriel Jeantet, *Pétain contre Hitler*, Paris, La Table Ronde, 1966 (hereafter cited as Jeantet), pp. 280–98.

into his government, their entry must be preceded – and not followed – by the proposed clarification of Franco-German relations. Otherwise, he warned, it 'would destroy the last vestiges of the government's authority over the police and administration, for, as the manifesto rightly pointed out, a large part of the French administration was orientated against collaboration and its representatives in France'. As if to emphasize his willingness, he repeatedly asked for another meeting with Hitler to discuss the consolidation of Franco-German relations, although he must have known that the Führer's attitude was unlikely to be any more sympathetic than it had been in April.[1] There is no knowing how long Laval might have been able to fence off the intrigues of the ultra-collaborationists. After all, they were divided amongst themselves, as they freely admitted in their manifesto.[2] But the question is an academic one, for the opposing intrigues of Pétain and his advisers produced a crisis which impelled the Germans to insist upon a transformation of the government along much the same lines as the authors of the manifesto had argued.

Pétain, as we have already seen, tried to get rid of Laval in April, but was prevented from doing so by Hitler's veto. The fall of Mussolini, with all that it implied for the eventual outcome of the war, seems to have determined him to try again. The day after the Italian dictator's overthrow, the Marshal told Krug von Nidda that 'Laval had neglected domestic politics,' adding cryptically that 'today more than ever, future eventualities must be guarded against.' He was careful to stress Laval's excellence as foreign minister, but the very emphasis which he placed upon this led Krug to wonder whether he was considering replacing him as prime minister.[3] Two days later, he was reassured by Lucien Romier, the minister of state and one of Pétain's closest confidants, that the Marshal wanted to retain Laval as both head of government and foreign minister, but wondered whether he ought to remain minister of the interior as well.[4]

In secret, the Marshal went much further than this. On 31 August he despatched a secret emissary to Algiers to make contact with both

[1] Schleier to Foreign Ministry, 4 October 1943, GFM/242/158828–32.
[2] One of the most important ultra-collaborationist leaders, Jacques Doriot, had not even signed the manifesto.
[3] Schleier to Foreign Ministry, 26 July 1943, GFM/242/158419–22.
[4] Schleier to Foreign Ministry, 28 July 1943, ibid., 158468–9.

Giraud and de Gaulle.[1] At the same time, he asked Admiral Auphan (who, it will be recalled, had left the government at the time of the North African landings) to prepare a plan of action to fit the new political situation. Auphan presented his plan to Pétain on 13 September. It called, among other things, for the replacement of Laval, the suspension of the S.T.O., the dissolution of the collaborationist parties, the relaxation of anti-Jewish measures, and contacts with the Giraudist Resistance. Auphan also provided a draft scheme for streamlining the government and the text of a proposed letter to Hitler announcing Laval's dismissal and the government's intention of implementing a new policy. He realized that the Germans would probably oppose the whole plan, even to the extent of arresting everyone involved and appointing a *Gauleiter* for France, but he did not think this mattered provided Pétain stuck it out and nominated a 'regency council' which would exercise his powers if he was prevented from doing so.[2]

Little time was lost in implementing this last proposal. On 27 September, a revised draft (the fifth) of Constitutional Act No. 4 was prepared, setting up a seven-man regency council in the event of Pétain's being unable to exercise his functions. The council would hand over its powers to the National Assembly if the Marshal's incapacity proved permanent. Not surprisingly, Admiral Auphan was one of the members. So were the former finance minister, Yves Bouthillier, and Professor Gidel, the rector of Paris university, who were already working at the Marshal's request on the draft of a new constitution. Two strange choices, however, were General Weygand, who was in detention in Germany and knew nothing of what was going on, and Léon Noël, the former French ambassador to Poland, who had repeatedly rejected appeals for help from Pétain throughout the summer, advising him to resign and leave the political arena to General de Gaulle. Like

---

[1] Jeantet, pp. 1–5. Jeantet writes that the emissary was instructed to tell Giraud and de Gaulle that they were now the beneficiaries of the oath of allegiance taken by French officers to Pétain and that, when Paris was liberated, the latter would hand over his powers to them and retire to the country. Jeantet's book is very obviously designed to whitewash Pétain and, in the absence of corroborative evidence, it would be unwise to accept his account of the content of the mission uncritically. However, there is no reason to doubt the mission's existence. At Pétain's trial in 1945, General Lacaille testified that, in October 1943, the Marshal made another attempt to get in touch with Giraud through the intermediary of a Trappist priest, Father Bursby (*Procès Pétain*, p. 226).

[2] Jeantet, pp. 269–79.

Weygand, Noël first learned of his nomination to the regency council after the liberation.[1]

Just over a fortnight later, on 12 October, Pétain saw General Neubronn, Field-Marshal von Rundstedt's representative in Vichy, and told him that Laval must go, 'or else the outbreak of anarchy in France would be inevitable'. He proposed to take over as head of the government himself.[2] On the same day, General Brécard, acting on Pétain's behalf, saw Colonel Knochen of the S.S. in Paris and asked him whether Hitler's veto on the replacement of Laval still stood.[3]

It was not until 26 October, however, that Pétain plucked up enough courage to confront Laval in person. According to the latter's contemporary account to Krug von Nidda, the Marshal declared that 'France found herself in a state of anarchy and was heading towards revolution. This was the government's fault. He, Laval, was unpopular. He had disappointed French expectations concerning German cooperation and he [Pétain] asked him to resign.' When the prime minister demanded a more detailed explanation, Pétain alluded to the ultra-collaborationist manifesto, without making it clear exactly what he meant. Laval retorted, somewhat contradictorily, that while the Marshal could certainly hand over the government to Déat and de Brinon, or to members of his own entourage, he (Laval) had his share of the responsibility and he would not tolerate any such combinations. Moreover, he added, unaware of Pétain's contacts with Neubronn and the S.S., the Germans would have to be informed of any proposed changes in the government. Laval, who had long been planning a government reshuffle of his own which would bring in a number of ex-members of parliament,[4] told Krug that he thought the best way of tackling the crisis was to proceed with his plans and, in addition, to purge the Marshal's entourage. 'If Pétain sticks to his guns,' Krug reported, 'Laval wants, if need be, to make an official approach to the Führer by personal letter through me. Laval is convinced that the Führer continues to have confidence in him.'[5]

The next phase of the crisis opened on 12 November, when Pétain

[1] Ibid., pp. 11–13; Noël in C.E. *Témoignages*, Vol. IV, pp. 1152–3; Bouthillier in ibid., Vol. VIII, pp. 2548–51.
[2] Neubronn memorandum, 12 October 1943, GMR/T–501/120/ 000378–9.
[3] Schleier to Foreign Ministry, 19 October 1943, GFM/242/158941–42.
[4] Schleier to Foreign Ministry, 26, 28 July 1943, GFM/242/158419–22, 158468–9.
[5] Schleier to Foreign Ministry, 27 October 1943, ibid., 158967–8.

informed Laval that he was about to issue a new constitutional act and explain it to the nation in a broadcast speech the following day. The new act was yet another revision of constitutional act No. 4, which stated that the Marshal's constituent powers would revert to the National Assembly in the event of his dying before the ratification of the new constitution. His speech announced that the draft of this constitution had been completed,[1] but that he was concerned at what would happen if he died before completing his task. 'Today I embody French legitimacy,' he planned to say. 'I intend to preserve it as a sacred trust and to return it, upon my death, to the National Assembly whence I received it, if the new constitution is not ratified. . . . I do not want my death to inaugurate an era of disorders which would imperil the unity of France. This is the purpose of the constitutional act which will be promulgated in the *Journal Officiel*.'[2] There was no conflict of purpose between this latest revision of constitutional act No. 4 and the earlier draft setting up a regency council. When Bouthillier had been shown the text of the latter, he had pointed out that it could not possibly be published because the Germans would immediately arrest all those who had been nominated to the council. What was needed was a document which would have the same effect, but which could be made public.[3]

Laval's initial reaction to both the act and the speech were favourable. He knew, of course, that the purpose of the act was to prevent him from becoming Pétain's successor, but he was confident of his ability to swing the National Assembly behind him as he had done in July 1940. 'As a member of parliament and a republican,' he subsequently boasted to Krug von Nidda, 'he would feel in his element in front of the National Assembly.' He merely asked for a delay in which to prepare public opinion and obtain German clearance. Pétain, however, refused to agree to any delay. The Germans would be informed out of courtesy, he explained, but it was 'pointless to request their authorization'. When it came to the point, they were told that the act was a reply to the establishment of a provisional consultative assembly by the Gaullists in Algiers.[4]

[1] For the text of the draft constitution, see Fernet, pp. 287–300.
[2] The texts of the act and the speech are printed in Jeantet, pp. 21–2 and Noguères, pp. 567–8.
[3] Bouthillier in C.E. *Témoignages*, Vol. VIII, p. 2551.
[4] Ménétrel notes in Jeantet, p. 300; Schleier to Foreign Ministry, 13, 14 November 1943, GFM/246/163173–8, 163191–7.

Although Laval's optimism was sufficiently contagious for both Krug and Schleier to recommend that permission be given to broadcast the speech, the authorities in Berlin took a different view. At 6 p.m. on 13 November, six hours after the Marshal had recorded the speech and one-and-a-half hours before it was due to go out over the air, de Brinon telephoned Vichy from Paris with the news that the Germans forbade the broadcast and would even use force to prevent it.[1] Upon receipt of the German message, Pétain summoned Krug von Nidda and told him that unless and until the broadcast was permitted, he was unable to fulfil his duties. In other words, he was going on strike.[2] This deadlock probably prompted Laval to change his mind about Pétain's proposals and, over the next few days, he made repeated attempts to persuade the Marshal to withdraw them and accept a compromise.[3] But all his efforts were in vain; the Marshal stood firm.

Krug von Nidda had told Pétain that the ban on his broadcast was only temporary and that the German government would let him have its considered views within 48 hours.[4] In fact, it was three weeks before Berlin made its definitive attitude known. One reason for the delay was to give the Germans time to reinforce their security forces in and around Vichy to guard against any untoward reaction. How seriously they regarded the situation was shown by the fact that they put the famous S.S. commander Otto Skorzeny, who had been responsible for Mussolini's dramatic rescue from an Italian prison, in charge of operations.[5] To deliver the message, which was couched in the form of a long letter from Ribbentrop to Pétain, they chose none other than Otto Abetz. Indeed, the crisis was to mark his return to the German embassy in Paris.[6]

Ribbentrop's letter began with a justification of the German refusal

[1] Schleier to Foreign Ministry, 13 November 1943, GFM/246/163173–8; Ménétrel notes in Jeantet, p. 301; de Brinon, p. 182.
[2] Schleier to Foreign Ministry, 14 November 1943, GFM/246/163179–82; Noguères, p. 572.
[3] For further details, see Schleier to Foreign Ministry, 14, 15, 17 (twice), 19 November 1943, GFM/246/163198–201, 163218–20, 163228–9, 163240–41; Ménétrel notes in Jeantet, pp. 302–3, 310.
[4] Schleier to Foreign Ministry, 14 November 1943, GFM/246/163179–82. In the light of the available evidence, it is impossible to say whether Krug was acting on his own initiative or not in this case.
[5] Abetz to Foreign Ministry, 28 November, 1 December 1943, ibid., 163280, 163281; Otto Skorzeny, *Geheim-Kommando Skorzeny*, Hamburg, Hansa Verlag Joseph Toth, 1950, pp. 170–71.
[6] Abetz, p. 269.

to agree to a revision of the constitution along the lines proposed by Pétain, together with a more general indictment of the policy of the Vichy government. But its heart contained what amounted to three ultimata: 'From now on, all proposed alterations to laws must be submitted for approval to the German government in good time. In addition, M. Laval must be entrusted without delay with the task of remodelling the French cabinet in a way acceptable to the German government and which will guarantee collaboration. . . . Finally, the leadership of the French state is responsible for the immediate removal from the administration of all elements hindering the serious task of reconstruction, and for their replacement by trustworthy people.' The German foreign minister did not believe that Pétain would fail to recognize the needs of the situation, but he warned him that the Führer had authorized him to say that, if he rejected the German demands, 'he leaves it entirely to your judgment to draw the conclusions which seem to you appropriate.'[1]

Abetz delivered Ribbentrop's letter on 4 December. The following day Pétain gave him a written declaration in which he stated that he would resume his duties forthwith and 'would provide explanations and define his position' in a subsequent letter.[2] This did not satisfy Ribbentrop, however. Pétain had not accepted the German demands, he cabled Abetz on 6 December, and he saw in the proposed letter a 'tendency to delay things or to shuffle off our demands which we must not tolerate under any circumstances'. Abetz was to inform the Marshal that 'the German government expects . . . his complete and unconditional acceptance . . . of its three . . . demands without delay'. This acceptance must be communicated in writing.[3]

In spite of Abetz's optimistic commentary, Pétain's promised letter, which was addressed to Hitler, only confirmed Ribbentrop's suspicions. It accepted the need to remodel the government, but requested that the new members be 'good Frenchmen [who] have not displayed

[1] Ribbentrop to Pétain, 29 November 1943, printed in Walter Stucki, *Von Pétain zur Vierten Republik*, Berne, Verlag Herbert Land & Cie, 1947 (hereafter cited as Stucki), pp. 160–64. Stucki was the Swiss minister in Vichy and his book is an extremely well-documented account of the régime's final months which is particularly valuable in that the German foreign office material is noticeably thin from about November 1943 onwards.

[2] Hemmen to Foreign Ministry, 4 December 1943, GFM/246/163286–8; Abetz to Foreign Ministry, 5 December 1943, ibid., 163293–4. The text of the declaration is printed in Noguères, p. 588.

[3] Ribbentrop to Abetz, 6 December 1943, GFM/246/163312–16.

hostility towards me in the past'. This would have excluded most of the ultra-collaborationists for a start. Moreover, there was no mention whatever of a purge of the administration or of a willingness to submit proposed amendments to laws to the German authorities.[1] 'I see in the letter,' Ribbentrop cabled Abetz, '. . . a considerable degree of evasion on the Marshal's part and a wilful avoidance of an unequivocal attitude towards our demands.' More assurances were required, he said, and on 15 December Abetz was instructed to raise the unsettled issues with Laval and to give him lists of those persons the Germans wanted removed from the government and administration. These included Lucien Romier, Jean Jardel, the Marshal's secretary of state, and General Campet, the head of his military secretariat. Dr Ménétrel was to be given one last chance, on condition that he confined himself strictly to his medical duties in future.[2]

By the time Abetz saw Laval on 19 December, the latter had already obtained a written pledge from Pétain that he would submit all legislative amendments to the Germans for their approval.[3] But it was not until the 29th, when he was again in Vichy, that Abetz was able to extract a written undertaking from the Marshal that he would not try to blackball any new appointments to the government or stand in the way of any dismissals the Germans deemed necessary. The occasion was the accrediting of Cecil von Renthe-Fink, who had been appointed Hitler's 'special diplomatic representative' – or, more crudely, watchdog – to Pétain.[4] When the two Germans arrived in Vichy, they found the Marshal still trying to create difficulties over the government changes, and they would not agree to hold the accrediting ceremony until he abandoned his opposition.[5]

The evidence shows, however, that it was Laval as much as Pétain who was seeking to prevent the entry of the ultra-collaborationists into

[1] Abetz to Foreign Ministry, 11 December 1943, ibid., 163345–9. The text of Pétain's letter, also dated 11 December 1943, is printed in Noguères, pp. 594–6, and Stucki, pp. 165–6.
[2] Ribbentrop to Abetz, 13, 15 (twice) December 1943, GFM/246/163360, 163381–3, 163385–90.
[3] Abetz to Foreign Ministry, 19 December 1943, ibid., 163408–12. The text of Pétain's declaration is printed in Noguères, p. 597.
[4] Ribbentrop to Abetz, 7 December 1943, GFM/246/163307/9. Pétain subsequently described Renthe-Fink as 'my nanny' (Stucki, p. 23).
[5] Abetz to Foreign Ministry, 29 (twice), 30 December 1943, GFM/246/163472–3, 163477–8, 163482–9; Renthe-Fink to Foreign Ministry, 31 December 1943, ibid., 163490–92. The text of Pétain's undertaking is printed in Noguères, pp. 597–8.

the government. Discussions had taken place between the various German agencies in Paris and the ultra-collaborationist leaders as far back as 7, 8, and 9 December, and a list of names was informally communicated to Laval a few days later.[1] According to one report, he returned to Vichy 'in a state of near collapse' as a result of the German demands. Typically, however, he did not reject them outright. Instead, the report continued, 'he simply hopes and will try to manœuvre so that the collaborationists will refuse to take part and he will be "kept on as a lesser evil" as a result.'[2]

These tactics worked quite well in respect of Marcel Déat, the leader of the *Rassemblement National Populaire*. At first, Laval offered him a post in Germany, looking after the interests of prisoners-of-war and workers. When Déat rejected this somewhat transparent attempt to get rid of him, Laval came up with the ministry of labour, which was one of the most unpopular jobs in the government on account of the compulsory labour service. When he realized that he was not going to be offered anything else, Déat sought to expand the scope of the portfolio to include other social questions. Laval resisted this pressure and it was not until March 1944 that Déat finally entered the government as minister of labour and national solidarity, as a result of German insistence.[3] Déat did not help his own cause by insisting upon certain conditions for his participation in the government, including the right to continue running and writing for his newspaper, *L'Œuvre*, to carry on as leader of the R.N.P., and to refuse to come to Vichy for cabinet meetings.[4] It was a similar rigidity which kept members of Doriot's rival party, the *Parti Populaire Français*, out of the government. Doriot himself was on the eastern front, fighting in the L.V.F., and the German foreign ministry blocked his request for leave during the crisis in case his arrival in France made matters worse. It was suggested, however, that some members of his party should join the

[1] Abetz to Foreign Ministry, 9, 12 December 1943, GFM/246/163324–8, 163354–5.
[2] Unsigned *Abwehr* report, 24 December 1943, GMR/T-501/189/000960–70. The source is stated to be Captain Brunnet of the ministry of information.
[3] Ibid.; Georges Albertini (secretary of the R.N.P.) in *La Vie de la France*, Vol. III, p. 1293; Jean Tracou, *Le Maréchal aux Liens*, Paris, André Bonne, 1948 (hereafter cited as Tracou), pp. 187–92 (Tracou was head of Pétain's civilian secretariat during the first half of 1944); Laval in *Procès Pétain*, p. 214, col. 2; J.O., *Lois et Décrets*, 17 March 1944, p. 818, col. 3.
[4] Georges Albertini, loc. cit.; unsigned *Abwehr* report, 14 January 1944, GMR/T-501/189/000955–6.

new government, to which the P.P.F. leaders in France indignantly retorted that they could decide nothing without Doriot.[1]

Laval had no such luck in preventing the appointment of Joseph Darnand, whom the S.S. insisted must replace René Bousquet as head of the French police. Darnand was head of the *Milice*, a paramilitary organization which had been founded under the government's auspices in January 1943. The date of its foundation suggests that it may well have been intended as a counterweight to the collaborationist parties which Laval had been refused permission to dissolve. If so, it was to prove a broken reed, for Darnand soon fell out with Laval and joined the very 'opposition' he had been intended to offset.[2] Even though Laval argued that Darnand's nomination would not only lead to the resignation of other extremely efficient police officers but might even endanger his own life,[3] he was forced to comply with the German demand, and Darnand was named secretary-general for the maintenance of order on 30 December 1943.[4] The most Laval could do was to flank the new man with two trusted subordinates – André Parmentier as director-general of the police and Jean-Marcel Lemoine as secretary of state for the interior – in the hope that they might be able to exercise some moderating influence upon him.[5] But even this was something of a forlorn hope. As a result of subsequent discussions with Oberg, a further decree was issued, giving Darnand the most extensive powers.[6]

It is arguable that, even at this late stage, Laval's subsequent reputation would have benefited if he had resigned rather than share power with men like Déat and Darnand. A journalist friend certainly advised

---

[1] Hencke memorandum, 7 January 1944, GFM/246/163565–6; Saint-Paulien (pseudonym for Maurice-Yvan Sicard), *Histoire de la Collaboration*, Paris, L'Esprit Nouveau, 1964, p. 410 (Sicard was a high-ranking member of the P.P.F. leadership).

[2] For the *Milice*, see the special report of the control section of the German armistice commission, dated 1 December 1943, GMR/T–77/829/5567063–76. For tension between Darnand and Laval, see unsigned *Abwehr* reports, 19 March, 14 April 1943, ibid., T–501/189/001018, 001014; *Abwehrnebenstelle* Bordeaux to *Abwehrleitstelle*, Paris, 9 December 1943, ibid., 000973–5.

[3] He was uneasy about the right-wing extremists among Darnand's followers. As we have seen (above, p. 281), he believed that such people had tried to kill him in 1941.

[4] J.O., *Lois et Décrets*, 31 December 1943, p. 3339, col. 2; Abetz to Foreign Ministry, 19, 21, 23 December 1943, GFM/246/163408–12, 163417–19, 163421–3.

[5] André Parmentier in *La Vie de la France*, Vol. I, pp. 565–6; Amédée Bussière in ibid., p. 578; Felix Olivier-Martin in ibid., Vol. II, p. 1051.

[6] J.O., *Lois et Décrets*, 21 January 1944, p. 238, col. 2; Abetz to Foreign Ministry, 24 January 1944, GFM/246/163675–6.

him to do so. He maintained that the prime minister 'could no longer justify the policy he was pursuing in the interests of France when, alongside him, he had men who had sold out body and soul to German national socialism'. But Laval did not agree. 'As far as I'm concerned,' he replied, 'if Déat and Darnand are forced on me, that's a more powerful reason for staying. Just tell me, what would they do if I wasn't there? They would give in all along the line to the Germans. So, I must stay to stop them from giving in all along the line. It will be even tougher, but it's a case of necessity.'[1] He certainly cared nothing for popularity. 'I don't give a damn for it,' he told an audience of mayors in February 1944, 'because if I was popular today in the job I hold, I would not be worthy of fulfilling my duty.'[2] It was the same old story: he was indispensable and he could save France in spite of herself.

But France was gradually sliding towards civil war. Resistance activity was increasing as the inevitable Allied invasion of France approached. Towards the end of February 1944, Abetz reported that the number of killings by the Resistance in the first half of the month exceeded the total for the whole of December 1943 and that four-fifths of the victims were French. In the more remote parts of France, where it was at its strongest, engagements with the Resistance began to take on the character of pitched battles. In the Ain *département*, for example, a large-scale operation in February required the use of artillery and resulted in the killing of 75 Resisters, the capture of 456, and the destruction of 64 arms dumps. The French government was inextricably involved in the repression of its fellow-countrymen. Abetz noted that 'the energetic assistance of the French *Milice* under the personal leadership of . . . Darnand and the introduction of French summary courts have contributed to further successes in the struggle against [Resistance] bands.' The establishment of summary courts was indeed a sinister departure. 'This law . . . is without precedent in our history,' Laval admitted to the cabinet. 'Even Fouché did not go so far.'[3]

---

[1] René Chateau in *La Vie de la France*, Vol. III, p. 1268.
[2] Speech to mayors of Montpellier district, 5 February 1944 (unpublished text kindly communicated to me by M. René de Chambrun).
[3] Abetz to Foreign Ministry, 25 February 1944, GFM/246/163867-70; *Militärbefehlshaber Frankreich/Kommandostab/Abteilung Ia*, action report for January–February 1944, GMR/T-501/144/000265; J.O., *Lois et Décrets*, 21 January 1944, p. 238, cols. 1–2; Tracou, p. 103.

The first half of 1944 also saw the final struggle over labour recruitment. After the 'pause' of October 1943, Sauckel and the Nazi leadership worked out a new programme at the beginning of 1944 which entailed the despatch of no less than a million French workers to Germany at the rate of 91,000 a month, beginning in February.[1] When Sauckel brought this programme to Paris, however, he found that the German agencies there were unanimously opposed to any attempt to implement it by compulsion, at least for the moment. '. . . Before an Anglo-Saxon invasion attempt has been repulsed,' he was warned on 14 January, 'only a tiny percentage of such a transfer would be achieved, even with the goodwill of the French government, and the vast majority of French workers who had been forcibly conscripted for labour service in Germany would not only be lost to the pool of labour working for German interests inside France, but would join the terrorist and dissident bands.'[2]

But this did not deter Sauckel from putting the programme before Laval the following day. He also presented the French prime minister with draft laws which extended the scope of the compulsory labour service and introduced the death penalty for officials who tried to sabotage recruitment. Laval bought time on the question of the million workers by agreeing to the draft legislation. On 1 February, two important laws were promulgated. The first extended the scope of the compulsory labour law of September 1942 to make all men between the ages of 16 and 60 and single or childless women between the ages of 18 and 45 eligible for conscription. The previous limits had been 18 to 50 for men and 21 to 35 for unmarried women only. The major concession which the French did obtain was the continuation of the ban on women being sent to Germany. The second law instituted various penalties, including death in the last resort, for officials who attempted to sabotage any government legislation.[3] A few days later, the French government came forward with another proposal which was clearly designed to head off the demand for a million workers. This was for a 'priority programme' which would run until the middle

---

[1] Lammers memorandum, 4 January 1944, Sauckel to Lammers, 5 January 1944, ND 1292–PS.

[2] Abetz to Foreign Ministry, 15 January 1944, GFM/246/163599–602.

[3] Sauckel to Hitler, 25 January 1944, ND 556(55)–PS; François Chasseigne in *La Vie de la France*, Vol. I, pp. 186–7; 'Colleagues of Bichelonne' in ibid., pp. 51–2; J.O., *Lois et Décrets*, 2 February 1944, pp. 358–9.

of March and would involve sending the equivalent of the 45,000 workers who had failed to return to Germany after their leave had expired, plus an unknown number of foreigners who were working in France, but whose total was said to be 'considerably more than 45,000'. But the Germans were not going to fall for that. Instead, they put forward their own idea of a 'priority programme': 273,000 workers by the end of April. This was accepted by Laval on 9 February.[1]

At the same time, the Germans did not seem to be attaching quite the same importance to the overall target of one million for the whole of 1944. Indeed, Sauckel had told the French negotiators that 'the figure . . . was a programme which they should strive to fulfil, but for which he did not at present expect a guarantee from the French government'. He went even further with Laval, telling him that 'after the prompt completion of the three-month "priority programme", further workers from France could perhaps be dispensed with, depending on the military situation.'[2] This was, however, an empty concession, for Sauckel had finally realized that he was not even going to get his 273,000 workers as things stood, let alone a million. After describing some of the subterfuges to which his agents in France, Italy, and Belgium had to resort to recruit labour, he told a meeting of the central planning committee on 1 March that 'all these methods, however grotesque they may sound, have to be used to overcome the fact that there is not executive power in these countries to bring the workers to Germany'.[3]

In the same speech, he referred to the 'protected enterprises' (*Sperrbetriebe*), which had been set up as a result of the Speer–Bichelonne agreement of the previous autumn,[4] as a special problem as far as France was concerned. 'In France,' he declared, 'the protected enterprise is nothing but a protection from the clutches of Sauckel.' Later in the month, he wrote to Hitler suggesting that there were as many as $5\frac{1}{2}$ million protected workers in France: $1\frac{1}{2}$ million in the *S–Betriebe* and another $4\frac{1}{2}$ million in other occupations exempted from the labour service, including $2\frac{3}{4}$ million in agriculture. 'In this situation,' he maintained, 'it is essential for me to have a free hand once more to carry out . . . a rational overall labour policy . . .' He also complained about

---

[1] Abetz to Foreign Ministry, 4, 9 February 1944, GFM/246/163747–51, 163793–4.
[2] Ibid.
[3] Sauckel speech, 1 March 1944, ND 124–R.
[4] See above, p. 374.

'the completely insufficient executive resources' at his disposal. Speer immediately leaped to the defence of his 'protected enterprises' and, at top-level meetings with Hitler on 6 and 7 April, it was agreed that they should remain, although some attempt should be made to comb out superfluous labour in them in order to appease Sauckel.[1]

The latter, therefore, had no alternative but to go back to the French. At the beginning of May, he repeated his demand for a million workers. Marcel Déat, who was by then the minister of labour, said that the only way to achieve this total was to create a new national labour service and call up everyone without exception. This was agreed by Laval in conversations with Sauckel on 10 and 11 May, but by the time the first decree had been signed which would have called up the entire 1944 age-group, the Allied landings in Normandy had taken place and it was decided that 'the publication and implementation of this decree will be postponed until a time when the military situation permits the employment of the agreed measures'. Such a time, of course, never came and from January to July 1944 only 42,000 of Sauckel's proposed million workers left for Germany – less than the number who had failed to return after their leave had expired.[2]

One thing which undoubtedly sustained Laval throughout those increasingly gloomy months of 1944 was what Abetz described as 'his hope that he would one day perform a great historical role as a peacemaker'.[3] Right up until the Allied invasion, he thought that the German army would not be defeated.[4] He really did believe, as he told an audience of mayors in February 1944, that 'only one army in the world is at present capable . . . of erecting a dam against bolshevism – the German army.'[5] In the circumstances he could not believe, as he told Tracou, that 'the Anglo-Saxons would play the bolshevist game to the end'. As for the Germans, he claimed that he repeatedly told them, 'There's nothing you can do in the west. Whatever you did, even if you built a large fleet, Britain and the United States would build a bigger one. Colonies are closed to you, the French ones the same as

[1] Sauckel to Hitler, 17 March 1944, Speer to Hitler, 5 April 1944, ND 3819–PS; unsigned memorandum, 9 April 1944, ibid., 124–R.
[2] Abetz to Foreign Ministry, 9, 12 May, 8 June 1944, GFM/255/166101–2, 166120–21, 166237–8; 'Collaborators of Bichelonne' in La Vie de la France, Vol. I, p. 54.
[3] Abetz to Foreign Ministry, 14 February 1944, GFM/246/163806–10.
[4] Stucki, pp. 24–5; Tracou, p. 302.
[5] Speech to mayors of Montpellier district, 5 February 1944 (unpublished text kindly communicated to me by M. René de Chambrun).

the rest. Your natural sphere of expansion is in the east. All right then, make peace in the west and agree to the sacrifices necessary to make it.'[1]

He clearly saw himself as the man capable of initiating the negotiations, telling Abetz in February that he was ready to act as a mediator whenever the Germans considered it appropriate. The ambassador curtly replied that the question of peace talks would only arise after a German victory and that 'then, a good many other ways apart from a French mediation would be available'.[2] Undaunted, the French prime minister returned to the charge on 3 May, asking Abetz point-blank whether France's moral potential could not be put to use on Germany's behalf and whether the contacts which he had with the enemy powers could not be used, if need be, as a preliminary to talks and for purposes of information'. This time Abetz was more polite but equally categorical. He replied that, in his opinion, 'the German government was not interested in talks taking place with the enemy powers' and he asked Laval to adhere to his earlier advice and steer clear of the entire subject.[3]

What were Laval's 'contacts with the enemy powers'? In his memoirs, Abetz refers to an attempt by Laval to enlist his support for a peace move involving the king of Sweden through the intermediary of Nordling, the Swedish consul-general in France. But the contemporary documents give an entirely different picture of this episode. From them it appears that the initiative came from the German side. Nordling was approached by two men – one German and one Italian – who claimed to be acting on behalf of the German foreign ministry. In fact, they seem to have been working for the S.S. Laval was only informed of their approach subsequently and refused to have anything to do with them when he had been told that they did not represent the foreign ministry.[4] Abetz also mentions an alleged mission by one Joseph de Claussais to Stockholm in April 1944 to sound out the Russians on the possibility of a compromise peace.[5] But there is no mention whatever of

[1] Tracou, pp. 118, 124.

[2] Abetz to Foreign Ministry, 14 February 1944, GFM/246/163806–10.

[3] Abetz to Foreign Ministry, 3 May 1944, ibid., 255/166065.

[4] Abetz, p. 273;–Abetz to Foreign Ministry, 30 January, 4 February, 22 March 1944, GFM/246/163706–7, 163742–4, 255/165895–6. Tracou also mentions this episode (p. 134) but misdates it.

[5] Abetz, p. 273.

this in the documents and, in view of Laval's strong anti-communist line, it would seem most unlikely that he would have favoured a compromise peace on the eastern front.

Nevertheless, it may well be that the Americans were in touch with Laval, not for purposes of peacemaking but to prevent General de Gaulle from coming to power in France after the liberation. At the turn of the year, an American journalist had approached François Piétri, the Vichy ambassador in Spain, with a message which the latter passed on to Laval. Its upshot was that President Roosevelt was fearful of what might happen in France if General de Gaulle took over after the liberation, and wanted to discuss the situation with a representative of the Vichy government outside the usual diplomatic channels.[1] Laval told Abetz of the approach and admitted that it was the first attempt by the United States government to get in touch with him. He added that 'obviously he was not getting involved'.[2] Piétri, however, continued to write to him with suggestions as to how he could meet the American wishes. He proposed the summoning of parliament and the formation of a government of 'personalities who, until now, have remained in the background'. He also asked Laval to consider whether he ought not to resign in such circumstances. In March, Laval told him to drop the subject.[3]

Early in June, however, Piétri received two more visitors. They were Jacques Lemaigre-Dubreuil and Jean Rigault, both prominent supporters of General Giraud who had lost their influence when the Gaullists took over the Algiers committee of national liberation. At the end of May, they had crossed into Spain from French North Africa via Tangier, apparently with the assistance of the American authorities.[4] The message they brought was as follows: 'Washington greatly fears a dictatorship by General de Gaulle, whom the British are backing up to the hilt. It must be stopped by the force of legality. This legality is parliament, which, when all is said and done, has only been suspended and not suppressed by the Marshal, and more particularly the senate, which is [parliament's] continuous and stable element. It is imperative that the Marshal hands over his powers to [parliament] in

[1] François Piétri. *Mes Années d'Espagne 1940–48*, Paris, Plon, 1954, p. 244.
[2] Abetz to Foreign Ministry, 17 January 1944, GFM/246/163612–13.
[3] Piétri, op. cit., pp. 244–5.
[4] Mohr to Foreign Ministry, 24 May 1944, GFM/255/166170.

such a way that, when the time comes, the Algiers committee will be confronted by a *fait accompli* and a ready-formed provisional government.'[1]

Laval did not receive this message until after D-Day and, when he did, he immediately informed the Germans.[2] At the beginning of July, they sent Roland Nosek of the S.S. to Madrid to meet the two men. His report tallied closely with what Piétri had already told Laval. Lemaigre-Dubreuil apparently feared that the Americans might be moving towards the recognition of General de Gaulle's provisional government in view of the latter's forthcoming visit to the United States. He believed that 'a declaration by influential politicians who had the respect of both camps was the only means of holding up his recognition'. In particular he thought that if Jeanneney and Herriot, the highly-respected presidents of the senate and chamber of deputies, could be prevailed upon to say that they would form 'a legal and democratically-based coalition government which included the Vichy group' after the liberation, the United States would withhold recognition from de Gaulle. Nosek commented that 'it is not clear how far this plan . . . is based upon American instructions, but from what Lemaigre-Dubreuil said, it is probable that he turned up as a front man for influential American political personalities'. Abetz, to whom Nosek reported, was all for doing what Lemaigre-Dubreuil suggested. After all, he argued, it was not in Germany's interest either for the Americans to recognize de Gaulle. A French emissary had just gone to Madrid and Abetz proposed that he should be authorized to accept Lemaigre-Dubreuil's proposals.[3]

The French emissary was one Michel Harispe, a former *Cagoulard*, and Lemaigre-Dubreuil was even more forthcoming with him than he had been with Nosek. Now he was not only proposing the formulation of a new French government, but also 'the complete neutralization of the whole of metropolitan France'. He claimed that the Allies would withdraw their troops from France if the Germans did likewise. This was particularly true of the Americans, 'for, in this event, American public opinion would no longer be interested in the European war and America would concentrate the entire war effort against Japan.' He

---

[1] Piétri, op. cit., p. 249.
[2] Abetz to Foreign Ministry, 14 June 1944, GFM/255/166272-3.
[3] Abetz to Foreign Ministry, 7 July 1944, ibid., 4120/E071207-8.

also expressed considerable interest in what was going on on the eastern front and asked Harispe to find out all he could about contacts between the Russians and the Germans. He said that 'the Americans were worried because the Germans did not display any concern about the development of the military situation on the eastern front. He knew that the United States would conclude peace with Germany if Germany concluded an armistice or peace treaty with the Soviet Union. In this event, the United States would only wage war against Japan.' Finally, he reverted to the question of the French government. Neither Pétain nor Laval could be members of it, he said. But 'if Pétain was needed as a symbolic figurehead for the future government, he had no objections on condition that he, Lemaigre-Dubreuil, retained control. . . .'[1]

How genuine was the Lemaigre-Dubreuil mission? To what extent was it a personal initiative and to what extent was it inspired by the United States government? There was certainly no love lost between the Americans and General de Gaulle in 1944. The American secretary of state, Cordell Hull, wrote in his memoirs that 'Mr Roosevelt had carried into 1944 the deep-seated suspicions he and I entertained regarding de Gaulle . . .' and he mentioned a cabinet meeting which took place 'about 20 May' in which 'the President said that ambassador Winant [in London] had raised with him the question of dealing with de Gaulle. He added that he had told Winant that if anyone could give him a certificate proving that de Gaulle was a representative of the French people he would deal with him, but that otherwise he had no idea of changing his mind.'[2] There is no doubt that he would have been very happy if someone other than de Gaulle had proved capable of rallying the French people, and either he, or one of his subordinates, may not have been above trying to create him.

Moreover, the timing of Lemaigre-Dubreuil's arrival in Spain is highly significant. He arrived just in time for D-Day. He also showed himself remarkably well informed about Allied war plans, blandly telling Harispe that an Allied invasion of southern France was imminent. It took place on 15 August. What really throws doubt upon the genuineness of the mission is all the talk about the neutralization of France, Russo-German peace feelers, and American readiness to concentrate upon the war against Japan, none of which accords with what

[1] Bargen to Foreign Ministry, 11 July 1944 (twice), ibid., E071205–6, E071209.
[2] Cordell Hull, *Memoirs*, Vol. 2, London, Hodder & Stoughton, 1948, pp. 1427, 1431

we know of Roosevelt's strategy and pursuit of Germany's 'unconditional surrender'. However, it is perhaps significant that this material appears only in Harispe's report. The latter was a representative of the French government, and some of the statements which he attributed to Lemaigre-Dubreuil bore a remarkable resemblance to the illusions which Laval consistently entertained regarding the United States. It may be that Laval saw an opportunity to use the Lemaigre-Dubreuil mission to give the Germans the impression that they were also official American views. If the Germans had seen fit to explore the matter further, we might have got nearer the truth, but on 14 July Ribbentrop ordered all contacts with Lemaigre-Dubreuil to be broken off.[1]

The advent of D-Day provided Laval with many other worries apart from his relations with the Allies. It was the signal for an immediate stepping-up of what now amounted to the guerrilla war between the Resistance on the one hand and the occupation authorities and their more zealous French collaborators on the other. Large-scale operations were mounted in the *Massif Central* and the German regional command noted in its war diary that 'the French attach importance to their participation in the struggle against the Resistance'.[2] The fanaticism of the *Milice* was matched only by that of the *Waffen*-S.S. divisions which took part in the fighting. This was the time of the infamous massacres at Oradour-sur-Glane and Tulle, when General von Neubronn confessed to the Swiss minister that 'he was ashamed to wear the German uniform' and Marshal Pétain told Renthe-Fink, 'You burn villages, you massacre children, you desecrate churches, you cover your country in shame. You are a nation of savages.'[3] On 6 August he addressed a long letter to Laval in which he complained of the attitude of the *Milice*. By its actions, he wrote, 'the *Milice* has succeeded in imposing an atmosphere of police terror which has been unknown in our country until now.'[4] The only thing that was wrong about this complaint was that it came a little late in the day.

Laval had already made it clear that he wanted no part of any bloodshed. In a broadcast speech on D-Day itself, he told the French people, 'We are not in the war. You must not take part in the fighting.

---

[1] Hilger to Bargen, 14 July 1944, GFM/4120/E071231.
[2] War Diary of *Hauptverbindungsstab 588*, 21 June 1944, ND 257-F.
[3] Stucki, p. 38; Tracou, p. 309. For events at Oradour and Tulle, see the documents prepared by the Vichy government and included in ND 673-F.
[4] The letter is printed in Noguères, pp. 653-6.

If you do not observe this rule, if you show proof of indiscipline, you will provoke reprisals the harshness of which the government would be powerless to moderate. You would suffer, both physically and materially, and you would add to your country's misfortunes. You will refuse to heed the insidious appeals which will be addressed to you. Those who ask you to stop work or invite you to revolt are the enemies of our country. You will refuse to aggravate the foreign war on our soil with the horror of civil war. . . . At this moment fraught with drama, when the war has been carried on to our territory, show by your worthy and disciplined attitude that you are thinking of France and only of her.'[1] This speech, with its theme of neutralism, was as much a criticism of the ultra-collaborationists as of the Resistance. They certainly did not share the view that France was not in the war and, at a meeting in Paris on 13 June, the leaders of all the groups were unanimous in asking that all French volunteers on the eastern front be brought back to fight the Allies in France.[2] When their most effective voice, Philippe Henriot, the secretary of state for information and propaganda,[3] was killed by the Resistance on 28 June, they determined upon one final bid to take over the government.

On 9 July, Admiral Platon arrived in Vichy bearing a manifesto on 'the political situation', which was signed, among others, by himself, Déat, de Brinon, Jean Bichelonne, the minister of industrial production, and Abel Bonnard, the minister of education. Doriot, too, had temporarily sunk his long-standing differences with Déat to sign the document. Complaining that 'rightly or wrongly, the most recent declarations of the head of state and the head of the government have been unanimously interpreted as the sign of a profound *malaise*,' the manifesto called for the accomplishment of 'gestures and actions'. 'These gestures and actions,' it claimed, 'will give the country the impression that, at long last, the government knows what it wants. These gestures and actions will show it that strength, faith, and intelligence are on the government's side and not on that of its enemies. Thousands of public servants and millions of Frenchmen will rally to authority when it is displayed.' More particularly, the manifesto demanded 'a formal and continuous statement of its position by the government', its

---

[1] Struwe to Foreign Ministry, 6 June 1944, GFM/255/166226-8.
[2] Abetz to Foreign Ministry, 14 June 1944, ibid., 166253-5.
[3] Henriot was one of the extremists forced on Laval and Pétain as a result of the November crisis.

return to Paris, its enlargement through 'the entry of indisputable elements', the reform of the cabinet so that it took decisions, and 'severe punishments up to and including the death penalty for all those whose action encourages civil war or jeopardizes the European position of France'.[1] The fact that such sentiments could be expressed in all seriousness a month after D-Day shows the extent to which the ultra-collaborationists had lost touch with reality.

Platon told Pétain that the majority of ministers refused to abide by 'Laval's neutral and *attentiste* policy'. They were going to resign and force him out. Platon himself would head the new government, with Déat as minister of state and Benoist-Méchin as foreign minister. According to Tracou, the Marshal listened to all this in silence and then told the admiral, 'My friend, you would do better to stay in the country and keep out of all this.'[2] Laval's reaction was rather more emphatic. 'I am determined to lance this abscess,' he declared. 'I shall immediately put this fool Platon under house arrest in the country and call a cabinet meeting in Vichy tomorrow. Those who don't come will be treated as having resigned. As for the signatories of the manifesto, if they don't retract I shall kick them out of the government. And if the Germans intervene, I shall hand in my resignation to the Marshal.'[3]

If we are to believe the published minutes, Laval put up a brilliant performance at the cabinet meeting, which took place on 12 July. All the ministers were present, with the notable exception of Déat. The prime minister read out the text of the manifesto and commented, 'I believe that the signatories of this document do not agree with my statements of 6 June. They ask the French government to carry out some gestures, some actions. Such as? They also ask for the government to be enlarged. With whom? . . . I immediately call upon those ministers who have signed this document and ask them to be so good as to explain.' Bichelonne, de Brinon, and Bonnard did not create a very good impression. They all denied that they had anything to do with the actual drafting of the manifesto and Bichelonne even maintained that he had only signed it 'out of weariness'. De Brinon claimed that it reflected 'a concern which is common enough in Paris', while Bonnard maintained that it expressed 'a general psychological state' in

[1] The text of the manifesto is printed in Tracou, pp. 325–7, and Stucki, pp. 167–9. The latter version contains the full list of signatories.
[2] Tracou, pp. 327–8.
[3] Ibid., p. 328.

the capital. The most serious single issue which any of them raised was Laval's attitude to the murder of his First World War acquaintance, Georges Mandel, by the *Milice*.[1] It is not clear whether they expected Laval to condone the murder, but he told them in no uncertain terms that he had no intention of doing so. '. . . I have no blood on my hands and I never will have,' he declared. '. . . I have no responsibility for these events. I am not covering these actions. These are methods which I utterly deplore. Georges Mandel is dead. I am sorry that he was killed in such circumstances.' He referred to the similar case of Jean Zay, the *Front Populaire*'s minister of education, who had also been murdered by the *Milice*. 'Two is enough, more than enough,' he said. '. . . Let anyone who disagrees with me say so.' No one replied. 'I note the cabinet's unanimity,' he declared, 'in favour of refusing to hand over any hostages in future and [to condone] reprisals of this nature.'

Having demolished his opponents' somewhat feeble arguments, he launched into a long attack upon the manifesto. Should the government return to Paris? It was the Germans who wanted it to remain in Vichy. Déat had complained that the cabinet never discussed political issues. 'The one time we do discuss them, I note he isn't here.' The government should be enlarged. With whom? Admiral Platon? 'M. Platon forgets that his letters are opened. He wrote to his brother a few days ago and this is what I read in his letter: "I find it painful that a head of the government states we are not in the war. This man does not deserve to be shot, but hanged. He will be." M. Platon is a fine man. He had a fine record at Dunkirk, but he would do better to keep out of politics.' He then came to the main issue. 'They want France to enter the war on Germany's side. With what weapons? M. Déat says he's not neutral. Alright then, let him join up. It's easy. M. Déat would also like the L.V.F. and the *Waffen*-S.S. to go and fight in Normandy. I opposed this and I pointed out to the Germans that if people saw large numbers of French troops on one side and a few hundred soldiers

---

[1] Mandel had been interned in Buchenwald by the Germans. In 1944, Abetz suggested to Laval that he, Blum, and Reynaud be shot by the Vichy government in retaliation for a collaborationist who had been shot by the Algiers committee. He was transferred to France and shot out of hand by the *Milice* while being taken from one prison to another. For further details, see John Sherwood, 'The Tiger's Cub: The Last Years of Georges Mandel', in James Joll (ed.), *The Decline of the Third Republic* (St Antony's Papers, No. 5), London Chatto & Windus, 1959, especially pp. 123-5.

in the German ranks on the other, the real feelings of the French people would explode in an obvious fashion. Today, therefore, I maintain my position in full. My only opponents are a few maniacs who are, moreover, in no hurry to go and fight themselves.' Did any minister believe, he concluded, that France could have any other policy but his own?

De Brinon protested that it was not a question of entering the war on the German side. Even the Germans themselves did not want that. All he and his friends wanted was for Laval to command. He was convinced that, if the prime minister had shown firmness, he could have kept Déat out of the government. The mention of Déat's name produced an immediate outburst from Laval. 'He must stop his activities,' he cried. 'Either he resigns or he replaces me. I can no longer work with him. If he comes to power, it will mean catastrophe and civil war will be precipitated.' Calming down, he asked whether everyone present agreed with his speech of 6 June and especially with the words 'we are not in the war'. There was a silence which he took as indicating approval. He then drafted a communiqué which included the statement that the cabinet 'noted that France could have no other policy than that defined by the head of the government on 6 June last'.[1] The meeting was over and the victory was Laval's. According to Tracou, de Brinon, Bonnard, and Bichelonne left the room with their heads bowed.[2]

Having spiked the ultra-collaborationists' guns – if only for the moment – Laval was free to attempt his own last-minute *coup*. He outlined his ideas to Marshal Pétain at the castle of Lonzat near Vichy, where the Germans now insisted the latter should stay for security reasons. Any hope of an agreement with the Gaullists, Laval argued, was an illusion. Their advent to power would mean 'civil war . . . and revolution'. He believed in legality and thought he could count upon the support of Herriot, whom he described as 'just the man for the situation'. 'He is on as good terms with Stalin as he is with the Americans,' he went on. '. . . What's more, he has the ear of parliament.' Laval said that he would shortly be going to Paris where he would endeavour to persuade the Germans to agree to the reconvening of the National Assembly and the granting of freedom of action to Pétain.[3]

---

[1] The minutes of the cabinet meeting are printed in Tracou, pp. 329–38.
[2] Ibid., p. 338. This detail is not included in the minutes.
[3] Ibid., pp. 356–8; Stucki, p. 52.

Laval's plan was an almost exact replica of that which had been put forward by Lemaigre-Dubreuil a few weeks earlier, and was undoubtedly inspired by it. It has been said that Laval received fresh confirmation from André Enfière, a close friend of Herriot's, that the Americans were still in favour of an interim government to prevent de Gaulle from coming to power. This message is supposed to have been given Enfière by Allen Dulles, the O.S.S. representative in Berne.[1] There is, however, no mention of Dulles or the Americans in Enfière's own account of these events[2] or in available contemporary documents. The story may be true, but, even if it is not, Laval had reason to believe as a result of the Lemaigre-Dubreuil mission that the Americans would not look unfavourably upon the reconvening of the national assembly. What he himself hoped to gain from it is not clear. He told one acquaintance that he intended to defend his policies during the occupation before the assembly,[3] possibly in the belief that the members of parliament would respond to his talents just once more. At best, he may have been trying to save his country from what seemed to him a genuine threat of civil war and restore his somewhat tattered reputation in the process. At worst, he may only have been seeking to save his own skin.

He certainly realized that things were getting desperate. 'I have learned,' he told Stucki on 6 August, 'that the Germans intend to "render the Marshal and myself secure". I am determined that I will only submit to the most extreme pressure and I will resign my post as head of the government the moment this pressure is applied.' He did not intend to run the government from any other French town, he continued, let alone from Germany. If he ever had to leave Vichy, except for short trips to Paris, he wanted Stucki and his government to know that he would no longer be prime minister, but 'a common or garden prisoner'.[4]

Laval left for Paris with his wife and daughter on 9 August. According to his later account, he had a long conversation with Abetz on the 11th and persuaded him to agree to the liberation of Herriot who, though not mentally ill, was being detained in an asylum near Nancy.

---

[1] Tracou, p. 366. It is interesting to note that de Gaulle accepts Tracou's version without question. See de Gaulle, Vol. II, p. 290.

[2] André Enfière in *La Vie de la France*, Vol. II, pp. 1054–77.

[3] René Lebret in ibid., Vol. III, p. 1211.

[4] Stucki, pp. 48–9.

Abetz told him to go and fetch the president of the chamber himself. The ambassador's decision was taken entirely on his own initiative, without the consent of Berlin. He says so in his memoirs, and this is confirmed by the sole surviving contemporary document on the whole affair; a telegram from Ribbentrop on 12 August instructing him to refrain from all discussion concerning the reconvening of the national assembly.[1]

If we are to believe Herriot's subsequent account, Laval's sudden arrival at the asylum near Nancy on 12 August was like a bolt from the blue. Nevertheless, he agreed to accompany the prime minister back to the capital and they arrived there on the 13th. As the chamber of deputies was occupied by the Germans, Herriot was put up at the Hôtel de Ville.[2] It is at this point that the accounts of this episode begin to diverge slightly. According to Herriot, when Laval broached his plan, he replied that 'that was his business, but in any event it was not mine because the president of the national assembly is the president of the senate. I begged him to knock at some other door.'[3] According to Laval, on the other hand, Herriot's reaction was rather more positive in that he suggested that the prime minister should contact M. Blondeau, the head of the senate secretariat, with a view to locating M. Jeanneney, the president of the senate. Laval took this advice and, after some initial reluctance, M. Blondeau is said to have agreed to go and see M. Jeanneney near Grenoble where he was living, telephone contact being impossible.[4]

In the meantime, Laval was desperately trying to persuade Pétain to come to Paris to crown the whole enterprise, but the Marshal refused to budge without guarantees for his safety.[5] On 11 August he signed a document appointing Admiral Auphan his representative to negotiate with the Allies and de Gaulle. If, when he came to exercise this mission, Pétain was no longer a free agent, the admiral was instructed to open the sealed envelope which contained the draft constitutional act of September 1943 setting up the regency council.[6]

---

[1] Tracou, p. 365; *Laval Parle*, pp. 155–7; Abetz, p. 297; Ribbentrop to Abetz, 12 August 1944, GFM/4141/E071579–80.
[2] Herriot in *Procès Pétain*, p. 113; *Laval Parle*, p. 157.
[3] Herriot, loc. cit.
[4] *Laval Parle*, p. 157; Guérard, pp. 154–5. (The latter version clearly derives from Laval.)
[5] See the extracts from General Bridoux's diary in *La Vie de la France*, Vol. III, pp. 1698–1702; Stucki, pp. 54–5.
[6] Ibid., p. 171.

On the evening of 16 August, the blow fell. Laval was having dinner when the telephone rang. It was the Hôtel de Ville with the news that the Germans had just re-arrested Herriot.[1] The order had come from the S.S. in Berlin, who were now all-powerful after the failure of the generals' attempt on Hitler's life the previous month, but Ribbentrop cannot have been opposed to it.[2] Laval rushed round to the Hôtel de Ville, upbraided Nosek, the S.S. officer who had been ordered to carry out the arrest, and insisted that Abetz be fetched at once. The following morning, in what he subsequently described as an attempt to gain time, he gave the German ambassador a letter in which he threatened to resign unless the order to re-arrest Herriot was rescinded.[3] But before Abetz had time to report this to Berlin, he received fresh instructions from Ribbentrop to the effect that, in view of the military situation, the French government must be transferred immediately to Belfort in the east of France. Déat, Darnand, and de Brinon had already left. At 7 p.m. on 17 August Laval called a meeting of all those ministers who were present in Paris and, at its conclusion, sent Abetz a message in which he stated that 'the French government does not agree to trans-fer its seat from Vichy to Belfort, whatever the reasons you invoke'. Abetz replied that the German government's decision was irrevocable and that, in the light of the French government's attitude, he had no alternative but to use force. Laval replied that he had no choice but to submit, but asked Abetz to 'realize that, in these circumstances, I can no longer exercise my functions'. Thus, the threat which he had uttered to gain time on the issue of Herriot's re-arrest had been implemented on that of the forcible transfer of the government, as he had promised Stucki it would. After entrusting the fate of the capital to various local dignitaries and after a sad farewell to his daughter, Laval left Paris late that night with his wife in a German convoy.[4] He was no longer prime minister and no longer a free man. He was never to be a free man again.

---

[1] François Hulot in *La Vie de la France*, Vol. II, p. 1041.
[2] Abetz, p. 297; Knochen in *La Vie de la France*, Vol. III, p. 1782.
[3] André Enfière in ibid., Vol. II, pp. 1075–6; *Laval Parle*, pp. 158–9.
[4] Ibid., pp. 159–60; Amédée Bussière in *La Vie de la France*, Vol. I, pp. 594–6; Stucki, pp. 90–91. The exchanges of letters between Abetz and Laval concerning the transfer of the government can be found on GFM/108/430–32. The letters in which Laval delegated powers to look after Paris are printed in *Laval Parle*, p. 275, and in Amédée Bussière's testimony cited above.

EPILOGUE

Captivity, Trial, and Death

August 1944 – October 1945

Laval's party arrived in Belfort at 9 a.m. on 18 August. Three days later, almost to the hour, they were joined by Marshal Pétain and his entourage, who had been compelled to leave Vichy in similar circumstances.[1] Like Laval, the Marshal had informed the Germans that his forcible abduction made it impossible for him to perform his duties,[2] but the latter were determined that some kind of pro-German French government should continue to exist. On 24 August Abetz drafted a memorandum setting out the tasks of such a government[3] while, at the same time, Fernand de Brinon was summoned to Hitler's military headquarters in east Prussia to discuss the matter with Ribbentrop. The German foreign minister took the view that it was pointless to rely any longer upon Pétain and suggested the formation of a government which excluded him. De Brinon claimed to have replied that 'the Marshal represented the sole legal power and that nothing could be done without him'. Hitler shared Ribbentrop's opinion, however, and on 25 August he summoned Laval, Darnand, and Déat to his presence.[4]

But for Laval, at any rate, the voice of the Führer had long since lost its Siren-like appeal. In spite of Abetz's sinister threat that there were 'still two million Frenchmen in Germany . . . [and] that the Führer is capable of frightful reactions', he refused to go. In a formal letter to the ambassador, he explained why. 'You are aware,' he wrote, 'of the

---

[1] Jean Lalanne (prefect of Belfort) in *La Vie de la France*, Vol. III, pp. 1620–21. For the details of Pétain's removal from Vichy, see Stucki, pp. 57–89; Renthe-Fink memorandum, 24 August 1944, GFM/108/233–45; Schellenberg to Foreign Ministry, 27 August, 1944, ibid., 4141/E071583–5.

[2] Pétain's declaration is printed in Louis Noguères, *La Dernière Etape: Sigmaringen*, Paris, Fayard, 1956 (hereafter cited as Noguères, *Sigmaringen*), p. 29.

[3] Abetz memorandum, 24 August 1944, GFM/7067/E525231–5.

[4] Debeney memorandum, 4 September 1944, in Noguères, *Sigmaringen*, p. 72. Cf. de Brinon's post-war account in de Brinon, pp. 241–2.

situation in which the Marshal and the French government find themselves as a result of the conditions in which they were taken to Belfort. Circumstances therefore make it morally impossible for me to go to the [Führer's] headquarters. Such a journey would appear to the French people as a contradiction of the position I have adopted and of which I have informed you, and they would not understand in what capacity I undertook the journey.'[1] He could not, he further explained to a member of the S.S., undertake 'negotiations which would mean the end of his political career'.[2] It was a mark of his astonishing self-confidence that he still believed he had one.

Undeterred by his refusal, the Germans pressed on without him and, towards the end of September, a 'French delegation for the defence of national interests' was formed under the chairmanship of de Brinon. It included Déat and Darnand but not Doriot, who, even in this pantomime situation, could not see his way to co-operating with his old rivals. Laval contemptuously dismissed the efforts to form a 'government' from the ranks of the ultra-collaborationists as 'pointless play-acting'.[3] The justice of the remark was underlined by the fact that, by the time the 'French delegation' came into existence, it was no longer in a position to administer a square centimetre of French territory.

In view of the speed of the Allied advance, orders were issued on 7 September to transfer the remnants of the Vichy government from Belfort to Germany. Their destination was the castle of Sigmaringen, the former residence of the Hohenzollern royal family, perched high above the River Danube in Württemberg.[4] There Laval rigorously abstained from any political activity and, like most enforced exiles, his main concern seems to have been his home and family.[5] In the middle of December, plans were made to transfer him to Logau, near Görlitz in Lower Saxony, right in the path of the advancing Red army. Indeed,

---

[1] Testimony of Paul Marion; Laval letter to Abetz, 25 August 1944, both cited in Noguères, *Sigmaringen*, p. 41.

[2] Schellenberg to Foreign Ministry, 5 September 1944, GFM/4141/E071595.

[3] Kaltenbrunner to Foreign Ministry, 7 September 1944, ibid., E071596. For further details on the 'French delegation' and its activities, see Noguères, *Sigmaringen*, *passim*; Aron, pp. 711–29.

[4] Reinebeck to Hofmann, 7 September 1944, GFM/4141/E071589; Abetz to Foreign Ministry, 10 September 1944, ibid., E071590–92.

[5] For accounts of Laval at Sigmaringen, see Gérard Rey in *La Vie de la France*, Vol. III, pp. 1252–9; Michel Letan, *Pierre Laval, de l'Armistice au Poteau*, Paris, Editions de la Couronne, 1947, pp. 117–50. Both men were eye-witnesses (see Mallet, Vol. II, p. 362).

14*

it has been suggested that Ribbentrop deliberately devised this plan as a punishment for his refusal to co-operate in the formation of a French government-in-exile. The idea was subsequently abandoned, however, and instead he was transferred to Wieflingen, only a few miles from Sigmaringen. The owner of the property in which Laval stayed was a farmer and the 'squire of Châteldon' seems to have appreciated the work of his German counterpart.[1]

This relatively pleasant interlude was, however, only a brief one. By April 1945, General Patton's army was approaching Sigmaringen and the third *Reich* was on the point of collapse. The French exiles were forced to seek their own salvation. Pétain returned to France, via Switzerland, determined to face the music. De Brinon surrendered to the Americans. Déat vanished into thin air until 1955, when it was announced that he had just died in an Italian monastery. Laval sought entry into Spain, evidently in the belief that his energetic activity on behalf of the nationalists during the civil war would favourably dispose General Franco towards him. 'It is neither the statesman nor the friend who is asking your help and assistance,' he telegraphed Lequerica, the former Spanish ambassador in France and now his country's foreign minister, 'but simply the man. . . . I ask you in my own name as well as in that of my wife and my faithful friend, Maurice Gabolde, for permission to enter Spain and await better days. Today, it is a tired and worn-out old man who is writing to you and, in memory of our long friendship, I thank you in advance.'[2] It was ten days before Lequerica replied and, in the meantime, Laval had tried unsuccessfully to enter both Switzerland and Liechtenstein.[3] According to Robert Aron, the Spanish foreign minister authorized Laval's entry into Spain provided he did not stay for longer than three months and provided he agreed to be interned during that period.[4] Laval's own account to one of his lawyers conveys a somewhat different impression. It states that when the *Junkers 88* aircraft containing Laval, his wife, Maurice Gabolde, and another ex-minister, Abel Bonnard, landed at Barcelona airport on 1 May 1945, it was met by a Spanish colonel who offered Laval the choice of another 'plane to take him to either Portugal or Eire. When

---

[1] Bobrik to *Sicherheitsdienst*, 14 December 1944, 13 January 1945, GFM/4141/E071609, E071611; Guérard, pp. 9–10; Baraduc, p. 34.
[2] Aron, p. 731. The telegram was sent on 17 April 1945.
[3] *Neue Zürcher Zeitung*, 24 April 1945.
[4] Aron, p. 732.

Laval replied that he wanted to stay, the colonel replied that, in that event he was under orders to intern the whole party. They were taken to the fortress of Monjuich, just outside Barcelona.[1]

De Gaulle's government immediately began to press for Laval's extradition, with the support of Britain and the United States.[2] Franco's government was on none too good terms with the victorious Allies; harbouring the most notorious member of the Vichy government threatened to make matters worse. Laval himself was uncertain as to what he should do. On 5 June he penned a desperate appeal to General de Chambrun, the father of his son-in-law René. 'I don't know where the children are,' he wrote. 'Paris? The United States? Some people have even told me Italy. I await your reply, which you will have agreed together, telling me . . . whether I can return immediately or not, or whether I should delay my return. I simply must have this advice, which you can give me based upon all the information in your possession. I will act according to your opinion.'[3] Laval's letter did not reach the General until 27 June. In his reply, which was dated 30 June, the latter strongly advised Laval to stay where he was.[4] Unfortunately, this letter never reached Laval. It was not delivered by the Spanish authorities to whom it had been entrusted,[5] which strongly suggests that the Spanish government had already made up its mind to hand him over. But it was not until 31 July that the same *Junkers 88* which had brought him to Barcelona landed at Linz in the American zone of Austria. The United States authorities immediately took him to Innsbruck, where he was handed over to the French.[6] The following day he was flown to Paris and imprisoned at Fresnes. Madame Laval occupied a cell in another part of the prison. 'Until that moment,' she subsequently told one of her husband's lawyers, 'we had never been separated.'[7]

---

[1] Baraduc, p. 36.

[2] *New York Times*, 1 June 1944 (statement by U.S. acting secretary of state, Joseph Grew); *Times*, 7 June 1944 (statement by U.K. minister of state, Richard Law).

[3] The letter is printed in Baraduc, p. 39.

[4] General de Chambrun's reply is printed in ibid., pp. 40–42.

[5] Ibid., p. 38; Mallet, Vol. II, p. 358.

[6] *New York Times*, 1 August 1945.

[7] Baraduc, p. 104. Madame Laval was released from Fresnes on 25 September (ibid., pp. 102, 112–13). 'I do not know why my wife was arrested,' Laval subsequently commented; 'she has always been Anglophile and de Gaullist, and we had frequent discussion on this subject' (*Times*, 3 October 1945).

Under the terms of an ordinance of 18 November 1944, General de Gaulle had set up a high court of justice to try all members of 'the governments or pseudo-governments which had their seat on metropolitan territory' between June 1940 and August 1944 'for crimes or offences committed in the exercise of or connected with their functions'.[1] Marshal Pétain's trial had begun on 23 July 1945 and, barely thirty-six hours after his arrival in France, Laval was called upon to testify at it. His evidence took up two whole afternoons (3 and 4 August) and covers 39 closely printed pages of the *Journal Officiel*. Considering that he had no documents and was relying mainly upon memory, it was a remarkable performance. It also showed how much time he had been devoting to the preparation of his own defence during his various internments, for large sections of his testimony dealt with his foreign policy during 1934–35 and he had to be reminded more than once that this was Pétain's trial and not his own. It is pointless to speculate how far his evidence influenced the verdict of 'guilty' returned against Pétain, for the latter would almost certainly have been found guilty whatever anyone had said.[2] For the historian, however, Laval's testimony is extremely valuable and much of it has subsequently been confirmed from other sources.

Whatever its faults, the Pétain trial had at least permitted the presentation and discussion of a vast amount of relevant material. Laval's own trial illustrated nothing but the inadequacies of the judicial system and the poisonous political atmosphere of the purge-trial era in France. He himself firmly believed that, if he could only secure a fair hearing, he would be able to convince his fellow-countrymen that he had been acting in their best interests all along. 'Father-in-law wants a big trial which will illuminate everything,' René de Chambrun told Laval's lawyers. 'If he is given time to prepare his defence, if he is allowed to speak, to call witnesses and to obtain from abroad the information and documents which he needs, he will confound his accusers.'[3] At the same time, Laval more than suspected what would really happen. 'Do you want me to tell you the set-up?' he asked one of his lawyers on 24 August. 'There will be no pre-trial hearings and no

---

[1] The text of the ordinance is printed in de Gaulle, Vol. III, pp. 408–9.

[2] Pétain himself refused to say anything at his trial, denying the competence of the court to try him.

[3] Albert Naud, *Pourquoi je n'ai pas defendu Pierre Laval*, Paris, Fayard, 1948 (hereafter cited as Naud), p. 16.

trial. I will be condemned – and got rid of – before the elections.'[1] He was not far wrong.

It soon became evident which way the wind was blowing. On 21 August Laval's two senior counsel, Albert Naud and Jacques Baraduc, were promised that the *instruction*, or pre-trial hearings, would be 'a long-winded affair' lasting into November. They were given a detailed scheme which provided for at least twenty-five sessions. Only five took place, however, before they were informed, through the press, that the *instruction* was over. Vigorous protests elicited a few more sessions at the end of September, but many important questions were left undiscussed. When the defence sought to obtain the trial documents which had been promised them, they were told that the examining magistrate had gone on holiday and had taken with him the key of the safe in which they were kept. When it came to the choice of members of the jury, instead of their being chosen by lot as the law required, some mysterious coincidence dictated that only the exact number needed turned up for the ballot. On this same occasion the president of the high court, M. Mongibeaux, announced that the trial must be completed before the general election – scheduled for 21 October – whatever happened. Finally, public opinion was in a violently hostile mood. A poll showed that no less than 78 per cent of those questioned wanted Laval to be sentenced to death.[2]

Formally charged with plotting against the security of the state and intelligence with the enemy, Laval began his trial at 1.30 p.m. on Thursday, 4 October 1945. The president began by reading out a letter from Naud and Baraduc in which they stated that, in view of the shortcomings of the *instruction* and other factors, they had asked the president of the bar association to discharge them from the task of defending Laval. 'We fear,' they commented, 'that the haste which has been employed to open the hearings is inspired, not by judicial preoccupations, but motivated by political considerations.' Laval's junior counsel, Yves Jaffré, although not nominated by the bar, agreed with their decision. None of Laval's lawyers were in court. Their absence and their letter were intended as a protest of which he thoroughly

---

[1] Baraduc, p. 31.

[2] This paragraph is based upon the statement issued by Baraduc and Naud to the foreign press on 30 October 1945 and reproduced in *Laval Parle*, pp. 13–15. For the failure to communicate the trial documents, see Naud, pp. 49–50. For the public opinion poll, see *Daily Telegraph*, 28 September 1945.

approved. It had no effect, however, for the court decided to carry on without them.[1]

The first day's debates set the tone for the rest of the trial. They were taken up with the *interrogatoire*, or detailed examination of the charges by the president and the public prosecutor. Mongibeaux, the president, was quite unable to control the court and permitted members of the jury to shout abuse at the accused while, at the same time, rebuking the latter whenever he stepped out of line. Mornet, the public prosecutor, was vicious but clumsy, and Laval seized every opportunity to score debating points off him. Both Mongibeaux and Mornet, indeed, had been members of the judiciary during the Vichy period, a fact of which Laval did not hesitate to remind them. It was not long before the thread of the *interrogatoire* was completely lost in a jumble of accusations, protests, and quibbles. At the end of the hearing, after a series of increasingly heated exchanges between Mongibeaux and Laval about the inadequacy of the *instruction*, the former threatened to expel the accused from the courtroom. Banging his briefcase on the table in front of him, Laval shouted angrily, 'Condemn me straight away; it will be clearer.' 'Guards, remove the accused!' ordered Mongibeaux. At this point, a young man in the audience applauded Laval, an incident which produced an astonishing outburst from the jury. 'Arrest him!' cried one member. 'It's the fifth column! . . .' shouted another. 'He deserves twelve bullets in his hide, just like Laval!' howled a third. Upon this edifying note, the first day's proceedings came to an end.[2]

The following afternoon, M. Mongibeaux was pleased to note that the accused's three lawyers were with him in court. In a letter to Naud and Baraduc, *Maître* Poignard, the president of the bar association, had advised them to resume their duties, but he also agreed to accompany them while the letter, which contained some sharp criticisms of the trial procedure, was read out to the court. Naud and Baraduc followed this up with a strong plea for the adjournment of the trial pending a more thorough *instruction*, but this was rejected by the court and the hearings continued. 'The day passed without incident,' Naud subsequently wrote. 'Laval finished up by being terribly verbose and

[1] *Procès Laval*, pp. 7–26; Naud, pp. 59–61.
[2] *Procès Laval*, pp. 26–97. The young man who applauded was one of the sons of Pierre Cathala, Laval's friend and former ministerial colleague.

boring. His interminable expositions on the birth of the Vichy régime were listened to by an icy jury, upon whom no argument seemed to have any effect. The public withdrew, disappointed in this hearing, which had begun in a high state of excitement and ended in somnolence.'[1]

This relatively peaceful atmosphere was completely shattered on 6 October. Mornet, the public prosecutor, excelled himself by remarking at one point, 'I can truthfully say that if, on the morrow of the liberation . . . Pierre Laval had been arrested and brought before a military court . . . his condemnation, followed by you know what, would not have been a judicial mistake.' 'That would have deprived me of the pleasure of hearing you,' Laval retorted with biting sarcasm.[2] Mongibeaux was no better, and he drew laughter from the audience when, during the course of one of his interrogations, he remarked that he did not want to assume the air of a prosecutor. Finally, Laval rounded on him in a scene which can only be described by quoting from the full stenographic record:

LAVAL: . . . *Monsieur le Président*, you supply the questions and the answers at one and the same time. Very well, I think it would be better if we left it at that as far as the serenity and majesty of your justice are concerned.

MONGIBEAUX: In your position, do you think you are assured of impunity?

LAVAL: I do not think I am assured of impunity, but there is one thing which is above us all, above you and above me, and that is truth and the justice of which you ought to be the embodiment.

BEDIN (a member of the jury): Justice will be done!

Another member of the jury: Yes, justice will be done!

MONGIBEAUX: Someone will have the last word: the high court.

LAVAL: You keep it!

MONGIBEAUX: You do not wish to answer any more of my questions?

LAVAL: No.

MONGIBEAUX: Consider carefully the attitude you are adopting. You do not wish to answer any more of my questions?

[1] Ibid., pp. 91–192; Naud, p. 221.
[2] Ibid., p. 201.

LAVAL: No, *Monsieur le Président*, not in view of your aggressive attitude and the way in which you question me. You supply the questions and the answers.

MONGIBEAUX: The hearing is adjourned. Remove the accused!

Members of the jury (to Laval): You're the trouble-maker!
Swine!
Twelve bullets!
He hasn't changed!

LAVAL: No, and I shan't change now.

MONGIBEAUX: (standing by his chair): Please! We are not at a public meeting!

LAVAL: The jury – before judging me – it's fantastic!

A member of the jury: You've already been judged, and France has judged you too![1]

After the adjournment, Mongibeaux announced that the part of the *interrogatoire* dealing with the charge of plotting against the security of the state was concluded and that he now proposed to deal with the charge of intelligence with the enemy. '*Monsieur le Président*,' Laval replied, 'the insulting way in which you questioned me earlier and the demonstrations in which some members of the jury indulged show me that I may be the victim of a judicial crime. I do not want to be an accomplice; I prefer to remain silent.' Mongibeaux thereupon called the first of the prosecution witnesses, but they had not expected to give evidence so soon and none were present. Mongibeaux therefore adjourned the hearing for the second time so that they could be located. When the court reassembled half an hour later, Laval was no longer in his place.[2]

For the remainder of his trial, Laval resolutely boycotted the hearings. On 8 October Paul-Henri Teitgen, the Christian Democrat minister of justice in de Gaulle's cabinet, made a personal appeal to Laval's lawyers to persuade him to change his mind. He freely admitted the scandalous conduct of the jury and of Mongibeaux and Mornet, but professed himself unable to do anything to curb them. 'I asked seven magistrates to preside over the high court,' he said. '. . . Only M. Mongibeaux accepted, doubtless because he had just been made presi-

---

[1] *Procès Laval*, pp. 205–7.
[2] Ibid., pp. 207–8.

dent of the court of appeal. As for the public prosecutor, I had to have
one who had not taken the oath of allegiance to Vichy. I searched in
vain and only managed to find M. Mornet. Even his case is doubtful.'
'As far as the jury is concerned,' he went on, raising his eyes and his
arms in a gesture of despair, 'you realize that I have no influence over
them.' Nevertheless, he did promise that all the trial documents would
be communicated to the defence, that the latter could call as many
witnesses as they liked, and that if the trial was not over by the date of
the elections, it would be adjourned until afterwards. All this, however,
was conditional upon Laval's resuming his place in court. Naud was in
favour of accepting the minister's offer; Baraduc thought it was a trap.
They agreed to leave the decision to Laval, who was against acceptance. 'If I do not go before the court again,' he wrote to Teitgen, 'I
shall be condemned. If I wish to pursue my defence I shall be condemned just the same.' The only remedy, he suggested, lay with the
government, which could order a continuation of the *instruction* or a
re-trial.[1]

In the meantime, the hearings had gone on as usual. On 6 October
ex-President Lebrun had testified concerning the events of June–July
1940.[2] On the 8th, the court heard General Doyen on Laval's policy
towards Germany during the last five months of 1940, the former
secretary of the senate, M. de Lapommeraye, on the national assembly
of July 1940, and the secretary of the national federation of labour
deportees on the compulsory labour service. None of them added much
that was new.[3] In the absence of any of the thirty-three witnesses the
defence had planned to call, the rest of the day was given over to the
almost inaudible reading out of transcripts of some of the pre-trial
hearings.[4] On the following day, two more prosecution witnesses were

[1] For the interview with Teitgen and its aftermath, see Naud, pp. 249–57; Baraduc,
pp. 143–6; Jaffré, pp. 263–7. There is one major discrepancy between the accounts of
Laval's three lawyers. Naud states that Laval was initially prepared to respond to Teitgen's
appeal, but that he was dissuaded from doing so by a false rumour that the government had
'arranged' for four members of the jury not to turn up, so that the trial would have to be
postponed. Both Baraduc and Jaffré, on the other hand, state categorically that Laval
opposed Teitgen's offer from the beginning, and Laval's letter to the minister, quoted by
Jaffré, would seem to confirm this. Jaffré, whose book appeared after Naud's, denies the
story of the missing jurymen. Baraduc, whose book was published at about the same time
as Naud's, makes no mention of it.
[2] *Procès Laval*, pp. 209–17.
[3] Ibid., pp. 219–38.
[4] Ibid., pp. 238–55.

called. The first, ex-ambassador Léon Noël, courageously refused to testify in the absence of the accused and his lawyers. The second, the director of Hachette's, spoke about the fortunes of his firm during the occupation. If anything, his evidence suggested that Laval had done quite a good job of protecting it against continuous German attempts to take it over.[1] There then followed the closing speech for the prosecution in which Mornet predictably demanded the death penalty.[2] There was, of course, no closing speech for the defence, but Mongibeaux did read out a letter from Laval which contained a detailed rebuttal of Doyen's evidence. Laval's most telling point was that Doyen had not resigned from the chairmanship of the French delegation to the armistice commission at Wiesbaden until June 1941. 'How could he have accepted to take part over such a long period in a policy which he so harshly condemns today?' Laval asked. 'I never noticed any indignation on the part of General Doyen while he was at Wiesbaden.'[3] But there was never any doubt about the verdict. After listing his alleged crimes in detail, the final judgment concluded, 'For these reasons, and in view of articles 87 and 75 of the penal code and the ordinance of 18 November 1944, [the court] sentences Laval to death, declares him convicted of national unworthiness and, as a result, sentences him to national degradation and the confiscation of all his goods.'[4]

Laval was transferred to the condemned block at Fresnes on 10 October, where he was placed in chains. In the last few days that remained to him, his family and his lawyers made desperate attempts to gain support for a re-trial, approaching such figures as Léon Blum, François Mauriac, and even the British ambassador, Duff Cooper.[5] On 12 October his three lawyers had an audience with General de Gaulle. Naud began by pointing out that, as a member of the Resistance, he had had nothing in common with Laval from a political point of view, but that the trial had been conducted in a scandalous fashion. Without saying a word, the General turned to Baraduc, who outlined the deficiencies of the *instruction*, and then to Jaffré, who said that the execution of a former prime minister after such a disgraceful trial would set a

---

[1] Ibid., pp. 257–62.
[2] Ibid., pp. 262–302.
[3] Ibid., pp. 302–5.
[4] Ibid., pp. 305–9.
[5] For accounts of these last few days, see Naud, pp. 258–75; Baraduc, pp. 155–87; Jaffré, pp. 273–306.

dangerous precedent. When they had all finished, de Gaulle shook their hands and they were ushered out. As they waited in the ante-chamber, they saw Gaston Palewski, the head of the General's secretariat, called into the room they had just left, emerge a moment later, and re-enter with a copy of a French legal handbook. De Gaulle, it seems, was unable to make up his mind and Laval's lawyers were told that he intended to consult M. Teitgen.[1]

Since the publication of the third volume of the General's memoirs in 1959, we have had the text of their exchange of letters. 'The Laval affair must be settled,' de Gaulle wrote to Teitgen. 'He has not requested a reprieve. The point to be settled, therefore, is the following: should there be a re-trial or not? If yes, the government must draw up a text. If not, justice must take its course.' Teitgen, who was campaigning in the provinces, replied the following day. 'I honestly believe,' he wrote, '1. that the events which took place during the hearings at the Laval trial, while they were clearly regrettable, were desired and provoked by the accused who, knowing what he deserved, sought every means to postpone his judgment; 2. that the procedure which was followed in the absence of the defaulting accused was that prescribed by the law; 3. that the sentence was basically justified; 4. that, as a result, this sentence must be carried out.'[2] In view of his comments to Laval's lawyers only five days before, Teitgen's performance was a shabby one. Indeed, it was paralleled only by de Gaulle himself, who, by publishing this correspondence in his memoirs, clearly intended to shuffle off responsibility on to Teitgen, without mentioning the fact that, before he even saw Naud, Baraduc, and Jaffré, he had told a press conference that there could be no question of a re-trial.[3]

The execution was fixed for the morning of Monday, 15 October. It was a hideous affair and, in its way, a fitting sequel to the travesty of justice that had been his trial. For Laval attempted to cheat the firing squad by taking poison from a phial which had been stitched inside the lining of his jacket since the war years. He did not intend, he explained in a suicide note, that French soldiers should become accomplices in a judicial crime. If the poison had not been so old, it would undoubtedly have worked, but, as it was, repeated stomach-pumpings revived him.

[1] For the audience with de Gaulle, see Naud, pp. 265–7; Baraduc, pp. 173–4; Jaffré, pp. 290–92.
[2] De Gaulle, Vol. III, pp. 617–18.
[3] Le Monde, 13–14 October, 1945.

Those present then witnessed the frightful spectacle of the condemned man, tormented by an agonizing thirst but unable to keep down any of the water proffered him, being half-carried to the execution stake in one of the courtyards at Fresnes. There, at twenty-three minutes past noon, he was shot.[1] He 'died bravely', as de Gaulle remarks with smug self-righteousness in his memoirs.[2] But it was his widow who made the most fitting comment upon his execution. 'It is not the French way to try a man without letting him speak,' she told an English newspaper. 'That's the way he always fought against – the German way.'[3]

[1] For accounts of Laval's execution, see Naud, pp. 276–84; Baraduc, pp. 188–200; Jaffré, pp. 308–18.

[2] Charles de Gaulle, op. cit., p. 251.

[3] *Evening Standard*, 16 October 1945.

Conclusion

The scandal of Laval's trial and execution has tended to obscure the almost complete opprobrium in which he was held in 1945. Five years of Allied propaganda – a sample of which is illustrated earlier – had rammed home the image of a shifty, toad-like traitor, and Vincent Auriol, who was shortly to be elected the first President of the Fourth Republic, could write of him in all seriousness, 'Everything about him is black: his clothes, his face, his soul.'[1] If his trial had been conducted properly, the verdict would undoubtedly have been the same and he would have gone to his death with even less sympathy than he in fact received.

More than twenty years later, it is both possible and desirable to reconsider his place in history. It would be pointless to attempt this by reference to the charges made at his trial, although this is what many of his would-be defenders have done, seeking to prove that, by dint of continued opposition to and thwarting of German demands, he is almost entitled to be considered as a member of the Resistance. This kind of argument makes the fatal mistake of trying to defend him on his opponents' ground. It would make far more sense to admit, from the very outset, that he was a loyal collaborator and argue that this was justified from the point of view of French interests as long as the Germans had a chance of winning the war.

Even so, he was no more 'guilty' of collaboration than many others, and a good deal less so than some. Why then, was he one of the few to be executed?[2] The answer can only be on grounds of *Realpolitik*. By his public speeches and exhortations during the occupation, and particularly during the difficult years of 1942–44, Laval had become identified with the Vichy régime to an even greater extent than Pétain himself.[3] In the final volume of his war memoirs, General de Gaulle

---

[1] Vincent Auriol, *Hier . . . Demain*, Vol. I, Paris, Charlot, 1945, p. 100.

[2] The others included Fernand de Brinon and Joseph Darnand.

[3] Robert Aron is almost certainly right when he says that Laval 'will perhaps end up by paying more dearly for [his words] than for the deeds which they concealed' (Aron, p. 58).

wrote that 'condemnation of Vichy in the person of its leaders dissociated France from a policy which had been one of national renunciation.'[1] As the most representative figure of the régime, Laval naturally received the severest condemnation. He himself had no illusions about what would happen. His parting words to Jacques Barnaud in November 1942 should be recalled in this context. 'If the Germans are beaten, General de Gaulle will return. He will be supported . . . by 80 or 90 per cent of the French people and I shall be hanged.'[2]

In that same statement he had said that, if he were not Laval, he would like to be de Gaulle, and there are indeed some striking parallels between the ideas of the two men. Laval's vision of European unity, for example, bears a remarkable similarity to that of de Gaulle's. 'We must organize our continent,' he declared during the course of the fullest exposition of his views on the subject,[3] 'and Europe will be weak or it will be strong. For it to survive, it must be constructed according to certain principles. . . . The organization of all the countries which comprise our continent must be such that neither the conquerors nor the conquered are ever again tempted to rise up against one another. On the material plane, the countries must help one another and harmonize their economic interests so that the needs of each can be satisfied without recourse to the competition and violence which have too often been the rule in the past. The new Europe will last if the germs of revenge are forever eradicated from it. Previously, peace was the result of compromise, balance, or compulsion. The European peace of tomorrow must be the result of association and of harmony. On the moral, cultural, and political plane, the individuality of the peoples must be respected. No country shall be able to impose its customs, its religion, or its régime upon the others, but, make no mistake about it, all the régimes will have one thing in common: they will rest upon a popular basis. . . . The love which I have for my country makes me hope for this new Europe, in which all peoples will discover the full flowering of their genius, for France has nothing to fear from their free competition. The ideal which I am expressing must be realized. It is in France's interests, it is in the interests of the other countries, and it is also in Europe's interests. For if the peoples know

---

[1] De Gaulle, Vol. III, p. 251.
[2] See above, p. 352.
[3] His broadcast speech of 5 June 1943. For the full text, see *Le Petit Parisien*, 7 June 1943.

that their country will be respected, they will work in brotherhood.'
What more eloquent plea could there be for *l'Europe des patries?*

Similarly, at the core of Laval's conception of Europe lay a belief
in a Franco-German *rapprochement*, just as it lies at the core of de
Gaulle's. Admittedly, in Laval's time, Germany was the dominant
partner, but this was a matter of necessity and not of design. When
Laval had originally spoken to the Americans and the Germans about
organizing the continent of Europe in 1931, there was no doubt in his –
or their – minds about which country was going to take the lead. There
is much less difference between the Franco-German *entente* about
which Laval waxed so enthusiastic after Montoire and the 'Paris–Bonn
axis' of our own time than many have cared to admit.

Both, of course, were in part directed against Britain. De Gaulle,
while perhaps not quite so irrational in his dislike of Britain as Laval,
none the less shares the latter's suspicions of that country's 'divide and
rule' attitude towards the European continent. Indeed, both men
reflect a basic tradition in French foreign policy which British policy-
makers ignore at their peril.

It is when we come to Laval's attitude towards the two super-
powers, the United States and the Soviet Union, that the parallel
between him and de Gaulle breaks down. There was none of de Gaulle's
suspicion of the United States in Laval. On the contrary, and as a result
no doubt of the influence of his son-in-law René de Chambrun,[1] Laval
always thought and expressed himself in terms highly favourable to the
United States.[2] He ardently hoped that France would prove to be a
bridge between America and the united Europe of which he dreamed,
and he never abandoned this hope, even in the face of Roosevelt's
bitter hostility.

For the Soviet Union, on the other hand, Laval had nothing but fear
and hatred. Unlike de Gaulle's, his Europe did not extend to the Urals.
Indeed, in the words of the American ambassador to France in 1931,
'he envisioned a future where . . . Russia would be thrust back into
Asia,'[3] which was presumably where he, in common with Hitler, felt

[1] René de Chambrun, as a descendant of Lafayette, is an honorary citizen of the state of
Maryland and has considerable interests and connections in the United States. For his influence upon Laval, see Robert Murphy, *Diplomat Among Warriors*, New York, Doubleday,
1964, pp. 59–60.
[2] An exception was his broadcast speech of 20 November 1942. But even this was skilfully
drafted – with René de Chambrun's help – to avoid a complete rupture. See above, pp. 351–52.
[3] See above, p. 23.

that she belonged. The nature of Russia's régime was, of course, the reason for his attitude. There can be few things more antipathetic to the individualistic French peasant who has made good, which is essentially what Laval was, than Communism. In his view, anything was preferable to it. Even in 1945, after all the trials and tribulations of the occupation, he could still say to one of his lawyers, '. . . Bolshevism is even worse than Hitlerism, and a statesman worthy of the name, even when he is at grips with a formidable and demanding occupying power, does not have the right not to be concerned at even greater perils which may arise in the future.'[1] He could never understand why the British and Americans apparently failed to realize that, by destroying Hitler's Germany with the aid of Stalin's Russia, they would build up an even more dangerous enemy for themselves.

In the light of post-war events, many of his fears seem justified. The collapse of Nazi Germany did indeed lead to a tremendous outflow of Soviet power and, even before the war's end, Churchill could write the following indictment of Anglo-American policy with which Laval would have heartily concurred: 'The proposed withdrawal of the United States army to the occupational lines which were arranged between the Russians and Americans . . . would mean the tide of Russian domination sweeping forward 120 miles on a front of 300 or 400 miles. This would be an event which, if it occurred, would be one of the most melancholy in history. . . . What would in fact be the Russian frontier would run from the North Cape in Norway, along the Finnish–Swedish frontier, across the Baltic to a point just east of Lübeck, along the at present agreed line of occupation and along the frontier between Bavaria and Czechoslovakia to the frontiers of Austria . . . and half-way across that country to the Isonzo river, behind which Tito and Russia will claim everything to the east. Thus the territories under Russian control would include the Baltic provinces, all of Germany to the occupational line, all Czechoslovakia, a large part of Austria, the whole of Yugoslavia, Hungary, Rumania, Bulgaria, until Greece in her present tottering condition is reached. It would include all the great capitals of Middle Europe, including Berlin, Vienna, Budapest, Belgrade, Bucharest, and Sofia. The position of Turkey and Constantinople will certainly come immediately into discussion . . . *This constitutes an event in the history of Europe to which*

[1] Jaffré. p. 182.

there has been no parallel, and which has not been faced by the Allies in their long and hazardous struggle.'[1]

Less than two years later, many of Churchill's fears had been realized, and there was the threat of even direr possibilities. In Europe, American Under-Secretary of State Dean Acheson told an audience of influential congressmen on 27 February 1947, 'it was clear that the Soviet Union, employing the instruments of Communist infiltration and subversion, was trying to complete the encirclement of Germany. In France, with four Communists in the Cabinet, one of them minister of defence, with Communists controlling the largest trade union and infiltrating government offices, factories, and the armed services, with nearly a third of the electorate voting Communist, and with economic conditions worsening, the Russians could pull the plug any time they chose. In Italy a similar if less immediately dangerous situation existed, but it was growing worse. In Hungary and Austria the Communists were tightening the noose on democratic governments. If Greece and the eastern Mediterranean should fall to Soviet control, the material and psychological effects in the countries that were so precariously maintaining their freedoms and democratic institutions would be devastating, and probably conclusive.'[2] Only a massive injection of countervailing American power, in the shape of the Truman doctrine and the Marshall plan, succeeded in saving the situation.

The accuracy of Laval's predictions concerning the nature of Soviet expansionism and incipient inter-continental rivalry have led some of his admirers to represent him as a great statesman who lived before his time. Alas, statesmen who live before their time rarely merit the epithet 'great', for it is of the essence of statesmanship to realize the limitations imposed by one's environment. Laval was never able to do this, particularly in the sphere of Franco-German relations.[3] Thus he failed to see that there was no basis for a *rapprochement* with Hitler's Germany on terms that were anything other than a humiliation for France.[4] The

---

[1] Churchill minute to Eden, 4 May 1945, printed in Winston S. Churchill, *The Second World War*, Vol. VI, *Triumph and Tragedy*, London, Cassell, 1954, p. 438 (emphasis added).

[2] Joseph M. Jones, *The Fifteen Weeks*, New York, Harcourt Brace, 1964, pp. 140–41.

[3] But the same was true in other matters. In 1935, for example, he did not understand that Italian ambitions in Abyssinia could not be reconciled with British public opinion or the Covenant of the League of Nations.

[4] Since the body of this book was completed, a brilliant new study of Germany's war-time policy towards France has appeared which proves this contention up to the hilt. It is: Eberhard Jäckel, *Frankreich in Hitlers Europa*, Stuttgart, Deutsche Verlags-Anstalt, 1966.

Nazi 'new order' was no partnership, but a master–slave relationship, and any hope that National Socialism would mellow with time or be replaced, short of defeat, by something less predatory and nihilistic was illusory. Laval's vision of Europe was a noble one, but it was incapable of realization until Hitler and Nazism were completely eradicated. In this, the British and Americans were right and he was wrong.

This is something which he would have found impossible to admit, for in common with the Duce, whom he once admired, he liked to believe that he was infallible. The sources are replete with his castigations of the folly of everyone except himself and expressions of his determination to do what he considered to be the right thing regardless of the feelings, wishes, or advice of anyone else. As he said to General Weygand in November 1942, he intended 'to make the French people happy in spite of themselves'.[1] At his trial in 1945, he complained with some bitterness, 'I have to be wrong for them to be right.'[2] Unfortunately, the reverse was probably even more apt. 'They' – i.e. everyone else – had to be wrong for him to be right.

Burdened with this unbounded faith in his own ability, Laval persisted in his illusions until they collapsed around his ears, from the Italian alliance, through Hitler's goodwill and the impossibility of Germany's defeat, to the chimera of a negotiated peace. In the circumstances, it is more than unfair that he has gone down in history with the reputation of a devious intriguer, for the greatest flaw in his character was not deviousness, but a frightening tendency towards over-simplification. Perhaps the paradox can best be explained in his own words, which might also serve as his epitaph. 'I have always had simple ideas in politics. People take me for a shyster, but they don't know me. What I do is so simple that it looks to those who don't understand like something very complicated.'[3]

---

[1] See above, p. 343.

[2] Jaffré, p. 226.

[3] Speech to mayors of the Lyon region, 22 April 1944 (unpublished text kindly communicated to me by M. René de Chambrun).

APPENDIX

BIBLIOGRAPHY

INDEX

Appendix:
French Governments, 1931–1944

A · *THE THIRD REPUBLIC*

1. *Laval Government* (27 January 1931–16 February 1932)
   Prime Minister: Pierre Laval
   Foreign Affairs: Aristide Briand (succeeded 14 January 1932 by Pierre Laval)
   Interior: Pierre Laval (succeeded 14 January 1932 by Pierre Cathala)
   Finance: Pierre-Etienne Flandin
   War: André Maginot (succeeded 14 January 1932 by André Tardieu)

2. *Tardieu Government* (20 February–10 May 1932)
   Prime Minister: André Tardieu
   Foreign Affairs: André Tardieu
   Interior: Albert Mahieu
   Finance: Pierre-Etienne Flandin
   Defence: François Piétri

1932 Elections

3. *Herriot Government* (3 June–14 December 1932)
   Prime Minister: Edouard Herriot
   Foreign Affairs: Edouard Herriot
   Interior: Camille Chautemps
   Finance: Germain-Martin
   War: Joseph Paul-Boncour

4. *Paul-Boncour Government* (18 December 1932–28 January 1933)
   Prime Minister: Joseph Paul-Boncour
   Foreign Affairs: Joseph Paul-Boncour
   Interior: Camille Chautemps
   Finance: Henri Chéron
   War: Edouard Daladier

425

5. *Daladier Government* (31 January–24 October 1933)
Prime Minister: Edouard Daladier
Foreign Affairs: Joseph Paul-Boncour
Interior: Camille Chautemps
Finance: Georges Bonnet
War: Edouard Daladier

6. *Sarraut Government* (26 October–23 November 1933)
Prime Minister: Albert Sarraut
Foreign Affairs: Joseph Paul-Boncour
Interior: Camille Chautemps
Finance: Georges Bonnet
War: Edouard Daladier

7. *Chautemps Government* (26 November 1933–27 January 1934)
Prime Minister: Camille Chautemps
Foreign Affairs: Joseph Paul-Boncour
Interior: Camille Chautemps
Finance: Georges Bonnet
War: Edouard Daladier

8. *Daladier Government* (30 January–7 February 1934)
Prime Minister: Edouard Daladier
Foreign Affairs: Edouard Daladier
Interior: Eugène Frot
Finance: François Piétri (succeeded 4 February 1932 by Paul
Marchandeau)
War: Jean Fabry (succeeded 4 February 1932 by Joseph
Paul-Boncour)

9. *Doumergue Government* (9 February–8 November 1934)
Prime Minister: Gaston Doumergue
Foreign Affairs: Louis Barthou (succeeded 13 October 1934 by Pierre
Laval)
Interior: Albert Sarraut (succeeded 13 October 1934 by Paul
Marchandeau)
Finance: Germain-Martin
War: Marshal Philippe Pétain

10. *Flandin Government* (8 November 1934–31 May 1935)
Prime Minister: Pierre-Etienne Flandin

Foreign Affairs: Pierre Laval
Interior: Marcel Régnier
Finance: Germain-Martin
War: General Maurin

11. *Bouisson Government* (1–4 June 1935)
Prime Minister: Fernand Bouisson
Foreign Affairs: Pierre Laval
Interior: Fernand Bouisson
Finance: Joseph Caillaux
War: General Maurin

12. *Laval Government* (7 June 1934–22 January 1936)
Prime Minister: Pierre Laval
Foreign Affairs: Pierre Laval
Interior: Joseph Paganon
Finance: Marcel Régnier
War: Jean Fabry

13. *Sarraut Government* (24 January–4 June 1936)
Prime Minister: Albert Sarraut
Foreign Affairs: Pierre-Etienne Flandin
Interior: Albert Sarraut
Finance: Marcel Régnier
War: General Maurin

1936 Elections

14. *Blum Government* (5 June 1936–21 June 1937)
Prime Minister: Léon Blum
Foreign Affairs: Yvon Delbos
Interior: Roger Salengro (succeeded 24 November 1936 by Marx Dormoy)
Finance: Vincent Auriol
Defence: Edouard Daladier

15. *Chautemps Government* (22 June 1937–10 March 1938)
Prime Minister: Camille Chautemps
Foreign Affairs: Yvon Delbos
Interior: Marx Dormoy (succeeded 18 January 1938 by Albert Sarraut)

Finance: Georges Bonnet (succeeded 18 January 1938 by Paul Marchandeau)

Defence: Edouard Daladier

16. *Blum Government* (13 March–8 April 1938)
Prime Minister: Léon Blum
Foreign Affairs: Joseph Paul-Boncour
Interior: Marx Dormoy
Finance: Léon Blum
Defence: Edouard Daladier

17. *Daladier Government* (10 April 1938–20 March 1940)
Prime Minister: Edouard Daladier
Foreign Affairs: Georges Bonnet (succeeded 13 September 1939 by Edouard Daladier)
Interior: Albert Sarraut
Finance: Paul Marchandeau (succeeded 2 November 1938 by Paul Reynaud)
Defence: Edouard Daladier

18. *Reynaud Government* (21 March–16 June 1940)
Prime Minister: Paul Reynaud
Foreign Affairs: Paul Reynaud (succeeded 18 May 1940 by Edouard Daladier, who was in turn succeeded 5 June 1940 by Paul Reynaud)
Interior: Henri Roy (succeeded 18 May 1940 by Georges Mandel)
Finance: Lucien Lamoureux (succeeded 5 June 1940 by Yves Bouthillier)
Defence: Edouard Daladier (succeeded 18 May 1940 by Paul Reynaud)
N.B. Marshal Philippe Pétain entered the Government as Deputy Prime Minister on 18 May 1940

19. *Pétain Government* (16 June–10 July 1940)
Prime Minister: Marshal Philippe Pétain
Foreign Affairs: Paul Baudouin
Interior: Charles Pomaret (succeeded 27 June 1940 by Adrien Marquet)
Finance: Yves Bouthillier
Defence: General Maxime Weygand
N.B. Pierre Laval entered the Government as Minister of State on 23 June 1940. On 27 June 1940, he became Deputy Prime Minister.

B · *THE VICHY RÉGIME*

Throughout the period, Marshal Pétain was Chief of State. From 12 July 1940 to 17 April 1942 he was also Prime Minister. From 18 April 1942 to 17 August 1944 the Prime Minister was Pierre Laval. Bearing this in mind, the Vichy régime passed through at least four fairly distinct phases as follows:

1. *12 July–13 December 1940*
   Deputy Prime Minister: Pierre Laval
   Foreign Affairs: Paul Baudouin (succeeded 24 October 1940 by Pierre Laval)
   Interior: Adrien Marquet (succeeded 6 September 1940 by Marcel Peyrouton)
   Finance: Yves Bouthillier
   Defence: General Maxime Weygand (until 6 September 1940)
   War: General Huntziger (from 6 September 1940)

2. *14 December 1940–9 February 1941*
   Foreign Affairs: Pierre-Etienne Flandin
   Interior: Marcel Peyrouton
   Finance: Yves Bouthillier
   War: General Huntziger

3. *10 February 1941–17 April 1942*
   Deputy Prime Minister: Admiral François Darlan
   Foreign Affairs: Admiral François Darlan
   Interior: Marcel Peyrouton (succeeded 17 February 1941 by Admiral François Darlan, who was in turn succeeded 11 August 1941 by Pierre Pucheu)
   Finance: Yves Bouthillier
   War: General Huntziger (until November 1941)
   Defence: Admiral François Darlan (from 11 August 1941)

4. *18 April 1942–17 August 1944*
   Foreign Affairs: Pierre Laval
   Interior: Pierre Laval
   Finance: Pierre Cathala
   War: General Bridoux

Bibliography

A · *UNPUBLISHED SOURCES*

Sûreté Nationale Reports (Archives Nationales, Paris): F7/13337; F7/13372; F7/13574; F713575.

Prefecture of Police Reports (Archives de la Préfecture de Police, Paris): Ba/1535 (3); Ba/1535 (7); Ba/1535 (75); Ba/1535 (79); Ba/1536 (89).

Henry L. Stimson Collection (Sterling Memorial Library, Yale University, New Haven, Conn.): Stimson Diary, 1931–2.

Miscellaneous Italian Records Collection (St Antony's College, Oxford): Job 148 (Ministero della Cultura Popolare file, Landini-Luciano correspondence); Job 321/3 (Ministero degli Esteri file, '*Francia: Situazione politica nel 1935*').

German Foreign Ministry and Chancellery Archives (Photostat copies in the Foreign Office Library, London): Serial Nos.

68 Handakten Schmidt (Dolmetscher): Aufzeichnungen
108 Handakten Renthe-Fink
110 Akten Staatssekretär betreffend Frankreich: 11.42–12.42
112 „   „   deutsch-französische Beziehungen: 2.42–4.42
117 „   „   betreffend Frankreich: 12.42
121 „   „   deutsch-französische Beziehungen: 6.40–12.40
128 „   „   betreffend Frankreich: 1.43
170 „   „   „   „   2.43–5.43
221 „   „   deutsch-französische Beziehungen: 1.41–5.41
242 „   „   betreffend Frankreich: 6.43–10.43
246 „   „   „   „   11.43–2.44
255 „   „   „   „   3.44–6.44
364 Handakten von Etzdorf: Geheime Kommandosachen und Geheime Reichssachen. Politische Berichte . . . Frankreich
386 Akten Staatssekretär deutsche-französisch Beziehungen: 6.41–9.41
422 „   „   „   „   „   5.42–6.42
434 „   „   betreffend Frankreich: 7.42–9.42
443 „   „   „   „   10.42–11.42
471 Abteiling Inland II (Geheim): Material der Wako, Wiesbaden
473 „   „   „   „   „   „   „   über Verhältnisse in Frankreich

431

899 Handakten Ritter (Frankreich): 2.42–7.42

1002 Handelspolitische Abteilung. Handakten Wiehl: Wirtschaftsdelegation Wiesbaden

1107 Goebbels Papers

1247 Handakten von Etzdorf: Aufzeichnungen Vertreter des Auswärtiges Amt

2406 Büro des Reichsaussenministers: Frankreich (1931–32)

2624 Pariser Botschaft: Geheimakten der politischen Registratur

3080 Büro des Reichsaussenministers: Österreich (1931–32)

3242 ,, ,, ,, Akten betreffend Kabinett Protokolle

3243 ,, ,, ,, Atken betreffend Reparation

3375 ,, ,, ,, Finanzkrise (1931)

3821 Pariser Botschaft (Geheim): . . . Einsatz französischen Arbeiter in Deutschland. . . .

4120 Abteilung Inland II (Geheim): Sicherheitsdienstmeldungen, Frankreich

4141 Abteilong Inland II (Geheim) Unterbringung der französischer Regierung Pétain. . . .

4620 Büro des Staatssekretärs: Politischer Schriftwechsel . . . mit Beamter des austwärtigen Dienstes

4644 Deutscher Botschaft Paris (Geheim): Der Höherer S.S. und Polizeiführer

5002 Boschaft Wien: Geheime Akten

5549 Abteilung Inland II (Geheim): Juden in Frankreich

5708 Politische Abteilung II: Frankreich. Bestrebungen zur Herbeiführung einer deutsch-französischer Verständigung

5724 Politische Abteilung II: Frankreich. Gegenseitig Besuche führender Staatsmänner. . . .

5726 Politische Abteilung II: Frankreich. Die deutsch-französische Studienkommission

7067 Nachlass Renthe-Fink: *Pétain Papiere*

7657 Presse Abteilung: Frankreich Allgemeines

9242 Alte Reichskanzlei, Auswärtige Angelegenheiten: Ausführung des Friedensvertrages – Baseler Bericht, Reparationskonferenz

9936 Oberkommando der Wehrmacht, Abteilung Landesverteidigung: Entwürfe zum Kriegstagebuch des Wehrmachtführungsstabes

F1, F7, F9, F18, F20 Loesch Papers. Files of the Reich Foreign Minister's Secretariat

K936 Politische Abteilung II: Frankreich. Politische Beziehungen Frankreich – Deutschland

K2083 Alte Reichskanzlei, Auswärtige Angelegenheiten Frankreich
    Politisches
K2086 Alte Reichskanzlei, Auswärtige Angelegenheiten Frankreich
    Berichte des deutsch-französischen Studienkommitees
L170 Alte Reichskanzlei, Auswärtige Angelegenheiten: Ausführung des
    Friedensvertrages 1930–31. . . .
P3 Abetz Papers

German Military Records (Microfilm copies available from the National
Archives, Washington, D.C.): Files

OKW/101	Oberkommando der Wehrmacht, Wehrwirtschafts- und Rüstungsamt: Protokolle. Berichte. 1942. (Microcopy T–77, Roll No. 638.)
OKW/117	Oberkommando der Wehrmacht, Wehrmachtführungsstab, Abteilung Landesverteidigung: Chefsachen LIV. Sammelmappe 'Attila', (Microcopy T–77, Roll No. 781.)
OKW/132	Oberkommando der Wehrmacht, Wehrmachtführungsstab, Abteilung Landesverteidigung: Untitled file on Franco-German collaboration. (Microcopy T–77, Roll No. 782.)
OKW/1063	Oberkommando der Wehrmacht, Amt Auslandsnachrichten und Abwehr, Abteilung Abwehr II: Allierte Landung in Französische Nordafrika am 8. November 1942. Ag. Ausland II A 5, Band 2. (Microcopy T–77, Roll. No. 896.)
OKW/1392	Deutscher General Vichy: Untitled file. (Microcopy T–77, Roll No. 842.)
DGV 70/23588	Deutscher General Vichy: Untitled file. (Microcopy T–501, Roll No. 120.)
DGV 70/23592	Deutscher General Vichy: Untitled file. (Microcopy T–501, Roll No. 121.)
47676	Militärbefehlshaber Frankreich/Kommandostab/Abteilung Ia: Einsatzbericht für die Monate Januar und Februar 1944. (Microcopy T–501, Roll No. 144.)
85142	Militärbefehlshaber Frankreich/Abwehrstelle Paris: IIIc A – Laval. (Microcopy T–501, Roll No. 189.)

Documents presented at the Nuremberg war crimes trials (Wiener Library, London).

Miscellaneous documents of the German occupation authorities in France (Centre de Documentation Juive Contemporaine, Paris).

Bell, P. M. H.: *Anglo-French Relations, May–December 1940*. M. Litt. thesis, University of Oxford, 1957 (Bodleian Library, Oxford).

Brüning, Heinrich: Letter to M. René de Chambrun, 3 January 1950 (photocopy in the author's possession).

Caujolle: See France, Haute Court de Justice.

Chambrun, Mme René de: Undated notes on Lord Templewood's *Nine Troubled Years* (copy in the author's possession).

Chambrun, René de: Memorandum for the French Public Prosecutor on his relations with Marshal Pétain, 22 January 1946 (copy in the author's possession); Letters to the author, 23 February, 3 November 1963, 13 September, 1965.

France, Haute Cour de Justice: *Procès de M. Pierre Laval. Enquête sur la Fortune, 1945. Rapport Caujolle* (copy in the possession of M. René de Chambrun).

Guénier, André: '*Réponses de M. André Guénier au questionnaire de Mr Geoffrey Warner,*' 13 September 1965 (in the author's possession).

Laval, Mme Pierre: '*Note dictée . . . en décembre 1945*' on the life of Pierre Laval (copy in the author's possession).

Laval, Pierre: Stenographic records of 12 confidential speeches made during the period 1942–44 (copy in the possession of M. René de Chambrun).

Markoff, Robert A.: *Opposition to the War in France, 1914–18*. Ph.D. thesis, University of Pennsylvania, 1962. (Microfilm copy available from University Microfilms. Ann Arbor, Michigan, No. 63–4164).

Palmer, A. W.: Letter to the author, 21 October 1963.

Wormser, Georges: '*Note sur le rôle de Pierre Laval lors de la formation du 2ème cabinet Clemenceau (Novembre 1917)*', 19 February 1963 (in the author's possession.

B · *PUBLISHED DOCUMENTS*

Benoist-Méchin, Jacques: *Le Procès Benoist-Méchin*, ed. J.-L. Aujol, Paris, Albin Michel, 1948.

British Broadcasting Corporation: *Daily Digest of Foreign Broadcasts*, April 1942.

Ciano, Galeazzo: *L'Europa verso la Catastrofe*, Milan, Mondadori, 1948.

Flandin, Pierre-Etienne: *Le Procès Flandin devant la Haute Cour de Justice, 23–26 juillet 1946*, Paris, Librairie de Médicis, 1947.

France, Commission d'Enquête Parlementaire: *Les Evénements survenus en France de 1933 à 1945. Rapport de M. Charles Serre, Député, au nom de la Commission d'Enquête Parlementaire*, 2 volumes; *Témoignages et Documents*

Receuillis par la Commission d'Enquête Parlementaire, 9 volumes. Paris, Presses Universitaires de France, n.d.

France: *La Délégation Française auprès de la Commission Allemande d'Armistice*, 5 volumes, Paris, Alfred Costes-Imprimerie Nationale, 1947–59.

France, Haute Court de Justice: *Procès du Maréchal Pétain. Compte Rendu in extenso des Audiences*, Paris, Imprimerie des Journaux Officiels, 1945.

France: *Journal Officiel de la République Française – Débats Parlementaires* and *Lois et Décrets*, Paris, Imprimerie des Journaux Officiels, 1914–44.

France, Ministère des Affaires Etrangères: *Documents Diplomatiques Français, 1932–39*, 2nd Series, Vol I, Paris, Imprimerie Nationale, 1963.

Germany, Auswärtiges Amt: *Documents on German Foreign Policy, 1918–45*, Series C, Vols. III, IV: Series D, Vols. III, IX, X, XI, XII, London, H.M.S.O., 1959, 1962, 1951, 1956, 1957, 1961, 1962.

Germany, Oberkommando der Wehrmacht: *Kriegstagebuch des Oberkommandos der Wehrmacht, 1940–45*, Vol II (1942), Part 2, ed. A. Hillgruber, Frankfurt-am-Main, Bernard & Graefe Verlag für Wehrwesen, 1963.

Hitler, Adolf: 'Führer Naval Conferences' in *Brassey's Naval Annual 1948*, London, William Clowes & Son, 1948.

Hitler, Adolf: *Hitlers Weisungen für die Kriegführung, 1939–45*, ed. W. Hubatsch, Frankfurt-am-Main, Bernard & Graefe Verlag für Wehrwesen, 1962.

Hitler, Adolf: *Reden und Proklamationen*, ed. M. Domarus, Vol. II, Munich, Süddeutscher Verlag, 1965.

Hoover Institution: *La Vie de la France sous l'Occupation (1940–44)*, 3 volumes, Paris, Plon, 1957.

International Military Tribunal: *Trial of the Major War Criminals before the International Military Tribunal, Nuremberg, 14 November 1945 – 1 October 1946*, 42 volumes, Nuremberg, International Military Tribunal, 1947–49.

Italy, Ministero degli Affari Esteri: *I Documenti Diplomatici Italiani*, 8th Series, Vol XIII; 9th Series, Vols. I, II, III, IV, Rome, La Libreria dello Stato, 1953, 1954, 1957, 1959, 1960.

Laval, Pierre: *Le Procès Laval. Compte Rendu Sténographique*, Paris, Albin Michel, 1946.

Mussolini, Benito: *Opera Omnia di Benito Mussolini*, ed. E. and D. Susmel, Vols. XXVII, XXIX, Florence, La Fenice, 1959.

Noguères, Louis: *La Dernière Etape: Sigmaringen*, Paris, Fayard, 1956.

Noguères, Louis: *Le Véritable Procès du Maréchal Pétain*, Paris, Fayard, 1955.

Pétain, Philippe: *Quatre Années au Pouvoir*, Paris, La Couronne Littéraire, 1949.

Les Procès de la Collaboration : Fernand de Brinon, Joseph Darnand, Jean Luchaire, Paris, Albin Michel, 1948.

Roatta, Mario: *Il Processo Roatta*, Rome, Donatello de Luigi, 1945.

Royal Institute of International Affairs: *Documents on International Affairs 1935*, 2 volumes, Oxford University Press for the Royal Institute of International Affairs, 1936.

United Kingdom, Foreign Office: *Correspondence showing the course of certain diplomatic discussions directed towards securing an European settlement, June 1934–March 1936* (Cmd. 5143), London, H.M.S.O., 1936.

United Kingdom, Foreign Office: *Documents on British Foreign Policy*, 2nd Series, Vols. II, III, London, H.M.S.O., 1947, 1948.

United Kingdom: *Parliamentary Debates*, December 1935.

United States, Department of State: *Foreign Relations of the United States, 1931*, Vol. I; *1935*, Vol. I; *1940*, Vol. II; *1942*, Vols. I, II, Washington, U.S. Government Printing Office, 1946, 1953, 1957, 1960, 1962.

C · *MEMOIRS AND DIARIES*

Abetz, Otto: *Das Öffene Problem: ein Rückblick auf zwei Jahrzehnte deutscher Frank reichpolitik*, Cologne, Greven Verlag, 1951.

Abetz, Otto: *Pétain et les Allemands. Mémorandum d'Abetz*, Paris, Editions Gaucher, 1948.

Alfieri, Dino: *Due Dittatori di Fronte*, Milan, Rizzoli, 1948.

Aloisi, Pompeo: *Journal, 25 juillet 1932 – 14 juin 1936*, translated from the Italian by Maurice Vaussard, Paris, Plon, 1957. (N.B. An Italian edition has not yet appeared.)

Auphan, Admiral Gabriel: '*Histoire de mes "Trahisons"* ', in *Les Grimaces de l'Histoire*, Paris, Les Iles d'Or, 1951.

Auriol, Vincent: *Hier . . . Demain*, Vol. I, Paris, Charlot, 1945.

Avon, Earl of: *Facing the Dictators*, London, Cassell, 1962.

Baraduc, Jacques: *Dans la Cellule de Pierre Laval*, Paris, Editions Self, 1948.

Bardoux, Jacques: *Journal d'un Témoin de la Troisième*, Paris, Fayard, 1957.

Barré, General Georges: *Tunisie, 1942–43*, Paris, Editions Berger-Levrault, 1950.

Barthe, Edouard: *La Ténébreuse Affaire du 'Massilia'*, Paris, Imprimerie Dupont, 1945.

Baudouin, Paul: *Neuf Mois au Gouvernement*, Paris, La Table Ronde, 1948.

Beck, Count Joseph: *Dernier Rapport: Politique Polonaise, 1926–39*, Neuchâtel, Editions de la Baconnière, 1951.

Blum, Léon: *L'Œuvre de Léon Blum, 1940–45*, Paris, Albin Michel, 1955.

Bois, Elie J.: *Le Malheur de la France*, London, The Continental Publishers & Distributors Ltd. (Hachette), 1941.

Bonnet, Georges: *La Défense de la Paix*, Vol. I, *De Washington au Quai d'Orsay*, Geneva, Les Editions du Cheval Ailé, 1946.

Boothby, Sir Robert: *I Fight to Live*, London, Gollancz, 1947.

Bourgin, Hubert: *Le Parti contre la Patrie*, Paris, Plon, 1924.

Bouthillier, Yves: *Le Drame de Vichy*, Vol. I, *Face à l'Ennemi, Face à l'Allié*; Vol. II, *Finances sous la Contrainte*, Paris, Plon, 1950, 1951.

Brinon, Fernand de: *Mémoires*, Paris, L.L.C., 1949.

Bryant, Sir Arthur: *The Turn of the Tide*, London, Collins, 1957.

Butcher, Harry C.: *Three Years with Eisenhower*, London, Heinemann, 1946.

Cavallero, Marshal Ugo: *Comando Supremo: Diario 1940–43*, Bologna, Cappelli, 1948.

Charles-Roux, François: *Cinq Mois Tragiques aux Affaires Etrangères*, Paris, Plon, 1949.

Charles-Roux, François: *Huit Ans au Vatican, 1932–40*, Paris, Flammarion, 1948.

Chautemps, Camille: *Cahiers Secrets de l'Armistice*, Paris, Plon, 1963.

Churchill, Winston S.: *The Second World War*, Vol. II, *Their Finest Hour*; Vol. VI, *Triumph and Tragedy*, London, Cassell, 1949, 1954.

Ciano, Galeazzo: *1937–38 Diario*, Bologna, Cappelli, 1948.

Ciano, Galeazzo: *Diario 1939–43*, 2 volumes, Milan, Rizzoli, 1946.

Clark, General Mark W.: *Calculated Risk*, New York, Harper, 1950.

Collette, Paul: *J'ai tiré sur Laval*, Caen, Ozanne, 1946.

Coudenhove-Kalergi, Richard: *An Idea conquers the World*, London, Hutchinson, 1953.

Darlan, Alain: *L'Amiral Darlan Parle*, Paris, Amiot-Dumont, 1952.

Dawes, Charles G.: *Journal as Ambassador*, New York, The Macmillan Company, 1939.

Desgranges, Abbé: *Journal d'un Prêtre-Député*, Paris-Geneva, La Palatine, 1960.

Eden, Anthony: See Avon, Earl of.

Edge, Walter E.: *A Jerseyman's Journal*, Princeton, Princeton University Press, 1948.

Fabry, Jean: *J'ai Connu, 1934–45*, Paris, Editions Descamps S.E.P.H.L., 1960.

Fernand-Laurent: *Un Peuple Ressuscite*, New York, Brentano's, 1943.

Fernet, Admiral Jean: *Aux Côtés du Maréchal Pétain*, Paris, Plon, 1953.

Flandin, Pierre-Etienne: *Politique Française, 1919–40*, Paris, Les Editions Nouvelles, 1947.

François-Poncet, André: *Souvenirs d'une Ambassade à Berlin*, Paris, Flammarion, 1946.

Frossard, Ludovic-Oscar: *De Jaurès à Léon Blum: Souvenirs d'un Militant*, Paris, Flammarion, 1943.

Gamelin, General Maurice: *Servir*, Vol. II, *Le Prologue du Drame, 1930–Août 1939*; Vol. III, *La Guerre, Septembre 1939–Mai 1940*, Paris, Plon, 1947.

Gaulle, General Charles de: *Mémoires de Guerre*, Vol. I, *L'Appel, 1940–42*; Vol. II, *L'Unité, 1942–44*; Vol. III, *Le Salut, 1944–46*, Paris, Plon, 1954, 1956, 1959.

Giraud, General Henri: *Mes Evasions*, Paris, Julliard, 1946.

Goebbels, Franz-Joseph: *Goebbels Tagebücher*, ed. Louis P. Lochner, Zürich, Atlantis Verlag, 1948.

Guariglia, Rafaele: *Ricordi, 1922–46*; Naples, Edizioni Scientifiche Italiane, 1949.

Guérard, Jacques: *Criminel de Paix*, Paris, Nouvelles Editions Latines, 1953.

Halder, General Franz: *Kriegstagebuch*, Vol. II, Stuttgart, W. Kohlhammer Verlag, 1963.

Herriot, Edouard: *Episodes, 1940–44*, Paris, Flammarion, 1950.

Herriot, Edouard: *Jadis*, Vol. II, *D'une Guerre à l'Autre, 1914–36*, Paris, Flammarion, 1952.

Hitler, Adolf: *Hitler's Secret Conversations, 1941–44*, New York, Signet Books, 1961.

Hitler, Adolf: *Mein Kampf*, New York, Reynal & Hitchcock, 1940.

Hoare, Sir Samuel: See Templewood, Viscount.

Hull, Cordell: *Memoirs*, Vol. II, London, Hodder & Stoughton, 1948.

Jaffré, Yves-Frédéric: *Les Derniers Propos de Pierre Laval*, Paris, André Bonne, 1953.

Jeantet, Gabriel: *Pétain contre Hitler*, Paris, La Table Ronde, 1966.

Jobert, Aristide: *Souvenirs d'un ex-Parlementaire*, Paris, Editions Eugène Fignière, 1933.

Jones, Thomas: *A Diary with Letters, 1931–50*, London, Oxford University Press, 1954.

Juin, Marshal Alphonse: *Mémoires*, Vol. I, *Alger–Tunis–Rome*, Paris, Fayard, 1959.

Lagardelle, Hubert: *Mission à Rome: Mussolini*, Paris, Plon, 1957.

Laroche, Jules: *La Pologne de Pilsudski: Souvenirs d'une Ambassade, 1926–35*, Paris, Flammarion, 1953.

Laval, Pierre: *Laval Parle: Notes et Mémoires rédigés par Pierre Laval dans sa cellule, avec une préface de sa fille et de nombreux documents inédits*, Geneva, Editions du Cheval Ailé, 1947.

Laval, Pierre: *The Unpublished Diary of Pierre Laval*, London, Falcon Press, 1948.

Leahy, Fleet-Admiral William D.: *I Was There*, London, Gollancz, 1950.

Lebrun, Albert: *Témoignages*, Paris, Plon, 1945.

Lémery, Henry: *D'une République à l'Autre*, Paris, La Table Ronde, 1964.

Liddell-Hart, Sir Basil H.: *Memoirs*, Vol. I, London, Cassell, 1965.

Malvy, Jean-Louis: *Mon Crime*, Paris, Flammarion, 1921.

Moulin de Labarthète, Henri du: *Le Temps des Illusions: Souvenirs (Juillet 1940-Avril 1942)*, Geneva, Editions du Cheval Ailé, 1946 .

Murphy, Robert: *Diplomat Among Warriors*, New York, Doubleday, 1964.

Naud, Albert: *Pourquoi je n'ai pas défendu Pierre Laval*, Paris, Fayard, 1948.

Paul-Boncour, Joseph: *Entre deux Guerres*, Vol. II, *Les Lendemains de la Victoire, 1919-34*; Vol. III, *Sur les Chemins de la Défaite, 1935-40*, Paris, Plon, 1945.

Peterson, Sir Maurice: *Both Sides of the Curtain*, London, Constable, 1950.

Piétri, François: *Mes Années d'Espagne*, Paris, Plon, 1954.

Peyrouton, Marcel: *Du Service Public à la Prison Commune*, Paris, Plon, 1950.

Pucheu, Pierre: *Ma Vie*, Paris, Amiot-Dumont, 1948.

Reynaud, Paul: *Au Cœur de la Mêlée*, Paris, Flammarion, 1951.

Reynaud, Paul: *La France a sauvé l'Europe*, Vol. II, Paris, Flammarion, 1947.

Reynaud, Paul: *Mémoires*, Vol. II, *Envers et Contre Tous*, Paris, Flammarion, 1963.

Robert, Admiral Georges: *La France aux Antilles de 1939 à 1943*. Paris, Plon, 1950.

Rossi, General Francesco: *Mussolini e lo Stato Maggiore: Avvenimenti del 1940*, Rome, Regionale, 1951.

Schmidt, Paul: *Statist auf diplomatischer Bühne, 1923-35*, Bonn, Athenäum-Verlag, 1949.

Sicard, Maurice-Yvan (pseud.: Saint-Paulien): *Histoire de la Collaboration*, Paris, L'Esprit Nouveau, 1964.

Simon, Viscount: *Retrospect*, London, Hutchinson, 1952.

Skorzeny, Otto: *Geheim-Kommando Skorzeny*, Hamburg, Hansa Verlag Joseph Toth, 1950.

Spears, Sir Edward L.: *Assignment to Catastrophe*, Vol II, *The Fall of France*, London, Heinemann, 1954.

Stehlin, General Paul: *Témoignage pour l'Histoire*, Paris, Robert Laffont, 1964.

Stimson, Henry L. and Bundy, McGeorge: *On Active Service in Peace and War*, London, Hutchinson, 1949.

Stucki, Walter: *Von Pétain zur Vierten Republik*, Berne, Verlag Herbert Lang & Cie., 1947.

Szembek, Jean: *Journal, 1933-39*, Paris, Plon, 1952.

Tabouis, Geneviève: *They Called Me Cassandra*, New York, Charles Scribner's Sons, 1942.

Templewood, Viscount: *Nine Troubled Years*, London, Collins, 1954.

15**

Thompson, Sir Geoffrey: *Frontline Diplomat*, London, Hutchinson, 1959.

Tissier, Pierre: *I Worked with Laval*, London, Harrap, 1942.

Tony-Révillon, M. M.: *Mes Carnets, Juin-Octobre 1940*, Paris, Odette Lieutier, 1945.

Tracou, Jean: *Le Maréchal aux Liens*, Paris, André Bonne, 1948.

Vansittart, Lord: *The Mist Procession*, London, Hutchinson, 1958.

Warlimont, General Walter: *Im Hauptquartier der deutschen Wehrmacht, 1939–45*, Frankfurt-am-Main, Bernard & Graefe Verlag für Wehrwesen, 1962.

Weygand, General Maxime: *En Lisant les Mémoires du Général de Gaulle*, Paris, Flammarion, 1955.

Weygand, General Maxime: *Mémoires*, Vol. III, *Rappelé au Service*, Paris, Flammarion, 1950.

D · SECONDARY WORKS

Allard, Paul: *Les Enigmes de la Guerre*, Paris, Editions des Portigues, 1933.

Arnoult, P. *et al.*: *La France sous l'Occupation*, Paris, Presses Universitaires de France, 1959.

Aron, Robert: *Histoire de Vichy*, Paris, Fayard, 1954.

Baldwin, A. W.: *My Father: The True Story*, London, Allen & Unwin, 1955.

Baraduc, Jacques: *Tout ce qu'on vous a caché*, Paris, Editions de l'Elan, 1949.

Beau de Loménie, Emmanuel: *La Mort de la Troisième République*, Paris, Editions du Conquistador, 1951.

Beloff, Max: 'The Sixth of February' in *The Decline of the Third Republic* (St Antony's Papers, No. 5), London, Chatto & Windus, 1959.

Bennett, Edward W.: *Germany and the Diplomacy of the Financial Crisis, 1931*, Cambridge (Mass.), Harvard University Press, 1962.

Binion, Rudolph: *Defeated Leaders*, New York, Columbia University Press, 1960.

Bodin, Louis, and Touchard, Jean: *Front Populaire 1936*, Paris, Armand Colin, 1961.

Bonnefous, Georges and Edouard: *Histoire Politique de la Troisième République*, Vols II, V, Paris, Presses Universitaires de France, 1957, 1962.

Bullock, Alan: *Hitler: A Study in Tyranny*, Harmondsworth, Penguin Books, 1962.

Butler, J. R. M.: *Grand Strategy*, Vol. II, London, H.M.S.O., 1957.

Campbell, Peter W.: *French Electoral Systems and Elections since 1798*, 2nd edn., London, Faber & Faber, 1965.

Colvin, Ian: *Vansittart in Office*, London, Gollancz, 1965.

Debû-Bridel, Jacques: *L'Agonie de la Troisième République*, Paris, Editions du Bâteau Ivre, 1948.

Detwiler, Donald: *Hitler, Franco und Gibraltar*, Wiesbaden, Franz Steiner Verlag, 1962.

Dhers, Paul: *Nouveaux Regards sur les Années Quarante*, Paris, Flammarion, 1958.

Docteur, Admiral: *La Grande Enigme de la Guerre: Darlan, Amiral de la Flotte*, Paris, Editions de la Couronne, 1949.

Dupeux, Georges: *Le Front Populaire et les Elections de 1936*, Paris, Armand Colin, 1959.

Feiling, Keith: *Neville Chamberlain*, London, Macmillan, 1946.

Ferrell, Richard: *American Diplomacy in the Great Depression*, New Haven, Yale University Press, 1957.

France, Statistique Générale et Institut de Conjoncture: *Mouvement Economique en France de 1929 à 1939*, Paris, Imprimerie Nationale, 1941.

Gehl, Jürgen: *Austria, Germany and the Anschluss, 1931–38*, London, Oxford University Press, 1963.

Geschke, Günter: *Die deutsche Frankreichpolitik 1940, von Compiègne bis Montoire*, Beiheft 12–13 der *Wehrwissenschaftlichen Rundschau*, Frankfurt-am-Main, Verlag E.S. Mittler & Sohn, October 1960.

Girard, Louis-Dominique: *Montoire: Verdun diplomatique*, Paris, André Bonne, 1948.

Hilberg, Raul: *The Destruction of the European Jews*, London, W. H. Allen, 1961.

Hytier, Adrienne D.: *Two Years of French Foreign Policy: Vichy, 1940–42*, Paris–Geneva, Librairie E. Droz, 1958.

Jäckel, Eberhard: *Frankreich in Hitlers Europa*, Stuttgart, Deutsche-Verlags-Anstalt, 1966.*

Johnson, C. O.: *Borah of Idaho*, New York, Longmans, 1936.

Jolly, Jean (ed.): *Dictionnaire des Parlementaires Français*, Vol. III, Paris, Presses Universitaires de France, 1963.

Jouvenel, Robert de: *La République des Camarades*, 2nd edn., Paris, Grasset, 1934.

Kammerer, Albert: *Du Débarquement Africain au Meurtre de Darlan*, Paris, Flammarion, 1949.

Kammerer, Albert: *La Passion de la Flotte Française*, Paris, Fayard, 1951.

Kammerer, Albert: *La Vérité sur l'Armistice*, 2nd edn., Paris, Editions Médicis, 1945.

Langer, William L.: *Our Vichy Gamble*, New York, Alfred A. Knopf, 1947.

Larmour, Peter J.: *The French Radical Party in the 1930's*, Stanford, Stanford University Press, 1964.

Letan, Michel: *Pierre Laval: de l'Armistice au Poteau*, Paris, Editions de la Couronne, 1947.

Lochner, Louis P.: *Herbert Hoover and Germany*, New York, The Macmillan Company, 1960.

Luther, Hans: *Der französische Widerstand gegen die deutsche Besatzungsmacht und seine Bekämpfung*, Tübingen, Institut für Besatzungsfragen, 1957.

Macartney, C. A. and Palmer, A. W.: *Independent Eastern Europe*, London, Macmillan, 1962.

Macleod, Iain: *Neville Chamberlain*, London, Frederick Muller, 1961.

Mallet, Alfred: *Pierre Laval*, 2 volumes, Paris, Amiot-Dumont, 1954.

Michel, Henri: *Histoire de la Résistance en France*, 3rd edn., Paris, Presses Universitaires de France, 1962.

Michel, Henri: *Vichy: Année 40*, Paris, Robert Laffont, 1966.*

Minart, Jacques: *Le Drame du Désarmement Français, 1918–1939*, Paris, La Nef de Paris, 1959.

Monneray, Henri (ed.): *La Persecution des Juifs en France et dans les autres Pays de l'Ouest*, Paris, Centre de Documentation Juive Contemporaine, 1947.

Montigny, Jean: *Toute la Vérité sur une Mois Dramatique de Notre Histoire*, Clermont-Ferrand, Editions Mont-Louis, 1540.

Mowat, Charles L.: *Britain between the Wars, 1918–40*, London, Methuen, 1955.

Noguères, Henri: *Le Suicide de la Flotte Française à Toulon*, Paris, Robert Laffont, 1963.

Pannetier, Odette: *Pierre Laval*, Paris, Denoël & Steele, 1936.

Privat, Maurice: *Pierre Laval*, Paris-Neuilly, Les Documents Secrets, 1931.

Robertson, Esmonde: *Hitler's pre-war Policy and Military Plans*, London, Longmans, 1963.

Schmitt, General Georges: *Les Accords Secrets Franco-Britanniques de Novembre-Décembre 1940: Histoire ou Mystification?* Paris, Presses Universitaires de France, 1957.

Scott, William E.: *Alliance against Hitler*, Durham (N.C.), Duke University Press, 1962.

Sherwood, John: 'The Tiger's Cub: The Last Years of Georges Mandel' in *The Decline of the Third Republic* (St Antony's Papers, No. 5), London, Chatto & Windus, 1959.

Soulié, Michel: *La Vie Politique d'Edouard Herriot*, Paris, Armand Colin, 1962.

Steinberg, Lucien: *Les Autorités Allemandes en France Occupée: Inventaire Commentée de la Collection de Documents conservés au Centre de Documentation Juive Contemporaine*, Paris, Centre de Documentation Juive Contemporaine, 1966.

Taylor, A. J. P.: *The Origins of the Second World War*, London, Hamish Hamilton, 1961.

Thomson, David: *Two Frenchmen: Pierre Laval and Charles de Gaulle*, London, The Cresset Press, 1951.

Torrès, Henri: *Pierre Laval*, London, Gollancz, 1941.

Toscano, Mario: '*Eden a Roma alla vigilia del conflitto italo-etiopico*' in *Pagine di Storia Diplomatica*, Vol. II, Milan, A. Giuffrè, 1963.

Toscano, Mario: *Le Origini Diplomatiche del Patto d'Acciaio*, 2nd edn., Florence, Sansoni, 1956.

Tournoux, J.-R.: *L'Histoire Secrète*, Paris, Plon, 1962.

Toynbee, Arnold J.: *Survey of International Affairs, 1931*, London, Oxford University Press for the Royal Institute of International Affairs, 1932.

Toynbee, Arnold J.: *Survey of International Affairs, 1935*, Vol. I, London, Oxford University Press for the Royal Institute of International Affairs, 1936.

Warner, Geoffrey: 'France' in S. J. Woolf (ed.), *European Fascism*, London, Weidenfeld & Nicolson, 1968.

Werth, Alexander: *The Destiny of France*, London, Hamish Hamilton, 1937.

Werth, Alexander: *France and Munich*, London, Hamish Hamilton, 1939.

Woodward, Sir E. L.: *British Foreign Policy in the Second World War*, London, H.M.S.O., 1962.

* The two books thus marked were first seen by me after the completion of the bulk of my manuscript. They are both studies of such importance, however, that they must be included in any bibliography of the subject.

E · *ARTICLES*

Askew, William C.: 'The Secret Agreement between France and Italy on Ethiopia, January 1935', *Journal of Modern History*, March 1953, pp. 47–48.

Bell, P. M. H.: '*Prologue de Mers-el-Kébir*', *Revue d'Histoire de la Deuxième Guerre Mondiale*, January 1959, pp. 15–36.

Dampierre, Robert de: '*Dix Années de Politique Française à Rome*', Part II, *La Revue des Deux Mondes*, 15 November 1953, pp. 258–83.

Dampierre, Robert de: '*Une Entente Italo-Yugoslave, Mars 1937*', *La Revue des Deux Mondes*, 1 September 1953, pp. 126–36.

Delattre, Gabriel: Article in *L'Aurore*, 3 October 1944.

Dhers, Paul: '*Le Comité de Guerre du 25 Mai 1940*', *Revue d'Histoire de la Deuxième Guerre Mondiale*, June 1953, pp. 165–83.

Garnier, Jean-Paul: '*Autour d'un Accord*', *Revue de Paris*, September 1961, pp. 102–14.

Kammerer, Albert: '*Le Véritable Montoire*', *Une Semaine dans le Monde*, 1 and 8 May 1948.

Lamoureux, Lucien: Memoirs in *La Bourbonnais Républicaine*, 26 June 1955, 10 July 1955, 25 September 1955, 2 October 1955.

Marin, Louis: '*Contributions à l'histoire des prodromes de l'Armistice*,' *Revue d'Histoire de la Deuxième Guerre Mondiale*, June 1951, pp. 1–26.

Schmitt, General Georges: '*La Matinée du 11 Novembre 1942 à Vichy*', *Revue d'Histoire de la Deuxième Guerre Mondiale*, October 1962, pp. 77–80.

Stambrook, F. G.: 'The German-Austrian Customs Union Project of 1931: A Study of German Methods and Motives', *Journal of Central European Affairs*, April 1961, pp. 15–44.

'The Struggle of the U.S.S.R. for Collective Security in Europe during 1933–35', Parts I–IV, *International Affairs* (Moscow), June 1963, pp. 107–16; July 1963, pp. 116–23; August 1963, pp. 132–39; October 1963, pp. 112–20.

Warner, Geoffrey: 'The Cagoulard Conspiracy', *History Today*, July 1960, pp. 443–50.

Warner, Geoffrey: 'Pierre Laval and the Fall of France', *History Today*, December 1961, pp. 817–27.

Warner, Geoffrey: 'The Stavisky Affair and the Riots of 6th February 1934', *History Today*, June 1958, pp. 377–85.

Watt, Donald C.: 'The Anglo-German Naval Agreement of 1935; An Interim Judgement', *Journal of Modern History*, June 1956, pp. 155–75.

Watt, Donald C.: 'The Secret Laval–Mussolini Agreement of 1935 on Ethiopia', *Middle East Journal*, Winter 1961, pp. 69–77.

F · *NEWSPAPERS AND PERIODICALS*

La Bataille Syndicaliste (Paris)
Daily Telegraph (London)
Department of State Bulletin (Washington, D.C.)
The Economist (London)
Evening Standard (London)
L'Humanité (Paris)
Le Journal de Saint-Denis (Saint-Denis)
Manchester Guardian (Manchester)
Le Monde (Paris)
Le Moniteur de Puy-de-Dôme (Clermont-Ferrand)
Neue Zürcher Zeitung (Zürich)
New York Times (New York)

News Chronicle (London)
Observer (London)
Le Petit Parisien (Paris)
Le Populaire (Paris)
Presse de Paris (Paris)
Le Temps (Paris)
The Times (London)

Index

447

454 · INDEX